Red Hat®
Linux® 7 Server

Red Hat® Linux® 7 Server

Mohammed J. Kabir

M&T Books
An imprint of IDG Books Worldwide, Inc.

Foster City, CA • Chicago, IL • Indianapolis, IN • New York, NY

Red Hat® Linux® 7 Server

Published by
M&T Books
An imprint of IDG Books Worldwide, Inc.
919 E. Hillsdale Blvd., Suite 400
Foster City, CA 94404
www.idgbooks.com (IDG Books Worldwide Web site)

ISBN: 0-7645-4786-0

Printed in the United States of America

10 9 8 7 6 5 4 3 2 1

10/RS/RS/QQ/FC

Distributed in the United States by IDG Books Worldwide, Inc.

Distributed by CDG Books Canada Inc. for Canada; by Transworld Publishers Limited in the United Kingdom; by IDG Norge Books for Norway; by IDG Sweden Books for Sweden; by IDG Books Australia Publishing Corporation Pty. Ltd. for Australia and New Zealand; by TransQuest Publishers Pte Ltd. for Singapore, Malaysia, Thailand, Indonesia, and Hong Kong; by Gotop Information Inc. for Taiwan; by ICG Muse, Inc. for Japan; by Intersoft for South Africa; by Eyrolles for France; by International Thomson Publishing for Germany, Austria, and Switzerland; by Distribuidora Cuspide for Argentina; by LR International for Brazil; by Galileo Libros for Chile; by Ediciones ZETA S.C.R. Ltda. for Peru; by WS Computer Publishing Corporation, Inc., for the Philippines; by Contemporanea de Ediciones for Venezuela; by Express Computer Distributors for the Caribbean and West Indies; by Micronesia Media Distributor, Inc. for Micronesia; by Chips Computadoras S.A. de C.V. for Mexico; by Editorial Norma de Panama S.A. for Panama; by American Bookshops for Finland.

For general information on IDG Books Worldwide's books in the U.S., please call our Consumer Customer Service department at 800-762-2974. For reseller information, including discounts and premium sales, please call our Reseller Customer Service department at 800-434-3422.

For information on where to purchase IDG Books Worldwide's books outside the U.S., please contact our International Sales department at 317-596-5530 or fax 317-572-4002.

For consumer information on foreign language translations, please contact our Customer Service department at 800-434-3422, fax 317-572-4002, or e-mail rights@idgbooks.com.

For information on licensing foreign or domestic rights, please phone +1-650-653-7098.

For sales inquiries and special prices for bulk quantities, please contact our Order Services department at 800-434-3422 or write to the address above.

For information on using IDG Books Worldwide's books in the classroom or for ordering examination copies, please contact our Educational Sales department at 800-434-2086 or fax 317-572-4005.

For press review copies, author interviews, or other publicity information, please contact our Public Relations department at 650-653-7000 or fax 650-653-7500.

For authorization to photocopy items for corporate, personal, or educational use, please contact Copyright Clearance Center, 222 Rosewood Drive, Danvers, MA 01923, or fax 978-750-4470.

Library of Congress Cataloging-in-Publication Data

Kabir, Mohammed J., 1971–
    Red Hat Linux 7 server / Mohammed J. Kabir.
        p.   cm.
    ISBN 0-7645-4786-0 (alk. paper)
    1. Linux.   2. Operating systems (Computers)
3. Web servers.   I. Title.
QA76.76.O63 K3145   2000
005.4'4769--dc21   00-048716

is a registered trademark or trademark under exclusive license to IDG Books Worldwide, Inc. from International Data Group, Inc. in the United States and/or other countries.

is a trademark of IDG Books Worldwide, Inc.

ABOUT IDG BOOKS WORLDWIDE

Welcome to the world of IDG Books Worldwide.

IDG Books Worldwide, Inc., is a subsidiary of International Data Group, the world's largest publisher of computer-related information and the leading global provider of information services on information technology. IDG was founded more than 30 years ago by Patrick J. McGovern and now employs more than 9,000 people worldwide. IDG publishes more than 290 computer publications in over 75 countries. More than 90 million people read one or more IDG publications each month.

Launched in 1990, IDG Books Worldwide is today the #1 publisher of best-selling computer books in the United States. We are proud to have received eight awards from the Computer Press Association in recognition of editorial excellence and three from Computer Currents' First Annual Readers' Choice Awards. Our best-selling *...For Dummies*® series has more than 50 million copies in print with translations in 31 languages. IDG Books Worldwide, through a joint venture with IDG's Hi-Tech Beijing, became the first U.S. publisher to publish a computer book in the People's Republic of China. In record time, IDG Books Worldwide has become the first choice for millions of readers around the world who want to learn how to better manage their businesses.

Our mission is simple: Every one of our books is designed to bring extra value and skill-building instructions to the reader. Our books are written by experts who understand and care about our readers. The knowledge base of our editorial staff comes from years of experience in publishing, education, and journalism — experience we use to produce books to carry us into the new millennium. In short, we care about books, so we attract the best people. We devote special attention to details such as audience, interior design, use of icons, and illustrations. And because we use an efficient process of authoring, editing, and desktop publishing our books electronically, we can spend more time ensuring superior content and less time on the technicalities of making books.

You can count on our commitment to deliver high-quality books at competitive prices on topics you want to read about. At IDG Books Worldwide, we continue in the IDG tradition of delivering quality for more than 30 years. You'll find no better book on a subject than one from IDG Books Worldwide.

John Kilcullen
Chairman and CEO
IDG Books Worldwide, Inc.

Eighth Annual Computer Press Awards ≥1992

Ninth Annual Computer Press Awards ≥1993

Tenth Annual Computer Press Awards ≥1994

Eleventh Annual Computer Press Awards ≥1995

IDG is the world's leading IT media, research and exposition company. Founded in 1964, IDG had 1997 revenues of $2.05 billion and has more than 9,000 employees worldwide. IDG offers the widest range of media options that reach IT buyers in 75 countries representing 95% of worldwide IT spending. IDG's diverse product and services portfolio spans six key areas including print publishing, online publishing, expositions and conferences, market research, education and training, and global marketing services. More than 90 million people read one or more of IDG's 290 magazines and newspapers, including IDG's leading global brands — Computerworld, PC World, Network World, Macworld and the Channel World family of publications. IDG Books Worldwide is one of the fastest-growing computer book publishers in the world, with more than 700 titles in 36 languages. The "...For Dummies®" series alone has more than 50 million copies in print. IDG offers online users the largest network of technology-specific Web sites around the world through IDG.net (http://www.idg.net), which comprises more than 225 targeted Web sites in 55 countries worldwide. International Data Corporation (IDC) is the world's largest provider of information technology data, analysis and consulting, with research centers in over 41 countries and more than 400 research analysts worldwide. IDG World Expo is a leading producer of more than 168 globally branded conferences and expositions in 35 countries including E3 (Electronic Entertainment Expo), Macworld Expo, ComNet, Windows World Expo, ICE (Internet Commerce Expo), Agenda, DEMO, and Spotlight. IDG's training subsidiary, ExecuTrain, is the world's largest computer training company, with more than 230 locations worldwide and 785 training courses. IDG Marketing Services helps industry-leading IT companies build international brand recognition by developing global integrated marketing programs via IDG's print, online and exposition products worldwide. Further information about the company can be found at www.idg.com. 1/26/00

Credits

ACQUISITIONS EDITOR
Debra Williams Cauley

PROJECT EDITOR
Neil Romanosky

TECHNICAL EDITOR
Joseph Riquelme

COPY EDITORS
Lisa Blake
Chris Jones

PROJECT COORDINATORS
Danette Nurse
Louigene A. Santos

MEDIA DEVELOPMENT MANAGER
Laura Carpenter

MEDIA DEVELOPMENT SUPERVISOR
Rich Graves

PERMISSIONS EDITOR
Laura Moss

MEDIA DEVELOPMENT SPECIALIST
Greg Stephens

MEDIA DEVELOPMENT COORDINATOR
Marisa Pearman

QUALITY CONTROL TECHNICIAN
Dina F Quan

GRAPHICS AND PRODUCTION
SPECIALISTS
Robert Bilhmayer
Jude Levinson
Michael Lewis
Victor Pérez-Varela
Ramses Ramirez

BOOK DESIGNER
Jim Donohue

ILLUSTRATOR
John Greenough

PROOFREADING AND INDEXING
York Production Services

COVER IMAGE
(c) Noma/Images.com

About the Author

Mohammed J. Kabir is the Chief Technology Officer and a co-founder of Intevo, Inc. His company (www.intevo.com) uses Linux as the platform for its INTEVO MAIL service. When he is not busy managing software projects or writing books, Kabir enjoys riding mountain bikes and watching sci-fi movies. Kabir studied computer engineering at California State University, Sacramento, and is also the author of *Apache Server Bible*, *Apache Server Administrator's Handbook*, and *CGI Primer Plus for Windows*. You can contact Kabir via e-mail at kabir@intevo.com or visit his personal Web site at http://www.nitec.com.

To my teachers at California State University, Sacramento

Preface

Welcome to *Red Hat Linux 7 Server*. Thanks to Red Hat, Linux has been gaining attention everywhere for the past few years. Now Linux is on the radar screen of virtually all IT professionals around the globe. Even commercial operating system giants have felt the impact of Linux. Once an operating system for the hobbyist, Linux has matured over the years and has become a serious server platform candidate for the world of IT. Those of us who keep our eyes and ears open for the new and rising stars in this field know that Linux is on a roll.

With the help of a world of Linux developers, Red Hat has helped this open source star take center stage in the server arena. All major vendors of hardware and software have started to show great interest in Linux; interestingly, some movers and shakers of the computer industry have even invested in and partnered with Red Hat Linux. Yes, finally they get it.

Is This Book for You?

There are many Linux- and Red Hat Linux–specific books for you to choose from. Some are good, and some are not so good. Many are focused on Linux as a personal operating system and discuss the details of how you can use Linux on your desktop computer. Some cover both Linux as a workstation and server platform and leave out important details. I wrote this book to help those who are interested in building a Linux server. In this book, you will find practical information about how you can manage users, disk quotas, processes, and networks, as well as how to set up a DNS server, an SMTP/POP3 e-mail server, a Web server, an FTP server, an NFS server, a Samba-based file and print server, an IRC server, a SQL server, and more. You will learn to enhance server and network security by using various tools and techniques and also learn to custom-compile the Linux kernel to fine-tune your server for higher performance.

Although there are many Linux distributions, the Red Hat Linux distribution has become my favorite. Therefore, it makes perfect sense to write this book using Red Hat Linux. Red Hat has done a wonderful job of giving Linux the professional look it needed to win the admiration of IT professionals worldwide.

This is not a book about how to use Linux as a desktop operating system. It is about the serious job of keeping your organization's server up and running with one of the technological marvels of this millennium. The book assumes no prior knowledge of Linux or any other UNIX or UNIX-like operating systems. However, it does assume that you enjoy having a stable server operating system that can run month after month without even a single reboot. Interested? Welcome aboard.

How This Book Is Organized

I have organized the book into eight parts.

Part 1: Getting Started

Part I is all about getting started with Red Hat Linux. The idea behind this part is to get your Red Hat Linux server installed and running. Because Red Hat Linux really shines in the installation area, you are likely to accomplish this goal in a very short time.

Part II: Working as a Superuser

Because you are reading this book, I assume you are also the superuser (administrator) of your Red Hat Linux server. In Part II, I discuss various details of the bootup and shutdown processes of Red Hat Linux server. I also explain the details of files and directory permissions, which is a must-know topic for any serious system administrator. Finally, the section provides a concise, everyday command reference for those who are new to Red Hat Linux. The command reference is likely to help you more than the typical man pages because it includes numerous examples.

Part III: Managing Users, Processes, and Networks

Part III deals with user administration, process management, and TCP/IP network basics and configuration. The chapter on user administration deals with user and group account management and how to implement disk quotas. You will find a chapter dedicated to process management that helps you learn about how processes are created, how to send signals to a running process, how to control process priority, how to monitor processes using various utilities, how to automate process execution via the cron facility, and how to log information from processes by using the syslog facility. The network administration chapter deals with basics of TCP/IP networking, how to classify IP networks, how to configure your server's network interfaces, how to create subnets, and so on.

Part IV: Setting Up Intranet/Internet Services

Part IV is the most important part of this book. It covers the common network services in great detail.

The Domain Name Service (DNS) chapter shows you how DNS works, how to configure BIND as a DNS server, how to perform load balancing using DNS, and so on.

The e-mail service chapter shows you how Simple Mail Transport Protocol (SMTP) mail service works, how to set up DNS for SMTP mail service, how to configure sendmail for SMTP mail service, and how to enable anti-spam measures. It also shows you how to set up a Post Office Protocol 3 (POP3) mail server and clients.

The Web service chapter shows how you can compile, configure, and install the famous Apache Web server for CGI scripts, Server Side Includes (SSI), virtual hosts, proxy service, secure transactions, and so on. From my experience, I know that Web service is one of the primary reasons many decide to use Red Hat Linux; therefore, I have specially prepared this chapter to provide you with all the information you need to create an elegant Web solution.

The FTP service chapter shows you how to configure wu-ftpd File Transfer Protocol (FTP) server for standard, anonymous, and guest FTP services. The in-depth coverage of this widely used FTP server provides you with valuable configuration options that enhance security and also provide a custom look and feel for your FTP users.

Finally, this part ends with a discussion on Internet Relay Chat (IRC) server and USENET news server. Although Internet Service Providers typically run news servers, private IRC servers are becoming very popular. A private IRC server can be a great resource for hosting company conferences over the Internet.

Part V: Setting Up Office Services

In Part V, you learn to use Linux in a office (LAN) environment.

The Samba service chapter shows you how to configure your Red Hat Linux server as a file and print server for the Windows computers in your LAN. You also learn to use Samba to access files and printers on other Windows computers.

The chapter on Network File System (NFS) shows you how to configure Red Hat Linux as an NFS server, which can provide mountable filesystems over the network. This chapter also introduces you to the rdist tool, which allows you to distribute files to other computers.

The last chapter in Part V shows you how to run MySQL, a SQL database server, on your Red Hat Linux server. It also provides useful examples of how you can create and access simple databases by using Perl scripts that run as both command-line scripts and CGI scripts.

Part VI: Securing and Monitoring

In Part VI, you learn various techniques for securing your Red Hat Linux server. The chapter on server security discusses issues such as shadow passwords, Pluggable Authentication Modules (PAMs), file/directory integrity checking tools, TCP wrapper, COPS, and so on.

The chapter on network security discusses issues such as use of nonroutable IP addresses for security purposes, masquerading IP addresses, packet filtering firewalls, proxy servers, and SATAN for monitoring network security holes.

Part VII: Tuning for Performance

Part VII deals with building custom kernels and designing large-scale, multi-server networks. The chapter on hacking the kernel discusses kernel compilation issues, and the chapter on the multi-server Web network discusses a real-world example of how you can use Red Hat Linux server to build a high-end Web network. The final two chapters in this part briefly discuss the configuration and use of the X Window System, respectively.

Part VIII: Appendixes

The two appendixes in Part VIII present various Linux resources and a detailed description of the contents and structure of the CD-ROM, respectively.

Tell Us What You Think

Both IDG Books Worldwide and I are very interested in finding out what you think of this book. Please feel free to register this book at the IDG Books Worldwide Web site (http://www.idgbooks.com) and give us your feedback. If you are interested in contacting me directly, send e-mail to kabir@intevo.com. I will do my best to respond promptly.

Acknowledgments

I'd like to thank Debra Williams Cauley, Neil Romanosky, Lisa Blake, and Chris Jones for working with me in updating this book. Many thanks to Bert Caridad and Terry Ewing for their contributions. Finally, I would also like to thank the IDG Books Worldwide team that made this book a reality. They are the people who turned a few files into a beautiful and polished book.

Contents at a Glance

Contents

Chapter 5

Part I

Getting Started

Chapter 1

Why Red Hat Linux?

IN THIS CHAPTER

◆ A brief history of Linux

◆ Information about various Linux distributions

◆ Why Red Hat Linux is the best Linux distribution

◆ Why to use Red Hat Linux as a server operating system

◆ How to get Red Hat Linux

WHEN IT COMES to server operating systems, you have two worlds to consider— UNIX and Windows 2000. There are other server-class operating systems, but these two dominate the market. Whenever someone talks about servers, the issue of UNIX versus Windows 2000/NT appears in the conversation. The umbrella word "UNIX" covers a lot of operating systems, Linux among them, even if Linux is not strictly a form of UNIX. The decision to choose UNIX over Windows NT or vice versa is often influenced by such factors as the buyer's background, the organization's IT capabilities, and its policies and politics. Because you are reading this book, I assume that you or your organization has already decided to choose the UNIX path either after a quick and intelligent thought cycle or after a long battle of UNIX versus Windows 2000/NT. Either way, here you are reading a book on Red Hat Linux. In this chapter, I plan to convince you that Red Hat Linux is the right choice for your server system. Before I go any further, take a brief look at the history of Linux.

The History of Linux

On October 5, 1991, Linus Benedict Torvalds, a graduate student from the University of Helsinki in Finland, announced in a Usenet newsgroup (`comp.os.minix`) that he had created a small UNIX-like operating system called Linux. The new operating system was inspired by another small UNIX operating system called Minix that was developed by Andy Tanenbaum. Although you would guess this announcement was about Linux version 0.01, it wasn't! In fact, Linux 0.01 was never announced. The reason was that 0.01 was not executable; Torvalds only provided the source of this version in the first Linux FTP site at `ftp://nic.funet.fi`.

The October 5 announcement from Torvalds referred to Version 0.02, which was capable of running the GNU Bourne Again Shell (bash) and the GNU C compiler

3

(gcc) and not much of anything else. Torvalds never knew that what he envisioned as an operating system for kernel hobbyists and hackers would turn into what is now known as Linux.

Linux started with Version 0.02, proceeded to Version 0.03, and then jumped to Version 0.10. As more and more programmers around the world started developing Linux, it reached Version 0.95. This indicated that the official release of Version 1.0 was very near. The official Version 1.0 was released in March 1992. As of this writing, the latest stable version of the Linux kernel is 2.2.3.

Today, Linux has stepped into the spotlight as a complete UNIX-like operating system. In recent days, Linux has received an enormous amount of media coverage on every side. It has become a breath of fresh air in the OS arena and is no longer the tiny hobbyist project that Torvalds initially created. Linux is not just a challenger to other so-called mainstream operating systems; in fact, it has become the one to beat.

Linux runs virtually all the respectable free software that organizations such as GNU make. It performs better than many expensive commercial operating systems. Although Intel *x*86 machines are the primary target platform, Linux has been ported to various other hardware platforms, including Sparc, Alpha, and Macintosh. In short, it is no longer thought of as the delightful dream of programmers who like to hack kernel code and want a low-cost, open-source operating system for such hacking at home. This has all changed. Linux is now everywhere.

In truth, most large organizations already have a heterogeneous server environment. Adding Linux to such an environment becomes a no-brainer due to the low-cost and open-source nature of the beast.

By now, many companies and individuals have taken the Linux kernel and bundled free and commercial software to create useful distributions of Linux. These distributions all share the same kernel code but provide value-added features in the installation, configuration, and application areas. Take a look at a few of the commonly available Linux distributions.

Other Major Linux Distributions

Many distributions other than Red Hat are available for Linux. Red Hat Linux is obviously my favorite and perhaps yours as well. The differences between the distributions are mainly in the following areas:

◆ Installation: Installation procedures range from completely manual to semiautomatic. One distribution may expect the user to create boot disks, but another such as Red Hat may supply disks or allow booting straight from a CD-ROM. One may have a minimal installation program, and another such as Red Hat may have a user-friendly menu-driven installation interface.

♦ Ease of configuration: A distribution may provide no configuration tools and expect you to edit configuration files manually to configure a system, whereas another may provide graphical user interface (GUI)-based tools to ease configuration tasks.

♦ Bundled software: One distribution may bundle hundreds of software packages in the main distribution, and another may bundle only a manageable set of software and provide the rest via FTP or other means.

♦ X Window system: One distribution may provide auto-probing of your video hardware to ease X Window system configuration, whereas another may require you to modify X Window system configuration files.

♦ Support: This is a big issue for commercial users. If you want commercial support for a distribution, you will find that the available choices are narrowed to only a very few.

Although this book is about Red Hat Linux, I think it is important for you to know how other Linux distributions differ from Red Hat Linux. In the following section, I briefly discuss a few popular Linux distributions from this point of view.

Caldera OpenLinux

If I had to choose a Linux distribution in the absence of Red Hat Linux, it would be Caldera's OpenLinux. I consider it the second-best Linux distribution for new users and businesses. The original Caldera distribution was created by the Linux Support Team (LST) in Germany, which later became part of Caldera.

This distribution is intended for businesses and offers a variety of commercial packages such as a secure Web server and the StarOffice Office Suite (a word processing program, a spreadsheet program, drawing programs, and so forth), DR-DOS (a DOS-like operating system that can be run using the DOSEMU emulator program), NetWare 3.x & 4.x Administration Utilities, and more. In many aspects, this is a very commercial version of Linux.

Because Caldera's target customers are mainstream businesses, it provides great support packages and also has one of the most powerful reseller programs. You can find more information on this distribution on the Internet at http://www.calderasystems.com/products/openlinux/.

Slackware Linux

Slackware is one the oldest distributions of Linux. Although I started my Linux experience with a Slackware distribution in the early days of Linux, I do not recommend this distribution for new Linux users because it requires a more hands-on, textual configuration than Red Hat Linux.

However, Slackware may be a great distribution for someone who wants to play kernel hacker or who likes a "do-it-yourself" approach to things. In short, it is not for the faint of heart. Slack, the cute, short name given to the distribution by its followers, does not use any packaging schemes, so all the packages come in tar files. This system could be quite a problem for new users, and it also poses a big problem when it comes to upgrading the operating system or other parts of the distribution. However, you can use a program called pkgtool to keep track of tar, tar.gz, and related files.

Slackware is distributed by Walnut Creek CDROM. You can find more information about it on the Internet at http://www.slackware.com/.

Debian GNU/Linux

Unlike Red Hat Linux, which is a commercial distribution of free Linux, the Debian GNU/Linux distribution itself is also free. Although Linux is primarily developed by programmers around the world, most Linux distributions are created by a tightly connected group of people. For example, Red Hat has its own staff to handle distribution issues. However, the Debian GNU/Linux distribution relies solely on a team of volunteers. The main distribution is larger than Red Hat because it includes packages that Red Hat considers contributed software and does not include in the official Red Hat distribution.

The Debian GNU/Linux distribution uses its own packaging scheme. It comes with the dpkg package manager for packages using the .dev format along with dselect and apt as the package management tools. Although the RPM technology developed by Red Hat has become the mainstream packaging solution for many Linux distributions and other UNIX software, the Debian packaging scheme does have some interesting features, such as the capability to download Debian GNU/Linux packages automatically, upgrade the distribution, and keep the software packages up to date.

Personally, I consider this distribution as the most relaxed and ideologically motivated Linux distribution. Because all developers are volunteers, there is no commercial pressure to release a version before it is really done. A new release is made public only if every milestone set forth by the team has been met. This also means that a release could be delayed if a volunteer gets involved in some other real-life matter. However, when a new release of Debian GNU/Linux comes out, it tends to have the fewest problems of any.

No official support is available from the nonprofit Debian Organization. You can find more information on this distribution on the Internet at http://www.debian.org/.

SuSE

SuSE, a distribution based in Germany, comes with a nifty, SwissArmy–type central administration and installation tool called YaST (Yet another Setup Tool.) An extensive set of packages comes as part of the main distribution. Many such packages are available for Red Hat as contributed software in ftp://contrib.redhat.com. Also note that this distribution includes cryptographic software such as ssh,

Apache-SSL, and PGP that have legal export restrictions in the U.S. This means that the SuSE distribution available in the U.S. is not the same as the non-U.S. version. This distribution also uses RPM packaging scheme.

You can find more information on this distribution on the Internet at http://www.suse.com/.

Other Linux distributions

Other mainstream Linux distributions include Eonova Linux, Linux-Mandrake, Stampede GNU/Linux, TurboLinux, and Xi Graphics maXimum cde/OS. Other specialized mini-Linux distributions focus on very low-end hardware to provide valuable single-purpose services. I personally find them very interesting because they often provide a quick and dirty way of getting much of the system administrative work done. In the following section I briefly discuss a few of these gems.

TRINUX
Trinux boots from several (two to three) floppies (or a MS-DOS/Windows 9.x partition) and runs entirely in RAM. It comes with the latest version of many network security tools such as NETWATCH, tcpdump, and netmon, which are very useful for TCP/IP port scanning and monitoring networks. Such a distribution of Linux turns an old x86 PC into a powerful network security management workstation. For more information on Trinux, go to the following URL: http://www.trinux.org.

LINUX ON A FLOPPY (LOAF)
LOAF fits on a single high-density (1.44MB) floppy disk and acts as simple network client system. More information on this distribution can be found at the following URL: http://www.ecks.org/loaf/.

LINUX ROUTER PROJECT
Linux Router Project is yet another single-floppy (1.44MB) Linux distribution; it turns an ordinary old x86 system into a router using the gated daemon. You can find the distribution at the following FTP site: ftp://sunsite.unc.edu/pub/Linux/distributions/linux-router/.

Linux distributions are available for several different processor architectures. In fact, Red Hat Linux has support for Alpha and SPARC, and Debian GNU/Linux has stable ports for Alpha and Motorola 68K architectures. Versions of Linux for PowerPC machines, such as PowerMacs, are available from MkLinux and LinuxPPC. Linux for UltraSPARC machines is available from UltraPenguin.

If you are interested in learning more about all the available Linux distributions, try the following URLs:

◆ http://www.linuxhq.com/dist-index.html

◆ http://www.linux.org/dist/index.html

Why Red Hat Is the Best

If you must ask the question "How do you know that Red Hat is the best?" the answer is: because Linus Torvalds himself uses it! Although it is true that Linus now uses Red Hat Linux, the true answer to the question should be clear from the following discussion.

As you may have realized from the discussion of the various distributions, practically the same Linux kernel code is used in all of them. What differentiates the mainstream distributions is the layer of ease of installation, ease of configuration, and breadth of user-level applications. Red Hat Linux's excellence in these respects makes it the most popular Linux distribution.

Red Hat is committed to making Linux usable for the masses. For Linux to be accepted by large numbers of computer users of the world, it must have a certain degree of user friendliness. Red Hat is working hard and fast to make Linux commonplace in the operating system arena. So far all indications are that it is making great progress in achieving its goals.

In fact, if you ask a serious Linux user who does not use Red Hat Linux about why she prefers a different distribution such as Slackware, chances are she will say that Red Hat tries to make things too simple in terms of installation and configuration. This ease-of-use apparently turns a few so-called gurus away from Red Hat Linux. That's unfortunate. If Linux is to be a successful operating system, it has to be user-friendly and usable by anyone from beginners to the most advanced users. Red Hat Linux does that just fine. If you crave total control and want to manually configure everything, go ahead! Red Hat Linux does not stop you from doing any such thing after you have installed it. Red Hat places no restrictions on compiling your kernel or configuring the network by hand. So the misconception that Red Hat hides configurations from the user is ill founded. It does make the installation very easy, such that anyone can install it. Once it is installed, you have all the choices to use GUI tools or manually configure anything you want.

The packaging scheme, Red Hat Package Management (RPM), was invented by the company and is surely one of the most interesting packaging schemes currently available for software distribution. As you may know, many other distributions also use RPM to manage packages.

By providing a simple and elegant method of installation, Red Hat targets everyone as potential Linux users, whereas the other distributions focus on particular classes of users. For example, Caldera OpenLinux apparently targets primarily small businesses to large enterprises, and Slackware Linux targets the veteran experts on UNIX or UNIX-like operating systems, but Red Hat targets both consumers and businesses.

Red Hat has succeeded in creating a great momentum for Linux. Because of its ease of installation, ease of configuration, and commercial support options, many people are running or considering Linux as an option. Even the biggest critics of Red Hat will credit the company with this achievement.

Efforts are under way to strengthen Red Hat Linux's position on all fronts. Red Hat has turned its official Web site (http://www.redhat.com) into a Linux portal to centralize all Linux happenings to a single Web-based source on the Internet. Because this is done in conjunction with other popular Linux Web sites, it is sure to become the single source of Linux information and software for millions of Linux users all around the world.

Such efforts are empowered by the involvement of various software and hardware giants such as IBM, HP, Informix Corporation, Oracle, Corel Corporation, SAP AG, Computer Associates International, Inc., and Intel. In fact, Compaq, IBM, Novell, and Oracle have taken equity positions in Red Hat to help bring Red Hat Linux to their customers. This should give you a good idea about where Red Hat is headed.

Now consider the benefits of the Red Hat Linux distribution. You get the most stable version of the Linux kernel, along with many GNU applications. Red Hat itself provides various configuration tools for both the X Window system and the character-based displays. The official Red Hat CD-ROMs also include various commercial applications that are either free for personal use or demo for commercial use.

Technical support has always been a big issue with corporations when it comes to software. Knowing that, Red Hat offers Response Link – a 24/7 technical support facility located at the company's headquarters. The available support packages include toll-free phone calls from anywhere in the U.S. and priority support services.

As you can see, Red Hat is in the Linux game for real and in a big way. It clearly offers the strongest, most viable distribution currently available in the market.

Red Hat Linux as a Server OS

In an ideal world, the best operating system wins all the server accounts. Unfortunately, we do not live in such a world. We live in a world where marketing is more important than the actual product. Many of us buy what we have heard of or know about from the media or by some other means. Most people are unsure about trying new ideas or backing one when their jobs are on the line. This truth allows a handful of operating system giants (you know who they are) to control the entire server market. Most IT managers are by default risk-averse even when the risk is slight. This reluctance to try the unknown is a big barrier for Linux to overcome if it is to become a giant in the server operating system market. Thanks to Red Hat, however, this attitude is changing rapidly. Because many computer giants have shown great interest in Red Hat Linux, it is becoming easier for IT professionals everywhere to put Linux in their proposals and even to try it out.

Those of us who are bold enough to try Linux as a server know that it is the ideal server platform. Like many people, I have run Linux servers for years with a very high degree of reliability. Many system administrators run Linux servers that have not been rebooted even once in over a year! That's how reliable Linux servers can be. The low cost, high reliability, and 24/7 support options makes Red Hat Linux a great server platform.

One of the reasons why Red Hat Linux excels over other server platforms such as Windows 2000 is that it takes advantage of the tried and proved software that the UNIX platform has to offer. For example, Red Hat Linux runs the most popular Web server, Apache, even though Apache was not primarily developed for Linux. Linux's strong ties with UNIX operating systems make it easy to port the greatest UNIX applications to Red Hat Linux much easier than to Windows 2000 (Windows NT). The granddaddy of SMTP mail server, sendmail, was ported to Red Hat Linux a long time ago. Server applications like these make Red Hat Linux a great choice. When you run the good old BIND DNS server on Linux, you know that the software has been around for a long time and therefore has a track record that you can count on.

Because Red Hat Linux runs virtually all great UNIX server applications, it automatically inherits many of the advantages of such software. This claim is one that Windows 2000 is not likely to be able to make. On top of this, it is often said that Linux does Windows platform–specific file services (SMB service) better than Windows platform itself! In other words, you are likely to create a more responsive and reliable file server from a Red Hat Linux system than from the Windows alternative.

You can also use economics to make your server platform decision easy to make. Using the Web and the Usenet as your research tool, find what kind of hardware that people (not the vendors) recommend to implement a server using anything other than Linux. The Windows 2000 hardware recommendation might scare a few people. You will find that RAM requirements are in triple digits of MB. The clock speed of the recommended CPU might be in multiple hundreds of MHz. Now some might argue that hardware prices have gone so low that these numbers won't scare many companies. This is true only if you are investing in a single server. What if you need to deploy several of these beasts to create an IT infrastructure? The figures soon add up and can hurt quite a bit. Also do not forget that many of the so-called commercial server operating systems have a hard limit on the number of users (or even network connections) that you can service using a license. And do not overlook the cost of maintenance and expensive support packages needed. When you add all these up, Red Hat Linux looks great.

A Red Hat Linux purchase gives you a great return on your hardware investment. Because Linux is primarily developed by people all around the world who do not always have the greatest and the latest hardware, it runs very well on even a very low-end system. This means that your hardware does not become obsolete as often as your hardware vendor wishes it. You can get a big bang for every hardware buck you have spent.

Hopefully you now know why Red Hat Linux can be a great server platform and you are eager to try it first hand. One of the most important things you must do as a future Red Hat Linux system administrator is to keep yourself up to date on developments in the Linux front. You can find out about many of the most commonly used Linux resources on the Internet in Appendix A.

The next step then is to get the Red Hat Linux distribution.

How to Get Red Hat Linux

You can acquire Red Hat Linux in any of several ways. For example, you can simply download Red Hat Linux from the official Red Hat Linux FTP server or any of its mirror FTP sites.

 TIP I never can get access to the Red Hat FTP server (`ftp://ftp.redhat.com`), as it appears to be very busy at all times. If your experience is the same, try `http://www.redhat.com/mirrors.html` for a list of mirror FTP sites near you.

If you have a fast Internet connection (that is, not a modem connection), you may want to download the latest version of Red Hat Linux that way.

The CD-ROM that accompanies this book includes Red Hat Linux 7.0. If this is still the latest version, go ahead and use it. If you find out that the enclosed Red Hat is not the latest version and you do not have a fast connection to the Internet, you can order the official Red Hat CD-ROM via Web, phone, or fax. Check the Red Hat Web site for details on how to place your order.

When you have a copy of the Red Hat Linux distribution, you are all set to proceed with installation, the subject of the next chapter.

Summary

In my personal experience, Red Hat Linux is a breath of fresh air because it is open-source, highly configurable, and very stable. Many users find that Red Hat Linux-based servers run even for years without needing a single reboot! That is a far cry from the NT environment, where daily or (if lucky) weekly or (if very lucky) monthly reboots are commonplace.

I hope you are now convinced that you have made the right decision and want to continue exploring and implementing the greatest server — Red Hat Linux server. Begin the journey by starting with the installation of Red Hat Linux in the next chapter. Good luck.

Chapter 2

Installation and Basic Configuration

IN THIS CHAPTER

- ◆ Understanding hardware requirements for Red Hat Linux
- ◆ How to prepare for installation
- ◆ How to install Red Hat Linux

IN THIS CHAPTER, you learn to install Red Hat Linux on your computer. Although Red Hat Linux runs on many hardware platforms, such as *x*86 PC clones, Alpha, and Sparc, I will focus on the *x*86-based installation because it is the dominant Linux platform. Installation tasks on other platforms vary slightly; you should consult the Red Hat Web site for the details (`http://www.redhat.com`).

Checking Your Hardware Requirements

From the beginning, Linux has required minimum hardware to run. This has not changed. Red Hat Linux runs on very minimal hardware, but just being able to run Linux is different than running it to create a server-class operation. To find out if your hardware is supported by Red Hat Linux, check the following Web site: `http://www.redhat.com/support/docs/rhl`.

Obviously, the better the hardware, the better the performance you get out of your Red Hat Linux system. However, be aware that all new hardware may not be supported right away! For example, if a video card with the fanciest features came out yesterday, do not expect it to be supported by Red Hat Linux tomorrow. Sometimes hardware manufacturers make it hard for Linux developers to get specific information needed to write driver modules, and hence it takes time for developers to support the latest features. After all, Linux is still primarily developed by loosely knit groups of people from all over the world, and not everyone has the time or financial support to try the latest hardware toys. The Red Hat company tries its best to support the newest gizmos, but even then it takes time. So the rule of thumb is to know what hardware others are using with Linux and how well it works. To find out how well a particular piece of hardware works with Red Hat Linux, you can check the hardware compatibility pages found in the preceding URL and also post your query to an appropriate Usenet Linux newsgroup. Describe the primary hardware you plan to use and see if anyone tells you any horror stories. Because this book is about creating a server-class Red Hat Linux system, here are some guidelines I often use to create such systems.

◆ CPU: The faster the better. However, buying the fastest processor available is not always necessary. For example, if all you want is to create a Web server running Apache on Red Hat Linux, you might want to consider a mid-range Pentium Pro or a lower-end Pentium II processor. No need to go out and get that Pentium III running at 400+ MHz. Of course, if you plan to run CPU-intensive applications via CGI or other means on the Web server, consider a very fast CPU; for most installations, a mid-range processor is the best choice.

◆ RAM: The more the merrier. This is one piece of hardware that you can go wild with and get as much as you can have. RAM is one of the most critical variables in the performance equation. That said, here is what I do when deciding how much RAM is needed for, say, a Web server. First decide how many requests you want to service per second. Sometimes it is hard to know this requests/second figure. Perhaps you have an idea about how many requests you want to be able to service per day. Say that you want the Web server to be able to service 3,456,000 requests/day. Now you can determine the requests/second figure as follows: 3,456,000 requests/day × 1 day/24 hours × 1 hour/3,600 seconds.

This gives you 40 requests/second. Now that you know how many requests/ second you will have, you also know that you need 40 Apache daemons to be able to service 40 requests simultaneously. In such a case your memory requirements for Apache alone would be 40 times the memory footprint of an Apache process.

This memory requirement could be approximately 40MB or more depending on how you configure Apache itself. For example, if you put the Perl interpreter inside Apache (mod_perl), add FastCGI support (mod_fastcgi), or add extra modules, each Apache process might require more memory. The more you know about your memory needs, the more intelligent you can be about your memory requirements. For most typical Web server deployment tasks, I personally recommend 256MB of fast 100-MHz (10 nanosecond) DRAM modules for newer computers.

◆ Hard Disk: How much hard disk space you need for your server is dictated by what you want to do with it. If you want the server to host a large number of files for your Web or LAN, determine the data size requirement and buy an appropriately sized hard disk. The size is really not the big issue, given that prices of large hard disks are falling on a regular basis.

However, what is important is the type of hard disk you choose for your server. You have two choices: IDE/EIDE or SCSI. If your server is going to be critical to your LAN or Internet operations, such as Web, FTP, or mail services, use multiple SCSI disks. SCSI provides much better throughput than its IDE/EIDE counterparts. I recommend use of wide SCSI hard disks that provide you approximately 20MB/sec performance. Using multiple wide-SCSI disks, you can minimize wait time inserted by your drive subsystem. In other words, when you use multiple SCSI disks, disk I/O-related bottlenecks can be reduced, which is a very good thing for a server. You might be tempted to get the ultra-wide SCSI disks and controllers, but be aware that appropriate drivers may not be available for the blazingly fast SCSI hardware you buy. Another important point about high-performance hard disks is that such disks may get hot really fast. Be sure to include appropriate cooling equipment; for instance, you can install extra fans in your unused drive bays to help reduce the risk of a disaster.

◆ Network Interface Card: A good server needs a good network interface card (NIC). Make sure you buy a high-performance NIC from a well-known vendor such as 3Com or Intel. Ideally, you want to get a card that allows you to disable Plug and Play (PNP) using a switch, since PNP does not quite work on Red Hat Linux just yet.

◆ Other hardware: Other important hardware includes a reasonably fast CD-ROM drive and a floppy disk drive. Most recent motherboards come with on-board IDE controllers and offer you the capability to connect four IDE devices. Because a CD-ROM is not frequently used on a server, you do not need the fastest one; just get one that works in the 10–20× speed range. Last but not least is the case. Make sure you get a server-class case and power supply for your system. I recommend that you get a case that comes with a redundant power supply and provides high wattage (300 watts or more).

Once you have your hardware ready for Red Hat Linux, you need to prepare for installation.

Preparing to Install Red Hat Linux

First, decide which Red Hat Linux you are going to use for your system. This book comes with the 7.*x* version of Red Hat Linux. If you are interested in installing the latest version of Red Hat, check the Red Hat Web site. If the version you have on the accompanying CD-ROM is still the latest, you can simply use this for your installation.

You can install Red Hat Linux via FTP, NFS, or SMB (Samba) services where the Red Hat CD-ROM is located in a remote computer. These methods are very error-prone. I highly recommend that you save time and effort by using a local CD-ROM drive and performing all installation tasks locally.

If you must install via FTP, NFS, or SMB services, make sure you have a local computer set up to provide the desired service and have the Red Hat CD-ROM mounted and exported for the intended Red Hat server computer. You could also make a copy of the entire Red Hat CD-ROM onto the hard disk to perform speedier installations.

Also note that you can install Red Hat from a DOS partition in your local hard disk. I recommend this type of installation if you cannot have a CD-ROM on the local system even for temporary installation tasks. Assuming that you have a way of accessing a remote computer on your LAN via NFS, SMB, FTP, or other means, do the following:

1. Create a RedHat directory in a partition that you will not use for your Red Hat Linux installation. In other words, say you have an MS-DOS partition that you would like to keep as is; use it for this purpose.

2. Create a subdirectory called base under the RedHat directory and copy the contents of the RedHat/base directory from the Red Hat CD-ROM on the remote computer.

3. Create another subdirectory called RPMS under the RedHat directory and copy the contents of the RedHat/RPMS directory from the Red Hat CD-ROM on the remote computer.

Because I think you can save a lot of trouble by doing a simple local CD-ROM-based install, I assume that you follow my advice and do just that. The rest of the chapter is based on this assumption.

The next step in preparing for a Red Hat Linux installation is to determine if you need a boot disk. If you bought the official Red Hat CD-ROM, you already have a boot disk and a supplementary disk supplied by Red Hat.

If you have a newer motherboard with a BIOS that supports booting the system from a CD-ROM, you do not need to use a boot disk. In this case, you have to recon-figure your BIOS setup to boot the system from the CD-ROM. Note that you need to change this setting (that is, booting from a CD-ROM) back to hard disk after you are done with installation. Most newer BIOS versions allow you to choose a chain of devices, from which they try to boot. For example, the BIOS may allow you to choose a sequence such as CD-ROM, C, A, which means that it tries to boot the system from the CD-ROM first, then from the hard disk, and finally from the A: floppy drive. Such an option allows you to keep the setting as is, because all you have to do to boot from the hard disk is to remove any CD-ROM from the CD-ROM drive.

On the other hand, if you use the CD-ROM accompanying this book as your dis-tribution, you need to make a boot disk from scratch. Here is how.

Creating a boot disk under MS Windows 9x/2000

You can create the boot disk under MS Windows 9*x*/2000 operating systems as follows:

1. Assuming your CD-ROM drive is called D: and you have the Red Hat CD-ROM mounted in the drive, run the following command from an MS-DOS shell window:

   `d:/dosutils/rawrite`

2. The `rawrite` utility will display the following prompt:

   `Enter disk image source file name:`

   `Please insert a formatted diskette into drive A: and press the enter key`

3. Enter \images\boot.img as the image source file. Now `rawrite` displays the following prompt.

   `Enter target diskette drive:`

4. Enter the appropriate drive letters. For example, if your floppy disk is in the A: drive, enter a: as the target drive.

5. Now you should put a blank, formatted floppy disk in the floppy drive and press Enter to continue.

6. The `rawrite` utility will write the boot.img image to the disk, and you are done.

 If you need to use a PCMCIA-based CD-ROM to install Red Hat Linux, you will also need to create a supplementary floppy disk using the technique just described. Enter only \images\supp.img as the image source filename in step 3.

Creating a boot disk under Linux

If you do not have an MS Windows system and would like to use another Linux system to create the boot disk, do the following:

1. Mount your Red Hat CD-ROM as usual. I assume that you have mounted it on /mnt/cdrom directory. Now change your current directory to the /mnt/cdrom/images directory where boot image is kept.

2. Assuming your floppy drive is /dev/fd0 (the default floppy device) and you are using a 1.44MB (3.5-inch, high-density) floppy disk, run the following command:

```
dd if=boot.img  of=/dev/fd0  bs=1440K
```

This should create the necessary boot disk. You can also create the supplementary floppy image disk by replacing the if=boot.img argument to if=supp.img in the preceding command. You only need the supplementary image for PCMCIA-based devices, which are typically used only on laptop/notebook computers.

Once you have created the boot disk, you are ready to install Red Hat Linux from the CD-ROM.

Installing Red Hat Linux

If you are booting the system from the CD-ROM, just insert your Red Hat CD in the drive and restart or start your intended server computer. In case you are using a boot floppy, insert it in the bootable floppy drive and restart or start the system.

When the system is booted, you will see a welcome screen from Red Hat. You will see a prompt such as this:

```
boot:
```

You have five choices.

◆ You can simply press the Enter key to start a normal installation or upgrade.

◆ Your second choice is to enter the word 'text' at the boot prompt to use text-based menu during installation or upgrade.

◆ The third choice is to enter the word "expert" at the boot prompt to perform the installation and upgrade in an expert user mode. In expert mode, the Red Hat installation program does not try to auto-detect your hardware but allows you to select various hardware components manually. You should choose to enter expert mode only if you are really an expert or having problem with auto-detection of certain hardware.

◆ The fourth choice is to enter "rescue" at the boot prompt. Use this option when you are trying to recover from a disaster. In such a case you need a rescue disk along with your standard boot disk. You can create the rescue disk in the same manner as you create the boot image disk or the supplementary image disk. Just replace the image filename with rescue.img in any of the boot image creation processes described previously.

♦ The fifth choice is to enter the word 'dd' if you are installing or upgrading a system that requires a special driver disk.

If you plan to perform an unattended installation where user interaction is not required, you can also enter `linux ks` at the boot: prompt. This allows the install program to use an installation mode called the Kickstart mode. This is a very advanced mode that requires that you create a custom configuration file called ks on the boot floppy disk or keep a file called *<IP address of the machine being set up>*-kickstart in the bootp server.

If you press the Enter key to start the default installation, Red Hat will use the X Windows System–based installation procedure. Since success of this installation process relies heavily on the quality of the video card and monitor that you use on the server system, I do not recommend this method for a server installation or upgrade tasks. Most people I know do not use a highend video card or monitor with a server system that is usually kept locked up in a rack or a server room. Also many times the default installation detected a very low, unusable resolution on many of the servers that I have experimented with.

Assuming that this is your first-time Red Hat Linux server install, the recommended option is to enter "text" at the boot prompt to start the installation process.

Understanding how the install program works

The installation program uses simple keys for navigation. You can use the up arrow, down arrow, Tab, spacebar, and Enter keys to do virtually all the work. You also have access to four virtual consoles, which you can select using the Alt+F1 through Alt+F4 keys. The default virtual console (Alt+F1) shows you the actual installation dialog windows, the second console (Alt+F2) gives a shell prompt where you enter commands, the third console (Alt+F3) displays the ongoing installation log messages, and the fourth console (Alt+F4) displays kernel messages.

Selecting a language, a keyboard, and an installation method

Once you have advanced past the initial greeting page, you are asked to choose the language you want to use; the default is English. Choose the appropriate language and press the Enter key to continue. The next screen asks you to select a keyboard type. The default is English. You can press Enter or select the appropriate keyboard type and continue. Press the Enter key again to continue past the greeting screen.

Choosing an installation type

Next, the install program offers you four installation type options – Workstation, Server System, Custom System, and Upgrade Existing Installation.

If you are planning on using the Red Hat Linux system as a personal workstation computer, you can choose the Workstation class. This option allows the installation program to remove all your existing Linux partitions and use the entire unpartitioned disk space to create a preconfigured system. The Workstation class system typically has a small swap partition (32MB) and a 16MB partition called /boot for kernel and related files. The rest of the unpartitioned disk space is used to create a single / (root) partition. Typically, you should have at least 600MB of disk space for a workstation class installation.

The second option is the Server class. This option is suitable for creating a server system. It uses a 64MB swap partition, a 16MB /boot partition for kernel and related files, a 256MB / (root) partition, a 512MB (or more) /usr partition for storing commonly used applications and utilities, a 512MB (or more) /home partition for user home directories, and a 256MB /var partition for system logs and queues. You should have approximately 1.6GB of disk space for such a system.

The third choice is the Custom class. This option enables you to choose whatever partitioning you want, using partitioning tools, and therefore is the most flexible. I use this option here.

After you have chosen the Custom class option, the installation program asks you to set up your disks.

Partitioning your disks

Partitioning your disks is a very important step, because you cannot safely change disk partitions without losing data. So be very careful with this step. The installation program displays the screen shown in Figure 2-1.

Here you are asked to choose a disk-partitioning tool. You have two choices — Disk Druid or the good old fdisk program.

The Disk Druid partitioning utility is more user-friendly than the fdisk program, so I recommend it for beginning users. Once you select this tool, your current disk partitions are displayed. Figure 2-2 shows a sample screen where the current disk partitions on my system are displayed.

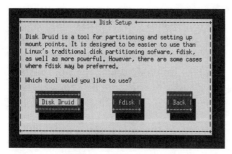

Figure 2-1: Choosing a disk-partitioning tool

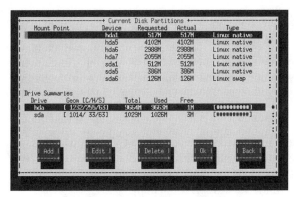

Figure 2-2: Viewing existing disk partitions

If you have partitions from your previous operating system such as MS Windows 9.x/NT, you can delete these partitions here or you can use unused partitions to create a dual-boot Red Hat Linux system. Because this book is dealing with a server installation as an example, assume that you only want to have Linux partitions. Study Figure 2-2 carefully and you can see the two disks in my system. These disks are named hda and sda. Red Hat Linux uses hdx (where x is a – z) for IDE disks and sdx (where x is a – z) for SCSI disks. Because my system has a single IDE hard disk, it is named hda; the single SCSI disk is named sda. If you have two IDE disks, they are named hda and hdb.

Red Hat Linux enables you to partition each disk, where each partition is labeled using the hd[a–z][N] scheme for IDE hard disks and sd[a–z][N] scheme for SCSI disks. Here N is the partition number. For example, hda1 is partition 1 on the first IDE disk, hda, and similarly, sda1 is the first partition of the first SCSI disk. You have to decide how you want to partition your disk(s.) Here are some pointers.

You need a / (root) partition to store your kernel and related files. This partition need not be very large. In fact, you can make it as small as 256MB, according to the Red Hat server class specification discussed earlier. Make sure that you choose Linux native as the partition type for the root partition.

Once you have decided the size of the / (root) partition, you need to decide on the size of the /usr partition. This is where all your applications will reside, so make sure this partition is fairly large. Your /usr partition should occupy at least 512MB. Make sure that you choose Linux native as the partition type for the /usr partition.

Next, you need to create a /home partition for user home directories. If you have a lot of users, you should decide how much space you want to allow per user, multiply it by the total number of users you expect to have, and create a suitable partition. Note that you can enforce a user's disk usage by adding disk quota support later. See Chapter 7 for details. Note that unlike the / directory or /usr directory, you can choose to name your user home partition anything you want. For example, if you are creating a Web server where you want to have a partition called /www for all user Web sites, you can also put user home directories under the same partition. In other words, you are not restricted to naming the partition /home. If you use a different name than /home as your user home partition, make sure you update the necessary configuration files for the useradd, userdel, usermod, and related programs (see Chapter 7 for details). Make sure that you choose Linux native as the partition type for the home directory partition.

Next, you should create a swap partition (partition type Linux swap) such that the partition size does not exceed twice the size of your physical RAM or 128MB, whichever is less. For example, if you have 32MB of RAM, you can create a 64MB swap partition.

If you have disks or disk space left, feel free to add as many extra partitions as you desire. Figure 2-3 shows the partitions I have chosen for my double-disk system.

Once you are done creating the partitions and mount-point assignments, you can select the OK button and continue with the next step.

Although I do not recommend the fdisk program for beginners, if you have chosen fdisk over Disk Druid, you see a screen showing all the available hard disks on your system, as shown in Figure 2-4.

![Current Disk Partitions screen]

Mount Point	Device	Requested	Actual	Type
/	hda1	517M	517M	Linux native
/www	hda5	4102M	4102M	Linux native
/intranet	hda6	2988M	2988M	Linux native
/usr	hda7	2055M	2055M	Linux native
/cdr	sda1	512M	512M	Linux native
/scratch	sda5	386M	386M	Linux native
	sda6	126M	126M	Linux swap

Drive Summaries
Drive	Geom [C/H/S]	Total	Used	Free	
hda	[1232/255/63]	9664M	9663M	1M	[##########]
sda	[1014/ 33/63]	1029M	1026M	3M	[#########]

[Add]   [Edit]   [Delete]   [Ok]   [Back]

Figure 2-3: A sample partition table

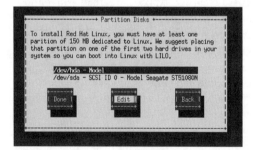

Figure 2-4: Choosing a hard disk to partition

Here you are given a chance to choose the hard disk you want to partition using the fdisk program. If you were to choose a hard disk and select the Edit option from the screen, you would see an interface such as the one shown in Figure 2-5.

```
This is the fdisk program for partitioning your drive. It is running
on /dev/hda.

The number of cylinders for this disk is set to 1232.
This is larger than 1024, and may cause problems with:
1) software that runs at boot time (e.g., LILO)
2) booting and partitioning software from other OSs
   (e.g., DOS FDISK, OS/2 FDISK)

Command (m for help): p

Disk /tmp/hda: 255 heads, 63 sectors, 1232 cylinders
Units = cylinders of 16065 * 512 bytes

  Device Boot    Start    End  Blocks    Id  System
/tmp/hda1           1     66  530113+   83  Linux native
/tmp/hda2          67   1232  9365895    5  Extended
/tmp/hda5          67    589  4200966   83  Linux native
/tmp/hda6         590    970  3060351   83  Linux native
/tmp/hda7         971   1232  2104483+  83  Linux native

Command (m for help): █
```

Figure 2-5: Using fdisk for partitioning disks

The fdisk program works with one disk at a time, and even though it provides a simple, inelegant user interface, it actually offers quite a bit more flexibility than the Disk Druid tool. Although I do not recommend fdisk for beginning users, it is worth taking a look at how fdisk works so that you can use it in a later time. Here I discuss some fdisk basics; if you are more interested in finishing up your install than learning about fdisk now, you can skip the rest of this section and go to the next section.

As you can see in Figure 2-5, fdisk has a simple, command prompt-oriented interface. It is also the default partitioning tool available after you have already installed Red Hat Linux. You can run fdisk from the command line using the following syntax:

```
fdisk hard disk device
```

For example:

```
fdisk /dev/sda
```

This command tells fdisk that you want to work on the first SCSI disk's partitions. Once you enter such a command, fdisk displays its command prompt "Command (m for help):" where you can enter m to get a help screen such as the following:

```
Command action
   a    toggle a bootable flag
   b    edit bsd disklabel
   c    toggle the dos compatibility flag
   d    delete a partition
   l    list known partition types
   m    print this menu
   n    add a new partition
   o    create a new empty DOS partition table
```

```
p    print the partition table
q    quit without saving changes
t    change a partition's system id
u    change display/entry units
v    verify the partition table
w    write table to disk and exit
x    extra functionality (experts only)
```

To view your existing partitions in the selected disk, enter p, which displays all your current partitions in a table format such as the following:

```
Disk /dev/sda: 33 heads, 63 sectors, 1014 cylinders
Units = cylinders of 2079 * 512 bytes

    Device Boot    Start      End    Blocks   Id  System
/dev/sda1              1      505    524916   83  Linux native
/dev/sda2            506     1014    529105+   5  Extended
/dev/sda5            506      886    396018   83  Linux native
/dev/sda6            887     1011    129906   82  Linux swap
```

As you can see here, the /dev/sda disk has been divided into four partitions, where the first partition is /dev/sda1, which starts at block 1 and ends at block 505. Each block is 1,024 bytes, or 1KB. So the first partition, /dev/sda1, consists of 524,916 blocks, or 524,916KB, or approximately 512MB.

To remove all existing partitions one by one, use the d command and enter the partition number you want to remove. Once you have removed one or more partitions, you can create new partitions as follows.

First, enter n as shown here to add a new partition:

```
Command (m for help): n
Command action
   e   extended
   p   primary partition (1-4)
```

You get two choices, as shown here. You can create either an extended partition or a primary partition. You need extended partitions only if you want to create more than four partitions. Because you only need /, /usr, /home, and a swap partition to get things going under Linux, you really do not need to create extended partitions. So create a primary partition by entering p at the prompt. The next prompt asks you to select a partition number:

```
Partition number (1-4): 1
```

Enter 1 for the first partition, 2 for the second, and so on. The next prompt asks you to select the starting block number. The range shown in the parentheses is the total blocks available for partitioning. If this is the first partition, you can choose 1 as the starting block as shown here:

```
First cylinder (1-1014): 1
```

To create a 512MB partition, you can enter the size in bytes, kilobytes, or megabytes. Because a value in megabytes is easy to deal with, I chose +512M for the last cylinder as shown here:

```
Last cylinder or +size or +sizeM or +sizeK ([1]-1014): +512M
```

Now to see if the partition has been created as requested, use the p command to see the partition information:

```
Disk /dev/sda: 33 heads, 63 sectors, 1014 cylinders
Units = cylinders of 2079 * 512 bytes

   Device Boot    Start      End    Blocks   Id  System
/dev/sda1                 1      505    524916   83  Linux native
```

As you can see, the first partition has been created as requested. The default partition type is Linux native; if you would like to change this, use the t command to toggle a partition's system ID flag. For example, to toggle a partition's system ID flag to Linux swap, I can use the following commands:

```
Command (m for help): t
Partition number (1-4): 1
Hex code (type L to list codes): 82
Changed system type of partition 1 to 82 (Linux swap)

Command (m for help): p

Disk /dev/sda: 33 heads, 63 sectors, 1014 cylinders
Units = cylinders of 2079 * 512 bytes

   Device Boot    Start      End    Blocks   Id  System
/dev/sda1                 1      505    524916   82  Linux swap
```

As you can see, I have first entered the t command to toggle the system ID of a partition and then selected the partition and entered 82 as the swap partition type. The l command can be used to list all the available partition types.

Note that if you use fdisk to create partitions, you must make a Linux native partition bootable. For example, to turn on /dev/sda1 as a bootable partition, I need to toggle the boot flag. At the prompt, I can enter the following:

```
Command (m for help): a
Partition number (1-6): 1
```

Now if I display the existing partition table using the p command, I see the following:

```
Disk /dev/sda: 33 heads, 63 sectors, 1014 cylinders
Units = cylinders of 2079 * 512 bytes

    Device Boot    Start      End    Blocks    Id  System
/dev/sda1    *         1      505    524916    83  Linux native
/dev/sda2             506     1014   529105+    5  Extended
/dev/sda5             506      886   396018    83  Linux native
/dev/sda6             887     1011   129906    82  Linux swap
```

As you can see, /dev/sda1 has "*" in the Boot column, showing that this partition is bootable.

Next, you are asked to pass any additional information to the kernel at boot, as shown in Figure 2-6.

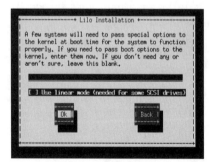

Figure 2-6: Adding kernel configuration options

In most cases, you do not need to provide any additional information here.

Selecting LILO installation options

As shown in Figure 2-7, you can install the Red Hat Linux boot loader either in the master boot record or in the first sector of the boot partition. If you have no other operating systems already installed, you can choose the master boot record. On the other hand, if you have an operating system already installed and want to keep it running, you will have to choose the first sector of the boot partition.

Figure 2-7: Selecting a location for LILO

 Remember that placing LILO in the master boot record gives LILO control over the boot process of your entire system. If you want to keep the system in a dual-boot setup with another operating system, chances are the other operating system has already installed its boot loader in the master boot record. So be careful about what you select here.

Next, you need to select the bootable partitions that you want LILO to manage. A dialog box such as Figure 2-8 displays all the partitions on your system (except for the swap) that can be used to boot operating systems, including Linux and others.

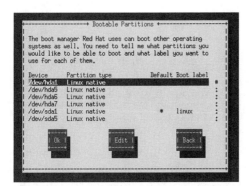

Figure 2-8: Configuring bootable partitions

The default bootable Red Hat Linux partition is marked with a "*" character. This partition is given a default boot label called "linux." In other words, when LILO starts up during the boot process, it allows you to type linux at the boot: prompt to boot Red Hat Linux. If you have another operating system coexisting on this system, you can select the partition it resides on and create a boot label for it. Select the partition involved and choose to edit the entry. You will see a dialog box similar to Figure 2-9.

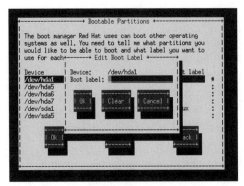

Figure 2-9: Configuring LILO boot labels

Enter the appropriate boot label name to identify the operating system easily. Once you are done editing the boot labels, select OK to continue.

Naming your server

Next the program asks you to enter a hostname for your server. This hostname should be a fully qualified name such as r2d2.nitec.com. In other words, you should have the host and the domain parts in the hostname. Select an appropriate hostname and press OK to continue.

Selecting mouse type

Next the program asks you to choose a mouse type as shown in Figure 2-10. If you do not plan on installing X Windows System or do not want to use a mouse you can leave the default as is and continue. If you are unsure about what type of mouse you have, keep the default as well.

Configuring the clock

Next, you are asked to configure the clock as shown in Figure 2-11.

If your (CMOS) hardware clock is set to Greenwich Mean Time (GMT), select the Hardware clock set to GMT option. Then choose the appropriate time zone the server resides in.

Figure 2-10: Configuring the mouse

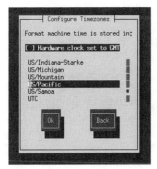

Figure 2-11: Configuring the clock

Setting a root password

The root account is the default superuser account on a Red Hat Linux system. You use this account to log into your new system. Figure 2-12 shows the root password entry dialog box.

Figure 2-12: Setting up the root user password

Choose a password for this account. You have to enter this password twice, and it is not displayed on the screen for security reasons. So make sure you know what you are typing as the password! Also do not forget to choose a good password. A good password is one that is not too easy to guess or crack. Do not ever use dictionary words in a password; always use one or more punctuation characters and numbers in the password. Also make sure you use a long password. Typically, anywhere from five to eight characters is acceptable.

Creating an optional user account

You can also create an optional user account if you wish in the next step. Since you can always create user accounts later with the useradd program, you can skip this step.

Configuring user authentication method

By default, Red Hat uses shadow passwords for user authentication. Typically, you do not need to change this method unless you are running a Network Information System (NIS), a Lightweight Directory Access Protocol (LDAP) server, or a Kerberos authentication server. If you run these types of external authentication server systems on your network, select the appropriate option to enable Red Hat Linux to authenticate users via the preferred method. In most cases you can use the default selection and move to the next step.

Selecting software to install

Next, the installation program asks you to choose packages, as shown in Figure 2-13.

Figure 2-13: Selecting components to install

For a server installation, you should select the server-related components; it is not a good idea to install everything on a server, because the more programs you have on the server, the more security holes they could create. I recommend installing only the components that you need to run on the server. However, you can always add or remove components later using the rpm command or the X Windows–based glint tool (see Chapter 23).

A server does not need to run the X Windows system, so you should not install any X Windows software unless you are curious and just want to see how it looks or works. In this sample installation process, I assume you don't install X Windows. See Chapter 22 for details on how you can install the X Windows system later.

If you would like to select individual packages with a component category, select the Select individual packages option. When you click the OK button, you see another screen, as shown in Figure 2-14.

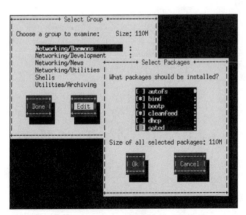

Figure 2-14: Selecting packages to install

To select packages within a component such as Networking/Daemons, select the component category and choose the Edit button, which will bring up the Select Packages dialog box shown in the preceding figure. Select the appropriate components. Once you have selected all the packages you want and unselected the packages you do not want, you can continue by clicking the OK button. The installation program displays a screen such as Figure 2-15.

This screen tells you that a complete installation log will be created in the /tmp/install.log file. Click the OK button to continue installation. The installation program displays a status screen, as shown in Figure 2-16.

If the status screen does not satisfy your curiosity, you can use the Alt+F1 to Alt+F4 keys to see exactly what the installation program is doing by switching to and from the virtual console. Once all the packages are installed, the installation program probes your system for a mouse.

Figure 2-15: Starting the installation process

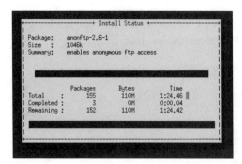

Figure 2-16: Installation in progress

Skipping X Windows System specifc configuration

The next few screens ask you about the monitor, video card, screen resolution, etc., which are configuration specific to X Windows System. I recommend that you accept the defaults and skip any probing requests by the installation program.

Creating a custom boot disk

As shown in Figure 2-17, the program asks you whether or not you want to create a custom boot disk.

Creating a boot disk should be mandatory because a custom boot disk is a must-have. It enables you to boot your system even if the boot loader program such as LILO fails to boot your system. You should not think twice about creating this disk.

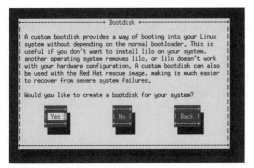

Figure 2-17: Choosing to create a custom boot disk

Use a brand new blank floppy disk to create the boot disk. This boot disk can be used in conjunction with the rescue disk that you can create using the rescue.img image. Note that if you decide to not create the custom boot disk only because you do not have a floppy handy, make sure you create it later using the mkbootdisk program.

The installation will complete with a dialog box shown in Figure 2-18.

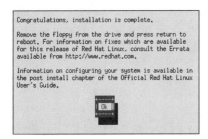

Figure 2-18: The installation completion message

Now you are ready to reboot the system for the first time. Remove the CD-ROM and any floppy disks from the drives and press OK to reboot.

Starting up Red Hat Linux for the first time

The system will reboot and display the boot prompt. You can either enter linux or press the Enter key to start Red Hat Linux for the first time. Of course, if you forget to do either, that's fine! LILO times out shortly afterwards and starts the default operating system – good old Linux!

Once the Linux kernel starts booting, you see a dialog box full of information. Do not despair if the information passes by too fast to read. You will have access to all this information soon. Be patient and let the system display a login prompt on the console.

Once the login prompt is displayed, log in as the user "root" using the password you entered earlier in the installation process. You should be logged into the system as root. Congratulations! You just became the superuser of your very own Red Hat Linux server. Your Linux system awaits your command.

If you want to see what went flying by during the bootup process, run the dmesg command to see the bootup messages. If the screen scrolls too much, use dmesg | more to see a page at a time.

 Linux has a feature not found in Microsoft-based systems: the capability to scroll back into the console's history. Shift+PageUp displays what just flashed by on your screen. But when you shift to a different virtual console, this history is lost. I've been frustrated by the fact that the login screen does a "clear screen" that destroys the last lines of the bootstrap display. For this reason, I suggest you modify /etc/inittab to refrain from running getty on virtual console 1. See Chapter 3 for details on how to modify /etc/inittab.

This is a good time to make sure the kernel detects your hardware as it should. Read the output of the dmesg program to find out. Now you are all ready to turn your new Red Hat Linux system into a full-blown Internet server.

Summary

In this chapter, you learned to install Red Hat Linux on your computer. I provided step-by-step guidelines to help you install this great operating system as painlessly as possible. There are many ways you can install Red Hat Linux on a system, but the most painless one involves a local CD-ROM and a boot disk. I recommended that you try the easy way because it is no fun to be stuck while installing an operating system. Hopefully, you are now up and ready to proceed with the rest of the book.

Part II

Working as a Superuser

Chapter 3

The Bootup and Shutdown Processes

IN THIS CHAPTER

- ◆ How to configure init
- ◆ How to boot up Linux
- ◆ How to shut down Linux
- ◆ How to manage init files

WHEN I FIRST STARTED using Linux back in the days when there was no Red Hat Linux, the very first thing I liked about Linux was the bootup process. I was tired of waiting for my Windows computers to go through the colorful logo screens and the dreaded blue screens without telling me what was going on. When a Windows computer fails to boot, you have to wear your Sherlock Holmes hat and investigate the cause from scratch. When a Linux computer fails to boot, however, you are likely to know where it got stuck, because the operating system displays virtually all the tasks it performs at bootup on the console. The same is true for the shutdown process. In Chapter 2 you learned about how the Linux kernel is booted from a floppy or a hard disk. Here you will learn how to customize the bootup and shutdown processes.

A Red Hat Linux kernel (that is, the core operating system) is typically stored in a compressed file. When the kernel is started by a boot loader program like LILO, it uncompresses itself, initializes the display device, and starts checking other hardware attached to your computer. As it finds your hard disks, floppy drives, network cards, and so forth, it loads the appropriate device driver modules. During this process it prints out text messages on your console screen. Listing 3-1 shows a shortened version of what my Red Hat 7.0 system displays during bootup.

Listing 3-1: Console messages during the bootup process

```
Linux version 2.2.16-21 (root@porky.devel.redhat.com) (gcc version
egcs-2.91.66 19990314/Linux (egcs-1.1.2 release)) #1 Wed Aug 9
11:45:35 EDT 2000
Detected 173424 kHz processor.
Console: colour VGA+ 80x25
```

```
Calibrating delay loop... 376.83 BogoMIPS
Memory: 63976k/66556k available (1020k kernel code, 416k reserved,
1080k data, 64k init, 0k bigmem)
Dentry hash table entries: 262144 (order 9, 2048k)
Buffer cache hash table entries: 65536 (order 6, 256k)
Page cache hash table entries: 16384 (order 4, 64k)
CPU: Intel Pentium III (Coppermine) stepping 01
Checking 386/387 coupling... OK, FPU using exception 16 error
reporting.
Checking 'hlt' instruction... OK.
POSIX conformance testing by UNIFIX
mtrr: v1.35a (19990819) Richard Gooch (rgooch@atnf.csiro.au)
PCI: PCI BIOS revision 2.10 entry at 0xfd880
PCI: Using configuration type 1
PCI: Probing PCI hardware
Linux NET4.0 for Linux 2.2
Based upon Swansea University Computer Society NET3.039
NET4: Unix domain sockets 1.0 for Linux NET4.0.
NET4: Linux TCP/IP 1.0 for NET4.0
IP Protocols: ICMP, UDP, TCP, IGMP
TCP: Hash tables configured (ehash 65536 bhash 65536)
Initializing RT netlink socket
Starting kswapd v 1.5
Detected PS/2 Mouse Port.
Serial driver version 4.27 with MANY_PORTS MULTIPORT SHARE_IRQ
enabled
pty: 256 Unix98 ptys configured
apm: BIOS version 1.2 Flags 0x03 (Driver version 1.13)
Real Time Clock Driver v1.09
RAM disk driver initialized:  16 RAM disks of 4096K size
PIIX4: IDE controller on PCI bus 00 dev 39
PIIX4: not 100% native mode: will probe irqs later
    ide0: BM-DMA at 0xfcf0-0xfcf7, BIOS settings: hda:DMA, hdb:pio
    ide1: BM-DMA at 0xfcf8-0xfcff, BIOS settings: hdc:DMA, hdd:pio
hda: IBM-DARA-212000, ATA DISK drive
hdc: MATSHITADVD-ROM SR-8174, ATAPI CDROM drive
ide0 at 0x1f0-0x1f7,0x3f6 on irq 14
ide1 at 0x170-0x177,0x376 on irq 15
hda: IBM-DARA-212000, 11509MB w/418kB Cache, CHS=1559/240/63
Floppy drive(s): fd0 is 1.44M
FDC 0 is a National Semiconductor PC87306
md driver 0.90.0 MAX_MD_DEVS=256, MAX_REAL=12
raid5: measuring checksumming speed
raid5: MMX detected, trying high-speed MMX checksum routines
    pII_mmx   :  1439.418 MB/sec
```

```
   p5_mmx    :  1511.808 MB/sec
   8regs     :  1112.901 MB/sec
   32regs    :   623.697 MB/sec
using fastest function: p5_mmx (1511.808 MB/sec)
scsi : 0 hosts.
scsi : detected total.
md.c: sizeof(mdp_super_t) = 4096
Partition check:
 hda: hda1 hda2 hda3 hda4
autodetecting RAID arrays
autorun ...
... autorun DONE.
Freeing unused kernel memory: 64k freed
Adding Swap: 264592k swap-space (priority -1)
```

If you are at the console when booting your system, you can press Shift+PageUp to scroll back the display to view boot messages. You can also view the boot messages at any time by running the dmesg program. The /var/log/messages files will also have many of the boot messages.

At this point, the kernel will mount the root file system (/) as read only and perform checks on the file system. If everything turns out to be okay, the root file system will be typically mounted as read/write.

If a problem arises and the kernel fails to mount the root partition or finds a severe problem with it, the kernel will panic and the system will halt. If the disk became corrupt for some reason, the kernel might provide you an option to run a file system checker program such as fsck.ext2 from a restricted shell.

Once the root file system is mounted, the kernel starts a program called init. This program starts all other programs. Once init completes running all the necessary programs, the system is up and running and the boot process is complete.

What init runs as part of the bootup process is highly customizable. I will cover init in detail in the following sections.

Configuring init

As mentioned before, init is the very first program that the kernel runs at the end of the boot sequence. The init program is available in two flavors — a UNIX System V-ish init or a BSD-ish init. The Red Hat distribution comes with the UNIX System V-flavored init. The difference between the two flavors is that System V-ish init uses run levels (discussed later in this section) and the BSD-ish init does not. Hence all the discussion about init will be limited to UNIX System V-ish init.

Since init is the first program run by the kernel, its process ID (PID) is 1. When it starts up, init reads a configuration file called /etc/inittab. The /etc/inittab file in a typical Red Hat Linux system is shown in Listing 3-2.

Listing 3-2: A typical /etc/inittab file

```
#
# inittab - This file describes how the INIT process should
#           set up the system in a certain run-level.
#
# Author: Miquel van Smoorenburg,
#           <miquels@drinkel.nl.mugnet.org>
#
# Modified for RHS Linux by Marc Ewing and Donnie Barnes
#

# Default runlevel. The runlevels used by RHS are:
#   0 - halt (Do NOT set initdefault to this)
#   1 - Single-user mode
#   2 - Multi-user, without NFS (The same as 3, if you
#                                do not have networking)
#   3 - Full multi-user mode
#   4 - unused
#   5 - X11
#   6 - reboot (Do NOT set initdefault to this)
#
id:3:initdefault:

# System initialization.
si::sysinit:/etc/rc.d/rc.sysinit

l0:0:wait:/etc/rc.d/rc 0
l1:1:wait:/etc/rc.d/rc 1
l2:2:wait:/etc/rc.d/rc 2
l3:3:wait:/etc/rc.d/rc 3
l4:4:wait:/etc/rc.d/rc 4
l5:5:wait:/etc/rc.d/rc 5
```

```
l6:6:wait:/etc/rc.d/rc 6

# Things to run in every runlevel.
ud::once:/sbin/update

# Trap CTRL-ALT-DELETE
ca::ctrlaltdel:/sbin/shutdown -t3 -r now

# When our UPS tells us power has failed, assume we have
# a few minutes of power left. Schedule a shutdown for
# 2 minutes from now.
#
# This does, of course, assume you have powerd installed and your
# UPS connected and working correctly.
#
pf::powerfail:/sbin/shutdown -f -h +2 "Power Failure; \
System Shutting Down"

# If power was restored before the shutdown kicked in, cancel it.
pr:12345:powerokwait:/sbin/shutdown -c "Power Restored; \
Shutdown Cancelled"

# Run gettys in standard runlevels
1:12345:respawn:/sbin/mingetty tty1
2:2345:respawn:/sbin/mingetty tty2
3:2345:respawn:/sbin/mingetty tty3
4:2345:respawn:/sbin/mingetty tty4
5:2345:respawn:/sbin/mingetty tty5
6:2345:respawn:/sbin/mingetty tty6

# Run xdm in runlevel 5
# xdm is now a separate servicex:5:respawn:/usr/bin/X11/prefdm -
nodaemon
```

This file defines how init behaves during server startup or shutdown events. Let's take a closer look at this file.

The init program ignores all of the blank and comment lines (that is, lines that start with a "#" sign) in the /etc/inittab file. The lines with colon-delimited fields are the init configuration lines. The syntax for such a line is as follows:

id:runlevels:action:process [arguments]

The first field is a unique label field to identify an entry in the file. An id can be 2–4 characters long. The second field (*runlevels*) defines which run levels this line applies to. The third field defines the action to be done, and the last field (*process*) defines the process to be run. You can also optionally specify command-line arguments for the process in the fourth field.

As mentioned before, a run level specifies a state of the system. The nine run levels are shown in Table 3-1.

TABLE 3-1 THE RUN LEVELS FOR INIT

Run Level	Description
0	Halt — used to halt the system
1	Single-user — used to set the system in a minimal configuration suitable for a single user
2	Not used
3	Multiuser — used to set the system in a configuration that supports multiple users
4	Not used
5	Used to start X Window System and the xdm, kdm, or gdmprograms via /etc/X11/prefdm script
6	Reboot — used to reboot the system
S or s	Used internally by scripts that run in run level 1
a, b, c	On-demand run levels — typically not used

Note that you can specify multiple run levels in a single init configuration line. For example, if you want init to run a process for both single-user and multiuser modes, you can specify a line such as:

```
id:13:action:process [arguments]
```

Table 3-2 shows possible actions.

TABLE 3-2 POSSIBLE ACTIONS FOR A SPECIFIC RUN LEVEL

Action	Description
Respawn	The process restarts whenever it terminates.
Wait	The process runs once and init will wait until it terminates.

Action	Description
Once	The process runs once.
Boot	The process runs during system boot and init ignores the run level field.
Bootwait	The process runs during system boot and init waits for the process to terminate.
Off	No action is taken. You can use off to disable a configuration line without removing it. However, you can just comment out the line with a leading "#" character instead.
Ondemand	Useful only when the run level is a, b, or c. The process runs whenever init is called with any of the three ondemand run levels. Typically not used.
initdefault	Sets the default run level for the system. The process field is ignored.
sysinit	The process runs once during system boot. A sysinit action takes precedence over boot or bootwait actions.
powerwait	The process runs when init receives a SIGPWR signal. Typically Uninterruptible Power Supply (UPS) monitoring software detects a power problem and issues such a signal to init. In such a case init waits until the process terminates.
powerfail	Same as powerwait, but init does not wait for the process to complete.
powerokwait	The process runs when init receives a SIGPWR signal and a text file called /etc/powerstatus contains an "OK" string. Typically, a UPS monitoring program creates this file and sends the SIGPWR signal to init to indicate that the power problem has been fixed.
ctrlaltdel	The process runs when init receives a SIGINT signal.
kbrequest	The process runs when init receives a KeyboardSignal from the keyboard handler.

The System V flavor of init, which is what Red Hat Linux init is, uses the following directory structure:

```
/etc
 +-rc.d
   +-init.d (dir)
   +-rc0.d  (dir)
```

```
+-rc1.d  (dir)
+-rc2.d  (dir)
+-rc3.d  (dir)
+-rc4.d  (dir)
+-rc5.d  (dir)
+-rc6.d  (dir)
+-rc.sysinit  (script)
+-rc.local    (optional script, supplied with Red Hat Linux)
+-rc.serial   (optional script)
+-rc (script)
```

The /etc/rc.d/rc.sysinit script

As you already know, when a Red Hat Linux system boots, the kernel runs init, which in turns runs the /etc/rc.d/rc.sysinit script before processing any other scripts for the desired run level. It runs this script before anything else because of the following line in the /etc/inittab file:

```
si::sysinit:/etc/rc.d/rc.sysinit
```

Notice that the run level field is empty because init recognizes sysinit as a system initialization action. The rc.sysinit script does many things, including setting the host name, enabling the swap partition, checking the file systems, loading kernel modules, and more. Typically, you do not need to modify this script.

The /etc/rc.d/init.d directory

The init.d subdirectory stores all the scripts needed for all the run levels. Keeping all the scripts in one location makes it easier to manage them. Each script starts/stops a particular service – the Domain Name Service (DNS), the Web service, or the like. All of these scripts follow a special command-line argument syntax. For example, to start the Network File System (NFS) service, you can run the following script:

```
/etc/rc.d/init.d/nfs start
```

To stop the same service, you can run the same script as follows:

```
/etc/rc.d/init.d/nfs stop
```

As you can see, the nfs script takes start and stop as arguments. This is true for all the scripts in this directory, which are symbolically linked to the rc[0–6].d directories as needed.

The /etc/rc.d/rc script

When init is told to change run level to one of the seven commonly used run levels, it runs a script specified in one of the following lines in the /etc/inittab file:

```
l0:0:wait:/etc/rc.d/rc 0
l1:1:wait:/etc/rc.d/rc 1
l2:2:wait:/etc/rc.d/rc 2
l3:3:wait:/etc/rc.d/rc 3
l4:4:wait:/etc/rc.d/rc 4
l5:5:wait:/etc/rc.d/rc 5
l6:6:wait:/etc/rc.d/rc 6
```

As you can see, for each run level (0-6) a script called /etc/rc.d/rc is run with the run level as the argument to the script. This script is responsible for starting and stopping all the services for the desired run level. For example, say that init is told to change the run level to 3. It runs the /etc/rc.d/rc script with an argument of 3 in a command line similar to this one:

```
/etc/rc.d/rc 3
```

The /etc/rc.d/rc script is shown in Listing 3-3.

Listing 3-3: The script /etc/rc.d/rc

```
#!/bin/bash
#
# rc            This file is responsible for starting/stopping
#               services when the runlevel changes. It is also
#               responsible for the very first setup of basic
#               things, such as setting the hostname.
#
# Original Author:
#               Miquel van Smoorenburg,
<miquels@drinkel.nl.mugnet.org>
#

# Source function library.
. /etc/init.d/functions

# Now find out what the current and what the
# previous runlevel are.
argv1="$1"
set `/sbin/runlevel`
```

```
runlevel=$2
previous=$1
export runlevel previous

# See if we want to be in user confirmation mode
if [ "$previous" = "N" ]; then
    if grep -i confirm /proc/cmdline >/dev/null || [ -f
/var/run/confirm ] ; then
        rm -f /var/run/confirm
        CONFIRM=yes
        echo "Entering interactive startup"
    else
        CONFIRM=
        echo "Entering non-interactive startup"
    fi
fi

# Get first argument. Set new runlevel to this argument.
[ -n "$argv1" ] && runlevel="$argv1"

# Tell linuxconf what runlevel we are in
[ -d /var/run ] && echo "/etc/rc$runlevel.d" > /var/run/runlevel.dir

# Is there an rc directory for this new runlevel?
if [ -d /etc/rc$runlevel.d ]; then
    # First, run the KILL scripts.
    for i in /etc/rc$runlevel.d/K*; do
        # Check if the script is there.
        [ ! -f $i ] && continue

        # Don't run [KS]??foo.{rpmsave,rpmorig} scripts
        [ "${i%.rpmsave}" != "${i}" ] && continue
        [ "${i%.rpmorig}" != "${i}" ] && continue
        [ "${i%.rpmnew}" != "${i}" ] && continue

        # Check if the subsystem is already up.
        subsys=${i#/etc/rc$runlevel.d/K??}
        [ ! -f /var/lock/subsys/$subsys ] && \
            [ ! -f /var/lock/subsys/${subsys}.init ] && continue

        # Bring the subsystem down.
        if egrep -q "(killproc |action )" $i ; then
            $i stop
```

```
        else
            action "Stopping $subsys: " $i stop
        fi
    done

    # Now run the START scripts.
    for i in /etc/rc$runlevel.d/S*; do
        # Check if the script is there.
        [ ! -f $i ] && continue

        # Don't run [KS]??foo.{rpmsave,rpmorig} scripts
        [ "${i%.rpmsave}" != "${i}" ] && continue
        [ "${i%.rpmorig}" != "${i}" ] && continue
        [ "${i%.rpmnew}" != "${i}" ] && continue

        # Check if the subsystem is already up.
        subsys=${i#/etc/rc$runlevel.d/S??}
        [ -f /var/lock/subsys/$subsys ] || \
            [ -f /var/lock/subsys/${subsys}.init ] && continue

        # If we're in confirmation mode, get user confirmation
        [ -n "$CONFIRM" ]  &&
          {
            confirm $subsys
            case $? in
              0)
                :
              ;;
              2)
                CONFIRM=
              ;;
              *)
                continue
              ;;
            esac
          }

        # Bring the subsystem up.
        if egrep -q "(daemon |action )" $i ; then
            $i start
        else
            if [ "$subsys" = "halt" -o "$subsys" = "reboot" -o
"$subsys" = "single" -o "$subsys" = "local" ]; then
```

```
                    $i start
            else
                action "Starting $subsys: " $i start
            fi
        fi
    done
fi
```

This script primarily does the following things:

1. It checks to see if a subdirectory exists for the run level specified in the argument. In other words, if the script runs with an argument of 3, it checks to see if the /etc/rc.d/rc3.d/ directory exists or not. If it exists, the script continues to the next step.

2. In this step the script determines whether or not any of the programs (often called services) that are supposed to run in the new run level are already running. If a service is already running, the script kills the service so that it can restart it in the next step. To kill a running service, the script runs the necessary "K" script with the "stop" argument.

3. In this final step the rc script runs all the "S" scripts with the "start" argument.

The /etc/rc.d/rc[0–6].d directories

The rc0.d to rc6.d subdirectories are used for run levels 0 to 6. These directories contain symbolic links to scripts in the /etc/rc.d/init.d directory. Take a look at the rc3.d directory in my Red Hat Linux 7.0 system. This directory lists the symbolic links shown in Listing 3-4.

Listing 3-4: A directory listing of /etc/rc.d/rc3.d of my Red Hat Linux system

```
lrwxrwxrwx  15 Aug 17 06:18 K01pppoe -> ../init.d/pppoe
lrwxrwxrwx  13 Aug 17 06:15 K20nfs -> ../init.d/nfs
lrwxrwxrwx  15 Aug 17 06:18 K20rwhod -> ../init.d/rwhod
lrwxrwxrwx  13 Aug 22 21:04 K35smb -> ../init.d/smb
lrwxrwxrwx  18 Aug 17 06:03 K45arpwatch -> ../init.d/arpwatch
lrwxrwxrwx  15 Aug 17 06:12 S05kudzu -> ../init.d/kudzu
lrwxrwxrwx  18 Aug 17 06:09 S08ipchains -> ../init.d/ipchains
lrwxrwxrwx  17 Aug 17 06:03 S10network -> ../init.d/network
lrwxrwxrwx  16 Aug 17 06:02 S12syslog -> ../init.d/syslog
lrwxrwxrwx  17 Aug 17 06:16 S13portmap -> ../init.d/portmap
lrwxrwxrwx  17 Aug 17 06:15 S14nfslock -> ../init.d/nfslock
lrwxrwxrwx  14 Aug 17 06:02 S16apmd -> ../init.d/apmd
lrwxrwxrwx  16 Aug 17 06:03 S20random -> ../init.d/random
```

```
lrwxrwxrwx  15 Aug 17 06:03 S25netfs -> ../init.d/netfs
lrwxrwxrwx  16 Aug 17 06:16 S35identd -> ../init.d/identd
lrwxrwxrwx  13 Aug 17 06:03 S40atd -> ../init.d/atd
lrwxrwxrwx  15 Aug 17 06:02 S40crond -> ../init.d/crond
lrwxrwxrwx  16 Aug 17 06:12 S45pcmcia -> ../init.d/pcmcia
lrwxrwxrwx  16 Aug 22 20:52 S50xinetd -> ../init.d/xinetd
lrwxrwxrwx  20 Aug 17 06:03 S56rawdevices -> ../init.d/rawdevices
lrwxrwxrwx  13 Aug 17 06:14 S60lpd -> ../init.d/lpd
lrwxrwxrwx  18 Aug 17 06:03 S75keytable -> ../init.d/keytable
lrwxrwxrwx  14 Aug 17 06:09 S80isdn -> ../init.d/isdn
lrwxrwxrwx  18 Aug 17 06:19 S80sendmail -> ../init.d/sendmail
lrwxrwxrwx  13 Aug 17 06:09 S85gpm -> ../init.d/gpm
lrwxrwxrwx  23 Aug 22 19:53 S90vmware -> /etc/rc.d/init.d/vmware
lrwxrwxrwx  13 Aug 17 06:03 S90xfs -> ../init.d/xfs
lrwxrwxrwx  17 Aug 17 06:02 S95anacron -> ../init.d/anacron
lrwxrwxrwx  19 Aug 17 06:14 S99linuxconf -> ../init.d/linuxconf
lrwxrwxrwx  11 Aug 17 06:03 S99local -> ../rc.local
```

Notice that scripts from the /etc/rc.d/init.d directory are linked two ways. Some scripts are linked as:

```
K{two-digit number}{script name}
```

Other scripts are linked as:

```
S{two-digit number}{script name}
```

All the scripts prefixed with a letter "K" run with the "stop" argument, and the other kind run with the "start" argument. The two-digit number is used to set the execution order. Thus a script called S01foo runs before S10bar. The /etc/rc.d/rc script runs the "S" and "K" scripts.

Once the rc script is finished, the processing done by init also finishes and the system becomes available in the new run level.

The /etc/rc.d/rc.local script

The rc.local script is typically run once at the end of the run levels 2, 3, and 5. You can add anything that needs to be run once per boot in this file.

The /etc/rc.d/rc.serial script

Like the rc.local script, rc.serial is typically run once at the end of run level 1 or 3 to initialize serial ports.

Now let's look at what init does when a system is started.

Booting Up Your System

During the bootup process, init first runs the rc.sysinit script and then runs the script for the default run level. Set the default run level in /etc/inittab using a line such as the following:

```
id:3:initdefault:
```

Here the default run level is set to 3. This means that init runs the script needed to put the system in multiuser mode.

If you take a second look at Listing 3-2, you will notice that the following line specifies what rc script needs to be run for run level 3.

```
l3:3:wait:/etc/rc.d/rc 3.
```

The rc script is run with an argument of 3. As mentioned before, this script runs all the scripts whose names start with "S" in the /etc/rc.d/rc3.d directory. It also supplies "start" as an argument to each of the "S"-prefixed scripts. When all the "S" scripts are run, the rc script finishes and the system becomes available in the default run level.

You can override the default run level at the LILO prompt. For example, if you want to boot the system in single-user mode, specify linux single to boot in single-user mode. If you use a label other than "linux" to boot Linux, you have to specify yourlabel single instead, where yourlabel is the name of the appropriate label.

Now let's look at how init works during a system shutdown event.

Shutting Down Your System

You can run init manually and tell it to change system run level by providing the desired run level in the command line. For example,

```
init 1
```

tells init to change current run level to 1. In other words, this instruction halts the system. If you are running in a multiuser mode (run level 3), the preceding command is less than ideal, because it does not inform the users on the system that the system is going to halt.

Typically, the shutdown command is used to shut down a system. It broadcasts a warning message to all logged-in users that the system is changing run level. It also provides you with an option to schedule the shutdown event.

The shutdown command works by telling init to change the current run level of the system to either halt (0) or reboot (6). For example,

```
shutdown -h now
```

This command signals init to change run level to 0 (halt) immediately.

Canceling a shutdown

The shutdown command enables you to schedule a shutdown event at a later time. For example,

```
shutdown +10
```

schedules a shutdown exactly 10 minutes after the command is entered at the shell prompt. Now a need might arise to cancel the shutdown event; in such a case you issue another shutdown command with a -c option. For example,

```
shutdown -c
```

cancels any scheduled shutdown event.

Rebooting your server

You can also run init manually to reboot your server. For example:

```
init 6
```

If you are running in a multiuser mode (run level 3), this command is not the best approach, because it does not inform the users on the system that system is going to reboot. Instead, you can use the shutdown command to reboot the server. For example:

```
shutdown -r +10
```

This command reboots the server in 10 minutes. All the users receive a message saying that the system is going to reboot shortly. This allows them to finish up and save their work.

When you use a delayed shutdown command like the one just described, the users who are logged in see the warning message it broadcasts, but shutdown does not prevent anyone from logging in during the shutdown countdown period. In order to prevent new logins, you can create a text file called /etc/nologin with an appropriate message stating that a shutdown has already been scheduled and people should try to log in at a later time. Do not forget to rename or delete the file after you reboot. If you are remotely rebooting a server, be absolutely sure to remove or rename this file prior to the actual shutdown. No normal user accounts are allowed to log in when this file is present. In fact you might want to add rm –f /etc/nologin at the end of the /etc/rc.local script and make sure that init runs it at the end of run level 3.

To reboot immediately, you can run:

```
shutdown -r  now
```

Rebooting using Ctrl+Alt+Delete

If you are on the system console, you can use the traditional Ctrl+Alt+Del key combination to reboot your server. This is possible because of the following line in /etc/inittab:

```
ca::ctrlaltdel:/sbin/shutdown -t3 -r now
```

This line allows init to trap the Ctrl+Alt+Del key combination and call the shutdown script to reboot immediately.

 Anyone who has physical access to your system console can shut down the system by pressing the Ctrl+Alt+Delete keys. To protect yourself from such a shutdown, you can create a file called /etc/shutdown.allow that will contain a list of users (one username per line) who are allowed to shut down the system. The root account does not need to be listed in this file.

Automatic shutdown on power failure

If you use a UPS to provide backup power for your system, you can use init to shut down the system gracefully when your UPS power is nearly drained. The default /etc/inittab includes the following line:

```
pf::powerfail:/sbin/shutdown -f -h +2 "Power Failure; \
System Shutting Down"
```

This line tells init to run shutdown in case of a power failure. The powerfail action is activated when a UPS program or powerd (a power monitoring daemon) sends the SIGPWR signal to init. The default setting allows the system to run on UPS power for two minutes before it halts. If your UPS is capable of sustaining power for a greater or lesser time, you should modify this value.

Because it is quite possible for power to come back before your UPS power is reasonably drained, init can be called to cancel a previously scheduled shutdown event. Do this with the following line in /etc/inittab:

```
pr:12345:powerokwait:/sbin/shutdown -c "Power Restored; \
Shutdown Cancelled"
```

When init receives a SIGPWR signal and a file called /etc/powerstatus contains an "OK" string in it, the powerokwait action is activated.

Managing init Files

As you already know, System V-ish init uses a lot of files, symbolic links, and directories. To simplify management of init files, a few tools are available. I discuss two such commonly used tools.

Using chkconfig to manage run levels

The chkconfig utility enables you to maintain the various symbolic links necessary for starting/stopping services in a run level. It can manage run level configuration for all the scripts in the /etc/rc.d/init.d directory. Here is how it works.

LISTING MANAGEABLE SERVICES
To view the services that will start or stop and in which run levels, run the following command:

```
chkconfig --list
```

This command lists all the chkconfig manageable services and tells you which services are going to be started (on) or stopped (off) for each run level. You can also check the run level configuration for a particular service by specifying the service name (that is, the script name in /etc/rc.d/init.d) in the command line. For example:

```
chkconfig --list httpd
```

The preceding command shows the following output in my Red Hat Linux server:

```
httpd 0:off 1:off 2:off 3:on 4:on 5:on 6:off
```

As you can see, the httpd service is on for run levels 2, 3, 4, and 5, and off for 0, 1, and 6.

ADDING A NEW SERVICE

If you just added a new script in the /etc/rc.d/init.d directory and want to make the service it offers available for a particular run level, you can run the chkconfig command as follows:

```
chkconfig --add service_name [--level runlevel]
```

For example:

```
chkconfig --add named
```

This command adds a service called named to the current run level. In other words, it creates a symbolic link that has an S {two-digit number} prefix in the current run level directory pointing to the /etc/rc.d/init.d/named script. If you want to add the service to a different run level than the current one, you can specify the run level with --level option. For example:

```
chkconfig --level 4 --add named
```

This command adds the named service to run level 4.

DELETING AN EXISTING SERVICE

To remove an existing service from a run level, use the following command:

```
chkconfig --del service_name [--level runlevel]
```

For example:

```
chkconfig --del named
```

This command removes the named service from the current run level. To remove the service from a different run level than the current one, use the --level option. For example:

```
chkconfig --del named --level 5
```

This command removes the named service from run level 5.

Using ntsysv to manage run levels

The `ntsysv` utility enables you to turn on/off various services in any run levels using a simple menu interface. When you run the command without any argument, it displays a screen similar to the one shown in Figure 3-1.

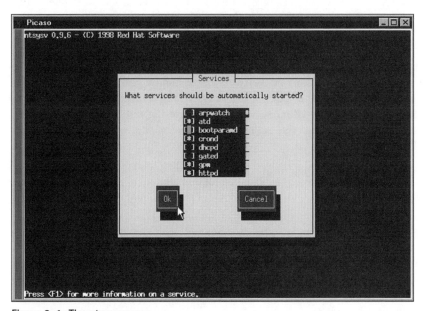

Figure 3-1: The ntsysv screen

The scrollable screen shows the state of all the services in the current run level. To turn on a service, you need to select it; to turn off a service, you just deselect it. Once you have made all the changes, you can save the changes by clicking the OK button or you can abort your changes by clicking the Cancel button. If you want to work on a different run level configuration, just supply the run level with the --level option. For example:

```
ntsysv --level 1
```

This command lets you work on the run level 1 configuration.

Using linuxconf to manage run levels

You can also use the linuxconf tool to configure run levels. Follow these instructions:

1. Select the Control → Control Panel → Control Service activity option.

2. Enable or disable one or more services.

3. Accept the changes.

4. Activate the changes before you quit linuxconf.

Creating a new service for a run level

If you install server software packages from well-known vendors, most likely they will provide you with a nice RPM package that also includes the necessary service script to go in /etc/rc.d/init.d. Sometimes, however, you find useful software that does not come with all the bells and whistles, and you end up customizing it or at least modifying how it works on your system. In such a case, you might need to create a service script for your new software. Here I show you how you can easily create a new service script that goes in the /etc/rc.d/init.d directory.

First take a look at an existing service script from the /etc/rc.d/init.d directory. Listing 3-5 shows one such script called httpd. This script is used to start/stop the Apache Web server.

Listing 3-5: /etc/rc.d/init.d/httpd

```
#!/bin/sh
#
# Startup script for the Apache Web Server.
#
# chkconfig: 345 85 15
# description: Apache is a World Wide Web server.  \
#              It is used to serve HTML files and CGI.
# processname: httpd
# pidfile: /var/run/httpd.pid
# config: /etc/httpd/conf/httpd.conf

# Source function library.
. /etc/rc.d/init.d/functions

# See how we were called.
case "$1" in
  start)
     echo -n "Starting httpd: "
     daemon httpd
```

```
        echo
        touch /var/lock/subsys/httpd
        ;;
    stop)
        echo -n "Shutting down http: "
        [ -f /var/run/httpd.pid ] && {
            kill `cat /var/run/httpd.pid`
            echo -n httpd
        }
        echo
        rm -f /var/lock/subsys/httpd
        rm -f /var/run/httpd.pid
        ;;
    status)
        status httpd
        ;;
    restart)
        $0 stop
        $0 start
        ;;
    reload)
        echo -n "Reloading httpd: "
        [ -f /var/run/httpd.pid ] && {
            kill -HUP `cat /var/run/httpd.pid`
            echo -n httpd
        }
        echo
        ;;
    *)
        echo "Usage: $0 {start|stop|restart|reload|status}"
        exit 1
esac

exit 0
```

As you can see, this sh script is really a simple case (conditional) statement. Now I show you an example of how you can create a new service script from an existing service script. Assume that your new service is called webmonitor and the executable is stored in /usr/sbin/webmonitor.

 It is a convention to use the same name for both the script and the executable program.

Here is how you create the /etc/rc.d/init.d/webmonitor script:

1. Copy an existing script from /etc/rc.d/init.d as /etc/rc.d/init.d/webmonitor. For simplicity and ease of understanding, I assume that you copied the /etc/rc.d/init.d/httpd script shown in Listing 3-5.

2. Using your favorite text editor (such as vi), search and replace all instances of "httpd" with the string "`webmonitor.`"

3. If you keep the executable in any directories other than /sbin, /usr/sbin, /bin, or /usr/bin, you have to change the `daemon webmonitor` line to reflect the path of the webmonitor executable. For example, if you keep the executable in the /usr/local/web/bin directory, you have to change the `daemon webmonitor` line to `daemon /usr/local/web/bin/webmonitor`.

4. If /usr/sbin/webmonitor does not create a PID file (/var/run/webmonitor.pid), then you have to replace the `kill `cat /var/run/webmonitor.pid`` line with `killproc webmonitor` and remove the `rm -f /var/run/webmonitor.pid line`.

5. Run `chmod 750 /etc/rc.d/init.d/webmonitor` to change the file permissions so that the root user can read, write, and execute the script.

That's all you need to do to create the new webmonitor service. You can now use the`chkconfig`, `ntsysv`, or `linuxconf` utility to add this new service to a desired run level.

Summary

In this chapter, you learned about how a Red Hat Linux system boots up and shuts down. You learned about init, which is started by the kernel and in turn starts all the processes (that are primarily various services) in the default run level.

Chapter 4

Understanding UNIX Files and Devices

IN THIS CHAPTER

◆ How to administer file, directory, and link permissions and ownership

◆ How to establish a permission policy for a multiuser system

ONE OF THE BIGGEST REASONS why many people dislike UNIX or UNIX-like operating systems is the way they handle files and directories. Many people simply find the concepts associated with UNIX files and directories to be nonintuitive. While working as a system administrator, I learned that almost 90 percent of user problems are associated with file and directory permissions and ownership issues. Many users just do not understand the underlying concept of file ownership and access permissions. This is not their fault—most of these people come to an OS like Linux from a background in Microsoft Windows 3.x or 9x (or some similar system) where the concept of file ownership or access permission is unheard of (Windows NT/2000 is an exception). So as a system administrator for an Internet server you will likely face many user problems dealing with files. Hence you have no choice but to become the wizard of files and directories. This chapter will show you how you can achieve such mastery.

Understanding File/Directory Permissions

Like all UNIX and UNIX-like operating systems, Linux associates a file or directory with a user and a group. Consider an example:

```
-rw-rw-r— 1 sheila  intranet  512 Feb 6 21:11 milkyweb.txt
```

The preceding line is produced by the `ls -1 milkyweb.txt` command on my Red Hat Linux system. You might already know that the `ls` program lists files and directories. The `-1` option shows the complete listing for the milkyweb.txt file. Now consider the same information in a tabular format in Table 4-1.

TABLE 4-1 OUTPUT OF A SAMPLE LS –1 COMMAND

Information Type	ls Output
File access permission	–rw–rw–r –
Number of links	1
User (file owner)	sheila
Group	intranet
File size (in bytes)	512
Last modification date	Feb 6
Last modification time	21:11
Filename	milkyweb.txt

Here, the milkyweb.txt file is owned by a user called sheila. She is the only regular user who can change the access permissions of this file. The only other user who can change the permissions is the superuser. The group for this file is intranet. Any user who belongs to the intranet group can access (read, write, or execute) the file based on current group permission settings (established by the owner).

To become a file owner, a user must create the file. Under Red Hat Linux, when a user creates a file or directory, its group is also set to the default group of the user, which happens to be the private group with the same name as the user. To make this a bit clearer, say that I've logged into my Red Hat Linux system as kabir and using a text editor like vi created a file called todo.txt. If I do an ls -1 todo.txt command, the following output appears:

```
-rw-rw-r— 1 kabir    kabir    4848 Feb 6 21:37 todo.txt
```

As you can see, the file owner and the group name are the same. This is because under Red Hat Linux, user kabir's default (private) group is also called kabir. This might be a bit confusing, but it is done to save you some worries, and of course you can change this behavior quite easily. However, the point here is that when a new file is created, the file owner is the file creator, and the group is the owner's default group.

As a regular user, you cannot reassign a file or directory's ownership to someone else. For example, I cannot create a file as user kabir and reassign its ownership to a user called sheila. Wonder why this is so? A wise person's answer will be security, of course. If a regular user were allowed to reassign file ownership to others, someone could create a nasty program that deleted files, change its ownership to the superuser, and wipe out the entire file system. Only the superuser can reassign file or directory ownership.

Changing ownership of files/directories using chown

As a superuser you can change the file/directory ownership using the chown command. To change the ownership of a file or directory, run the command as follows:

```
chown  newuser file or directory
```

For example:

```
chown  sheila kabirs_plans.txt
```

This command makes user sheila the new owner of the file kabirs_plans.txt.

If the superuser would also like to change the group for a file or directory, she can use the chown command as follows:

```
chown  newuser.newgroup file or directory
```

For example:

```
chown  sheila.admin kabirs_plans.txt
```

The preceding command not only makes sheila the new owner but also resets the group of the file to be admin.

If the superuser wants to change the user and/or group ownership of all the files or directories under a given directory, she can use the -R option to run the chown command in recursive mode. For example:

```
chown  -R sheila.admin /home/kabir/plans/
```

The preceding command changes the user and group ownership of the /home/kabir/plans/ directory and all the files and subdirectories within it.

Although you have to be the superuser to change the ownership of a file, you can still change a file or directory's group as a regular user using the chgrp command.

Changing group of files/directories using chgrp

The chgrp command lets you change a file or directory's group ownership as long as you are also part of the new group. In other words, you can change groups only if you belong to both the old and new groups. For example:

```
chgrp httpd  *.html
```

If I run the preceding command to change the group for all the HTML files in a directory, I must also be part of the httpd group. You can find out what groups you are in using the `groups` command without any argument. Like the `chown` command, `chgrp` also uses `-R` to recursively change group names of one or more files or directories.

Now that you know how users are associated with files and directories, take a look at how access permissions work with files and directories. There are two ways of looking at the file/directory permissions.

Understanding access permissions using octal numbers

Although using octal numbers is my favorite method for understanding file/directory access permissions, I must warn you that it involves bits. If you feel you are mathematically challenged, you can skip this section and go to the next section, which explains the same permissions using a much simpler access string.

Because I am going to use a not-so-frequently-used numbering system called the octal number system to explain access permissions, here is a small memory refresher on octal numbers. The octal number system uses eight digits as opposed to the commonly used ten digits of the decimal system. The octal digits are 0–7, and each digit can be represented by three bits (in binary system). Table 4-2 shows the binary equivalent for each octal digit.

TABLE 4-2 OCTAL TO BINARY CONVERSION

Octal	Binary
0	000
1	001
2	010
3	011
4	100
5	101
6	110
7	111

This table will become useful in understanding file/directory permission. Figure 4-1 shows how you can think of the permissions as four octal digits. Here the first octal digit is the leftmost or most significant one.

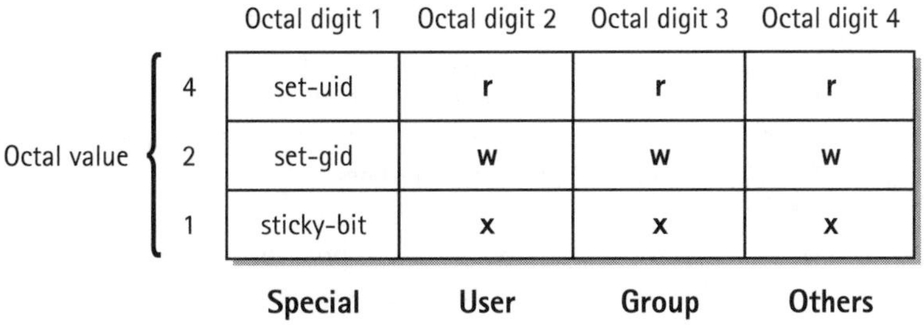

		Octal digit 1	Octal digit 2	Octal digit 3	Octal digit 4
	4	set-uid	r	r	r
Octal value	2	set-gid	w	w	w
	1	sticky-bit	x	x	x
		Special	**User**	**Group**	**Others**

Figure 4-1: A permission diagram using four octal digits

As you can see in the figure, the first octal digit is used for special permission settings, the second digit is used for setting permissions for the file owner, the third digit is used for setting permissions for the group, and finally, the fourth digit is used for setting permissions for everyone else. When any of these digits are omitted, it is considered to be a zero. Table 4-3 shows a few sample permission values.

TABLE 4-3 SAMPLE PERMISSION VALUES

Permission Value	Explanation
0400	Only read (r) permission for the file owner. This is equivalent to 400, where the missing octal digit is treated as a leading zero.
0440	Read (r) permission for both the file owner and the users in the group. This is equivalent to 440.
0444	Read (r) permission for everyone. This is equivalent to 444.
0644	Read (r) and write (w) permissions for the file owner. Everyone else has read-only access to the file. This is equivalent to 644; the number 6 is derived by adding 4 (r) and 2 (w).
0755	Read (r), write (w), and execute (x) permissions for the file owner and read (r) and execute (x) permissions to the file for everyone else. This is equivalent to 755; the number 7 is derived by adding 4 (r) + 2 (w) + 1 (x).

Continued

TABLE **4-3** SAMPLE PERMISSION VALUES *(Continued)*

Permission Value	Explanation
4755	Same as 755 in the last example except for the fact that this file is set-UID. When an executable file with set-UID permission is run, the process runs as the owner of the file. In other words, if a file is set-UID and owned by the user gunchy, any time it is run, the running program will enjoy the privileges of the user gunchy. So if a file is owned by root and the file is also set to be set-UID, anyone who can run the file essentially has the privileges of the superuser. If a set-UID root file can be altered by anyone but root, it is a major security hole. Please be very careful when setting the set- UID bit.
2755	Similar to 755 but also sets the set-GID bit. When such a file is executed, it essentially has all the privileges of the group of the file.
1755	Similar to 755 but also sets the sticky bit. The sticky bit is formally known as the save text mode. This is an infrequently used feature that tells the OS to keep an executable program's image in memory even after it exits. This is an external attempt to reduce the start-up time of a large program. Instead of setting the sticky bit, you should try to recode the application for better performance when possible.

To come up with a suitable permission setting, you need to determine what type of access the user, the group, and everyone else should have and consider if the set-UID, set-GID, or sticky bit is necessary. Once you have determined the need, you can construct each octal digit using 4 (read), 2 (write), and 1 (execute) or a custom value by adding any of these three values. Although the octal number based permissions may seem a bit hard at the beginning, with practice their use can become second nature.

Understanding access permissions using access strings

Now we will look at permissions using the access string method, which is (supposedly) simpler than the numeric method discussed earlier. Figure 4-2 shows the access string version of the permissions diagram.

Special	User (u)	Group (g)	Others (o)
set-uid (s)	read (r)	read (r)	read (r)
set-gid (s)	write (w)	write (w)	write (w)
sticky-bit (t)	execute (x)	execute (x)	execute (x)

Special   User (u)   Group (g)   Others (o)

All (a)

Figure 4-2: The permissions diagram using access strings

Each type of permission is represented with a single character (in parentheses). To create a permission string, you need to specify the following:

◆ Whom does it affect? Your choices are: u (user), g (group), o (others), or a (all).

◆ What type of permission needs to be set? Your choices are: r (read), w (write), x (execute), s (set-UID or set-GID), or t (sticky bit).

◆ What is the action type? In other words, are you setting the permission or removing it? When setting the permissions, you need to use"+" to specify an addition and "–" to specify a removal.

For example, to allow the file owner read access to the file, you will need to specify a permission string such as u+r; or to allow everyone to read and execute a file, you will need a permission string such as a+rx. Similarly, to make a file set-UID, you need u+s; to set it as set-GID, you need g+s.

Now that you know multiple ways of manipulating file and directory permissions, look at how you can use your newfound administrative skills with the chmod command.

Changing access privileges of files/directories using chmod

The chmod utility allows you to change (permission) modes, and hence it is called chmod. You can use either the octal or the string method with this nifty utility. For example:

```
chmod 755 *.pl
```

The preceding command changes permissions for files ending with extension .pl. Each of the .pl files is set as read, write, and execute (7 = 4 [read] + 2 [write] + 1 [execute]) by the owner. The files are also set to be readable and executable (5 = 4 [read] + 1 [execute]) by the group and others.

You can accomplish the same using the string method as follows:

```
chmod a+rx,u+w *.pl
```

Here a+rx is used to allow read (r) and execute (x) permissions for all (a), and u+w is used to allow the file owner (u) to write (w) to the file. Note that when you use multiple access strings, you need to separate each pair of by a comma. Also note that no space is allowed between the permissions strings.

If you would like to change permissions for all the files and subdirectories within a directory, you can use the -R option to perform a recursive permission operation. For example:

```
chmod -R 750 /www/mysite
```

Here the 750 octal permission is applied to all the files and subdirectories of the /www/mysite directory.

Special notes on directory permissions

The permission settings for a directory are similar to those for regular files, but not identical. Here are some special notes on directory permissions:

◆ Read-only access to a directory will not allow you to cd into that directory; to do that, you will need execute permission.

◆ Execute-only permission will allow you to access the files inside a directory as long as you know their names and you are allowed to read the files.

◆ To be able to list the contents of a directory using a program like ls and also to able to cd into a directory, you need both read and execute permissions.

◆ If you have write permission for a directory, you can create, delete, or modify any files or subdirectories within that directory even when someone else owns the file or subdirectory.

Now consider a special type of file called a symbolic link and the permission issues it presents.

Managing Permissions for Links

Apart from the regular files and directories, you will encounter another type of file quite frequently — links.

Links are pointer files that point to other files. A link allows you to create multiple names for a single file or directory. There are two types of links: hard and soft (symbolic) links. You will learn more about links in the next chapter. Here I am going to discuss the special permission issues that arise from the use of links.

Changing permissions or ownership of a hard link

If you change the permission or the ownership of a hard link, it also changes the permission of the original file. For example, take a look at the following `ls -l` output:

```
-rw-r-r-  1 root              21 Feb  7 11:41 todo.txt
```

Now if the root user creates a hard link (using the command line `Len todo.txt plan`) called plan for todo.txt, the `ls -l` output will look as follows:

```
-rw-r-r-  2 root              21 Feb  7 11:41 plan
-rw-r-r-  2 root              21 Feb  7 11:41 todo.txt
```

As you can see, the hard link, plan, and the original file, todo.txt, have the same file size (shown in the fourth column) and also share the same permission and ownership settings. Now if the root user runs the following command:

```
chown  sheila plan
```

to give the ownership of the hard link to a user called sheila, will it work as usual? Take a look at the `ls -l` output after the preceding command:

```
-rw-r-r-  2 Sheila   root    21 Feb  7 11:41 plan
-rw-r-r-  2 Sheila   root    21 Feb  7 11:41 todo.txt
```

As you can see, the `chown` command changed the ownership of plan, but the ownership of todo.txt (the original file) has also changed. So when you change the ownership or permissions of a hard link, the effect also applies to the original file.

Changing permissions or ownership of a soft link

Changing the ownership of a symbolic link or soft link does not work the same way. For example, take a look at the following `ls -l` output:

```
lrwxrwxrwx  1 sheila   root     8 Feb  7 11:49 plan -> todo.txt
-rw-r-r-  1 sheila   root    21 Feb  7 11:41 todo.txt
```

Here you can see that the plan file is a symbolic (soft) link for todo.txt. Now suppose the root user changes the ownership of the symbolic link as follows:

```
chown kabir plan
```

The ls -l output shows

```
lrwxrwxrwx   1 kabir    root        8 Feb  7 11:49 plan -> todo.txt
-rw-r—r—  1 sheila    root       21 Feb  7 11:41 todo.txt
```

Now the question is, can user kabir write to todo.txt using the symbolic link (plan)? The answer is no, unless the directory where these files are stored is owned by kabir. So changing a soft link's ownership does not work in the same way as with hard links. However, if you change the permission settings of a soft link, the file it points to gets the new settings. For example:

```
chmod 666 plan
```

This changes the todo.txt file's permission as shown here in the ls -l listing:

```
-rw-rw-rw-   1 kabir    kabir      25 Feb  7 11:52 plan
-rw-r-r—  1 sheila    root       21 Feb  7 11:41 todo.txt
```

So be cautious with links, because the permission and ownership settings on these special files are a bit nonintuitive.

Creating a Permission Policy for a Multiuser Server

As mentioned before, most user problems on UNIX and UNIX-like systems are related to file permissions. If something that was working yesterday and day before yesterday all of a sudden stops working today, you should first suspect a permission problem. One of the most common causes of permission problems is the root account. Many inexperienced system administrators often access files and programs via a superuser (root) account. When a program is run using the root user account, the files that such a program creates can often be set with root ownership. In this section, I will discuss a few permission policies that you might want to implement, especially if you have many users on a single system.

Setting users' configuration file permissions

Each user's home directory houses some semihidden files that start with a period (or dot). These files are often used to execute commands at user login. For example, all the shells (csh, tcsh, bash, and so on) available to a user read their settings from a dot file like .cshrc or .bashrc. If a user is not careful to keep file permissions set properly, another not-so-friendly user can cause problems for the naive user. For example, if one user's .cshrc file is writable by a second user, the latter can play a silly trick such as putting a logout command at the beginning of the .cshrc file so that the first user will be logged out as soon as she logs in. Of course, the silly trick could develop into other tricks that will violate a user's file privacy in the system. Therefore you might want to watch for such situations on a multiuser system. You can run the COPS program discussed in Chapter 18 to detect many permission problems. If you have only a handful of users, you can also quickly perform simple checks like the following:

```
find /home -type f -name ".*rc" -exec ls -l {} \;
```

This command will display permissions for all the dot files (ending in "rc" to list only .cshrc, .bashrc, and so on) in the /home directory hierarchy. If your users' home directories are kept in /home, this will quickly show you which users might have a permission problem.

Setting default file permissions for users

As a system administrator, you can define the default permission settings for all the user files that get on your system. To set the default permissions for new files, you can use the umask command as follows:

```
umask mask
```

To understand how umask works, consider an example:

Say that umask is set to 022. When a new file is created, typically the file creation function requests a permission setting of 0666. However, in such a case the final permission settings for the file are derived by the system as shown in Figure 4-3.

As you can see in the figure, the requested permission, 0666, is ANDed with the complement of the current mask (that is, 022 becomes 755) so that the result is 0644, which allows the file owner read and write access but gives everyone else only read access.

To create a default mask for file permissions, you can embed the umask command in a global shell resource file in /etc so that when a user logs in and runs a shell, the global resource file for that shell will be executed. This in turn will execute the umask command and provide a default mask for the user session. For example, if your users use the /bin/csh or /bin/tcsh shell, you can put a desirable umask command in the /etc/csh.cshrc file for this purpose.

The default umask for Red Hat Linux is 002, which is set in /etc/profile file. Since Red Hat Linux creates a private group (of the same name as the username) for each new user, the default 002 umask allows the user and her private group to be able to access the files or directories she creates.

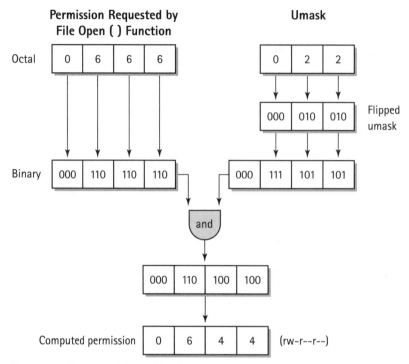

Figure 4-3: How umask is used by the system

Setting executable file permissions

Only the owner should have write permission for program files run by regular users. For example, the program files in /usr/bin should have permission settings such that only root can read, write, and execute; the settings for everyone else should include only read and execute. Allowing others besides the owner to write into a program file can create serious security holes. For example, if someone other than the root can write to a program like /usr/bin/zip, a malicious user can replace the real zip program with a Trojan horse program that will compromise system security, damaging files and directories as it pleases. So, you should always check the program files on your systems to make sure they have proper permissions. Run COPS frequently to detect permission-related problems. See Chapter 18 for details on COPS.

Setting default file permissions for FTP

If many of your users FTP their files on the server, you can control the default umask for the FTP server such that one user's file is not accessible by another. For example, if you would like to set permissions so that only the user and her group can read a file uploaded on a Web server via FTP, you can modify the in.ftpd line in the /etc/inetd.conf file. This line by default looks like:

```
ftp   stream tcp nowait root   /usr/sbin/tcpd  in.ftpd -l -a
```

To set a default umask for all files uploaded via FTP, you need to add an a -u argument with the appropriate umask value. For example, to set 640 (rw-r — —-) permission for each file uploaded, you can set the to 026. So change the preceding line as follows:

```
ftp   stream tcp nowait root   /usr/sbin/tcpd  in.ftpd -l -a -u026
```

Restart the inetd server (killall -HUP inetd) and FTP a file via a user account to see if the permissions are set as expected.

This feature is very handy for systems that act as Web servers for many different clients. If you do not want one client to see another client's files, use this option along with a special ownership setting. For example, say that you keep all your Web client files in the /www partition or directory, where each client site has a directory of its own (for example, /www/myclient1, /www/myclient2, and so on). Now you probably already gave each client an FTP account to upload files in these directories. To stop a client from seeing another's files, use as described with the FTP server and also reset the ownership of each client site as follows:

```
chwon -R client.Web server user   /www/client dir
```

For example, if you run your Web server as "httpd" and have a client user called myclient, then the preceding command will look like this:

```
chown -R myclient.httpd /www/myclient
```

This will change the ownership of the /www/myclient directory along with all its subdirectories and files to myclient (user) and httpd (group). This is done to allow the client user to own, modify, and delete her files and also to allow the Web server to read the files in the directory. However, to disallow everyone else, you must change the permissions as follows:

```
chmod -R 2770   /www/client dir
```

For the current example, the actual command is as follows:

```
chmod -R 2770   /www/myclient
```

This command sets all the files and subdirectory permissions for /www/myclient to 2770, which allows the files and directories to be readable, writable, and executable by the owner (myclient) and the Web server user (httpd). It also ensures that when new files are created, they have their permissions set to allow the Web server user to read the file. Do this with the set-GID (2) digit.

Working with Files and Directories

In this section I will show you how to work with files using various utility programs available on your Red Hat Linux system.

Viewing files and directories

You are probably already familiar with ls. This is probably the most widely used program on any UNIX or UNIX-like platform. The most widely used options for ls are -l (long listing), -a (all files including filenames starting with a period), -1 (single-column filenames-only listing), and -R (recursive listing).

Navigating your way into directories

You are also likely to know the cd command, which is really a built-in shell command. If you do not provide any directory name as an argument, the cd command will return you to the home directory of the user account you are currently using. Any time you are in doubt about where you are in the file system, you can use the pwd command, which displays your current directory name.

Determining file type

Unlike Microsoft Windows operating systems, Linux does not rely on file extensions to determine file types. You can use the file utility to determine a file's type. For example:

```
file /usr/bin/file
```

This command shows what type of file /usr/bin/file (itself) is. Here is an example of output:

```
/usr/bin/file: ELF 32-bit LSB executable, Intel 80386, \
version 1, dynamically linked, not stripped
```

Viewing the access statistics of a file or directory

The stat program gives you statistics on a file or directory. For example:

```
stat /tmp
```

shows stats on the /tmp directory. Here is an example of output:

```
File: "/tmp"
  Size: 2048        Filetype: Directory
  Mode: (1777/drwxrwxrwt)        Uid: (   0/   root) Gid:
(   0/   root)
Device: 3,0   Inode: 16321    Links: 22
Access: Sun Feb  7 02:00:35 1999(00000.00:01:11)
Modify: Sun Feb  7 02:01:01 1999(00000.00:00:45)
Change: Sun Feb  7 02:01:01 1999(00000.00:00:45)
```

Copying files and directories

Use the cp command to copy files from one location to another. For example:

```
cp  /some/important.txt  /new/place/
```

This command copies a file called important.txt from the /some directory to the /new/place directory. You can specify a new destination filename as well. Commonly used options for cp include -f, which allows you to force copying a file to a location where another file exists with the same name. For example:

```
cp  -f /some/important.txt /new/place/
```

This command copies the important.txt file even if a file by that name is already in the /new/place directory.

To copy a directory along with all its files and subdirectories, use:

```
cp -r source-directory destination-directory
```

For example:

```
cp -r /tmp/foo   /zoo/foo
```

Moving files and directories

To move files or directories, use the mv command. For example:

```
mv  /file1  /tmp/file2
```

This command moves /file1 to /tmp/file2. Similarly, you can move a directory along with all its contents as well. Note that mv does not move directories across different file systems. To do this, use cp with the -r option to copy the directory to the new file system and then remove the directory (see the text that follows) from the current location.

Deleting Files and Directories

To delete a file or directory, use the rm command. For example:

rm *filename*

This command removes the file. If you are using the /bin/tcsh shell, you may have an alias called rm set as follows:

alias rm   rm -i

In such a case the -i prompt tells the command to prompt you before actually deleting anything. Thus, if you prefer to be prompted, you can use the -i option. On the other hand, you can use the -f option to force a removal.

To remove a directory, you will need to specify the -r option. For example:

rm -rf *directory*

This command removes all the files and subdirectories within the specified directory.

Finding files

To locate a file, you can use various commands. To locate the exact path of a program, you can use the which command. For example:

which   httpd

This command will show you the fully qualified pathname of the httpd program if it is available. Some shells have a built-in command, and others use /usr/sbin/which instead.

You can locate a file or directory by a partial or full name using the locate program. For example:

locate   netpr.pl

This command will query the updatedb database and return all occurrences of the netpr.pl file. For to work properly, you must make sure that you have a cron job set up to run updatedb on a daily or weekly basis.

Another very powerful program that you can use for locating files or directories is find. It is fairly complex program, discussed in detail in Chapter 5.

Overriding the default file permission mask

The system administrator can set a default permission mask in a global resource file for the shell you are using. For example, if you are using the /bin/tcsh shell, the system administrator can set default file permissions for you in the /etc/csh.cshrc file using the umask command. If you want to override the default permission mask, however, you can run umask from the command line to change the default mask. For example:

umask 222

This will set the default permission mask to be read, read, and read for everyone. In other words, it turns off the write permission for user, group, and others. This will also override whatever the system default was for your shell. However, this change is temporary; when you log out and log back in, the system default will be effective again. If you basically dislike the system's permission mask, voice your opinion to the system administrator and also put the appropriate umask command in your shell's resource file. For example, if you prefer the mask to be 222 all the time and use /bin/tcsh as a shell, you can put this command in your ~/.cshrc file so that every time you log in, the umask overrides the system's default.

Using ext2 FileSystem–Specific Permissions

The ext2 file system used for Red Hat Linux provides some unique features. One of these features allows a file to be immutable for even the root user. For example:

chattr +i filename

The preceding command will set the "i" attribute of a file in an ext2 file system. When this attribute is set, the file cannot be modified, deleted, or renamed by anyone. No links can be added to point to this file either. This attribute can be set or cleared only by the root user. So you can use this attribute to protect against accidents involving files. When you need to clear the attribute, you can run:

chattr -i filename

A few other interesting features of the ext2 system, such as the undelete attribute, are not yet implemented but will become available in a future ext2 file system version. If you start using the chattr command, sometimes you will notice that you can't modify or delete a file although you have the permission to do so. This happens when you forget that you had previously set the immutable attribute of the file using chattr; because this attribute does not show up in ls output, it can be confusing. To see which files have what ext2 attributes, you can use the lsattr program.

Summary

In this chapter, you learned about file and directory permissions. You learned to determine permissions using both numeric and string methods. You also learned to use various utilities to set and remove file and directory permissions. You further learned to use various utilities to work with files and directories.

Chapter 5

Everyday Commands

IN THIS CHAPTER

- ◆ How the Linux command line works

- ◆ How to use the online manual (man) pages

- ◆ How various Linux commands work

LINUX, LIKE ANY OTHER UNIX operating system, has hundreds of commands. It is virtually impossible to remember all the details of each command; therefore, manual pages (also known as man pages) were created. You can look up details of a command in its man page. However, man pages are often very cryptic and too long. Most of them do not come with good examples. Sometimes the amount of details can be mind boggling. Also, if you do not know the name of the command, you cannot find information on it, right? This is why I have created this chapter. Here you will find commonly used commands that you are likely to use on a daily basis. I have organized the chapter in sections so that you can find related commands under a general heading. For example, if you are looking for a command that works on files or directories, you can simply go to "General File and Directory Commands," or if you are looking for a command that compresses files, you can simply take a look at the commands under "File Compression and Archive-Specific Commands."

Understanding the UNIX Command Line

Much of your work with Linux will consist of entering commands one after another. These commands follow established rules commonly known as the command line syntax. If you do not follow the syntax correctly, a command may execute incorrectly, and problems can result.

When you type a command, the entire line is known as the command line. Most commonly, you use commands one at a time. However, the command line can have multiple commands if the commands are separated with a semicolon. We can clear the screen first and then list the contents of the current directory with one command line by typing:

```
clear; ls
```

When you enter a command, you type the name of the command, possibly followed by other information. The items that follow the name of the program are arguments. For example, we enter the following as the command line:

```
wc -1 doc.txt
```

There are two arguments in this example, the –l and the doc.txt. It is up to the program to determine how to use the arguments.

There are two types of arguments: options and parameters. Options come right after the program name and are usually prefixed with a dash (minus sign character). The parameters come after the options. From the preceding example, the -1 is an option telling wc to count the number of lines; doc.txt is a parameter indicating which file to use.

When entering commands at the command line, remember the arguments are case sensitive just as filenames in UNIX are. Overall, the general syntax of a UNIX command is:

```
command_name options parameters
```

Basics of wildcards

When you use directory and file commands, you can use special characters called wildcards to specify patterns of filenames. For example, to list all of the files in the current directory that end in .c, use:

```
ls *.c
```

The asterisk is a wildcard. The shell interprets the pattern and replaces it with all of the filenames that end in .c. Table 5-1 shows commonly used wildcards.

TABLE 5-1 COMMONLY USED WILDCARD CHARACTERS

Wildcard	Meaning
*	Match any sequence of one or more characters.
?	Match any single character.
[ ]	Match one of the enclosed characters or range.

Table 5-2 shows a few examples of wildcard usage so that you can get a grasp of how wildcards work.

TABLE 5-2 EXAMPLES OF WILDCARD USAGE

Example	Meaning
Jo*	Files that begin with Jo
Jo*y	Files that begin with Jo and end in y
Ut*l*s.c	Files that begin with Ut, contain an l, and end in s.c
?.h	Files that begin with a single character followed by .h.
Doc[0-9].txt	Files with the names Doc0.txt, Doc1.txt, . . . , Doc9.txt
Doc0[A-Z].txt	Files with the names Doc0A.txt, Doc0B.txt, . . . , Doc0Z.txt

---

As you can see, using wildcards can make selecting multiple items easy.

Basics of regular expressions

Various UNIX commands use regular expressions. They provide a convenient and consistent way of specifying patterns to be matched. They are similar to wildcards, but they are much more powerful. They provide a wider scope of pattern selecting. Several different UNIX commands use regular expressions, including ed, sed, awk, grep, and, to a limited extent, vi and emacs.

The special characters in Table 5-3 are typical of regular expressions in general. Understand these special characters, and you need to learn only a few variations as they arise.

TABLE 5-3 SPECIAL CHARACTERS FOR REGULAR EXPRESSIONS

Symbol	Meaning
.	Match any single character except newline.
*	Match zero or more of the preceding characters.
^	Match the beginning of a line.
$	Match the end of a line.
\<	Match the beginning of a word.

Continued

TABLE 5-3 SPECIAL CHARACTERS FOR REGULAR EXPRESSIONS *(Continued)*

Symbol	Meaning
\>	Match the end of a word.
[ ]	Match one of the enclosed characters or range of characters.
[^]	Match any characters not enclosed.
\	Take the following symbol literally.

First, within a regular expression, any character that does not have a special meaning stands for itself. For example, to search for lines that contain "foo" in the file data.txt, use:

```
grep foo data.txt
```

To search for only lines in data.txt that begin with the word "foo," use:

```
grep '^foo' data.txt
```

The use of single quotes tells the shell to leave these characters alone and to pass them to the program. Single quotes are necessary whenever using any of the special characters.

The dollar sign indicates you want to match a pattern at the end of the line:

```
grep 'hello$' data.txt
```

Any lines ending with "hello" result in a match using the preceding regular expression.

To look for a pattern that begins a word, use \<.

```
grep '\<ki' data.txt
```

The preceding expression searches for words that begin with "ki" in the file data.txt. To find the pattern "wee," but only at the end of a word, use:

```
grep 'wee\>' data.txt
```

From Table 5-3, notice that the period matches any single character except newline. This comes in handy if we are searching for all the lines that contain the letters "C" followed by two letters and end in "s"; here, the regular expression is:

```
grep 'C..s' data.txt
```

This expression matches patterns like: "Cats," "Cars," and "Cris" if they are in the file data.txt.

If you want to specify a range of characters, use a hyphen to separate the beginning and end of the range. When you specify the range, the order must be the same as in the ASCII code. For example, to search for all the lines that contain a "B" followed by any single lowercase letter, use:

```
grep 'B[a-z]' data.txt
```

It is also possible to specify more than one range of characters in the same pattern.

```
grep 'B[A-Za-z]' data.txt
```

The preceding example selects all lines that contain the letter "B" followed by an uppercase or lowercase letter.

How to Use Online man Pages

The online man (short for manual) pages are divided into eight major sections, as in Table 5-4. Other sections may come with your flavor of UNIX, but most, if not all UNIXes, contain eight major sections. Section 1 contains the description of the bulk of UNIX commands. Most users can get by fine with only this section of the manual. Sections 2, 3, 4, and 5 of the UNIX manual are of interest only to programmers. Section 8 is only for system administrators.

TABLE 5-4 SECTIONS OF MAN PAGES

Section	Topic
1	Executable programs or shell commands
2	System calls (functions the kernel provides)
3	Library calls (functions within system libraries)
4	Special files (usually in /dev)
5	File formats (that is, /etc/passd)
6	Games
7	Miscellaneous information
8	Maintenance commands

Modern-day UNIX systems cover much more detail than their ancestors. It is common to see sections broken into subsections. For instance, section 6 is a reference for games. However, you may find a section 6a (for adventure games), a section 6c (for classic games), and so on.

The man command allows you to view the online manuals. The syntax for this command is as follows:

```
man [-k] [section] keyword
```

The keyword is usually the name of the program, utility, or function. The default action is to search in all of the available sections following a predefined order and to show only the first page found, even if the keyword exists in several sections.

Because commands may appear in several sections, the first page found might not be the man page you are looking for. The command printf is a good example.

Say we are writing a program and would like to know more about the ANSI C library function printf (). Just by typing

```
man printf
```

we get information about printf. However, the man pages for this printf are for the shell command printf. Obviously, this is the wrong information. A reasonable solution is to list all of the sections covering printf (if it exists in multiple sections) and to select the correct one. We can search the keywords of the man pages with the -f option:

```
man -k printf
fprintf        printf (3b)     - formatted output conversion
fprintf        printf (3s)     - print formatted output
printf         printf (1)      - write formatted output
printf         printf (3b)     - formatted output conversion
printf         printf (3s)     - print formatted output
```

The printf we are interested in is a library function. It is in section 3 (from Table 5-4) or, more specifically, in section 3b or 3s from the output. To specify a particular section of a man page, we pass it to man at the command line:

```
man 3b printf
```

Now this is the correct information we are looking for!

General File and Directory Commands

In this section, you will learn about file- and directory-specific commands you are likely to use on a daily basis.

cat

Syntax:

```
cat  file  [>|>]  [destination file]
```

The `cat` command displays the contents of a file to stdout. It is often helpful to examine the contents of a file by using the `cat` command. The argument you pass to `cat` is the file you wish to view. To view the total content of a filename:

```
cat name
Kiwee
Joe
Ricardo
Charmaine
```

`cat` can also merge existing multiple files into one:

```
cat name1 name2 name3 > allnames
```

This example combines the files name1, name2, and name3 to produce the final file allnames. We establish the order of the merge by the order in which we enter the files at the command line.

Using `cat`, we can append a file to another file. For instance, if we had forgotten to add name4 in the previous command, we can still produce the same results by executing the following:

```
cat name4 >> allnames
```

chmod

Syntax:

```
chmod  [-R] permission-mode  file or directory
```

We use this command to change the permission mode of a file or directory. The permission mode is specified as a three- or four-digit octal number. For example:

```
chmod 755  myscript.pl
```

The preceding command changes the permission of myscript.pl script to 755 (rwxr-xr-x), which allows the file owner to read, write, and execute and allows only read and execute privileges for everyone else. Here is another example:

```
chmod -R 744 public_html
```

The preceding command changes the permissions of the public_html directory and all its contents (files and subdirectories) to 744 (rwxr − r −), which is a typical permission setting for personal Web directories we access using `http://server/ ~username` URLs under Apache Server. The `-R` option tells `chmod` to recursively change permissions for all files and directories under the named directory.

chown

Syntax:

```
chown [ -fhR ] Owner [ :Group ] { File . . . | Directory. . . }
```

The `chown` command changes the owner of the file the File parameter specifies to the user the Owner parameter specifies. The value of the Owner parameter can be a user ID or a login name in the /etc/passwd file. Optionally, we can also specify a group. The value of the Group parameter can be a group ID or a group name in the /etc/group file.

Only the root user can change the owner of a file. You can change the group of a file only if you are a root user or if you own the file. If you own the file but are not a root user, you can change the group only to a group of which you are a member. Table 5-5 discusses the details of the `chown` options.

TABLE 5-5 CHOWN OPTIONS

Option	Description
-f	Suppresses all error messages except usage messages.
-h	Changes the ownership of an encountered symbolic link but not that of the file or directory the symbolic link points to.
-R	Descends directories recursively, changing the ownership for each file. When a symbolic link is encountered and the link points to a directory, the ownership of that directory is changed, but the directory is not further traversed.

The following example changes the owner of the file to another user:

```
chown bert hisfile.txt
```

clear

Syntax:

```
clear
```

The `clear` command clears your terminal and returns the command line prompt to the top of the screen.

cmp

Syntax:

```
cmp [-ls] file 1 file2
```

This command compares the contents of two files. If there are no differences within the two files, `cmp` by default is silent.

To demonstrate, file1.txt contains:

```
this is file 1
the quick brown fox jumps over the lazy dog.
```

and file2.txt contains:

```
this is file 2
the quick brown fox jumps over the lazy dog.
```

The only difference between the two files is the first line, last character. In one file, the character is a "1," and the other file has a "2":

```
cmp file1.txt file2.txt
file1.txt file2.txt differ: char 14, line 1
```

The results of `cmp` correctly identify character 14, line 1 as the unequal character between the two files. The `-l` option prints the byte number and the differing byte values for each of the files.

```
cmp -l file1.txt file2.txt
14 61 62
```

The results of the preceding example show us that byte 14 is different, with the first file having an octal 61 and the second file having an octal 62.

Finally, the `-s` option displays nothing. The `-s` option only returns an exit status indicating the similarities between the files. It returns a 0 (zero) if the files are identical and a 1 if the files are different. Last, the `-s` option returns a number >1 (greater than 1) when an error occurs.

cp

Syntax:

```
cp  [-R] source file or directory  file or directory
```

Use the cp command to make an exact copy of a file. The cp command requires at least two arguments. The first argument is the file you wish to copy, and the second argument is the location or filename of the new file. If the second argument is an existing directory, cp copies the source file into the directory.

```
cp main.c main.c.bak
```

The preceding example will copy the existing file main.c and creates a new file called main.c.bak in the same directory. These two files are identical, bit for bit.

cut

Syntax:

```
cut  [-cdf list]  file
```

The cut command extracts columns of data. The data can be in bytes, characters, or fields from each line in a file. For instance, a file called names contains information about a group of people. Each line contains data pertaining to one person:

```
Fast  Freddy:Sacramento:CA:111-111-1111
Joe   Smoe:Los Angeles:CA:222-222-2222
Drake Snake:San Francisco:CA:333-333-3333
Bill  Steal:New York:NY:444-444-4444
```

To list the names and telephone numbers of all individuals in the file, the options -f and -d should suffice:

```
cut -f 1,4 -d : names
Fast  Freddy:111-111-1111
Joe   Some:222-222-2222
Drake Snake:333-333-3333
Bill  Steal:444-444-4444
```

The -f list option specifies the fields you elect to display. The -d options define each field. In the preceding example, -d : indicates that a colon separates each field. Using : as the field delimiter makes fields 1 and 4 the name and phone number fields.

To display the contents of a particular column, use the -c list option.

```
cut -c 1-5 names
Fast
Joe
Drake
Bill
```

The preceding example shows how to list columns 1 through 5 in the filename names and nothing else.

diff

Syntax:

```
diff [-iqb] file1 file2
```

We use the diff command to determine differences between files and/or directories. By default, diff does not produce any output if the files are identical.

The diff command is different from the cmp command in the way it compares the files. The diff command is used to report differences between two files, line by line. The cmp command reports differences between two files character by character, instead of line by line. As a result, it is more useful than diff for comparing binary files. For text files, cmp is useful mainly when you want to know only whether two files are identical.

To illustrate the difference between considering changes character by character and considering them line by line, think of what happens if we add a single newline character to the beginning of a file. If we compare that file with an otherwise identical file that lacks the newline at the beginning, diff reports that a blank line has been added to the file, and cmp reports that the two files differ in almost every character.

The normal output format consists of one or more hunks of differences; each hunk shows one area where the files differ. Normal format hunks look like this:

```
change-command
< from-file-line
< from-file-line. . .
--
> to-file-line
> to-file-line. . .
```

There are three types of change commands. Each consists of a line number or comma-separated range of lines in the first file, a single character indicating the kind of change to make, and a line number or comma-separated range of lines in the second file. All line numbers are the original line numbers in each file. The types of change commands are:

- ◆ `'lar'`: Add the lines in range r of the second file after line l of the first file. For example, '8a12,15' means append lines 12–15 of file 2 after line 8 of file 1; or, if changing file 2 into file 1, delete lines 12–15 of file 2.

- ◆ `'fct'`: Replace the lines in range f of the first file with lines in range t of the second file. This is like a combined add and delete but more compact. For example, '5,7c8,10' means change lines 5–7 of file 1 to read as lines 8–10 of file 2; or, if changing file 2 into file 1, change lines 8–10 of file 2 to read as lines 5–7 of file 1.

- ◆ `'rdl'`: Delete the lines in range r from the first file; line l is where they would have appeared in the second file had they not been deleted. For example, '5,7d3' means delete lines 5–7 of file 1; or, if changing file 2 into file 1, append lines 5–7 of file 1 after line 3 of file 2.

For example, a.txt contains

```
a
b
c
d
e
```

and b.txt contains

```
c
d
e
f
g
```

The diff command produces the following output:

```
1,2d0
< a
< b
5a4,5
> f
> g
```

The diff command produces output that shows how the files are different and what we need to do for the files to be identical. First, notice how 'c' is the first common character between the two files. The first line reads 1,2d0. This is interpreted as deleting lines 1 and 2 of the first file, lines a and b. Next, the third line reads 5a4,6. The 'a' signifies append. If we append lines 4 through 6 of the second file to line 5 of the first file, the files are identical.

The `diff` command has some common options. The -i option ignores changes in case. `diff` considers upper and lowercase characters equivalent. The `-q` option gives a summary of information. Simply put, the `-q` option reports if the files differ at all.

```
diff -q a.txt b.txt
Files a.txt and b.txt differ
```

The `-b` option ignores changes in whitespace. The phrase "the foo" is equivalent to "the foo" if we use the `-b` option.

du

Syntax:

```
du [-ask] filenames
```

This command summarizes disk usage. If you specify a directory, du reports the disk usage for that directory and any directories it contains. If do not specify a filename or directory, du assumes the current directory. du -a breaks down the total and shows the size of each directory and file. The `-s` option will just print the total. Another useful option is the `-k` option. This option prints all file sizes in kilobytes. Here are some examples of the various options:

```
du -a
247     ./util-linux_2.9e-0.1.deb
130     ./libncurses4_4.2-2.deb
114     ./slang1_1.2.2-2.deb
492     .

du -s
492     .
```

emacs

The emacs program, a full-screen visual editor, is one of the best editors. It is known for its flexibility and power as well as for being a resource hog. The power of emacs is not easily obtained. There is a stiff learning curve that requires patience and even more patience. There can be as many as four sequential key combinations to perform certain actions.

However, emacs can do just about anything. Aside from the basic editing features, emacs supports the following: syntax highlighting; macros; editing multiple files at the same time; spell checking; mail; FTP; and many other features.

When reading about emacs, you'll often see words like meta-Key and C-x. The meta key is the meta key on your keyboard (if you have one) or most commonly the Esc key. C-x is the syntax for Ctrl plus the X key. Any "C-" combination refers to the Ctrl key.

The two most important key combinations to a new emacs user are the C-x C-c and C-h C-h combinations. The first combination exits emacs. You'd be surprised to know how many people give up on emacs just because they cannot exit the program the first time they use it. Also, C-h C-h displays online help, where you can follow the tutorial or get detailed information about a command. Table 5-6 shows emacs's most commonly used commands:

TABLE 5-6 COMMON EMACS COMMANDS

Commands	Effects
C-v	Move forward one screenful.
M-v	Move backward one screenful.
C-p	Move the cursor to the previous line.
C-n	Move the cursor to the next line.
C-f	Move the cursor right one position.
C-b	Move the cursor left one position.
M-f	Move forward a word.
M-b	Move backward a word.
C-a	Move to beginning of line.
C-e	Move to end of line.
M-a	Move back to beginning of sentence.
M-e	Move forward to end of sentence.
\<Delete\>	Delete the character just before the cursor.
C-d	Delete the next character after the cursor.
M-\<Delete\>	Kill the word immediately before the cursor.
M-d	Kill the next word after the cursor.
C-k	Kill from the cursor position to end of line.
M-k	Kill to the end of the current sentence.
C-x	Undo the previous command.

Commands	Effects
C-x C-f	Open another file.
C-x C-s	Save the current file.
C-x C-w	Save the current file as another name.
C-x s	Save all the buffers that have recently changed.
C-x C-c	Exit emacs.

fgrep

The fgrep command is designed to be a faster-searching program (as opposed to grep). However, it can search only for exact characters, not for general specifications. The name fgrep stands for "fixed character grep." These days, computers and memory are so fast that there is rarely a need for fgrep.

file

Syntax:

file *filename*

The file command determines the file's type. If the file is not a regular file, this command identifies its file type. It identifies the file types directory, FIFO, block special, and character special as such. If the file is a regular file and the file is zero-length, this command identifies it as an empty file.

If the file appears to be a text file, file examines the first 512 bytes and tries to determine its programming language. If the file is an executable a.out, file prints the version stamp, provided it is greater than 0.

```
file main.C
main.C:          c program text
```

find

Syntax:

```
find [path] [-type fd1] [-name pattern] [-atime [+-]number of days]
[-exec command {} \;] [-empty]
```

The `find` command finds files and directories. For example:

```
find  .  -type d
```

The `find` command returns all subdirectory names under the current directory. The `-type` option is typically set to d (for directory) or f (for file) or l (for links).

```
find  .  -type f -name "*.txt"
```

This command finds all text files (ending with .txt extension) in the current directory, including all its subdirectories.

```
find  .  -type f -name "*.txt" -exec grep -l 'magic' {} \;
```

This command searches all text files (ending with the .txt extension) in the current directory, including all its subdirectories for the keyword "magic," and returns their names (because `-l` is used with grep).

```
find . -name "*.gif" -atime -1 -exec ls -l {} \;
```

This command finds all GIF files that have been accessed in the past 24 hours (one day) and displays their details using the `ls -l` command.

```
find . -type f -empty
```

This displays all empty files in the current directory hierarchy.

grep

Syntax:

```
grep [-viw] pattern file(s)
```

The `grep` command allows you to search for one or more files for particular character patterns. Every line of each file that contains the pattern is displayed at the terminal. The `grep` command is useful when you have lots of files and you want to find out which ones contain words or phrases.

Using the `-v` option, we can display the inverse of a pattern. Perhaps we want to select the lines in data.txt that do not contain the word "the":

```
grep -vw 'the' data.txt
```

If we do not specify the `-w` option, any word containing "the" matches, such as "toge[the]r." The `-w` option specifies that the pattern must be a whole word. Finally, the -i option ignores the difference between upper and lowercase letters when searching for the pattern.

Much of the flexibility of `grep` comes from the fact that you can specify not only exact characters but also a more general search pattern. To do this, use what we describe as "regular expressions."

head

Syntax:

```
head [-count | -n number] filename
```

This command displays the first few lines of a file. By default, it displays the first 10 lines of a file. However, you can use the preceding options to specify a different number of lines.

```
head -2 doc.txt
# Outline of future projects
# Last modified:  02/02/99
```

The preceding example illustrates how to view the first two lines of the text file doc.txt.

ln

Syntax:

```
ln [-s] sourcefile target
```

`ln` creates two types of links: hard and soft. Think of a link as two names for the same file. Once we create a link, we cannot distinguish it from the original file. We cannot remove a file that has hard links from the hard disk until we remove all links. We create hard links without the `-s` option.

```
ln ./www ./public_html
```

However, a hard link does have limitations. A hard link cannot link to another directory, and a hard link cannot link to a file on another file system. Using the `-s` option, we can create a soft link, which eliminates these restrictions.

```
ln -s /dev/fs02/jack/www /dev/fs01/foo/public_html
```

Here we create a soft link between the directory www on file system 2 and a newly created file public_html on file system 1.

locate

Syntax:

```
locate keyword
```

The `locate` command finds the path of a particular file or command. `locate` finds an exact or substring match. For example:

```
locate foo
/usr/lib/texmf/tex/latex/misc/footnpag.sty
/usr/share/automake/footer.am
/usr/share/games/fortunes/food
/usr/share/games/fortunes/food.dat
/usr/share/gimp/patterns/moonfoot.pat
```

The output locate produces contains the keyword "foo" in the absolute path or does not have any output.

ls

Syntax:

```
ls [-1aRl] file or directory
```

The `ls` command allows you to list files (and subdirectories) in a directory. It is one of the most popular programs. When we use it with the `-1` option, it displays only the file and directory names in the current directory; when we use the `-l` option, a long listing containing file/directory permission information, size, modification date, and so on is displayed; the `-a` option allows you to view all files and directories (including the ones that have a leading period in their names) within the current directory; the `-R` option allows the command to recursively display contents of the subdirectories (if any).

mkdir

Syntax:

```
mkdir directory . . .
```

To make a directory, use the `mkdir` command. We have only two restrictions when choosing a directory name: (1) File names can be up to 255 characters long, and (2) directory names can contain any character except the /.

```
mkdir dir1 dir2 dir3
```

The preceding example creates three sub-directories in the current directory.

mv

Syntax:

```
mv [-if]sourcefile targetfile
```

Use the mv command to move or rename directories and files. The command performs a move or rename depending on whether the targetfile is an existing directory. To illustrate, we would like to give a directory called foo the new name of foobar.

```
mv foo foobar
```

Because foobar does not already exist as a directory, foo becomes foobar. If we issue the following command,

```
mv doc.txt foobar
```

and foobar is an existing directory, we peform a move. The file doc.txt now resides in the directory foobar.

The -f option removes existing destination files and never prompts the user. The -i option prompts the user whether to overwrite each destination file that exists. If the response does not begin with "y" or "'Y," the file is skipped.

pico

Syntax:

```
pico [filename]
```

This full-screen text editor is very user-friendly and highly suitable for users who migrate from a Windows or DOS environment.

pwd

Syntax:

```
pwd
```

This command prints the current working directory. The directories displayed are the absolute path. None of the directories displayed are hard or soft symbolic links.

```
pwd
/home/usr/charmaine
```

rm

Syntax:

```
rm [-rif] directory/file
```

To remove a file or directory, use the rm command. Here are some examples:

```
rm doc.txt
rm ~/doc.txt
rm /tmp/foobar.txt
```

To remove multiple files with rm, we can use wildcards or type each file individually. For example,

```
rm doc1.txt doc2.txt doc3.txt
```

is equivalent to:

```
rm doc[1-3].txt
```

rm is a powerful command that can cause chaos if we use it incorrectly. For instance, you have your thesis that you've worked so hard on for the last six months. You decide to rm all of your docs, thinking you are in another directory. After finding out a backup file does not exist (and you are no longer in denial), you wonder if there were any ways to have prevented this.

The rm command has the -i option that allows rm to be interactive. This tells rm to ask your permission before removing each file. For example, if you entered:

```
rm -i *.doc
rm: remove thesis.doc (yes/no)? n
```

The -i option gives you a parachute. It's up to you to either pull the cord (answer no) or suffer the consequences (answer yes). The -f option is completely the opposite. The -f (force) option tells rm to remove all the files you specify, regardless of the file permissions. Use the -f option only when you are 100 percent sure you are removing the correct file(s).

To remove a directory and all files and directories within it, use the -r option. rm -r will remove an entire subtree.

```
rm -r documents
```

If you are not sure what you are doing, combine the -r option with the -i option:

```
rm -ri documents
```

The preceding example asks for your permission before it removes every file and directory.

sort

Syntax:

```
sort [-rndu] [-o outfile] [infile/sortedfile]
```

The obvious task this command performs is to sort. However, sort also merges files. The sort command reads files that contain previously sorted data and merges them into one large, sorted file.

The simplest way to use sort is to sort a single file and display the results on your screen. If a.txt contains:

```
b
c
a
d
```

To sort a.txt and display the results to the screen:

```
sort a.txt
a
b
c
d
```

To save sorted results, use the -o option: sort -o sorted.txt a.txt saves the sorted a.txt file in sorted.txt. To use sort to merge existing sorted files and to save the output in sorted.txt, we use:

```
sort -o sorted.txt a.txt b.txt c.txt
```

The -r option for this command reverses the sort order. Therefore, a file that contains the letters of the alphabet on a line is sorted from z to a if we use the -r option.

The -d option sorts files based on dictionary order. The sort command considers only letters, numerals, and spaces and ignores other characters.

The -u option looks for identical lines and suppresses all but one. Therefore, sort produces only unique lines.

stat

Syntax:

```
stat file
```

This program displays various statistics on a file or directory. For example:

```
stat foo.txt
```

This command displays the following output:

```
  File: "foo.txt"
  Size: 4447232      Filetype: Regular File
  Mode: (0644/-rw-r—r—)  Uid: ( 0/root)  Gid: (0/root)
Device:  3,0   Inode: 16332     Links: 1
Access: Mon Mar  1 21:39:43 1999(00000.02:32:30)
Modify: Mon Mar  1 22:14:26 1999(00000.01:57:47)
Change: Mon Mar  1 22:14:26 1999(00000.01:57:47)
```

You can see the following displayed: file access; modification; change date; size; owner and group information; permission mode; and so on.

strings

Syntax:

```
strings filename
```

The `strings` command prints character sequences at least four characters long. We use this utility mainly to describe the contents of nontext files.

tail

Syntax:

```
tail [-count | -fr] filename
```

The `tail` command displays the end of a file. By default, `tail` displays the last 10 lines of a file. To display the last 50 lines of the file doc.txt, we issue the command:

```
tail -50 doc.txt
```

The `-r` option displays the output in reverse order. By default, `-r` displays all lines in the file, not just 10 lines. For instance, to display the entire contents of the file doc.txt in reverse order, use:

```
tail -r doc.txt
```

To display the last 10 lines of the file doc.txt in reverse order, use:

```
tail -10r doc.txt
```

Finally, the `-f` option is useful when you are monitoring a file. With this option, `tail` waits for new data to be written to the file by some other program. As new data are added to the file by some other program, tail displays the data on the screen. To stop tail from monitoring a file, press Ctrl+C (the intr key) because the `tail` command does not stop on its own.

touch

Syntax:

```
touch file or directory
```

This command updates the timestamp of a file or directory. If the named file does not exist, this command creates it as an empty file.

umask

See the section on default file permissions for users in Chapter 4.

uniq

Syntax:

```
uniq [-c] filename
```

The `uniq` command compares adjacent lines and displays only one unique line. When used with the `-c` option, `uniq` counts the number of occurrences. A file that has the contents:

```
a
a
a
b
a
```

produces the following result when we use it with `uniq`:

```
uniq test.txt
a
b
a
```

Notice how we remove the adjacent a's but not all a's in the file. This is an important detail to remember when using uniq. If you would like to find all the unique lines in a file called test.txt, you can run the following command:

```
sort  test.txt  | uniq
```

This command sorts the test.txt file and puts all similar lines next to each other, allowing `uniq` to display only unique lines. For example, say that you want to find quickly how many unique visitors come to your Web site; you can run the following command:

```
awk '{print $1}' access.log | sort | uniq
```

This displays the unique IP addresses in a CLF log file, which is what Apache web server uses.

vi

The vi program is a powerful full-screen text editor you can find on almost all UNIX systems because of its size and capabilities. The vi editor does not require much in the way of resources to utilize its features. In addition to the basic edit functions, vi can search, replace, and concatenate files, and it has its own macro language, as well as a number of other features.

There are two modes in vi. It is important to learn and understand these modes; learning them makes your life a whole lot easier.

The first mode is the input mode. In input mode, text is entered in the document. You can insert or append text.

The second mode is the command mode. When vi is in command mode, you can move within the document, merge lines, search, and so on. You can carry out all functions of vi from command mode except enter text. You can enter text only in input mode.

A typical vi newbie assumes he is in input mode and begins typing his document. He expects to see his newly inputted text, but what he really sees is his current document mangled because he is in command mode.

When vi starts, it is in command mode. You can go from command mode to input mode by using one of the following commands: [aAiIoOcCsSR]. To return to command mode, press the Esc key for normal exit, or press Interrupt (the Ctrl+C key sequence) to end abnormally.

Table 5-7 shows a summary of common vi commands and their effects in command mode.

TABLE 5-7 SUMMARY OF COMMON VI COMMANDS

Commands	Effects
Ctrl+D	Moves window down by half a screenful.
Ctrl+U	Moves window up by half a screenful.
Ctrl+F	Moves window forward by a screenful.
Ctrl+B	Moves window back by a screenful.
k or up arrow	Moves cursor up one line.
j or down arrow	Moves cursor down one line.
l or right arrow	Moves cursor right one character.
h or left arrow	Moves cursor left one character.
Return	Moves cursor to beginning of next line.
– (minus)	Moves cursor to beginning of previous line.
w	Moves cursor to beginning of next word.
b	Moves cursor to beginning of previous word.
^ or 0	Moves cursor to beginning of current line.
$	Moves cursor to end of current line.
A	Inserts text immediately after the cursor.
o	Opens a new line immediately after the current line.
O	Opens a new line immediately before the current line. Note this is an uppercase letter o, not a zero.
x	Deletes character under the cursor.
dw	Deletes a word (including space after it).
D or d	Deletes from the cursor until the end of line.
d^	(d caret) Deletes from the beginning of the line to the space or character to the left of the cursor.
dd	Deletes the current line.

Continued

TABLE 5-7 SUMMARY OF COMMON VI COMMANDS *(Continued)*

Commands	Effects
U	Undoes last change. Note that 2 undos will undo the undo (nothing changes).
:w	Writes the changes for the current file and continues editing.
:q!	Quits vi without saving any changes.
:ZZ	Saves current file and exits vi.

wc

Syntax:

```
wc [-lwc] filename
```

The wc (word count) command counts lines, characters, and words. If we use the wc command without any options, the output displays all statistics of the file. The file test.txt contains the following text:

```
the quick brown fox jumps over the lazy dog
wc test.txt
        1        9       44 test.txt
```

The results tell us there is one line with nine words containing 44 characters in the file test.txt. To display only the number of lines, we use the -l option. The -w option displays only the number of words. Finally, the -c option displays only the total number of characters.

whatis

Syntax:

```
whatis keyword
```

This command displays a one-line description for the keyword entered in the command line. The whatis command is identical to typing man -f. For instance, if you want to display the time but you are not sure whether to use the time or date command, enter:

```
whatis time date
```

```
time           time (1)        - time a simple command
date           date (1)        - print the date and time
```

Looking at the results, you can see that the command you want is date. The time command actually measures how long it takes for a program or command to execute.

whereis

The whereis command locates source/binary and manuals sections for specified files. The command first strips the supplied names of leading pathname components and any (single) character file extension, such as .c, .h, and so on. Prefixes of s. resulting from use of source code control are also dealt with.

```
whereis ls
ls: /bin/ls /usr/man/man1/ls.1.gz
```

The preceding example indicates the location of the command in question. The ls command is in the /bin directory, and its corresponding man pages are at /usr/man/man1/ls.1.gz.

which

Syntax:

```
which command
```

The which command displays the path and aliases of any valid, executable command.

```
which df
/usr/bin/df
```

The preceding example shows us that the df command is in the /usr/bin directory. which also displays information about shell commands.

```
which setenv
setenv: shell built-in command.
```

File Compression and Archive-Specific Commands

The commands in this section compress, archive, and package files.

compress

Syntax:

```
compress [-v] file(s)
```

The compress command attempts to reduce the size of a file using the adaptive Lempel-Ziv coding algorithm. A file with a .Z extension replaces a compressed file. Using any type of compression for files is significant because smaller file sizes increase the amount of available disk space. Also, transferring smaller files across networks reduces network congestion.

The -v (verbose) option displays the percentage of reduction for each file you compress and tells you the name of the new file. Here is an example of how to use the compress command:

```
ls -alF inbox
-rw----   1 username cscstd    194261 Feb 23 20:12 inbox
compress -v inbox
inbox: Compression: 37.20%-replaced with inbox.Z

ls -alF inbox.Z
-rw----   1 username cscstd    121983 Feb 23 20:12 inbox.Z
```

gunzip

Syntax:

```
gunzip [-v] file(s)
```

To decompress files to their original form, use the gunzip command. gunzip attempts to decompress files ending with the following extensions: .gz, -gz, .z, -z, _z, .Z, or tgz.

The -v option displays a verbose output when decompressing a file.

```
gunzip -v README.txt.gz
README.txt.gz:           65.0%-replaced with README.txt
```

gzip

Syntax:

```
gzip [-rv9] file(s)
```

The gzip command is another compression program. It is known for having one of the best compression ratios but for a price. It can be considerably slow. Files compressed with gzip are replaced by files with a .gz extension.

The -9 option yields the best compression sacrificing speed. The -v option is the verbose option. The size, total, and compression ratios are listed for each file. Also, the -r option recursively traverses each directory compressing all the files along the way.

```
ls -alF README.txt
-rw-r—r—  1 root       root             16213 Oct 14 13:55 README.txt

gzip -9v README.txt
README.txt:                65.0%—replaced with README.txt.gz

ls -alF README.txt.gz
-rw-r—r—  1 root       root              5691 Oct 14 13:55 README.txt.gz
```

rpm

Syntax:

```
rpm -[ivhqladefUV] [—force] [—nodeps] [—oldpackage] package list
```

This is the Red Hat Package Manager program. It allows you to manage RPM packages, making it very easy to install and uninstall software.

To install a new RPM package called precious-software-1.0.i386.rpm, run:

```
rpm -i precious-software-1.0.i386.rpm
```

You can make rpm a bit more verbose by using -ivh instead of just the -i option. If you have installed the package and for some reason would like to install it again, you need to use the --force option to force rpm.

If you are upgrading a software package, you should use the -U option. For example:

```
rpm -Uvh precious-software-2.0.i386.rpm
```

This command upgrades the previous version of the precious-software package to version 2.0. However, if you have installed a newer version and want to go back to the previous version, rpm detects this condition and displays an error message saying that the installed version is newer than the one you are trying to install. In such a case, should you decide to proceed anyway, use the --oldpackage option with the -U option to force rpm to downgrade your software.

To find a list of all available packages installed on your system, run:

```
rpm -qa
```

To find out which package a program such as sendmail belongs to, run:

```
rpm -q sendmail
```

This returns the RPM package name you use to install sendmail. To find out which package a specific file such as /bin/tcsh belongs to, run:

```
rpm -qf /bin/tcsh
```

This displays the package name of the named file. If you are interested in finding the documentation that comes with a file, use the -d option along with the -qf options. To list all files associated with a program or package, such as sendmail, use the -l option, as shown here:

```
rpm -ql sendmail
```

To ensure that an installed package is not modified in any way, you can use the -V option. For example, to verify that all installed packages are in their original state, run the following:

```
rpm -Va
```

This option becomes very useful if you learn that you or someone else could have damaged one or more packages.

To uninstall a package such as sendmail, run:

```
rpm -e sendmail
```

If you find that removing a package or program breaks other programs because they depend on it or its files, you have to decide if you want to break these programs or not. If you decide to remove the package or the program, you can use the --nodeps option with the -e option to force rpm to uninstall the package.

tar

Syntax:

```
tar [c] [x] [v] [z] [f filename]   file or directory names
```

The tar command allows you to archive multiple files and directories into a single .tar file. It also allows you to extract files and directories from such an archive file. For example:

```
tar cf source.tar *.c
```

This command creates a tar file called source.tar, which contains all C source files (ending with extension .c) in the current directory.

```
tar cvf source.tar *.c
```

Here the v option allows you to see which files are being archived by tar.

```
tar cvzf backup.tar.gz  important_dir
```

Here all the files and subdirectories of the directory called important_dir are archived in a file called backup.tar.gz. Notice that the z option is compressing this file; hence, we should give the resulting file a .gz extension. Often, the .tar.gz extension is shortened by many users to be .tgz as well.

To extract an archive file, backup.tar, you can run:

```
tar xf backup.tar
```

To extract a compressed tar file (such as backup.tgz or backup.tar.gz), you can run:

```
tar xzf backup.tgz
```

uncompress

Syntax:

```
uncompress [-v] file(s)
```

When we use the compress command to compress a file, the file is no longer in its original form. To return a compressed file to its original form, use the uncompress command.

The uncompress command expects to find a file with a .Z extension, so the command line "uncompress inbox" is equivalent to "uncompress inbox.Z."

The -v option produces verbose output.

```
uncompress -v inbox.Z
inbox.Z: —replaced with inbox
```

unzip

Syntax:

```
unzip file(s)
```

This command decompresses files with the .zip extension. We can compress these files with the unzip command, Phil Katz's PKZIP, or any other PKZIP-compatible program.

uudecode

Syntax:

```
uudecode file
```

The `uudecode` command transforms a uuencoded file into its original form. `uudecode` creates the file by using the "target_name" the uuencode command specifies, which we can also identify on the first line of a uuencoded file.

To convert our uuencoded file from the following entry back to its original form:

```
uudecode a.out.txt
```

As a result, we create the executable file a.out from the text file a.out.txt.

uuencode

Syntax:

```
uuencode in_file target_name
```

The `uuencode` command translates a binary file into readable form. We do this by converting the binary file into ASCII printable characters. One of the many uses of `uuencode` is transmitting a binary file through e-mail. A file we have uuencoded appears as a large e-mail message. The recipient can then save the message and use the `uudecode` command to retrieve its binary form.

The target_name is the name of the binary file we create when we use the uuencode.

This example uuencodes the executable program a.out. The target name that uudecode creates is b.out. We save the uuencoded version of a.out in the file a.out.txt.

```
uuencode a.out b.out > a.out.txt
```

zip

Syntax:

```
zip [-ACDe9] file(s)
```

This compression utility compresses files in a more popular format, enabling compatibility with systems such as VMS, MS-DOS, OS/2, Windows NT, Minix, Atari, Macintosh, Amiga, and Acorn RISC OS. This is mainly because of zip's compatibility with Phil Katz's PKZIP program. Files compressed with zip have the .zip extension.

The `zip` command has an array of options that are toggled by its switches. This command can create self-extracting files, add comments to ZIP files, remove files from an archive, and password-protect the archive.

These are a few of the features zip supports. For a more detailed description, see your local man page.

File Systems – Specific Commands

The commands in this section deal with file systems.

dd

Syntax:

```
dd if=input file [conv=conversion type] of=output file [obs=output
block size]
```

This program allows you to convert file formats. For example:

```
dd if=/tmp/uppercase.txt   conv=lcase of=/tmp/lowercase.txt
```

This command takes the /tmp/upppercase.txt file and writes a new file called /tmp/lowercase.txt and converts all characters to lowercase (lcase). To do the reverse, you can use conv=ucase option. However, dd is most widely used to write a boot image file to a floppy disk that has a file system that mkfs has already created. For example:

```
dd if=/some/boot.img   conv=lcase of=/dev/fd0 obs=16k
```

This command writes the /some/boot.image file to the first floppy disk (/dev/fd0) in 16KB blocks.

df

Syntax:

```
df  [-k] FileSystem | File
```

The df command summarizes the free disk space for the drives mounted on the system. Hard disk space is an important resource in a computer, and we should monitor it carefully. Mismanagement of hard disk space can cause a computer to crawl on its knees and can cause some unhappy users.

```
df

Filesystem      512-blocks      Free %Used   Iused %Iused Mounted on
/dev/hd4          49152        25872  48%     2257    19% /
```

```
/dev/hd2           1351680     243936    82%    19091    12% /usr
/dev/hd9var          49152      12224    76%     2917    48% /var
/dev/hd3             57344      52272     9%      125     2% /tmp
/dev/lv00            57344      55176     4%       19     1% /tftpboot
/dev/hd1            163840      16976    90%     1140     6% /home
/dev/fs01          8192000    6381920    23%    20963     3% /home/fs01
/dev/fs02          8192000    1873432    78%       72     1% /home/fs02
```

To view the disk space summary for the current file system:

```
df .
Filesystem    512-blocks      Free %Used     Iused %Iused Mounted on
/dev/fs01        8192000   6381920   23%     20963      3% /home/fs01
```

Notice that the db output is printed in 512-byte blocks. It may seem odd to think of blocks with this size if you are used to 1K blocks or more precisely 1,024-byte blocks. The -k option displays the summary with 1,024-byte blocks instead:

```
df -k .

Filesystem    1024-blocks      Free %Used     Iused %Iused Mounted on
/dev/fs01        4096000   3190960   23%     20963      3% /home/fs01
```

With the -k option in mind, the results are very different. If you interpret the output incorrectly, you may run out of disk space sooner than you think.

edquota

See the section on assigning disk quotas to users in Chapter 7 for details.

fdformat

Syntax:

```
fdformat  floppy-device
```

This program does a low-level format on a floppy device. For example:

```
fdformat /dev/fd0H1440
```

This formats the first floppy disk (/dev/fd0) as a high-density 1.44MB disk.

fdisk

See Chapter 2 for details.

mkfs

Syntax:

```
mkfs [-t fstype] [-cv] device-or-mount-point [blocks]
```

This command allows you to make a new file system. For example:

```
mkfs -t ext2 /dev/hda3
```

The preceding command creates an ext2-type file system on the /dev/hda3 partition of the first IDE hard disk. The -c option allows you instruct mkfs to check bad blocks before building the file system; the -v option produces verbose output.

mkswap

See Chapter 2 for details.

mount

Syntax:

```
mount -a [-t fstype] [-o options] device  directory
```

This command mounts a file system. Typically, the mount options for commonly used file systems are stored in /etc/fstab. For example:

```
/dev/hda6  /intranet  ext2  defaults 1 2
```

If the preceding line is in /etc/fstab, you can mount the file system stored in partition /dev/hda6 as follows:

```
mount  /intranet
```

You can also mount the same file system as follows:

```
mount  -t ext2 /dev/hda6 /intranet
```

We use the -t option to specify file system type. To mount all the file systems specified in the /etc/fstab, use the -a option. For example:

```
mount  -a -t ext2
```

The preceding command mounts all ext2 file systems. Commonly used options for -o option are ro (read-only) and rw (read/write). For example:

```
mount  -t ext2 -o ro /dev/hda6 /secured
```

The preceding command mounts /dev/hda6 on /secured as a read-only file system.

quota

See the section on monitoring disk usage in Chapter 7 for details.

quotaon

See the section on configuring your system to support disk quotas in Chapter 7 for details.

swapoff

Syntax:

```
swapoff -a
```

This command allows you to disable swap devices. The -a option allows you to disable all swap partitions specified in /etc/fstab.

swapon

Syntax:

```
swapon -a
```

This command allows you to enable swap devices. The -a option allows you to enable all swap partitions specified in /etc/fstab.

umount

Syntax:

```
umount  -a [-t fstype]
```

This command unmounts a file system from the current system. For example:

```
umount  /cdrom
```

The preceding command unmounts a file system whose mount point is /cdrom and the details of whose mount point are specified in /etc/fstab.

The -a option allows you to unmount all file systems (except for the proc file system) specified in the /etc/fstab file. You can also use the -t option to specify a particular file system type to unmount. For example:

```
umount  -a -t iso9660
```

This command unmounts all iso9660-type file systems, which are typically CD-ROMs.

DOS-Compatible Commands

If you need access to MS-DOS files from your Linux system, you need to install the Mtools package. Mtools is shipped with Red Hat as an RPM package, so installing it is quite simple. See the rpm command for details on how to install an RPM package.

Mtools is a collection of utilities that allow you to read, write, and move around MS-DOS files. It also supports Windows 95–style long filenames, OS/2 Xdf disks, and 2m disks. The following section covers the common utilities in the Mtools package.

mcopy

Syntax:

```
mcopy [-tm] source-file-or-directory  destination-file-or-directory
```

We use the mcopy utility to copy MS-DOS files to and from Linux. For example:

```
mcopy  /tmp/readme.txt   b:
```

The preceding command copies the readme.txt file from the /tmp directory to the b: drive. The -t option enables you to automatically translate carriage return/line feed pairs in MS-DOS text files into new line feeds. The -m option allows you to preserve file modification time.

mdel

Syntax:

```
mdel msdosfile
```

This utility allows you to delete files on an MS-DOS file system.

mdir

Syntax:

```
mdir [-/] msdos-file-or-directory
```

This utility allows you to view an MS-DOS directory. The `-/` option allows you to view all the subdirectories as well.

mformat

Syntax:

```
mformat [-t cylinders] [-h heads] [-s sectors]
```

This utility allows you to format a floppy disk to hold a minimal MS-DOS file system. I find it much easier to format a disk by using an MS-DOS machine than to specify cylinders, heads, sectors, and so on.

mlabel

Syntax:

```
mlabel [-vcs] drive:[new label]
```

This utility displays the current volume label (if any) of the name drive and prompts for the new label if you do not enter it after the drive: in the command line. The `-v` option prints a hex dump of the boot sector of the named drive; the `-c` option clears the existing volume label, and the `-s` shows the existing label of the drive.

System Status – Specific Commands

The commands we discuss in this section deal with status information on system resources.

dmesg

Syntax:

```
dmesg
```

This program prints the status messages the kernel displays during bootup.

free

Syntax:

```
free
```

This program displays memory usage statistics. An example of output looks like this:

```
            total    used    free   shared  buffers  cached
Mem:        127776   124596  3180   30740   2904     107504
-/+ buffers/cache:   14188   113588
Swap:       129900   84      129816
```

shutdown

Syntax:

```
shutdown [-r] [-h] [-c] [-k]  [-t seconds] time [message]
```

This command allows a superuser or an ordinary user listed in the /etc/shutdown. allow file to shut the system down for a reboot or halt. To reboot the computer now, run:

```
shutdown -r now
```

To halt the system after the shutdown, replace the -r with -h. The -k option allows you to simulate a shutdown event. For example:

```
shutdown -r -k now System going down for maintenance
```

This command sends a fake shutdown message to all users. The -t option allows you to specify a delay in seconds between the warning message and the actual shutdown event. In such a case, if you decide to abort the shutdown, run shutdown again with the -c option to cancel it.

Note that you can use the HH:MM format to specify the time. For example:

```
shutdown -r 12:55
```

This reboots the system at 12:55. You can also use +minutes to specify time. For example:

```
shutdown -r +5
```

This starts the shutdown process five minutes after you print the warning message.

uname

Syntax:

```
uname [-m] [-n] [-r] [-s] [-v] [-a]
```

This command displays information about the current system. For example:

```
uname -a
```

This command displays a line such as the following:

```
Linux picaso.nitec.com 2.0.36 #1 Tue Oct 13 22:17:11 EDT 1998 i586
unknown
```

The -m option displays the system architecture (for instance, i586); the -n option displays the host name (for instance, picaso.nitec.com); the -r option displays the release version of the operating system (for instance, 2.0.36); the -s option displays the operating system name (for instance, Linux); and the -v option displays the local build version of the operating system (for instance, #1 Tue Oct 13 22:17:11 EDT 1998).

uptime

Syntax:

```
uptime
```

This command displays current time, how long the system has been up since the last reboot, how many users are connected to the server, and the system load in the last 1, 5, and 15 minutes.

User Administration Commands

The commands in this section deal with user administration.

chfn

See the section on modifying an existing user account in Chapter 7.

chsh

See the section on modifying an existing user account in Chapter 7.

groupadd

See the section on creating a new group in Chapter 7.

groupmod

See the section on modifying an existing group in Chapter 7.

groups

Syntax:

```
groups [username]
```

This command displays the list of group(s) the named user currently belongs to. If no username is specified, this command displays the current user's groups.

last

Syntax:

```
last [-number] [username]  [reboot]
```

This command displays a list of users who have logged in since /var/log/wtmp was created. For example:

```
last julie
```

This command shows the number of times user julie has logged in since the last time /var/log/wtmp was created.

```
last -10 julie
```

This command shows only the last 10 logins by julie.

```
last reboot
```

This displays the number of times the system has been rebooted since /var/log/ wtmp file was created.

passwd

Syntax:

```
passwd username
```

This command allows you to change a user's password. Only a superuser can specify a username; everyone else must type passwd without any argument, which allows the user to change his or her password. A superuser can change anyone's password using this program.

su

Syntax:

```
su  [-]  [username]
```

You can use the su command to change into another user. For example:

```
su john
```

This command allows you to be the user john as long as you know john's password, and this account exists on the server you use.

The most common use of this command is to become root. For example, if you run this command without any username argument, it assumes that you want to be root and prompts you for the root password. If you enter the correct root password, su runs a shell by using the root's UID (0) and GID (0). This allows you effectively to become the root user and to perform administrative tasks. This command is very useful if you have only Telnet access to the server. You can telnet into the server as a regular user and use it to become root to perform system administrative tasks. If you supply the – option, the new shell is marked as the login shell. Once you become the root user, you can su to other users without entering any password.

useradd

See the section on creating new user account in Chapter 7.

userdel

See the section on deleting or disabling a user account in Chapter 7.

usermod

See the section on modifying an existing user account in Chapter 7.

who

Syntax:

```
who
```

This command displays information about the users who are currently logged into a system. You can also use the w command for the same purpose.

whoami

Syntax:

```
whoami
```

This command displays your current username.

User Commands for Accessing Network Services

The commands we discuss in this section allow you to access various network services.

finger

Syntax:

```
finger user@host
```

This program allows you to query a finger daemon at the named host. For example:

```
finger kabir@blackhole.integrationlogic.com
```

This command requests a finger connection to the finger daemon running on the `blackhole.integrationlogic.com` server. If the named host does not allow finger connections, this attempt fails. On success, the finger request displays information about the named user. If the user has a .plan file in the home directory, most traditional finger daemons display this file. Because finger has been used by hackers to cause security problems, most system administrators disable finger service outside their domains.

ftp

Syntax:

```
ftp ftp hostname or IP address
```

This is the default FTP client program. You can use this to FTP to an FTP server. For example:

```
ftp  ftp.cdrom.com
```

This opens an FTP connection to `ftp.cdrom.com` and prompts you to enter a username and a password. If you know the username and password, you can log into the FTP server and upload or download files. Once you are at the FTP prompt, you can enter "help" or "?" to get help on FTP commands.

lynx

Syntax:

```
lynx [-dump] [-head] [URL]
```

This is the most popular interactive text-based Web browser. For example:

```
lynx http://www.integrationlogic.com/
```

This command displays the top page of the site. It is a very handy program to have. For example, say you want quickly to find what kind of Web server the site uses without asking the Webmaster. You can run the following command:

```
lynx -head http://www.integrationlogic.com/
```

This displays the HTTP header the lynx browser receives from the Web server. An example of output is shown here:

```
HTTP/1.1 302 Moved
Date: Tue, 02 Mar 1999 06:47:27 GMT
Server: Apache/1.3.3 (Unix)
Location: http://www.integrationlogic.com/index.shtml
Connection: close
Content-Type: text/html
```

As you can see, this header shows that www.integrationlogic.com runs on the Apache 1.3.3 Web server on a UNIX platform. Note that not all Web sites give their Web server platform information, but most do. If you would like to avoid the interactive mode, you can use the -dump option to dump the page on the screen (STDOUT). For example,

```
lynx -dump -head http://www.integrationlogic.com/
```

This dumps the header to stdout. The -dump feature can be quite handy. For example:

```
lynx -dump -head http://webserver/new.gif > new.gif
```

This allows you to save new.gif on the Web server host on a local file called new.gif.

The interactive mode allows you to browse a text browser-friendly site in a reasonably nice manner.

mail

Syntax:

```
mail user@host [-s subject]  [< filename]
```

This is the default SMTP mail client program. You can use this program to send or receive mail from your system. For example, if you run this program without any argument, it displays a "&" prompt and shows you the currently unread mail messages by listing them in a numeric list. To read a message, enter the index number, and the mail is displayed. To learn more about mail, use the "?" command once you are at the "&" prompt.

To send a message to a user called kabir@integrationlogic.com with the subject header "About your Red Hat book," you can run:

```
mail  kabir@integrationlogic.com  -s "About your Red Hat book"
```

You can then enter your mail message and press Ctrl+D to end the message. You can switch to your default text editor by entering ~v at the beginning of a line while you are in the compose mode.

If you have already prepared a mail message in a file, you can send it using a command such as:

```
mail  kabir@nitec.com  -s "About your Red Hat book" << feedback.txt
```

This sends a message with the given subject line; the message consists of the contents of the feedback.txt file.

pine

Syntax:

```
pine
```

This is a full-screen SMTP mail client that is quite user-friendly. If you typically use mail clients via telnet, you should definitely try this program. Because of its user-friendly interfaces, it is suitable for your Linux users who are not yet friends with Linux.

rlogin

Syntax:

```
rlogin [-l username] host
```

This command allows you to log remotely into a host. For example, to log into a host called `shell.myhost.com`, you can run:

```
rlogin shell.myhost.com
```

Because rlogin is not safe, I recommend that you use it only in a closed LAN environment. The `-l` option allows you to specify a username to use for authentication. If you would like to log remotely into a host without entering a password, create a .rhosts file in the user's home directory. Add the hostname or IP address of the computer you use to issue the rlogin request. Again, because many consider this a security risk, I do not recommend wide use of rlogin.

talk

Syntax:

```
talk username tty
```

If you need to send a message to another user, e-mail works just fine. But if you need to communicate with another user in real-time, like a telephone conversation, use the `talk` command.

To talk to another user who is logged in:

```
talk ronak@csus.edu
```

The user you request has to accept your talk request. Once the user accepts your talk request, you can begin talking (or typing) to each other. The talk program terminates when either party executes Ctrl+C (the intr key).

telnet

Syntax:

```
telnet hostname or IP address  [port]
```

This is the default Telnet client program. You can use this program to connect to a Telnet server. For example:

```
telnet  shell.myportal.com
```

This command opens a Telnet connection to the `shell.myportal.com` system if the named host runs a Telnet server. Once a connection is opened, the command prompts you for username and password and, on successful login, allows you to access a local user account on the Telnet server.

wall

Syntax:

```
wall
```

This command allows you to send a text message to everyone's terminal as long as he or she has not disabled write access to the tty via the `mesg n` command. Once you type wall, you can enter a single or multiline message and can send it by pressing Ctrl+D.

Network Administrator's Commands

The commands we discuss in this section allow you to gather information on network services and on the network itself.

host

Syntax:

```
host  [-a] host IP address
```

By default, this program allows you to check the IP address of a host quickly. If you use the `-a` option, it returns various sorts of DNS information about the named host or IP address.

hostname

Syntax:

```
hostname
```

This program displays the host name of a system.

ifconfig

Syntax:

```
ifconfig [interface] [up | down] [netmask mask]
```

This program allows you to configure a network interface. You can also see the state of an interface using this program. For example, if you have configured your

Red Hat Linux for networking and have a preconfigured network interface device, eth0, you can run:

```
ifconfig eth0
```

You should see output similar to the following:

```
eth0 Link encap:Ethernet HWaddr 00:C0:F6:98:37:37
     inet addr:206.171.50.50  Bcast:206.171.50.63 Mask:255.255.255.240
     UP BROADCAST RUNNING MULTICAST  MTU:1500  Metric:1
     RX packets:9470 errors:0 dropped:0 overruns:0 frame:0
     TX packets:7578 errors:0 dropped:0 overruns:0 carrier:0 collisions:0
     Interrupt:5 Base address:0x340
```

Here ifconfig reports that network interface device eth0 has an Internet address (inet addr) 206.171.50.50, a broadcast address (Bcast) 206.171.50.63, and network mask (255.255.255.240). The rest of the information shows the following: how many packets this interface has received (RX packets); how many packets this interface has transmitted (TX packets); how many errors of different types have occurred so far; what interrupt address line this device is using; what I/O address base is being used; and so on.

You can run ifconfig without any arguments to get the full list of all the up network devices.

You can use ifconfig to bring an interface up. For example:

```
ifconfig eth0 206.171.50.50 netmask 255.255.255.240 \
broadcast 206.171.50.63
```

The preceding command starts eth0 with IP address 206.171.50.50. You can also quickly take an interface down by using the ifconfig command. For example:

```
ifconfig eth0 down
```

This command takes the eth0 interface down.

netcfg

See the section on using netcfg to configure a network interface card in Chapter 9.

netstat

Syntax:

```
netstat [-r] [-a] [-c] [-i]
```

This program displays the status of the network connections both to and from the local system. For example:

```
netstat -a
```

This command displays all the network connections on the local system. To display the routing table, use the -r option. To display network connection status on a continuous basis, use the -c option. To display information on all network interfaces, use the -i option.

nslookup

Syntax:

```
nslookup [-query=DNS record type] [hostname or IP] [name server]
```

This command allows you to perform DNS queries. You can choose to query a DNS server in an interactive fashion or just look up information immediately. For example:

```
nslookup -query=mx integrationlogic.com
```

This command immediately returns the MX records for the integrationlogic. com domain.

```
nslookup -query=mx integrationlogic.com ns.nitec.com
```

This command does the same, but instead of using the default name server specified in the /etc/resolv.conf file, it uses ns.nitec.com as the name server. You can also use -q instead of -query. For example:

```
nslookup -q=a  www.formtrack.com
```

This command returns the IP address (Address record) for the named hostname. You can run nslookup in interactive mode as well. Just run the command without any parameters, and you will see the nslookup prompt. At the nslookup prompt, you can enter "?" to get help. If you are planning on performing multiple DNS queries at a time, interactive mode can be very helpful. For example, to query the NS records for multiple domains such as ad-engine.com and classifiedworks. com, you can just enter the following command:

```
set query=ns
```

Once you set the query type to ns, you can simply type ad-engine.com and wait for the reply; once you get the reply, you can try the next domain name; and so on.

If you would like to change the name server while at the nslookup prompt, use the server command. For example:

```
server ns.ad-engine.com
```

This will make nslookup use `ns.ad-engine.com` as the name server. To quit interactive mode and return to your shell prompt, enter exit at the nslookup prompt.

ping

Syntax:

```
ping [-c count] [-s packet size] [-I interface]
```

This is one of the programs network administrators use most widely. We use it to see if a remote computer is reachable via the TCP/IP protocol. Technically, this program sends an Internet Control Message Protocol (ICMP) echo request to the remote host. Because the protocol requires a response to an echo request, the remote host is bound to send an echo response. This allows the ping program to calculate the amount of time it takes to send a packet to a remote host. For example:

```
ping blackhole.nitec.com
```

This command sends ping messages to the `blackhole.nitec.com` host on a continuous basis. To stop the ping program, you need to press Ctrl+C, which causes the program to display a set of statistics. Here is an example of output of the ping requests the preceding command generates:

```
PING blackhole.nitec.com (209.63.178.15): 56 data bytes
64 bytes from 209.63.178.15: icmp_seq=0 ttl=53 time=141.5 ms
64 bytes from 209.63.178.15: icmp_seq=1 ttl=53 time=162.6 ms
64 bytes from 209.63.178.15: icmp_seq=2 ttl=53 time=121.4 ms
64 bytes from 209.63.178.15: icmp_seq=3 ttl=53 time=156.0 ms
64 bytes from 209.63.178.15: icmp_seq=4 ttl=53 time=126.4 ms
64 bytes from 209.63.178.15: icmp_seq=5 ttl=53 time=101.5 ms
64 bytes from 209.63.178.15: icmp_seq=6 ttl=53 time=98.7 ms
64 bytes from 209.63.178.15: icmp_seq=7 ttl=53 time=180.9 ms
64 bytes from 209.63.178.15: icmp_seq=8 ttl=53 time=126.2 ms
64 bytes from 209.63.178.15: icmp_seq=9 ttl=53 time=122.3 ms
64 bytes from 209.63.178.15: icmp_seq=10 ttl=53 time=127.1 ms
-- blackhole.nitec.com ping statistics--
11 packets transmitted, 11 packets received, 0% packet loss
round-trip min/avg/max = 98.7/133.1/180.9 ms
```

The preceding output shows 10 ping requests to the `blackhole.nitec.com` host. Because the program is interrupted after the 11th request, the statistics show that ping has transmitted 11 packets and has also received all the packets, and therefore no packet loss has occurred. This is good in that packet loss is a sign of poor networking between the ping requester and the ping responder. The other interesting statistics are the round-trip minimum (min) time, the average (avg) time, and the maximum (max) time. The lower these numbers are, the better the routing is between the involved hosts. For example, if you ping a host on the same LAN, you should see the round-trip numbers in the one-millisecond range.

If you would like to have ping automatically stop after transmitting a number of packets, use the `-c` option. For example:

```
ping -c 10 blackhole.nitec.com
```

This sends 10 ping requests to the named host. By default, ping sends a 64-byte (56 data bytes + 8 header bytes) packet. If you are also interested in controlling the size of the packet sent, use the `-s` option. For example:

```
ping -c 1024 -s 1016 reboot.nitec.com
```

This command sends a packet 1,024 (1016 + 8) bytes long to the remote host.

 By sending large packets to a remote host running weak operating systems (you know what they are), you might cause the host to become very unusable to the user(s) on the remote host. This could be considered as an attack by many system administrators and therefore is very likely to be illegal in most parts of the world. So be very careful when you start experimenting with ping and someone else's computer.

route

Syntax:

```
route add -net network address netmask dev device
route add -host hostname or IP dev device
route add default gw hostname or IP
```

This command allows you to control routing to and from your computer. For example, to create a default route for your network, use the route command as follows:

```
route add -net network address netmask   device
```

For example, to create a default route for 206.171.50.48 network with a 255.
255.255.240 netmask and eth0 as the interface, you can run:

```
route add -net 206.171.50.48 255.255.255.240 eth0
```

To set the default gateway, you can run the route command as follows:

```
route add  default gw gateway address device
```

For example, to set the default gateway address to 206.171.50.49, you can run
the following command:

```
route add  default gw 206.171.50.49 eth0
```

You can verify that your network route and default gateway are properly set up
in the routing table by using the following command:

```
route -n
```

Here is an example of output of the preceding command:

```
Kernel IP routing table
Destination   Gateway Genmask         Flags Metric Ref Use Iface
206.171.50.48 0.0.0.0 255.255.255.240 U     0      0   6   eth0
127.0.0.0     0.0.0.0 255.0.0.0       U     0      0   5   lo
0.0.0.0       206.171.50.49  0.0.0.0 UG     0      0   17  eth0
```

 TIP Make sure you have IP forwarding turned on in /etc/sysconfig/network and also in the kernel to allow routing packets between two different network interfaces.

tcpdump

Syntax:

```
tcpdump expression
```

This is a great network debugging tool. For example, to trace all the packets
between two hosts brat.nitec.com and reboot.nitec.com, you can use the following command:

```
tcpdump host brat.nitec.com and reboot.nitec.com
```

This command makes tcpdump listen for packets between these two computers. If reboot.nitec.com starts sending ping requests to brat.nitec.com, the output looks something like the following:

```
tcpdump: listening on eth0
09:21:14.720000 reboot.nitec.com> brat.nitec.com: icmp: echo request
09:21:14.720000 brat.nitec.com> reboot.nitec.com: icmp: echo reply
09:21:15.720000 reboot.nitec.com> brat.nitec.com: icmp: echo request
09:21:15.720000 brat.nitec.com> reboot.nitec.com: icmp: echo reply
09:21:16.720000 reboot.nitec.com> brat.nitec.com: icmp: echo request
09:21:16.720000 brat.nitec.com> reboot.nitec.com: icmp: echo reply
09:21:17.730000 reboot.nitec.com> brat.nitec.com: icmp: echo request
09:21:17.730000 brat.nitec.com> reboot.nitec.com: icmp: echo reply
```

If you are having a problem connecting to an FTP server, you can use tcpdump on your LAN gateway system to see what is going on. For example:

```
tcpdump port ftp or ftp-data
```

This displays the FTP-related packets originating and arriving in your network.

As you can see, this allows you to debug a network problem at a low level. If you are experiencing a problem in using a service between two hosts, you can use tcpdump to identify the problem.

traceroute

Syntax:

```
traceroute host or IP address
```

This program allows you to locate network routing problems. It displays the routes between two hosts by tricking the gateways between the hosts into responding to an ICMP TIME_EXCEEDED request. Here is an example of a traceroute from my local system to the blackhole.nitec.com host:

```
traceroute to blackhole.nitec.com (209.63.178.15), 30 hops max, 40
byte packets
 1 router (206.171.50.49)  4.137 ms  3.995 ms  4.738 ms
 2 PM3-001.v1.NET (206.171.48.10) 32.683 ms  33.295 ms  33.255 ms
 3 HQ-CS001.v1.NET (206.171.48.1) 42.263 ms  44.237 ms  36.784 ms
 4 ix.pxbi.net (206.13.15.97) 106.785 ms  63.585 ms  101.277 ms
 5 ix.pxbi.net (206.13.31.8) 86.283 ms  64.246 ms  69.749 ms
 6 ca.us.ixbm.net (165.87.22.10) 71.415 ms  72.319 ms  85.183 ms
 7 mae.elxi.net (198.32.136.128) 101.863 ms  80.257 ms  67.323 ms
 8 y.exli.net (207.173.113.146) 71.323 ms  104.685 ms  110.935 ms
```

```
 9 z.exli.net (207.173.113.217) 69.964 ms  137.858 ms  85.326 ms
10 z1.exli.net (207.173.112.251) 81.257 ms  107.575 ms  78.453 ms
11 209.210.249.50 (209.210.249.50) 90.701 ms  91.116 ms  109.491 ms
12 209.63.178.15 (209.63.178.15)  83.052 ms  76.604 ms  85.406 ms
```

Each line represents a hop; the more hops there are, the worse the route usually is. In other words, if you have only a few gateways between the source and the destination, chances are that packets between these two hosts are going to be transferred at a reasonably fast pace. However, this won't be true all the time because it takes only a single, slow gateway to mess up delivery time. Using traceroute, you can locate where your packets are going and where they are perhaps getting stuck. Once you locate a problem point, you can contact the appropriate authorities to resolve the routing problem.

Process Management Commands

The commands we discuss in this section show you how to manage processes, i.e., running programs in your system.

bg

Syntax:

```
bg
```

This built-in shell command is found in popular shells. This command allows you to put a suspended process into background. For example, say that you decide to run du -a / | sort -rn > /tmp/du.sorted to list all the files and directories in your system according to the disk usage (size) order and to put the result in a file called /tmp/du.sorted. Depending on the number of files you have on your system, this can take a while. In such a case, you can simply suspend the command line by using Ctrl+Z and type bg to send all the commands involved in the command line to background, thus returning your shell prompt for other use.

 TIP If you wish to run a command in the background from the start, you can simply append "&" to the end of the command line.

To find out what commands are running in the background, enter jobs and you see the list of background command lines. To bring a command from the background, use the fg command.

fg

Syntax:

```
fg [%job-number]
```

This built-in shell command is found in popular shells. This command allows you to put a background process into foreground. If you run this command without any argument, it brings up the last command you put in the background. If you have multiple commands running in the background, you can use the jobs command to find the job number and can supply this number as an argument for fg to bring it to the foreground. For example, if jobs shows that you have two commands in the background, you can bring up the first command you put in the background by using:

```
fg %1
```

jobs

Syntax:

```
jobs
```

This built-in shell command is found in popular shells. This command allows you to view the list of processes running in the background or currently suspended.

kill

See the section on signaling a running process in Chapter 8.

killall

See the section on signaling a running process in Chapter 8.

ps

See the section on using ps to get process status in Chapter 8.

top

See the section on monitoring processes and system load in Chapter 8.

Task Automation Commands

The commands we discuss in this section show you how to run unattended tasks.

at

See the section on scheduling processes section in Chapter 8.

atq

See the section on scheduling processes in Chapter 8.

atrm

See the section on scheduling processes in Chapter 8.

crontab

See the section on scheduling processes in Chapter 8.

Productivity Commands

The commands we discuss in this section help you increase your productivity.

bc

Syntax:

```
bc
```

This is an interactive calculator that implements a calculator-specific language as well. Personally, I am not all that interested in learning the language, but I find this tool very useful in doing quick calculations. When you run the command without any arguments, it takes your input and interprets it as calculator programming statements. For example, to multiply 1,024 by 4, you can simply enter 1024*4 and the result is displayed. You can reuse the current result by using the period character.

cal

Syntax:

```
cal [month] [year]
```

This nifty program displays a nicely formatted calendar for the month or year specified in the command line. If you do not specify anything as an argument, the calendar for the current month is displayed. To see the calendar for an entire year, enter the year in 1–9999 range. For example:

```
cal 2000
```

This command displays the following calendar for the year 2000:

```
                                     2000

          January                  February                   March
 Su Mo Tu We Th Fr Sa     Su Mo Tu We Th Fr Sa     Su Mo Tu We Th Fr Sa
                    1            1  2  3  4  5            1  2  3  4
  2  3  4  5  6  7  8      6  7  8  9 10 11 12      5  6  7  8  9 10 11
  9 10 11 12 13 14 15     13 14 15 16 17 18 19     12 13 14 15 16 17 18
 16 17 18 19 20 21 22     20 21 22 23 24 25 26     19 20 21 22 23 24 25
 23 24 25 26 27 28 29     27 28 29                 26 27 28 29 30 31
 30 31
           April                     May                      June
 Su Mo Tu We Th Fr Sa     Su Mo Tu We Th Fr Sa     Su Mo Tu We Th Fr Sa
                    1         1  2  3  4  5  6               1  2  3
  2  3  4  5  6  7  8      7  8  9 10 11 12 13      4  5  6  7  8  9 10
  9 10 11 12 13 14 15     14 15 16 17 18 19 20     11 12 13 14 15 16 17
 16 17 18 19 20 21 22     21 22 23 24 25 26 27     18 19 20 21 22 23 24
 23 24 25 26 27 28 29     28 29 30 31              25 26 27 28 29 30
 30
           July                    August                  September
 Su Mo Tu We Th Fr Sa     Su Mo Tu We Th Fr Sa     Su Mo Tu We Th Fr Sa
                    1         1  2  3  4  5                        1  2
  2  3  4  5  6  7  8      6  7  8  9 10 11 12      3  4  5  6  7  8  9
  9 10 11 12 13 14 15     13 14 15 16 17 18 19     10 11 12 13 14 15 16
 16 17 18 19 20 21 22     20 21 22 23 24 25 26     17 18 19 20 21 22 23
 23 24 25 26 27 28 29     27 28 29 30 31           24 25 26 27 28 29 30
 30 31
          October                  November                 December
 Su Mo Tu We Th Fr Sa     Su Mo Tu We Th Fr Sa     Su Mo Tu We Th Fr Sa
  1  2  3  4  5  6  7            1  2  3  4                        1  2
  8  9 10 11 12 13 14      5  6  7  8  9 10 11      3  4  5  6  7  8  9
 15 16 17 18 19 20 21     12 13 14 15 16 17 18     10 11 12 13 14 15 16
 22 23 24 25 26 27 28     19 20 21 22 23 24 25     17 18 19 20 21 22 23
 29 30 31                 26 27 28 29 30           24 25 26 27 28 29 30
                                                   31
```

ispell

Syntax:

```
ispell filename
```

This program allows you to correct spelling mistakes in a text file in an interactive fashion. If you have a misspelling in the file, the program suggests a spelling and gives you options to replace it with a correctly spelled word. This is the spell checker for text files.

mesg

Syntax:

```
mesg [y | n]
```

This program allows you to enable or disable public write access to your terminal. For example:

```
mesg y
```

The preceding command enables write access to your terminal so that another user on the same system can use the write command to write text messages to you. The n option allows you to disable write access. If you do not wish to be bothered by anyone at any time, you can add mesg n to your login script (.login) file.

write

Syntax:

```
write username tty
```

This program allows you to write text messages to the named user if he or she has not disabled write access to her tty. For example:

```
write  shoeman
```

This command allows you to type a text message on screen, and when you finish the message by pressing Ctrl+D, the message is displayed on the user shoeman's terminal. If the user is logged in more than once, you have to specify the terminal name as well. For example:

```
write  shoeman ttyp0
```

This allows you to write to shoeman and to display the message on terminal ttyp0. If someone has multiple terminals open, you might want to run the w or who command to see which tty is most suitable.

Shell Commands

In this section, you will find some very basic shell commands.

alias

Syntax:

```
alias   name of the alias = command
```

This is a built-in shell command available in most popular shells. This command lets you create aliases for commands. For example:

```
alias dir   ls -l
```

This command creates an alias called dir for the `ls -l` command. To see the entire alias list, run `alias` without any argument.

history

Syntax:

```
history
```

This is a built-in shell command available in most popular shells. This command displays a list of commands you have recently entered at the command line. The number of commands that history displays is limited by an environment variable called "history." For example, if you add "set history = 100" to your .login file, whenever you log in, you allow the history command to remember up to 100 command lines. You can easily rerun the commands you see in the history by entering their index number with a "!" sign. For example, say that when you enter the history command, you see the following listings:

```
1  10:25   vi irc-bot.h
2  10:25   vi irc-bot.c
3  10:26   which make
```

To run the `vi irc-bot.c` command again, you can simply enter "!2" in the command line.

set

Syntax:

```
set   var = value
```

This is a built-in shell command available in most popular shells. It allows you to set environment variables with specific values. For example:

```
set foo = bar
```

Here a new environment variable foo is set to have "bar" as the value. To see the list of all environment variables, run set by itself. To view the value of a specific environment variable, such as path, run:

```
echo $path
```

This shows you the value of the named environment variable. If you use this command quite often to set a few special environment variables, you can add it to .login or .profile or to your shell's dot file so that the special environment variables are automatically set when you log in.

source

Syntax:

```
source filename
```

This is a built-in shell command available in most popular shells. This command lets you read and execute commands from the named file in the current shell environment.

unalias

Syntax:

```
unalias    name of the alias
```

This is a built-in shell command available in most popular shells. This command lets you remove an alias for a command. For example:

```
unalias dir
```

This command removes an alias called dir. To remove all aliases, use "*" as the argument.

Printing-Specific Commands

This section discusses commands that help you print from your Linux system.

lpq

Syntax:

```
lpq [-al] [-P printer]
```

The lpq command lists the status of the printers. If you enter lpq without any arguments, information about the default printer is displayed.

```
lpq
  Printer: lp@rembrandt  'Generic dot-matrix printer entry'
  Queue: no printable jobs in queue
  Status: server finished at 21:11:33
```

The -P option specifies information about a particular printer. The -a option returns the status of all printers.

With the -1 option, lpq reports the job identification number, the user name that requests the print job, the originating host, the rank in queue, the job description, and the size of the job.

lpr

Syntax:

```
lpr [-i indentcols] [-P printer] [filename]
```

This command sends a file to the print spool to be printed. If you give no filename, data from standard input is assumed.

The -i option allows the option of starting the printing at a specific column. To specify a particular printer, we can use the -P printer option.

```
lpr main.c
```

The preceding example attempts to print the file main.c.

lprm

Syntax:

```
lprm [-a] [jobid] [all]
```

The lprm command sends a request to lpd to remove an item from the print queue. We can specify the print jobs the job ID or username is to remove, or they can include all items.

To remove all jobs in all print queues:

```
lprm -a all
```

To remove all jobs for the user "kiwee" on the printer "p1":

```
lprm -Pp1 kiwee
```

Summary

In this chapter, you learned about many useful commands that most system administrators need on a daily basis. One thing to remember is that the syntax shown here is for the most common use and not representative of the complete set of available options for a command. The goal of the chapter is to help you get started in learning various useful commands using simple examples.

Part III

Managing Users, Processes, and Networks

Chapter 6

Using Linuxconf

IN THIS CHAPTER

◆ What is Linuxconf?

◆ How to install and configure Linuxconf

◆ How to use Linuxconf via console, shell, X Windows, and the Web

THIS PART OF THE BOOK is focused on various administration aspects of the Red Hat Linux operating system. The rest of the chapters in this part cover specific topics such as user, process, and network administration. In this chapter, I discuss Linuxconf – a centralized administration facility bound to become a major selling point for the Linux operating system.

Before considering the details of Linuxconf, you need to know why it was created. For a long time, most people have thought of UNIX and UNIX-like operating systems such as Linux as cryptic. Why? Well, virtually all of them require the use of the command line and cryptic configuration files to manage most everything. No common and simple administrative interface has been available to manage such systems. This has created a high learning curve to use and administer such operating systems. Interestingly, people who overcome the hurdle of learning to use the command line and the configuration files for administering these operating systems end up enjoying the way things work. They often state that one of the strongest features of UNIX and UNIX-like operating systems is that these systems allow them to get down and dirty at a level that competing systems such as Microsoft Windows and the Mac OS have never offered. So you have people who love Linux the way it is; unfortunately, these are the same people who keep Linux moving forward. These are the same people who often append signature files to their e-mail that read something like "UNIX is not unfriendly; it is just picky about who it is friends with." So if they do not think an easier administrative user interface is needed, who is going to build one? Well, this is how things were until a few years ago.

Finally, a group of individuals and Red Hat decided to do something about it. They wanted to create a more marketable Linux system. If the average user could easily administer Linux, certainly marketability would increase a great deal. So they started the Linuxconf project. The purpose of the project has been to create a flexible, easy-to-use administration facility for Linux that provides a familiar look and feel and comes with sufficient documentation in the form of help files. Because users could access a Linux system in many ways, such as via a console/shell or via X Windows, the Linuxconf project also needed to provide multiple ways of accessing the administrative user interface. In fact, Linuxconf now offers system administration via console/shell, X Windows, and even the Web!

I personally feel that Linuxconf will greatly help market Linux as a great operating system for mass use. It will help remove a substantial part of the widespread fear that anything that is UNIX or UNIX-like, such as Red Hat Linux, is hard to manage or use. However, I also know that the traditional command line way of doing administration is not likely to go away any time soon; after all, once someone masters the command line, it is practically impossible to fall in love with middleware such as Linuxconf.

Because we live in a world in which we seek both command line and friendlier administrative interfaces, I have decided to cover both types in this book. In this chapter, I provide an introduction to Linuxconf, and when necessary, I mention Linuxconf-specific configuration procedures in other chapters, side by side with the traditional way of doing things.

What Is Linuxconf?

Actually, Linuxconf is not just a pretty user interface for administering Linux systems. It is much more than that. First of all, because we can access Linux in multiple ways, such as via Telnet, console, X Windows, or the Web, there are three Linuxconf interfaces. Second, Linuxconf is also an activator. In other words, it allows you to activate the configuration you create for your Linux system. Last but not least, when you configure something via Linuxconf, it performs validity checking to ensure that the modified configuration does not cause any problems.

Technically, Linuxconf is a C++ application that provides a core set of functionalities accessible via an Application Programming Interface (API) for external modules. Each module provides a set of functions for a certain service. For example, the Apache Web server management is implemented in the Apache module. Modules are stored in the /usr/lib/linuxconf/modules directory. Currently, many modules are distributed with the RPM package version of Linuxconf. For example, Table 6-1 shows all the modules shipped with Linuxconf version 1.1.6.

TABLE 6-1 MODULES SHIPPED WITH LINUXCONF VERSION 1.1.6

Module	Description
dhcpd	The Dynamic Host Configuration Protocol server configuration module
firewall	The firewall configuration module, which allows you packet filtering at the kernel level, IP masquerading, port redirections, and IP accounting
mailconf	Sendmail SMTP server configuration

Module	Description
motd	The message of the day file (/etc/motd) configuration module
mrtg	The Mrtg (Multi-router Traiffic Grapher) configuration module
netadm	The network configuration module
pppdialin	The PPP-related configuration module
rarp	The Linux kernel's RARP table configuration module
squid	The Squid proxy configuration module
status	The system status module
treemenu	An internal module
usermenu	An internal
wuftpd	The wu-ftpd, FTP server, configuration module
opensshd	The open sshd configuration module
syslogconf	The syslog configuration module
uucp	The uucp configuration module
kernelconf	The kernel configuration module
inittab	The /etc/inittab file configuration module
fetchmailconf	The fetchmail configuration module
ircdconf	The IRC client configuration module
modemconf	The modem configuration module
shellmod	The shell configuration module
managerpm	The RPM package management module
vregistry	The virtual registry configuration module
isapnpconf	The ISA plug and play configuration module

You may be wondering what Linuxconf can configure and manage. Well, the idea is to manage everything. Because we use external modules to manage things, it is easy for developers around the world to develop Linuxconf modules for their software. This means that once Linuxconf becomes the primary administration software because of mass use, almost everything configurable will include a Linuxconf module. Currently, Linuxconf manages the following: system time; time zone; CMOS clock; LILO; basic network configuration; the file system; user accounts; disk quota configuration; dial-up configuration; routing; the DNS server; the NFS server; the SMTP (sendmail) server; the routed router; NIS client configuration; RARP configuration; UUCP; firewalls, and so on. However, not everything is managed completely.

Installing Linuxconf

Installing Linuxconf is quite simple. If you do not install Linuxconf during your Red Hat Linux installation, you can install it any time from the RPM package shipped with the official Red Hat CD-ROM or the CD-ROM included with this book. For example, I install the following RPM packages as follows:

```
rpm   -ivh gnome-linuxconf-0.33-6.i386.rpm
rpm   -ivh linuxconf-1.19r2-2.i386.rpm
```

The above RPM packages installs Linuxconf and the GNOME version of the Linuxconf interface.

Also, you can download the RPM package from the official Linuxconf FTP site at `ftp://ftp.solucorp.qc.ca/pub/linuxconf/devel/`.

Now take a look at how to configure Linuxconf for your system.

Configuring Linuxconf

As I mentioned previously, we can use Linuxconf in multiple ways. Linuxconf automatically chooses between the text (for console or remote shell) and graphics mode (for X Windows). For example, if you log into your system console and run /sbin/linuxconf from the command line, you see a screen similar to the one in Figure 6-1.

Figure 6-1: The text interface for Linuxconf

Figure 6-1 shows the top-level menu entries – Config, Control, and Status. Here is how the navigation works in text mode.

To expand a particular branch of the menu, select it using the arrow keys, and press the Enter key. For example, to expand the Networking branch under the Config section, I can select Networking and press Enter. The result is in Figure 6-2.

Figure 6–2: Expanding the Networking section under the Config section in Linuxconf

As you can see, there are multiple branches (Networking, Users accounts, File systems, boot mode) under Config. To close a branch, select the Quit button, and press Enter. To quit Linuxconf, use the Tab key to select the Quit button again, and press Enter. Linuxconf probes the running servers and configuration and determines if anything needs to be activated. If something needs to be activated because you made some changes to something, you see a screen with the choices in Figure 6-3.

Figure 6–3: Linuxconf choices on quit

In such a case, if you would like to see what Linuxconf does to synchronize the running system with the current configuration, select the "Preview what has to be done" option, and press Enter. Another screen appears with a to-do list as in Figure 6-4.

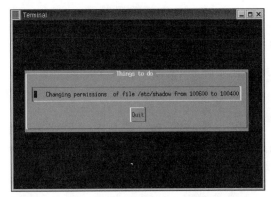

Figure 6-4: Linuxconf's things to do list

If you decide to let Linuxconf activate the listed changes, quit of the preview screen, select the Activate the changes option, and press Enter. Linuxconf activates whatever is necessary and exits.

If you would like to use Linuxconf's graphical user interface (GUI) from X Windows, run /usr/bin/gnome-linuxconf or /sbin/linuxconf from an X-terminal window or via your Window manager. The tree menu appears much nicer in the GUI version, as in Figure 6-5.

As with the text-based interface, when you decide to quit the GUI, Linuxconf asks you to activate any changes you make. You are also able to preview or quit without activating the current configuration.

Unfortunately, the Web-based Linuxconf interface is the worst-looking interface among the three. It is unfortunate in that the Web-based one could be the jazziest. Because my favorite interface is the GUI, I use the GUI interface throughout the book for Linuxconf-related discussions.

By default, you cannot access the Web-based Linuxconf interface. In the following section, I show you how to enable it.

Setting up Web-based remote access for Linuxconf

Remote system administration is nothing new to Linux. System administrators have been using shell accounts to manage faraway servers via Telnet or SSH for a long time. What Web-based remote administration hopes to provide is a better interface for the same thing. By providing a familiar and consistent look and feel, it is likely to make it easier for novice administrators to manage remote systems. Web-based remote administration is also the current trend for almost all major software; the good news is that Linux is no exception.

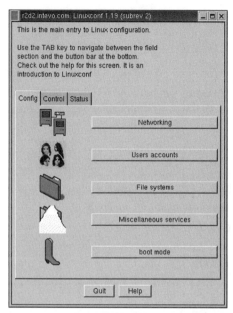

Figure 6-5: The graphical interface for Linuxconf

The advantages of being able to administer via a Web browser from any platform at any time are limitless. This is especially helpful for those who manage a large number of Linux systems in an organization. If you allow your Linux system to be managed from anywhere, however, you create a big security risk – anyone can now try to break into your system via the Web-accessible Linuxconf interface. This is why you must restrict Web-based Linuxconf access only to your trusted network.

The Web-based Linuxconf is an inetd-run service. When you install the Linuxconf RPM package, you add a line such as this to your /etc/services file:

```
linuxconf   98/tcp
```

The rpm installation also drops in /etc/xinetd.d/linuxconf-web file. By default, this file looks as follows:

```
# default: off
# description: The Linuxconf system can also be accessed via a web \
#              browser.  Enabling this service will allow connections to \
#              Linuxconf running in web UI mode.
service linuxconf
{
        socket_type      = stream
        wait                 = yes
        user                 = root
        server               = /sbin/linuxconf
```

```
server_args       = --http
disable               = yes
}
```

To enable the Web interface, change the `disable = yes` line to `disable = no`. This allows xinetd to run Linuxconf in HTTP mode when a request for connection is made on TCP/IP port 98. In other words, when you use a browser on your Linux system to access `http://localhost:98/`, the inetd daemon starts /sbin/linuxconf using the –http option.

By default, Linuxconf runs as a root user process. Therefore, if a security hole is discovered in Linuxconf, it is likely to allow root privileges to anyone. Linuxconf is over 80,000 lines of C++ code. Frankly, I don't feel too comfortable running a large root user program via the Web. You have to make your own decision about using it via the Web.

As I mention previously, Linuxconf allows Web-based access only from the local host. If you would like to enable remote administrative access to Linuxconf via the Web, you need to follow these steps:

1. Run linuxconf from your console or X Windows.

2. Select the Config menu. Click the Networking button. Select the Misc. menu, and click the Linuxconf network access button. You should see a window such as the one in Figure 6-6.

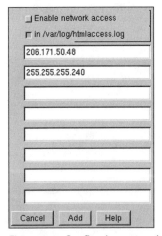

Figure 6-6: Configuring network access for Linuxconf

3. Select the Enable network access check box.

4. Select the "Log access in /var/log/htmlaccess.log" check box to allow logging of Linuxconf access requests via network.

5. In the network or host entry box, enter the name of the host you would like to permit for Linuxconf access via the Web. You can also enter the IP or network address here. If you would like to allow any host on your local area network (LAN) to be able to manage this system remotely, you can use the network address here. Figure 6-6 shows that I use a network address of 206.171.50.48. To enable all machines in my network, I have to specify the netmask 255.255.255.240 in the optional netmask entry box. The netmask is optional because Linuxconf can compute the netmask from your network address. If you plan to add multiple hosts but not your entire network, you can just add their IP addresses. By default, the screen allows you to enter two IP address and two optional netmasks. If you need more space, click the Add button to get extra entry boxes for additional hosts.

6. Once you enter the hostnames or IP address or the network/netmask pair, click the Accept button.

7. Click the Quit button to exit Linuxconf and to activate the current configuration when asked.

This should allow the named hosts (or IP addresses) to access Linuxconf via the Web.

As I mention previously, Linuxconf uses both internal code functions and external modules to perform the actual configuration. Currently, the Linuxconf RPM package ships with virtually all the available modules. This is likely to change because, ideally, Linuxconf modules really should ship with individual packages. For example, the Apache package for Red Hat should include a Linuxconf module. If you do not use the Apache Web server, you do not need the Apache module in your Linuxconf configuration. The more modules you have, the more cluttered the Linuxconf interface looks. If application developers ship modules themselves, you have only what you need. Hopefully, that's the way Linuxconf will go soon. Until this happens, you can manually configure the modules you need.

Configuring Linuxconf modules

You can add new modules or deactivate existing modules. Modules are kept in the /usr/lib/linuxconf/modules directory. To add a new module, download the necessary RPM package from a Linuxconf FTP site. The list of FTP sites carrying Linuxconf files is available at `http://dns.solucorp.qc.ca/linuxconf/available.html`.

Once you download the new Linuxconf module, use the `rpm -ivh module_package` command to install it. Once installed, the module automatically appears in the module list in Linuxconf. It is also automatically activated.

To deactivate a module, do the following:

1. Run linuxconf.

2. From the Control menu, click the Control files and systems button. Then click the Configure Linuxconf modules button. You see a screen similar to that in Figure 6-7.

3. Scroll down the module list, and locate the module you would like to deactivate. Toggle the check box so that the module becomes inactive.

4. Click the Accept button.

5. If you have nothing else to do in Linuxconf, click the Quit button. The system asks you to activate the changes. Click Activate the changes to complete the process.

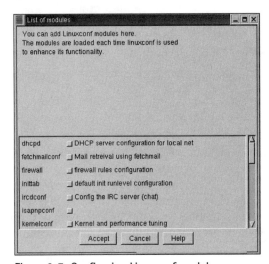

Figure 6-7: Configuring Linuxconf modules

Linuxconf also allows you to create privileged user accounts you can use to administer a certain aspect of your Linux system. This feature should be a great help when you have co-administrators in your organizations. Perhaps you would like to off-load some of the simpler administrative tasks to junior administrators. In such a case, you can create normal user accounts with restricted sets of privileges. We discuss this in the following section.

Defining user privileges

Linuxconf allows you to associate certain administrative privileges with normal users. Consider this example: Say that you have a normal user account pikeb and would like to assign some administrative privileges to this account. Do the following:

1. Run linuxconf from your root account.

2. Click the User accounts button from the Config menu.

3. Select User accounts from the Normal (users) menu. You see a list of all normal users on your system. Locate the target user (kabir in this example), and double-click the line of the user's record. You see a screen similar to the one in Figure 6-8.

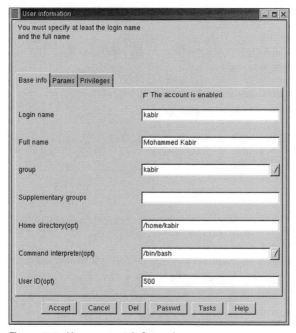

Figure 6-8: User account information

4. As you can see in Figure 6-8, the Base Info tab window is shown first. Click the Privileges tab to configure available privilege options. Figure 6-9 shows the available privilege windows.

As you can see in Figure 6-9, four privilege tab windows are within the Privileges tab window. The first is the General system control tab window. This window provides the options shown in Table 6-2.

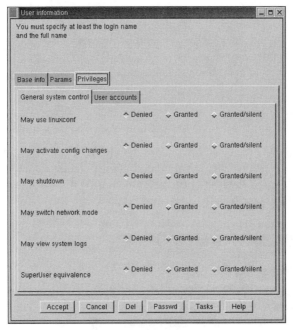

Figure 6-9: User Privilege options

TABLE 6-2 GENERAL SYSTEM CONTROL OPTIONS

Privilege Option	Explanation
May use linuxconf	If you want the user to be able to run Linuxconf, you must grant the user this privilege.
May activate config changes	Grant this privilege if you want the user to activate any changes to the current system configuration.
May shutdown	Grant this privilege if you want the user to be able to shut down the system.
May switch network mode	Grant this privilege if you want the user to enable/disable network connectivity.
May view system logs	Grant this privilege if you want the user to see system log files.
SuperUser equivalence	Grant this privilege only to user(s) who need to have superuser (root) access.

5. To grant any of the privileges shown in Table 6-2, you need to click the appropriate Granted or Granted/silent option. The difference between "Granted" and "Granted/silent" is that the latter does not require the user to authenticate using a password. I recommend not using the silent mode for anything.

6. Click the Accept button, and exit Linuxconf by clicking the Quit button and activating the changes you just made.

After you exit Linuxconf, log into your system as the user, and run Linuxconf. Test your new privileges. Make sure they are what you want them to be. Once you are sure that the user in question has all the right privileges, you are done. Give the lucky (we hope) user the good news.

Now take a look at a really cool Linuxconf feature that lets you create multiple system profiles for your Red Hat Linux system.

Using multiple system configuration profiles

A long time ago, Microsoft released MS-DOS 6.*xx* with updated AUTOEXEC.BAT and CONFIG.SYS syntax so that one could create customizable boot configurations. Being able to create multiple configurations for a single system allows MS-DOS users to make better use of resources. Linuxconf's multiple system profiling feature is quite similar to what Microsoft offered for its OS. The only difference is that Linuxconf offers a more advanced version of system profiling.

Linuxconf defines a system profile as a set of subsystems. A subsystem is a special group of configuration files. For example, mail is a subsystem that has configuration files such as /etc/aliases, /etc/mail/virtusertable, /var/lib/mailertable, and so on. Linuxconf stores each defined subsystem in a subdirectory of /etc/linuxconf/ archive. In other words, if a subsystem is defined, it is given a family name as the subdirectory is created. For example, if mail is the family name of a subsystem in a configuration, /etc/linuxconf/archive/mail contains mail-related configuration files for this system profile. This technique comes in very handy when you want to share configuration files among two or more system profiles. For example, if the mail subsystems of two of your system profiles are the same, you can just instruct Linuxconf to use the same profile.

By default, Linuxconf offers two system profiles: Office and Home. You can find the list of available system profiles in Linuxconf. Click the Control menu, select the Control files and systems option, and then select the Configure system profiles option. You see the list of available configurations as in Figure 6-10.

To determine which system profile Linuxconf is using, select the Control menu, click the Control panel button, and then click the Switch system profile button. You see the list of available configurations as in Figure 6-11.

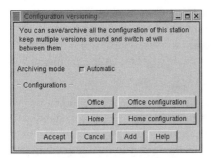

Figure 6-10: Available (default) system profiles

Figure 6-11: Determining the current system profile

You can also create your own system profiles. Here is how:

1. Select the Control menu, click the Control files and systems button, and click the Configure system profiles button. You see a window similar to the one in Figure 6-10.

2. Click the Add button to add a new system profile. The system asks you to enter a name for the new system profile as in Figure 6-12. A name is a single word and cannot have any space characters. Enter the name of your choice, and click Accept.

3. The system now asks you to enter a title for your new profile. This can be anything you want; you use it only to help distinguish the profile from the others. Enter something meaningful in terms of your needs.

4. Now you need to provide the archiving family names (that is, /etc/ linuxconf/archive/subsystem-family-name) for various subsystems such as crond; PPP/SLIP/PLIP; DNS server; firewalling rules; wu-ftpd server; gated; inet; httpd; lpd, and so on. You can also provide a default archiving family name to use when you do not explicitly define an archiving

family name for a certain subsystem. If you do not set a default family name or do not provide an explicit family name, the subsystem's data are stored in the /etc/conf.linuxconf file. If you would like to use an existing subsystem from another profile, you can just enter the existing family name for that profile.

If multiple archives share a subsystem, any changes to the subsystem's configuration files are effective in all system profiles using that subsystem.

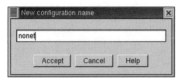

Figure 6-12: Adding a name for the new system profile

5. Once you specify all archiving family names, click the Accept button. Your new profile is added to the list of available profiles. Click the Accept button again.

6. To use your newly created profile, select the Control menu, click the Control panel button, and then click the Switch system profile button. Now click your profile to switch to it. Once you switch to your new profile, it is automatically archived when you switch back to another profile. If you would like to archive it manually, click the Control menu, select the Control panel option, and then select the Archive configurations option.

As you already know, we can use Linuxconf to configure and activate virtually everything in your system. However, we cannot configure everything fully just yet. One of the primary weaknesses of the current version of Linuxconf is its lack of appropriate documentation. Because I am not totally convinced that Linuxconf is ready for prime time, I discuss Linuxconf-specific configuration details wherever appropriate throughout the book. In other words, instead of discussing various issues, such as how to configure sendmail or NFS via Linuxconf, in this chapter, I discuss the appropriate Linuxconf-specific configurations in sendmail- or NFS-specific chapters; these chapters also show you the traditional means of configuring these services.

Summary

In this chapter, I introduced you to Linuxconf. You learned to install and to configure it for your Red Hat Linux system. Linuxconf is a great new tool for managing Linux systems via console, shell accounts, X Windows, and the Web. It is not only an easy-to-use system configuration application but also a configuration activator. It allows you to create multiple system configurations and to switch among them without the hassle of manual configuration backup and restore operations. I have no doubt that Linuxconf will contribute greatly to making the Linux user base much wider. In the rest of the book, I use Linuxconf whenever appropriate.

Chapter 7

User Administration

IN THIS CHAPTER

♦ How to create superuser or privileged accounts

♦ How to add, modify, and delete users and groups by using command line tools and Linuxconf

♦ How to implement disk quotas for users

MANAGING USERS IS A BIG part of a system administrator's everyday workload. In this chapter, you learn about the various aspects of user administration.

Becoming the Superuser

You already know that the root account is the superuser account on any UNIX system. In fact, if you installed Red Hat Linux yourself, you have already used this account to log into your system for the first time. You probably also know that because the root account is the superuser, it has access to everything on the system. The root user can start and stop any program as well as create and delete any file at will (not a good thing). So what more is there to learn about the superuser account? Well, let's find out.

First of all, many novice system administrators think that the user root is the only superuser. This is not true at all. The username "root" is not what makes an account a superuser. Take a look at the following lines from an example /etc/ passwd file.

```
root:dcw12Y6bSUfyo:0:0:root:/root:/bin/tcsh
bin:*:1:1:bin:/bin:
daemon:*:2:2:daemon:/sbin:
kabir:.HoiviYBP4/8U:0:0:Mohammed Kabir:/home/kabir:/bin/tcsh
sheila:gTwD/qLMFM9M.:501:501::/home/sheila:/bin/tcsh
apache:!!:502:502::/usr/local/apache:/bin/false
```

Can you guess how many superuser accounts are in this password file? The answer is two: they are root and kabir. To understand why, you have to remember that that the /etc/passwd file has the following format:

```
username:password:UID:GID:fullname:home-dir:shell
```

Now notice the UID (user ID) and GID (group ID) fields of the root account. They are both set to 0 (zero). If you look back at the line for the ordinary-looking user kabir, you see that his UID and GID are also set to 0. This is what turns a user into a superuser. In other words, any user with a UID and GID of zero is equivalent to a root.

As you can see, you can turn any ordinary user account into a superuser account. In most situations, you do not want to do this because having multiple superuser accounts can mean additional security risks. But I have seen organizations use multiple superuser accounts that have multiple system administrators working on the same systems. They do this to ensure a little more accountability in such an environment. For example, if the kabir and root accounts in the password file described previously are for two different system administrators, it is a bit easier to tell who does what as the superuser by looking at various log files than if the two system administrators share the default root account. I have seen the use of multiple superuser accounts in one other not-so-desirable situation – when someone has hacked a system. In such a case, the hacker creates an ordinary-looking superuser account by setting the UID and GID values to 0. This allows the hacker to log back in and become a superuser without knowing the root user's password. This trick works on systems where the system administrator is a novice or just too busy to keep an eye open for such things.

Let's face it, no system administrator has the time (in the context of a real for-profit organization) to keep watching for hackers on a daily basis, so you might want to employ some scripts as your helpers in such a case. For example:

```
/bin/grep '0:0' /etc/passwd | awk 'BEGIN {FS=":"} {print $1}' | mail
-s "`date +"%D %T"`" root
```

This is a really small script that uses a few standard commands to check the /etc/passwd file for users with UID and GID values set to 0. It can mail the root user a list of such accounts. If you run this script via cron by placing it in a file in /etc/cron.daily, it sends you an e-mail message every day that shows you the list of superusers. You can then quickly check this e-mail every day to know which accounts have superuser privileges. Of course, a smart hacker can find out about this and be able to change the script to feed you fake information. But my personal experience shows that most hackers are thrill seekers who hardly spend the time to investigate things for themselves. In my experience, most so-called hackers just find an exploit program on the Internet, compile, and run it to get access; they often lack the smartness to go through the checks that a careful system administrator might put in place.

Now that you know you can turn any user account into a superuser account, you might think that any user can log into a Red Hat Linux system quite easily; this is not true. The Red Hat Linux system by default uses the Pluggable Authentication Module (PAM) for login authentication. The PAM requires you to allow superuser access only from terminals considered secure. By default, the PAM configuration file for login, /etc/pam.d/login, contains a line such as the following:

```
auth        required        /lib/security/pam_securetty.so
```

This line states that the security restrictions the pam_securetty.so module enforces need to be satisfied before the module permits a login. This particular module considers a superuser login attempt satisfactory only if the superuser attempts the login from a TTY listed in the /etc/securetty file. So if you decide to turn an ordinary user into a superuser and attempt to log in via Telnet (which uses a pseudo-TTY device), you cannot log in. But you can easily change this by adding the pseudo-TTY devices (typically, ttyp1 to ttyp12) in the /etc/securetty file. This is not recommended because it creates a security risk. Instead, if you must use multiple superuser accounts. Because of administrative and accountability reasons, you should do the following:

1. Create multiple superuser accounts.

2. Create one ordinary user account per superuser.

3. Instruct each superuser to log into the system as an ordinary user and to change to the superuser account using the su command (discussed next).

You can use the su command to substitute UIDs and GIDs. For example, you can log in as an ordinary user and change to the root account by running su without any argument. You are prompted for the root password; if you know the root password, su starts a new shell and logs you in as the root user.

Remember that superusers (UID = 0, GID = 0) have full access to everything, and these are therefore very sensitive accounts. In the following section, I show you how you can delegate superuser privileges to ordinary user accounts without turning them into full-scale superusers.

Assigning Privileges to Ordinary Users

Using the sudo command, you can allow ordinary users to execute commands a superuser typically runs. Say that you are the chief system administrator for your organization and you've just been blessed with two new assistant system administrators. You want to distribute some of your routine administrative tasks to these two. Now should you create two superuser accounts with UIDs and GIDs set to 0 so that these two administrators can have full access to everything as you do? That depends on how confident you are in their ability to be as careful as you are when working as the ultimate user. Because confidence requires time to build, I guess you want to allow them access only to what they need access to. Assuming you agree with me, you need to configure sudo to allow these fellows to run privileged commands as regular users. Here is how.

The sudo command allows users specified in the /etc/sudoers file to run superuser commands. For example, an ordinary user permitted to run superuser commands via sudo can run:

```
sudo vi /etc/passwd
```

This allows this user to modify the /etc/passwd file. The sudo program is very configurable, so you can custom-tailor what an ordinary user listed in /etc/sudoers can or cannot do. The /etc/sudoers files have the following types of lines:

- ◆ Blank and comment lines (starting with "#" characters) are ignored.

- ◆ We use optional host alias lines to create short names for the list of hosts. A host alias line must start with the Host_Alias keyword, and commas must separate the hosts in the list. For example:

```
Host_Alias REDHAT=wormhole,blackhole
```

Here wormhole and blackhole are two hosts we can call REDHAT.

- ◆ We use optional user alias lines to create short names for the list of users. A user alias line must start with the User_Alias keyword, and commas must separate the users in the list. For example:

```
User_Alias ASSISTANTS=mike,brian
```

- ◆ We use optional command alias lines to create short names for the list of commands. A command alias must start with the

```
Cmnd_Alias CMDS=/bin/rm,/bin/chmod,/bin/chown
```

- ◆ We use optional run-as aliases to create short names for the list of users. We can use such an alias to tell sudo to run commands as one of the aliased users. For example:

```
Runas_Alias OP=root,operator
```

- ◆ Required user access specification lines appear. The syntax for the user access specification is as follows:

```
user  host=[run as user]  command list
```

You can specify a real username as user or use the User_Alias to specify a list. Similarly, you can use a real hostname or a Host_Alias for host. By default, all commands executed via sudo are run as root. If you would like run a command by using a different user, you can specify the username (or a Runas_Alias). You can specify a command (or a Cmnd_Alias), for example:

```
kabir  wormhole= /sbin/shutdown
```

Here, the user kabir is allowed to run the /sbin/shutdown command on a host called wormhole. Note that you can insert a "!" in front of a command or a command alias to deny the command or command alias as permitted.

It is possible to define multiple aliases in a single line, for example:

```
UserAlias ASSISTANTS=mike,brian:INTERNS=monika,paula,jones
```

Here, we define two aliases (ASSISTANTS and INTERNS) in a single line where a colon character separates the alias definitions. This syntax also applies to other alias types.

There are two special keywords: ALL and NOPASSWD. The ALL keyword means "everything," and we use NOPASSWD to state that no password should be required. Listing 7-1 shows an example /etc/sudoers file.

Listing 7-1: An example /etc/sudoers file

```
# sudoers file.
#
# This file MUST be edited with the 'visudo'
# command as root.
#
# See the man page for the details on how to
# write a sudoers file.
#

# Host alias specification

# User alias specification
User_Alias   SENIORADMIN=kabir
User_Alias   ASSISTANTS=mike,john
# User privilege specification

SENIORADMIN ALL=ALL
ASSISTANTS  ALL=ALL
```

This /etc/sudoers file defines two user aliases: SENIORADMIN and ASSISTANTS. The first alias has only one user (kabir), and the second alias has two users (mike and john). The example /etc/sudoers file shown above can be explained as follows:

The users in user alias SENIORADMIN can run sudo on ALL hosts as root (default), and these users can run ALL commands as well. Because user kabir is the only user in this group, this effectively states that kabir can run all commands via sudo. In other words, the user kabir can do anything the user root can do.

The second user specification states that users in the user alias ASSISTANTS be allowed the same access privileges as users in the first specification.

Now let's go back to the first example, where we have two assistants who do need full superuser access yet. Say that you (user ID = yourid) want these two users (sysad1, sysad2) to have privileges to run only the shutdown command. In such a case, your /etc/sudoers file might look like:

```
# User alias specification
User_Alias   SENIORADMIN=yourid
User_Alias   ASSISTANTS=sysad1,sysad2

# User privilege specification
SENIORADMIN ALL=ALL
ASSISTANTS   ALL=/sbin/shutdown
```

Now say that after a while you become confident that these two users can handle other superuser privileges in a responsible manner, so you want to give them full access, except the privilege to run the su command. The /etc/sudoers now looks as follows:

```
# User alias specification
User_Alias   SENIORADMIN=yourid
User_Alias   ASSISTANTS=sysad1,sysad2

# User privilege specification
SENIORADMIN ALL=ALL
ASSISTANTS   ALL=ALL,!/bin/su
```

As you can see from the user specifications for the ASSISTANTS, they are allowed to run ALL commands via sudo except the /bin/su command. As you can see, the sudo command can be very useful when creating users with partial superuser privileges. Now that you know a great deal about how to create and manage superuser accounts, consider the management issues related to regular users.

When it comes to creating, modifying, and removing user accounts, you have two choices: manage users using command line tools, or use Linuxconf. Because the first method is traditional and the second method is the up-and-coming way of doing things, I show you both ways.

Managing Users with Command Line Tools

As Linux becomes more popular than ever, the Red Hat company and the Linux community are making it very easy to use Linux. The linuxconf project is a good example. However, we still need the traditional way of managing a UNIX box so that people versed in other UNIX operating systems can easily manage Linux systems as well. In this section, I show you the traditional way of handling user administration by using various command line tools.

 Commands discussed in the following sections work with shadow passwords as well. You learn about shadow passwords in Chapter 18.

Creating a new user account

Creating a new user account is quite easy. To create a user from your command line, you can run the useradd command. For example, to create a user called newuser, you can run this command as follows:

```
useradd newuser
```

This adds a new entry in /etc/passwd (and in /etc/shadow if you use shadow passwords: see Chapter 18 for details) using system defaults. For example, when I run the preceding command on my Red Hat system, /etc/passwd shows a new line such as the following:

```
newuser:!!:506:506::/home/newuser:/bin/bash
```

If you remember the /etc/passwd fields from earlier discussion, you see that the password field (the second field) is set to !!. This means the password is not set and the user cannot log in just yet. You need to create a password for this user by running the passwd command as follows:

```
passwd newuser
```

The program asks you to enter the password twice. Once the password you enter is accepted, it is encrypted and added to the user's entry in the /etc/passwd file.

The useradd automatically selects the UID and the GID values. Basically, it just increments the last user UID in /etc/passwd by one and the last GID in /etc/group by one to create the UID and GID, respectively, for the new user. We create the home directory in the default top-level home directory. Similarly, we select the login shell from a system default. You will learn to set these defaults in a later section. If you would like to override a system default, you can specify a command line option. To override the default home directory, use the -d newdirectory option (where newdirectory is the name of your directory). For example:

```
useradd newuser -d /www/newuser
```

This creates the new user (newuser) and sets the user's home directory to /www/newuser. Note that `useradd` creates only the final directory and not the entire path. For example, if you specify –d /some/new/dir/myuser as the option, `useradd` creates myuser only if /some/new/dir/ exists.

When you create the new home directory, you copy files in the /etc/skel directory to the new home directory. These files are typically dot configuration files for the default shell. For example, if the default shell is /bin/bash, you should have default versions of .bashrc, .bash_profile, and .bash_login in the /etc/skel directory so that you can automatically set up the new user's home directory with these files. You will learn more about this in a later section in this chapter.

The `useradd` that comes with Red Hat Linux creates a private group for the user with the same name as the username. For example, if you run `useradd kabir`, you create a new user named kabir in the /etc/passwd file and a new group called kabir in the /etc/group file. This method allows the new user to be totally isolated from other users and therefore ensures greater privacy for the user. Whenever the new user creates a file, by virtue of this private group, only the new user has access to it. The user has to change the file permissions explicitly to allow someone else to see the file.

However, if your user account philosophy clashes with this private-group idea, you can override it using the -g group option (where group is the name of your group). For example:

```
useradd mjkabir -g users
```

Here, `useradd` creates the new user (mjkabir) with the default group set to the users.

 TIP You can use the `groups username` command to find which user belongs to what group.

If you would like to make the new user a member of additional groups on your system, you can use the -G comma-separated list of groups option. For example:

```
useradd mjkabir -G wheel,admins
```

Here, you add the new user (mjkabir) to the wheel and admins groups in the /etc/group file.

Creating a new group

To create a new group, use the `groupadd` command. For example:

```
groupadd mygroup
```

This adds a new group called mygroup in the /etc/group and in the /etc/gshadow file if you are using shadow passwords. By default, the groupadd program creates the group with a GID above 499 because 0–499 are (sort of) reserved for system-level accounts such as root, bin, and mail. So if your /etc/group file has the last group GID set to 511, the new group you create with this program has a GID of 512, and so on. If you would like specifically to set the GID of your new group, use the -g GID option. Also, if you would like to create a group with a GID in the 0–499 range, use the -r option with the -g GID option to force groupadd to create the new group as a system group. Note that if the group or GID you are trying to use with the program is already in use in /etc/group, you get an error message.

Modifying an existing user account

Dealing with forgotten user passwords is the most common task a system adminis-trator performs. Here, you learn to change various details of a user account.

CHANGING A PASSWORD

To change or set a user's password, use the passwd command. For example:

```
passwd kabir
```

This allows you to change user kabir's password. You are asked to enter the pass-word twice to confirm it. Make sure you choose good passwords for your users. Do not use simple-to-remember passwords such as common dictionary words. Note that users can also run the passwd program to change their own passwords. When ordinary users run the passwd program, no username argument is required because the program allows them to change only their own passwords.

CHANGING THE SHELL

If the default shell is not appropriate for a user, you may change it to any shell you list in /etc/shells. Use the chsh command to change a user's shell. For example:

```
chsh brian
```

This command allows you to change user brian's current shell. If you specify any shell or program name that is not in /etc/shells, the user is not able to log in. Note that users can change their own shells by using this command as well. Ordinary users do not need to specify usernames as an argument because the only shells they can change are their own.

Note that you can also use the usermod command to modify shell information as follows:

```
usermod -s new shell path username
```

where *new shell path* and *username* are the correct values.

CHANGING THE HOME DIRECTORY

To change the home directory of an existing user, run the usermod command as follows:

```
usermod -d new home directory username
```

where *new home directory* and *username* are the correct values.

For example, if a user called keller has /home/keller as her home directory and you would like to move it to /home2/keller, you can run the command as follows:

```
usermod -d /home2/keller keller
```

This sets the new directory as her home directory. However, if you would like to move her home directory contents to the new location, use the -m option as follows:

```
usermod -d -m /home2/keller keller
```

CHANGING A UID

To change the UID of a user, use the usermod command as follows:

```
usermod -u UID username
```

where *UID* and *username* are the correct values.

For example:

```
usermod -g 500 myfrog
```

This command changes the UID for user mrfrog to 500. Note that all files and directories the user owns within his or her home directory automatically reflects the UID change. However, if the user owns files outside his or her own home directory, you have to change ownership manually by using the chown command. (See Chapter 5 for details on how to use the chown command.)

CHANGING A DEFAULT GROUP

To change the default group for a user, use the usermod command as follows:

```
usermod -g group name or GID username
```

where *group name* or *GID* and *username* are the correct values.

For example:

```
usermod -g 777 myfrog
```

This command changes the default group for user mrfrog to 777.

CHANGING AN ACCOUNT EXPIRATION DATE

If you are using shadow passwords, you can change the expiration date of a user account by using the usermod command, as follows:

```
usermod -e MM/DD/YY username
```

where *MM/DD/YY* and *username* are the correct values.

For example:

```
usermod -e 12/31/99 kabir
```

This command resets the account expiration date for user kabir to 12/31/99.

CHANGING FINGER INFORMATION

If you run a finger daemon, you can also change the finger information, such as full name and phone numbers. Run the chfn command to change a user's finger information. For example:

```
chfn jennifer
```

This allows you to change user jennifer's finger information, which is stored in the /etc/passwd file. A user can change her own finger information by using this program as well. A user can also create a .plan file in her home directory that gets appended to the information the finger program shows.

Modifying an existing group

To modify an existing group name or GID, use the groupmod command. To rename a group to a new name, use the following syntax:

```
groupmod -n new group  current group
```

For example:

```
groupmod -n experts novices
```

Here, the existing novices group is renamed to experts. To change the GID, use the -g new GID option. For example:

```
groupmod -g 666 troublemakers
```

This command changes the current GID of the troublemakers group to 666.

Deleting or disabling a user account

To delete an existing user, use the userdel command. For example:

```
userdel snake
```

This deletes a user called snake. If you would like to remove the user's home directory and all contents within the directory, use the -r option. Note that userdel does not delete the user if the user is currently logged in. Ask the user to log out by sending a write message (write username); if asking is not an option, use the killall command to terminate all processes associated with the user, and then run the userdel command.

If you would like temporarily to disable a user account, you can do one of the following:

◆ Use the usermod -s new shell username command to change the shell to /bin/false (make sure it is in your /etc/shells). This disallows the user from logging into the system.

◆ If you are using the shadow passwords, you can use the usermod -e MM/DD/YY username command to cause the user account to expire.

If you would like to disable all user account access for a temporary reason, you can create a file called /etc/nologin with a message explaining why you are not allowing access. The login program does not allow any nonroot account to log in as long as this file is in place.

If you administer the server via Telnet or any other means, such as secure shell (ssh) access, do not create /etc/nologin; you will not be able to log into your system. By default, root or superuser accounts are not allowed to log in directly from a nonsecured TTY (that is, any TTY not specified in /etc/securetty), so you can't log in as an ordinary user and then su to a privileged user account.

Creating default user settings

The default settings for creating new users using the useradd command come from /etc/default/useradd. An example of this file is in Listing 7-2.

Listing 7-2: An example /etc/default/useradd file

```
# useradd defaults file
GROUP=100
```

```
HOME=/home
INACTIVE=-1
EXPIRE=
SHELL=/bin/bash
SKEL=/etc/skel
```

The GROUP=100 line specifies that the default group ID is 100. You use this value only when you disable (using the -n option) the default private group (that is, the group with the same name as the new user). You can specify a group name instead of the numeric value as well. The value you specify in this line must exist in /etc/group. You can change this value as follows:

```
useradd -D -g newsgroup name or GID
```

where *newsgroup name* and *GID* are the proper values.

The HOME=/home line specifies the default top-level home directory for new users. For example, when you create a new user called joe, the default home directory is /home/joe. You can change this to fit your needs. Make sure the directory already exists. You can change this value as follows:

```
useradd -D -d directory
```

The INACTIVE=-1 line specifies when (in days) the account becomes inactive after the password expires. This is useful only if you are using shadow passwords. The default value of –1 states that accounts are never inactive. You can change this value as follows:

```
useradd -D -f number of days
```

The EXPIRE= line specifies when an account should be disabled. This is useful only if you are using shadow passwords. By default, accounts never become disabled. You can change this value as follows:

```
useradd -D -e  MM/DD/YY
```

The defaults we use to create new users come from the /etc/login.def file. Listing 7-3 shows an example of this file.

The SHELL=/bin/bash line specifies the default login shell path. You can change this value as follows:

```
useradd -D -s /bin/tcsh
```

Note that the useradd program does not check if the path you specify is a valid shell or even if it exists. Make sure the path you specify is a valid shell and is in the /etc/shells file.

The SKEL=/etc/skel line specifies the directory where we keep various user configuration files such as dot files for shells, X Windows, and so forth. We copy the files in this directory to the new home directory of a new user account. Normally, you do not want to change this path to some other directory. On the other hand, if you do want to change it, you have to modify the /etc/default/user-add file by using an editor, or you can just create a symbolic link /etc/skel that points to the desired directory.

If you are using the shadow passwords, you use another default configuration file called /etc/login.defs to create user accounts. Listing 7-3 shows an example of this file.

Listing 7-3: An example /etc/login.defs file

```
# *REQUIRED*
#   Directory where mailboxes reside, _or_ name
#   of file, relative to the home directory.
#   If you _do_ define both, MAIL_DIR takes precedence.
#   QMAIL_DIR is for Qmail
#
#QMAIL_DIR     Maildir
MAIL_DIR   /var/spool/mail

#MAIL_FILE     .mail
# Password aging controls:
#
#   PASS_MAX_DAYS  Maximum number of days a
#                     password may be used.
#
#   PASS_MIN_DAYS  Minimum number of days allowed
#                     between password changes.
#
#   PASS_MIN_LEN   Minimum acceptable password length.
#
#   PASS_WARN_AGE  Number of days warning given before
#                     a password expires.
#
PASS_MAX_DAYS  99999
PASS_MIN_DAYS  0
PASS_MIN_LEN   5
PASS_WARN_AGE  7

#
# Min/max values for automatic uid
# selection in useradd
#
UID_MIN  500
```

```
UID_MAX   60000

#
# Min/max values for automatic gid
# selection in groupadd
#
GID_MIN   500
GID_MAX   60000

#
# Require password before chfn/chsh can make
# any changes.
#
CHFN_AUTH   yes

#
# Don't allow users to change their "real name"
# using chfn.
#
CHFN_RESTRICT   yes

#
# If defined, this command is run when removing a user.
# It should remove any at/cron/print jobs etc. owned by
# the user to be removed (passed as the first argument).
#
#USERDEL_CMD   /usr/sbin/userdel_local

#
# If useradd should create home directories for
# users by default On RH systems, we do. This option is
# ORed with the -m flag on useradd command line.
#
CREATE_HOME   yes
```

Because the comments (that is, the lines that start with the "#" character) in this file are sufficient to explain configuration details, I do not discuss these details here.

Managing Users with linuxconf

Now take a look at how we can use linuxconf to do all the things we have covered. I use the X Windows-based interface here.

Adding a new user account

To access the user administrative interface in linuxconf, do the following:

Select the Config → User accounts → Normal → User accounts option from the left side of the window. You see a tab, as in Figure 7-1.

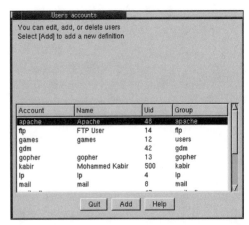

Figure 7-1: The linuxconf user administration tab

To add a new user, click the Add button on the right side of the window. A new window, as in Figure 7-2, appears.

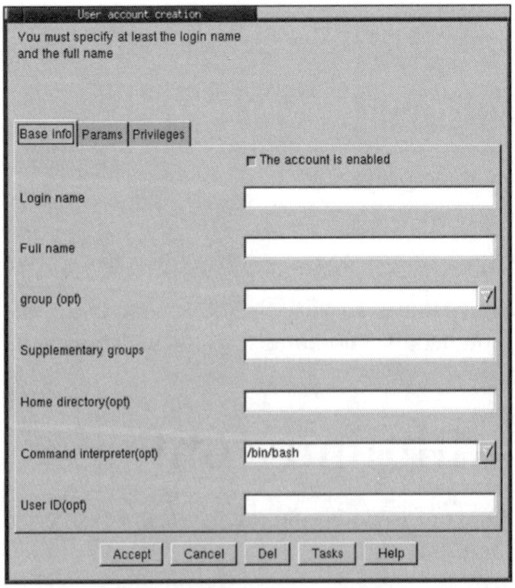

Figure 7-2: Adding a new user account

As you can see, this window has multiple tabs. The first tab is the Base info tab. Here you have to enter the following: Login name (username); Full name, group name (optional); Supplementary groups (optional); Home directory (optional); Command shell (optional); and User ID (optional). You can also choose to create this account but to not enable it just yet by unselecting the "This account is enabled" check box.

You can use the other tabs (Extra, Mail aliases, and Privileges) to set up additional information about this account. The privilege options in the Privileges tab window are applicable only to linuxconf. In other words, if you assign privileges to an ordinary account, the privilege is applicable only if the user is able to run linuxconf. For example, if you would like this user to be able to run linuxconf, you can choose to allow this in the Privileges tab window. Figure 7-3 shows the Privileges tab window.

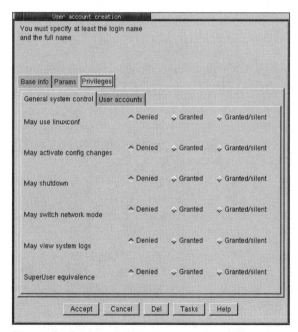

Figure 7-3: Adding privileges to a new user account

Once you select the appropriate privileges (if any), click Accept to add the user. Note that the user is not added until you tell linuxconf to activate the configuration via the Control → Control Panel → Activate configuration option or until you allow it to activate the configuration before you quit the application.

Modifying an existing user account

To modify a user account in linuxconf, select the Config → User accounts → Normal → User accounts option from the left side of the window. You see a tab window, as in Figure 7-1. Now click the account name on the right side, and you see a tab window similar to Figure 7-2 but which has all account information preloaded. You can modify anything you want and can use the Control → Control Panel → Activate configuration option to activate the changes immediately or to activate them when you quit the application.

Deleting or disabling an existing user account

To delete or disable a user account, select the Config → User accounts → Normal → User accounts option from the left side of the window. You see a tab as in Figure 7-1. Now click the account name on the right side, and you see a tab window similar to Figure 7-2 but which has all account information preloaded. To delete this account, click the Del button; to disable it, unselect the "This account is enabled" check box.

Adding, modifying, and deleting groups

To add, modify, or delete groups, do the following:

◆ Select the Config → User accounts → Normal → Group definitions option from the left side of the screen. You see a tab as in Figure 7-4.

◆ To add a new group, click Add. This brings up a new window as in Figure 7-5. Enter the name and, optionally, the GID, members, and so on, and click Accept. The new group is effective when you activate the changes you make in linuxconf.

◆ To modify an existing group, click an existing group name from the window in Figure 7-4. A new tab appears with the select group's information preloaded. Make necessary changes, and click Accept. The modified group is effective when you activate the changes you make in linuxconf.

◆ To delete a group, click an existing group name from the window in Figure 7-4. A new tab window appears with the selected group's information preloaded. Click Delete. The deletion is effective when you activate the changes you make in linuxconf.

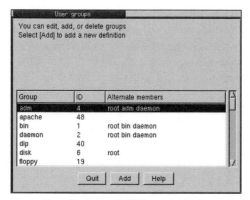

Figure 7-4: Adding, modifying, or deleting a group

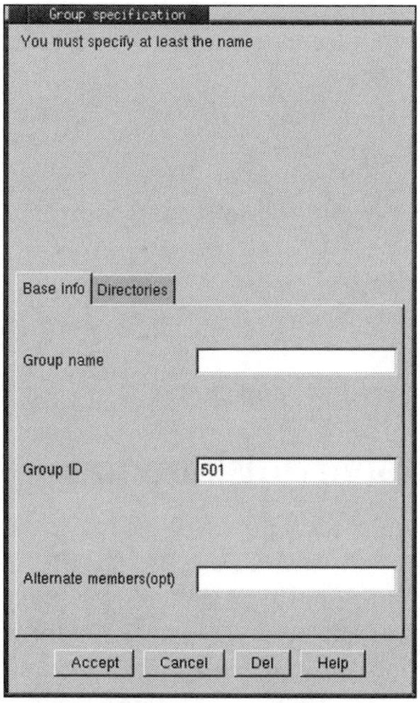

Figure 7-5: Adding a new group

Although linuxconf tries to make user administration quite simple, it often falls apart when you change something in your system. For example, when I upgraded my SMTP mail transport agent (sendmail), the user administration aspect of the linuxconf stopped being nice. It could not locate a program (makemap) that comes with sendmail, and therefore it kept asking me about it (even after I specified the path to the program) every time I wanted to add, modify, or delete a user. As I state in a previous chapter on linuxconf, this program is a good idea, and it should be considered as something in the making that will soon (hopefully) be a fully functional, centralized configuration management system – a dream come true for a Red Hat Linux administrator.

Now that you know how to add, modify, and delete user accounts, look at how you can control disk usage by each user.

Using Disk Quotas for Users

Disk space on a multiuser system can be quite a scarce resource. Experience shows that as soon as you plug in a new drive with lots of space, users tend to use it up quite rapidly. So the more you add, the more you need. The best way to ensure that you have enough disk space for your system is to enforce disk quotas. Here is how.

Installing disk quota software

The official Red Hat CD-ROM comes with the quota software. For example, to install the quota software for an *x*86 machine, I can run the following command from the CD-ROM's /RedHat/RPMS directory:

```
rpm -ivh quota-version.i386.rpm
```

Once you install the quota software, you are ready to configure it.

Configuring your system to support disk quotas

First, decide which partitions you want to bring under disk quotas. Typically, these are the partition(s) for user home directories and Web space. Also, decide if you would like to enforce quotas per user, per group, or both. Here I assume you want to enable disk quotas for the /home and /www partitions and you want to enforce only the per-user disk quota for the /home partition and the per-group disk quota for the /www partition. Also, I assume you have a /etc/fstab file that looks like the following:

```
/dev/sda1    /home  ext2    defaults  1 2
/dev/sda5    /www   ext2    defaults  1 2
```

To enforce user-level disk quotas on /home, you have to modify the first line as follows:

```
/dev/sda1    /home  ext2    defaults,usrquota  1 2
```

Similarly, to enable group-level disk quotas on /www, you must modify the second fstab line as follows:

```
/dev/sda5    /www    ext2    defaults.grpquota  1 2
```

 You can also use both usrquota and grpquota for a single partition if you plan to enforce quotas for both users and groups.

Once you complete these modifications, you need to modify the /etc/rc.d/rc.local script as follows:

```
# Check quota and then turn quota on.
if [ -x /sbin/quotacheck ]; then
     echo "Checking quotas. This may take some time..."
     sbin/quotacheck -avug
     echo " Done."
  fi
if [ -x /sbin/quotaon ]; then
     echo "Enabling disk quota .."
     /sbin/quotaon -avug
     echo " Done."
  fi
```

When you run this script after you load the file systems, you enable quota checking and then turn on the disk quota feature.

Now you need to create quota files for each file system you have placed under quota control. So create the quota files as follows:

```
touch /home/quota.user
touch /www/quota.group
```

Make sure these two files have read and write permissions for only the root user. Now you have completed the system-level quota configuration; before you continue with the quota assignments for users and groups, you should reboot the system. This runs the quotacheck program, which creates disk usage information in the quota files.

Assigning disk quotas to users

Once you have rebooted the system with the new quota configuration, you are ready to assign disk quotas for each user. To assign disk quotas per user, use the `edquota` command. For example, to allocate a disk quota for a user named kabir, run:

```
edquota -u kabir
```

This brings up the default text editor (such as vi or whatever is set in $EDITOR environment variable) with contents similar to those shown here:

```
Quotas for user kabir:
/dev/sda5: blocks in use: 0, limits (soft = 0, hard = 0)
          inodes in use: 0, limits (soft = 0, hard = 0)
```

Here the user kabir has used 0 blocks (in KB) on disk partition /dev/sda5 (under usrquota control), and the limits (soft or hard) are not set yet. Similarly, this user has not owned any files (incodes), and no limit (soft or hard) has been set yet.

As you can see, you can set limits for the amount of space (in blocks) a user can consume and at the same time control how many files the user can own. The soft limit specifies the maximum amount of disk space (blocks) or files (inodes) a user can have on the file system. The hard limit is the absolute amount of disk space (in blocks) or files (inodes) a user can have.

For example, say that you want to allow user kabir to have a soft limit of 1MB (1,024KB) and a hard limit of 4MB (4,096KB) for disk space. Also say that you want to allow this user a soft limit of 128 files/directories (inodes) and a hard limit of 512 files/directories. You can set the quota limit by using `edquota -u kabir`, as follows:

```
Quotas for user kabir:
/dev/sda5: blocks in use: 0, limits (soft = 1024, hard = 4096)
          inodes in use: 0, limits (soft = 128, hard = 512)
```

Once you save the configuration, the user can no longer exceed the hard limits. If the user tries to exceed either of these (disk space and inode count), an error message is displayed. For example:

```
[kabir@picaso /home]$ mkdir eat_space
mkdir: cannot make directory `eat_space': Disc quota exceeded
```

Here, the user kabir tries to create a new directory in /home; because he has exceeded the quota limit, the preceding error message is displayed.

If you have a lot of users to assign quotas to, the preceding method can be quite time consuming. To aid you with such a situation, the edquota program includes a -p prototype user option that allows you to copy the prototype user's disk quota configuration for others. For example, say you want to use the quota configuration you just created for user kabir for three other users (sheila, jennifer, and mrfrog). You can run:

```
edquote -p kabir  -u sheila jennifer mrfrog
```

Now all three users have the same quota configuration as kabir.

Placing groups under disk quota control is very similar. The edquota syntax for configuring a group's quota requirements is as follows:

```
edquota -g group name
```

To enforce the soft limit for either user or group quotas, you need to configure the grace period by using the edquota -t command. When you run this command, your editor displays something similar to the following:

```
Time units may be: days, hours, minutes, or seconds
Grace period before enforcing soft limits for users:
/dev/sda5: block grace period: 0 days, file grace period: 0 days
```

You can specify the grace period in days, hours, minutes, or even seconds. For example:

```
Time units may be: days, hours, minutes, or seconds
Grace period before enforcing soft limits for users:
/dev/sda5: block grace period: 7 days, file grace period: 5 hours
```

Here, the grace period for the disk space limit (in blocks) is seven days, and the grace period for the number of files (inodes) is only five hours.

Monitoring disk usage

To find the amount of disk space a user is using, you can run the quota command as follows:

```
quota -u username
```

For example:

```
quota -u kabir
Disk quotas for user kabir (uid 500):
Filesystem blocks quota limit grace files quota limit    grace
/dev/sda5   0       1024  4096           1     128   512
```

You can run the same command to monitor the disk usage of a group as well. The syntax is as follows:

```
quota -g group
```

When you find users or groups over their limits, you can send them e-mail messages to bring down disk usage to acceptable limits.

Summary

In this chapter, you learned a great deal about superuser accounts. You learned that a superuser may not necessarily need to have access to the root account to do his or her job. You learned to create custom-tailored superuser accounts using sudo, which allows you to delegate system administration to assistants or novice system administrators. You learned to manage ordinary user accounts and groups. I discussed various ways of creating, modifying, and deleting user accounts and groups. You also learned about the option of using disk quotas as a user resource management tool.

Chapter 8

Process Administration

IN THIS CHAPTER

- ◆ How processes get started
- ◆ How to send various signals to a running process
- ◆ How to run processes in the foreground and the background
- ◆ How to set process priority using nice
- ◆ How to monitor processes on your system
- ◆ How to log process-generated messages with syslog
- ◆ How to automate process execution using at and cron

YOUR RED HAT LINUX SYSTEM is really a repository of programs of various types, such as system daemons, user applications, and utilities. When you run any of these programs, an instance of the program is normally loaded into your computer's memory. At this point, it becomes a running process in your system. A process utilizes your computer's CPU, physical and virtual memory, and disks to perform something useful. Because processes consume your system resources, they are an important part of your system's performance. The more processes you run, the more resources you need. Being able to manage processes in your system is an important administrative skill. In this chapter, you will learn to control, monitor, and automate processes.

How Processes Get Started

As you know from Chapter 3, when a computer starts, its firmware (BIOS) runs a bootstrap program (typically found on a bootable disk). The bootstrap program then loads the kernel. The kernel in turn runs the init program. So the very first process in your system is an instance of the init program. It starts other processes according to the system's run level, which is specified in the /etc/rc.d/rc.sysinit file. Because we give every process a process identification (PID), the init process gets a PID of 1. We use the PID number to manage processes in a system. The init process typically runs system initialization programs such as swapon, mount, and setserial once and then starts one or more daemon processes. A daemon process is an instance of a program that typically runs forever or exits only when signaled to do so. For example, the sendmail STMP mail server runs as a daemon process. Typically, it runs forever and services mail requests as they come; ideally, it should exit only when signaled by the kernel.

When we configure a Red Hat Linux computer to run as a server, the init process typically starts a daemon process called xinetd. This process is responsible for providing many of the widely used network services such as Telnet and FTP. This process is known as the Internet Super Server. It runs and listens for connection requests on various ports specified in /etc/services. When it receives a request for a certain service, it starts the appropriate daemon process listed in a file within the /etc/xinetd.d directory for that service. For example, when you request a Telnet connection from a remote computer to a Red Hat Linux server, the xinetd process receives a request on TCP port 23. It then starts the Telnet daemon (/usr/sbin/in. telnetd) process. The Telnet daemon starts a /bin/login process and uses a pseudo-terminal device to exchange information between the login process and the remote Telnet client. The login process runs a shell process (such as /bin/bash, /bin/tcsh. /bin/csh, or /bin/sh) when the user successfully authenticates herself. The shell process then allows the user to run other processes. As you can see, it's all about processes. In fact, the processes it is running at the time define the state of any system at a given moment. Therefore, it is vital for a system administrator to know how to control processes. In the following section, you will learn to do just that.

Controlling and Monitoring Processes

As I mentioned previously, the init process typically starts daemon processes at boot. You can control which daemons run at boot time by reconfiguring init configuration files and scripts (see Chapter 3 for details). Except for daemon processes, processes you run are user processes or interactive processes. You run an interactive process via a shell. Every standard shell provides a command line where a user enters the name of a program. When a user enters a valid program name in the command line, the shell creates a copy of itself as a new process and replaces the new process with the named program from the command line. In other words, the shell runs the named program as another process.

To get information about all running processes on your system, you need to run a utility called ps.

Using ps to get process status

This nifty utility produces a report of all the processes in a system. For example, when I run ps from a login shell, it shows the following output:

```
PID    TTY STAT TIME COMMAND
31795 p7  S    0:00 -tcsh
31811 p7  R    0:00 ps
```

As you can see, ps provides a tabular report. Here, ps shows that I am running two processes: the -tcsh shell (really the /bin/tcsh shell run as a login shell) and the ps process itself. Table 8-1 explains the meaning of the common output fields for ps.

TABLE 8-1 OUTPUT FIELDS FOR PS

Field	Explanation
USER or UID	Process owner's username.
PID	Process ID.
%CPU	CPU utilization of the process. Because the time base over which this is computed varies, it is possible for this to exceed 100 percent.
%MEM	Percentage of memory (in kilobytes) utilization of the process.
SIZE	Size (in kilobytes) of virtual memory the process uses.
RSS	Resident set size or size of real memory (in kilobytes) the process uses.
TTY	Terminal (tty) associated with the process. Usually, the tty name is shortened. For example, p7 is displayed for /dev/ttyp7.
STAT	State of the process. Process states are represented by characters such as R (running or ready to run); S (sleeping); I (idle); Z (zombie); D (disk wait); P (page wait); W (swapped out); N (lowered priority by nice); T (terminated); < (execution priority raised by superuser), and so on.
START	Process start time or date.
TIME	Total CPU time the process uses.
COMMAND	Command line being executed.
NI	The nice priority number.
PRI	Process priority number.
PPID	Process ID (PID) of the parent process.
WCHAN	Name of the kernel function where a process is sleeping. The name of the function is retrieved from the /boot/System.map file.
FLAGS	A numeric flag associated with the process.

The ps utility also accepts a number of command line arguments. Table 8-2 shows commonly used options.

TABLE 8-2 COMMONLY USED PS OPTIONS

Options	Description
A	Show processes belonging to all users.
E	Show process environment variables after the command line being executed.
L	Show output in long format.
U	Show user name and process start time.
W	Show output in wide format. Normally, output is truncated if it cannot fit in a line. Using this option, you can prevent it.
Txx	Show processes associated with *xx* tty device.
X	Show processes without controlling tty.

Now let's look at a few examples.

To see all the processes you are running at any time, run:

```
ps u
```

An example of the output of the preceding command is shown here:

```
USER   PID %CPU %MEM  SIZE   RSS TTY STAT START TIME COMMAND
kabir   18  0.0  0.8  1556  1040  p5 S    08:41 0:00 -tcsh
kabir  135  0.0  0.8  1560  1040  p7 S    09:03 0:00 -tcsh
kabir  852 53.8  0.6  1604   788  p5 R    09:33 0:04 perl ./eatcpu.pl
kabir  855  0.0  0.3   848   484  p7 R    09:34 0:00 ps u
```

This shows all processes running for a user called kabir. The first two lines show that kabir is running two tcsh shell sessions. The third line is very interesting, as it shows a Perl script called eatcpu.pl utilizing approximately 53.8 percent of the CPU. Notice the STAT flags. The Perl script and the ps are the only running (or runnable) processes here. By looking at the TTY field, you can tell which process is attached to which tty.

Now let's look at another example:

```
ps au
```

Here, the au option tells `ps` to display all processes (excluding the one not associated with any controlling tty). To find out what processes a particular user owns, you can run:

```
ps au | grep username
```

where *username* is the name of the actual user.

For example, `ps au | grep sheila` shows all the interactive processes (that is, processes associated with a tty) a user named sheila is running. Typically, normal users are not allowed to run daemon processes or processes not associated with a tty. However, if you just want to find if any such processes exist for any user, you can run:

```
ps aux
```

The x option tells `ps` to list processes detached from terminals. You can identify these processes by looking at the TTY field, which displays a "?" character instead of a shortened name of a tty device such as p7 (/dev/ttyp7).

To find the PID of a process's parent, you can run:

```
ps 1 PID
```

where PID is the PID of the process.

For example, if you would like to find the parent of a process with PID 123, you can run ps 1 123, and the parent's PID is listed in the PPID field of the report.

To determine what initial environment variables are available to processes, you can run:

```
ps e
```

This appends the environment information to the COMMAND field.

A regular (non-superuser or root) user cannot use the e option to see the environment information of another user's processes. This is a security feature. Only root or superuser-equivalent users can view environment information of all the processes.

As you can see, `ps` allows you to find various items of information about processes on your system. Now you can use the information it provides to control them.

Signaling a running process

Linux, and all UNIX, provides a way to send various signals to processes. A signal is an exception typically used to tell the process to do something other than usual. For example, if you need to kill a process, you can send it a signal to terminate. The command to signal a process is called `kill`. It is a confusing name because you can use kill to send any valid signal, not just to send a signal to kill the process.

USING KILL

The `kill` command can be a built-in shell command for many popular shells, such as csh and tcsh. However, there is also an external kill program, which is typically in the /bin directory. Both versions work the same way. To find what signals you can send to processes via kill, you can run:

```
kill --l
```

You should see a list similar to the following:

```
 1) SIGHUP       2) SIGINT       3) SIGQUIT      4) SIGILL
 5) SIGTRAP      6) SIGIOT       7) SIGBUS       8) SIGFPE
 9) SIGKILL     10) SIGUSR1     11) SIGSEGV     12) SIGUSR2
13) SIGPIPE     14) SIGALRM     15) SIGTERM     17) SIGCHLD
18) SIGCONT     19) SIGSTOP     20) SIGTSTP     21) SIGTTIN
22) SIGTTOU     23) SIGURG      24) SIGXCPU     25) SIGXFSZ
26) SIGVTALRM   27) SIGPROF     28) SIGWINCH    29) SIGIO
30) SIGPWR
```

The built-in `kill` command in the GNU Bourne-Again Shell (/bin/bash) produces the preceding output. Other shells or the /bin/kill might print the output a bit differently. For example, /bin/kill –l produces the following output:

```
HUP INT QUIT ILL TRAP IOT UNUSED FPE KILL USR1 SEGV USR2 PIPE ALRM
TERM STKFLT CHLD CONT STOP TSTP TTIN TTOU IO XCPU XFSZ VTALRM PROF
WINCH
```

Careful readers notice that these two `kill` commands differ in the -l output they produce. In fact, if you use /bin/csh (C shell) or /bin/tcsh (enhanced C shell) and run the built-in `kill` command with -l option, you get another listing that does not match either of these. Say I want to know which signals are really available under Red Hat Linux. Because I also want to provide you with an interactive demonstration of how you can use kill to send various signals to a process, I write a Perl script called gen_signal_demo.pl, as shown in Listing 8-1, to identify the signals available on my Red Hat Linux system.

Listing 8-1: gen_signal_demo.pl

```perl
#!/usr/bin/perl
#
# Chapter 8
#
# Written by kabir@intevo.com
#
# Purpose: to generate a Perl script that installs
#          signal handlers for all possible signals.
#          This script is used to demonstrate in an
#          interactive way how signals are caught.
#
# Notes: I don't attempt to stop the script from not
#        installing useless signal handlers for
#         uninterruptible signals (KILL, STOP).
#
#        This script is strictly for demonstration use.
#
# Syntax:  gen_signal_demo.pl > signal_demo.pl
#---------------------------------


# First generate the #!/usr/bin/perl line for the
#
print <<SBANG;
#!/usr/bin/perl

SBANG

foreach $signal (keys %SIG){

print <<SIG;
   \$SIG{$signal} = sub { print "Caught a $signal signal.\\n"; };
SIG

   }

print <<MAIN;

print "Hello, my PID is \$\$.\\n";
print "Use kill -signal \$\$ command to experiment on me.\\n";

# Set a 10 sec. alarm event.
alarm(10);
```

```
# Loop forever.
while(1){
  sleep(1);  # Sleep for a second.
  }

MAIN
```

This relatively small Perl script generates another Perl script. Run the script as follows:

```
gen_signal_demo.pl > signal_demo.pl
```

The generated script has signal handlers for all signals available on your system. If you look at the generated script, you will notice that it defines signal handlers by using the following construct:

```
$SIG{shortened signal name}   = sub { # handler code };
```

For example:

```
$SIG{INT} = sub { print "Caught a INT signal.\n"; };
```

Here, the SIGINT handler is defined. It prints "Caught a INT signal.\n" when you signal the script with SIGINT. Run the signal_demo.pl script as follows:

```
./signal_demo.pl
```

The output looks something like the following:

```
Hello, my PID is XXXX
Use kill --signal XXXX command to experiment on me.
```

The real PID of the process replaces the *XXXX* string. Before you use the `kill` command to send various signals to this program, browse Table 8-3 to find more information on each signal.

TABLE 8-3 **AVAILABLE SIGNALS**

#	Name (short name)	Description
1	SIGHUP (HUP)	Hang up. This signal is often used to instruct a process to reload configuration files.

#	Name (short name)	Description
2	SIGINT (INT)	Interrupt.
3	SIGQUIT (QUIT)	Quit.
4	SIGILL (ILL)	Illegal instruction.
5	SIGTRAP (TRAP)	Trace trap.
6	SIGIOT (IOT)	IOT instruction.
7	SIGBUS (BUS)	Bus error.
8	SIGFPE (FPE)	Floating-point exception.
9	SIGKILL (KILL)	Kill. This signal cannot be caught (that is, handled in a process), blocked, or ignored.
10	SIGUSR1 (USR1)	User-defined signal 1.
11	SIGSEGV (SEGV)	Segmentation violation.
12	SIGUSR2 (USR2)	User-defined signal 2.
13	SIGPIPE (PIPE)	Write on a pipe with no one to read it.
14	SIGALRM (ALRM)	Alarm clock.
15	SIGTERM (TERM)	Software termination signal. This is often sent before a KILL signal is issued. This allows a process to catch this signal and to prepare to exit.
16	SIGSTKFLT	Stack fault on coprocessor.
17	SIGCHLD (CHLD)	Child status has changed.
18	SIGCONT (CONT)	Continue after STOP signal. This signal cannot be blocked.
19	SIGSTOP (STOP)	Stop. This signal cannot be caught (that is, handled in a process), blocked, or ignored.
20	SIGTSTP (TSTP)	Stop signal generated from keyboard, typically by using Ctrl+Z.
21	SIGTTIN	Background read attempted from control terminal.
22	SIGTTOU	Background write attempted to control terminal.
23	SIGURG	Urgent condition present on socket.
24	SIGXCPU	CPU time limit exceeded. See man setrlimit (2).

Continued

TABLE 8-3 *Continued*

#	Name (short name)	Description
25	SIGXFSZ	File size limit exceeded. See man setrlimit (2).
26	SIGVTALRM	Virtual time alarm. See man setitimer (2).
27	SIGPROF	Profiling timer alarm. See man setitimer (2).
28	SIGWINCH	Window size change.
29	SIGIO	I/O is possible on a descriptor. See man fcntl (2).
30	SIGPWR	Power failure.
31	UNUSED	Not used.

Once you get the signal_demo.pl script running, use another virtual console, login shell, or xterm (if you are on X Windows) to send signals to the process. When you run the script, it displays the PID, so there's no need to do a ps to locate the PID of this process. Send any of the signals just listed to the process, and see the message it prints. For example, if the PID of this process is 12345 and you run:

```
kill --HUP 12345
```

it displays:

```
Caught a HUP signal.
```

Note that the script schedules an alarm event (using the alarm function) to occur after 10 seconds of execution. This prints:

```
Caught a ALRM signal.
```

When you send a KILL signal by using `kill -KILL 12345`, the process exits because a signal handler cannot catch this signal. Similarly, if you send a STOP signal to the process, it is suspended. When it is suspended, you see a message such as:

```
Suspended (signal)
```

You can run ps to see that the STAT field shows a T flag, which means the process is terminated. This is a bit misleading because the process really stops, not terminates. To bring the process back to running mode, you can send it a CONT signal. An interesting thing about the suspended mode is that the process is still able to receive any pending signals that are sent during its suspended stage. In other words, if you suspend this process by using the STOP signal and then send an HUP signal while the process is still suspended, kernel sends the HUP signal to the process when it runs again in response to a CONT signal.

You seldom use most of the signals in Table 8-3 outside system programs. As a system administrator, you are likely to use only HUP, INT, TERM, STOP, and KILL. If you are not fond of typing or prefer numbers to letters, you can use signal numbers with kill as well. For example, to issue a KILL signal, you can either do kill –KILL PID or kill –9 PID. Better yet, you can kill a process by name by using the killall utility.

USING KILLALL

This nifty utility lets you kill a process by name. For example, if you have a process called signal_demo.pl and would like to kill it without typing its PID, you can run:

```
killall --KILL signal_demo.pl
```

When you do not provide a signal name, killall automatically sends the SIGTERM signal. However, be careful when using killall; it kills all instances of the named command. Sometimes, the convenience of not having to know the PID can go sour. For example, look at the following ps output:

```
 PID  TTY STAT TIME COMMAND
 1246 p8 S    0:00 -tcsh
 2160 p6 S    0:00 -tcsh
 2365 p1 S    0:00 -bash
 2459 p6 S    0:00 vi bar.txt
 2460 p8 S    0:00 vi foo.txt
 2463 p1 R    0:00 ps
```

Say that for some reason you want to kill the vi process used for editing the foo.txt file. If you run killall vi foo.txt expecting it to terminate only this instance of vi, you are surprised to find that all of your vi sessions have terminated. This occurs because killall expects command names as arguments and sends signals to all instances of a named program.

 Be extremely cautious when running the killall command as a superuser because it removes every instance of the named command from the entire system, which includes all users.

Now that you know how to send signals to running processes, let's look at how you can control process priority.

Controlling process priority

Linux has two priority numbers associated with each process. For example, if you run ps -l, you see two fields, PRI and NI. The PRI field shows the actual process priority, which the operating system dynamically computes. Among other factors, the operating system takes the NI number into account when it computes and updates the PRI number. We call the NI number the nice number or the requested process execution priority number. The owner or the superuser can set this number to influence the actual execution priority number (PRI). You can use the /bin/nice utility to change the NI number. The functionality of this utility is often built into popular shells such as /bin/csh, /bin/tcsh, and others.

USING nice TO CHANGE PROCESS PRIORITY

By default, the built-in shell version of nice or the /bin/nice utility allows a user to decrease process priority only. Only the superuser is allowed to increase the priority of a process. The valid range of process priority is from -20 to 20, where the lower the number, the higher the priority. In other words, -20 is the highest NI priority, and 20 is the lowest. Before you can set the priority of a process, run which nice to determine if you are going to run the built-in shell version of nice or the /bin/nice utility. This is necessary because the syntax varies between these two versions. For example, suppose you want to run a Perl script called foo.pl at the lowest priority (20), and the shell version of the nice command is:

```
nice +10 foo.pl
```

and the /bin/nice version of the same command is:

```
nice -10 foo.pl
```

If you are a superuser and want to increase the priority of the foo.pl script to -10, the built-in shell version of the command looks like:

```
nice -10 foo.pl
```

and the /bin/nice version of the same command looks like:

```
nice-10 foo.pl
```

If this is too confusing to you, you can use another utility called snice to handle process priority upgrades or downgrades. Here is how:

◆ Use ps to find the PID of the process whose priority you want to change.

◆ To upgrade priority, run snice -n PID, where n is the new priority number. For example, snice -5 1234 increases the priority of the process 1234 (the PID) by 5. Note that, as with nice, only a superuser can increase priority.

♦ To downgrade priority, run `snice +n PID`, where n is the new priority number. For example, `snice +5 1234` decreases the priority of process 1234 (the PID) by 5. As with nice, any user can lower priority of the processes he or she owns.

As with snice, you can use the renice utility to change the priority of a process. The preceding steps for snice also apply to renice.

To make sure the priority changes are taking effect, you can run `ps -l` to determine the value of NI field.

RUNNING A PROCESS IN THE FOREGROUND OR THE BACKGROUND

In most cases, when you run a process from a console, shell, or xterm, you run the program in the foreground. When a process runs in the foreground, you have to wait for it to finish. However, instead of waiting for a process to finish, you can run it in the background by specifying a "&" character at the end of the command line. This becomes very handy when you are running a process that takes a long time to finish and you'd rather do something useful while it works. For example, say you want to use the du command to get an idea of which files are taking up the most disk space in your system. You can run it in the background as follows:

```
du > /tmp/du.out &
```

Here, output is directed to a file /tmp/du.out because you do not want du output to interrupt you while you are working on something else.

TIP If you would like to leave a program running in the background after you log off from a shell session, you can use the nohup program. It immunizes a command from SIGHUP and SIGTERM signals and allows the process to continue without a tty. See the man page for details.

Now let's look at how you can monitor process load in your system.

Monitoring Processes and System Load

Being able to monitor the state of the processes in a system at any time is very important for system administration. As a Red Hat Linux system administrator, you have a few tools to help you in the monitoring processes. I discuss them here.

Using top

The `top` utility is one of my favorite process-monitoring tools. Using `top`, you can monitor process activity in real time. Figure 8-1 shows a `top` session running on an X-terminal window.

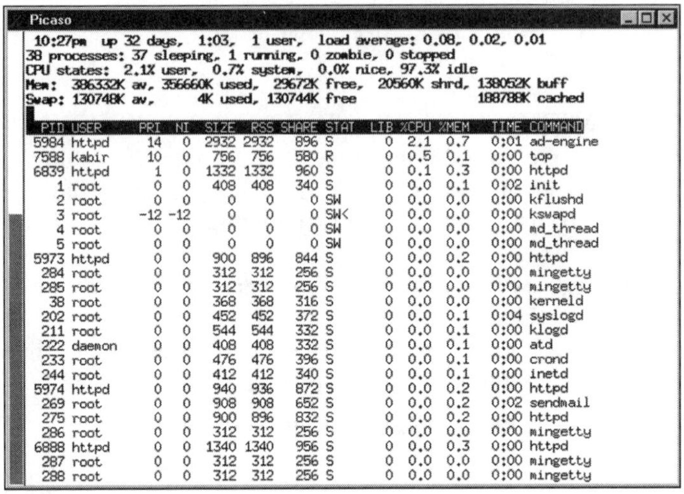

Figure 8-1: A top session running on an X terminal

The screen is updated automatically to provide a fresh, new look at the running state of the system. The first line is the uptime line, which shows the current time of the system, how long the system has been up since the last reboot, how many users are on the system, and three load average numbers. The load averages are the average numbers of processes ready to run during the last 1, 5, and 15 minutes. The second line is the process statistics line, which shows the total number of processes running at the time of the last `top` screen update. This line also shows the number of sleeping, running, zombie, and stopped processes. The third line displays CPU statistics (which include the percentage of CPU time the user uses) and system, nice, and idle processes. The fourth line provides memory statistics, which include total available memory, free memory, used memory, shared memory, and memory used for buffers. The fifth line provides virtual memory or swap statistics, which include total available swap space, used swap space, free swap space, and cached swap space. The rest of the lines are similar to a `ps`-generated report.

Using `top`, you can identify which processes are using most of your resources. All you need to do is look at the few entries in the ps-like output. For example, Figure 8-1 shows that a process called ad-engine is consuming 2.1 percent of the CPU time and 0.7 percent of the memory, which makes it the `top` process. The second most resource-consuming process is the `top` utility itself! When you run `top` to monitor other processes, `top` itself takes some resources to run. However, you still get a good idea about the percentage of resources a process consumes.

Using vmstat

The vmstat utility also provides interesting information about processes, memory, I/O, and CPU activity. When you run this utility without any arguments, the output looks similar to the following:

```
procs          memory            swap     io  system      cpu
r b w  swpd free  buff cache si  so bi bo in  cs us sy id
0 0 0     8 8412 45956 52820  0   0  0  0 104 11 66  0 33
```

The procs fields show the number of processes waiting for run time (r), the number of processes blocked (b), and the number of processes swapped out (w).

The memory fields show the amounts of swap, free, buffered, and cached memory in KB.

The swap fields show the amount (in KB/sec) of memory swapped in (si) from disk and the amount of memory swapped out (so) to disk.

The io fields show the number of blocks sent (bi) and received (bo) to and from block devices per second.

The system field shows the number of interrupts (in) and context switches (cs) per second.

The cpu field shows the percentage of total CPU time in terms of user (us), system (sy), and idle (id) time.

If you would like vmstat to update information automatically, you can run it as vmstat nsec, where nsec is the number of seconds you want it to wait before another update.

Using uptime

To get quick statistics on the state of your system because of process load, you can run the uptime utility. It shows the current time of the system, how long the system has been up since the last reboot, how many users are on the system, and three load average numbers. The load averages are the average number of processes ready to run during the last 1, 5, and 15 minutes.

Logging Processes

A process log is a system administrator's best friend. Log files often provide the system administrator with a great deal of clues about what's going on with a certain process. Almost all widely used server software packages — sendmail, Apache, named, and so on — write logs. There are two trends when it comes to writing logs. Some server programs write custom log files, and some use a facility called syslog, which is a logging facility the syslogd daemon provides. Typically, init starts syslogd at run level 3 (multiuser). The syslog facility provides a centralized logging environment for processes that wish to write logs.

Configuring syslog

Typically, syslog is already configured on most systems. The default Red Hat installation installs syslogd and its /etc/syslog.conf configuration file, which is in Listing 8-2.

Listing 8-2: The syslogd configuration file, /etc/syslog.conf

```
# Log all kernel messages to the console.
# Logging much else clutters up the screen.
kern.*    /dev/console

# Log anything (except mail) of level info or higher.
# Don't log private authentication messages!
*.info;mail.none;authpriv.none  /var/log/messages

# The authpriv file has restricted access.
authpriv.*  /var/log/secure

# Log all the mail messages in one place.
mail.* /var/log/maillog

# Everybody gets emergency messages.
*.emerg *

# Save mail and news errors of level err and
#higher in a  special file.
uucp,news.crit  /var/log/spooler
```

The configuration file is quite simple. The blank lines and the lines starting with "#" are ignored. The structure of a syslogd configuration line is as follows:

```
facility.priority    destination
```

where facility can be one of the following keywords: auth, Authpriv, cron, daemon, kern, lpr, mail, news, syslog, user, uucp, and local0–local7. A priority can be one of the following keywords in ascending order of severity: debug, info, notice, warning, err, crit, alert, emerg, none. You can also use "*" as a wildcard for the facility or the priority part of the line to indicate all facilities or all priorities, respectively. You can use a comma-separated list of multiple facilities with the same priority in a line. For example:

```
uucp,news.crit  /var/log/spooler
```

Here, log entries (often called messages) of critical (crit) priority from uucp and news facilities (that is, uucp and the news server program) are written to /var/log/spooler file.

You can also use a semicolon-separated list of multiple facility.priority pairs to assign a single destination to them. For example:

```
*.info;mail.none;authpriv.none   /var/log/messages
```

Here, all informative (info) log entries from all facilities are written to the /var/log/messages file with the exception of the informative messages from the mail and authpriv facilities.

The default syslogd configuration makes it write the log files in the /var/log directory.

Monitoring logs using tail

If you are experiencing problems with a server process, find out if it writes log files. If it writes log files of its own or uses the syslog facility, you can monitor the log files by using the tail utility as the process runs. This utility allows you to monitor growing log files by viewing the last part of a file. For example, to monitor the /var/log/messages file, you can run:

```
tail --f  /var/log/messages
```

This allows you to view the file as new entries are written to it. If you would like to limit the number of lines you see, use the --line number option. For example, to view only the last three lines of the same file as the last example, you can run `tail -f --line 3 /var/log/messages`.

Note that syslogd-produced log files can grow very large in a very active system. Therefore, it is important that you rotate your log files by using the logrotate facility. In fact, by default, the RPM package for syslogd installs a logrotate configuration file called syslog in /etc/logrotate.d directory. The logrotate setup rotates the log files on a weekly basis and keeps compressed backups of back logs as well.

Now take a look at how you can schedule processes for unattended execution.

Scheduling Processes

Like all other forms of UNIX and UNIX-like operating systems, Red Hat Linux provides you with two popular process-scheduling facilities. In this section, you learn to use both of these services.

Using at

The at utility allows you to queue a command for execution at a later time. For example, to run the disk usage summary generator utility called du at 8:40 p.m., you can run at as follows:

```
at 20:40
```

The at command displays a prompt such as "at>" where you can enter the du command as follows:

```
at> du -a > /tmp/du.out
```

Here, the output of du is directed to a file. After you enter the command (the du command in this example), at displays the prompt again. You can press Ctrl+D to exit. You see a message similar to the one here:

```
at> <EOT>
warning: commands will be executed using /bin/sh
job 1 at 1999-12-06 20:40
```

This means that at has scheduled the at daemon (atd) to run du –a > /tmp/du.out job at 8:40 p.m., 12/06/1999. Note that you can use a variety of time formats to specify the time of execution. For example, instead of saying at 20:40, you can say at 8:40 p.m.. You can also specify the date with the time. For example, 8:40 p.m. feb 23, 10 a.m. + 5 days, 12:30 P.M. tomorrow, midnight, and noon are all valid time specifications.

To verify that your job is in the job queue, run the atq command. It shows the currently scheduled job in the queue. All scheduled jobs are stored in /var/spool/at directory.

 If you are the root user on a system, you see commands that will be run by examining the files in the /var/spool/at spool directory.

If you want to stop the scheduled job, you can run the atrm command to remove your job. You need to know the job sequence number to remove a job with atrm. To find what jobs you have scheduled, run the atq command, and delete any job by using atrm job#. For example, to remove job #1, run atrm 1.

The scheduled job is run via the atd daemon process, which init starts for run level 3 (multiuser mode). If you would like to restrict use of the at facility, you can create a /etc/at.allow file and list all users allowed to run it. Remember to enter a single username per line. Any user not in the allow file does not have access to the at facility. On the other hand, if you want to deny only a few users but to allow the rest, you can create a similar file called /etc/at.deny. All usernames in this file are denied access to at.

Although at provides you with process scheduling capabilities, another facility called cron is more widely used than at, as it offers a more structured way for creating unattended process execution schedules for repetitive tasks.

Using cron

You need to schedule many tasks (processes) in a Linux system for unattended execution on a regular basis. For example, to rotate the log files syslogd creates, or to remove old files from the /tmp directory, you need to run a process daily or weekly. The cron facility allows you to create a recurring task schedule. In fact, it was not so long ago that there was no atd daemon, and all at jobs were run via a program called atrun, which in turn was run via the cron facility.

The cron facility includes the crond daemon, which the init process starts. The crond daemon reads task schedules from /etc/crontab and files in the /var/spool/ cron directory. The latter stores schedule files (often called crontab or cron table) for normal users allowed to run cron jobs. As a superuser, you can specify a list of users allowed to run creon jobs in /etc/cron.allow file. Similarly, you can explicitly deny cron access to users by specifying their names in /etc/cron.deny file. Both files use a simple, one username per line format. If you allow users to run cron jobs, they can use the crontab utility to create job schedules. For example, if you allow users to run cron jobs, they can run crontab –e to create and edit their cron job entries. A cron job specification has the following format:

```
minute(s) hour(s) day(s) month weekday username command argument(s)
```

Table 8-4 describes the first five time-specification fields.

TABLE 8-4 CRON TIME-SPECIFICATION FIELDS

Fields	Description	Range
Minutes(s)	One or more minutes in an hour. You can specify a comma-separated list of minutes.	0–59
Hour(s)	One or more hours in a day. You can specify a comma-separated list of hours.	0–23, where 0 is midnight
Day(s)	One or more days in a month. You can specify a comma-separated list of days.	1–31
Month(s)	One or more months in a year. You can specify a comma-separated list of months.	1–12
Weekday(s)	One or more days in a week. You can specify a comma-separated list of days.	1–7, where 1 is Monday

For any of the fields in Table 8-4, you can use "*" as a wildcard. Now let's look at an example:

```
01 * * * * root /some/script
```

This states that /some/script runs every first minute of every hour, every day, every month, and every weekday. The script runs as the root user. To run this script every 10 minutes, you can define a cron job such as the following:

```
0,10,20,30,40,50 * * * * root /some/script
```

To run the same script only once a month, you can schedule a cron job as follows:

```
01 1 1 * * root /some/script
```

Here, the script runs at 1:01 A.M. on the first day of every month.

The default cron job for the system is /etc/crontab, which includes a few interesting cron job entries such as the following:

```
SHELL=/bin/bash
PATH=/sbin:/bin:/usr/sbin:/usr/bin
MAILTO=root

# run-parts
01 * * * * root run-parts /etc/cron.hourly
02 4 * * * root run-parts /etc/cron.daily
22 4 * * 0 root run-parts /etc/cron.weekly
42 4 1 * * root run-parts /etc/cron.monthly
```

You use these cron jobs to run the run-parts script in /usr/bin directory. This script runs every hour, every day, every week, and every month using the four cron job specifications in the preceding listing. It takes a directory name as an argument and runs all scripts or programs in the directory. For example, consider the first cron entry in the preceding listing. It states that the run-parts script should run at the first minute of every hour. The script is fed the argument /etc/cron.hourly. Because the script runs all the files in this directory, the entire process effectively works as if all the files in the /etc/cron.hourly directory are set up as cron jobs. This trick allows you to put new files in the /etc/cron.hourly directory and to schedule it automatically for an hourly run. Similarly, the other three cron entries allow you to run any program on a daily, weekly, or monthly basis by just placing them in the /etc/cron.daily, /etc/cron.weekly, or /etc/cron.monthly directory. This makes it easy to create cron jobs for almost everything without having to configure a cron entry.

For example, say you want to synchronize your system time with a remote time server on a daily basis. You decide to use the rdate utility to set the time via the Internet. The command to run is:

```
/usr/bin/rdate --s  time.server.host.tld
```

Because the default /etc/crontab contains a cron entry that allows you to schedule daily cron jobs by just placing the script or program in the /etc/cron.daily directory, you can create a simple shell script such as the following and place it in the /etc/cron.daily directory:

```
#!/bin/sh
/usr/bin/rdate --s time.server.host.tld
```

Your job is done. Every day at 4:02 a.m., your script runs with all other scripts and programs in the /etc/cron.daily directory.

As you can see, setting up cron jobs is much more systematic than using at commands to queue tasks, and, therefore, cron is preferred over at. In fact, I recommend that you disable the at facility by removing the atd entry from your /etc/rc.d/rc3.d directory.

Summary

In this chapter, you learned how processes get created; how to use signals to control them; how you can use various utilities such as ps, top, vmstat, and uptime to monitor processes; how you can log messages from server processes via the syslog facility; and how you can automate unattended process execution by using the at and cron services.

Chapter 9

Network Administration

WHAT GOOD IS A RED HAT LINUX server without a TCP/IP network? In this chapter you will learn about the basics of TCP/IP networking and also learn to configure your Red Hat Linux system for such a network.

Basics of TCP/IP Networking

If you are not new to TCP/IP networking, you may skip or quickly browse this section.

TCP/IP is the most widely used communication protocol for networking computers. Each computer in a TCP/IP network has one or more network interfaces. Each network interface has a unique address – an IP address. Figure 9-1 shows two very simple TCP/IP networks.

Notice that the first network in the figure has two computers connected. Each computer is connected to the network via a network interface. In this example, each computer is connected via a Network Interface Card (NIC). Notice that each NIC has a unique IP address. The second example network in the same figure shows two computers, each with multiple network interfaces, and each of these interfaces has its own unique IP address. So the point here is that each network interface must have a unique IP address. However, because each host computer might have multiple network interfaces, multiple IP addresses may point to the same host.

An IP address is a four-byte-long number that is typically written in a special dot (that is, period) format: a dot separates every pair of bytes. For example:

```
192.168.10.1
```

Figure 9-2 shows this IP address in hex, binary, and decimal number formats.

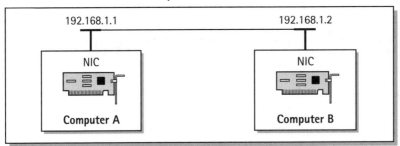

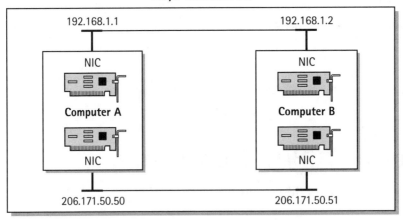

Figure 9-1: An example of two simple TCP/IP networks

192.168.10.1

byte 8 bits	byte 8 bits	byte 8 bits	byte 8 bits	**4 bytes** **32 bits**

00–FF	00–FF	00–FF	00–FF	**Hex**
C0	A8	A	1	

00–255	00–255	00–255	00–255	**Decimal**
192	168	10	1	

00000000 –11111111	00000000 –11111111	00000000 –11111111	00000000 –11111111	**Binary**
11000000	10101000	00001010	00000001	

Figure 9-2: An IP address in hex, binary, and decimal formats

As you can see in the figure, each byte (eight bits) can be any number between 0 and 255. Therefore, the total number of possible IP addresses is 2^{32}, or 4,294,967,296. This is quite a large number, so when TCP/IP was originally designed the designers thought we would never run out of IP addresses. Alas! The way the Internet revolution is going on, it appears that very soon our home appliances will require IP addresses to communicate with a central home computer. Is it too far-fetched to think of a microwave with an IP address exchanging recipes with an Internet server? Not really. In any event, the current IP numbering scheme, called IPv4, is no longer sufficient, so a new numbering scheme, IPv6 or IP Next Generation or IPng, is likely to become a reality soon. IPng is a new version of IP designed to be an evolutionary step from IPv4. IPng addresses are 16 bytes (128 bits) long.

The total number of possible addresses using Ipng is 2^{128}, or 340,282,366,920, 938,463,463,374,607,431,768,211,456. As you can see, IPng will surely serve us for many centuries. However, because support for IPng in the Linux kernel is still at the experimental stage, I recommend that you keep your eyes and ears open on this. For now, you need to worry only about the current IPv4 scheme. The current IP number scheme allows us to create classes of IP networks. We discuss these classes in the following section.

Classifying IP Networks

As mentioned previously, we use IP numbers to identify network interfaces on host computers. These numbers are not randomly assigned. Each IP number carries two types of information. To understand what these are, consider an analogy. All of us are familiar with the concept of an area code in a phone number. For example, (916) 555-5555 is a U.S. phone number, where 916 is the area code for the city of Sacramento, California. When someone in New York, New York, dials the preceding number, the phone company's computer routes the call to a phone in Sacramento, California. This routing of calls uses the area code of the number to determine the path of the connection. IP addresses work the same way. You can think of an IP address as:

IP = { Network Address } + {Interface address of the host computer}

For example, 192.168.2.10 is an IP address in the 192.168.2.0 network, and the interface address, which is often called the host address, is .10. In other words, this IP address points to the network interface .10 in the 192.168.2.0 network. Which part of the IP address we use to identify the network depends on the class of the network. Notice that when you are writing a network address, you write the interface identifier bytes as zeros.

As you know, the 32-bit IP address covers a range from 0.0.0.0 to 255.255. 255.255 (2^{32}) addresses. They are classified (with exceptions) as follows:

Class A networks

Any IP address that ranges from 0.0.0.0 to 127.255.255.255 is a class A IP network. Figure 9-3 shows the possible range of IP addresses in this class.

Class A IP network

Network	Total address space	Usable address space
0.0.0.0	0.0.0.0. – 0.255.255.255	0.0.0.1 to 0.255.255.254
1.0.0.0	1.0.0.0. – 1.255.255.255	1.0.0.1 to 1.255.255.254
2.0.0.0	2.0.0.0. – 2.255.255.255	2.0.0.1 to 2.255.255.254
3.0.0.0	3.0.0.0. – 3.255.255.255	3.0.0.1 to 3.255.255.254
...	...	...
126.0.0.0	126.0.0.0 – 126.255.255.255	126.0.0.1 to 126.255.255.254
127.0.0.0	127.0.0.0 – 127.255.255.255	127.0.0.1 to 127.255.255.254

Figure 9-3: Class A network addresses

In this class, the leftmost byte of the IP address determines the network address. We use the rest of the three bytes to identify the network interface on a host. So you can think of the class as $n.x.x.x$, where n is 0 to 127 and $x.x.x$ can be any three-byte number from 0.0.0 to 255.255.255. In other words, there are 2^{24} (16,777,216) IP addresses per class A network. Notice that the first network is 0.0.0.0. There are two special class A networks.

The 0.0.0.0 network is reserved and used to indicate the default route for a network; we use the 127.0.0.0 network as a loopback network. Each computer should use 127.0.0.1 as the loopback interface IP address. We use this address to test network software without having a physical network. For example, you can run telnet 127.0.0.1 to test the Telnet client in a single, non-networked computer. In such a case, the Telnet client program connects to the local host computer. You also notice that the /etc/hosts file contains an entry that assigns this IP address to a hostname called localhost – the only hostname in the loopback network. Because these special class A networks have special meanings and are not used to identify any physical class A networks, technically there are only 126 class A networks. Also note that 10.0.0.0 network is reserved.

Class B networks

Any IP address that ranges from 128.0.0.0 to 191.255.255.255 is a class B network. Figure 9-4 shows the possible range of IP addresses in this class.

Class B IP network

Network	Total address space	Usable address space
128.0.0.0	128.0.0.0 – 128.0.255.255	128.0.0.1 to 128.0.255.254
128.1.0.0	128.0.0.0 – 128.1.255.255	128.1.0.1 to 128.1.255.254
•••	•••	•••
128.255.0.0	128.255.0.0 – 128.255.255.255	128.255.0.1 to 128.255.255.254
•••	•••	•••
191.255.0.0	191.255.0.0 – 191.255.255.255	191.255.0.1 to 191.255.255.254

Figure 9-4: Class B Network Addresses

In this class, the leftmost two bytes determine the network. So you can think of this class as $n1.n2.x.x$, where $n1$ can be 128 to 191, $n2$ can be 0 to 255, and $x.x$ can be any two-byte number between 0.0 and 255.255. There are 2^{16} (65,536) IP addresses per class B network. Between 128.0.0.0 and 191.255.0.0, there are 2^{14} (16,384) class B networks. Note that the 172.16.0.0 to 172.31.0.0 class B networks are reserved.

Class C networks

Any IP address that ranges from 192.0.0.0 to 223.255.255.255 is a class C IP network. Figure 9-5 shows the possible range of IP addresses in this class.

In this class, the leftmost three bytes determine the network. So you can think of this class as $n1.n2.n3.x$, where $n1$ can be 192 to 223, $n2$ can be 0 to 255, $n3$ can be 0 to 255, and x can be a single-byte number between 0 to 255. There are 2^8 (256) IP addresses per class C network. Between 192.0.0.0 and 223.255.255.0, there are 2^{21} (2,097,152) class C networks. Note that addresses below 223.255.255.255 (that is, 224.0.0.0 to 255.255.255.255) are reserved.

Figure 9-6 demonstrates one of the easiest ways to determine quickly which IP address is in which network.

Class C IP network

Network	Total address space	Usable address space
192.0.0.0	192.0.0.0 – 192.0.0.255	192.0.0.1 to 192.0.0.254
192.0.1.0	192.0.1.0 – 192.0.1.255	192.0.1.1 to 192.0.1.254
•••	•••	•••
192.0.255.0	192.0.255.0 – 192.0.255.255	192.0.255.1 to 192.0.255.254
192.1.0.0	192.1.0.0 – 192.1.0.255	192.1.0.1 to 192.1.0.254
•••	•••	•••
192.255.255.0	192.255.255.0 – 192.255.255.255	192.255.255.1 to 192.255.255.254
193.0.0.0	193.0.0.0 – 193.0.0.255	192.255.255.1 to 192.255.255.254
•••	•••	•••
223.255.255.0	223.255.255.0 – 223.255.255.255	223.255.255.1 to 223.255.255.254

Figure 9-5: Class C network addresses

Leftmost byte of an IP address

Binary	Hex	Decimal	
0000 0000	00	0	Class A
0111 1110	7F	126	

Binary	Hex	Decimal	
1000 0000	80	128	Class B
1011 1111	BF	191	

Binary	Hex	Decimal	
1100 0000	C0	192	Class C
1101 1111	DF	223	

Figure 9-6: A cheat sheet for recognizing IP networks

You can simply look at the leftmost byte of an IP address and determine the class of the network. For example, the IP addresses in the class A network always have the leftmost byte set to 0 to 126 (127 is the loopback network). Similarly, the IP addresses in the class B network have the leftmost byte set to 128 to 191. And finally, the IP addresses in class C network have the leftmost byte set to 192 to 223.

You should also know that the first and the last IP addresses in any network (A, B, or C) are not usable as IP addresses for network interfaces. For example, 206.171.50.0 is a class C network where the range is 206.171.50.0 to 206.171.50.255. However, the 206.171.50.0 address is the network address, and the 206.171.50.255 address is the broadcast address for that network; therefore, we should assign it to any network interface.

By now, you know a great deal about IP addresses; you should be able to identify what class an IP address belongs to quite easily. Now take a look at how you can configure the network interface on your Red Hat Linux server.

Configuring a Network Interface

Because this book deals primarily with the server aspects of the Red Hat Linux operating system, it is a safe guess on my part that you will be connecting the Red Hat Linux computer to an Ethernet. Such an Ethernet could be your very own Local Area Network (LAN) or a LAN at an ISP (for instance, colocated servers). I will also assume that you have already installed an Ethernet adapter card (that is, a Network Interface Card, or NIC) that works with Red Hat Linux. To find out which NICs are compatible with your version of Red Hat Linux, see the hardware compatibility section of the Red Hat Web site. In general, most popular NIC cards work fine with Red Hat Linux.

 You might have already configured your network at the Red Hat Linux installation phase, but I still recommend that you read this section because you may need to change your network configuration at a later time.

You can configure your network in several ways. First I will discuss the command line method, as it is the most powerful (in the sense that you do not need to rely on any special tool other than your favorite text editor).

Using traditional methods to configure network interface cards

The traditional way is my favorite method of doing all types of configuration because it forces me to know exactly what is needed to configure something. My motto: Once you know how to do things the "old-fashioned" way, you can do them any way you like.

CONFIGURING A NEW NETWORK INTERFACE

Before you do anything, run the dmesg program (or view the /var/log/dmesg file) to find if the current Linux kernel is recognizing your network card. If it is not, read the module configuration section in Chapter 2. On the other hand, if the Linux kernel recognizes your card, you should see some lines in the dmesg output pertaining to the kernel's discovery of your network device. For example, when I run the following command on a Red Hat Linux system with a generic (NE2000 compatible) Ethernet card:

```
dmesg | grep --I eth
```

it prints the following output:

```
NE*000 ethercard probe at 0x340: 00 c0 f6 98 37 37
eth0: NE2000 found at 0x340, using IRQ 5.
```

This tells me that the kernel has found my NE2000-compatible network card and is using Interrupt Request Line (IRQ) 5, as well as the I/O address space starting at 0x340. Also note that this device is called eth0 (that is, Ethernet device 0). Once you have confirmed that the kernel is recognizing your network device, you are ready to configure it. In this example, I assume that you want to configure the first Ethernet device, eth0, and that you want a persistent configuration.

What I mean by a persistent configuration is one you use every time you start your computer. You can do this with the help of the /etc/rc.d/init.d/network script. When this script links (where the name of the link is S*xx*network; *xx* is any number) from the default run level directory (which could be /etc/rc.d/rc3.d), the /etc/rc.d/init.d/network script runs at boot time. This script loads the network interfaces by using files stored in the /etc/sysconfig directory. Now take a look at how to configure eth0 so that it automatically starts up at boot.

The very first file you have to modify is /etc/sysconfig/network. Listing 9-1 shows an example of this file.

Listing 9-1: The /etc/sysconfig/network file

```
NETWORKING=yes
FORWARD_IPV4=yes
HOSTNAME=picaso.nitec.com
DOMAINNAME=nitec.com
GATEWAY=206.171.50.49
GATEWAYDEV=eth0
```

The NETWORKING=yes line states that you want to enable networking support.

The FORWARD_IPV4=yes should be set to yes if you would like to allow forwarding of IP packets to and from your Red Hat Linux server. This is required only if a Red Hat Linux computer is going to act as a gateway or router (discussed in a later section) for a network. For example, if you are planning on installing proxy server software on your computer to allow Web access for other computers on your LAN, you should set the FORWARD_IPV4 option to yes. On the other hand, if you are just planning on using this computer as a colocated Web server on a ISP network, you can turn IP forwarding off by setting this option to no.

The next two lines specify the hostname of the computer and the domain name of your network. The hostname you specify here must include the domain name you specify in the DOMAINNAME line. In other words, don't specify a hostname that uses a different domain name from the name you state in the DOMAINNAME line.

The next two lines specify the information you need to determine the default gateway for a computer. A default gateway is a computer (or a router) that transfers packets to and from your computer. For example, if you intend to connect your Red Hat Linux computer to your LAN, where you have an ISDN router that connects the LAN to the Internet, specify the IP address of the ISDN router's network interface as the default gateway. The GATEWAYDEV is important when you have multiple network interfaces. If you have only one Ethernet device, you should always set this to eth0. If you have multiple Ethernet devices (eth0, eth1, and so on), you have to use the interface name connected to the default gateway.

Once you configure the /etc/sysconfig/network file, you are ready to create the network interface file in the /etc/sysconfig/network-scripts directory. The network interface file uses ifcfg-interface as the naming convention. For example, the network interface filename for eth0 is ifcfg-eth0. An example of this file is in Listing 9-2.

Listing 9-2: The /etc/sysconfig/network-scripts/ifcfg-eth0 file

```
DEVICE=eth0
IPADDR=206.171.50.50
NETMASK=255.255.255.240
NETWORK=206.171.50.48
BROADCAST=206.171.50.63
ONBOOT=yes
```

Before you can configure the information in this file, you have to obtain from your Internet service provider the network address, the network mask, the IP address for the network interface on the host, and the broadcast address. You will learn more about the network mask and broadcast address in a later section.

The first line in this file specifies the device name. The second line specifies the network mask (netmask) number. The third line specifies the IP address of the network. The fifth line specifies broadcast address. Set he ONBOOT option, shown in the sixth line, to yes if you want the network interface to be "up" (that is, started) after boot.

Once you configure these two files, you are ready to bring up the network. The easiest way to bring up the interface you just configured is to run:

```
/etc/sysconfig/network--scripts/ifup  eth0
```

The ifup script takes the device name as the argument and starts it. It also creates a default route for the network. Once you have run this command, you can use the ifconfig program to see if the interface is up and running. To see if device eth0 is up, run:

```
ifconfig eth0
```

You should see output similar to the following:

```
eth0 Link encap:Ethernet HWaddr 00:C0:F6:98:37:37
inet addr:206.171.50.50  Bcast:206.171.50.63 Mask:255.255.255.240
UP BROADCAST RUNNING MULTICAST  MTU:1500  Metric:1
RX packets:9470 errors:0 dropped:0 overruns:0 frame:0
TX packets:7578 errors:0 dropped:0 overruns:0 carrier:0 collisions:0
Interrupt:5 Base address:0x340
```

Here ifconfig reports that network interface device eth0 has an Internet address (inet addr) 206.171.50.50, a broadcast address (Bcast) 206.171.50.63, and a network mask 255.255.255.240. The rest of the information shows the following: how many packets this interface has received so far (RX packets); how many packets this interface has transmitted so far (TX packets); how many errors of different types have occurred so far; what interrupt address line this device is using; what I/O address base is being used; and so on.

You can run ifconfig without any arguments to get the full list of all the up network devices. Note that the ifup script uses ifconfig to bring an interface up. For example:

```
ifconfig eth0 206.171.50.50 netmask 255.255.255.240 \
broadcast 206.171.50.63
```

The preceding command starts eth0 with IP address 206.171.50.50. You can also quickly take an interface down by using the ifconfig command. For example:

```
ifconfig eth0 down
```

This command takes the eth0 interface down. Once you have the interface up and running, you should try to contact a computer in your network. You can use the ping IP address command to see if you can use your new interface to contact a host on the same network.

If your /etc/resolv.conf file was not set up properly during installation, you are not able to ping a host by using its hostname. The /etc/resolv.conf file looks like the following:

```
search nitec.com
nameserver 206.171.50.50
```

This is set up during Red Hat Linux installation. If you have specified an invalid IP address for the name server, your computer is not able to contact the name server. So if you have your network interface up but you are unable to ping a host by using the hostname, try using the IP address of the host (really the network interface address). If you can ping the other host on your network, your interface is set up properly; just correct the nameserver line by fixing the IP address of the name server.

However, if you cannot ping a host by using either the IP address or the hostname, you might have a routing problem. If you have not used the ifup script as shown earlier and instead have used ifconfig to bring up the interface, you need to create a default route to your network and a default gateway manually. To create a default route for your network, use the route command as follows:

```
route add --net network address netmask device
```

For example, to create a default route for the 206.171.50.48 network with a 255.255.255.240 netmask and eth0 as the interface, I can run:

```
route add --net 206.171.50.48 255.255.255.240 eth0
```

To set the default gateway, you can run the route command as follows:

```
route add default gw gateway address device
```

For example, to set the default gateway address to 206.171.50.49, I can run the following command:

```
route add default gw 206.171.50.49 eth0
```

You can verify that your network route and default gateway are properly set up in the routing table by using the following command:

```
route --n
```

Here is an example of output of the preceding command:

```
Kernel IP routing table
Destination    Gateway Genmask          Flags Metric Ref Use Iface
206.171.50.48 0.0.0.0 255.255.255.240 U     0      0   6   eth0
127.0.0.0      0.0.0.0 255.0.0.0        U     0      0   5   lo
0.0.0.0        206.171.50.49  0.0.0.0 UG    0      0   17  eth0
```

At this point, you should use the ping program to ping hosts inside and outside your network. If you are successful, your network is up. If you still do not get any replies from your ping attempts, you should go back to the beginning of this section and ensure that you have followed all steps as suggested.

Here you learned how to configure a network interface so that a single IP address is associated with it. I told you earlier that each interface must have its unique IP address; ever wonder if you can associate multiple IP addresses to the single interface? Yes, you can, using the IP alias module for the Linux kernel. Here is how.

ALIASING MULTIPLE IP ADDRESSES WITH A SINGLE NETWORK INTERFACE

The first step in creating an IP alias is to determine if you have the IP alias module loaded with the kernel. The simplest way to check this is to run the lsmod command and see if ip_alias.o is listed anywhere in the output. If you do not see this module and you have not custom-compiled your kernel to include this module as part of the kernel, you can try to load the module by using the following command:

```
/sbin/insmod  /path/to/ip_alias.o
```

where */path/to/ip.alias.o* is the real path to ip_alias.o module. You can use locate ip_alias.o to locate the path in your system. Typically, the path is /lib/modules/*kernel version number*/ipv4/ip_alias.o. Once you have loaded the ip_alias.o module, run lsmod to ensure that it is loaded. Now, to create an alias for the eth0 device, do the following:

◆ Copy your existing /etc/sysconfig/network-scripts/ifcfg-eth0 file to /etc/sysconfig/network-scripts/ifcfg-eth0:0 to create an alias device named eth0:0.

◆ Modify the file so that the lines are similar to the ones in Listing 9-3. Of course, your network, netmask, and IP address will vary. Make sure you change only the DEVICE and IPADDR line. You should set the DEVICE line to eth0:0 and IPADDR to the IP address you want to use as an alias to what you have assigned for eth0.

Listing 9-3: The /etc/sysconfig/network-scripts/ifcfg-eth0:0 file

```
DEVICE=eth0:0
USERCTL=no
ONBOOT=yes
BOOTPROTO=
BROADCAST=206.171.50.63
NETWORK=206.171.50.48
NETMASK=255.255.255.240
IPADDR=206.171.50.58
```

◆ To start the alias device, run ifconfig eth0:0 up, and you should see output similar to what is here:

```
lo Link encap:Local Loopback
    inet addr:127.0.0.1  Bcast:127.255.255.255  Mask:255.0.0.0
    UP BROADCAST LOOPBACK RUNNING  MTU:3584  Metric:1
    RX packets:501 errors:0 dropped:0 overruns:0 frame:0
    TX packets:501 errors:0 dropped:0 overruns:0 carrier:0
      collisions:0

eth0 Link encap:Ethernet  HWaddr 00:C0:F6:98:37:37
    inet addr:206.171.50.50 Bcast:206.171.50.63
Mask:255.255.255.240
    UP BROADCAST RUNNING MULTICAST  MTU:1500  Metric:1
    RX packets:2 errors:0 dropped:0 overruns:0 frame:0
    TX packets:2 errors:0 dropped:0 overruns:0 carrier:0
collisions:4
    Interrupt:5 Base address:0x340

eth0:0 Link encap:Ethernet  HWaddr 00:C0:F6:98:37:37
    inet addr:206.171.50.58  Bcast:206.171.50.63
Mask:255.255.255.240
    UP BROADCAST RUNNING  MTU:1500  Metric:1
    RX packets:9 errors:0 dropped:0 overruns:0 frame:0
    TX packets:9 errors:0 dropped:0 overruns:0 carrier:0
collisions:0
```

As you can see, the eth0:0 device is up and running. You can create an alias of any other Ethernet device in the same way. So what can you do with an IP alias? Here are few practical uses of IP aliases.

◆ Say that you have two machines providing Web services and all of a sudden one of the machines becomes unavailable because of some problem. Or perhaps you want to take the machine down for a couple of days for some upgrade work. In such cases, you can use an IP alias to service the unavailable machine's IP address. You can simply add virtual Web sites to service the Web sites you hosted on the broken or unavailable system until it is functional again.

◆ Many older Web browsers do not use the name-based virtual hosting feature (see Chapter 12). In such a case, you can use IP aliases to create virtual IP-based Web sites.

Now take a look at how you can avoid the traditional process and do it the easy way.

Although the following method may be very easy compared to the steps in the traditional method, I highly recommend the latter because a network administrator must know how things work from the inside out. I recommend using the following method only once you have mastered the traditional way of doing things.

Using netcfg to configure a network interface card

You need to have X Windows working on your system in order to use netcfg. This program allows you to configure all aspects of the basic network configuration. You must run this as a superuser from X Windows. The initial window, in Figure 9-7, displays the current hostname, domain name, and name server configuration.

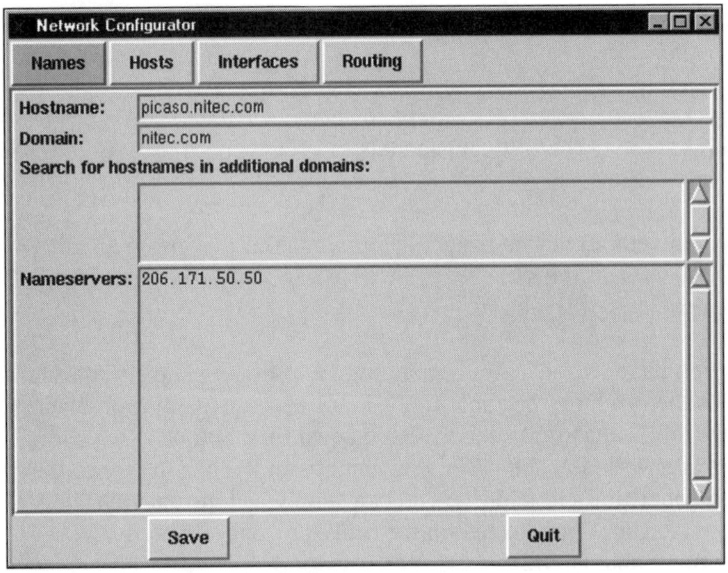

Figure 9-7: The Network Configurator Names window

To change the host name, the domain name, or the name servers, click Names. You can simply modify the values and click Save. Note that the program does not display any status message when you click Save, and so it is a bit confusing at first. Also note that the domain name displayed in the program comes from the search list (first entry in the list) in the /etc/resolv.conf file. If you do not have any search list set up in this file, netcfg does not display a domain name.

To add, modify, or remove a network interface, click Interfaces. You see a screen, as in Figure 9-8, displaying the current network interfaces.

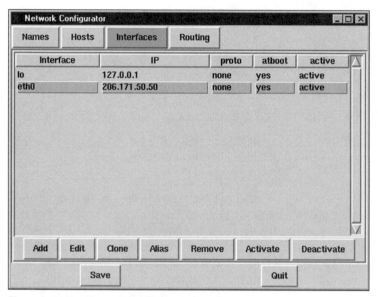

Figure 9-8: The Network Configurator Interfaces window

To add a new network interface, do the following:

◆ Click Add to bring up a dialog box as in Figure 9-9.

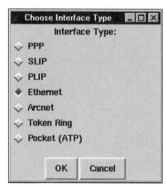

Figure 9-9: Adding a new network interface

◆ Click Ethernet to create a new Ethernet network interface configuration. Once you click OK, you see a dialog box as in Figure 9-10.

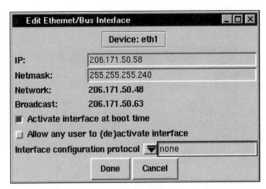

Figure 9-10: Entering information about the new interface

◆ Enter the IP address and the net mask for this new device. The netcfg program automatically calculates the network and broadcast address from the information you provide. If you would like this interface to be active at boot, click Activate interface at boot time. You should leave the Allow any user to (de)activate interface option unchecked because allowing just anyone to activate/deactivate your network interfaces is really a bad idea. If you are not using DHCP or BOOTP servers to dynamically assign IP addresses for this interface, select none as the interface configuration protocol. Click Done to complete the configuration; you are asked to confirm that you want to save the configuration. Save the configuration by clicking OK. The new interface appears in the interface list in the next screen.

◆ If you would like to activate the interface right away, click Activate. The screen should update the status of interface to be active. However, netcfg might show the interface as active when it is really not. This happens when you try to configure a nonexistent network card. One of the easiest ways to check the interface is to run the `ifconfig interface name` command from the command line to see which interfaces are up and running.

You just activated the new interface; now you need to set up a default gateway (discussed in a later section) as follows:

◆ Click Routing to bring up the window in Figure 9-11.

◆ Enter the default gateway IP address. The gateway device name should be the device you just configured.

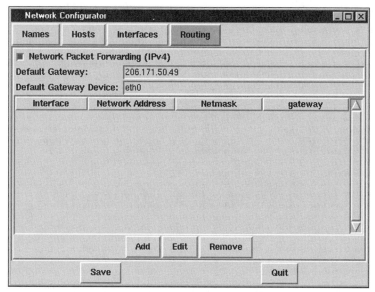

Figure 9-11: Configuring a default gateway

♦ If you would like to set up this device to forward IP packets to and from computers on your network, set the Network Packet Forwarding (IPV4) option.

♦ Save the new settings, and quit the program.

Now you have configured the new interface and have also set up a default gateway. Test your new interface by pinging a computer on your network by using the ping *IP address* command. If you can ping a remote host, you have successfully configured the new interface.

To modify an existing network interface, do the following:

♦ Click Interfaces. Double-click the existing network interface line. This brings up a dialog box as in Figure 9-10. Make changes as appropriate.

♦ Once you have made changes and have saved the changes, deactivate the interface first, and then activate it.

If you are using X Windows on a remote terminal to run the netcfg program, do not deactivate the interface used for providing network connectivity to your terminal. In other words, if you deactivate the interface needed for your remote X connection, your X session will not work, and you will not be able to activate the interface without local access.

To delete an existing network interface, do the following:

◆ Click Interfaces. Select the existing network interface.

◆ Click Delete to complete the process. The statements in the preceding Caution apply here.

When setting up the network interface by using either the traditional or the netcfg method, you must provide a default gateway IP address. In the following section, I discuss why you need a default gateway.

Why Use a Default Gateway?

Take a look at Figure 9-12. It shows two networks: network A (192.168.1.0) and network B (192.168.2.0).

Network A 192.168.1.0

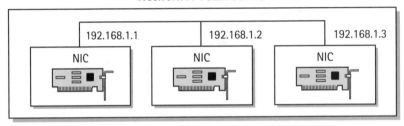

Network B 192.168.2.0

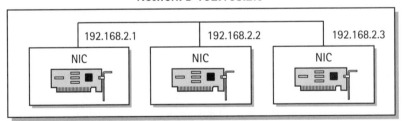

Figure 9-12: Two distinct IP networks

These two networks are completely separate. The computers in either network can see the hosts in the same network just fine. A user using the 192.168.1.1 computer in network A can ping the other two computers by using their network interface IP addresses. However, he or she cannot access any of the host computers on network B. Why? There is no way for the packets in network A to go to network B. How can these two networks be joined? You guessed right – by using a gateway computer or a router. Figure 9-13 shows how we can do this.

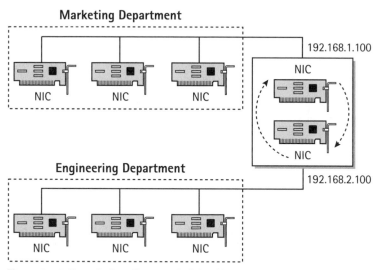

Figure 9-13: Two distinct IP networks joined by a gateway

The new computer in the network is the gateway computer. It has two network interfaces. The network interface attached to the A network has an IP address 192.168.1.100, and the interface attached to the B network has an IP address of 192.168.2.100. The computer is set up to forward IP packets between these two networks. For example, when the 192.168.1.1 computer wants to send a packet to 192.168. 2.1, it forwards the IP packet to the 192.168.1.100 gateway computer. This gateway machine places a modified version of the packet on its other interface (192.168.2.100), which becomes available to the destination computer. When the destination computer wants to respond, it follows a similar process so that the gateway computer is able to send the packet to the source computer on network A.

You need the gateway computer only if you want to communicate with two different networks. Note that the gateway computer need not be a PC or a workstation; it can be a specialized computer hardware such as a router.

Now that you know how to join two different networks by using a gateway, take a look at how to split networks by creating subnetworks or subnets.

Dividing a Network into Subnetworks

Take a look at the network in Figure 9-14.

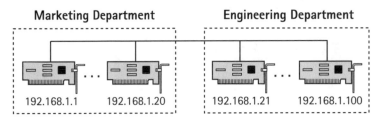

Network/netmask: 192.168.1.0/255.255.255.0

Figure 9-14: A large network shared by 100 users

This network has 100 host computers connected to a single network, 192.168.1.0. Because all computers share the same physical network cable, the traffic load is likely to be quite heavy at peak hours. For example, if all marketing people start using the network at the same time as the engineers in the engineering department, things become very slow, as every host has to share the network bandwidth. So what's the solution? Subnetworks. Take a look at Figure 9-15.

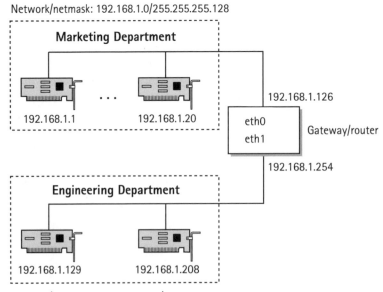

Network/netmask: 192.168.1.128/255.255.255.128

Figure 9-15: Splitting a large network into subnetworks

Here we divide the 192.168.1.0 network into two networks – 192.168.1.0 and 192.168.1.128. Both of these subnetworks are connected to each other using a gateway (or router) with two network interfaces. When we configure each host computer on each of these two networks properly, we separate the network traffic between these networks. For example, when a user in the marketing department wants to communicate with another computer in the same department, the network traffic between these two computers remains in their network. The same is true for the engineering side. However, when users from different departments want to communicate with each other's computers, it is allowed. The gateway computer forwards such internetwork traffic to and from these networks. The result is a speedier network because not all users are on the same, large network anymore. Now see how you can implement such a solution.

When a full network such as 192.168.1.0 needs to be divided into subnets, there needs to be a way for the computer to determine which IP address belongs to which network. For example, the computer with the network interface 192.168.1.1 in the marketing department needs to know if 192.168.1.129 is in the same network or if it should send packets destined for 192.168.1.129 to the gateway computer for further forwarding tasks. The way it can determine if an IP address belongs to its own subnet is by using a mask called a network mask or netmask.

Before you can create a subnet from a network, you need to understand how to create a netmask. For example, say you want to determine the network mask for the network 192.168.1.0. This address in binary format looks like:

```
11000000.10101000.00000001.00000000
```

Because this is a class C address, the network bits are the first 24 bits (three bytes). To create the mask, you must set these bits to 1s and the remaining (host interface) bits to 0s. So the netmask looks as follows:

```
11111111.11111111.11111111.00000000
```

In decimal format, this looks like 255.255.255.0. When creating a netmask, all you need to remember is that the network bits are all 1s and the host bits are all 0s. For example, the netmask for the class A network 10.0.0.0 is 255.0.0.0, and, similarly, the netmask for the class B network 129.1.0.0 is 255.255.0.0.

In a TCP/IP network, when a computer wants to send a packet to an IP address, it determines whether the IP address is local by performing a bitwise AND operation. For example, to determine if 192.168.1.1 is local to a network with subnet mask 255.255.255.0, a host computer does the following:

```
    Binary                                   Decimal
    11000000.10101000.00000001.00000001 => 192.168.1.1
AND 11111111.11111111.11111111.00000000 => 255.255.255.0
    _ _ _ _ _ _ _ _ _ _ _ _ _ _ _ _ _ _ _ _ _ _ _ _ _
    11000000.10101000.00000001.00000000 => 192.168.1.0
```

As you can see, a bitwise AND operation returns the network address (192.168.1.0) of the IP address 192.168.1.1. Because a host computer knows to what network it belongs, it can very easily determine how to handle packets for such an IP address.

Because you are likely to deal with class C networks a lot, I use this class in all examples in this section.

When a class C network is left in its entirety, the netmask is 255.255.255.0. To divide the network into subnets, we need to create a new netmask. We do this by setting one or more bits in the host interface part of the default class netmask (255.255.255.0) to 1s. Consider the ongoing example class C network – 192.168.1.0. By setting the most significant bit in the host interface number part of the address to 1, we get:

```
11111111.11111111.11111111.10000000 => 255.255.255.128
```

This is a new netmask that splits the class in half. All IP addresses from 192.168.1.0 to 192.168.1.127 belong to the 192.168.1.0 network, and the rest of the IP addresses, 192.168.1.128 to 192.168.1.255, belong to the 192.168.1.128 network. Both networks use the 255.255.255.128 netmask. For example, to determine which network an IP address called 192.168.1.10 belongs to, we can perform the following bitwise AND operation:

```
Binary                                     Decimal
    11000000.10101000.00000001.00001010 => 192.168.1.10
AND 11111111.11111111.11111111.10000000 => 255.255.255.128
    _ _ _ _ _ _ _ _ _ _ _ _ _ _ _ _ _ _ _ _ _ _ _
    11000000.10101000.00000001.00000000 => 192.168.1.0
```

As you can see, the netmask 255.255.255.128 tells us that the given IP address belongs to the 192.168.1.0 network. Now see which network an IP address called 192.168.1.200 belongs to:

```
Binary                                     Decimal
    11000000.10101000.00000001.11001000 => 192.168.1.200
AND 11111111.11111111.11111111.10000000 => 255.255.255.128
    _ _ _ _ _ _ _ _ _ _ _ _ _ _ _ _ _ _ _ _ _ _ _
    11000000.10101000.00000001.10000000 => 192.168.1.128
```

As you can see again, the same netmask gives us a different network address (192.168.1.128) for the given IP address. Using this netmask, you have effectively separated the 192.168.1.0 networks into two subnets – 192.168.1.0 and 192.168.1128.

Because a full class C network has 256 possible IP addresses, the separate subnets have 128 IP addresses. However, not all of them are ever usable as host (interface) IP addresses. In a full class C network such as 192.168.1.0 (with netmask

255.255.255.0), we use 192.168.1.0 as the network address and 192.168.1.255 as the broadcast address. We use a broadcast address to communicate with all host computers in the network, so these two addresses are in a sense reserved. Therefore, in a full class C network, you have 254 (255 – network IP address – broadcast IP address) possible IP addresses. Similarly, when a network is subdivided, each subnet gets a network address and a broadcast address; therefore, when a class C network is divided into two subnets, four IP addresses become unusable for host addressing. In our example, this looks like the following:

```
Network: 192.168.1.0
Netmask: 255.255.255.128
First usable host IP address: 192.168.1.1
Last usable host IP address: 192.168.1.126
Broadcast address: 192.168.1.127

Network: 192.168.1.128
Netmask: 255.255.255.128
First usable host IP address: 192.168.1.129
Last usable host IP address: 192.168.1.254
Broadcast address: 192.168.1.255
```

You might wonder how many subnets you can create out of a full class A, B, or C network. The formula is as follows: number of subnets $= 2^{(\text{host bits} - 1)}$

For example, the number of host bits in a class C network is 8 (the last byte), so technically, you can create 2^7 (128) equal-sized subnets from a single class C network. However, because of the loss of IP addresses (as network and broadcast addresses), most network administrators do not make more than 16 subnets out of a class C network.

If you are new to the subnetting concept, you might find the ipcalc tool quite useful. For example, say you want to make sure your subnet calculations are as expected. You can use this tool to reassure yourself that your numbers are right. Say you want to confirm that the subnets used in Figure 9-15 are correct. You can supply any IP in the 192.168.1.1–254 range to ipcalc along with the subnet mask to determine which network the IP address belongs to. Here are two examples:

```
ipcalc --broadcast --network 192.168.1.1 255.255.255.128
BROADCAST=192.168.1.127
NETWORK=192.168.1.0

ipcalc --broadcast --network 192.168.1.129  255.255.255.128
BROADCAST=192.168.1.255
NETWORK=192.168.1.12
```

In the first example, the ipcalc program is told to display the broadcast address (using the --broadcast argument) and the network address (using the --network argument) of an IP address 192.168.1.1 using the 255.255.255.128 netmask. It returns the broadcast address as 192.168.1.127 and the network address as 192.168.1.0. This is correct. In the second example, the program is asked to display the same information for an IP that belongs to the other half of the network, and it displays the correct addresses.

Now that you know a great deal about how to create subnets, take a look at what's involved in creating the example subnets in Figure 9-15.

Gateway computer configuration

The gateway computer in Figure 9-15 must have two network interfaces. One of the interfaces has to be connected to each of the subnets. The /etc/sysconfig/network file for this computer is in Listing 9-4.

Listing 9-4: The /etc/sysconfig/network file

```
NETWORKING=yes
FORWARD_IPV4=yes
HOSTNAME=gateway.nitec.com
DOMAINNAME=nitec.com
```

The most important setting here is FORWARD_IPV4=yes, which enables IP forwarding in the kernel.

TIP You must have IP forwarding support built into the kernel. You can use the cat/proc/sys/net/ipv4/ip_forward command to see if IP forwarding is enabled in a running kernel. If the output is 1, then IP forwarding is set; a value of 0 signifies that IP forwarding is off. You can also turn it on or off by pushing a value of 1 or 0 by using the echo n > /proc/sys/net/ipv4/ip_forward command, where n is either 1 or 0.

Listings 9-5 and 9-6 show the two interface (eth0 and eth1) files.

Listing 9-5: The /etc/sysconfig/network-scripts/ifcfg-eth0 file

```
DEVICE=eth0
IPADDR=192.168.1.126
NETMASK=255.255.255.128
NETWORK=192.168.1.0
BROADCAST=192.168.1.127
ONBOOT=yes
```

Listing 9-6: The /etc/sysconfig/network-scripts/ifcfg-eth1 file

```
DEVICE=eth1
IPADDR=192.168.1.254
NETMASK=255.255.255.128
NETWORK=192.168.1.128
BROADCAST=192.168.1.255
ONBOOT=yes
```

Once you set these files and the interfaces are up and running (either via a reboot or using the ifup command), you need to create two default routes for the two networks using the following route commands:

```
route add --net 192.168.1.0   255.255.255.128 eth0
route add --net 192.168.1.128 255.255.255.128 eth1
```

Each of the preceding route commands makes sure that packets destined for the named network are transmitted via the named interface device.

Host computer configuration

You must configure each host computer on each subnet so that each computer knows the network address, the local subnet mask, and the gateway information. For example, assuming that all host computers are also Linux workstations and each has a single Ethernet interface device (eth0), the /etc/sysconfig/network file on any of the host computers on the 192.168.1.0 network is in Listing 9-7.

Listing 9-7: The /etc/sysconfig/network file

```
NETWORKING=yes
FORWARD_IPV4=yes
HOSTNAME=marketing--1.nitec.com
DOMAINNAME=nitec.com
GATEWAY=192.168.1.126
GATEWAYDEV=eth0
```

The interface file on this computer looks like the example in Listing 9-8.

Listing 9-8: The /etc/sysconfig/network-scripts/ifcfg-eth0 file

```
DEVICE=eth0
IPADDR=192.168.1.1
NETMASK=255.255.255.128
NETWORK=192.168.1.0
BROADCAST=192.168.1.127
ONBOOT=yes
```

In a similar fashion, you need to set up the computers in the 192.168.1.128 network. Each computer in this network uses GATEWAY=192.168.1.254 line in the /etc/sysconfig/network file and uses NETWORK=192.168.1.128 and BROADCAST= 192.168.1.255 in its /etc/sysconfig/network-scripts/ifcfg-eth0 files.

Of course, if any of these computers are non-Linux systems, such as Windows 9*x*/2000 or NT systems, you have to use the appropriate network configuration tool to set these values.

Once you have the gateway computer and at least one host set up in each network, you are ready to test the subnets. The easiest way to test subnets is to use the ping program. Here is a simple testing and trouble-shooting guideline.

To remove all DNS-related issues from the testing, I recommend you use only IP addresses during a network test as follows:

1. First, use the ping program to ping a host computer in the same subnet. For example, run ping 192.168.1.2 from the 192.168.1.1 computer. If you do not get ping replies, check the network configuration files (/etc/sysconfig/network and /etc/sysconfig/network-scripts/ifcfg-eth0). Correct any problem you notice, and restart the interface by first taking it down using ifconfig eth0 down and then bringing it up using /etc/sysconfig/network-scripts/ifup eth0. Once you are able to ping a host in the same subnet, proceed to the next step.

2. After you have ensured that you can ping a host from another computer in the same subnet for both subnets, ping the gateway computer from each subnet. If you cannot perform this operation, check the gateway computer's network configuration files, and correct any errors or typos. Once you can ping the gateway computer from each subnet, you should proceed to the next step.

3. Now try to ping a host in the other subnet. If you can't ping the host in the other subnet, try using traceroute *IP address* to determine if the packets are even making it to the gateway machine. If traceroute shows that the packets are making it to the gateway but not being forwarded to the destination, the problem is at the gateway. You should ensure that IP forwarding is on. Run cat /proc/sys/net/ipv4/ip_forward on the gateway computer to see if the returned value is 1 or 0. If it is not 1, IP forwarding is either off in the /etc/sysconfig/network file or not enabled in the kernel. In such a case, fix this problem and retry.

At this point, you should be able to send ping requests from any of the two subnets. Once this is true, you have two working subnets.

Summary

In this chapter, you learned the basics of TCP/IP networking and in-depth details of various classes of IP addresses; also, you learned to set up network interfaces, IP aliases, and functional subnetworks that help increase network performance.

Part IV

Setting Up Intranet/Internet Services

Chapter 10

DNS Service

IN THIS CHAPTER

- How Domain Name Service works
- How to configure a DNS client
- How to set up a DNS server using BIND
- How to manage DNS for virtual domains
- How to balance load with round robin DNS

DOMAIN NAME SERVICE (DNS) is the heart of the Internet. Understanding how DNS works and how to turn your Red Hat Linux system into a DNS server is very important for a system administrator. However, discussing all the details of DNS in a single chapter is impossible. In this chapter, I will cover only the basic and practical aspects of DNS. The goal of this chapter is to help you understand how DNS works and how to implement a DNS server for your Red Hat Linux system.

How Does DNS Work?

You may already know that the Internet uses the Internet Protocol (IP). In other words, every computer (that is, resource) on the Internet has a unique IP address, and all traffic to and from every computer is communicated via IP. A close parallel can be found in the public telephone network. Everyone who has a telephone has a unique phone number. To make a phone call, you need to know the destination party's phone number. Similarly, to communicate on the Internet, you need an IP number. But in general, people dislike remembering large numbers and most are limited how many they can remember. An easier way to communicate became necessary. DNS fills that void.

The easiest way to understand how DNS works is to look at an example. Let's say that you want to access the `http://www.integrationlogic.com/` Web site to see what products and services Integration Logic, Inc., offers. Obviously, you start up your favorite Web browser and enter `http://www.integrationlogic.com/` as the URL. If this is the first time you are requesting this Web site, DNS gets involved. Figure 10-1 shows how a simple diagram of how this process works.

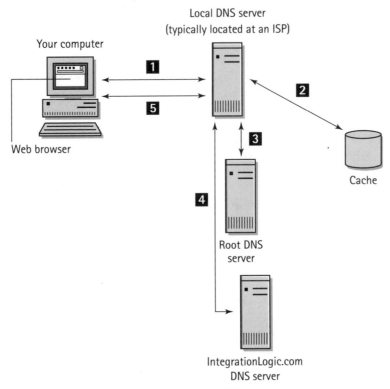

Figure 10-1: A simple diagram showing how DNS works

Your Web browser contacts the local DNS server (typically, it is your ISP's DNS server) to locate the IP address for www.integrationlogic.com (1). The local DNS server checks its cache to find the IP address for the site (2). If this DNS server never got a request for www.integrationlogic.com before, the cache has no information about it. In such a case the local DNS server contacts another DNS server (typically, a root DNS server) to locate the IP address of the DNS server responsible for the integrationlogic.com domain (3). If www.integrationlogic.com really exists, then the root DNS server returns the address of the DNS server that is the DNS authority for this domain. Now the local DNS server asks the DNS server for the integrationlogic.com domain to return the IP address for the www.integrationlogic.com site (4). Because the www.integrationlogic.com site really exists, the integrationlogic.com domain's DNS server returns the IP address of this site. The local DNS server finally returns the IP address to the Web browser and caches the IP for future use (5).

This entire process might seem a bit confusing to many, but it is really simple and transparent to the end user. The average user typically does not have a clue about this and rightfully so. As you can see now, DNS is really a system of resolving Internet host (computer) names to IP addresses. Well, what happens if you happen to know the IP address of a system and want to know the hostname? This is why DNS was designed – to resolve both IP addresses and hostnames in both directions. In reality, DNS serves more functions than just IP-to-host or host-to-IP name resolutions; you will learn about many of the popular and practical use of DNS in the later parts of this chapter.

When it comes to DNS, you have to make a decision: Do you need to run a DNS server, or can you configure your system as a DNS client for a remote (typically an ISP's) DNS server? The answer lies in the following questions:

◆ Do you want to provide DNS for one or more of your Internet domains?

◆ Do you want to improve performance of the DNS service for frequently requested Internet resources?

If your answer is yes to either of the preceding questions, you should consider running a local DNS server. However, whether or not you decide to run a DNS server on your Red Hat Linux system, you still need to configure it as a DNS client for a local or remote DNS server.

Now consider how to configure your Red Hat Linux system as a DNS client computer.

Configuring a DNS Client (Resolver)

If you plan on accessing other Internet host computers from your Red Hat Linux system, you need to configure it as a DNS client system. The client part of DNS is called the resolver. It is a set of routines in the C library that allows any program to perform DNS queries. The resolver comes standard with Red Hat Linux. In this section, you will learn to configure the resolver.

Typically, the Red Hat installation program asks you about your DNS server and automatically configures the necessary resolver configuration file. However, it is often necessary to change the resolver configuration to reflect any changes to the DNS server you use. For example, if you configure your resolver during Red Hat installation and later change your ISP, you need to configure it again manually. Here is how.

If you are planning on using your ISP's DNS server for resolving names and IP addresses, ask your ISP to give you the hostname and the IP address of its DNS servers. Once you have the required information, you can configure the resolver.

First you need to modify the resolver configuration file called /etc/resolv.conf. Listing 10-1 shows a typical /etc/resolv.conf file for a domain called nitec.com.

Listing 10-1: The resolver configuration file /etc/resolv.conf

```
# Default Domain
domain nitec.com

# Default search list
```

```
search nitec.com

# First name server
nameserver 206.171.50.50

# Second name server
nameserver 206.171.50.55
```

Like many other common Linux configuration files, this file has a very simple format. Any blank line or lines starting with "#" are ignored. The only meaningful lines are the ones with a domain, search, or name server directive.

The domain directive enables you to specify the default domain name for the system. If you do not have this line set to the domain name of your system, the default domain name is automatically extracted from the hostname of your system.

The search directive is used to influence how the resolver searches for hostnames that are not fully qualified. For example, if I want to enter a ping www command in a shell on the system with the preceding resolver configuration file, the ping program asks the resolver to resolve www. Because www is a partial hostname, the resolver creates a full hostname using the search list (for instance, www.nitec.com) and tries to resolve an IP for that host. For example, if I set the search directive to integrationlogic.com in the preceding listing and make the same ping request, the resolver returns the IP address for www.integrationlogic.com. If you do not provide a search directive, the default domain name is automatically applied when partial hostnames need to be resolved.

The name server directive specifies the domain name server that the resolver should use to query. You can (and should) specify multiple name server directives in the configuration file. Each domain name server is queried in order of appearance in the configuration file. For example, if a program requests the resolver to resolve a hostname called www.ad-engine.com, the resolver first tries to resolve the name to an IP using the 206.171.50.50 domain name server. If the 206.171.50.50 domain name server fails to return a response (that is, if the query times out), then the second domain name server, 206.171.50.55, is contacted. Currently, you are allowed to list only three name server directives in the configuration file. It is generally a good idea to have at least two name server directives set to two different name servers.

 You can set the name server directive to any domain name server's IP address on the Internet. However, you should use only the closest name server IP addresses in order to reduce delay in domain name resolution. Also, never use someone's domain name server IP address in your resolver configuration file without permission. It is considered rude and might have legal consequences if your resolver places a heavy load on someone's name server.

So far you have learned how to configure the DNS resolver on your system to use remote DNS servers. It is also possible to hard-code one or more IP addresses to their respective hostnames in the /etc/hosts file. This file has a very simple format as follows:

```
IP address   hostname   short-cut   hostname
```

Here is an example of an /etc/hosts file:

```
206.171.50.50 picaso.nitec.com  picaso
127.0.0.1     localhost         localhost
```

The resolver can use this file to resolve an address when the remote DNS servers are not available. Also, if you have a small network and do not want to run a local DNS server, you may use this file to resolve local hostnames. However, when both the remote DNS server and the /etc/hosts file are available, the resolver needs to know in which order to process DNS queries. You can set the order in the /etc/host.conf file using the order directive. For example:

```
order hosts,bind
```

If your /etc/host.conf file has this order directive, then the resolver first attempts to use the /etc/hosts file to service the query. If the file does not contain an entry that can be used, the DNS servers specified in the /etc/resolv.conf file are used.

 TIP If you have a large user base, you can improve DNS-related performance by using a local DNS server over an /etc/hosts file, because reading the file for each new DNS request can be quite slow.

Once you have set up the files just described, your DNS resolver configuration is complete. The easiest way to test your DNS configuration is to try to ping a computer on the Internet. If the ping program fails because of an unknown hostname, double-check your DNS resolver configuration for typos.

Running your own DNS server has quite a few administrative benefits. For example, if you own one or more Internet domains, you can add, delete, or modify DNS records as you please. In the following section you learn how to set up a DNS server on your Red Hat Linux system.

Setting Up a DNS Server

Red Hat Linux comes with the Berkeley Internet Name Domain (BIND) server software. If you have not installed it during the operating system installation phase, you can install the RPM version of the software. For example, to install the 8.2.2-P5 version of BIND software for the Intel x86 platform, I located the bind-8.2.2_P5-24.i386.rpm package in the Red Hat Linux CD-ROM's RPMS directory and ran the following command:

```
rpm -ivh bind-8.2.2_P5-24.i386.rpm
```

The RPM package of the BIND software just described comes with three programs: /usr/sbin/named (the name server itself), /usr/sbin/named-xfer (the accessory program for the name server), /usr/sbin/ndc (a program to control the name server), and /usr/doc/bind-8.2.2/named-bootconf.pl (an accessory Perl script to convert older configuration files to the new format). Once you have installed the BIND software, you are ready to configure DNS.

Understanding the basics of DNS configuration

The primary configuration file for BIND domain name server, "named," is /etc/named.conf. At startup, the named server reads this configuration file to determine how it should function.

THE /ETC/NAMED.CONF FILE

This file consists of comments, statements, and blank lines.

COMMENTS   A comment line can be a single line that starts with two forward slash characters. For example:

```
// This is a comment line in named.conf
```

Or it can be a line that starts with a "#" character as follows:

```
# This is a comment line in named.conf
```

Or it can be a multiline comment that starts with /* and ends with */. For example:

```
/*
    This is a multiline comment in named.conf

*/
```

Apart from the comments and blank lines, which are ignored by named, the real configuration lines are called statements, which have the following syntax:

```
keyword {
        // details of the statement
        };
```

Named can make use of many types of statements. I will discuss only the most commonly used here.

OPTIONS STATEMENT   The options statement enables you to set up global options for the name server. You should use only a single options statement in the named.conf file. If no options statement is specified, a default options statement with each option set to its default is used. Many options can go inside the options statement block, enclosed by the { }. The commonly used options are as follows:

```
options {
   directory path_name;
   statistics-interval number;
   forwarders { [ in_addr ; [ in_addr ; ... ] ] };
   forward ( only | first );
   };
```

The directory option enables you to specify the working directory path of the name server. If a directory is not specified, the working directory defaults to ".", the directory from which the server was started. The directory specified should be an absolute path. Also note that when you specify a relative directory as part of another statement block, the relative directory is assumed to be relative to the working directory.

The statistics-interval option allows you to control the frequency of statistics produced by the name server. By default the name server writes statistics to the default log (using syslogd in /var/messages) every hour. If you want to change this default behavior, add this option and specify the desired interval between statistics logging in number of minutes. If you find the statistics to be not useful enough to warrant regular reporting and would like to reduce your log file size a bit, set the number to zero to disable this feature.

If you would like your name server to forward DNS queries to other name servers, you can set a list of IP addresses of the remote name servers using the forwarders option. For example:

```
forwarders { 206.171.50.10; 206.177.175.10; };
```

Here two IP addresses of two different name servers are listed. Each pair of IP addresses needs to be separated by a semicolon. The default forwarder list is empty, and therefore no forwarding is performed; all queries are answered by the name server itself.

The forward option is useful only if the forwarders list is not empty. This option controls how the name server behaves. If you set this option to "first" (the default), then the name server sends all the queries to the forwarders. If the forwarders time out or cannot answer the query, the name server then tries to do the lookup by itself.

If you set the forward option to "only," then the name server queries only the forwarders and does not try to look up the answer itself.

For most sites, the options statement will look something like the following:

```
options {
  directory "/var/named"
  };
```

In other words, the most common use of the options statement is just to specify the working directory of the server. The working directory is where you keep all the domain- or zone-specific files.

ZONE STATEMENT   Apart from the options statement, the zone statement is the only other type of statement that you find in virtually any site's named.conf configuration. To set up a name service for an Internet domain, you need to create a zone statement in the /etc/named.conf file. Three commonly used zone statements look as follows:

```
zone domain_name {
  type master;
  file path_name;
  };

zone domain_name {
  type slave;
  masters { ip_addr; [ ip_addr; ... ] };
  file path_name;
  };

zone "." {
  type hint;
  file path_name;
  };
```

The first zone statement is used for a master (primary) zone. For example, if you want your name server to be the authoritative name server for a particular domain, you should set up a master zone. For example:

```
zone "ad-engine.com" {
  type master;
```

```
file "ad-engine.db";
};
```

Here the name server is configured as the primary name server for the ad-engine.com domain. Notice that the file option is used to specify the filename of the zone- or domain-specific configuration. If the filename you specify here is relative to the working directory of the server, it must reside inside the working directory.

If you are setting up multiple name servers for a particular domain, you can set only one to be the master or authoritative name server using the "type master" option. The rest of the name servers (as many as you wish) must be set up as the slave name servers. For example:

```
zone "ad-engine.com" {
  type slave;
  masters { 206.171.50.10; };
  file "ad-engine.db";
};
```

Here the current name server is being set up as a slave name server for the ad-engine.com domain. The masters list specifies one or more IP addresses that the slave contacts to update its copy of the zone. If the file option is specified, then the replica of the zone's configuration is written to the file. Use of "file" is recommended, because it often speeds server startup.

You can specify as many zone statements as you need in the /etc/named.conf file. However, you should never specify multiple zone configurations for each zone or domain. For example, you should not set up a name server to be the master and the slave name server for the same zone.

Finally, the other commonly used zone statement is the third kind. This is a special zone statement. The domain name is "." and the type of name server is "hint" or cache. This special zone is used to specify a set of root name servers. When the name server starts up, it uses this list (hints) to find a root nameserver and get the most recent list of root name servers.

Now take a look at the zone- or domain-specific configuration.

DOMAIN- OR ZONE-SPECIFIC CONFIGURATIONS

For each Internet domain or zone, you need two configuration files. One configuration file is for setting up the forward DNS (hostname-to-IP) translation, and another one is for setting up the reverse DNS (IP-to-hostname) translation. For example:

```
zone "ad-engine.com" {
  type master;
  file "ad-engine.db";
};
```

```
zone "50.171.206.in-addr.arpa" {
   type master;
   file "db.206.171.50";
   };
```

I have the preceding two zone statements in /etc/named.conf. These two zone statements set up my name server as the authoritative master (primary) name server for the `ad-engine.com` domain. In other words, all hostname-to-IP translations (also known as forward DNS) for the `ad-engine.com` are handled by this name server. And the second zone statement sets up the name server as the master (primary) name server for the 206.171.50.0 network. In other words, all IP-to-hostname translations (also known as reverse DNS) for this network are also handled by this name server. The first zone statement states that the `ad-engine.com` domain's forward zone configuration information is kept in the ad-engine.db file, and the second zone statements states that the reverse DNS configuration for the 206.171.50.0 network is stored in the file named "db.206.171.50."

Both of these files consist of DNS resource record (RR) and optional comment lines. A DNS resource record has the following syntax:

```
{name}    {TTL}    addr-class    record-type    record-specific-data
```

The name field is always the name of the domain record, and it must always start in column 1. Traditionally, only the first DNS resource record sets the *name* field. For all the other resource records in a zone file, the name may be left blank; in that case, it takes on the name of the previous resource record. The second field, *TTL*, is an optional Time to Live field. This specifies how long this data is stored in the database. Leaving this field blank means that the default time to live is specified in the Start of Authority resource record (see the next heading). The third field, *addr-class*, is the address class. The only widely used address class is IN for Internet addresses and other information. The fourth field, *record-type*, states the type of the resource record. The fifth field, *record-specific-data*, is the data for the record type in the fourth field. The commonly used resource records are discussed in the text that follows.

SOA: START OF AUTHORITY   The SOA or Start of Authority record is used to indicate the start of a zone. The syntax for the SOA record is as follows:

```
@    IN    SOA    nameserver.  contact-email-address (
                  serial_number       ; Serial
                  refresh_number      ; Refresh
                  retry_number        ; Retry
                  expire_number       ; Expire
                  minimum_number )    ; Minimum
```

The first field is the name field. This field is always set to "@" and need not be repeated in any other resource record in the same file. The *nameserver* field is used to specify the hostname of the current name server, and the *contact-email-address* field is used to specify the e-mail address of the system administrator for the domain. The rest of the SOA record-specific data is used to set a serial number and various default values.

The *serial_number* is the version number of this zone file. Although you can use any positive number as your serial number, the common practice is to use a "YYYYMMDDNNN"-formatted number. Here YYYY is the four-digit year, MM is the two-digit month, DD is the two-digit day of the month, and NNN is a three-digit number. So a serial number such as "19990215001" tells you that the last time the zone file was modified was 02/15/1999 and there were two revisions on that date (000–001). Every time you update a zone file, you must increment the serial number or else the change will not take effect.

The *refresh_number* indicates how often, in seconds, a secondary name server is to check with the primary name server to see if an update is needed. Note that if you update your master (or primary) zone file on the master name server and fail to update the serial number, the secondary name server will not update its copy of the zone information. The *retry_number* indicates how long, in seconds, a secondary server should wait before retrying a failed zone transfer due to an external problem. The *expire_number* is the upper limit, in seconds that a secondary name server is to use the zone data before it expires. The *minimum_number* is the limit (in seconds) to be used for the Time to Live (TTL) field on resource records that do not specify one in the zone file. It is also an enforced minimum on time to live if it is specified on some resource record (RR) in the zone. There must be exactly one SOA record per zone. Here is a sample SOA record for a domain called ad-engine.com:

```
@   IN   SOA   ns.ad-engine.com. kabir.ad-engine.com. (
                1999020100   ; Serial
                7200         ; Refresh -  2 hours
                3600         ; Retry   -  1 hour
                43200        ; Expire  - 12 hours
                3600 )       ; Minimum -  1 hour
```

Here the name server hostname for ad-engine.com is ns.ad-engine.com, and the contact e-mail address is kabir@ad-engine.com. Notice that the "@" part of the e-mail address is replaced with a "." character in the SOA record.

The refresh rate is set to 7,200 seconds (two hours). So a secondary name server for ad-engine.com will poll the primary server to see if the serial number for the zone has increased or not. The commonly used values range from 2 to 12 hours and depend on how frequently you change a zone's configuration. The retry rate is set to 3,600 seconds (one hour). If network trouble stops a secondary name server from contacting the primary server at the end of the refresh cycle (after every two hours in this case), then the secondary should wait another hour before retrying to communicate with the primary server. The expire rate is set to 43,200 seconds (12 hours). This allows the secondary to treat its copy of the zone data as valid for 12 hours if it can't contact the primary server. This value is particularly important if you have set up a secondary DNS on a different network. You should set it high enough so that in case the primary name server or its network fails, the secondary can provide DNS service for the longest outage period.

In this example, the secondary name server will provide DNS service for 12 hours after it has failed to communicate with the primary server and will stop DNS service for that zone after the specified time. However, it will still try to communicate with the primary name server on a regular basis. The minimum elapsed time is the default TTL value for resource records. This specifies how long a resource record stays valid in a name server's cache. For example, when a name server queries the ad-engine.com name server for a certain DNS record, it will keep the answer for the query in its cache for 3,600 seconds (1 hour). If you change your DNS information frequently, you should set this to a low number; otherwise, set it to a high number.

NS: NAME SERVER   The Name Server record is used to specify the name server responsible for a domain. The syntax is as follows:

```
IN   NS   name-server-hostname.
```

Notice that the name and TTL fields (of the resource record) are not specified, because the name needs to be specified only in SOA records using the "@" character, and the TTL value is also specified in SOA records using the minimum number. For example:

```
IN   NS   ns.ad-engine.com.
```

This resource record specifies that ns.ad-engine.com is the name server for the current zone file. You can specify multiple NS records. In fact you should have at least two NS records (one for the master and one for the slave name server). Also notice the period after the end of the name server hostname. You must insert a period after all full hostnames in a zone file.

A: ADDRESS   The Address record specifies an IP address for a specific hostname. An A record translates a hostname to an IP address. The syntax is as follows:

```
hostname  IN  A  IP-address
```

For example:

```
www.ad-engine.com.  IN  A  206.171.50.51
```

You should have at least one A record per host. You can also use a shortcut for the hostname. For example,

```
www IN  A  206.171.50.51
```

is the same as the previous A record if the zone is `ad-engine.com`. In other words, if you do not specify a full hostname, the domain name is appended to the short name. Thus `www` becomes `www.ad-engine.com`.

PTR: DOMAIN NAME POINTER   The Domain Name Pointer record is used to translate an IP address to a hostname. This is also called the reverse Domain Name Service. The syntax for PTR record is as follows:

```
IP-address  IN PTR  hostname.
```

For example:

```
206.171.50.51 IN PTR www.ad-engine.com.
```

Here the IP address 206.171.50.51 is associated with the host `www.ad-engine.com`. You can use a shortened version as follows:

```
51 IN PTR www
```

Typically, an ISP does the primary reverse DNS for a network.

CNAME: CANONICAL NAME   The Canonical Name record, CNAME, specifies an alias (hostname) for the canonical (official) hostname. The syntax is as follows:

```
Alias  IN CNAME Canonical-hostname.
```

For example:

```
webserver.ad-engine.com. IN CNAME www.ad-engine.com.
```

Here webserver.ad-engine.com is an alias for www.ad-engine.com. The shortened version is as follows:

```
webserver IN CNAME www
```

Note that when the `webserver.ad-engine.com` needs to be resolved to an IP address, the IP address of the `www.ad-engine.com` is returned. Therefore you must make sure that at least one A record exists for the canonical hostname.

MX: MAIL EXCHANGE   The Mail Exchange record is used to specify a hostname that is set up as the SMTP mail server for a domain. The syntax is as follows:

```
IN  MX  preference-value  mail-server-hostname.
```

For example:

```
IN  MX  0  mail.ad-engine.com.
```

The preference number is useful only if you have more than one mail server. For example:

```
IN  MX  10  fast-mail-server.ad-engine.com.
IN  MX  20  slow-mail-server.ad-engine.com.
```

Here the lower preference number indicates a higher precedence.

Now that you have learned the basics of DNS resource records, you are ready to create primary, secondary, and cache-only DNS servers.

Master/primary DNS server

Let's assume that I have named running on the ns.nitec.com host I just registered a domain called classifiedworks.com with Internic, and I want to set up named on ns.nitec.com to provide primary DNS for this new domain. Here is how.

First, I need to create the following zone statement in the /etc/named.conf file:

```
zone "classifiedworks.com" {
  type master;
  file "classifiedworks.db";
  };
```

This statement states that my name server is the master name server for the classifiedworks.com domain. Now I need to create a zone file called classifiedworks.db in the name server's working directory (specified by the options { directory path_name}; statement. Listing 10-2 is an example of such a zone file for the classifiedworks.com domain.

Listing 10-2: A zone file for the classifiedworks.com domain

```
@    IN  SOA  ns.nitec.com. kabir.nitec.com. (
            1999020100  ; Serial
            7200        ; Refresh -  2 hours
            3600        ; Retry   -  1 hour
            43200       ; Expire  - 12 hours
            3600 )      ; Minimum -  1 hour
```

```
    IN  NS  ns.nitec.com.
    IN  MX  10 mail.nitec.com.

www IN  CNAME www.nitec.com.
ftp IN  A   206.171.50.55
```

Here I have set up SOA and NS records to state that ns.nitec.com is the name server for the classifiedworks.com domain. Because I want to receive mail for this domain on the mail.nitec.com host, I set up an MX record that does just that. I set up an alias called www.classifiedworks.com for www.nitec.com. And finally, I set up an A record for ftp.classifiedworks.com to point to 206.171.55.

Using the various resource records, you can configure the zone file as you need. Once the zone file is configured and stored in the working directory of the DNS server, the primary name server configuration for the domain is complete.

Slave/secondary DNS server

Configuring a slave or secondary DNS server is quite simple. The only file you need to update by hand is the /etc/named.conf file. For example, say that I want to use a DNS server called ns2.nitec.com as the secondary name server for the classified works.com domain. The very first thing I need to do is create a zone statement such as the following in the /etc/named.conf file of the ns2.nitec.com named server:

```
zone "classifiedworks.com" {
  type slave;
  file "classifiedworks.db";
  };
```

Because this is a slave or secondary server, I do not need to create the classified works.db file by hand. I can just grab the file from the primary name server for the classifiedworks.com domain using a program called named-xfer, which comes with the named distribution. Because I know the name of the primary name server for the classifiedworks.com domain to be ns.nitec.com, I can run the named-xfer command as follows:

```
named-xfer -z classifiedworks.com -f classifiedworks.db \
-s 0 ns.nitec.com
```

Here the -z option specifies the zone name, the -f option specifies the zone file name, and the -s option specifies the name server where the information currently resides.

Once you run this program, a file called classifiedworks.db will be created in the current directory. Once I move the file to the working directory of the named server on the ns2.nitec.com machine, the secondary DNS configuration for the classifiedworks.com domain is complete.

Reverse DNS server

If you own your network IP addresses, you will have to do reverse DNS for them. For example, if you own an IP network called 206.171.50.0 and use it in your forward DNS configuration for a domain called `nitec.com`, you will have to set up a reverse DNS zone for this network. Here is how.

First, modify the /etc/named.conf file to include a new zone as follows:

```
zone "50.171.206.in-addr.arpa" {
  type master;
  file "db.206.171.50";
  };
```

Notice the special zone name (`50.171.206.in-addr.arpa`) used in the preceding zone configuration. To create a reverse DNS zone name, you must reverse your network number and append `in-addr.arpa` at the end of the name.

Now you need to create db.206.171.50 in the working directory of the named server. Note that the filename for the reverse DNS zone can be anything, but it is customary to use the db.*network-address* names. This file is similar to the other zone files I have shown so far; the only difference is that it will have PTR records instead of A, CNAME, and so on. Listing 10-3 shows an example of the db.206.171.50 file.

Listing 10-3: An example of a reverse DNS zone file (db.206.171.50)

```
@    IN  SOA  ns.nitec.com. kabir.nitec.com. (
            1999020100   ; Serial
            7200         ; Refresh -  2 hours
            3600         ; Retry   -  1 hour
            43200        ; Expire  - 12 hours
            3600 )       ; Minimum -  1 hour

     IN  NS  ns.nitec.com.

51.50.171.206.in-addr.arpa.   IN  PTR ns.nitec.com.
52.50.171.206.in-addr.arpa.   IN  PTR mail.nitec.com.
53.50.171.206.in-addr.arpa.   IN  PTR www.nitec.com.
```

Here the PTR records are provided to map three different IP addresses to three different hostnames. You can also specify the preceding PTR records in shortened form as follows:

```
51  IN  PTR ns.nitec.com
52  IN  PTR mail.nitec.com
53  IN  PTR www.nitec.com
```

In most cases, your ISP will own the IP addresses for your network and should be prepared to provide master reverse DNS service. However, there is one special network for which you must provide reverse name service. This special network is 127.0.0, which is used for the local loopback interface IP (127.0.0.1). Because no one has authority over this loopback network, everyone must provide reverse DNS service themselves. This is why you will always need to have a special zone statement in your /etc/named.conf file that looks like the following:

```
zone "0.0.127.in-addr.arpa" {
  type master;
  file "named.local";
  };
```

You will also have to have the named.local zone file in the working directory of your name server. This file is shown in Listing 10-4.

Listing 10-4: The named.local file

```
@     IN  SOA  localhost. root.localhost. (
               1999020100  ; Serial
               7200        ; Refresh -  2 hours
               3600        ; Retry   -  1 hour
               43200       ; Expire  - 12 hours
               3600 )      ; Minimum -  1 hour

      IN  NS  localhost.

1     IN  PTR localhost.
```

Cache-only/slave DNS server

Technically, all DNS servers are cache enabled, or in other words, DNS servers use cache by default. However, if you do not want to provide DNS service for any Internet domains and desire only to improve DNS query performance for your network, you can run a cache-only DNS server. Such a server will have an /etc/named.conf file as shown in Listing 10-5.

Listing 10-5: A cache-only DNS server's /etc/named.conf

```
zone "." {
  type hint;
  file "named.ca";
  };

zone "0.0.127.in-addr.arpa" {
  type master;
```

```
file "named.local";
};
```

The first zone statement specifies that the name server use the named.ca file to determine root name server names at startup. And the second zone statement provides the reverse name service for the local loopback network. That's all you need to create a cache-only name server.

So far you have learned to create various name server configurations; now look at how you can control the named name server.

Controlling the DNS server

The named distribution comes with a nifty program called ndc that provides a simple command line interface for controlling the name server.

STARTING THE NAME SERVER

Your name server should start automatically at boot. If it does not start automatically, you need to take the following steps:

1. Log into your name server system as root and change directory to /etc/rc.d/init.d. Make sure that you have a script called "named" in this directory. If you are missing this script, you should reinstall the BIND distribution RPM from your Red Hat CD-ROM.

2. Once you have confirmed that you have the /etc/rc.d/init.d/named script, change directory to your default system run level (see /etc/inittab) rc directory. For most systems the default run level is 3; if yours is also the same, change directory to /etc/rc.d/rc3.d/.

3. Make a symbolic link called SXXnamed that points to the /etc/rc.d/init.d/ named script. Replace XX in SXXnamed with a high number such as 55 or 85 to ensure that the system does not try to start the name server before network interfaces are set up properly. For example, to make a symbolic link called S55named to point to the named script, you can run:

   ```
   ln -s /etc/rc.d/init.d/named S55named
   ```

   Once you have created this link, your system will start the name server every time you boot your system. If, however, you prefer to run the name server manually, you can use the ndc program as follows:

   ```
   ndc start
   ```

RELOADING NEW NAME SERVER CONFIGURATION

After you modify any of the zone files or the /etc/boot.conf file, you must restart the name server to make the changes effective. You can force the name server to reload the new configuration as follows:

```
ndc reload
```

Do not forget to modify the serial number in the SOA record for any zone file you modify, or else the name server will not load the new configuration. To restart the name server by killing it first, you can use restart instead of reload in the preceding line.

STOPPING THE NAME SERVER
If for any reason you need to stop the name server, just run the ndc command as follows:

```
ndc stop
```

VIEWING NAME SERVER STATISTICS
You can use the ndc program to generate various name server statistics in the working directory of the name server. Run:

```
ndc stats
```

This command will create a file called named.stats in the name server's working directory. This statistics file will show various items of information including the number of queries per resource record.

Every time you modify your DNS information, do not forget to test the configuration using a name server query tool. In the following section I will discuss how you can test your name server configurations.

Testing Your DNS Server

Many tools are available for manually querying name servers. If you would like to have a few commonly used query tools, install the bind-utils RPM distribution from your Red Hat CD-ROM. The bind-utils distribution comes with dig, dnsquery, host, nslookup, and more. My favorite and the most widely used is the nslookup utility, and so I will demonstrate this for testing DNS configurations.

Say that you just registered a new domain with Internic and have already set up the necessary DNS configuration on your name server.

After restarting the name server, you want to test the configuration via nslookup.

When you run nslookup from the command line, it shows the hostname and IP address of the name server it is going to use by default. If you are running nslookup on the name server system, you should see the name and IP of the name server. If you don't see the name server's information, make sure your /etc/resolv.conf file is configured properly. On the other hand, if you are running nslookup on a computer other than the name server, you will have to tell the program to use the name server you want to test. Note you need to do this only if Internic has not yet released the new domain's name server information to the root name servers. To tell nslookup to use a different name server than the default, you enter server *hostname* (where hostname is the hostname of the server you want to test) from the nslookup command prompt. Once you have entered this command, nslookup will use the specified name server host for all queries.

The nslookup utility allows you to perform any type of DNS query using a simple syntax. For example, to locate the name server for a domain, you can run the following command from within the nslookup program:

```
set query=ns
domain.tld
```

The first line tells nslookup to perform a NS (Name Server Record) query for the next domain (domain.tld). Similarly, you can perform queries for A, MX, CNAME, and so on. If the responses you get do not look right, you should go back to the zone file and make sure you have no typos. One common mistake is not to end a full hostname with a period.

Managing DNS for Virtual Domains

A single name server can provide name service for many domains. This feature allows a single system to host a large number of Internet domains. In fact, that's how most Internet service provider (ISP) companies provide Web sites for their customers. Because such a domain is hosted on another domain (for example, the ISP's own domain), they are called *virtual domains*. Virtual domains are quite common these days. It almost seems as if everyone I know has a domain of their own. If you need to create a lot of virtual domains for your customers on a daily basis, you might want to automate the process as much as you can. Listing 10-6 shows a Perl script called makesite that I often use to create a virtual domain.

Listing 10-6: The makesite script

```
#!/usr/local/bin/perl -w

use strict;

#
# Purpose: makesite creates virtual sites.
# It uses a set of templates to create DNS, and HTTPD
# configurations files.
#
# Note: this is a very *simple* script.
#
###########################################################
```

```perl
use Time::localtime;

my $site              = $ARGV[0] or &syntax;
my $MAKESITE_DIR      = '/scratch/dns/makesite';
my $USER              = 'httpd';
my $GROUP             = 'httpd';
my $PERMISSION        = '2770';
my $BASE_DIR          = '/tmp';
my $HTDOCS            = 'htdocs';
my $CGIBIN            = 'cgi-bin';
my $NAMED_PATH        = '/var/named';
my $NAMED_FILE_EXT    = '.db';
my $NAMED_TEMPLATE    = "$MAKESITE_DIR/named.template";
my $NAMED_CONF        = '/etc/named.conf';
my $HTTPD_CONF        = '/usr/local/apache/etc/httpd.conf';
my $VHOST_TEMPLATE    = "$MAKESITE_DIR/httpd.template";
my $LOG_FILE          = "$BASE_DIR/makesite.log";

my $dir = $site;
my @domain_types = qw(com net org edu);
my ($domain_ext, $thesite_dir, $public_dir,
    $htdocs_dir, $cgibin_dir, $named_file,
    $dir_len, $temp_len);

my $tm = localtime(time);
my $date = sprintf("%s-%02s-%02s-%02d-%02d", $tm->year+1900,
                                             $tm->mon+1,
                                             $tm->mday,
                                             $tm->hour,
                                             $tm->min);

my $serial = sprintf("%s%02d%02d000",        $tm->year+1900,
                                             $tm->mon+1,
                                             $tm->mday);

$site =~ y/[A-Z]/[a-z]/;

# Get the length with the EXT
$dir_len = length($dir);

foreach $domain_ext (@domain_types){ $dir =~ s/\.$domain_ext//g; }

# Get the new length without the EXT
$temp_len = length($dir);
```

```perl
# If the user has not entered an extension then show syntax.
&syntax if($temp_len == $dir_len);

$named_file = $NAMED_PATH . '/' . $dir . $NAMED_FILE_EXT ;
$thesite_dir = $BASE_DIR . '/' . $dir;
$htdocs_dir = $BASE_DIR . '/' . $dir . '/' . $HTDOCS;
$cgibin_dir = $BASE_DIR . '/' . $dir . '/' . $CGIBIN;

die "$thesite_dir already exist! Aborted!\n" if(-e $thesite_dir);

system("mkdir $thesite_dir");
system("mkdir $htdocs_dir");
system("mkdir $cgibin_dir");

&createNamedFile($named_file,$site,"$dir$NAMED_FILE_EXT");
&createIndexFile($htdocs_dir,$site);
&createVirtualHostConf( domain=>$site,
                        website=>"www.$site",
                        cgibin=>$cgibin_dir,
                        htdocs=>$htdocs_dir);

system("chown -R $USER.$GROUP $thesite_dir");
system("chmod -R $PERMISSION $thesite_dir");

open(FP,">$LOG_FILE") || die "Can't write to log file.\n";
print FP "$date created www.$site [$htdocs_dir] site.\n";
close(FP);

exit 0;

sub createNamedFile{
   my $file = shift;
   my $domain = shift;
   my $database = shift;
   my $line;

   open(OUT,">$file") || die "Can't write $file\n";
   open(FP,$NAMED_TEMPLATE) || die "Can't open $NAMED_TEMPLATE\n";
   while($line=<FP>){
     $line =~ s/<DOMAIN>/$domain/g;
     $line =~ s/<SERIAL>/$serial/g;
     print OUT $line;
     }
   close(FP);
   close(OUT);
```

```
    open(FP,">$NAMED_CONF") || die "Can't open $NAMED_CONF\n";
    print FP <<ZONE;

// $domain was created on $date
zone "$domain" {
        type master;
        file "$database";
};

ZONE
    close(FP);
    }


sub createIndexFile{
  my $htdocs = shift;
  my $domain = shift;

  open(FP,">$htdocs/index.html") || die "Can't write index.html \n";
  print FP <<INDEX_PAGE;
  <HTML>
  <HEAD> <TITLE> $domain </TITLE> </HEAD>
  <BODY BGCOLOR="white">
  <CENTER>
   This is $domain Web site
   <p> It was created on $date </p>
  </CENTER>
  </BODY>
  </HTML>
INDEX_PAGE

  close(FP);
  }


sub createVirtualHostConf{

  my %params = @_;
  my $line;
  open(OUT,">$HTTPD_CONF") || die "Can't open $HTTPD_CONF $!\n";

  open(FP,$VHOST_TEMPLATE) || die "Can't open $VHOST_TEMPLATE $!\n";
  while($line=<FP>){
    $line =~ s/<DOMAIN>/$params{domain}/g;
    $line =~ s/<CGI-BIN-DIR>/$params{cgibin}/g;
    $line =~ s/<HTDOCS-DIR>/$params{htdocs}/g;
    $line =~ s/<WWW-SITE>/$params{website}/g;
```

```
    print OUT $line;

    }
  close(FP);
  close(OUT);
  }

sub syntax{
    print <<SYNTAX;

    makesite <virtual Internet domain>
    Example: makesite nitec.com

SYNTAX
    exit 0;
    }
```

The purpose of this Perl script is to enable me to create a virtual Web site with proper DNS and Apache Web server configuration without doing many file editing tasks. For example, say that I want to create a new Web site called www.newdomain.com. If I were to do everything manually, I would have to do the following:

1. Add a new zone statement in the /etc/named.conf file for newdomain.com.

2. Add a new zone file for newdomain.com in the working directory of the name server. I would have to create this from scratch or copy and modify an existing domain file.

3. Create a Web site document root and CGI script directory for the domain in the appropriate Web space on the server.

4. Modify the Apache server configuration file so that Apache treats www.newdomain.com as a new Web site.

Because manually configuring these important files can be error prone, I decided to write the makesite script that does all of these steps. For example, to create the www.newdomain.com site with proper DNS and Apache configuration, I can run:

```
makesite newdomain.com
```

This command adds a zone statement such as the following in the /etc/named.conf file:

```
// newdomain.com was created on 1999-02-03-13-30

zone "newdomain.com" {
  type master;
```

```
file "newdomain.db";
};
```

This statement creates a newdomain.db file in /var/named (the working directory for my name server), which is shown in Listing 10-7.

Listing 10-7: The /var/named/newdomain.db file

```
@   IN   SOA   newdomain.com. hostmaster.newdomain.com. (
               19990206000   ; serial YYYYMMDDXXX
               7200          ; refresh
               3600          ; (1 hour) retry
               1728000       ; (20 days) expire
               3600)         ; (1 hour) minimal TTL

; Name Servers
  IN   NS   ns.nitec.com.
  IN   MX   10 mail.nitec.com.

; CNAME records
www   IN   CNAME   www.nitec.com.
```

The script then appends the following lines to the end of the Apache server configuration (httpd.conf) file:

```
#
# Domain Configuration for www.newdomain.com
#

<VirtualHost www.newdomain.com>
  ServerName www.newdomain.com
  ServerAdmin webmaster@newdomain.com

  DocumentRoot /tmp/newdomain/htdocs
  ScriptAlias /cgi-bin/ /tmp/newdomain/cgi-bin/

  ErrorLog logs/www.newdomain.com.error.log
  TransferLog logs/www.newdomain.com.access.log

</VirtualHost>

#
# End of Domain Configuration for www.newdomain.com
#
```

And finally the script creates the following directory structure and the index. html page for the Web site:

```
/www/newdomain
/www/newdomain/htdocs—the document root for the Web site
/www/newdomain/cgi-bin—the cgi-bin directory
```

The index.html page is stored in the /www/newdomain/htdocs/ directory. The script also sets up the permissions for the Web site directories so that only a specified user and group have read/write permissions.

Because the script does all the dirty work, I can create many virtual sites without constantly worrying about configuration problems. And finally when I am done making sites, I can restart the name server and the Web server to bring up all the sites online. This is really a simple yet useful tool. You will find this tool easy to use. The makesite script takes the domain name as the argument and uses two text template files to create the name server and the Web server configuration information. Listing 10-8 shows the named.template file used to create the name server configuration.

Listing 10-8: The named.template file

```
@   IN SOA <DOMAIN>.  hostmaster.<DOMAIN>. (
                    <SERIAL>    ; serial YYYYMMDDXXX
                    7200        ; refresh
                    3600        ; (1 hour) retry
                    1728000     ; (20 days) expire
                    3600)       ; (1 hour) minimal TTL

; Name Servers
    IN   NS  ns.nitec.com.
    IN   MX  10 mail.nitec.com.

; CNAME records
www  IN   CNAME  www.nitec.com.
```

If you look carefully, you will see the two special tags (<DOMAIN> and <SERIAL>) in this template file. The makesite script reads this template and replaces these tags with appropriate information. Because the idea is to create a virtual Web site with a proper DNS configuration, you do not need to create any A records. For example, the preceding configuration states that the www.<DOMAIN> (for instance, www.newdomain. com) is an alias of www.nitec.com. Using A records will make maintenance of many virtual Web sites time consuming if IP changes are required. I use the CNAME record so that if www.nitec.com host's IP needs to be changed, I do not need to modify the virtual domain's configuration files at all.

Listing 10-9 shows the httpd.template file used to create the Apache server configuration.

Listing 10-9: The httpd.template file

```
#
# Domain Configuration for <WWW-SITE>
#

<VirtualHost <WWW-SITE>
  ServerName <WWW-SITE>
  ServerAdmin webmaster@<DOMAIN>

  DocumentRoot <HTDOCS-DIR>
  ScriptAlias /cgi-bin/ <CGI-BIN-DIR>/

  ErrorLog logs/<WWW-SITE>.error.log
  TransferLog logs/<WWW-SITE>.access.log

</VirtualHost>

#
# End of Domain Configuration for <WWW-SITE>
#
```

As with the previous template, you will notice that a few custom tags are used in this file. These tags get replaced with appropriate information as well.

To use this Perl script in your own environment, first modify the following lines in the beginning of the script:

```
my $MAKESITE_DIR  = '/usr/local/src/makesite';
```

Change the directory path to the location of the makesite files.

```
my $USER  = 'httpd';
```

Change the username if you run your Apache Web server using another user id like 'nobody' or something else.

```
my $GROUP  = 'httpd';
```

Change the group name if you run your Apache Web server using another group like 'nobody' or something else.

```
my $PERMISSION  = '2770';
```

Change the permission value as you see fit. This value allows only the $USER and $GROUP to have full access in the Web site directory.

```
my $BASE_DIR  = '/www';
```

Change the value of the $BASE_DIR variable to the base directory of all of your Web sites.

```
my $HTDOCS  = 'htdocs';
```

Change the value of the $HTDOCS variable to the relative name of the document root directory name for httpd.conf file. The current setting creates $BASE_DIR/<sitename>$HTDOCS (default: /www/<sitename>/htdocs) as the document root for the Web site.

```
my $CGIBIN  = 'cgi-bin';
```

Change the value of the $CGIBIN variable to the relative directory name if you do not want the Apache ScriptAlias directive to be set to $BASE_DIR/<sitename>/$CGIBIN (default: /www/<sitename>/cgi-bin).

```
my $NAMED_PATH  = '/var/named';
```

Change the value of the $NAMED_PATH variable to the directory to the working directory of your name server.

```
my $LOG_FILE  = "$BASE_DIR/makesite.log";
```

Change the value of the $LOG_FILE variable to point to somewhere else if you do not want to write the makesite log file in the base directory. For example, you can set this to "/tmp/makesite.log" to write to the /tmp directory.

```
my $HTTPD_CONF  = '/usr/local/apache/etc/httpd.conf';
```

Change the value of the $HTTPD_CONF variable to point to the httpd.conf file of your Web server.

Once you have made the preceding changes, you should modify the named. template and httpd.template files as you see fit and store both of these files in the directory where you keep the makesite script. Finally make sure that the script is executable and that the Perl interpreter line (the #! bang line) is set up correctly. Hopefully, this will save you some work. If you know Perl programming, you can always fine-tune the script to your environment as much as you want.

Organizations that manage multiple virtual domains often have multiple servers. In the following section you will learn how to use a DNS trick to balance load over many servers.

Balancing Load Using the DNS Server

The idea is to share load among multiple servers of a kind. This sharing is typically used for balancing Web load over multiple Web servers. This trick is called round robin Domain Name Service.

Say that you have two Web servers, www1.yourdomain.com (192.168.1.10) and www2.yourdomain.com (192.168.1.20), and you would like to balance load for the www.yourdomain.com on these two servers using the round robin DNS trick. In your yourdomain.com zone file add the following lines:

```
www1   IN   A 192.168.1.10
www2   IN   A 192.168.1.20

www    IN   CNAME   www1
www    IN   CNAME   www2
```

Restart your name server and ping the www.yourdomain.com host. You will see the 192.168.1.10 address in the ping output. Stop and restart pinging the same host, and now you will see the second IP address being pinged. This is due to the fact that the preceding configuration tells the name server to cycle through the CNAME records for www. In other words, the www.yourdomain.com host is both www1.yourdomain.com and www2.yourdomain.com.

Now when someone enters www.yourdomain.com, the name server will give out the first address once, and then for the next request it will give out the second address and keep on cycling between these addresses.

One of the disadvantages of the round robin DNS trick is that there is no way for the name server to know which system is heavily loaded and which is not; it just blindly cycles. If one of the servers crashes or become unavailable for some reason, the round robin DNS will still return the broken server's IP on a regular basis. This could be quite chaotic because some people will be able to get to the sites and some won't.

If your load demands better management and it is important to check your server's health, your best choice is to get a hardware solution using the new director products such as the Web Director (http://www.radware.com/), Ace Director (http://www.alteon.com/), or Local Director (http://www.cisco.com/). I have used Web Director with great success.

Summary

In this chapter, you learned the basics of Domain Name Service (DNS) and how to set up the Berkeley Internet Name Domain (BIND) server for your Red Hat Linux system. You learned about the various resource records and how to create primary/master, secondary/slave, cache-only, and reverse DNS servers. You learned how to automate creation of multiple virtual domains. You also learned the round robin DNS trick that enables you to create a somewhat load-balanced solution where multiple servers are involved.

Chapter 11

E-mail Service

IN THIS CHAPTER

- ◆ How SMTP mail works
- ◆ How to set up DNS for SMTP mail service
- ◆ How to set up sendmail for SMTP mail service
- ◆ How to test sendmail configuration
- ◆ How to secure sendmail
- ◆ How to take antispam measures
- ◆ How to set up a POP mail server
- ◆ How to set up SMTP/POP mail clients

CAN YOU PICTURE THE Internet without e-mail? Most people can't. E-mail service is the most widely used Internet service. In this chapter, you will learn how e-mail works and how to create an e-mail server on Red Hat Linux.

Figure 11-1 shows a basic flow diagram of how e-mail works.

As you can see in the figure, a user with an e-mail client application sends an e-mail message to an e-mail server. The sender's e-mail server then locates the e-mail server responsible for the recipient's e-mail service. The sender's e-mail server transfers the e-mail to the recipient's e-mail server. The recipient accesses the e-mail via an e-mail client application that requests her e-mail server to provide any unread e-mail messages. Now the recipient can reply to the sender using the same client/server method used for the sender.

The communication protocol used between the client and the server are typically Post Office Protocol (POP) and Simple Mail Transport Protocol (SMTP). The POP protocol is used to retrieve e-mail from the e-mail server, and SMTP is used to send e-mail to the server. The local SMTP server then sends the message to the SMTP server responsible for the recipient. However, if the e-mail client is on the SMTP server itself, POP protocol is not needed. As you can see, the transfer of e-mail messages is done to and from servers via SMTP protocol. Let's take a closer look at how SMTP works.

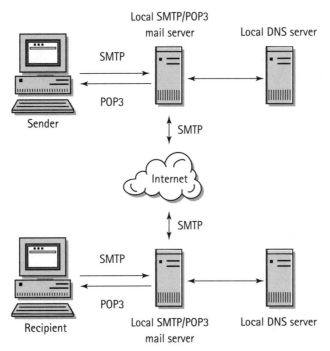

Figure 11-1: A basic flow diagram of how e-mail works

How SMTP Mail Works

Just as the name suggests, the Simple Mail Transport Protocol is simple by design. An SMTP server listens to TCP port 25 for connections. Another SMTP server (or a client) connects to this port and initiates an e-mail transaction using simple SMTP commands. In fact, you can use the Telnet client program from any computer to connect to a known SMTP server as follows:

```
telnet  smtp server hostname or IP address  25
```

Here I will show you how to emulate an e-mail client via Telnet and send an e-mail message to someone. Because I am already running an SMTP server on one of my Red Hat Linux servers called blackhole.nitec.com, I can simply run telnet picaso.nitec.com 25 to connect to the local SMTP server. Here is an interactive SMTP session.

When I Telneted to port 25 of an SMTP server called picaso.nitec.com, it displayed the following message:

```
220 picaso.nitec.com ESMTP Sendmail 8.10.1/8.10.1/Rbl-Orbs-Dul; Sun,
21 Feb 1999 10:08:00 -0800
```

This is a greeting message from the SMTP server on `picaso.nitec.com`. Once the greeting message has been sent, the server waited for my commands. The very first SMTP command I entered is the following:

```
helo nitec.com
```

This generated the following response from the server:

```
250 picaso.nitec.com Hello IDENT:kabir@picaso.nitec.com
[206.171.50.50], pleased to meet you
```

To get some help on available SMTP commands, I entered:

```
help
```

The server responded with the following help message:

```
214-This is Sendmail version 8.10.1
214-Topics:
214-    HELO    EHLO    MAIL    RCPT    DATA
214-    RSET    NOOP    QUIT    HELP    VRFY
214-    EXPN    VERB    ETRN    DSN
214-For more info use "HELP <topic>".
214-To report bugs in the implementation send email to
214-    sendmail-bugs@sendmail.org.
214-For local information send email to Postmaster at your site.
214 End of HELP info
```

Now I could use these commands to create an e-mail message. First, I told the server my return e-mail address using the `MAIL` command as follows:

```
MAIL From: someone@out-there.com
```

The server responded with the following acknowledgment message:

```
250 someone@out-there.com... Sender ok
```

Then I gave it the recipient's e-mail address using the RCPT command:

```
RCPT To: kabir@nitec.com
```

Again, the server responded with the following acknowledgment message:

```
250 kabir@nitec.com... Recipient ok
```

Once I had given the sender and recipient's e-mail addresses to the server, it was time to enter the content of the e-mail message. I used the DATA command as follows:

```
data
```

The server responded with the following message:

```
354 Enter mail, end with "." on a line by itself
```

I entered the following e-mail message:

```
Date: 01 Jan 2000 12:00:01
From: alter-ego
To: kabir@nitec.com
Subject: Ping!

How are you on the first day of the new century?
Is your computer still working?

Later
Yourself from the future.
.
```

I terminated the message using a single period on a line by itself. The server acknowledged the message using the following response:

```
250 JAA01145 Message accepted for delivery
```

I entered the QUIT command to complete the message transaction as follows:

```
quit
```

Finally, the server responded with the following message, and my connection to the server was closed as follows:

```
221 blackhole.nitec.com closing connection
Connection closed by foreign host.
```

Because the e-mail message I created here went to my user account kabir@nitec.com, I retrieved it with my e-mail client program a few seconds after the message was composed via Telnet, as described previously. The actual message along with the headers are shown here:

```
Return-Path: <someone@out-there.com>
```

```
        Received: from reboot.nitec.net (kabir@reboot.nitec.com
[206.171.50.51] by picaso.nitec.com (8.10.1/8.10.1) with SMTP ID
KAA01163 for kabir@nitec.com; Sun, 21 Feb 1999 10:03:52 -0800

       Message-ID: <199902211803.KAA01163@blackhole.nitec.com>
             Date: 01 Jan 2000 12:00:01
             From: alter-ego@your-future.com
               To: kabir@nitec.com
          Subject: Ping!
           Status:
  X-Mozilla-Status: 0000
 X-Mozilla-Status2: 00000000
           X-UIDL: 36cdb3b500000032

How are you on the first day of the new century?
Is your computer still working?

Later
Yourself from the future.
```

As you can see, the e-mail I received from the server is exactly what I composed earlier via Telnet. Normally, your e-mail client program does the composing part of the SMTP.

 Read the RFC 821 document for details on the SMTP protocol.

As you can see, the entire process is quite simple once you have an SMTP server up and running. Before you can get your own SMTP server running on your Red Hat Linux server, you need to create an appropriate DNS configuration for e-mail delivery. Here is how.

Setting Up DNS Mail Service

You may recall from Chapter 10 (DNS Service) that you use Mail Exchange (MX) records to identify SMTP mail server resources in a DNS configuration for a domain. Say that you want to designate a host called mail.yourdomain.com as your SMTP mail server for the domain yourdomain.com. The Start of Authority (SOA) record for yourdomain.com must include a line such as:

```
IN  MX  preference-value mail-server-hostname.
```

Here, *preference-value* is a positive (integer) number and useful only when you have multiple SMTP mail servers. If you have just a single SMTP mail server, this number can have any value. For example:

```
IN  MX  5  mail.yourdomain.com.
```

Here the single SMTP mail server `mail.yourdomain.com` has been set to preference level 5. Here is an example of the multiserver scenario:

```
IN  MX  10  fast-mail-server.ad-engine.com.
IN  MX  20  slow-mail-server.ad-engine.com.
```

Here the preference number plays a vital role. When an SMTP mail server from anyone on the Internet wishes to send mail to `someone@ad-engine.com`, it first performs a DNS query to locate the MX record for `ad-engine.com`. The MX record returned to the SMTP mail server will be as just shown in the preceding code. The SMTP mail server then selects `fast-mail-server.ad-engine.com` as the preferred mail server for the delivery because it has the higher priority (that is, the lower preference number) of the two available servers. It then tries to initiate an SMTP connection (using port 25) with the `fast-mail-server.ad-engine.com` computer. If the `fast-mail-server.ad-engine.com` server is not available for any reason, the `slow-mail-server.ad-engine.com` server will be selected for delivery. So having multiple MX records provides you with redundancy in your mail delivery system, which is very important if e-mail is a critical part of your organization.

 Always use a hostname in an MX record that has its own A record. In other words, do not use host aliases in MX records. See RFC 1123 for details.

Once you have set up DNS with appropriate MX records, test the configuration via `nslookup -q=mxyourdomain` command. If you have configured DNS properly, you see the MX records you just created. Once this is taken care of, you are ready to set up the SMTP mail service.

Setting Up SMTP Mail Service

The very first step in setting up an SMTP service is to decide which SMTP mail server you would like to use for your Red Hat Linux system. Many SMTP mail server products are available. However, sendmail stands out among the rest because of its long history of worldwide deployment. It is also the default SMTP mail server for

Red Hat Linux. Hence I use sendmail as the SMTP server for this chapter. Look at how you can install sendmail on your system.

Installing sendmail

Like any other server software you install on your Red Hat system, sendmail also comes in RPM packages. However, you do need to install multiple RPM packages; they are:

- ◆ sendmail-*<version>.<architecture>*.rpm – the main distribution

- ◆ sendmail-cf-*<version>.<architecture>*.rpm – the mail sendmail configuration file distribution

- ◆ sendmail-config-*<version>.<architecture>*.rpm – the auxiliary configuration files distribution

- ◆ sendmail-doc-*<version>.<architecture>*.rpm – the documentation distribution

Installing these packages is quite simple; just run `rpm -ivh` *package name* to install each package.

If you have installed a previous version of sendmail during Red Hat Linux installation, remove the sendmail packages before you install a new version; they might not be exactly compatible. To uninstall an RPM package, use the `rpm -e package name` command. You can also locate the exact package name of an RPM package using the `rpm -q partial package name` command.

Once you install the packages, you are ready to configure sendmail. The primary configuration file for sendmail is /etc/sendmail.cf.

Starting and stopping sendmail

Although you have not yet configured the sendmail server, you can still run it. To start sendmail manually, you can run the following command:

```
/usr/sbin/sendmail -q<queue processing interval>
```

You have to replace queue processing interval with a time. Typically, time is specified in minutes or hours. For example, to have sendmail process the mail queue every 15 minutes, you can use `-q15m`, or to process the queue every hour, you can use `-q1h`. You can also specify seconds (s), days (d), or weeks (w). For example, you can specify -q1h30m so that sendmail processes the query every hour and a half.

 If you do not have a full-time Internet connection, you may use /usr/sbin/ sendmail –bd –o DeliveryMode=d to start sendmail in deferred mode, which avoids use of DNS until it is run again via /usr/sbin/sendmail –q. If you connect periodically, you can put /usr/sbin/sendmail –q in a cron job so that when your connection is up, the queue is processed automatically.

If you want sendmail to start automatically after each boot, make sure you create a symbolic link (starting with Sxx where xx is a number) from your default run level directory to the /etc/rc.d/init.d/sendmail script. For example, to run sendmail after each boot for a multiuser system (run level 3), I can create the following symbolic link:

```
ln -s /etc/rc.d/init.d/sendmail  /etc/rc.d/rc3.d/S85sendmail
```

This symbolic link makes sure that sendmail starts automatically after each boot. If you take a look at this script, you will see that sendmail is started with the –bd option, which starts it as a daemon, a background process. You may wish to modify the /etc/rc.d/init.d/sendmail script to reflect the queue interval requirements for your site. You might also want to add the following code just before the line (daemon /usr/sbin/sendmail –bd) in the script to automatically run newaliases and makemap on the configuration files at boot:

```
newaliases
for i in virtusertable access domaintable mailertable
do
  if [ -f /etc/mail/$i ] ; then
     echo "Making $i database for sendmail..."
     makemap hash /etc/mail/$i < /etc/mail/$i
     sleep 1
  fi
done
sleep 1
```

This ensures that all the configuration databases are rebuilt each time you start the server process.

You can use the /etc/rc.d/init.d/sendmail script to start, stop, and restart sendmail quite easily as well. To stop sendmail, run:

```
/etc/rc.d/init.d/sendmail stop
```

To restart sendmail, run:

```
/etc/rc.d/init.d/sendmail restart
```

You can also force sendmail to process its queue immediately using the –q option. For example:

```
/usr/sbin/sendmail -q
```

This command forces the immediate processing of the entire queue. If you prefer to process the queue partially, you can use the –qSstring option to process queues for only those messages that have the named string as part of the sender address. For example:

```
/usr/sbin/sendmail -qSkabir
```

will force sendmail to process all the queued mail for sender kabir. This could be handy when you have lots of mail waiting in a queue. You can also use –qRstring to force sendmail to process messages that have the named string as part of the recipient address.

You can run the `mqueue` command to identify the messages currently in the queue.

Understanding and configuring /etc/sendmail.cf

The /etc/sendmail.cf file is really not meant for humans. It is meant for the sendmail daemon, and therefore the syntax is optimized for the daemon as well. If you are new to sendmail, the configuration file may scare you as it has many administrators over many years. The /etc/sendmail.cf configuration file is considered the most complex configuration file a UNIX administrator has to deal with in her professional career. I feel the same way.

A complete book can be (and has been) written about the configuration that goes in /etc/sendmail.cf. However, not every administrator needs to know the details of /etc/sendmail.cf configuration. In fact, in most cases you do not even need to modify this configuration file, as it comes well equipped with commonly required configurations. Here I provide a brief overview of the configuration file that will help you understand how things are set up in the file and also enable you to follow instructions found at the sendmail Web site (`http://www.sendmail.org`) to implement certain features as needed. In other words, the information you find in this chapter is enough to get you up and running and also provide you with enough know-how to follow clearly written instructions in implementing configuration changes. What you will not learn here is how to create your own configuration rules, which requires extensive understanding of the inner working of the sendmail configuration.

The sendmail.cf file contains the following types of configuration information:

- ◆ Blank lines are ignored.

- ◆ Comment lines, designated by a leading "#" sign, are also ignored.

- ◆ Lines starting with C, D, F, H, O, P, V, K, M, S, or R are configuration lines.

- ◆ Lines starting with a leading whitespace character are continuation lines.

In the following sections I discuss various configurations in brief so that you have an idea about which one does what.

S AND R: ADDRESS REWRITE RULES

An "S" line is used to mark the start of a new rewrite rule. The syntax for such a line is Srule, where rule is the rule name/number. For example S3 marks the start of rule set 3.

An "R" line defines an address rewrite rule. A rewrite rule can be simply thought of as a statement such as the one that follows:

```
If (current e-mail address matches rule's left-hand-side pattern)
then
    Replace current address
            with the rule's right-hand-side pattern
end
```

It has the following syntax:

```
R<LHS>    <RHS>    <optional comments>
```

Here, *LHS* is the left-hand-side pattern, and *RHS* is the right-hand-side pattern of the rule. For example:

```
R$*  < $* > $* <@>       $: $1 < $2 > $3
```

Here, the left-hand-side pattern is $* < $* > $* <@>, and the right-hand-side pattern is $: $1 < $2 > $3. Both left- and right-hand-side patterns are composed of various metasymbols such as $*, $+, $-, $=x, and $~x.

Rewrite rules are quite complex and in most cases will not require any changes on your part. However, if you are planning on writing your own rewrite rules, you should read the Sendmail Installation and Operation Guide bundled with the sendmail documentation.

D: DEFINE MACRO

The "D" lines define a macro. The syntax is as follows:

```
D<macro name>   <string>
```

For example:

```
DP   someword
```

This is same as $P = someword, and whenever $P is referenced elsewhere, it is expanded to someword.

Typically, you do not need to add, delete, or remove any "D" macro definitions.

C AND F: DEFINE CLASSES

The "C" lines are similar to "D" lines. The syntax for such a line is as follows:

```
C<class name> <string> <string> . . .
```

For example:

```
CA   str1 str2 str3
```

Here the A class is a list of str1, str2, and str3 strings. The "F" lines are same as "C" lines except for the fact that an "F" line is used to specify a class that is read from a file. For example:

```
Fw/etc/mail/sendmail.cw
```

Here the w class is a list of all the domain names in the /etc/mail/sendmail.cw file. This file must contain a single entry per line. The only other "F" line you will notice in your sendmail.cf file is:

```
FR-o /etc/mail/relay-domains
```

Here the class R is a list of all domain names in /etc/mail/relay-domains. Notice the -o option, which makes the line optional. In other words, sendmail will not complain if this file is empty. Typically, you do not need to make any changes here. However, if you want sendmail to complain if no relay domains are defined, you can remove the -o option from the preceding FR line.

M: DEFINE MAILER

An "M" line is used to create a mailer definition. The syntax for such a line is as follows:

```
Mmailer name field = value, field = value, . . .
```

For example:

```
Msmtp,   P=[IPC], F=mDFMuX, S=11/31, R=21/31, E=\r\n, L=990,
         T=DNS/RFC822/SMTP
```

Here mailer SMTP is being defined. Typically, you do not need to make any changes in standard mailer definitions.

H: DEFINE HEADER

An "H" line is used to create a header definition. The syntax for such a line is as follows:

```
H[?flags?]<header name>: <header template>
```

For example:

```
H?P?Return-Path: <$g>
HReceived: $?sfrom $s $.$?_($?s$|from $.$_)
        $.by $j ($v/$Z)$?r with $r$. id $i$?u
        for $u; $|;
        $.$b
H?D?Resent-Date: $a
H?D?Date: $a
H?F?Resent-From: $?x$x <$g>$|$g$.
H?F?From: $?x$x <$g>$|$g$.
H?x?Full-Name: $x
H?M?Resent-Message-Id: <$t.$i@$j>
H?M?Message-Id: <$t.$i@$j>
```

Each of the preceding "H" lines defines a mail header. You should not make any changes in header definitions.

O: SET OPTION

The "O" lines are used to set global options for sendmail. The syntax for such a line is as follows:

```
O option name = value
```

Table 11-1 shows all the options available in the latest version (8.9.x) of sendmail.

TABLE 11-1 SENDMAIL OPTIONS

Option	Explanation
AliasFile=/etc/mail/aliases	Sets the name of the alias database file. Change only if you keep the alias database some place other than /etc/mail/aliases.
AliasWait=30m	Default timeout in minutes for aliases to load at startup. Do not change.
AutoRebuildAliases=True	If set to True, sendmail tries to rebuild the aliases database if necessary and possible. Do not change.
BlankSub=.	Sets the blank substitution character. Do not change.
CheckAliases=False	If set to True, checks the right-hand side of an alias in the aliases database for validity. Default is set to False. No change recommended.
ClassFactor=1800	Used to compute priority of a message. Do not change.
ConnectionCacheSize=2	The maximum number of open connections that will be cached at any time.
ConnectionCacheTimeout=5m	The maximum time (in minutes) that a cached connection will be kept open during idle period.
ConnectionRateThrottle=20	Allows no more than specified number of daemon processes for incoming connections per second. Setting this to 0 will allow unlimited (i.e., as many as are permitted by your system resources) number of daemon processes per second.
DefaultUser=8:12	Default user and group for mailers. The UID 8 is default for user 'mail' in /etc/passwd and GID 12 is default for group 'mail' in /etc/group file. Change not recommended.
DeliveryMode=background	Runs sendmail in the background. No change required.
EightBitMode=pass8	Sets how eight-bit data are handled. Keep the default.

Continued

TABLE 11-1 SENDMAIL OPTIONS *(Continued)*

Option	Explanation
ForkEachJob=FALSE	When set to TRUE, a separate process if forked to service each message in the queue. No change required.
ForwardPath=$z/.forward.$w+$h:$z/.forward+$h:$z/.forward.$w:$z/.forward	Sets the path for searching for the .forward file for each user. No change required.
HelpFile=/usr/lib/sendmail.hf	Sets the location of the help file.
HoldExpensive=False	When set to True, expensive mailers (marked using F=e flag in "M" line for the mailer) are not allowed to connect immediately. Keep the default.
HostStatusDirectory=.hoststat	Sets the directory name for the host status information. The default value sets the directory to be /var/spool/mqueue/.hoststat. No change required.
HostsFile=/etc/hosts	Sets the name of the hosts file. No change required.
LogLevel=8	Sets the default log level. No change required.
MatchGECOS=False	When this is set to True, sendmail will perform fuzzy search in the /etc/passwd file to locate a "similar" username in the GECOS field of each password entry. Default is recommended.
MaxDaemonChildren=40	Maximum number of forked child processes at any time.
MaxHopCount=30	Maximum number of times a message can be processed before it is rejected.
MaxMessageSize=5000000	Maximum size of a message in bytes. Messages larger then this size will not be accepted.
MeToo=False	When an alias contains the sender herself, sendmail automatically removes the sender from the expansion. If this option is set to True, the sender will receive the mail in such a case. You might want to set this to True because it could reduce some tech-support calls from users who wish to receive mail even if it originated from themselves.

Option	Explanation
MinFreeBlocks=100	Minimum number of free blocks that must be present before sendmail will accept a message. This enables you to ensure that someone cannot wipe out your disk space by mail bombing (i.e., sending multiple copies of large mail messages) to your server. You might want to increase this number to a higher number than the default.
MinQueueAge=10m	A message must be in the queue for at least the specified number of minutes before it is processed.
NoRecipientAction= add-to-undisclosed	When a message does not contain an appropriate recipient header, the specified action is taken. The default value creates a "To: undisclosed-recipients" header.
OldStyleHeaders=True	Toggle old/new header format. No change required.
OperatorChars=.:%@!^/[]+	List of token delimiter characters. No change required.
PrivacyOptions=needvrfyhelo, restrictmailq,restrictqrun, goaway	See the section on ensuring privacy under "Securing sendmail" in this chapter for details.
QueueDirectory=/var/spool/ mqueue	The fully qualified pathname of the queue directory.
QueueLA=8	When the system's load average exceeds the specified number, do not send messages but instead queue them.
QueueSortOrder=Host	Sets the queue sort order. The default value allows sendmail to sort the queue using the hostnames of the recipients. You can change this to "Priority" to sort mail using priority header, or you can set this to "Time" to sort by submission time.
RecipientFactor=30000	This value is used to penalize the priority of a message that has a large number of recipients.
RefuseLA=12	When the system's load average exceeds the specified value, refuse incoming connections.
RetryFactor=90000	This value is used to lower message retry priority. No change recommended.

Continued

TABLE 11-1 SENDMAIL OPTIONS *(Continued)*

Option	Explanation
RunAsUser=mail	This value sets the username sendmail uses for all its child processes. In other words, sendmail child processes that are forked to service the actual requests do not run as the superuser; this therefore enhances security. No change recommended.
SendMimeErrors=True	When set to True, error messages are set using MIME formats. No change required.
SevenBitInput=False	When set to True, a message is converted into seven-bit data. Do not change the default value.
O SmtpGreetingMessage= $j Sendmail $v/$Z; $b	Sets the greeting message that sendmail issues when a connection is made. If you do not like to tell the world about the version of sendmail you use, remove the $v/$Z variables from this line. This might provide fewer clues for someone who is trying to exploit any security holes.
StatusFile=/var/log/sendmail.st	The fully qualified pathname of the status file.
SuperSafe=True	Toggle super safe mode. Default setting is recommended.
TempFileMode=0600	Sets the default mode for the temporary files in the queue.
Timeout.command=30m	Default timeout value for SMTP commands.
Timeout.connect=3m	Default timeout value for connection.
Timeout.datablock=1h	Default timeout value for data blocks.
Timeout.datafinal=1h	Default timeout value for final "." in the data.
Timeout.datainit=5m	Default timeout value for the DATA command.
Timeout.fileopen=60s	Default timeout value for opening .forward and :include: files.
Timeout.helo=5m	Default timeout value for the HELO command.
Timeout.hoststatus=10m	After the specified timeout period host becomes stale.
Timeout.initial=5m	Default timeout value for the initial greeting message.

Option	Explanation
Timeout.mail=10m	Default timeout value for the MAIL command.
Timeout.misc=2m	Default timeout value for the NOOP or VERB commands.
Timeout.queuereturn. non-urgent=7d	Value specifies time to elapse before nonurgent message is returned to sender.
Timeout.queuereturn.normal=5d	Value specifies time to elapse before normal message is returned to sender.
Timeout.queuereturn.urgent=2d	Value specifies time to elapse before urgent message is returned to sender.
Timeout.queuereturn=5d	Value specifies time to elapse before a message is returned to sender.
Timeout.queuewarn. non-urgent=12h	Value specifies time to elapse before a warning is sent to the sender about yet-undelivered nonurgent message.
Timeout.queuewarn.normal=6h	Value specifies time to elapse until a warning is sent to the sender about yet-undelivered normal message.
Timeout.queuewarn.urgent=2h	Value specifies time to elapse until a warning is sent to the sender about yet-undelivered urgent message.
Timeout.queuewarn=6h	Value specifies time to elapse until a warning is sent to the sender about yet-undelivered message.
Timeout.quit=2m	Default timeout value for the QUIT command.
Timeout.rcpt=30m	Default timeout value for the RCPT command.
Timeout.rset=5m	Default timeout value for the RSET command.
UnixFromLine=From $g $d	Defines the format used for UNIX-style From line. Do not change the default.
UnsafeGroupWrites=True	When set to True, files such as .forward and :include: are considered unsafe when they are writable by a group. Do not change the default.
UseErrorsTo=False	When set to True and an error occurs, sendmail will use the ErrorsTo header (if available) to report the error. Do not change the default.

P: PRECEDENCE DEFINITIONS

A "P" line is used to set values for the "Precedence:" header field. The syntax for such a line is as follows:

```
Pfield name = value
```

For example:

```
Pfirst-class=0
```

V: CONFIGURATION VERSION LEVEL

A "V" line is used for compatibility with older versions of a configuration. You do not need to make any changes to such a line.

K: KEY FILE DECLARATION

A "K" line is used to define a map. The syntax for such a line is as follows:

```
Kmap name mapclass arguments
```

For example:

```
Kaccess hash -o /etc/mail/access.db
```

Now take a look at the other sendmail configuration files in the /etc/mail directory.

Configuring /etc/mail/* files

I discuss the sendmail configuration files found in the /etc/mail directory in this section.

RESTRICTING ACCESS TO YOUR SENDMAIL SERVER USING /etc/mail/access

This configuration file can be used to create an access restriction database for your sendmail server. You can control access to your sendmail server on a per-domain, subdomain, IP address, or network basis. The configuration lines in this file have the following format:

```
host or user  access control option
```

Here, host or user can be a fully or partly qualified host name, domain name, IP address, network address, or e-mail address such as wormhole.nitec.com, nitec.com, 192.168.1.10, 192.168.1.0, spammer@somewhere.com, or what have you. The available configuration options are shown in Table 11-2.

TABLE 11-2 CONFIGURATION OPTIONS FOR THE /etc/mail/access DATABASE

Option	Description
OK	Accept mail even if other configuration rules would want to reject mail from the specified host or the user.
RELAY	Act as an SMTP mail relay for the specified host. In other words, accept mail intended for users on the specified domain and also allow users on the specified domain to send mail via the server. Do not reject mail from the specified domain even if other rules would like you to do so.
REJECT	Reject all (incoming/outgoing) mail for the specified domain.
DISCARD	Discard the message completely using the $#discard mailer. Discarded messages are accepted but silently kept undelivered so that the sender thinks they have been delivered.
501 <message>	Do not accept mail if sender address partially or fully matches the specified *user@host*.
553 <message>	Do not accept mail if sender address does not contain host name.
550 <message>	Do not accept mail for specified domain name.

Here is an example /etc/mail/access configuration:

```
Any-spam-maker.com       REJECT
client-domain.com        RELAY
annoying-company.com     DISCARD
dumbguy@dumb-net.com     501 You can't use this mail server.
```

Here all mail from any-spam-maker.com will be rejected; all incoming and outgoing mail to and from client-domain.com will be relayed; all mail from annoying-company.com will be accepted but silently discarded, and any mail from dumbguy@dumb-net.com will be rejected with the "You can't use this mail server" message.

Note that sendmail does not directly use the /etc/mail/access configuration file. It uses a DBM database version of the file. To create the necessary DBM file for your /etc/mail/access file, run the following command:

```
makemap hash /etc/mail/access < /etc/mail/access
```

This command creates the necessary DBM database file (such as /etc/mail/access.db) in the same directory. You do not need to restart the sendmail daemon any time you modify this file.

CREATING ALIASES FOR USERS WITH /etc/mail/aliases

This configuration file enables you to create an alias database for users. For example, say that you would like to create an alias called carol.godsave for a user called carol. You can do that using this configuration file, which has the following format:

```
alias name: comma-separated list of users
```

To create the carol.godsave alias, you can add a line in this configuration file as follows:

```
carol.godsave: carol
```

When sendmail receives mail for carol.godsave@yourdomain.com, it will be delivered to the carol account on your mail server. One of the commonly used functions of aliases is to create local groups. For example:

```
web-developers: keith, cynthea, jason
```

The preceding line defines an alias, web-developers, which can be used to send e-mail messages to the specified users.

The default /etc/mail/aliases file already contains a set of default aliases. Make sure you change them as needed. Also note that if you have a user with the same name as an alias, the e-mail will be sent to the user(s) specified in the alias. For example:

```
root: kabir
```

When mail is sent to root@nitec.com, even though there is a user account called root on the mail server, the mail will still be sent to user kabir. You can also chain aliases. For example:

```
root: kabir
kabir: mohammed
```

Here the alias root resolves to the alias kabir, which resolves to mohammed. So mail sent to root@localhost on my system can go to the mailbox of a user called mohammed.

Note that sendmail does not directly use the /etc/mail/aliases configuration file. It uses a DBM database version of the file. To create the necessary DBM file for your /etc/mail/aliases file, run the following command:

```
newaliases
```

This command creates the necessary DBM database file (such as /etc/mail/ aliases.db) in the same directory. You do not need to restart the sendmail daemon any time you modify this file.

Running `newaliases` is equivalent to running the sendmail `-bi` command.

MAPPING DOMAINS USING /etc/mail/domaintable

This configuration file can be used to create a domain name mapping database such as:

```
Yet-another-domain.com yourdomain.com
```

Here `yet-another-domain.com` has been mapped to yourdomain.com. So when mail is received for *user@yet-another-domain.com*, it is translated to *user@ yourdomain.com*. Note that the destination domain (`yourdomain.com`) must be a fully qualified domain name. Also note that the domain mapping in the domain table is reflected into headers; that is, this is done in ruleset 3.

Note that sendmail does not directly use the /etc/mail/domaintable configuration file. It uses a DBM database version of the file. To create the necessary DBM file for your /etc/mail/domaintable file, run the following command:

```
makemap hash /etc/mail/domaintable < /etc/mail/domaintable
```

This command creates the necessary DBM database file (such as /etc/mail/ domaintable.db) in the same directory. You do not need to restart the sendmail daemon any time you modify this file.

REROUTING MAIL FOR DOMAINS USING /etc/mail/mailertable

This configuration file can be used to create a database to override default mail routing for certain domains. The format of this file is as follows:

```
source-domain mailer:replacement-domain or user@host
```

For example:

```
visitor-01.mydomain.com  local:visitor1
```

When mail for `visitor-01.mydomain.com` arrives, it is rerouted to the local user visitor1. Note that you can use only the mailers that are specified in the /etc/sendmail.cf file using an "M" line. A quick look in the /etc/sendmail.cf file shows qsmtp, procmail, smtp, esmtp, smtp8, relay, usenet, uucp, uucp-ol, suucp, uucp-new, uucp-om, uucp-uuom, local, and prog to be defined as mailers.

Note that you can also specify partial domain names as the source domain name. For example:

```
.mydomain.com  smtp:mail-hub.mydomain.com
```

Here mail for `*.mydomain.com` hosts will be relayed to `mail-hub.mydomain.com` server via the SMTP mailer.

 You must have appropriate MX record for source domain or mail will never be delivered.

Consider another example:

```
ad-engine.com  smtp:kabir@integrationlogic.com
```

Here all mail for `ad-engine.com` will be delivered to user `kabir@integrationlogic.com` via the SMTP mailer as long as `ad-engine.com` is listed in the /etc/mail/sendmail.cw file.

Note that sendmail does not directly use the /etc/mail/mailertable configuration file. It uses a DBM database version of the file. To create the necessary DBM file for your /etc/mail/mailertable file, run the following command:

```
makemap hash /etc/mail/mailertable < /etc/mail/mailertable
```

This command creates the necessary DBM database file (for instance, /etc/mail/mailertable.db) in the same directory. You do not need to restart the sendmail daemon any time you modify this file.

SETTING UP MAIL RELAYS USING /etc/mail/relay-domains

The latest version of sendmail (v 8.9.x) denies unauthorized relaying of mail by default. In other words, if sendmail is not explicitly told to accept mail destined for another domain, it will refuse to do so. For example, say that you run the latest version of sendmail on a host called `mail.mydomain.com`. If someone from anywhere tries to use `mail.mydomain.com` to deliver mail to another SMTP server, your sendmail server will refuse such requests by default. This is done to eliminate mail relay abuse by people who send unsolicited e-mail messages.

To allow legitimate domains to use your sendmail server as a relay, you need to specify them in this file. You should add your own domain and any other friendly domains for which you want to allow relay operation. For example:

```
nitec.com
integrationlogic.com
ad-engine.com
```

You can also use IP addresses in the form of a network address or a full IP. To test the relay configuration, run:

```
echo '$=R' | sendmail -bt
```

This command should display all the allowed domains.

SETTING UP LOCAL DELIVERY DESTINATIONS: /etc/mail/sendmail.cw

You can use this file to specify the names of hosts and domains for which the sendmail server will receive e-mail. An example of this file is shown here:

```
nitec.com
ad-engine.com
classifiedworks.com
```

Here each line specifies a domain name that the sendmail server services.

CREATING VIRTUAL MAIL SERVERS USING /etc/mail/virtualtable

If you would like to provide mail support for multiple domains, you can set up virtual mail service using sendmail. For example, say that you would like to provide virtual mail service for a domain called yourclient.com. Here is how:

1. Add the domain (yourclient.com) in the /etc/mail/sendmail.cw file so that sendmail will accept mail for this host.

2. Add the domain (yourclient.com) in the /etc/mail/relay-domains file so that sendmail will relay messages for this domain.

To map the virtual domain users to one or more local accounts, use the /etc/mail/virtusertable file as follows:

```
virtual e-mail address   real e-mail address
```

Here are some examples:

```
webmaster@yourclient.com   mike
```

```
mike@yourclient.com        mike
info@yourclient.com        jason
jason@yourclient.com       jason
```

Here e-mail for virtual e-mail addresses such as `webmaster@yourclient.com` and `mike@yourclient.com` goes to local user mike, and similarly, mail for `info@yourclient.com` and `jason@yourclient.com` goes to another local user, jason. This provides `yourclient.com` with a mail server they didn't have. To the rest of the world, it appears that `yourclient.com` has a mail server. If you also do the `yourclient.com` domain's DNS service for this domain, you can make the entire process look very professional by doing the following things:

◆ Add an A record in the `yourclient.com` domain's DNS that points to your sendmail server. For example, if your sendmail server host's IP address is 192.168.1.10, you can add the following line in the DNS configuration file for the `yourclient.com` domain.

```
mail.yourclient.com.  IN   A   192.168.1.10
```

◆ Add an MX record in the `yourclient.com` domain's SOA record that points to `mail.yourclient.com`. For example:

```
IN   MX 5 mail.yourclient.com.
```

This makes the rest of the (unsuspecting) world think that `yourclient.com` has a real mail server, as long as you have sendmail set up with the virtual configuration discussed previously.

Web site clients of ISPs often request virtual mail service. In other words, people or companies that pay an ISP to do Web site hosting (`www.client-domain.com`) also often request to have virtual mail service. In such a case, creating a single /etc/mail/virtusertable is often unmanageable. For example, if you are hosting hundreds of domains, /etc/mail/virtusertable will be a point of human error every time you or your assistant administrator modify the file. In such a case, you can create a more manageable solution. For example, say you need two virtual mail services for two clients called `client-a.com` and `client-b.com`. Here is what you do:

◆ Create a separate virtual e-mail map file for each domain. Use a naming convention such as domain.ftr (.ftr is short for fake-to-real).

◆ Create an /etc/mail/client-a.ftr file, which contains the content of what will normally go in /etc/mail/virtusertable for this domain. For example, this file could look like the following:

```
user1@client-1.com  client1
webmaster@client-1.com   unix@home-town-isp.com
@client-1.com  client1
```

In this sample file, the `user1@client-1.com` address has been mapped to the local account client1, the `webmaster@client-1.com` has been mapped to a remote ISP account, and all other possible e-mail addresses for the domain have been mapped to the local account. The last entry is quite useful and often requested. It allows the `client-1.com` domain to use whatever e-mail address they want on their Web site or other business publications and advertising, and still get the mail in the right place. For example, if `www.client-1.com` publishes an e-mail address called `info@client-1.com`, anyone sending mail to that account is happily serviced by the client1 user.

◆ Now create the /etc/mail/client-b.ftr file for the second client. This file is likely to be similar to the previous example, but suppose that the `client-b.com` owner wants all e-mail addresses to be automatically mapped to her existing accounts in your home town ISP mail server. In such a case this map file will look as follows:

```
@client-b.com   %1@home-town-isp.com
```

◆ Now that you have two virtual user map files, you can create the final /etc/mail/virtusertable file using the following commands:

```
touch /etc/mail/virtusertable
cat *.ftr > /etc/mail/virtusertable
```

Here the first command creates the /etc/mail/virtusertable file if it does not already exist. The second command concatenates all the .ftr files to /etc/mail/virtusertable. This effectively creates the final /etc/mail/virtusertable.

◆ Now you can run the makemap program to create the database version of the file as follows:

```
makemap hash /etc/mail/virtusertable <
/etc/mail/virtusertable
```

As you can see in the preceding example, creating multiple virtual user map files can help you to keep track of individual domains quite easily. Any time you want to change a domain specific map, just modify the domain's ftr file and create the final /etc/mail/virtusertable file using the technique discussed here.

Because most mail client programs enable users to set outgoing "From:" lines to whatever they wish, you may not need to do anything to map outgoing traffic for virtual sites. However, if you wish to make sure outgoing mail from users of virtual mail sites translates to their virtual domains, you can use the /etc/mail/generic-stable file.

Take, for example, a virtual mail site called `classifiedworks.com`, for which you have an .ftr file such as /etc/mail/classifiedworks.ftr, which has the following line:

```
sales@classifiedworks.com   sheila
```

Here the `sales@classifiedworks.com` address is mapped to a local user called sheila. Now when sheila sends mail using the sendmail server, you want her mail to appear as `sheila@classifiedworks.com` and not `sheila@yourdomain.com`. In such a case, create a /etc/mail/genericstable file with the following line:

```
sheila   sales@classifiedworks.com
```

As you can see here we are reversing the content of virtusertable file. In the spirit of keeping domain-specific information separate, you may wish to create a separate reverse map file per domain. Let's say this file will have an extension called .rtf (real to fake). Once you have created such a file for each domain you do virtual mail service for, you can create a combined /etc/mail/genericstable file as follows:

```
touch /etc/mail/genericstable
cat *.rtf > /etc/mail/genericstable
```

Now run the makemap program to create the database version of this file:

```
makemap hash /etc/mail/virtusertable < /etc/mail/virtusertable
```

In summary, for each virtual mail domain, create a .ftr file that maps fake e-mail addresses to real ones and make another file to map real addresses to fake e-mail addresses. Once these files are made, you combine them to create a /etc/mail/virtusertable (for *.ftr) and /etc/mail/genericstable file (for *.rtf). Then run makemap as just shown to create the database versions of these files. This completes the process as long as you have each of the virtual domains listed in /etc/mail/sendmail.cw and /etc/mail/relay-domains files.

Testing Your sendmail Configuration

As you can see, you have quite a few configuration files to deal with to get sendmail working the way you want. Because there is a lot to configure, chances are high that something won't work exactly the way you want. Therefore I recommend that you do the following:

- ◆ Always back up your configuration before making any changes.
- ◆ Every time you make a change to your sendmail configuration, test it before proceeding too far.

Here you will see a few examples of how you can do testing on typical configuration issues.

Testing sendmail address rewrite rules

You can test how the sendmail rules behave. To perform such testing, run sendmail as follows:

```
sendmail -bt
```

This command runs sendmail in address mode and provides you with a prompt to interact with it. At the prompt you can enter a test command such as:

```
<rewrite rule #s>  <test address>
```

For example, to see what sendmail's rewrite rule 0 will do with kabir@nitec.com, run:

```
0 kabir@nitec.com
```

The output on my sendmail system is shown here:

```
ADDRESS TEST MODE (ruleset 3 NOT automatically invoked)
Enter <ruleset> <address>
> 0 kabir@nitec.com
rewrite: ruleset   0  input: kabir @ nitec . com
rewrite: ruleset 199  input: kabir @ nitec . com
rewrite: ruleset 199 returns: kabir @ nitec . com
rewrite: ruleset  98  input: kabir @ nitec . com
rewrite: ruleset  98 returns: kabir @ nitec . com
rewrite: ruleset 198  input: kabir @ nitec . com
rewrite: ruleset 198 returns: $# local $: kabir @ nitec . com
rewrite: ruleset   0 returns: $# local $: kabir @ nitec . com
```

As you can see, the kabir@nitec.com address is delivered using the local mailer. Consider another example. Say that you have the following /etc/mail/domaintable map:

```
ad-engine.com   nitec.com
```

So any mail destined for ad-engine.com should be rerouted to nitec.com. Here is a test:

```
ADDRESS TEST MODE (ruleset 3 NOT automatically invoked)
Enter <ruleset> <address>
> 3,0 kabir@nitec.com
rewrite: ruleset   3  input: kabir @ nitec . com
rewrite: ruleset  96  input: kabir < @ nitec . com >
```

```
rewrite: ruleset  96 returns: kabir < @ ad-engine . com . >
rewrite: ruleset   3 returns: kabir < @ ad-engine . com . >
rewrite: ruleset   0  input: kabir < @ ad-engine . com . >
rewrite: ruleset 199  input: kabir < @ ad-engine . com . >
rewrite: ruleset 199 returns: kabir < @ ad-engine . com . >
rewrite: ruleset  98  input: kabir < @ ad-engine . com . >
rewrite: ruleset  98 returns: kabir < @ ad-engine . com . >
rewrite: ruleset 198  input: kabir < @ ad-engine . com . >
rewrite: ruleset  90  input: < ad-engine . com > kabir < @ ad-
engine . com . >
rewrite: ruleset  90  input: ad-engine . < com > kabir < @ ad-
engine . com . >
rewrite: ruleset  90 returns: kabir < @ ad-engine . com . >
rewrite: ruleset  90 returns: kabir < @ ad-engine . com . >
rewrite: ruleset  95  input: < > kabir < @ ad-engine . com . >
rewrite: ruleset  95 returns: kabir < @ ad-engine . com . >
rewrite: ruleset 198 returns: $# esmtp $@ ad-engine . com . $: kabir
< @ ad-engine . com . >
rewrite: ruleset   0 returns: $# esmtp $@ ad-engine . com . $: kabir
< @ ad-engine . com . >
```

Here the address kabir@nitec.com is rewritten as kabir@ad-engine.com, and sendmail shows that it will deliver it via ESMTP (expensive SMTP) mailer because ad-engine.com is not listed in /etc/mail/sendmail.cw. If it were, the preceding test would show the following output:

```
ADDRESS TEST MODE (ruleset 3 NOT automatically invoked)
Enter <ruleset> <address>
> 3,0 kabir@ad-engine.com
rewrite: ruleset   3  input: kabir @ ad-engine . com
rewrite: ruleset  96  input: kabir < @ ad-engine . com >
rewrite: ruleset  96 returns: kabir < @ ad-engine . com . >
rewrite: ruleset   3 returns: kabir < @ ad-engine . com . >
rewrite: ruleset   0  input: kabir < @ ad-engine . com . >
rewrite: ruleset 199  input: kabir < @ ad-engine . com . >
rewrite: ruleset 199 returns: kabir < @ ad-engine . com . >
rewrite: ruleset  98  input: kabir < @ ad-engine . com . >
rewrite: ruleset  98 returns: kabir < @ ad-engine . com . >
rewrite: ruleset 198  input: kabir < @ ad-engine . com . >
rewrite: ruleset 198 returns: $# local $: kabir
rewrite: ruleset   0 returns: $# local $: kabir
```

Notice that I used 3,0 as the rule set because ruleset 3 is involved in the domain-table translation and the ruleset 0 is involved in parsing the address.

Testing /etc/mail/* database files

Any time you modify your files /etc/mail/access, /etc/mail/aliases, /etc/mail/ domaintable, /etc/mail/mailertable, /etc/mail/virtusertable, and so on, you should make sure sendmail can perform lookups properly. For example, say that you just created the following alias in the /etc/mail/alias file:

```
root: kabir
```

After running the newaliases command, you want to find out if sendmail can do appropriate alias lookups. To test a database lookup, run sendmail -bt and at the address test mode prompt, enter the following:

```
/map database name key
```

For example, to test the /etc/mail/aliases database for the alias root, I can run

```
/map aliases root
```

which shows the following output:

```
map_lookup: aliases (root) returns kabir
```

Using sendmail to see the SMTP transaction verbosely

You can also use sendmail to see how it delivers a message to the destination. For example:

```
sendmail -vt
```

Here the -vt option tells sendmail to be verbose and scan for To:, From:, Cc:, and Bcc: headers in the input. Once the preceding command is run, it waits for user input. At this point you can enter something like this:

```
To: kabir@integrationlogic.com
From: someone@somewhere.com
Subject: Testing sendmail

This is a test.
```

.

After entering a short message as shown here, press Ctrl+D to exit message entry mode. Sendmail will then display an SMTP transaction similar to the one shown here:

```
kabir@integrationlogic.com... Connecting to
mail.integrationlogic.com. via esmtp...
220 wormhole.integrationlogic.com ESMTP Sendmail 8.10.1/8.10.1; Sun,
21 Feb 1999 19:57:00 -0500
>> EHLO picaso.nitec.com
250-wormhole.integrationlogic.com Hello picaso.nitec.com
[206.171.50.50], pleased to meet you
250-EXPN
250-VERB
250-8BITMIME
250-SIZE
250-DSN
250-ONEX
250-ETRN
250-XUSR
250 HELP
>> MAIL From:<kabir@picaso.nitec.com> SIZE=77
250 <kabir@picaso.nitec.com>... Sender ok
>> RCPT To:<kabir@integrationlogic.com>
250 <kabir@integrationlogic.com>... Recipient ok
>> DATA
354 Enter mail, end with "." on a line by itself
>> .
250 TAA16439 Message accepted for delivery
kabir@integrationlogic.com... Sent
(TAA16439 Message accepted for delivery)
Closing connection to mail.integrationlogic.com.
>> QUIT
221 wormhole.integrationlogic.com closing connection
```

The lines that start with >> are sent by the local sendmail server (picaso.nitec.com) to the remote sendmail server (mail.integrationlogic.com). As you can see, this is very close to the transaction I demonstrated earlier via a Telnet connection.

Using the sendmail debug flag

You can use the -dX option (where X is a debug level) along with -bv to see what action sendmail takes for a particular address. For example:

```
sendmail -bv -d0 kabir@nitec.com
```

This produces the following output on my sendmail server:

```
Version 8.10.1
 Compiled with: MAP_REGEX LOG MATCHGECOS MIME7TO8 MIME8TO7
NAMED_BIND NETINET NETUNIX NEWDB NIS QUEUE SCANF SMTP USERDB XDEBUG

============ SYSTEM IDENTITY (after readcf) ============
     (short domain name) $w = picaso
 (canonical domain name) $j = picaso.nitec.com
        (subdomain name) $m = nitec.com
            (node name) $k = picaso.nitec.com
========================================================

kabir@nitec.com... deliverable: mailer local, user kabir
```

As you can see, the –d0 option causes sendmail to display various items of information about sendmail itself. The last line in the preceding output shows how sendmail will handle the given address. If you specify –d without any debug level number, you will see all the debugging information you ever wanted.

Using a test configuration file

When you are playing around with sendmail.cf, it is a good idea to create a test version of the /etc/sendmail.cf file and modify only the test copy. This way, you do not lose any working configuration. Here is how you can test a new configuration.

♦ Create a copy of /etc/sendmail.cf with a new name. Here I assume you call the test configuration /etc/sendmail-test.cf.

♦ To run sendmail with your new test configuration file, use the –C option. For example, /usr/sbin/sendmail –Csendmail-test.cf uses /etc/sendmail-test.cf.

♦ If you would like to use a different queue (that is, other than /var/spool/ mqueue) for the test configuration, use the –oQ option. For example, /usr/sbin/sendmail –Csendmail-test.cf –oQ/var/spool/test-mqueue uses the /var/spool/test-mqueue directory for the test configuration.

At this point, you should have sendmail configured as expected. Now consider a few security issues concerning your sendmail configuration.

Securing sendmail

Being one of the oldest mail servers, sendmail has had its share of security holes and blame. The recent version of sendmail has been released with strict security in mind.

Securing your configuration files

Beginning with version 8.9.*x*, sendmail has tightened the restrictions on configuration file permissions. For example, if I run `chmod -R 664 /etc/mail/*` to change the file permissions for the configuration files and then try to restart sendmail, I get the following error messages:

```
Starting sendmail: /etc/sendmail.cf: line 93: fileclass: cannot open
/etc/mail/sendmail.cw: Group writable directory

WARNING: Group writable directory /etc/mail
/etc/mail/virtusertable.db: could not create: Permission denied

WARNING: Group writable directory /etc/mail
/etc/mail/access.db: could not create: Permission denied

WARNING: Group writable directory /etc/mail
/etc/mail/domaintable.db: could not create: Permission denied

WARNING: Group writable directory /etc/mail
/etc/mail/mailertable.db: could not create: Permission denied
```

In general, you should do the following to make sure sendmail is safe to run in your system:

◆ Ensure that the /etc/sendmail.cf and /etc/mail/* files and directories are readable by only the superuser or the username you specified in the RunAsUser line in the /etc/sendmail.cf file. All these files and directories should be writable by the superuser only.

◆ Do not enable group write permission for any of the configuration files, directories, or any other file that sendmail needs to read.

Under no circumstances should you enable group write access for any of the configuration files. Although sendmail allows you to disable the file permission and ownership-related security features using the DontBlameSendmail option, I highly recommend that you fix the permission/ownership problem rather than disable the checks in sendmail. If you want to keep the security checks as they are, ensure that user home directories where .forward files are kept are not writable by any group. The .forward file itself should have a 644 (rw-r−r−) permissions setting. You should also make sure that any directory in the path of a file that sendmail reads has the group write access disabled. If you must use the DontBlameSendmail option to introduce security holes, read the documentation supplied with sendmail to know how to use this feature.

Once you have made sure that file/directory-level permissions are set properly and sendmail does not spit out any warning or error message because of permission/

ownership of files and directories, you should also make sure logging is properly enabled. By default, sendmail will write logs via syslogd, and therefore you should write the following line in your /etc/syslog.conf file.

```
mail.*              /var/log/maillog
```

You can change the log filename to your liking; typically this file is named mail-log or mail.log. Also make sure you that you have an entry such as the following in /etc/logrotate.d/syslog file.

```
/var/log/maillog {
    postrotate
        /usr/bin/killall -HUP syslogd
    endscript
  }
```

This command restarts syslogd after logrotate processes the /var/log/maillog file.

Ensuring a stricter mode of operating and privacy

You can force sendmail to enforce stricter adherence to the SMTP protocol when clients connect to your server, and you can also control how users interact with sendmail. This is done using an option line such as the following:

```
O PrivacyOptions=needvrfyhelo,restrictmailq,restrictqrun,goaway
```

The values for PrivacyOptions are shown in Table 11-3.

TABLE 11-3 PRIVACYOPTIONS FOR SENDMAIL

Option	Explanation
public	Allow open access.
needmailhelo	Client must use HELO or EHELO before issuing a MAIL command.
needexpnhelo	Client must use HELO or EHELO before issuing an EXPN command.
noexpn	Client cannot use EXPN command.
needvrfyhelo	Client must use HELO or EHELO before issuing a VRFY command.
novrfy	Client cannot use VRFY command.
notrn	Client cannot use ETRN command.

Continued

TABLE 11-3 PRIVACYOPTIONS FOR SENDMAIL *(Continued)*

Option	Explanation
noverb	Client cannot use VERB command.
restrictmailq	Restrict use of mailq command. When this option is set only the superuser and the owner and group users of the queue directory can run the mailq command.
restrictqrun	Restrict –q option. When this option is set, only the superuser and the owner of the queue directory can use this option.
noreceipts	Do not return success code upon success.
goaway	Do not allow SMTP status queries.
authwarnings	Insert X-Authentication-Warning: headers in messages.

You should take one other kind of security measure to protect sendmail from being abused. It is discussed in the following section.

Taking Antispam Measures

In this day and age of bulk unsolicited e-mail, your sendmail server may be vulnerable to abuse by outsiders. People who send out unsolicited e-mail messages to thousands of people often use someone else's mail server to do their dirty work. This is called the third-party mail relay vulnerability.

Dealing with third-party mail relay vulnerability

Until recently, sendmail allowed mail relaying for anyone by default. In other words, someone who is totally unrelated to you or your organization could use your sendmail server as an SMTP mail relay to send mail to someone else you don't know about. In such a case, both the sender and the recipient are unknown or unrelated to you or your organization. This was permissible formerly, as it provided mail administrators debugging capabilities to locate mail connectivity problems. However, the bulk e-mailers, or spammers, are now rampant on the Internet, and they seek out unprotected relays to do their large mailing jobs. This abuses your system resources and also subjects you or your organization to legal complications. Many U.S. states are now passing laws against unsolicited e-mail, and the parties involved may be financially responsible for damages.

If your mail server becomes involved in a legal matter related to unsolicited e-mail, handling the matter and proving your innocence might take additional legal and financial resources on your part. Also, if your server becomes involved in such a mailing, many recipients will simply assume that you are actively involved in this matter and are more than likely to send you hundreds of angry e-mail messages. They may also report you to a spammers blacklist. This could damage your reputation or that of your organization, and also interfere with your mail connectivity operations as many mail servers will check the spammers blacklist before they agree to exchange mail with your domain. Find out if your sendmail is vulnerable to such a relay attack.

One of the easiest ways to check your mail server for relay vulnerabilities is to go to the URL `http://maps.vix.com/tsi/ar-test.html` provided by Mail Abuse Prevention System (MAPS) Transport Security Initiative Web site. You can enter the hostname of your mail server in the target host entry box and click the GO button to determine if your mail server is vulnerable to relay attacks. Figure 11-2 shows that I am about to test my mail server at `mail.nitec.com`.

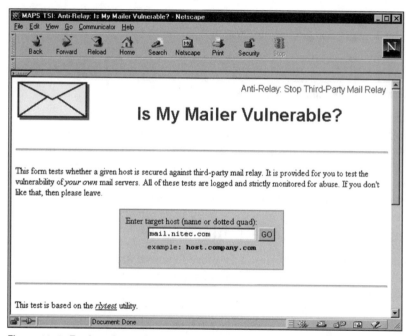

Figure 11-2: Testing picaso.nitec.com for third-party relay vulnerability

The site tests a host to determine whether it will relay third-party e-mail messages. The results of the test in Figure 11-3 show that `mail.nitec.com` does not relay.

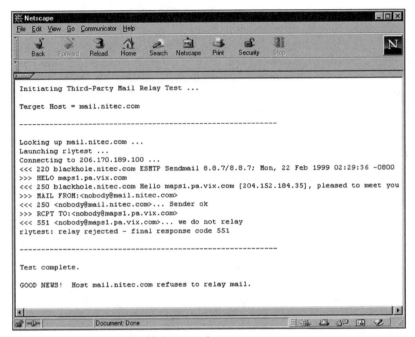

Figure 11-3: Output of the third-party relay test

As you can see, `mail.nitec.com` does not allow third-party relaying. Note that if you want to permit one or more domains to use your sendmail server for relay purposes, add them to the /etc/mail/relay-domains file. Also, if you would like to block known spammers from sending junk e-mail messages, use the /etc/mail/ access file to explicitly deny them access to your mail server.

Sending spammers to the black hole

You can use the Mail Abuse Prevention System's Realtime Blackhole List (RBL) to automatically block known spammers from using your sendmail server. The Web site for RBL is at: `http://maps.vix.com/`.

You can think of RBL as a database of known spammers. By querying the database, you can find out who the spammers are and reject mail services for those domains.

To understand how RBL works, consider an example. Assume that you want to know if a certain domain with IP address 127.0.0.2 is listed in RBL. Run:

```
nslookup -q=a 2.0.0.127.rbl.maps.vix.com
```

which will display the IP address for the preceding host (`2.0.0.127.rbl. maps.vix.com`) to be 127.0.0.2. Here you have taken the IP address 127.0.0.2 and turned it into a special host name by reversing the IP octets and appending rbl.maps.vix.com to the end to produce 2.0.0.127.rbl.maps.vix.com. Then you looked up an A (address) record for this host, which returned the IP address (127.0.0.2) you already knew. In other words, if you know the IP address of a possible spammer, you can simply perform the preceding test to see if you get an IP address in return. If you do get the same IP address back from such a lookup, it signifies that this IP is listed in RBL. You can perform another lookup to get a text record (txt) as follows:

```
nslookup -q=txt 2.0.0.127.rbl.maps.vix.com
```

This will display:

```
2.0.0.127.rbl.maps.vix.com        text = "Blackholed - see
<URL:http://maps.vix.com/cgi-bin/lookup?127.0.0.2>"
```

If the IP address you use to create the special hostname is not listed in RBL, you do not get any response for either the A (address) or TXT (text) records and can assume that this IP is not listed. Because RBL supplies the 127.0.0.2 IP address for testing purposes, it is listed in the RBL and hence you get the preceding responses in name server queries.

So MAPS RBL is a DNS-based spam checking and blocking system you can query to determine if a certain IP address is blocked as spammer or not. You can use RBL two ways. You can simply sign an agreement with MAPS RBL, transfer the entire database onto a local host, and create a local RBL for your own use. Or you can query the master RBL database on a case-by-case basis. The latest version of sendmail (8.9.*x*) comes with RBL. The Red Hat Linux RPM available for the latest version enables RBL in /etc/sendmail.cf, so you do not have to do anything to configure it. Here is how you can test the RBL configuration in your sendmail. Run:

```
sendmail -bt
```

At the address test mode prompt, enter:

```
.D{client_addr}127.0.0.1
Basic_check_relay <>
```

The output looks like the following:

```
ADDRESS TEST MODE (ruleset 3 NOT automatically invoked)
Enter <ruleset> <address>
> .D{client_addr}127.0.0.1
> Basic_check_relay <>
rewrite: ruleset 190    input: < >
rewrite: ruleset 190 returns: OKSOFAR
```

This output tells you that the rewrite result was OKSOFAR because the address 127.0.0.1 (loopback address) is not blocked in RBL. Now duplicate the preceding test using 127.0.0.2 (the RBL-supplied test IP, which *is* blocked in RBL). You should see output similar to the following:

```
ADDRESS TEST MODE (ruleset 3 NOT automatically invoked)
Enter <ruleset> <address>
> .D{client_addr}127.0.0.2
> Basic_check_relay <>
rewrite: ruleset 190    input: < >
rewrite: ruleset 190 returns: $# error $@ 5 . 7 . 1 $: "Mail from "
127 . 0 . 0 . 2 " refused by blackhole site rbl.maps.vix.com. Email
from your server is blocked.  Contact your local Systems
Administrator or ISP."
```

As you can see, this IP is blackholed, or blacklisted, in RBL, and therefore send-mail will not allow this IP to relay messages.

You can also perform a real test using an autoresponder that Russell Nelson has put together. According to the autoresponder owner, you must send mail to nelson-rbl-test@crynwr.com from the server whose RBL blocking you wish to test. Expect one reply from ns.crynwr.com with the SMTP conversation. If you get another reply from linux.crynwr.com, your RBL setup is not working.

 TIP If you want to know which mail transactions are rejected because of RBL, you can simply run grep "maps.vix.com" /var/log/maillog to see the rejected requests.

Setting Up POP Mail Service

The Post Office Protocol (POP) is widely used to retrieve mail stored by an SMTP server. Like SMTP, this protocol is also very simple. Consider how a POP client retrieves mail from a POP server.

How does it work?

I will use a Telnet client to demonstrate this as I did for SMTP. Because POP server listens to TCP port 110, I can Telnet to my POP server, blackhole.nitec.com, as follows:

```
telnet blackhole.nitec.com 110
```

I am greeted with the following message from the POP server:

```
+OK POP3 blackhole.nitec.com v4.47 server ready
```

Then I type the following POP command to tell the server which user's mailbox I want to open.

```
USER kabir
```

It responds with the following message:

```
+OK User name accepted, password please
```

Then I enter the password for the user kabir using the following POP command:

```
PASS mypwd1
```

The POP server responds with the following message:

```
+OK Mailbox open, 3 messages
```

As you can see, I have three messages on the server. I produce a listing of the messages using the following POP command:

```
LIST
```

The POP server replies as follows:

```
+OK Mailbox scan listing follows
1 1387
2 588
3 590
```

To retrieve one of these messages (#3), I enter the following POP command:

```
RETR 3
```

The server return the message with the following response code:

```
+OK 590 octets
Return-Path: <kabir@nitec.com>
Received: from nitec.com (picaso.nitec.com [206.171.50.51])
        by blackhole.nitec.com (8.8.7/8.8.7) with ESMTP id KAA01647
        for <sales@nitec.com>; Mon, 22 Feb 1999 10:05:39 -0800
Message-ID: <36D19B4D.969597E6@nitec.com>
```

```
Date: Mon, 22 Feb 1999 10:00:45 -0800
From: Mohammed Kabir <kabir@nitec.com>
X-Mailer: Mozilla 4.5 [en] (WinNT; I)
X-Accept-Language: en
MIME-Version: 1.0
To: sales@nitec.com
Subject: TEST 2
Content-Type: text/plain; charset=us-ascii
Content-Transfer-Encoding: 7bit
Status:

THIS IS TEST 2
.
```

As you can see, the entire POP transaction is quite simple. Now see how you can set up your system with POP support.

 Read RFC 1939 to learn more about POP3.

Installing a POP3 server

The latest version of the POP protocol is 3, hence you want to install a POP3 server. The IMAP package included in your Red Hat CD-ROM includes a POP3 server. So to install POP3, just install the IMAP package using the usual RPM-ivh *package name* command.

Configuring POP3 service

Once you have installed the server, you need to modify the /etc/inetd.conf file so that you have a line such as the following:

```
pop-3   stream  tcp     nowait  root    /usr/sbin/tcpd  ipop3d
```

If you have a pop-2 line, you can comment it out, as POP2 is not widely used and most recent POP clients support POP3. Once you have set up the preceding line in /etc/inetd.conf, you need to check the /etc/services file to make sure you have the following lines:

```
pop-3   110/tcp  # PostOffice V.3
pop     110/tcp  # PostOffice V.3
```

Once you have checked these two files, you can restart the inetd daemon using killall –HUP inetd to allow it to listen for POP3 requests on TCP port 110. When requests for POP3 connections come to the system, the inetd daemon will launch the ipop3d daemon to handle the requests. Your POP3 server is now ready to service requests. However, if you would like to enhance system security, you might want to limit access to your POP3 server using the /etc/hosts.allow and /etc/hosts.deny files used by the TCP wrapper (tcpd). See Chapter 18 for details.

Configuring SMTP/POP Mail Clients

Once you have both SMTP and POP3 servers configured, you need to set up mail client software for your users. If your users access their mail by Telneting to the mail server, you need to install one or more mail client packages such as mail, pine, and procmail. People who use Telnet to access their mail can use the mail forwarding feature quite easily.

For example, if a user wants to send her mail to a different account or to another mail server, she can add a .forward file in her home directory to make sendmail deliver mail to the requested address. The format of the .forward file is quite simple. To forward all mail for a user called mrfrog to mrfrog@freemail-domain.net, you edit ~mrfrog/.forward such that the mrfrog@freemail-domain.net address is in a line by itself. Also make sure that the file permissions for .forward allow only the owner to read and write the file; everyone else should have only read access to it.

In most cases, however, users access mail via a Windows machine running a POP3 client. To enable users to configure a typical Windows POP3/SMTP mail client, all you need to supply each user is the following information:

- ◆ Username
- ◆ Password
- ◆ Incoming POP3 mail server IP or host name
- ◆ Outgoing SMTP mail server IP or host name

Note that you will have to permit such clients to use your sendmail server as a relay, or else the client will not be able to send mail out. For example, if your mail server is accessed via America Online, you will have to add aol.com to your /etc/mail/relay-domains.

Commercial Alternatives

Although I think that the open source sendmail server is quite suitable for almost all situations, your organization may have requirements that will not permit use of sendmail as the primary mail server software. For example, if the software policy for your organization requires that all software in use by your organization be commercially supported by a vendor, you may have to use a commercial version of sendmail, as it is directly supported by Sendmail, Inc. Here are some alternatives to the open source sendmail server.

Sendmail Pro

Sendmail Pro is the commercial version of the open source sendmail server. It comes with enhancements and provides commercial-grade support that you expect from a reliable vendor. You can find more information on this product at the following URL: http://www.sendmail.com/.

Don't confuse http://www.sendmail.org/ with http://www.sendmail.com/. The first is a Web site maintained by the Sendmail Consortium, and the second is the Web site for Sendmail, Inc.

qmail

This qmail package claims to be the modern replacement for the open source sendmail. From what I've heard from other system administrators, it is a breeze to set up and also provides great integration with mailing list software. You can download an RPM package version of this software from the following URL: http://www.qmail.org/.

If you want to use a mailing list software package with sendmail, you should consider Majordomo, which can be found at http://www.greatcircle.com/majordomo/.

Summary

In this chapter, you learned to set up your Red Hat Linux server as an SMTP and POP3 mail server. You learned how SMTP and POP3 work; how to use sendmail server software to create a robust SMTP mail server; and how to use the POP3 server in the IMAP package to create a POP3 server for users to retrieve mail messages.

Chapter 12

Web Service

IN THIS CHAPTER

- How to compile, configure, and install the Apache Web server
- How to configure Apache for CGI support
- How to configure Apache for server-side includes
- How to support virtual Web service using Apache
- How to use Apache as a proxy server
- How to use HTTP authentication with Apache
- How to monitor the Apache server
- How to log hits and errors with Apache
- How to enhance your Web site security
- How to use SSL with Apache for secure transactions

FOR THE PAST FEW YEARS, approximately 50 percent of the world's Web sites have been running on the Apache Web server. Apache has been the number one Web server since 1996. According to surveys by a well-known company called Netcraft (http://www.netcraft.com/), Apache and its derivative Web servers have a clear lead over commercial Web servers such as those from Microsoft and Netscape. So it is no surprise that Red Hat ships Apache as the default Web server in the official CD-ROM distribution. In this chapter you will learn how to configure and manage the Apache Web server.

I must confess that covering all aspects of Apache in a single chapter is virtually impossible because of size constraints. Therefore I discuss only the major configuration and management issues related to Apache. If you require a more in-depth coverage of the Apache Web server, please consider *The Apache Server Bible* or *Apache Server Administrator's Handbook*, published by IDG Books Worldwide. The author of both of these books is also yours truly!

System Requirements for Apache

Apache can be run on just about any computer capable of running a recent version of the Red Hat Linux operating system. However, just being able to run Apache might not be a practical goal, especially if you are planning on running a high-performance Web server. In order to create a stable platform for Apache, you should pay attention to the following system requirements.

The ANSI C compiler

If you plan on compiling Apache on your Red Hat Linux system, you need to have an ANSI C compiler. I recommend the GNU C compiler (gcc) from the Free Software Foundation (FSF) that is already included with your Red Hat distribution. However, make sure that you have gcc version 2.7.2.*x* or above. On the other hand, if you plan on installing just prebuilt binary files, you do not need to have a C compiler on the target system. I highly recommend compiling your own copy of Apache because then you can customize as you see fit.

Sufficient disk space

The standard Apache source distribution is roughly 5–6 megabytes (MB). The Apache Group recommends that you have 12MB of temporary disk space for compilation purposes. However, you do not need the source if you are going to install just a prebuilt binary distribution. The size of binary distributions will vary depending on the operating system, but it is unlikely to exceed the 5–6MB limit. So either way, for the Apache software itself you need roughly 5–6MB of disk space.

If you plan to install other third-party modules such as mod_fastcgi, mod_perl, or mod_php, you will need additional disk space.

Although Apache itself might take little disk space, you may have to carefully consider log space requirements if you install Apache on a high-traffic site. A high-traffic site is likely to produce a great number of server log entries that could require a lot of disk space. For example, a typical log entry might take approximately 80 bytes of disk space. If you expect to get about a hundred thousand hits every 24 hours, for example, your Apache access log file might grow by eight million bytes per day. So plan ahead and allocate enough log space for Apache.

Sufficient RAM

Sufficient RAM is probably the most important preinstallation requirement. Apache runs in a "pool-of-servers" mode, which means that multiple instances of Apache server processes (httpd) run to service requests. Each of these server processes uses approximately the same amount of RAM. The number of the server processes that are running on your system is configurable via Apache directives such as MinSpareServers, MaxSpareServers, StartServers, and so on. You have to calculate how much RAM you need by multiplying the number of maximum server processes you want to run at any given time with the amount of RAM required by each server process. The formula looks like:

```
RAM for Apache = Maximum number of Apache processes allowed
                 X
                 RAM required by a single Apache process
```

This gives you a rough but fairly good idea about how much RAM you need. My Red Hat 5.2 Linux system running the standard Apache server (that is, built straight out of the source distribution) takes approximately 1.5MB per Apache server process. So if I want to run at most ten Apache processes (set using the MaxSpareServers directive), I need 15MB of RAM just for Apache plus whatever is required by the OS and other server processes running on the system.

Remember that the memory requirements per Apache server process vary from platform to platform, and also it is likely that you will increase the memory requirements when adding third-party modules into your Apache processes. For example, mod_perl certainly makes your Apache process larger. In fact, each mod_perl-enabled Apache process has copies of your Perl CGI scripts in it, which increases the RAM requirements. So if you plan on using mod_perl with Apache, make sure you have plenty of RAM. In such a case, do not forget to calculate the amount of memory required by the CGI scripts that you plan to use with mod_perl.

Other requirements

Some of the support scripts, such as dbmmanage and apxs, use the Perl 5 interpreter. I recommend that you download the latest Perl interpreter from the following Web site: http://www.perl.com/.

Apache 1.3 also can take advantage of the Dynamic Shared Object (DSO) mechanism for loading and unloading modules at runtime. Although DSO support is available for Linux, I personally do not use DSO options when compiling Apache, because DSO support apparently slows down the execution of the server by about five percent or so.

Getting Apache from the Net

Although the official copy of Red Hat Linux comes with an RPM-packaged version of a prebuilt Apache Web server, you may still want to download the latest version from the official Apache Web site at the following URL: http://www.apache.org/.

If you are not in the United States, it might be faster to get Apache source and binaries from a nearby Apache mirror site. Use the URL http://www.apache.org/dyn/closer.cgi to locate a good mirror site near you. Here I assume that you are getting the software from the official Apache Web site. The software (both source and binaries) can be found at http://www.apache.org/dist/.

You will see many recent versions of Apache distributions archived using various compression programs. For example:

```
Apache_1.3.12.tar.gz
Apache_1.3.12.tar.Z
```

These are samples of Apache Version 1.3.12 source distribution. The difference is in the size, due to differences in compression technique. Download one of these files. No matter which format you choose to download, all you need are the tar utility and the gnuzip or gzip utility to decompress the files. For example, to decompress the Apache 1.3.12.tar.gz file on my Red Hat 5.2 system, I use the following command:

```
tar xvzf apache_1.3.12.tar.gz
```

Or I could use:

```
gzip -d apache_1.3.12.tar.gz
tar xvf apache_1.3.12.tar
```

which decompresses and extracts all the files in a subdirectory while keeping the relative path for each file intact.

The binaries are usually kept in a different directory where each operating system has a subdirectory of its own. It's a good idea to compile the Apache source yourself instead of using someone else's binary. When you use a downloaded binary file, you are letting someone else (possibly someone you don't know) decide which modules and features are enabled in your Web server. Occasionally, downloaded binary files may not work at all on your system, because there could be incompatibilities between the library files required by the binary and what is available on your system. If this is acceptable or if compiling is not an option for you, make sure the site from which you download the binaries is reputable. In this chapter, I assume that you would like to compile your own copy. I discuss the process involved in creating a custom Apache server in the following sections.

Creating a Custom Apache Server

Once you have extracted the source into a directory of your choice, you are ready to configure and compile your custom copy of Apache. You can configure Apache manually, or you can use the new Autoconf-style interface called APACI. I prefer the APACI method because it is quicker and requires less knowledge of Apache configuration details; in other words, you have to read fewer README and INSTALL files to get the job done. Hence it is also the recommended method.

Configuring Apache source using APACI

In the top-level directory of the source distribution, you will find a script called configure, which is what you need for configuring Apache using APACI. You can run this script as follows:

```
./configure --help
```

This enables you to see all the available options.

The first step in configuring Apache is to determine where you want to install it. For example, to install Apache in a directory called /usr/local/apache, you can run the configuration script as follows:

```
./configure --prefix=/usr/local/apache
```

This installs all Apache files under the specified directory. However, if for some reason you need to install certain files outside the directory, you can use the – prefix options:

`--exec-prefix=DIR`: Installs architecture-dependent files in DIR.

`--bindir=DIR`: Installs executables in DIR.

`--sbindir=-DIR`: Installs sys-admin executables in DIR.

`--libexecdir=DIR`: Installs program executables in DIR.

`--mandir+DIR`: Installs manual (man) pages in DIR.

`--sysconfdir=DIR`: Installs configuration files in DIR.

`--datadir=DIR`: Installs read-only data files in DIR.

`--includedir=DIR`: Installs include files in DIR.

`--localstatedir=DIR`: Installs modifiable data files in DIR.

`--runtimedir=DIR`: Installs runtime data in DIR.

`--logfiledir=DIR`: Installs logfile data in DIR.

`--proxycachedir=DIR`: Installs proxy cache data in DIR.

`--compat`: Installs according to the Apache 1.2 installation paths.

For example, if you keep your logs in a separate partition called /logs and you want Apache to write logs there, you can run the configure script as follows:

```
./configure --prefix=/usr/local/apache --logfiledir=/logs
```

If you want to be 100 percent sure about which directory each file is going to be installed in, use the --layout option. For example:

```
./configure --prefix=/usr/local/apache  --layout
```

This command shows the following output:

```
Configuring for Apache, Version 1.3.12

Installation paths:
prefix: /usr/local/apache
exec_prefix: /usr/local/apache
bindir: /usr/local/apache/bin
sbindir: /usr/local/apache/bin
libexecdir: /usr/local/apache/libexec
mandir: /usr/local/apache/man
sysconfdir: /usr/local/apache/etc
datadir: /usr/local/apache/share
includedir: /usr/local/apache/include
localstatedir: /usr/local/apache/var
runtimedir: /usr/local/apache/var/run
logfiledir: /usr/local/apache/var/log
proxycachedir: /usr/local/apache/var/proxy

Compilation paths:
HTTPD_ROOT: /usr/local/apache
SUEXEC_BIN: /usr/local/apache/sbin/suexec
SHARED_CORE_DIR: /usr/local/apache/libexec
DEFAULT_PIDLOG: var/run/httpd.pid
DEFAULT_SCOREBOARD: var/run/httpd.scoreboard
DEFAULT_LOCKFILE: var/run/httpd.lock
DEFAULT_XFERLOG: var/log/access_log
DEFAULT_ERRORLOG: var/log/error_log
TYPES_CONFIG_FILE: etc/mime.types
SERVER_CONFIG_FILE: etc/httpd.conf
ACCESS_CONFIG_FILE: etc/access.conf
RESOURCE_CONFIG_FILE: etc/srm.conf
```

The --layout option enables you to verify the directory structure before it is actually used. If you are upgrading Apache from 1.2 and you want to keep the old directory structure, you can use --compat, which uses the old-style directory structure.

TIP   If you find yourself constantly overriding the default layout, you can create a custom layout in the configure.layout file. The simplest way to create a custom layout is to edit the configure.layout file in the top-level Apache source distribution. Copy the existing Apache layout starting with the <Layout apache> line and ending with </Layout>. Then change the directory paths as you please and replace the layout name from Apache to whatever you like. You can then use this layout with the - -with-layout=<*name of your custom layout*> option.

The next step in configuring Apache is to decide if you want to use the standard module configuration provided by the developers of Apache. If this is your first time compiling Apache, you might stick to the standard configuration just to get used to the entire process.

The standard or default configuration file for APACI-based configuration is stored in the src subdirectory. It is called Configuration.apaci and is shown in Listing 12-1.

Listing 12-1: The default configuration file without the comments and blank lines

```
EXTRA_CFLAGS= `$(SRCDIR)/apaci`
EXTRA_LDFLAGS=
EXTRA_LIBS=
EXTRA_INCLUDES=
EXTRA_DEPS=

Rule SHARED_CORE=default
Rule SHARED_CHAIN=default
Rule SOCKS4=no
Rule SOCKS5=no
Rule IRIXNIS=no
Rule IRIXN32=yes
Rule PARANOID=no
Rule WANTHSREGEX=default

AddModule modules/standard/mod_env.o
AddModule modules/standard/mod_log_config.o
AddModule modules/standard/mod_mime.o
AddModule modules/standard/mod_negotiation.o
AddModule modules/standard/mod_status.o
```

```
AddModule modules/standard/mod_include.o
AddModule modules/standard/mod_autoindex.o
AddModule modules/standard/mod_dir.o
AddModule modules/standard/mod_cgi.o
AddModule modules/standard/mod_asis.o
AddModule modules/standard/mod_imap.o
AddModule modules/standard/mod_actions.o
AddModule modules/standard/mod_userdir.o
AddModule modules/standard/mod_alias.o
AddModule modules/standard/mod_access.o
AddModule modules/standard/mod_auth.o
AddModule modules/standard/mod_setenvif.o
```

There are three types of information in this file. The EXTRA_* lines are used by the configure script to add extra flags in the Makefile, which, in turn, is needed to compile Apache. The Rule lines are used by the script to turn certain functions on or off. And the AddModule lines enable Apache modules that should be part of your Apache executable.

MAKEFILE CONFIGURATION OPTIONS

For most systems, you do not need to modify any of these extra flags. Also note that the configure script tries to figure out which C compiler you use on your system. In case you think it might fail to find your compiler for some reason, you can uncomment the #CC= line and send it to your compiler:

```
CC = gcc.
```

In such a case, you also might have to supply extra compiler flags in the following lines:

```
EXTRA_CFLAGS=
EXTRA_LDFLAGS=
```

If your system requires special libraries or include files, you can specify them using the following lines:

```
EXTRA_LIBS=
EXTRA_INCLUDES=
```

Note that the configure script automatically sets code optimization to –02. If you want a different setting, first uncomment the following line:

```
#OPTIM=-02
```

Then, change the value to the value you desire, if your C compiler supports it. For most installations, the default settings work just fine, just as they did for me on a Red Hat 5.2 Linux system.

RULES CONFIGURATION OPTIONS

As with the Makefile flags, you should not need to modify the `Rules` lines. However, if you must modify these rules, you can use the configure script. To enable a rule, use the `--enable-rule=NAME` option, where `NAME` is the name of the rule. For example:

```
./configure --prefix=/usr/local/apache --enable-rule=SOCKS4
```

Similarly, you can disable a rule using the `--disable-rule` option.

The first two `Rule` lines (`SHARED_CORE`, `SHARED_CHAIN`) relate to Dynamic Shared Object (DSO) support and should be left as is.

The SOCKS4 functionality is turned off by default. SOCKS is a control system in which all TCP/IP network application data flow through the SOCKS daemon. This enables SOCKS to collect, audit, screen, filter, and control the network data. Most people use it as a software-based firewall. If you want to make Apache SOCKS4-compliant, you need to turn this feature on by setting it to Yes using the `--enable-rule=SOCKS4` option in the command line of the configure script. Also, make sure you modify the `EXTRA_LIBS` setting in the Makefile configuration area, to point to your SOCKS4 library file. Similarly, if you want SOCKS5 support, turn it on by setting it to Yes using the `--enable-rule=SOCKS5` option in the command line of the configure script.

The `IRIXNIS` rule is for people who want to use Apache on a Silicon Graphics system running IRIX and NIS. The `IRIXN32` option is also meaningful for systems running IRIX operating system. It tells Apache to use n32 libraries instead of o32 libraries.

The `PARANOID` rule allows you to see if any Apache module is executing any shell scripts during configuration. Apache 1.3 allows modules to execute custom shell scripts when the configure script is run. This rule is turned off by default. If you want to enable it, set this to Yes using the `--enable-rule=PARANOID` option in the command line of the configure script.

The `WANTHSREGEX` option is automatically set to Default. This command specifies that you want to use the regular expression package included with Apache. If you'd rather use your own system's regular expression package, however, you can set this option to No using the `--disable-rule=WANTHSREGEX` option in the command line of the configure script.

MODULES CONFIGURATION OPTIONS

Add the default set of modules to the standard Apache using the `AddModule` lines. The modules are listed in reverse priority order. If you plan to add other modules, do not manually modify this file. I recommend using the configure script to add, remove, enable, or disable modules.

To enable a module that is not already enabled by default, you can use the `--enable-module=NAME` option. To disable a module, use the `--disable-module=NAME` option. For example, to disable CGI module you can use:

```
./configure—prefix=/usr/local/apache—disable-module=cgi
```

Or, to enable the user-tracking module, you can run configure as follows:

```
./configure—prefix=/usr/local/apache—enable-module=usertrack
```

Once run the configure script successfully using one or more of the options discussed previously, you are ready to compile and install Apache.

Compiling and installing Apache

Compiling and installing Apache is very simple once you have run the configure script. Just run the `make` command from the top-level directory of your Apache source distribution. If everything goes well, you will not see any error messages. In such a case, you can install Apache by running the `make install` command. If you get error(s) when running `make`, note the error message(s) and go through the configuration steps again. If you still have problems, go to the Apache Web site and read the FAQ to find out if there is something you need to do to get Apache running. In my experience, the standard Apache source distribution compiles on Red Hat without a single hitch. So if Apache is not working at this point, double-check your steps before you seek help from Usenet newsgroups such as `comp.infosystems.www.servers.unix` and `linux.redhat`.

Once you have compiled and installed Apache, you can run Make Clean to remove all the object files that get created during compilation.

Compiling and installing Apache support tools

When you configure Apache with the configure (or config.status) script, it automatically installs a set of support tools. So you do not need to do anything extra to install any of the support tools. The only exception is the logresolve.pl script. You need to install this Perl script manually. Also, if you do not want to install any of the support tools, you can supply the `--without-support` option when running the configure (or config.status) script. I highly recommend leaving the default alone because the support tools are very helpful in administering various aspects of Apache. In the following section, you learn more about these support tools.

APACHECTL

Using this script, you can now control Apache. To learn about the command line options it accepts, just run it without any command line options or use the help option as follows:

```
/path/to/apache/bin/apachectl help
```

To start the server, just run the script as follows:

```
/path/to/apache/bin/apachectl start
```

To stop the server, just run the script as follows:

```
/path/to/apache/bin/apachectl stop
```

To restart the server, just run the script as follows:

```
/path/to/apache/bin/apachectl restart
```

To perform a graceful restart, run the script as follows:

```
/path/to/apache/bin/apachectl graceful
```

For the curious, the command sends a SIGHUP signal, and the command sends a SIGUSR1 signal to Apache. Because the latter is user defined (that is, defined by the Apache developers), it is much more agreeable to the running server.

To get the full status of the running server, run the script as follows:

```
/path/to/bin/apachectl fullstatus
```

You get a page full of information showing various server status data. It is probably a good idea to redirect the status information to a file, because it is likely to be more than a screenful. Here is how you can redirect the data to a file called /TMP/STATUS:

```
/path/to/apache/sbin/dir/apachectl fullstatus > /tmp/status
```

To test the server configuration files for syntax errors, you can run the apachectl script as follows:

```
/path/to/apache/sbin/dir/apachectl configtest
```

AB
This utility enables you to run benchmarks on your Web server. Just run the program without any options to find out about the command line options it takes.

APXS
This utility helps in compiling modules for dynamic loading. It is not useful unless you have Dynamic Module Support (DSO) enabled on your Apache server, and your operating system supports DSO.

LOGRESOLVE.PL

This Perl script does not get installed automatically, but you can manually copy it in an appropriate place from the src/support directory of your Apache source distribution. This script resolves IP addresses found in an Apache log file to their hostnames. This script also spawns child processes and uses the parent process to provide caching support to speed up DNS lookups, which are often very slow.

LOGRESOLVE

This utility works practically the same way as the logresolve.pl script. However, this executable program gets installed by default. To learn about the command line syntax, just run it with -h option.

HTPASSWD

This utility enables you to create username/password pairs for per-directory authentication schemes. To see the usage syntax, run the program without any arguments. Unlike the previously mentioned support tools, this utility gets installed in the bin directory of your Apache server installation directory.

DBMMANAGE

This utility enables you to manage DBM-based username/password pairs for DBM-based authentication schemes. To see the usage syntax, run the program without any arguments. This utility is also installed in the bin directory of your Apache server installation directory.

HTDIGEST

This utility enables you to create username/password pairs for MD5 digest-based authentication schemes. To see the usage syntax, run the program without any arguments. This utility is also installed in the bin directory of your Apache server installation directory.

Customizing Apache with optional or third-party modules

I recommend that you try out the standard Apache first before you add any third-party modules. You can thus make sure that everything is working before you add any third-party code to the picture. Once you have the standard Apache running on your system, you can customize it as you please. In such a case, you no longer need to run the configure script in the same manner you did the first time. A script called config.status is automatically created when you run the configure script. The config.status script maintains a history of the options you supplied to configure script. For example, if you run the configure script once as follows:

```
./configure --prefix=/usr/local/apache --disable-module=cgi
```

then the config.status script will look like this:

```
#!/bin/sh
##
##  config.status -- APACI auto-generated
##                   configuration restore script
##
##  Use this shell script to rerun the APACI
##  configure script for restoring your configuration.
##  Additional parameters can be supplied.
##

./configure \
"--prefix=/usr/local/apache" \
"--disable-module=cgi" \
"$@"
```

Let's say that now you want to enable the usertrack module. You can run configure again as follows:

```
./configure --prefix=/usr/local/apache \
--disable-module=cgi -enable-module=usertrack
```

Or you can run:

```
./config.status --enable-module=usertrack
```

As you can see, config.status makes configure easier to work with. I recommend you use it for all future compilations. Also note that if you decide to start fresh, you can just delete config.status and run configure to create a brand new config.status script.

ADDING FASTCGI SUPPORT

Before you can add FastCGI support to your Apache, you have to download the latest FastCGI module (mod_fastcgi.c) from the FastCGI Web site, http://www.fastcgi.com/.

The first step is to extract the FastCGI module distribution. Then, copy or move the distribution to the SRC/MODULES/FASTCGI directory of your Apache source distribution. Then, change directories to your top-level Apache source distribution directory and run the configuration script as follows:

```
./configure \
-activate-module=src/modules/fastcgi/libfastcgi.a
```

If you have previously compiled Apache using APACI and want to keep the existing configuration along with the new mod_fastcgi.c module update, run the following command instead:

```
./config.status \
-activate-module=src/modules/fastcgi/libfastcgi.a
```

Now, rebuild the Apache server executable (httpd) by running the make command. If you get no error messages, run the make command again with the install option to reinstall the Apache executable.

Once you have built the new Apache executable, you should check to verify that the mod_fastcgi.c module is included in the executable. The easiest way to verify this is to run the following command:

```
/path/to/your/apache/httpd -l
```

Make sure you use the appropriate path instead of /path/to/your/apache as shown earlier. You should see mod_fastcgi.c listed in the output produced by the -l option. If you don't see it, you have missed one or more steps in compiling Apache, so go back and verify your steps.

ADDING AN EMBEDDED PERL INTERPRETER IN APACHE

Make sure you have the latest Perl installed on your system. Check the version number of your installed Perl using the perl -v command and verify with the latest version available at http://www.perl.com/. If you don't have the latest version, I recommend that you download and install it. I am using version 5.005_002 for this book.

Once you have installed the latest Perl on your target system, you need to download the latest version of mod_perl from http://perl.apache.org/.

Also, many of the tests used for verifying a mod_perl installation use the LWP Perl modules, so it might be a good idea to install LWP modules along with LWP's prerequisite modules. If you have installed Perl properly, you can install the LWP modules quite easily using the CPAN module. Run CPAN as follows:

```
perl -MCPAN -install LWP
```

Once you have completed these prerequisite tasks, you can install the mod_perl module.

There are two parts to installing mod_perl support into your Apache server. First, you must update your Perl distribution with mod_perl and then update Apache distribution with mod_perl. To make things simpler, I will also assume that you have downloaded and decompressed the mod_perl source distribution from http://perl. apache.org/ into a directory such that both Apache source and mod_perl source share the same top-level directory as their parent directory. In other words, both

Apache source and mod_perl source distributions are subdirectories of a single parent directory. For the installation example discussed here, let's assume that the Apache server is in /usr/local/build/apache-1.3.12 and the mod_perl source distribution is in /usr/local/build//usr/local/build/mod_perl-1.16. (Note that your version numbers for both Apache and mod_perl may vary.) Now change directories to the source distribution (/usr/local/build//usr/local/build/ mod_perl-1.16), and run the following command:

```
perl Makefile.PL APACHE_SRC=../apache-1.3.12/src \
DO_HTTPD=1  \
USE_APACI=1  \
PREP_HTTPD=1  \
EVERYTHING=1
```

This command builds the Perl side of mod_perl and also prepares the Apache side of mod_perl. Once you have run the preceding command, you can run the following commands, as long no error messages stop you:

```
make
make test
make install
```

Now you have to complete the Apache side of the mod_perl installation. If you are compiling Apache for the first time, you can run the following command from the Apache source distribution directory:

```
./configure -prefix=/path/to/where/you/want/to/install/apache \
—activate-module=src/modules/perl/libperl.a
```

If you have already compiled Apache, however, you should use the following command instead:

```
./config.status—activate-module=src/modules/perl/libperl.a
```

This command preserves all the previous options that you supplied to configure command. Once you have run either version of the two preceding commands, you are ready to run the following commands:

```
make
make test
make install
```

These commands install Apache with mod_perl support. You can verify that mod_perl is part of your Apache executable (httpd) by using the httpd -l command.

ADDING PHP SUPPORT

Before you can install PHP support, make sure you have already compiled Apache at least once. When you are ready, download the latest PHP distribution from http://www.php.net/, extract it into an appropriate directory, and enter the top-level PHP distribution directory, running its own configure script as follows:

```
./configure \
--with-apache=/path/to/your/apache/distribution/directory
```

Once you have configured it with Apache, run the command followed by a if you do not get any compilation errors. This builds PHP on your system, and then you can proceed with the Apache part of this installation.

Change directories to your Apache source distribution and run the configure (or config.status) script as follows:

```
./configure -activate-module=src/modules/php3/libphp3.a
```

Once you have run the preceding command, run followed by a to install the PHP support in Apache.

Once you compile and install Apache, you are ready to get it up and running. In the following section, you learn how to do just that.

Getting Apache Up and Running

Every Apache source distribution comes with the following set of default configuration files:

- ◆ access.conf
- ◆ httpd.conf
- ◆ srm.conf
- ◆ magic
- ◆ mime.types

The last two files, magic and mime.types, should be left as is in most cases. The magic file is used for a special module called mod_mime_magic, and the mime.types file controls which MIME types are sent to the client for a given file extension. If for some reason you need to create additional MIME types for your server, I recommend you use the AddType directive instead of modifying this file.

The httpd.conf, access.conf, and the srm.conf files are the ones that you have to customize to create an appropriate Web server configuration. Although these are three different files, they share the same structure. In fact, you can put all the directives in httpd.conf and keep the other two files empty. In a future version, Apache

Group is likely to drop the requirements for configuration files to just one. However, because traditionally there have been three files, I assume that you go with the tradition as well. These text files have two types of information: optional comments and server directives. Lines that contain a # symbol as the first character are comments; these comments have no purpose for the server software, but act as a form of documentation for the server administrator. You can add as many comment lines as you want; the server simply ignores all comments when it parses these files.

Except for the comments and blank lines, the server treats all other lines as either complete directives or parts of directives. While editing these files, you need to make certain decisions regarding how you want the server to behave. In the following sections, you learn what these directives mean and how you use them to customize your server.

Configuring httpd.conf

The httpd.conf file is the primary configuration file. It tells the server how it is to run. Listing 12-2 shows the default httpd.conf file. I removed the comments because it is easier to understand the configuration when you can see it in one piece.

Listing 12-2: The default httpd.conf without comments

```
ServerType standalone
Port 80
User nobody
Group nobody

ServerName wormhole.nitec.com
ServerAdmin kabir@wormhole.nitec.com
ServerRoot /usr/local/apache

ErrorLog /usr/local/apache/var/log/error_log
LogLevel warn

LogFormat "%h %l %u %t \"%r\" %>s %b \"%{Referer}i\" \"%{User-
Agent}i\"" combined
LogFormat "%h %l %u %t \"%r\" %>s %b" common
LogFormat "%{Referer}i -> %U" referer
LogFormat "%{User-agent}i" agent
CustomLog /usr/local/apache/var/log/access_log common
PidFile /usr/local/apache/var/run/httpd.pid
ScoreBoardFile /usr/local/apache/var/run/httpd.scoreboard

HostnameLookups off
UseCanonicalName on
```

```
Timeout 300
KeepAlive On
MaxKeepAliveRequests 100
KeepAliveTimeout 15
MinSpareServers 5
MaxSpareServers 10
StartServers 5
MaxClients 150
MaxRequestsPerChild 30
```

Now let's take a close look at each of these directives.

RUNNING APACHE AS A STAND-ALONE OR INETD SERVER

The first directive in the default httpd.conf configuration file is ServerType. This directive specifies how the Web server is run. The server can be run using one of two methods: stand-alone or inetd. It may appear that the stand-alone and inetd methods are virtually identical in their functionality, but there's a big difference. The difference lies in the performance of the server. An inetd-run server process exits as soon as it finishes servicing a request. In the stand-alone mode, the child Web server processes linger for a certain amount of time before they cease to exist. This gives them a chance to be reused by future requests. Because the overhead of launching a new process per request is absent in the stand-alone mode, this mode is more efficient. So the default value (stand-alone) should work for most sites. If you have decided to stick with this default value, you can skip the rest of this section. If you prefer to run Apache as an inetd server, however, then set this directive to inetd value.

Next you need to create a file called /etc/xinetd.d/www as follows:

```
service www
{
        flags           = REUSE
        port            = 80
        socket_type     = stream
        protocol        = tcp
        wait            = no
        user            = root
        server          = /usr/sbin/httpd
        log_on_failure  += USERID
}
```

Once you have created the /etc/xinetd.d/www file, you need to modify the /etc/services file, which has a record structure as follows:

service name port number/protocol name service entry in inetd.conf

The line to add in the /etc/services is:

```
www 80/tcp httpd
```

The preceding entry states that www (i.e. httpd) service is available on port 80. If you want to use a different port for your Web (HTTP) service, replace 80 with a number for a port that is not already being used by another service. Because all port numbers below 1024 are reserved for standard services, you want to use a port address higher than 1024 (for example, 8080) and lower than 65535.

Now you need to tell the xinetd server to reconfigure itself as follows:

```
killall -USR1 xinetd
```

This enables the xinetd server to reread the configuration files you modified. Now your xinetd configuration is complete.

Once you assign the Apache directive ServerType to inetd and configure the /etc/xinetd.d/www and /etc/services files, the User and Group directives in the httpd.conf file have no effect. However, make sure the user name you used in the /etc/inetd.conf file has access privileges both to your Web directories and to the storage location for the log files of the server.

 TIP I recommend that you run Apache as an inetd server only if your system has very little RAM to spare, or if you do not expect to have a high-traffic Web site.

A PORT FOR THE STAND-ALONE SERVER The Port directive has no effect if you choose to run your Apache server as an inetd process. On the other hand, if you kept the default ServerType setting (stand-alone), you can use this directive to tell Apache the port address to listen to.

The default HTTP port is 80, and you should use this in typical Web sites. If you are not the root user of the system, however, and you want to run the Web server, you need a port number greater than 1023 and lower than 65535. All ports below 1024 are considered standard reserved ports and require inetd-level (root-level) access to start a service. If you are just experimenting with Web servers on a non-root account on a system, you can use a port higher than the mentioned range, as long as it has not already been taken. If you try to use a port address that is already in use by another server, you get an error message when you try to start the server. Also, note that if you use any port other than the standard HTTP port 80, you have to supply a port number along with all URL requests to the server. For example, if you set this directive as Port 8080, you need to request resources (such as a page called MYPAGE.HTML) on this server as follows:

```
http://www.domain.tld:8080/mypage.html
```

A USER AND A GROUP FOR THE STAND-ALONE SERVER   Like the Port directive, the User and the Group directives in the httpd.conf file are meaningful only for a stand-alone server. The syntax for these directives is as follows:

```
User  [username  |   #UID]
Group [group name |   #GID]
```

These two directives are very important for security reasons. When the primary Web server process launches a child server process to fulfill a request, it changes the child's UID and GID according to the values set for these directives.

Running the child processes as root user processes opens a potential security hole for attack by hackers. Allowing interaction with a root user process risks a potential breach of security in the system; hence, I do not recommend this user capability. Rather, I highly recommend that you run the child server processes as a very low-privileged user belonging to a very low-privileged group. The user named nobody (usually UID = –1) and the group named nogroup (usually GID = –1) are low privileged. You should consult your /etc/group and /etc/passwd files to determine these settings.

If you run the primary Web server as a non-root (regular) user, it cannot change the UIDs and GIDs of child processes, because only root user processes can change the UIDs or GIDs of other processes. Therefore, if you run your primary server as the user named foobar, then all child processes have the same privileges of foobar. Similarly, whatever group ID you have is also the group ID for the child processes.

 If you plan to use the numeric format for user and/or group IDs, you need to insert a # symbol before the numeric value, which can be found in the /etc/passwd and /etc/group files.

COMMON DIRECTIVES FOR BOTH INETD AND STAND-ALONE SERVERS

The stand-alone and inetd-based servers share the following common directives:

```
CustomLog path/to/logfile
```

This directive sets the log file path for storing logs for successful access requests. It also sets the log format for logging the access requests. The default log format is called "common," which is discussed in the LogFormat directive section earlier. If you choose to use a different log format such as combined, then make sure you change the default value from common to combined.

```
ErrorLog path/to/logfile
```

This directive specifies the log file used for logging error messages. If you set this directive to a relative path (that is, a path that does not start with a slash character), then the path is assumed to be relative to the ServerRoot directory. For example, if your ServerRoot directory is set as /usr/local/apache and ErrorLog is set to var/logs/error_log, then the ErrorLog path is the equivalent of the following:

```
ErrorLog /usr/local/apache/var/log/error_log
```

Whatever directory you keep the logs in, make sure that only the primary server process has write access in that directory. This is a major security issue; allowing other users or processes to write to the log directory can lead to someone unauthorized taking over your primary Web server process UID, which is normally the root account.

```
HostnameLookups on | off
```

When this directive is set to off, it tells Apache not to do DNS lookups to determine host names of requesting clients. Since DNS lookups are time consuming, the default value off is a very good idea. Turning this on may cause clients to time out if their ISP has not properly set up the client's reverse-DNS settings.

```
LogFormat format
```

The LogFormat specifies the format for server log files and also assigns a nickname to that format. The default httpd.conf contains multiple LogFormat directives but uses only one with the CustomLog directive. For example:

```
LogFormat "%h %l %u %t \"%r\" %>s %b \"%{Referer}i\" \"%{User-Agent}i\"" combined
```

This log format nicknamed "combined" specifies all the Common Log Format (CLF) fields and adds the referrer and the user-agent fields. The next format in the default configuration is as follows:

```
LogFormat "%h %l %u %t \"%r\" %>s %b" common
```

This format is simply the Common Log Format, and hence it is nicknamed "common." The last two LogFormat directives in the default httpd.conf file are:

```
LogFormat "%{Referer}i -> %U" referer
LogFormat "%{User-agent}i" agent
```

These two directives create nicknames for log formats that store only the referrer and user-agent information. By default, the "common" format is used with the CustomLog directive. However, because most log analysis programs accept the combined format, you may want to set that as the default. After all, more log information is always better for determining who is accessing your site and how.

```
LogLevel  [emerg | alert | crit | errors | warn | debug ]
```

This directive specifies the level of logging for the ErrorLog directive. The default value, warn, is normally sufficient. It tells Apache to log all emergency (emerg) error conditions, alert (alert) conditions, critical (crit) errors, and all the warnings (warn). If you plan to do a great deal of debugging, you might want to set this to debug, which catches just about all types of errors, warnings, and informative messages from the server. Also remember that the more disk I/O the server performs, the slower it gets. So keeping the LogLevel at debug is not ideal for production servers.

```
ServerAdmin e-mail address
```

This directive sets the e-mail address of the server admin. The e-mail address displays when the server generates an error message page. Typically it is set as follows:

```
ServerAdmin webmaster@domain.tld
ServerName hostname
```

This directive sets the server's Internet host name. Normally, you want to enter a host name such as www.yourcompany.com. Be sure, however, that the host name you enter here has proper DNS records that point it to your server machine.

```
ServerRoot path
```

This directive specifies the top-level directory where the server's configuration, error, and log files are kept. This is the parent directory for all server-related files. If you compiled and installed Apache using APACI interface, the default ServerRoot is set to the value of the PREFIX value you supplied as the parameter to the configure script. For example, if you run the configure script from your Apache distribution directory as follows:

```
./configure  --PREFIX=/usr/local/apache
```

then ServerRoot is set to /usr/local/apache by default. However, if you compiled Apache manually, you might have to change the default value to point to an appropriate directory.

```
Timeout number
```

This directive is set to the number of seconds that the server waits for the client. The default value should be just fine.

`UseCanonicalName on | off`

When set to on, this directive tells Apache to use ServerName- and Port directive-specified values when creating self-referencing URLs. On the other hand, when it is set to off, the server will construct self-referencing URLs using the server name and port information the client supplied. If the client does not supply any such information, the server then uses ServerName- and Port-specified values. Most sites do not use self-referencing URL addresses, so this is not going to be an important directive for most of us.

DIRECTIVES FOR A STAND-ALONE SERVER

The following directives in the default httpd.conf file are meaningful only for Apache running in the stand-alone mode.

`KeepAlive on | off`

This directive enables or disables the KeepAlive feature built into Apache. Simply speaking, KeepAlive is a feature that allows persistent connection between the server and the client. Having a persistent connection helps speed up the delivery of the content, because no time is lost in establishing new connections for each request. Keep the default as is because it is a part of the HTTP 1.1 specification.

`KeepAliveTimeout`

This directive specifies the maximum time (in seconds) the server waits for a subsequent connection before it disconnects from the client. Keep the default as is.

`MaxClients number`

This directive sets the limit on the number of simultaneous requests that can be supported. The maximum possible value is 256. If you feel that you need to handle more than 256 simultaneous connections, you have to edit the src/include/httpd.h header file and set the HARD_SERVER_LIMIT constant to the desired limit. Once you compile the new server, you will be able to set this directive to the desired limit.

`MaxKeepAliveRequests number`

This directive specifies the maximum number of requests to be serviced per KeepAlive connection. You should keep the default as is. Note that setting the value to zero disables the KeepAlive feature.

`MaxRequestsPerChild number`

This directive sets the limit on the number of requests a child server process services before it dies. If you set the value to zero, the child server processes never dies. Keep the default as is.

`MaxSpareServers` *number*

This directive specifies the maximum number of spare (idle) servers that Apache runs. You should experiment with this directive only if you are running Apache to host very busy Web sites.

This directive is useless with the Windows version of Apache.

`MinSpareServers` *number*

This directive sets the minimum number of spare (idle) servers that the primary server keeps around. You should experiment with this directive only if you are running Apache to host very busy Web sites. Apache can automatically adjust to load, so I recommend that you do not use a large number here.

This directive is useless with the Windows version of Apache because it does not use a pool of servers to service requests.

`PidFile` *path/filename*

This directive specifies a filename for storing the primary server's process ID information. Scripts can easily determine the process ID of the primary server using this file. For example, if the PidFile is set as follows:

`PidFile /usr/local/apache/var/run/httpd.pid`

I can restart the Apache server using the kill command as follows:

`kill -HUP `cat /usr/local/apache/var/run/httpd.pid``

Make sure that only the primary server process has write access in the directory containing this file. This is a major security issue; allowing other users or processes to write to this directory can lead to someone unauthorized taking over your primary Web server process UID, which is normally the root account.

`ScoreBoardFile` *path/filename*

This directive is set to a filename that the primary server uses to communicate with its child server processes. This is needed for only a few OS platforms. If you have to use a ScoreBoardFile, then you may see improved speed by placing it on a RAM disk. Consult your OS manuals.

`StartServers` *number*

This directive sets the initial number of child server processes that Apache launches at startup. Apache can automatically adjust to load, so there is no real need to change the default.

 This directive is useless with the Windows version of Apache.

Configuring srm.conf

The srm.conf file is the resource configuration file; it tells the server the resources you want to offer from your Web site, and where and how to offer them. Listing 12-3 shows the default srm.conf file without comments.

Listing 12-3: The default srm.conf without comments

```
DocumentRoot /usr/local/apache/share/htdocs
UserDir public_html

DirectoryIndex index.html
FancyIndexing on
AddIconByEncoding (CMP,/icons/compressed.gif) x-compress x-gzip
AddIconByType (TXT,/icons/text.gif) text/*
AddIconByType (IMG,/icons/image2.gif) image/*
AddIconByType (SND,/icons/sound2.gif) audio/*
AddIconByType (VID,/icons/movie.gif) video/*
AddIcon /icons/binary.gif .bin .exe
AddIcon /icons/binhex.gif .hqx
AddIcon /icons/tar.gif .tar
AddIcon /icons/world2.gif .wrl .wrl.gz .vrml .vrm .iv
AddIcon /icons/compressed.gif .Z .z .tgz .gz .zip
AddIcon /icons/a.gif .ps .ai .eps
AddIcon /icons/layout.gif .html .shtml .htm .pdf
AddIcon /icons/text.gif .txt
AddIcon /icons/c.gif .c
AddIcon /icons/p.gif .pl .py
AddIcon /icons/f.gif .for
AddIcon /icons/dvi.gif .dvi
AddIcon /icons/uuencoded.gif .uu
AddIcon /icons/script.gif .conf .sh .shar .csh .ksh .tcl
AddIcon /icons/tex.gif .tex
AddIcon /icons/bomb.gif core
AddIcon /icons/back.gif ..
```

```
AddIcon /icons/hand.right.gif README
AddIcon /icons/folder.gif ^^DIRECTORY^^
AddIcon /icons/blank.gif ^^BLANKICON^^

DefaultIcon /icons/unknown.gif
ReadmeName README
HeaderName HEADER
IndexIgnore .??* *~ *# HEADER* README* RCS
AccessFileName .htaccess
TypesConfig /usr/local/apache/etc/mime.types

DefaultType text/plain

AddEncoding x-compress Z
AddEncoding x-gzip gz

AddLanguage en .en
AddLanguage fr .fr
AddLanguage de .de
AddLanguage da .da
AddLanguage el .el
AddLanguage it .it

LanguagePriority en fr de
Alias /icons/ /usr/local/apache/share/icons/

BrowserMatch "Mozilla/2" nokeepalive
BrowserMatch "MSIE 4\.0b2;" nokeepalive downgrade-1.0 force-
response-1.0
BrowserMatch "RealPlayer 4\.0" force-response-1.0
BrowserMatch "Java/1\.0" force-response-1.0
BrowserMatch "JDK/1\.0" force-response-1.0
```

The directives in srm.conf are discussed in the following sections.

```
AccessFileName filename filename filename . . .
```

This directive sets the directory access control filename. Some Web administrators change the default (.htaccess) to enhance security, because the .htaccess name is widely known. If you are planning on changing the name, make sure you choose a name that starts with a period so that it does not show up in directory listings. Also note that the default access.conf file prohibits Apache from looking into any directory level access control file. If you plan to use such access control files, make sure you modify the access.conf file accordingly. For example, the default access.conf file has the following configuration segment:

```
<Directory />
  Options FollowSymLinks
  AllowOverride None
</Directory>
```

This configuration uses the AllowOverride directive to prohibit Apache from looking into the AccessFileName-specified file. If you are interested in allowing Apache to look for an access control file in a certain subsection of your site, use the following configuration:

```
<Directory /path/to/your/dir>
  Options FollowSymLinks
  AllowOverride All
</Directory>
```

This configuration allows you to have an access control file such as .htaccess in the /path/to/your/dir directory or any of the subdirectories below it. It also enables you to override all the allowed directives. If you are interested in a more restricted setting, you may set AllowOverride to:

- AuthConfig: Allows the authorization directives, such as AuthDBM GroupFile, AuthDBMUserFile, AuthGroupFile, AuthName, AuthType, AuthUserFile, and require.

- FileInfo: Allows the document type directives, such as AddEncoding, AddLanguage, AddType, DefaultType, ErrorDocument, and LanguagePriority.

- Indexes: Allows the directory indexing directives, such as AddDescription, AddIcon, AddIconByEncoding, AddIconByType, DefaultIcon, Directory Index, FancyIndexing, HeaderName, IndexIgnore, IndexOptions, and ReadmeName.

- Limit: Allows the host access directives, such as allow, deny, and order.

- Options: Allows the directory options directives, such as Options and XbitHack.

AddEncoding *MIME-encoding file-extension file-extension* . . .

This directive assigns MIME encoding information with filename extensions. Keep the defaults as they are.

AddIcon *icon name name* . . .

This directive sets the icon filename for a specific file extension. When Fancy Indexing is on, Apache displays this icon next to each file matching the extension specified in this directive. Keep the default as is.

`AddIconByEncoding icon MIME-encoding mime-encoding . . .`

This directive sets the icon to display next to files with MIME-encoding for FancyIndexing. Keep the default as is.

`AddIconByType icon MIME-type MIME-type . . .`

This directive also sets the icon to display next to files with MIME-encoding for FancyIndexing. Keep the default as is.

`AddLanguage MIME-language file-extension file-extension . . .`

This directive assigns language-specific MIME encoding information with file-name extensions. Keep the defaults as they are.

`Alias URL-path path`

This directive enables you to create an alias for a physical directory. The default alias /icons/ points to the directory where the server's icon images are stored. If the path is incorrect, modify it as appropriate. The icon images are used to create fancy directory listings.

`BrowserMatch variable[=value] [. . .]`

This directive defines environment variables based on the User-Agent HTTP request header field. Keep the defaults as is.

`DefaultIcon url`

This directive sets the icon to display for files when no specific icon is known. Keep the default as is.

`DefaultType MIME-type`

This directive sets the default content type. When the server cannot determine a document's MIME type using the mapping information stored in mime.types or other means (such as AddType directives), it uses the value set by this directive. Keep the default as is.

`DirectoryIndex filename filename filename . . .`

This directive specifies the file the Apache server considers the index for the directory being requested. For example, when a URL such as `www.yourcompany.com` is requested, the Apache server determines that this is a request to access the / (document root) directory of the Web site. If the DocumentRoot directive is set as follows:

```
DocumentRoot /www/www.yourcompany.com/public/htdocs
```

then the Apache server looks for a file named /www/www.yourcompany.com/ public/htdocs/index.html. If the server finds the file, Apache services the request by returning the content of the file to the requesting Web browser. If the DirectoryIndex is assigned welcome.html instead of the default index.html, however, the Web server looks for /www/www.yourcompany.com/public/htdocs/welcome.html instead. If the file is absent, Apache returns the directory listing by creating a dynamic HTML page. You also can specify multiple index filenames in the DirectoryIndex directive. For example:

```
DirectoryIndex index.html index.htm welcome.htm
```

tells the Web server that it should check for the existence of any of the three files, and if any one is found, it should be returned to the requesting Web client.

Listing many files as the index may create two problems. First, the server now has to check for the existence of many files per directory request; this could make it a bit slower than usual. Second, having multiple files as indexes could make your site a bit difficult to manage from the organizational point of view. If your Web site content developers use various systems to create files, however, it may be a practical solution to keep both index.html and index.htm as index files. For example, a Windows 3.*x* machine is unable to create filenames with extensions longer than three characters, so a user working on such a machine may need to update all of his or her index.html files manually on the Web server. Using the recommended index filenames eliminates this hassle.

```
DocumentRoot path
```

This directive tells the server to treat the supplied directory name as the root directory for all documents. The default is typically set to Apache's own htdocs directory, where server documentation is kept. You have to change the default. This is a very important decision. For example, if the directive is set as follows:

```
DocumentRoot /
```

then every file on the system becomes accessible by the Web server. Of course, you can protect files by providing proper file permission settings, but setting the document root to the physical root directory of your system is definitely a major security risk. Instead, you want to point the DocumentRoot to a specific subdirectory of your file system. A potentially better option is to create a Web directory structure for your organization. For example, if you are planning to host more than one Web site (such as virtual hosts) using your Apache server, you may want to create a partition specifically for Web documents and scripts. I typically use a separate disk partition such as /www to store all the Web sites I manage. I keep each site as a subdirectory of the /www directory. However, it is often a good idea to go one step further. For example:

◆ Directory structure for www.nitec.com on port 80

```
/www/www.nitec.com/public
/www/www.nitec.com/public/htdocs   Document Root Dir
/www/www.nitec.com/public/cgi-bin  CGI Script Dir
```

◆ Directory structure for www.nitec.com on port 8080

```
/www/www.nitec.com/staging
/www/www.nitec.com/staging/htdocs   Document Root Dir
/www/www.nitec.com/staging/cgi-bin  CGI Script Dir
```

◆ Directory structure for www.nitec.com on port 9000

```
/www/www.nitec.com/dev
/www/www.nitec.com/dev/htdocs   Document Root Dir
/www/www.nitec.com/dev/cgi-bin  CGI Script Dir
```

This is the directory structure I use for the entire production of my company Web site (www.nitec.com). Having such a directory structure allows me to develop, stage, and produce the Web site in a systematic fashion. For example, when some new development work is done for the site, it is accessible from the www.nitec.com:9000 site. Then, once approved, the newly developed content moves to www.nitec.com:8080. Finally, the content moves to the public site.

Just because your document root points to a particular directory does not mean the Web server cannot access directories outside your document tree. You can easily enable it to do so using symbolic links (with proper file permission) or aliases. From an organizational and security perspective, I don't recommend using a lot of symbolic links or aliases to access files and directories outside your document tree. Nonetheless, it is sometimes necessary to keep a certain type of information outside the document tree, even if you need to keep the contents of such a directory accessible to the server on a regular basis.

If you have to add symbolic links to other directory locations outside the document tree, make sure that when you back up your files, your backup program is instructed to back up symbolic links properly.

FancyIndexing on | off

This directive sets the FancyIndexing option on or off for a directory. When a request for a directory is made and none of the files in the directory match any name specified in the DirectoryIndex directive, the server generates a dynamic directory listing if this feature is on. Also, note that FancyIndexing and IndexOptions directives override each other. Instead of using the FancyIndexing directive, you can use the IndexOptions directive as follows:

```
IndexOptions FancyIndexing
```

which also turns on FancyIndexing for server-generated directory listings.

```
HeaderName filename
```

This directive sets the filename embedded in the directory listings created by the server. This file is inserted before the actual listing, thus creating the effect of a header.

```
IndexIgnore filename filename filename . . .
```

This directive sets the filenames that will be ignored by the server when creating a dynamic directory listing. The filenames can be simple regular expressions separated by space characters. Keep the default.

```
LanguagePriority MIME-language MIME-language . . .
```

This directive sets the precedence of languages in order of decreasing preference. Keep the default as is if English (en) is your preferred language.

```
ReadmeName filename filename filename . . .
```

This directive sets the filename appended to the end of a directory listing created by the server. This file is inserted after the actual listing, thus creating the effect of a footer. This file must be in the requested directory.

```
TypesConfig filename
```

This directive sets the location of the MIME types configuration file. Keep the default unless you move the mime.types file.

```
UserDir directory
```

This directive tells Apache which directory to consider as the DocumentRoot for users on your system. This instruction applies only if you have multiple users on the system and want to allow each one to have his or her own Web directory. The default value is public_html, which means that if you set up your Web server's name to be www.yourcompany.com, and you have two users (joe and jenny), their personal Web site URLs and Web directories are as follows:

```
http://www.yourcompany.com/~joe    ~joe/public_html
http://www.yourcompany.com/~jenny  ~jenny/public_html
```

The tilde (~) character extends to a user's home directory. The directory specified by the UserDir directive resides in each user's home directory, and Apache must have read and execute permissions to read files and directories within the public_html directory. You can accomplish this with the following commands:

```
chown -R <user>.<Apache server's group name> \
  ~<user>/<directory assigned in UserDir>
chmod -R 2770 ~<user>/<directory assigned in UserDir>
```

For example, if the username is joe and Apache's group is called httpd, and public_html is assigned in the UserDir directive, the preceding commands look like this:

```
chown -R joe.httpd  ~joe/public_html
chmod -R 2770 ~joe/public_html
```

The first command, chown, changes ownership of the ~joe/public_html directory (as well as all files and subdirectories within it) to joe.httpd. In other words, it gives the user joe and the group httpd full ownership of all the files and directories in the public_html directory. The next command, chmod, sets the access rights to 2770; in other words, only the user (joe) and the group (httpd) have full read, write, and execute privileges in public_html and all files and subdirectories under it. It also ensures that when a new file or subdirectory is created in the public_html directory, the newly created file has the group ID set. This enables the Web server to access the new file without the user's intervention.

If you create user accounts on your system using a script (such as the /usr/sbin/useradd script on Linux systems), you may want to incorporate the Web site creation process in this script. Just add a mkdir command to create a default public_html directory (if that's what you assign to the UserDir directive) to be used as the Web directory. Add the chmod and chown commands to give the Web server user permission to read and execute files and directories under this public directory.

Configuring access.conf

The final configuration file you need to modify is the access.conf file. The access.conf file sets access permissions for items such as files, directories, and scripts on your Web site. Listing 12-4 shows the default access.conf file without comments.

Listing 12-4: The default access.conf

```
<Directory />
Options FollowSymLinks
AllowOverride None
</Directory>

<Directory /usr/local/apache/share/htdocs>
Options Indexes FollowSymLinks
AllowOverride None
order allow,deny
allow from all
</Directory>

<Directory /usr/local/apache/share/cgi-bin>
AllowOverride None
Options None
</Directory>
```

This is the only configuration file in which you need to modify directives that span multiple lines. The first directive you need to modify has the following syntax:

```
<Directory path> . . . </Directory>
```

You can enclose a group of directives between the `<Directory>` and `</Directory>` containers. The scope of the enclosed directives is limited to the named directory path (with subdirectories); however, you may use only directives that are allowed in a directory context. The named directory is either the full path to a directory or a wildcard string.

The first <Directory /> . . . </Directory> container configuration segment is very restrictive; it enables the server to follow only symbolic links and disables per-directory based access control files (.htaccess) for all directories starting with the root directory of the system. You should keep this configuration segment as is. The idea here is both to open things that need to be opened and to lock up everything else. For example, the next <Directory /usr/local/etc/httpd/htdocs> . . . </Directory> configuration segment allows directory indexing and the FollowSymLinks feature for the DocumentRoot directory.

You may need to change the directory /usr/local/etc/httpd/htdocs to whatever you set earlier as the argument for the DocumentRoot directive in the httpd.conf file. The default setting, which includes multiple directives such as Options and AllowOverride, tells the server the following:

◆ The named directory and all subdirectories under it can be indexed. In other words, if there is an index file, it is displayed; in the absence of an index file, the server creates a dynamic index for the directory. The Options directive specifies this.

- ◆ The named directory and all subdirectories under it can have symbolic links that the server can follow (that is, use as a path) to access information. The Options directive also specifies this.

- ◆ No options specified in the directory container can be overridden by a local access control file (specified by the AccessFileName directive in srm.conf; the default is .htaccess). This is specified in the AllowOverride directive.

- ◆ Access is permitted for all.

The default setting should be sufficient at this early stage. If your server is going to be on the Internet, however, you may want to remove the FollowSymLinks option from the Options directive line. Leaving this option creates a security risk. For example, if a directory in your Web site does not have an index page, the server displays an automated index that shows any symbolic links you have in that directory. This could cause the display of sensitive information or may even allow anyone to run an executable that resides in a carelessly linked directory.

The final configuration segment in Listing 12-4 disables all options and per-directory (.htaccess) overrides for a special directory called /usr/local/apache/share/cgi-bin. This directory is where the distributed CGI scripts are. The contents of the CGI script directory should not be directly available via a Web browser. Therefore, there is no need to allow any per-directory control on that directory. Hence, the default is to remove all options.

Controlling the Apache server

Apache 1.3.*x* comes with a nifty shell script called apachectl, which can be used to control the server in many ways. In this section, I will discuss this script in detail. However, before you can control Apache, you must become the superuser on your system, unless you have configured Apache to run on a port above 1023.

Note that if you set up the inetd configuration for httpd properly, you don't need to do anything to start or stop the Apache server, because inetd runs it when it receives a request for access on the HTTP port.

STARTING THE SERVER

To start the server, just run the apachectl script as follows:

```
/path/to/your/apache/sbin/dir/apachectl start
```

If you want your server to start up automatically after a system reboot, you should add the preceding line to your /etc/rc.local or a similar file in your rc.d directory. I use the script shown in Listing 12-5 for automatic Apache startup and shutdown at boot and reboot, respectively.

Listing 12-5: The httpd.sh script

```
#!/bin/sh
#
# httpd   This shell script starts and stops the Apache server
# It takes an argument 'start' or 'stop' to start and
# stop the server process, respectively.
#
# Notes: You might have to change the path information used
# in the script to reflect your system's configuration.
#
[ -f /usr/local/apache/sbin/apachectl ] || exit 0

# See how the script was called.
case "$1" in
  start)
        # Start daemons.
        echo -n "Starting httpd:"
        /usr/local/apache/sbin/apachectl start
        touch /var/lock/subsys/httpd
        echo
        ;;
  stop)
        # Stop daemons.
        echo -n "Shutting down httpd:"
        /usr/local/apache/sbin/apachectl stop

        echo "done"
        rm -f /var/lock/subsys/httpd
        ;;
  *)
        echo "Usage: httpd {start|stop}"
        exit 1
esac
exit 0
```

I put this script in the /etc/rc.d/init.d/ directory and made the following symbolic links:

```
/etc/rc.d/rc3.d/S80httpd -> /etc/rc.d/init.d/httpd.sh
/etc/rc.d/rc3.d/K80httpd -> /etc/rc.d/init.d/httpd.sh
```

When the system starts up, it loads the Apache server automatically. The script also stops the Apache server at system shutdown or reboot.

STOPPING THE SERVER
To stop the server, just run the apachectl script as follows:

*/path/to/your/*sbin/dir/apachectl stop

RESTARTING THE SERVER
To restart the server, just run the apachectl script as follows:

*/path/to/your/apache/*sbin/dir/apachectl restart

To perform a graceful restart, run the apachectl script as follows:

*/path/to/your/apache/*sbin/dir/apachectl graceful

For the curious, the restart command sends a SIGHUP signal and the graceful command sends a SIGUSR1 signal to Apache. Because the latter is user defined (that is, defined by the Apache developers), it is much more agreeable to the running server.

GETTING FULL STATUS OF THE SERVER
Before you can get the full status of the server, you will need to make sure you have the Lynx text-based Web browser installed on your system. You can get this nifty Web browser from the following URL: http://lynx.browser.org/.
Once you have Lynx installed, you can get the full status of the running server when you run the apachectl script as follows:

*/path/to/your/apache/*sbin/dir/apachectl fullstatus

You receive a page full of information showing various server status data. It is probably a good idea to redirect the status information to a file because it is most likely to be more than a full screen. Here is how you can redirect the data to a file called /tmp/status:

*/path/to/your/apache/*sbin/dir/apachectl fullstatus > /tmp/status

CHECKING SERVER CONFIGURATION FILES
To test the server configuration files for syntax errors, you run the apachectl script as follows:

*/path/to/your/apache/*sbin/dir/apachectl configtest

Testing the Apache server

Run your favorite Web browser and point it to the Web site running your newly configured Apache server. If you are running the Web browser on the same system running Apache, you can use the following URL: http://localhost/.

In all other cases, however, you need to specify the exact host name (such as www.yourcompany.com). If you have not made any changes to the default htdocs directory, you see a page that tells you "It Works!" This page is shipped with the Apache distribution and you need to change it with your own content.

Finally, you want to make sure the log files are updated properly. To check your log files, enter the log directory and run the following command:

```
tail -f [/path/to/access_log]
```

The tail part of the command is a utility that enables viewing of a growing file (when the -f option is specified). Now, use a Web browser to access the site, or, if you are already there, simply reload the page you currently have on the browser. You should see an entry added to the listing on the screen. Click the Reload button a few more times to ensure that the access file is updated accordingly. If you see the updated records, your access log file is working. Press Ctrl+C to exit the tail command session. If you do not see any new records in the file, you should check the permission settings for the log files and the directory in which they are kept.

Another log to check is the error log file. Use:

```
tail -f [/path/to/error_log]
```

to view the error log entries as they come in. Simply request nonexistent resources (such as a file you don't have) on your Web browser, and you see entries being added. If you observe this, the error log file is properly configured.

If all of these tests were successful, then you have correctly configured your Apache server. Congratulations!

Managing Your Apache Server

Now that you have a functioning Web server, you can work on the service aspect of your Web. In this section you learn about typical Web server management issues.

Configuring Apache for CGI scripts

In the early years of the Web, there were only static HTML pages, but now almost every Web site uses CGI scripts to provide dynamic, on-the-fly Web pages. Therefore CGI capabilities are virtually required for almost all Web server installations. The good news is that Apache makes it quite easy to support CGI scripts.

Configuring Apache to process CGI requests includes telling Apache where you store your CGI programs, setting up CGI handlers for specific file extensions, and indicating which file extensions should be considered CGI programs. It is a good idea to keep your CGI programs in one central directory. This permits better control of them. Scattering CGI programs all over the Web space might make the site unmanageable, and it also could create security holes that would be hard to track.

CREATING A CGI PROGRAM DIRECTORY

Making a central CGI program directory is just the beginning of setting up a secured CGI environment. It is best to keep this central CGI program directory outside of your DocumentRoot directory so that CGI programs cannot be accessed directly. Why? Well, when it comes to CGI programs, you want to provide as little information as possible to the outside world. This will ensure better security for your site(s). The less someone knows about where your CGI programs are physically located, the less harm that person can do.

The first step is to create a directory outside of your DocumentRoot directory. For example, if /www/mycompany/public/htdocs is the DocumentRoot directory of a Web site, then /www/mycompany/public/cgi-bin is a good candidate for the CGI program directory. To create the alias for your CGI program directory, you can use the ScriptAlias directive.

If you are setting up CGI support for the primary Web server, edit the httpd.conf file and insert a ScriptAlias line with the following syntax:

```
ScriptAlias  /alias/ /path/
to/the/CGI/program/directory/ending/with/slash/
```

For example:

```
ScriptAlias /cgi-bin/ /www/mycompany/public/cgi-bin/
```

If you are setting up CGI support for a virtual site, add a ScriptAlias line in the <VirtualHost . . . > container that defines the virtual host. For example:

```
NameVirtualHost 206.171.50.60
<VirtualHost 206.171.50.60>
ServerName blackhole.nitec.com
ScriptAlias /apps/ /www/nitec/blackhole/public/cgi-bin/
</VirtualHost>
```

Here the /apps/ alias is used to create a CGI program directory alias. If there is a CGI program called feedback.cgi in the /www/nitec/blackhole/public/cgi-bin directory, it can be accessed only via the following:

```
http://blackhole.nitec.com/apps/feedback.cgi
```

After you set up the ScriptAlias directive, make sure that the directory permission permits Apache to read and execute files found in the directory.

The directory pointed to by ScriptAlias should have very strict permission settings. No one but the CGI program developer or the server administrator should have full (read, write, and execute) permissions for the directory. Note that you can define multiple CGI program directory aliases, and the ScriptAlias-specified directory is not browseable (by default) for security reasons.

When requested, Apache attempts to run any executable (file permission-wise) file found in the ScriptAliased directory. For example:

```
http://blackhole.nitec.com/apps/foo.cgi
http://blackhole.nitec.com/apps/foo.pl
http://blackhole.nitec.com/apps/foo.bak
http://blackhole.nitec.com/apps/foo.dat
```

All of the preceding URL requests prompt Apache to attempt running the various foo files.

I am not particularly fond of the idea that any file in the ScriptAlias-specified directory can be run as a CGI program. I prefer a solution that enables me to restrict the CGI program names such that only files with certain extensions are treated like CGI programs. This is accomplished with the AddHandler handler. For example:

```
Alias /cgi-bin/ /path/to/cgi/dir/outside/doc/root/

<Directory /path/to/cgi/dir/outside/doc/root/>
  Options ExecCGI -Indexes
  AddHandler cgi-script .pl .cgi
</Directory>
```

The `Alias` directive line tells Apache to create an alias called cgi-bin for the */path/to/*cgi/dir/outside/doc/root/ directory. The `Options ExecCGI -Indexes` line tells Apache to permit CGI program execution from within this directory and not allow anyone to browse the contents of the directory. The `AddHandler cgi-script .pl .cgi` line tells Apache to treat the list of named extensions as CGI program extensions. In other words, whenever Apache encounters a URL requesting a file that contains one of the named extensions, Apache must execute that file as a CGI program).

ENABLING CGI-BIN ACCESS FOR YOUR USERS

Many Internet service providers (ISPs) offer Web sites with user accounts. These Web sites usually have URLs, such as `http://www.isp.net/~username`.

ISPs often get requests for cgi-bin access from the users. The term "cgi-bin access" is a general one used by many to indicate CGI facility on a Web server. Traditionally, the CGI program directory has been aliased as /cgi-bin/, and hence, this term was created. The other common term that became very popular is "home page," which refers to the top-level index page of a Web directory of a user.

In this section, I discuss the two ways to provide cgi-bin access for users on an Apache Web server. You need to implement only one of the following methods.

USING DIRECTORY OR DIRECTORYMATCH CONTAINERS   When the UserDir directive is set to a directory name, Apache considers it the top-level directory for a user Web site. For example:

```
ServerName www.yourcompany.com
UserDir public_html
```

Now when a request for `www.yourcompany.com/~username` arrives, Apache locates the named user's home directory (usually by checking the /etc/passwd file) and then appends the UserDir-specified directory to create the pathname for the top-level user Web directory. For example:

```
http://www.yourcompany.com/~joe
```

This URL makes Apache look for /home/joe/public_html (assuming /home/joe is joe's home directory). If the directory exists, the index page for that directory is sent to the requesting client.

One way to add CGI support for each user is to add the following configuration in one of your Apache configuration files:

```
<Directory ~ "/home/[a-z]+/public_html/cgi-bin">
  Options ExecCGI
  AddHandler cgi-script .cgi .pl
</Directory>
```

Or if you are using the latest Apache server, you can use the following configuration:

```
<DirectoryMatch  "/home/[a-z]+/public_html/cgi-bin">
  Options ExecCGI
  AddHandler cgi-script .cgi .pl
</DirectoryMatch>
```

In both methods, Apache translates `www.yourcompany.com/~username/ cgi-bin/` requests to /home/username/public_html/cgi-bin/ and permits any CGI program with the proper extension (.cgi or .pl) to execute.

Note that all usernames must be lowercase characters in order for this to work. If you have usernames that are alphanumeric, you have to use a different regular expression.

SCRIPTALIASMATCH   Using the ScriptAliasMatch directive, you also can support CGI program directories for each user. For example:

```
ScriptAliasMatch ~([a-z]+)/ \
cgi-bin/(.*)/home/$1/public_html/cgi-bin/$2
```

This directive matches username to $1, where $1 is equal to ~([a–z]+), and matches everything followed by /cgi-bin/ to $2, where $2 is equal to (.*).Then it uses $1 and $2 to create the actual location of the CGI program directory. For example:

```
http://www.yourcompany.com/~joe/ \
cgi-bin/feedback.cgi?book=dummies&author=kabir
```

Here ~([a–z]+) maps one or more lowercase characters following the tilde mark (~) to $1. In other words, the (and) pair enables us to capture everything between the tilde (~) and the trailing forward slash (/) after the username. So $1 is set to kabir and (.*) maps everything following the cgi-bin/ and the parenthesis pair in this regular expression, and enables us to put everything in $2. Thus $2 is set to search.cgi?book=dummies&author=kabir.

Now Apache can create the physical path of the CGI program directory using:

```
/home/$1/public_html/cgi-bin/$2
```

This regular expression results in the following path for the previous example:

```
/home/kabir/public_html/ \cgi-
bin/search.cgi?book=dummies&author=kabir
```

Because this is where the CGI program search.cgi is kept, it executes.

If you are like me – not fond of having the CGI program directory under public_html (that is, the UserDir-specified directory) – you can keep it outside by removing the public_html part of the expression as follows:

```
ScriptAliasMatch ~([a-z]+)/cgi-bin/(.*) /home/$1/cgi-bin/$2
```

This maps the example call:

```
www.yourcompany.com/~joe/ \cgi-
bin/feedback.cgi?book=dummies&author=kabir
```

to the following physical file:

```
/home/kabir/cgi-bin/search.cgi?book=dummies&author=kabir
```

Of course, if you are not too fond of keeping a user subdirectory world readable (that is, public_html), you can remedy this by creating a Web partition (or a directory) for your users and giving them individual directories to host their home pages.

CREATING NEW CGI EXTENSIONS USING ADDTYPE

You learned how to create CGI program extensions using the AddHandler directive previously; however, if you want to create new CGI program extensions in a particular directory, you can also use the .htaccess (or file specified by the AccessFile Name directive).

Before you can add new extensions using the per-directory access control file (.htaccess), you have to create a ⟨Directory⟩ container as follows:

```
<Directory /path/to/your/directory>
  Options ExecCGI
  AllowOverride FileInfo
</Directory>
```

The first directive inside the preceding directory container tells Apache that you want to enable CGI program execution in this directory. The second directive tells Apache to enable the FileInfo feature in the per-directory access control file (.htaccess). This feature enables you to use an AddType directive in the per-directory access control file.

To add a new CGI program extension (.wizard), all you need to do is create an .htaccess (or whatever you specified in the AccessFileName directive) file in the directory with the following:

```
AddType application/x-httpd-cgi .wizard
```

Now, rename an existing CGI program in that directory to have the .wizard extension, and request it via your browser. Make sure all of the file permission settings for the directory and the CGI programs are set to read and execute by Apache.

Configuring Apache for server-side includes

CGI scripts are not the only way to create dynamic contents: server-side includes (SSIs) is another option. Again, Apache makes adding SSI support for your Web sites easy.

Although the mod_include.c module, required for server-side include (SSI) support, is compiled by default in the standard Apache executable, the SSI parsing of HTML pages is not enabled by default. To enable SSI support for Apache, you need to perform the following steps:

1. Add a new handler for SSI pages.

2. Add a new file extension for SSI pages.

3. Enable SSI parsing for a directory.

When these steps are completed for a directory called chapter_08, under a virtual host called `apache.nitec.com`, the configuration appears as follows:

```
<VirtualHost 206.171.50.50>

ServerName apache.nitec.com
DocumentRoot /data/web/apache/public/htdocs
ScriptAlias /data/web/apache/public/cgi-bin

<Directory /data/web/apache/public/htdocs/chapter_08>
  AddHandler server-parsed .shtml
  AddType text/html .shtml
  Options +Include
</Directory>

</VirtualHost>
```

The use of Include in the Options directive enables all SSI commands. If you plan on disabling execution of external programs via SSI commands, you can use IncludesNOEXEC instead. This directive disables execution of external programs. However, it also disables loading of external files via the SSI command Include.

Now let's take a closer look at each step involved in enabling SSI support.

ADD A NEW HANDLER FOR SSI PAGES

Let's say that you want to use .shtml as the SSI file extension for all HTML pages containing one or more SSI commands. You need to tell Apache that the file extension .shtml should be treated as an SSI-enabled page. You can do that using the AddHandler directive as follows:

```
AddHandler server-parsed .shtml
```

The AddHandler directive tells Apache that an .shtml file needs to be handled by the server-parsed handler, which is found in the mod_include module.

If, for some reason, you have to use the .html and .htm extensions as the SSI extensions, do not use:

```
AddHandler server-parsed .html
AddType text/html .html

AddHandler server-parsed .htm
AddType text/html .htm
```

These directives would degrade your server performance. Apache would process all the .html and .htm files, which means that files without any SSI commands would be parsed, thereby increasing the delay in file delivery. Avoid using the .html or .htm extensions for SSI; if you must use them, however, then use the XbitHack directive. For example:

```
<Directory /some/path/>
  Options +Includes
  XbitHack on
</Directory>
```

The preceding configuration enables SSI parsing for each .html (and .htm) file in the /some/path/ directory as long as its owner has read and execute permissions for the file.

ADD A NEW FILE EXTENSION FOR SSI PAGES

Although Apache now knows how to handle the .shtml file, it needs to be told what to tell the Web browser about this file. Web servers send header information for each request to tell the Web browser what type of content is being sent as the response. Therefore, you need to tell Apache that when responding to an .shtml file request, it should tell the browser, by setting the content type, that the information being sent is still an HTML document. This way, the Web browser renders the content onscreen as usual. The MIME type for HTML content is text/html. The following line shows how to tell Apache to generate a text/html content type header when transmitting the output of an .shtml page:

```
AddType text/html   .shtml
```

For backward compatibility, documents with the MIME type text/x-server-parsed-html or text/x-server-parsed-html3 are also parsed (and the resulting output is given the MIME type text/html).

ENABLE SSI PARSING FOR A DIRECTORY

Both Apache and Web browsers know how to handle the new .shtml files; however, Apache is still not ready to parse the .shtml pages.

Using the Options directive, you need to tell Apache that you want to enable Includes support. First, however, you need to determine where to put this Options directive.

If you want to enable SSI support in the entire (primary) Web site, add the following directive in one of the global configuration files (such as access.conf):

```
Options +Includes
```

If you want to enable SSI support for a virtual Web site, you need to put the preceding directive inside the appropriate <VirtualHost . . .> container. Or if you want to be able to control this option from directory to directory, you can put this directive inside a <Directory . . .> container or in the per-directory access control file (.htaccess).

If you use a per-directory access control file (.htaccess) to enable SSI support, make sure the AllowOverride directive for the site owning that directory allows such an operation. The AllowOverride directive for such a site must allow the Includes option to be overridden. For example, if the AllowOverride is set to None for a site, no SSI parsing occurs.

If you do not use the + sign in the Options line in the preceding example, all the options except Includes are disabled.

USING SSI COMMANDS

SSI commands are embedded in HTML pages in the form of comments. The base command structure looks like this:

```
<!--#command argument1=value argument2=value argument3=value -->
```

The value is often enclosed in double quotes; many commands allow only a single attribute-value pair. Note that the comment terminator (-->) should be preceded by whitespace to ensure that it isn't considered part of the SSI command.

Now, let's examine the config, echo, exec, fcgi, flastmod, include, printenv, and set SSI commands.

```
config [errmsg="error message"] [sizefmt=["bytes" | "abbrev"]
[timefmt=format string]
```

The config command enables you to configure error messages and output formats. For example:

```
<!--#config errmsg="This is a custom SSI error message." -->
<!--#config errmsg_typo="This is a custom error message." -->
```

The first line is a valid config errmsg command that sets the error message to the string "This is a custom SSI error message." The second line is an invalid SSI command that causes a parse error; the error message, "This is a custom SSI error message" is displayed as a result. The message appears where the invalid command is found. It is possible to enter HTML tags or even insert client-side script in the string of the error message.

To configure the output format for the file size, use the config sizefmt= ["bytes" | "abbrev"] command. Acceptable format specifiers are "bytes" or "abbrev." For example:

```
<!-- config sizefmt="bytes" -->
```

This shows file sizes in bytes. To show files in kilobytes or megabytes, use:

```
<!-- config sizefmt="abbrev" -->
```

To configure the display format for time, use the `config timefmt=format string` command. The commonly used value of the format string can consist of the following identifiers:

%a: The abbreviated weekday name according to the current locale

%A: The full weekday name according to the current locale

%b: The abbreviated month name according to the current locale

%B: The full month name according to the current locale

%c: The preferred date and time representation for the current locale

%d: The day of the month as a decimal number (range 01 to 31)

%H: The hour as a decimal number using a 24-hour clock (range 00 to 23)

%I: The hour as a decimal number using a 12-hour clock (range 01 to 12)

%j: The day of the year as a decimal number (range 001 to 366)

%m: The month as a decimal number (range 01 to 12)

%M: The minute as a decimal number

%p: Either a.m. or p.m., according to the given time value or locale

%S: The second as a decimal number

%w: The day of the week as a decimal, Sunday being 0

%x: The preferred date representation for the current locale without the time

%X: The preferred time representation for the current locale without the date

%y: The year as a decimal number without a century (range 00 to 99)

%Y: The year as a decimal number including the century

%Z: The time zone name or abbreviation

%%: A literal % character

For example:

```
<!--#config timefmt="%m/%d/%Y" -->
```

This directive displays the time as 05/20/1998.

```
echo var="variable name"
```

The echo command prints one of the Include variables or any of the CGI environment variables. If the value of the variable is not available, it prints "(none)" as the value. Any dates printed are subject to the currently configured timefmt. For example:

```
<!--#config timefmt="%m/%d/%Y" -->
<!--#echo var="DATE_LOCAL" -->
```

These commands print a date such as 05/20/1998, due to the specified timefmt string.

```
exec [cgi="path/to/cgi/program"]   [cmd="path/to/other/program "]
```

The exec command enables you to execute an external program. The external program can be a CGI program or any other type of executable such as shell scripts or native-binary files. If you used the IncludesNOEXEC value for the Options directive, the exec command is disabled. The exec cgi command runs the named program as a CGI script, and the exec cmd command runs the named program using the sh (/bin/sh) shell as an external program.

```
fsize [ file = "path" ]  [ virtual="URL"]
```

This command prints the size of the specified file. When the first syntax (file= "path") is used, the path is assumed to be relative to the directory containing the current SSI document being parsed. You cannot use ../ in the path, nor can absolute paths be used. You cannot access a CGI script in this fashion. You can, however, access another parsed document. For example:

```
<!--#fsize file="download.zip">
```

If the second syntax is used, the virtual path is assumed to be a (%-encoded) URL path. If the path does not begin with a slash (/), then it is taken to be relative to the current document. You must access a normal file this way, but you cannot access a CGI script in this fashion.

```
flastmod [ file = "path" ]  [ virtual="URL"]
```

The flastmod command prints the last modification date of the specified file. The output is subject to the timefmt format specification. For example:

```
<!--#flastmod file="free_software.zip">
<!--#flastmod virtual="/download/free_software.zip">
```

If you are unclear about the syntax difference, see the previous section, the `fsize` command, as an example. To control how the modification date is printed, see the `config` command, earlier in this chapter.

```
Include [ file = "path" ]  [ virtual="URL"]
```

The include directive inserts the text of a document into the SSI document being processed. See the `fsize` command for the difference between file and virtual mode.

Any included file is subject to the usual access control. If the directory containing the parsed file has the option IncludesNOEXEC set, and including the document would cause a program to be executed, then it is not included. This option prevents the execution of CGI scripts. Otherwise, CGI scripts are invoked as they normally are, using the complete URL given in the command, including any query string. For example:

```
<!--#include file="copyrights.html" -->
```

This directive includes the copyrights.html file in the current document. Recursive inclusions are detected, and an error message is generated after the first pass.

```
printenv
```

The `printenv` command prints out a listing of all existing variables and their values. For example:

```
<!--#printenv -->
```

This command prints all the Include and CGI environment variables available. Use the `<PRE>` tag pair to make the output more readable. Also note that displaying the output of this command in a publicly accessible page might give away somewhat sensitive information about your system. Therefore use this command only for debugging purposes.

```
set var="name" value="something"
```

The `set` command sets the value of a user-defined variable. For example:

```
<!--#set var="home" value="index.shtml" -->
```

Note that any variable set using the preceding command is not persistent. In other words, every time a page that uses the `set` command is loaded, all the variables are set again.

USING SSI VARIABLES

In addition to the CGI environment variables, the SSI module makes a set of variables available to all SSI files. These variables are called the include variables. These can be used by SSI commands (echo, if, elif, and so on) and by any program invoked by an SSL command. The include variables are:

DATE_GMT: The current date in Greenwich Mean Time

DATE_LOCAL: The current date in the local time zone

DOCUMENT_NAME: The current SSI filename

DOCUMENT_URI: The (%-decoded) URL path of the document

LAST_MODIFIED: The last modification date of the current file – the date is subject to the config command's timefmt format

The include variables and the CGI variables are preset and available for use. Any of the preset variables can be used as arguments for other commands. The syntax for using defined variables is as follows:

```
<!--#command argument1="$variable1" argument2="$variable2" . . . -->
```

As you can see, the variable name is prefixed by a $ sign. Here's another example:

```
<!--#config errmsg="An error occurred in $DOCUMENT_NAME page." -->
```

When using variables in a var="variable" field, the $ sign is not necessary. For example:

```
<!--#echo var="DOCUMENT_NAME" -->
```

If you need to insert a literal dollar sign into the value of a variable, you can insert the dollar sign using backslash quoting. For example:

```
<!--#set var="password" value="\$cheese" -->
<!--#echo var="password" -->
```

This directive prints $cheese as the value of the variable "password."

Also, if you need to reference a variable name in the middle of a character sequence that might otherwise be considered a valid identifier on its own, use a pair of braces around the variable name. For example:

```
<!--#set var="uniqueid" value="${DATE_LOCAL}_${REMOTE_HOST}" -->
```

This command sets uniqueid to something like Tue May 20 06:47:48 1998_206.171.50.51, depending on the timefmt setting.

USING SSI FLOW CONTROL COMMANDS

As in programming languages, flow control is also available in the SSI module. Using flow control commands, you can create different output conditionally. The simplest flow control (that is, conditional) statement is:

```
<!--#if expr="test_expression" -->
<!--#endif -->
```

These directives evaluate the test expression and if the result of the test is true, then all the text up to the endif command is included in the output. The test_expression can be a string, which tests as true if the string is not empty, or it can be a comparison expression that involves two strings and a comparison operator such as = (equal), != (not equal), < (less than), > (greater than), <= (less than or equal to), or >= (greater than or equal to). Let's look at an example of a string by itself:

```
<!--#if expr="foobar" -->
   This test is successful.
<!--#endif -->
```

This directive always displays "This test is successful" because the expression is true when the test_expression is a non-null string. If expr="foobar" is changed to expr="" or expr="'''", however, then the text within the if-endif block will never be part of the output. Now let's look at an example of a string equality test:

```
<!--#set var="quicksearch" value="yes" -->
<!--#if expr="$quicksearch = yes" -->
  Quick search is requested.
<!--#endif -->
```

Here the variable called quicksearch is being set with the value yes and is later being compared with yes. Since the set value and the comparison value are equal, the "Quick search is requested" line is the output. If you require more complex flow control constructs, you can use the following forms:

```
<!--#if expr="test_condition1" -->

<!--#elif expr="test_condition2" -->

<!--#else -->

<!--#endif -->
```

The elif enables you to create an else-if condition. For example:

```
<!--#if expr="${HTTP_USER_AGENT} = /MSIE/" -->

  <!--#set var="browser" value="IE" -->
  <!--#include flie="vbscript.html" -->

<!--#elif expr="${HTTP_USER_AGENT} = /Lynx/" -->

  <!--#set var="browser" value="Lynx" -->
  <!--#include flie="simple-html.html" -->

<!--#else -->

  <!--#set var="browser" value="Navigator" -->
  <!--#include flie="javascript.html" -->

<!--#endif -->
```

Here, the HTTP_USER_AGENT variable is checked to see if it contains the string MSIE (a string used by Microsoft Internet Explorer browser). If it does contain this string, then the browser variable is set to "IE" and a file named vbscript.html is inserted in the current document. On the other hand, if the HTTP_USER_AGENT does not contain the MSIE string, it is assumed to be the other leading browser (Netscape Navigator), and so the browser variable is set to "Navigator" and the javascript.html file is inserted in the current document. By using the if-then-else construct, this example code sets a different value to the same variable and loads different files.

Hosting virtual Web sites

Serving more than one Web site per Web server is virtually a required feature for a high-end Web server. Apache supports two types of virtual hosts – IP-based virtual hosts and name-based virtual hosts. No matter what type of virtual host you choose to implement, proper Domain Name Service (DNS) configuration is a prerequisite. IP-based virtual host configuration requires unique IP addresses for each virtual host, and name-based virtual hosts are created using CNAME records. Because Chapter 10 covers DNS in great length, I do not discuss DNS specifics here. I assume that you know how to create an A or CNAME record in the DNS database.

APACHE CONFIGURATION FOR VIRTUAL HOSTS

You can configure Apache in two ways to enable it to support multiple hosts (the main server and the virtual servers). Either you can run multiple daemons, so that each host has a separate httpd daemon, or you can run a single daemon that supports all the virtual hosts and the primary server host. The second approach is widely used and preferable in most cases. Hence I will discuss only this method in the following section.

A single httpd daemon launches child processes to service requests for the primary Web site and all the virtual sites; by default, Apache listens to port 80 on all IP addresses of the local machine, and this is often sufficient. If you have a more complex requirement, such as listening on various port numbers or listening only to specific IP addresses, you can use the BindAddress or Listen directives.

Apache uses the special container <VirtualHost> in the httpd.conf file to handle all the virtual host–specific configurations. An example of a minimal virtual-host configuration might look like this:

```
<VirtualHost 192.168.0.50>
    DocumentRoot /www/apachehandbook/public/htdocs
    ServerName  www.apachehandbook.com
</VirtualHost>
```

The first line marks the start of a virtual-host (www.apachehandbook.com) configuration. The enclosed IP address needs to be a valid IP for www.apache handbook.com. If a nonstandard (that is, not 80) port address needs to be used, it can be supplied as follows:

```
<VirtualHost IP-address:port>
```

For example:

```
<VirtualHost 192.168.0.50:8080>
```

Any directive inside a <VirtualHost> container applies only to that virtual host. Any directive that has been used outside the <VirtualHost> directives applies to the primary server's configuration. Each virtual host inherits the primary server's configuration unless there is a conflict. In a case in which the same directive is used both in the main server configuration and in a virtual host configuration (that is, inside a <VirtualHost> container), the directive inside the virtual host configuration overrides the primary server's setting for only that particular virtual host. For example, if you have ServerName set to www.yourcompany.com in your primary-server configuration (that is, outside any <VirtualHost> container), and you have a ServerName directive in a <VirtualHost> container set to www.yourclient.com, then obviously you want the virtual host to respond to www.yourclient.com, right? That's exactly what happens; the directive within the virtual host section overrides the main server's corresponding directive. It may be easier to think of the main server configuration as the global default configuration for all virtual hosts that you create using the <VirtualHost>. So when configuring virtual hosts, you need to decide what to change in each of the virtual host configurations.

The directives either override the configuration given in the primary server or supplement it, depending on the directive. For example, the DocumentRoot directive in a <VirtualHost> section overrides the primary server's DocumentRoot, whereas AddType supplements the main server's MIME types.

Now, when a request arrives, Apache uses the IP address and port on which it arrived to find a matching virtual host configuration. If no virtual host matches the address and port, the request is handled by the primary server configuration. If it does match a virtual host address, Apache uses the configuration of that virtual server to handle the request.

In the previous example, the virtual-host configuration used is the same as the primary server, except that for the virtual host the DocumentRoot is set to /www/apachehandbook/ public/htdocs, and the ServerName is set to www.apache handbook.com. Directives commonly set in <VirtualHost> containers are DocumentRoot, ServerName, ErrorLog, and TransferLog.

You can put almost any configuration directive in the VirtualHost directive, with the exception of ServerType, StartServers, MaxSpareServers, MinSpareServers, MaxRequestsPerChild, BindAddress, Listen, PidFile, TypesConfig, ServerRoot, and NameVirtualHost. You may place User and Group directives inside VirtualHost containers if the suEXEC wrapper is used.

You can have as many <VirtualHost> containers as you want. The primary server can handle one or more of your virtual hosts, or you can have a <VirtualHost> for every available address and port and leave the primary server with no requests to handle.

APACHE CONFIGURATION FOR IP-BASED VIRTUAL HOSTS   Setting up IP-based virtual hosts in a single primary Apache server configuration is very simple. All you need to do is create a <VirtualHost> container per virtual IP address. For example, to create a virtual host called vhost1.domain.com (192.168.0.50) with /www/vhost1/ as the DocumentRoot directory, you add the following lines in the httpd.conf file:

```
<VirtualHost 192.168.0.50>
  DocumentRoot /www/vhost1
  ServerName vhost1.domain.com
</VirtualHost>
```

APACHE CONFIGURATION FOR NAME-BASED VIRTUAL HOSTS   Setting up name-based virtual hosts is also very easy. The very first step is to set the NameVirtualHost directive to the IP address of the name-based virtual hosts. This directive specifies an IP address that you use as a target for name-based virtual hosts. For example, say that you want to set up two virtual hosts such as www.client1.com and www.client2.com on an Apache server that listens to IP address 192.168.0.50. Here is an example configuration for such a setup:

```
NameVirtualHost 192.168.0.50
```

```
<VirtualHost 192.168.0.50>
  ServerName www.client1.com
  DocumentRoot /www/client1
</VirtualHost>

<VirtualHost 192.168.0.50>
  ServerName www.client2.com
  DocumentRoot /www/client2
</VirtualHost>
```

You need only a single NameVirtualHost directive per IP address for all the name-based virtual hosts using that IP address. When a request comes for one of these virtual hosts from an HTTP/1.1 compliant browser, Apache matches the ServerName with the hostname provided in the Host header of the request. Thus Apache determines which virtual host is requested.

Once you have created the virtual host configuration for Apache, you can start (or restart) the Apache server so the configuration can take effect. Also don't forget to create any directories that you might be using in a virtual host configuration before restarting your Apache server.

Starting with Apache 1.3.*x*, you can verify your virtual host configuration by running Apache using the -s option.

Using Apache as a proxy server

Proxy support in Apache comes from the mod_proxy module. This module is not compiled by default.

COMPILING THE PROXY MODULE

If you are using the APACI interface for compiling and installing Apache, then building a new Apache executable with the proxy module is as easy as performing the following steps in your Apache source distribution directory:

◆ If you are running the configure script for the first time, then enter the following command:

```
./configure -prefix=/dir/where/you/want/to/install/apache \
—enable-mode=proxy
```

◆ On the other hand, if you have already run the configure script before to compile Apache, run:

```
./config.status —enable-module=proxy
```

This way your previous configuration options are applied in creating a new configuration file. Now run the `make` command, and if it returns no error messages, run the `make install` command to install the newly compiled Apache executable in the appropriate directory.

PROXY MODULE DIRECTIVES

The proxy module for Apache comes with the set of directives needed to make use of the module. All of these directives are usable in both main server configuration or in any virtual server configuration context.

```
ProxyRequests on | off
```

This directive allows you to enable or disable the caching proxy service. However, it does not affect the functionality of the ProxyPass directive. The default value is "off."

```
ProxyRemote match remote-proxy-server-URL
```

This directive enables you to interface your proxy server with another proxy server. The value of match can be either the name of a URL scheme (http, ftp, and so on) or a partial URL.

The remove-proxy-server URL can be `http://remove-proxy-hostname:port`. Note that, currently, only the HTTP protocol is supported. In other words, you can specify only a proxy server that deals with the HTTP protocol; however, you can forward FTP requests from your proxy server to one that supports both HTTP and FTP protocols as follows:

```
ProxyRemote ftp http://ftp.proxy.nitec.com:8000
```

This directive sends all FTP requests that come to the local proxy server to `ftp://ftp.proxy.nitec.com`. The requests are sent via HTTP, so the actual FTP transaction occurs at the remote proxy server.

If you just want to forward all proxy requests for a certain Web site to its proxy server directly, you can do that with this directive. For example:

```
ProxyRemote http://www.isp.com/ http://web-proxy.isp.com:8000
```

This command sends all requests that match `www.isp.com` to `web-proxy.bigisp.com`. If you want to forward all of your proxy requests to another proxy, however, you can use the asterisk as the match phrase. For example:

```
ProxyRemote * http://proxy.domain.com
```

This directive sends all local proxy requests to the proxy server at `proxy.domain.com`.

```
ProxyPass relative-URL destination-URL
```

This directive enables you to map a Web server's document tree onto your proxy server's document space. For example:

```
ProxyPass /internet/microsoft       www.microsoft.com/
```

This directive found in the httpd.conf file of a proxy server called `proxy.nitec.com` permits users of the proxy server to access the Microsoft Web site using the URL:

```
http://proxy.nitec.com/internet/microsoft
```

This directive acts like a mirror of the remote Web site. Any request that uses the relative-URL is converted internally into a proxy request for the destination URL.

```
ProxyPassReverse relative-URL destination-URL
```

This directive is useful when you want to create a reverse proxy server using Apache. In such a reverse proxy setup, this directive fixes the Location headers that might be returned by the actual Web server. For example:

```
<Virtualhost 206.171.50.50>
   ServerName www.nitec.com
   ProxyRequests on
   ProxyPass / realserver.nitec.com/
   ProxyPassReverse / realserver.nitec.com/
</VirtualHost>
```

Here the `www.nitec.com` is the proxy server that gets all the pages from another server called `realserver.nitec.com`. The ProxyPass directive enables this feature. However, if a page on `realserver.nitec.com` sends a Location header in response, the ProxyPassReverse directive does not allow the proxy server `www.nitec.com` to be bypassed by the client.

```
ProxyBlock  partial or full host name . . .
```

This directive enables you block access to a named host or domain; for example:

```
ProxyBlock gates
```

This command blocks access to any host that has the word "gates" in its name. This way, access to `http://gates.ms.com` or `http://gates.friendsofbill.com` is blocked. You also can specify multiple hosts as follows:

```
ProxyBlock apple orange.com banana.com
```

This directive blocks all access to any host that matches any of the preceding words or domain names. The mod_proxy module attempts to determine the IP addresses for these hosts during server startup and caches them for matching later.

To block access to all hosts, use:

```
ProxyBlock *
```

This directive effectively disables your proxy server.

```
NoProxy Domain name| Subnet | IP Address | Hostname
```

This directive gives you some control over the ProxyRemote directive in an intranet environment. You can specify a domain name, subnet, IP address, or hostname not to be served by the proxy server specified in the ProxyRemote directive. For example:

```
ProxyRemote   *  http://firewall.yourcompany.com:8080
NoProxy          .yourcompany.com
```

Here all requests for `anything.yourcompany.com` (such as `www.yourcompany.com`) are served by the local proxy server, and everything else goes to the `firewall.yourcompany.com` proxy server.

```
ProxyDomain Domain
```

This directive specifies the default domain name for the proxy server. When this directive is set to the local domain name on an intranet, any request that does not include a domain name gets this domain name appended in the request. For example:

```
ProxyDomain    .nitec.com
```

When a user of the `nitec.com` domain sends a request for a URL such as `http://marketing/us.html`, the request is regenerated as the following URL:

```
http://marketing.nitec.com/us.html
```

Note that the domain name you specify must have a leading period.

```
ProxyReceiveBufferSize bytes
```

This directive sets the network buffer size for outgoing requests from the proxy server. It has to be greater than 512. However, to use the system's default buffer size, set this directive to 0.

CacheRoot *directory*

This directive allows you to enable disk caching. You specify a directory name where the proxy server can write cached files. The Apache server running the proxy module must have write permission for the directory. For example:

CacheRoot /www/proxy/cache

This directive tells Apache to write proxy cache data to the /www/proxy/cache directory. Note that you need to specify the size of the cache using the CacheSize directory before the proxy server can start using this directory for caching. You also may need to use other cache directives such as CacheSize, CacheMaxExpire, CacheDefaultExpire, CacheGcInterval, and CacheDirLength to create a usable disk caching proxy solution.

CacheSize *n kilobytes*

This directive specifies the amount of disk space (in K) that should be used for disk caching. The cached files are written in the directory specified by the CacheRoot directive. Note that it is possible for the proxy server to write more data than the specified limit, but the proxy server's garbage collection scheme deletes files until the usage is at or below this setting. The default setting (5K) is unrealistic; I recommend anywhere from 10MB to 1GB depending on your user load.

CacheGcInterval *n hours*

This directive specifies the time interval (in hours) when Apache checks the cache directories for deleting expired files. At this point Apache also enforces the disk space usage limit specified by the CacheSize directive.

CacheMaxExpire *n hours*

This directive specifies the time (in hours) when all cached documents expire. In other words, if you specify this directive as:

CacheMaxExpire 48

then all the cached documents will expire in 48 hours, or two days. This directive overrides any expiration date specified in the document itself; so if a document has a expiration date later than the maximum specified by this directive, the document is still removed. The default value is 24.

`CacheLastModifiedFactor` *floating point number*

This directive specifies a factor (default is 0.1) used to calculate expiration time when the original Web server does not supply an expiration date for a document. The calculation is done using the following formula:

```
expiry-period = (last modification time for the document) *
(floating point number)
```

So if a document was last modified 24 hours ago, then the default factor of 0.1 makes Apache calculate the expiration time for this document to be 2.4 hours. If the calculated expiration period is longer than that set by CacheMaxExpire, then the latter takes precedence.

`CacheDirLength` *length*

When disk caching is on, Apache creates subdirectories in the directory specified by the CacheRoot directive. This directive specifies the number of characters (the default is 1) used in creating the subdirectory names. You really do not need to change the default for this directive.

`CacheDirLevels` *levels*

This directive specifies the number of subdirectories that Apache creates to store cache data files. Default value is 3. See CacheDirLength for related information.

`CacheDefaultExpire` *n hours*

This directive provides a default time (in hours) used to expire a cached file when the last modification time of the file is unknown. Default value is 1. CacheMaxExpire does not override this setting.

`CacheForceCompletion` *percentage*

This directive tells the proxy server to continue transferring a document from the remote HTTP/FTP server even if the request is canceled. The percentage specified in the directive makes the proxy server determine if it should continue or not with the transfer. The default value is 90 percent, which tells the proxy server to continue transferring when 90 percent of the document is already cached. You can change the value from 1 to 100.

`NoCache` *Domain name| Subnet | IP Address | Hostname . . .*

The NoCache directive specifies a list of hosts, domain names, and IP addresses, separated by spaces, for which no caching is performed. You should use this directive to disable caching of local Web servers on an intranet. Note that the proxy server also matches partial names of a host. If you want to disable caching altogether, use the following:

```
NoCache *
```

To enable the proxy server, you need to set the ProxyRequests to On. After that, the additional configuration depends on what you want to do with your proxy server. Whatever you decide to do with it, any proxy configuration that you choose should go inside a special <Directory . . .> container that looks like the following:

```
<Directory proxy:*>
. . .
</Directory>
```

Any directives that you want to use to control the proxy server's behavior should go inside this container. The asterisk is a wildcard for the requested URL. In other words, when a request for www.nitec.com is processed by the Apache server, it looks like:

```
<Directory proxy:http://www.nitec.com/>
. . .
</Directory>
```

You also can use the <Directory ~ /RE/> container, which uses regular expressions. For example:

```
<Directory ~ proxy:http://[^:/]+/.*>
. . .
</Directory>
```

Now let's look at a few commonly used proxy configurations.

CACHING REMOTE WEB SITES

Because a great deal of Web content on both the Internet and intranets is likely to be static, caching them on a local proxy server could save valuable network bandwidth. A cache-enabled proxy server fetches requested documents only when the cache contains an expired document or when the requested document is not present in the cache. To enable caching on your proxy server, you need to specify caching directives inside a special directory container. For example:

```
<Directory proxy:*>
CacheRoot /www/cache
CacheSize 1024
```

```
CacheMaxExpire 24
</Directory>
```

This configuration defines a caching proxy server that writes cache files to the /www/cache directory. It is permitted to write 1,024K of data (1MB), and the cache must expire after each day (24 hours).

If you do not want to permit outside people to abuse your proxy, you can restrict proxy access either by host or by username/password authentication.

To control which hosts have access to the proxy server, you can create a configuration such as the following:

```
<Directory proxy:*>
AuthType Basic
AuthName Proxy
order deny,allow
deny from all
allow from myhost.nitec.com
</Directory>
```

This configuration denies access to all but myhost.nitec.com. If you want to use username/password authentication, you can use something similar to the following:

```
<Directory proxy:*>
AuthType Basic
AuthName Proxy
AuthUserFile /path/to/proxy/.htpasswd
AuthName Proxy
require valid-user
</Directory>
```

Create the .htpasswd file using the htpasswd utility that comes with Apache. It is also possible to restrict access for a protocol, for example:

```
<Directory proxy:http:*>
. . .
</Directory>
```

This directive enables you to control how HTTP requests are processed by your proxy server. Similarly, you can use the following to control how each of these protocols is handled by the proxy server:

```
<Directory proxy:ftp:*>
. . .
</Directory>
```

You can also create a virtual host exclusively for a proxy server. In that case, the directives should go inside the proxy host's `<VirtualHost>` container:

```
<VirtualHost proxy.host.com:*>
. . .
</VirtualHost>
```

MIRRORING A WEB SITE

A mirror Web site is a local copy of a remote Web site. For example, if you wanted to mirror the `www.apache.org` Web site so your users can connect to your mirror site for quick access to Apache information, you can use the proxy server to create such a mirror as follows:

```
ProxyPass / www.apache.org/
ProxyPassReverse / www.apache.org/
CacheRoot /www/cache
CacheDefaultExpire 24
```

This directive makes a proxy server a mirror of the `www.apache.org` Web site. For example, this configuration turns my proxy server blackhole.nitec.com into a www.apache.org mirror. Users who enter `http://blackhole.nitec.com` as the URL receive the Apache mirror's index page as if they had gone to `www.apache.org`.

 You must get permission before you mirror someone else's Web site as you may be infringing on copyrights.

CREATING A REVERSE PROXY SERVER

You need reverse proxy servers when the real HTTP/FTP server is behind a firewall or when a load-balancing scheme is speeding up or distributing delivery of the content. Creating a reverse proxy server is quite easy with the latest proxy module found in Apache 1.3.*x*. Say that you have a Web server with hostname `realserver.yourcompany.com` and you want to have everyone visit it via a reverse proxy server called `www.yourcompany.com` (11.22.33.44). You can create the following virtual host on `.yourcompany.com` server:

```
<VirtualHost 11.22.33.44>
   ServerName www.yourcompany.com
   ProxyPass / realserver.yourcompany.com/
   ProxyPassReverse / realserver.yourcompany.com/
   CacheRoot /www/cache
   CacheDefaultExpire 24
</VirtualHost>
```

This directive makes the proxy server a reverse proxy for `realserver.your company.com`. To your visitors, they are accessing `www.yourcompany.com`.

Authenticating Web users

Knowing how to create password-protected, restricted areas in a Web site is a must for any Web administrator. By default, Apache supports authentication schemes such as the host-based authentication and basic HTTP authentication.

USING HOST-BASED AUTHENTICATION

In this authentication scheme, access is controlled by the host name or the host's IP address. When a request is made for a certain resource, the Web server checks to see if the requesting host is allowed access to the resource and takes action based on the findings. The standard Apache distribution includes a module called mod_access, which provides this access control support using directives such as `allow`, `deny`, `order`, `allow from env=variablename`, and `deny from env= variablename`.

```
allow from host1 host2 host3 . . .
```

This directive enables you to define a list of hosts (containing one or more hosts or IP addresses) that are allowed access to a certain directory. When more than one host or IP address is specified, they should be separated with space characters. Table 12-1 shows the possible values for the directive.

TABLE 12-1 POSSIBLE VALUES FOR THE ALLOW DIRECTIVE

Value	Example	Description
All	`allow from all`	This reserved word allows access for all hosts. The example shows how to use this option.
A fully qualified domain name (FQDN) of a host	`allow from wormhole.nitec. com`	Only the host that has the specified FQDN is allowed access. The allow directive in the example allows access only to `wormhole. nitec.com`. Note that this compares whole components; `toys.com` would not match `etoys.com`.

Continued

TABLE 12-1 POSSIBLE VALUES FOR THE ALLOW DIRECTIVE *(Continued)*

Value	Example	Description
A partial domain name of a host	`allow from .mainoffice.nitec.com`	Only all the hosts that match the partial host name are allowed access. The example permits all the hosts in `.mainoffice.nitec.com` network to access the site. For example, `developer1.mainoffice.nitec.com` and `developer2.mainoffice.nitec.com` have access to the site. However, `developer3.baoffice.nitec.com` is not allowed access.
A full IP address of a host	`allow from 206.171.50.50`	Only the specified IP address is allowed access. The example shows a full IP address (all four octets of IP are present), 206.171.50.50, that is allowed access.
A partial IP address	Example 1: `allow from 206.171.50` Example 2: `allow from 130.86`	When not all four octets of an IP address are present in the allow directive, the partial IP address is matched from left to right, and hosts that have the matching IP address pattern (that is, it is part of the same subnet) are allowed access. In the first example, all hosts with IP addresses in the range of 206.171.50.1 to 206.171.50.255 have access. In the second example, all hosts from the 130.86 network are allowed access.
A network/netmask pair	`Allow from 206.171.50.0/255.255.255.0`	This enables you to specify a range of IP addresses using the network and the netmask address. The example allows only the hosts with IP addresses in the range of 206.171.50.1 to 206.171.50.255 to have access. This feature is available in Apache 1.3 or later.

Value	Example	Description
A network/nnn CIDR specification	`Allow 206.171. 50.0/24`	Similar to the previous entry, except the netmask consists of nnn high-order 1 bits. The example is equivalent to allow from 206.171. 50.0/255.255.255.0. This feature is available in Apache 1.3 or later.

```
deny from host1 . . .
```

This directive is the exact opposite of the allow directive. It enables you to define a list of hosts that are denied access to a specified directory. Like the allow directive, it can accept all the values shown in Table 12-1.

```
order deny, allow | allow, deny | mutual-failure
```

This directive controls how Apache evaluates both allow and deny directives. For example:

```
<Directory /mysite/myboss/rants>
  order deny, allow
  deny from myboss.mycompany.com
  allow from all
</Directory>
```

This example denies the host myboss.mycompany.com access and allows all other hosts to access the directory. The value for the order directive is a comma-separated list that indicates which directive takes precedence. Typically, the one that affects all hosts is given lowest priority. In the preceding example, because the allow directive affects all hosts, it is given the lower priority. When you set this directive to mutual-failure, only those hosts appearing on the allow list but not on the deny list are granted access. In all cases, Apache evaluates every allow and deny directive.

```
allow from env=variable
```

This directive, a variation of the allow directive, allows access when the named environment variable is set. This feature is useful only if you are using other directives such as BrowserMatch to set an environment variable. For example:

```
BrowserMatch "MSIE" ms_browser
<Directory /path/to/Vbscript_directory>
```

```
    order deny,allow
    deny from all
    allow from env=ms_browser
</Directory>
```

Here the Apache server sets the ms_browser environment variable for all browsers that provide the MSIE string as part of the User-Agent header. The allow directive allows only browsers for which the ms_browser variable is set.

```
deny from env=variable
```

This directive, a variation of the deny directive, denies access capability for all hosts for which the specified environment is set. For example:

```
BrowserMatch "MSIE" ms_browser
<Directory /path/to/Vbscript_directory>
  order deny,allow
  allow from all
  deny from env=ms_browser
</Directory>
```

Here access is blocked for all Web browsers that send MSIE string as part of the User-Agent header in a request.

USING HTTP-SPECIFIED BASIC AUTHENTICATION
Support for HTTP-specified basic authentication in Apache has been around for quite a while. By default, Apache provides authentication support using the mod_auth.c module.

USING STANDARD mod_auth
This module is compiled by default in the standard distribution. Standard mod_auth-based basic HTTP authentication uses user names, groups, and passwords stored in text files to confirm authentication. This confirmation works well when you are dealing with a small number of users. However, if you have a lot of users (thousands or more), use of mod_auth might have a performance penalty. In such a case you can use something more advanced, such as DBM files, Berkeley DB files, or even a SQL database. The default authentication module offers the following directives.

```
AuthUserFile filename
```

This directive sets the name of the text file that contains the user names and passwords used in the basic HTTP authentication. You must provide a fully quali-fied path to the file to be used. For example:

```
AuthUserFile /www/nitec/secrets/.htpasswd
```

This file is usually created using a support utility called htpasswd. The format of this file is very simple. Each line contains a single user name and an encrypted password. To enhance security, keep the AuthUserFile-specified file outside the document tree of your Web site.

AuthGroupFile *filename*

This directive specifies a text file to be used as the list of user groups for basic HTTP authentication. The filename is the absolute path to the group file. You can create this file using any text editor. The format of this file as follows:

groupname: *username1 username2 username3 . . .*

To enhance security, make sure the AuthGroupFile-specified file resides outside the document tree of your Web site.

AuthAuthoritative   on | off

If you are using more than one authentication scheme for the same directory, you can set this directive to on so that when a user name/password pair fails with the first scheme, it is passed on to the next (lower) level.

Now let's take a look at an example of basic authentication. This example shows you how to create a restricted directory that requires a user name and a password for access. To simplify the example, I assume the following are settings for a Web site called apache.nitec.com:

```
DocumentRoot /data/web/apache/public/htdocs
AccessFileName .htaccess
AllowOverride  All
```

Now let's also assume that you want to restrict access to the following directory, such that only a user named "reader" with the password "bought-it" is able to access the /www/IDGbooks/readers/ directory. Follow these steps to create the restricted access.

STEP 1: CREATING A USER FILE WITH HTPASSWD   The standard Apache distribution comes with a utility program called htpasswd, which creates the user file needed for the AuthUserFile directive. Use the program as follows:

```
htpasswd -c /data/web/apache/secrets/.htpasswd reader
```

The htpasswd utility asks for the password of "reader." Enter "bought-it" and then reenter the password again to confirm that you didn't make a typo. After you reenter the password, the utility creates a file called .htpasswd in the /data/web/ apache/secrets directory. Note the following:

♦ Use the `-c` option to tell htpasswd that you want to create a new user file. If you already have the password file and want to add a new user, you do not want this option.

♦ Place the user file outside the document root directory of the `apache. nitec.com` site, as you do not want anyone to download it via the Web.

♦ Use a leading period (.) in the filename so that it will not appear in the `ls` output unless the `-a` option is specified. This is a simple attempt to hide files from prying eyes.

To save future headaches, execute the following command:

```
cat /data/web/apache/secrets/.htpasswd
```

This directive should show a line similar to the following (the password won't be exactly the same as this example):

```
reader:hulR6FFh1sxK6
```

This display confirms that you have a user called "reader" in the .htpasswd file. The password "bought-it" is encrypted by the htpasswd program using the standard crypt() function.

STEP 2: CREATING AN .HTACCESS FILE   Using a text editor, add the following lines to a file named /www/IDGbooks/readers/.htaccess:

```
AuthName "IDG Readers Only"
AuthType  Basic
AuthUserFile /data/web/apache/secrets/.htpasswd
require user reader
```

The first directive, AuthName, sets the realm of the authentication. This is really just a label sent to the Web browser so the user receives some clue about the file or directory she is about to access. In this case, the "IDG Readers Only" string indicates that only IDG readers can access this directory. The second directive, AuthType, specifies the type of authentication to be used. Because only basic authentication is supported, AuthType is always set to "Basic." The next directive, AuthUserFile, specifies the filename for the user file. The path to the user file is provided here. The last directive, require, specifies that a user named "reader" is allowed access to this directory.

STEP 3: SETTING FILE PERMISSIONS   After the .htaccess and the .htpasswd files are created, make sure that only Apache can read the files. No users except the file owner and Apache should have access to these files.

STEP 4: TESTING   Next, use a Web browser to access the following URL: `http://apache.nitec.com/chapter 12`. Apache will send the 401 status header and WWW-Authenticate response header to the browser with the realm (set in AuthName) and authentication type (set in AuthType) information. The browser displays a pop-up dialog box that requests a user name and password.

It is a good idea to see if one can get in without a user name or password, so enter nothing in the entry boxes in the dialog and press the OK button. This action should result in an authentication failure. The browser receives the same authentication challenge again, so it displays another dialog box.

Choosing the Cancel button results in the browser showing the standard "Authentication Required" error message from Apache.

Pressing the Reload button on the browser requests the same URL again, and the browser receives the same authentication challenge from the server. This time enter "reader" as the user name and "bought-it" as the password and press the OK button. Apache now allows you to access the directory.

You can change the "Authentication Required" message by using the ErrorDocument directive:

```
ErrorDocument 401 /nice_401message.html
```

Insert this line in your srm.conf file and create a nice message in the nice_401message.html file to make your users happy.

Instead of allowing a single user called "reader" to access the restricted area, as demonstrated in the previous example, here you allow anyone belonging to group named "asb_readers" to access the same directory. Let's assume this group has two users: pikejb and bcaridad. Follow these steps to give the users in group asb_readers directory access.

STEP 1: CREATING A USER FILE USING HTPASSWD   Using the `htpasswd` utility, create the users pikejb and bcaridad.

STEP 2: CREATING A GROUP FILE   Using a text editor such as vi, create a file named /data/web/apache/secrets/.htgroup. This file has a single line, as follows:

```
asb_readers: pikejb bcaridad
```

STEP 3: CREATING AN .HTACCESS FILE IN /DATA/WEB/APACHE/PUBLIC/HTDOCS/ CHAPTER_10   Using a text editor, add the following lines to a file called /www/ IDGbooks/readers/.htaccess:

```
AuthName "IDG Readers Only"
```

```
AuthType   Basic
AuthUserFile /data/web/apache/secrets/.htpasswd
AuthGroupFile /data/web/apache/secrets/.htgroup
require group  asb_readers
```

This is almost the same configuration that I discussed in the previous example but with two changes. The first change is the addition of a new directive, AuthGroupFile, which points to the .htgroup group file created earlier. The next change is in the require directive line, which now requires a group called "asb_readers." In other words, Apache allows access to anyone that belongs to that group. Note that you could have just as easily used the following line:

```
require user pikejb bcaridad
```

instead of:

```
require group asb_readers
```

However, listing all users in the require line could become cumbersome and cause unnecessary headaches. Using group, you can easily add or remove multiple users. As in the previous example, make sure the .htaccess, .htpasswd, and .htgroup files are readable only by Apache, and that no one but the owner has write access to the files.

You can also mix Apache's host-based access control with the basic HTTP authentication scheme. For example:

```
AuthName "IDG Readers Only"
AuthType   Basic
AuthUserFile /data/web/apache/secrets/.htpasswd
AuthGroupFile /data/web/apache/secrets/.htgroup
require group  asb_readers
order deny, allow
deny from all
allow from .nitec.com
```

This configuration is the same as the last example, but it adds three host-based access control directives discussed in earlier sections. The first one is the order directive, which tells Apache to evaluate the deny directive before it does the allow directive. The deny directive tells Apache to refuse access from all hosts. The allow directive tells Apache to allow access from the apache-training.nitec.com domain. This effectively tells Apache that any hosts in the .nitec.com domain are welcome to this directory. Note that here Apache assumes that both host-based and basic HTTP authentications are required for this directory. If you want to allow access when a user enters a valid username/password pair or makes the request from the nitec.com domain, you need to add satisfy any at the end of the preceding configuration.

Monitoring server status

The module mod_status.c enables Apache administrators to monitor the server via the Web. An HTML page is created with server statistics. It also produces another page that is machine readable. The information displayed on both pages includes: server version and compilation date/time stamp; current time on the server system; time when the server was last restarted; server uptime; total number of accesses served so far; total bytes transferred so far; the number of idle servers and their status; averages giving the number of requests per second, the number of bytes served per second, and the number of bytes per request; CPU usage by each child server and total load placed on the server by Apache processes; and the list of virtual hosts and requests currently being processed.

This module is not compiled by default in the standard Apache distribution, so you need to compile it into your Apache executable (httpd) yourself. Once you have the mod_status module compiled and built into your Apache server, you need to define a URL location where Apache displays the information. In other words, you need to tell Apache which URL will bring up the server statistics on your Web browser.

Let's say that your domain name is yourdomain.com, and you want to use the following URL: www.mydomain.com/apache-status. Using the <Location . . .> container, you can tell the server that you want it to handle this URL using the server-status handler found in the mod_status module. The following lines do the job:

```
<Location /apache-status>
  SetHandler server-status
</Location>
```

Here, the SetHandler directive sets the handler (server-status) for the previously mentioned URL. This configuration segment should typically go in the access.conf file, but it really can go inside any of the three configuration files. Once you have added the configuration in one of the three files, you can restart the server and access the preceding URL from a browser. Note that the <Location . . .> container in this example enables anyone using this URL to see the server status; this may not be a good thing as far as security is concerned. To make sure that only machines on your domain can access the status page, you replace the preceding configuration with the following:

```
<Location /apache-status>
  SetHandler server-status
  order deny, allow
  deny from all
  allow from .yourdomain.com
</Location>
```

where you replace *yourdomain.com* with your own domain name. If you want only one or more selected hosts to have access to this page, you simply list the host names in the allow directive line.

 TIP You can have the status page update itself automatically if you have a browser that supports the refresh command. Access the page http:// www.yourdomain.com/server-status?refresh=N to refresh the page every N seconds. Replace N with the time interval in seconds you want the status page to refresh itself, in other words, if N is 120, then the statistics are refreshed every two minutes.

To simplify the status display, add ?auto at the end of the URL. This query string tells Apache to display simplified output.

Logging hits and errors

Knowing the running status of your server is helpful in managing the server, but knowing who or what is accessing your Web site(s) is also very important, as well as exciting. As Web server software started appearing in the market, many Web server log analysis programs started appearing as well. These programs became part of the everyday work life of many Web administrators. Along with all these came the era of log file incompatibilities that made log analysis difficult and cumbersome; no single analysis program worked on all log files. Then came the Common Log Format (CLF) specification. This specification enabled all Web servers to write logs in a reasonably similar manner, thus making log analysis easier from one server to another.

By default, the standard Apache distribution includes a module called mod_log_config,responsible for the basic logging, and it writes CLF log files by default. You can alter this behavior using the LogFormat directive. However, CLF covers logging requirements in most environments.

The CLF file contains a separate line for each request. A line is composed of several tokens separated by spaces:

host ident authuser date request status bytes

If a token does not have a value, then it is represented by a hyphen (-). Tokens have the following meanings:

◆ Host: This is the fully qualified domain name of the client, or its IP address.

◆ Ident: If the IdentityCheck directive is enabled and the client machine runs identd, then this is the identity information reported by the client.

- ◆ Authuser: If the requested URL required a successful Basic HTTP authentication, then the user name is the value of this token.

- ◆ Date: This is the date and time of the request.

- ◆ Request: This is the request line from the client, enclosed in double quotes (" ").

- ◆ Status: This is the three-digit HTTP status code returned to the client.

- ◆ Bytes: This is the number of bytes in the object returned to the client, excluding all HTTP headers.

The date field has the following format:

```
date = [day/month/year:hour:minute:second zone]
```

For example:

```
[02/Jan/1998:00:22:01 -0800]
```

Four directives are available in the mod_log_config module:

```
TransferLog filename | "| /path/to/external/program"
```

This directive sets the name of the log file or program where the log information is to be sent. By default, the log information is in the Common Log File (CLF) format. This format can be customized using the LogFormat directive.

When the TransferLog directive is found within a virtual host container, the log information is formatted using the LogFormat directive found within the context. If a LogFormat directive is not found in the same context, however, the server's log format is used.

The TransferLog directive takes either a log file path or a pipe to an external program as the argument. The log filename is assumed to be relative to the ServerRoot setting if no leading / character is found. For example, if the ServerRoot is set to /etc/httpd, then the following tells Apache to send log information to the /etc/httpd/logs/access.log file:

```
TransferLog logs/access.log
```

When the argument is a pipe to an external program, the log information is sent to the external program's standard input (STDIN).

Note that a new program is not started for a VirtualHost if it inherits the TransferLog from the main server. If a program is used, then it is run under the user who started httpd. This will be the root if the server was started by the root. Be sure that the program is secure.

```
LogFormat format [nickname]
```

This directive sets the format of the default log file named by the TransferLog directive. The default value is "%h %l %u %t \"%r\" %s %b." If you include a nickname for the format on the directive line, you can use it in other LogFormat and CustomLog directives rather than repeating the entire format string. A LogFormat directive that defines a nickname does nothing else – that is, it only defines the nickname; it doesn't actually apply the format.

`CustomLog file-pipe format-or-nickname`

Like the TransferLog directive, this directive enables you to send logging information to a log file or an external program. Unlike the TransferLog directive, however, it enables you to use a custom log format that can be specified as an argument.

The argument format specifies a format for each line of the log file. The options available for the format are exactly the same as for the argument of the LogFormat directive. If the format includes any spaces (which it will in almost all cases), enclose it in double quotes.

Instead of an actual format string, you can use a format nickname defined with the LogFormat directive.

Nicknames are available only in Apache 1.3 or later. Also, the TransferLog and CustomLog directives can be used multiple times in each server to make each request log to multiple files.

`CookieLog filename`

The CookieLog directive sets the filename for the logging of cookies. The filename is relative to the ServerRoot. This directive is included only for compatibility with mod_cookies and is therefore deprecated; use of this directive is not recommended. Use the user-tracking module's directive instead. The user-tracking module mod_usertrack is discussed later in this chapter.

CUSTOMIZING SERVER LOG FILES

Although CLF meets most log requirements, sometimes it is useful to be able to customize logging data. For example, you may want to log the type of browsers accessing your site so that your Web design team can determine what type of browser-specific HTML to avoid or use. Or perhaps you want to know which Web sites are sending (that is, referring) visitors to your sites. All this is accomplished quite easily in Apache. The default logging module, mod_log_config, supports custom logging.

Custom formats are set with the LogFormat and CustomLog directives of the module. The format argument to LogFormat and CustomLog is a string. This format string can have both literal characters and special % format specifiers. When literal values are used in this string, they are copied into the log file for each request. The

% specifiers, however, are replaced with corresponding values. The special % specifiers are:

- %b: Bytes sent, excluding HTTP headers

- %f: The filename of the request

- %{variable}e: The contents of the environment variable VARIABLE

- %h: The remote host that made the request

- %{ IncomingHeader }i: The contents of IncomingHeader – that is, the header line(s) in the request sent to the server. The i character at the end denotes that this is a client (incoming) header.

- %l: If the IdentityCheck directive is enabled and the client machine runs identd, then this is the identity information reported by the client.

- %{MODULE_NOTE }n: The contents of the note MODULE_NOTE from another module

- %{ OutgoingHeader }o: The contents of OutgoingHeader – that is, the header line(s) in the reply. The o character at the end denotes that this is a server (outgoing) header.

- %p: The port to which the request was served

- %P: The process ID of the child that serviced the request

- %r: The first line of the request

- %s: The status returned by the server in response to the request. Note that when the request gets redirected, the value of this format specifier is still the original request status. If you want to store the redirected request status, use %..>s instead.

- %t: The time of the request. The format of time is the same as in CLF format.

- %{format}t: The time, in the form given by format. (You can look at the strftime man page.)

- %t: The time taken to serve the request, in seconds

- %u: If the requested URL required a successful Basic HTTP authentication, then the user name is the value of this format specifier. The value may be bogus if the server returned a 401 status (Authentication Required) after the authentication attempt.

- %u: The URL path requested

- %v: The name of the server or the virtual host to which the request came

You can include conditional information in each of the preceding specifiers. The conditions can be presence (or absence) of certain HTTP status code(s). For example, let's say you want to log all referring URLs that pointed a user to a nonexistent page. In such a case, the server produces a 404 status (Not Found) header. So to log the referring URLs, you can use the format specifier:

```
'%404{Referer}i'
```

Similarly, to log referring URLs that resulted in an unusual status, you can use:

```
'%!200,304,302{Referer}i'
```

Notice the use of the ! character to denote the absence of the server status list.

Similarly, to include additional information at the end of the CLF format specifier, you can extend the CLF format, which is defined by the format string:

```
"%h %l %u %t \"%r\" %s %b"
```

For example:

```
"%h %l %u %t \"%r\" %s %b \"%{Referer}i\" \"%{User-agent}i\""
```

This format specification logs CLF format data and adds the Referer and User-agent information found in client-provided headers in each log entry.

USING ERROR LOGS

If you don't log errors, you can't determine what's wrong and where the error occurs. Interestingly, error logging is supported in the core Apache. The ErrorLog directive enables you to log all types of errors that Apache encounters. You can either specify a filename or use the syslog daemon (syslogd) to log all errors. For example:

```
ErrorLog /logs/error_log
```

With this directive, Apache writes error messages to the /logs/error_log file. To use the syslog facility, use:

```
ErrorLog syslog
```

Using the LogLevel directive, you can specify what type of messages Apache should send to syslog. For example:

```
ErrorLog syslog
LogLevel debug
```

Here, Apache is instructed to send debug messages to syslog. If you want to store debug messages in a different file via syslog, then you need to modify /etc/syslog. conf. For example:

```
*.debug    /var/log/debug
```

Add this line in /etc/syslog.conf, restart syslogd (killall –HUP syslogd), and Apache enables you to store all Apache debug messages to the /var/log/debug file. Also note that you can set LogLevel to any of the following settings:

- ◆ emerg: Emergency messages

- ◆ alert: Alert messages

- ◆ crit: Critical messages

- ◆ error: Error messages

- ◆ warn: Warnings

- ◆ notice: Notification messages

- ◆ info: Information messages

- ◆ debug: Messages logged at debug level also include the source file and line number where the message is generated to help debugging and code development.

 TIP If you want to see updates to your syslog or any other log files as they happen, use the tail utility with - f */path/to/log* option.

ANALYZING SERVER LOG FILES

Many third-party Web server log analysis tools are available. Most of these tools expect the log files to be in CLF format, so make sure you have CLF formatting in your logs. Here are some of those tools and where you can find them:

- ◆ WebTrends: http://www.webtrends.com/

- ◆ Wusage: http://www.boutell.com/wusage/

- ◆ wwwstat: http://www.ics.uci.edu/pub/websoft/wwwstat/

- ◆ http-analyze: http://www.netstore.de/supply/http-analyze/

- ◆ pwebstats: http://www.unimelb.edu.au/pwebstats.html

- ◆ WebStat Explorer: `http://www.webstat.com/`

- ◆ AccessWatch: `http://netpressence.com/accesswatch/`

The best way to find out which one will work for you is to try them out, or at least visit their Web sites for feature comparisons. Two utilities that I find very helpful are Wusage and wwwstat. Wusage is my favorite commercial log analysis application. It is highly configurable and produces great graphical reports using the company's well-known GD graphics library. I also like the free wwwstat program. It is written in Perl, so you need to have Perl installed on the system on which you want to run it.

MAINTAINING SERVER LOG FILES

On Apache sites with high hit rates or many virtual domains, the log files can become huge in a very short time, easily causing a disk crisis. When log files become very large, you should rotate them. You have two options for rotating your logs: You can use a utility that comes with Apache called rotatelog, or you can use logrotate.

USING ROTATELOG   Apache comes with a support tool called rotatelog. You can use this program as follows:

```
TransferLog "| /path/to/rotatelogs logfile rotation time in seconds"
```

For example, if you want to rotate the access log every 86,400 seconds (that is, 24 hours), use the following line:

```
TransferLog "| /path/to/rotatelogs /var/logs/httpd 86400"
```

Each day's access log information stores in a file called /var/logs/httpd.nnnn, where nnnn represents a long number.

USING LOGROTATE   Designed to ease the system administration of log files, logrotate enables the automatic rotation, compression, removal, and mailing of log files on a daily, weekly, monthly or size basis. Normally, logrotate is run as a daily cron job. You can create a file called /etc/logrotate.d/apache as follows:

```
/path/to/apache/access_log {
compress
rotate 5
mail webmaster@yourdomain.com
errors root@yourdomain.com
size=1024K
postrotate
kill -HUP 'cat /path/to/httpd.pid'
endscript
}
```

This configuration specifies that the */path/to/apache/access_log* file be rotated whenever it grows over one megabyte (1,024K) in size, and that the old log files be compressed and mailed to `webmaster@yourdomain.com` after going through five rotations, rather than being removed. Any errors that occur during processing of the log file are mailed to `root@yourdomain.com`.

Enhancing Web server security

The moment your Web server is accessible to the rest of the world, you open a window for others to get into your server. Most people use only what you provide on your Web site, but some may look for holes in this window to get to the information they are not supposed to access. Some of these people are vandals who want to create embarrassing situations, and some are information thieves. Either way, if anyone succeeds in finding that hole, you may find your Web sites mutilated with obscene materials, or you might even lose confidential data. Sometimes the attacks may not affect your site directly. The infiltrators may use your server and other resources to get to another network and thus put you at legal risk.

In order to reduce security risks, you have to be alert at all times. There is no finite number of things you can do to your Web server to make it 100 percent secure. Retaining a high degree of security is an ongoing process; you must keep yourself up to date on news in the computer security area and take preventive measures as needed. The very first step in securing your Web server is to read and implement the security techniques discussed in Chapter 18 and Chapter 19. Once you have implemented all of the applicable preventive measures discussed in those chapters, you are ready to tackle the following security issues specific to a Web server.

INSTALLING APACHE AND NOT A TROJAN HORSE

Apache is freely available software, so it is important that you obtain it from a reliable source. Do not ever download Apache binaries or source code from just any Web or FTP site. Always check with the official site, `www.apache.org`, first. In the future, Apache source will be PGP (Pretty Good Privacy) signed.

CREATING DEDICATED USER AND GROUP FOR APACHE

If you run Apache as a stand-alone server, make sure you create a dedicated user and group for Apache. Do not use the nobody user or the nogroup group, especially if your system has already defined these. Chances are your system is using them in other services or other places. This might lead to administrative and security problems. Instead, create a fresh new user and group for Apache, and use them with the directives mentioned.

PROTECTING SERVERROOT AND LOG DIRECTORIES

Make sure that the ServerRoot directories (especially the log directories and files) are not writeable by anyone but the root user. You do not need to give Apache user/group read or write permission in log directories. Enabling anyone other than the root user to write files in the log directory could lead to a major security hole.

DISABLING DEFAULT ACCESS

A strict security model dictates that there be no default access, so you should get into the habit of permitting no access at first. Permit only specific access to specific locations. To implement no default access, use the following configuration segment in one of your Apache configuration files:

```
<Directory />
  Order deny,allow
   Deny from all
</Directory>
```

This disables all access. Now, if you need to enable access to a particular directory, use the <Directory . . .> container again to open that directory. For example, if you want to permit access to /www/mysite/public/htdocs, add the following configuration:

```
<Directory /www/mysite/public/htdocs>
  Order deny,allow
  Allow from all
</Directory>
```

This method – opening only what you need – is a preventive security measure and I highly recommend it.

DISABLING USER OVERRIDES

If you don't want users to override server-configuration settings using the per-directory configuration file (.htaccess) in a directory, disable this feature as follows:

```
<Directory />
  AllowOverride None
  Options None
  allow from all
</Directory>
```

This prevents user overrides and, in fact, speeds up your server. The server speed increases because it no longer looks for the per-directory access control files (.htaccess) for each request.

REDUCING CGI RISKS

The biggest security risk on the Web comes in the form of CGI applications. CGI (Common Gateway Interface) is not inherently insecure, but poorly written CGI applications are a major source of Web security holes. Actually, the simplicity of the CGI specification makes it easy for many inexperienced programmers to write CGI applications. These inexperienced programmers, being unaware of the security aspects of internetworking, create applications that work but also create hidden back doors and holes on the system on which the applications run.

Here are the three most common security risks that CGI applications may create:

♦ Information leaks: Such leaks help hackers break into a system. The more information a hacker knows about a system, the better he or she gets at breaking into the system.

♦ Execution of system commands via CGI applications: In many cases remote users have succeeded in tricking an HTML form-based mailer script to run a system command or give out confidential system information.

♦ Consumption of system resources: A poorly written CGI application can be made to consume system resources such that the server becomes virtually unresponsive.

Of course, you should take careful steps in developing or installing CGI applications when your Apache server runs these applications as an unprivileged user, but even carefully written applications can be a security risk.

Most of the security holes created by CGI applications are caused by user input.

LIMITING CGI RISKS WITH WRAPPERS

The best way to reduce CGI-related risks is not to run any CGI applications at all; however, in the days of dynamic Web content, this could be suicide! Perhaps you can centralize all CGI applications in one location and closely monitor their development to ensure that they are well written.

In many cases, especially on Internet service provider systems, all of the users with Web sites want CGI access. In this case, it might be a good idea to run CGI applications under the user ID of the user who owns the CGI application. By default, CGI applications that Apache runs use the Apache user ID. If you run these applications using the owner's user ID, all possible damage is limited to what the user ID is permitted to access. In other words, a bad CGI application run with a user ID other than the Apache server user ID can damage only the user's files. The user responsible for the CGI application will now be more careful because the possible damage affects his or her content solely. In one shot, you get increased user responsibility and awareness and, at the same time, a limited area for potential damage.

To run a CGI application using a different user ID than the Apache server, you need a special type of program called a wrapper. A wrapper program enables you to run a CGI application as the user who owns the file rather than as the Apache server user. Some CGI wrappers do other security checks before they run the requested CGI applications. In the following sections, I cover two popular CGI wrappers.

SUEXEC

Apache comes with a support application called suEXEC that provides Apache users with the ability to run CGI and SSI programs under user IDs that are different from the user ID of Apache. suEXEC is a setuid wrapper program that is called when an

HTTP request is made for a CGI or SSI program . When such a request is made, Apache provides the suEXEC wrapper with the program's name and the user and group IDs. suEXEC runs the program using the given user and group ID.

Before running the CGI or SSI command, the suEXEC wrapper performs a set of tests to ensure that the request is valid. Among other things, this testing procedure ensures that the CGI script is owned by a user allowed to run the wrapper and that the CGI directory or the CGI script is not writable by anyone but the owner. Once the security checks are successful, the suEXEC wrapper changes the user ID and the group ID to the target user and group ID via setuid and setgid calls. The group-access list is also initialized with all groups of which the user is a member. suEXEC cleans the process's environment by establishing a safe execution PATH (defined during configuration), as well as passing through only those variables whose names are listed in the safe environment list (also created during configuration). The suEXEC process then becomes the target CGI application or SSI command and executes. This may seem like a lot of work, and it is – but taking these steps provides a greater security coefficient as well.

CONFIGURING AND INSTALLING SUEXEC If you want to install suEXEC support in Apache, you need to run the configure (or config.status) script as follows:

```
./configure-prefix=/path/to/apache \
        -enable-suexec \
        -suexec-caller=httpd \
        -suexec-userdir=public_html
        -suexec-uidmin=100 \
        -suexec-gidmin=100
        -suexec-safepath="/usr/local/bin:/usr/bin:/bin"
```

Here is the detailed explanation of this configuration.

```
-enable-suexec
```

This option enables suEXEC support.

```
-suexec-caller=httpd
```

This option changes httpd to the user ID you use for the User directive in the Apache configuration file. This is the only user that will be permitted to run the suEXEC program.

```
-suexec-userdir=public_html
```

This option defines the subdirectory under users' home directories where suEXEC executables are kept. Change the public_html to whatever you use as the value for the UserDir directive that specifies the document root directory for a user's Web site.

```
—suexec-uidmin=100
```

This option defines the lowest user ID (UID) permitted to run suEXEC-based CGI scripts. In other words, user IDs below this number are not be able to run CGI or SSI commands via suEXEC. You should take a look at your /etc/passwd file and make sure the range you chose does not include the system accounts that are usually lower than 100.

```
—suexec-gidmin=100
```

This option defines the lowest group ID permitted to be a target group. In other words, group IDs below this number are not be able to run CGI or SSI commands via suEXEC. You should take a look at your /etc/group file and make sure that the range you chose does not include the system account groups that are usually lower than 100.

```
—suexec-safepath="/usr/local/bin:/usr/bin:/bin"
```

This option defines the PATH environment variable that suEXEC executes for CGI applications and SSI commands.

ENABLING AND TESTING SUEXEC Once you have installed both the suEXEC wrapper and the new Apache executable in the proper location, restart Apache. When the Apache server starts up, it writes a message similar to this:

```
[notice] suEXEC mechanism enabled (wrapper: /usr/local/sbin/suexec)
```

This line tells you that the suEXEC is active. Now let's test suEXEC functionality. In the srm.conf file, add the following lines

```
UserDir public_html
AddHandler cgi-script  .pl
```

The first directive (UserDir) sets the document root of a user's Web site to be ~username/public_html where username can be any user on the system. The second directive associates the cgi-script handler with the .pl files. This is done to run Perl scripts with .pl extensions as CGI scripts. For this test, you need a user account. In this example, I use the host wormhole.nitec.com and a user called kabir. Copy the script shown in Listing 12-6 in a file called test.pl and put it in a user's public_html directory. In my case I put the file in the ~kabir/public_html directory.

Listing 12-6: A CGI script to test suEXEC support

```
#!/usr/bin/perl
#
# Make sure the preceding line is pointing to the
# right location. Some people keep perl in
# /usr/local/bin.

my ($key,$value);
print "Content-type: text/html\n\n";
print "<h1>Test of  suEXEC<h1>";

foreach $key (sort keys %ENV){
    $value = $ENV{$key};
    print "$key = $value <br>";
    }
exit 0;
```

To access the script via a Web browser, I request the following URL: `http://wormhole.nitec.com/~kabir/test.pl`.

A CGI script executes only after it passes all the security checks performed by suEXEC. suEXEC also logs the script request in its log file. The log entry for my request looks as follows:

```
[1998-12-23 16:00:22]: uid: (kabir/kabir) gid: (kabir/kabir) cmd:
test.pl
```

If you really want to know that the script is running under the user's UID, you can insert a sleep command (such as sleep(10);) inside the foreach loop that slows down the execution. It also enables you to run commands such as top or ps on your Web server console to find out the UID of the process running test.pl. You can change the ownership of the script using the chown command, try to access the script via your Web browser, and see the error message that suEXEC logs. For example, when I change the ownership of the test.pl script in the ~kabir/public_ html directory as follows:

```
chown root test.pl
```

I get a server error and the log file shows the following line:

```
[1998-12-23 16:00:22]: uid/gid (500/500) mismatch with directory
(500/500) or program (0/500)
```

Here the program is owned by user ID 0, and the group is still kabir (500), so suEXEC refuses to run it. As you can see, suEXEC is doing what it is supposed to do.

To ensure that suEXEC is going to run the test.pl program in other directories, I create a cgi-bin directory in ~kabir/public_html and put test.cgi in that directory. After determining that the user and group ownership of the new directory and file are set to user ID kabir and group ID kabir, I access the script using:

```
http://wormhole.nitec.com/~kabir/cgi-bin/test.pl
```

If you have virtual hosts and want to run the CGI programs and/or SSI commands using suEXEC, you must use User and Group directives inside the <VirtualHost . . .> container. Set these directives to user and group IDs other than those the Apache server is currently using. If only one, or neither, of these directives is specified for a <VirtualHost> container, the server user ID or group ID is assumed.

For security and efficiency reasons, all suexec requests must remain within either a top-level document root for virtual host requests or one top-level personal document root for userdir requests. For example, if you have four virtual hosts configured, you need to structure all of your virtual host document roots off of one main Apache document hierarchy to take advantage of suEXEC for virtual hosts.

CGIWRAP

CGIWrap is like the suEXEC program in that it permits users to use CGI applications without compromising the security of the Web server. CGI programs are run with the file owner's permission. In addition, CGIWrap performs several security checks on the CGI application and the application does not execute if any checks fail. CGIWrap is written by Nathan Neulinger; the latest version of CGIWrap is available from the primary FTP site on ftp://ftp.cc.umr.edu/pub/cgi/cgiwrap/. Use CGIWrap via a URL in an HTML document. As distributed, CGIWrap is configured to run user scripts located in the ~/public_html/cgi-bin/ directory.

CONFIGURING AND INSTALLING CGIWRAP   CGIWrap is distributed as a gzip-compressed tar file. You can uncompress it using gzip and extract it using the tar utility.

Run the Configure script, and it prompts you to answer many questions. Most of these questions are self-explanatory; however, a feature in this wrapper differs from suEXEC. It enables you to create allow and deny files that you can use to restrict access to your CGI applications. Both of these files have the same format, as shown in the following:

```
User ID
mailto:Username@subnet1/mask1,subnet2/mask2. . .
```

You can either have a single username (nonnumeric user ID) or a user `mailto:`
`ID@subnet/mask` line where one or more subnet/mask pairs can be defined, for
example:

```
mailto:Myuser@1.2.3.4/255.255.255.255
```

If this line is found in the allow file (you specify the filename), the user kabir's
CGI applications are permitted to be run by hosts that belong in the 206.171.50.0
network with netmask 255.255.255.0.

Once you run the Configure script, you must run the make utility to create the
CGIWrap executable.

ENABLING CGIWRAP   To use the wrapper application, copy the CGIWrap executable to the user's cgi-bin directory. Note that this directory must match what
you have specified in the configuration process. The simplest way to get things
going is to keep the ~username/public_html/cgi-bin type of directory structure for
the CGI application directory.

Once you copy the CGIWrap executable, change the ownership and permission
bits as follows:

```
chown root CGIWrap
chmod 4755 CGIWrap
```

Create hard links or symbolic links nph-cgiwrap, nph-cgiwrapd, or cgiwrapd to
CGIWrap in the cgi-bin directory as follows:

```
ln [-s] CGIWrap cgiwrapd
ln [-s] CGIWrap nph-cgiwrap
ln [-s] CGIWrap nph-cgiwrapd
```

On my Apache server, I specify only the cgi extension as a CGI application, and
therefore, I renamed my CGIWrap executable to cgiwrap.cgi to get it working. If
you have similar restrictions, you might try this approach or make a link instead.

Now you can execute a CGI application as follows:

```
http://www.yourdomain.com/cgi-bin/cgiwrap/username/scriptname
```

To access user kabir's CGI application test.cgi on the `wormhole.nitec.com` site,
for example, I use the following:

```
http://wormhole.nitec.com/cgi-bin/cgiwrap/kabir/test.cgi
```

If you wish to see debugging output for your CGI, specify cgiwrapd instead of CGIWrap, as in the following URL:

http://www.yourdomain.com/cgi-bin/cgiwrapd/username/scriptname

If the script is an nph-style script, you run it using the following URL:

```
http://www.yourdomain.com/cgi-bin/nph-cgiwrap/username/scriptname
```

REDUCING SERVER-SIDE INCLUDES RISKS

If you run external applications using SSI commands such as exec, the security risk is virtually the same as with the CGI applications. However, you can disable the exec command very easily under Apache, using the Options directive as follows:

```
<Directory />
  Options IncludesNOEXEC
</Directory>
```

This disables exec and includes SSI commands everywhere on your Web space; however, you can enable the exec commands whenever necessary by defining a narrower-scoping directory container. Following is an example:

```
<Directory />
  Options IncludesNOEXEC
</Directory>

<Directory /ssi>
  Options +Include
</Directory>
```

This configuration segment disables the exec command everywhere but the /ssi directory.

Using SSL for secured transactions

Electronic commerce on the Web is booming at an extraordinary rate. One prerequisite for an e-commerce site is to have secure transaction capabilities, which are provided by Secure Sockets Layer (SSL). Unfortunately, due to U.S.-enforced legal restrictions on the export of cryptography, Apache does not readily come with SSL support. However, you have several choices for third-party SSL software for Apache. Table 12-2 should help you pick the right one for your needs.

TABLE 12-2 SSL SOLUTIONS FOR APACHE

Software	Distribution	Restriction	Comments
Apache-SSL	Free	Copyright and patent laws may restrict commercial use in the U.S.A.	Not recommended, because this is not the cleanest solution. Apache-SSL is basically a set of patches for Apache and not so well documented.
mod_ssl	Free	Copyright and patent laws may restrict commercial use in the U.S.A.	A clean solution. Although partly based on Apache-SSL, it is much cleaner and better documented. Recommended by the author.
Red Hat Secure Server	Commercial	U.S. cryptography-related export restrictions apply for countries outside the U.S.A. and Canada.	The cheapest commercial solution. Based on mod_ssl.
Raven SSL	Commercial	None	A midrange (price-wise) module solution.
Stronghold Web Server	Commercial	None	The author's personal favorite SSL solution for serious e-commerce sites. It is the most expensive among the commercial options.

The mod_ssl module is a much cleaner approach than Apache-SSL, and it is free. Although partly based on Apache-SSL, it is yet another well-documented module by Ralf S. Engelschall. I recommend this if you are using the latest version of Apache.

GETTING mod_ssl

The mod_ssl module is not distributed with the standard Apache source distribution. You download it from the following Web site: http://www.engelschall. com/sw/mod_ssl/. Because this module depends on the SSLeay package (like Apache-SSL), you also need the SSLeay package from the following FTP site: ftp://ftp.psy.uq.oz.au/pub/Crypto/SSL/. If you are a U.S. citizen and plan on using the SSL support in the United States, you need to obtain the RSA Reference Implementation package from the following FTP site: `ftp://ftp.rsa.com/rsaref/`.

View the README file at the FTP site to locate the U.S. citizens–only directory where the rsaref20.tar.Z package is kept.

You also need a working Perl 5 interpreter, and you must make sure that you have the latest Apache source from the Apache Web site or one of its mirror sites.

COMPILING AND INSTALLING MOD_SSL   Extract all the source packages into an appropriate directory. I typically use /usr/local/src for such purposes. Once you have extracted each of the previously mentioned packages, you are ready to compile and install them with the following steps.

I assume that you have extracted the necessary packages into the following directories:

◆ /usr/local/src/apache_1.3.12 for the Apache source distribution

◆ /usr/local/src/mod_ssl-2.0.13-1.3.12 for the mod_ssl source distribution

◆ /usr/local/src/SSLeay-0.9.0b for the mod_ssl source distribution

◆ /usr/local/src/rsaref-2.0/ for the RSAref package for U.S. citizens only

Your version numbers might vary because this software is always being updated, so make sure you supply appropriate version numbers as you follow the instructions in this book.

BUILDING THE RSAREF LIBRARY
You do not need the RSAref package for mod_ssl if you are not in the United States. If you are in the United States and do not already have the librsaref.a library module, follow these steps:

1. Change directories to /usr/local/src/rsaref-2.0.

2. Run the following commands:

```
cp -rp install/unix local
cd local
make
mv rsaref.a librsaref.a
```

Once you have created the librsaref.a library file, you can compile SSLeay.

BUILDING SSLeay
Change directories to /usr/local/src/SSLeay-0.9.0b, and run the following command:

```
make -f Makefile.ssl links
```

If you are in the United States, you need to tell SSLeay about the rsaref library package. So run the following commands:

```
perl ./Configure gcc -DNO_IDEA -DRSAref -lRSAglue \
-L`pwd`/../rsaref-2.0/local/ -lrsaref
cp rsaref/rsaref.h include/
```

Everyone else should run the following command, which does not specify the RSAref library package:

```
perl ./Configure gcc  -DNO_IDEA
```

Now you compile and test the package by running the following commands:

```
make
make test
```

BUILDING mod_ssl AND APACHE

Change directories to /usr/local/src/mod_ssl-2.0.13-1.3.12, and run the configure script as follows:

```
./configure  \
—with-apache=../apache_1.3.12   \
—with-ssleay=../ SSLeay-0.9.0b \
—with-rsaref=../rsaref-2.0/local  \
—prefix=/usr/local/apache
```

You do not need the –with–rsaref option if you are not in the United States. Also make sure you use the appropriate–prefix value for your desired Apache destination.

If you already have a working server certificate and a private key, you can supply the following options to the configure script:

```
—with-key=/path/to/your/server.key
—with-crt=/path/to/your/server.crt
```

Now you can compile Apache as follows:

Change your document directory to /usr/local/src/apache_1.3.12, and run the following command:

```
make
```

If you do not have a real server certificate and private key, you can make a test certificate using the following command:

```
make certificate
```

Now run the following command to install the Apache server:

```
make install
```

You now have an SSL-enabled Apache server. All that remains is the Apache configuration.

CONFIGURING APACHE FOR MOD_SSL

The mod_ssl package installs a copy of the httpd.conf.default file in the etc subdirectory of your Apache installation directory. You can use this file to test and configure your Apache server. An example of this file is listed in Listing 12-7.

Listing 12-7: The default httpd.conf installed with mod_ssl

```
##
## httpd.conf—Apache HTTP server configuration file
##

ServerType standalone

Port 80
<IfDefine SSL>
Listen 80
Listen 443
</IfDefine>

HostnameLookups off

User nobody
Group nobody
ServerAdmin kabir@picaso.nitec.com
ServerRoot "/usr/local/apache"
ErrorLog /usr/local/apache/var/log/error_log
LogLevel warn
LogFormat "%h %l %u %t \"%r\" %>s %b \"%{Referer}i\" \"%{User-
Agent}i\"" combined
LogFormat "%h %l %u %t \"%r\" %>s %b" common
LogFormat "%{Referer}i --> %U" referer
LogFormat "%{User-agent}i" agent
CustomLog /usr/local/apache/var/log/access_log common
PidFile /usr/local/apache/var/run/httpd.pid
ScoreBoardFile /usr/local/apache/var/run/httpd.scoreboard
ServerSignature on
UseCanonicalName on

Timeout 300
```

```
KeepAlive on
MaxKeepAliveRequests 100
KeepAliveTimeout 15

MinSpareServers 5
MaxSpareServers 10
StartServers 5
MaxClients 150
MaxRequestsPerChild 30

<IfModule mod_ssl.c>
#   We disable SSL globally.
SSLDisable

SSLCacheServerPath      /usr/local/apache/sbin/ssl_gcache
SSLCacheServerPort      /usr/local/apache/var/run/ssl_gcache_port
SSLSessionCacheTimeout 300

<IfDefine SSL>
<VirtualHost _default_:443>

#   Set up the general virtual server configuration.
DocumentRoot /usr/local/apache/share/htdocs
ServerName picaso.nitec.com
ServerAdmin kabir@picaso.nitec.com
ErrorLog /usr/local/apache/var/log/error_log
TransferLog /usr/local/apache/var/log/access_log

# Enable SSL for this virtual host.
SSLEnable
SSLRequireSSL
SSLCertificateFile      /usr/local/apache/etc/ssl.crt/server.crt
SSLCertificateKeyFile  /usr/local/apache/etc/ssl.key/server.key
SSLVerifyClient none
MD5:DES-CBC3-SHA
SSLLogFile /usr/local/apache/var/log/ssl_misc_log
CustomLog /usr/local/apache/var/log/ssl_log "%t %h %{version}c \
%{cipher}c %{subjectdn}c %{issuerdn}c \"%r\" %b"
</VirtualHost>
</IfDefine>
</IfModule>
The first configuration segment in the file is as follows
<IfDefine SSL>
Listen 80
Listen 443
</IfDefine>
```

Here Apache is made to listen to port 80 and 443 only if a label called "SSL" is defined in the command line of the Apache executable (httpd). You can define the label when running the Apache executable directly as follows:

```
httpd -DSSL
```

or using the apachectrl script from the sbin subdirectory of your Apache installation as follows:

```
apachectl -sslstart
```

If this label is not defined, Apache listens only to port 80, which is set by the Port directive earlier in the configuration.

The mod_ssl related directives found in the default httpd.conf file are enclosed in a `<IfModule mod_ss.c>` . . . `</IfModule>` container. This container is used to make sure the enclosed directives are taken into consideration only if the mod_ssl.c module is compiled into the running Apache executable.

```
SSLDisable
```

Use this directive to disable SSL support everywhere, in order to later enable SSL support where needed. In this example, SSL support is enabled for the mail server listening on port 443 and not on port 80.

```
SSLCacheServerPath      /usr/local/apache/sbin/ssl_gcache
SSLCacheServerPort      /usr/local/apache/var/run/ssl_gcache_port
SSLSessionCacheTimeout 300
```

These three directives are used to set up path, port, and timeout values for the SSL session cache server. Then again the `<IfDefine Label>` container is used to make sure that the server was intended to run in SSL mode using the –DSSL or sslstart option provided at the command line. Next comes the virtual host configuration for the default server running on port 443. This is the SSL-enabled server. After the usual DocumentRoot, ServerName, ServerAdmin, ErrorLog, and TransferLog directives, the SSLEnable directive is used to turn on SSL support for this virtual host. Next the SSLRequireSSL directive is used to ensure that only SSL-based access is permitted for this virtual host.

```
SSLCertificateFile \
/usr/local/apache/etc/ssl.crt/server.crt

SSLCertificateKeyFile \
/usr/local/apache/etc/ssl.key/server.key
```

These two directives set the server's certificate and private key file path. If you already have a real certificate and private key for your server, you should use them here.

The next directive, SSLVerifyClient, is set to "none" to allow any SSL-capable client to access the site. If you want to allow only clients with client certificates, you can set this to "require."

The SSLLogFile and the CustomLog directives are used to write SSL-related logging data in a custom file. This custom file is really not needed in that most of the SSL data is automatically written to the error log file of the virtual host.

If you are interested in running your main server as an SSL-enabled server, you can just put the following directives outside any virtual host configuration:

```
Listen 443
SSLEnable
SSLRequireSSL
SSLCertificateFile      /usr/local/apache/etc/ssl.crt/server.crt
SSLCertificateKeyFile   /usr/local/apache/etc/ssl.key/server.key
SSLVerifyClient none
```

The directives used in mod_ssl are the same as the Apache-SSL directives.

TESTING APACHE BUILT WITH mod_ssl

Testing your mod_ssl-enabled server is quite simple. You just restart the server using the apchectl script with the "sslstart" or "startssl" option and access it as https://yourserver.domain.tld. Be sure to type "https" and not "http" to access your SSL-enabled site. If you are use a certificate created with the make certificate command, the Web browser displays warning dialog windows stating that the server is using SSL but the certificate is not issued by any known Certificate Authority. In such a case, you should apply for a real certificate from a known CA such as Verisign or Thawte.

GETTING A CA-SIGNED CERTIFICATE

To get a browser-recognizable certificate from one of the well-known Certificate Authorities, here are a few CAs that are likely to provide you with a certificate for Apache-SSL:

◆ VeriSign: http://www.verisign.com/

◆ Thawte Consulting: http://www.thawte.com/certs/server/request.html

◆ CertiSign Certificação Digital Ltda.: http://www.certisign.com.br/

◆ IKS GmbH: http://www.iks-jena.de/produkte/ca/

The certification process requires that you produce paper documents proving the authenticity of your business. Such documents also have to be accompanied by letters from high authorities in your organization. It is possible to get a certificate for your personal Web server; you do not have to have a legally founded company. For personal server certificates, most CAs require only proof of an existing bank account.

COMMERCIAL SSL SOLUTIONS

If you are in doubt about your legal ability to use a mod_ssl-based SSL solution and can afford the cost, I recommend getting either Stronghold or the Red Hat Secure server. I have personally evaluated and used the Stronghold server and found it to be a solid product. The Red Hat Secure Server is not available for evaluation.

Summary

In this chapter, you learned how to create a great Web service using the most popular Web server—Apache. I discussed how you could create a custom Apache server by compiling it from source. Custom compilation provides you with a greater flexibility than downloading and installing a stock binary copy made by someone else. You learned to get the Apache server up and running quickly by modifying the configuration files. You also learned to provide CGI support for both virtual Web sites and individuals users, to enable server-side includes, to support both IP-based and name-based virtual Web sites, to use Apache as a caching and a reverse proxy server, to use HTTP authentication to create restricted access areas in your Web sites, to monitor and log an Apache server, to enhance your Web site security using CGI wrappers like suEXEC and CGIWrap, and to use SSL with Apache using mod_ssl module.

Chapter 13

FTP Service

IN THIS CHAPTER

◆ How to configure wu-ftpd for standard FTP service

◆ How to configure wu-ftpd for anonymous FTP service

◆ How to configure wu-ftpd for guest FTP service

◆ How to configure wu-ftpd for virtual FTP service

◆ Learn about other FTP servers

TRANSFERRING FILES FROM ONE computer to another is a common activity on almost any network. Although various methods exist for transferring files over a TCP/IP network like the Internet, the most commonly used method is the File Transfer Protocol (FTP). In this chapter, you learn how to turn your Red Hat Linux server into an FTP server.

Using wu-ftpd: the Default FTP Server

The Red Hat Linux distribution ships with the Wuarchive-ftpd. More affectionately known as wu-ftpd, it is an FTP server developed at Washington University. The most popular FTP server on the Internet, wu-ftpd is used on thousands of FTP sites all around the world.

If you choose to install FTP service during the Red Hat Linux installation, the wu-ftpd server is installed by default. However, if you are not sure whether or not you have already installed the wu-ftpd server, you can just query the RPM database of installed packages as follows:

```
rpm -qa | grep wu--ftpd
```

The `rpm -qa` command lists all the installed RPM packages, and the piped `grep wu` command matches the wu-ftpd pattern in the package names outputted by the `rpm` command, thus enabling you to see if any package has the "wu-ftpd" string pattern in its name. For example, the preceding command shows "wu-ftpd-2.4. 2vr17-3" on my Red Hat machine. The version number on your system will vary, as a new version of the wu-ftpd is likely to be shipped with a later version of Red Hat Linux.

If you do not get any output for the preceding command, you currently do not have the wu-ftpd server installed and need to proceed with the installation as described in the text that follows. On the other hand, if you see a version of wu-ftpd already installed, you can skip the installation section and go right to the "Configuring FTP service" section.

Installing wu-ftpd server

When it comes to installing wu-ftpd server, you have two options: Install the pre-compiled RPM package version of wu-ftpd or get the source from the URL `ftp://ftp.academ.com/pub/wu-ftpd/private/` and compile it yourself. Because the Red Hat–provided wu-ftpd RPM package is quite suitable for most people, I do not describe the second process, which requires compiling it on your own. I highly recommend that you use the wu-ftpd RPM package unless you have a very special reason for compiling and installing from the source. In the latter case, make sure you read the bundled documentation with great care.

Here is how you can install the wu-ftpd RPM package.

INSTALLING FROM YOUR RED HAT CD-ROM

To install from your Red Hat CD-ROM:

1. Log into your Red Hat server as root.

2. Mount your Red Hat CD-ROM and change directory to RedHat/RPMS. Run the following command:

   ```
   ls | grep wu-ftpd
   ```

   to locate the RPM package for wu-ftpd server.

3. Once you have located the filename of the RPM package for wu-ftpd, you can run the following command to install the package:

   ```
   rpm -ivh name of the wu-ftpd package
   ```

   For example:

   ```
   rpm -ivh wu-ftpd-2.6.1-4.i386.rpm
   ```

   This command installs the 2.6.1-4 version of wu-ftpd for x86 computers. Your version number and system architecture may vary.

INSTALLING FROM A RED HAT FTP SERVER

If you do not have the Red Hat CD-ROM or you want to install the latest version over the Internet, you can run the following command:

```
rpm -ivh URL
```

For example, when I want to install the wu-ftpd-2.6.1-4.i386.rpm package from an anonymous FTP server called `ftp://ftp.cdrom.com/` that mirrors the Red Hat distribution, I run the following command:

```
rpm -ivh ftp://ftp.cdrom.com/pub/linux/redhat/redhat-\
7.0/i386/RedHat/RPMS/wu-ftpd-2.-6.1-4.i386.rpm
```

If you want to install from such a server, always make sure that you first determine the right URL by browsing the site via a Web browser. The URL will vary with your system architecture (i386, Alpha, Sparc, or what have you), as well as with the versions of Red Hat Linux and the wu-ftpd software.

Also note that if you are trying to install a newer version of wu-ftpd while keeping an older version, you have to supply the -- force option in the rpm command line.

Once you have installed wu-ftpd or confirmed that you have it installed as part of the Red Hat installation, you are ready to configure your new FTP server.

Configuring FTP service

Your FTP server configuration consists of the following files:

+ /etc/services
+ /etc/xinetd.d/wu-ftpd
+ /etc/ftpaccess
+ /etc/ftpconversions
+ /etc/ftpgroups
+ /etc/ftphosts
+ /etc/ftpusers

The wu-ftpd server, like many other TCP/IP-based servers, runs via the Internet super-server called "xinetd," which listens for an FTP connection on port 21; when such a connection request is detected, it launches the wu-ftpd server. At startup, xinetd looks at two files to determine which service (port) is associated with a server. These two files are /etc/services and the /etc/xinetd.d/wu-ftpd.

/etc/services

As you may already know, the /etc/services file describes the TCP/IP services available on your Linux server. The lines that matter for the FTP server configuration are:

```
ftp-data     .    20/tcp
ftp               21/tcp
```

These two lines tell xinetd which ports to use for the data and command functions of the FTP service respectively. The default port declarations are standard and should not be changed.

 The FTP specification (RFC 765) specifies the FTP data port (20) as one less than the command port (21). The data port value is really not derived from the declaration in /etc/services. However, including the data port declaration in the /etc/services file prevents it from being accidentally used for something else.

The preceding lines tell xinetd which ports belong to the FTP service, but it still needs to know which server software is responsible for the service. This is defined in files kept in the /etc/xinetd.d directory. The FTP service is defined in /etc/xinetd.d/wu-ftpd file.

/etc/xinetd.d/wu-ftpd

The default version of this file looks as follows:

```
# default: on
# description: The wu-ftpd FTP server serves FTP connections.
#It uses normal, unencrypted usernames and passwords
#for authentication.

service ftp
{
        socket_type             = stream
        wait                    = no
        user                    = root
        server                  = /usr/sbin/in.ftpd
        server_args             = -l -a
        log_on_success          += DURATION USERID
        log_on_failure          += USERID
        nice                    = 10
}
```
Here the service "ftp" is tied with the server software called in.ftpd, which is the name of the wu-ftpd executable.

The –l and –a server arguments are specified by default. The –l option specifies that each FTP session be logged via the syslog facility, and the –a option specifies that the access control configuration specified in /etc/ftpaccess be enabled. These two arguments are very useful and should not be removed. For other options, see the ftpd man page.

If you make any changes to /etc/xinetd.d/wu-ftpd or /etc/services, make sure you tell xinetd to reload the configuration by sending a SIGUSR1 signal as follows:

```
kill -USR1 PID of xinetd
```

or

```
killall -USR1 xinetd
```

/etc/ftpaccess

This file is the main configuration file for the FTP server and contains configuration information in the following format:

```
keyword   one or more options
```

The default /etc/ftpaccess file is shown in Listing 13-1.

Listing 13-1: The default /etc/ftpaccess file

```
class    all    real,guest,anonymous    *

email root@localhost

loginfails 5

readme   README*      login
readme   README*      cwd=*

message /welcome.msg              login
message .message                  cwd=*

compress          yes          all
tar               yes          all
chmod    no     guest,anonymous
delete   no     guest,anonymous
overwrite no     guest,anonymous
rename   no     guest,anonymous

log transfers anonymous,real inbound,outbound

shutdown /etc/shutmsg

passwd--check rfc822 warn
```

This file is the most important configuration file for the server, and hence I discuss it in great detail. You can specify five types of configuration information in this file.

ACCESS CONFIGURATION   You can specify access configuration using the class, deny, limit, noretrieve, loginfails, private, autogroup, and guestgroup keywords.

```
class
Syntax: class  classname>  typelist  addrglob
Default: class  all  real,guest,anonymous  *
```

The `class` keyword is used to define a class name and specify the type of users that belong to the class. It also specifies the IP addresses or the domain names from which the class members can access the FTP server. The arguments are as follows:

- *classname* is an arbitrary name for the class.

- *typelist* is a comma-separated list of user types. Three types of users are available: real, anonymous, and guest. A real user is someone who has a valid username and password in the /etc/passwd or /etc/shadow file. The anonymous and guest accounts are discussed in detail later in this chapter.

- *adrglob* can be an IP address of a host, a partial IP address with wildcards, (such as 206.171.50.*), a hostname such as blackhole.nitec.com, or a partial domain name with wildcards (such as *.nitec.com).

The default /etc/ftpaccess file contains a class definition called "all" that specifies that users of type real, guest, and anonymous can access the FTP server from anywhere. The wildcard character "*" is used to denote "anywhere." Now consider the following example:

```
class   all   real 206.171.50.*
```

Here FTP access is granted only to real users who access the server from the 206.171.50.0 network. Note that you can also use domain names instead of IP addresses. For example:

```
class   all   real *.nitec.com *.ad--engine.com
```

The preceding class definition allows real users to log in from any machine in the `nitec.com` and `ad--engine.com` domains.

Note that if you are not planning on allowing anonymous or guest accounts on your FTP server, you can remove the "guest" and "anonymous" keywords from the default typelist for the "all" class.

```
deny
Syntax: deny  addrglob  message_file
Default: none
```

This keyword is used to deny FTP service to hosts that match the IP addresses or domain names specified. For example:

```
deny  *.edu
```

This instruction tells the FTP server to deny access to anyone trying to access the server from a U.S. university. Here is another example:

```
deny  *.com  /etc/goaway.msg
```

This configuration denies FTP access to anyone in a .com domain and also displays the /etc/goaway.msg file.

```
limit
Syntax: limit class n times message_file
Default: none
```

This keyword limits the number of simultaneous user logins for the named class. The arguments are as follows:

- ◆ *n* is the number of users allowed access.

- ◆ *times* is when the limit should apply. The time can be specified in a 24-hour clock format. For example, 0700–1700 is a range that covers 7 A.M. to 5 P.M. The time format can also include days, as shown in Table 13-1.

TABLE 13-1 THE TIME FORMAT FOR LIMIT

Keyword	Meaning
Any	Any time
Wk	Any weekday
Sa	Saturday
Su	Sunday
Mo	Monday
Tu	Tuesday
We	Wednesday
Th	Thursday
Fr	Friday

You can combine the days as well. For example: SaSu07–17 covers the weekend from 7 A.M. to 5 P.M. Here is an example configuration that sets limits on access:

```
class   local   real        *.nitec.com
class   remote  anonymous    *

limit local  200  Any /etc/msgs/msg.toomany
limit remote 100  Any /etc/msgs/msg.toomany
```

The preceding configuration allows up to 200 users from the nitec.com domain to log in at any time. At the same time it allows only 100 anonymous users to access the system at any time.

```
noretrieve
Syntax: noretrieve filename filename . . .
Default: none
```

This keyword denies FTP users the ability to retrieve named files. For example:

```
noretrieve /etc/passwd
```

The preceding line denies anyone the ability to retrieve the /etc/passwd file. A message such as "/etc/passwd is marked unretrievable" is displayed. Note that if the filename does not include a fully qualified path name, all files with such names are marked unretrievable. For example:

```
noretrieve passwd core
```

This line prevents anyone from retrieving any file named passwd or core from any directory. Note that you cannot use wildcards in the filename.

```
loginfails
Syntax: loginfails number
Default: loginfails 5
```

This keyword defines the number of times a user can attempt to log in before getting disconnected. When a user fails to enter a valid username/password pair for a login for the specified number of times, an error message is logged and the user is disconnected.

```
private
Syntax: private yes or no
Default: none
```

The wu-ftpd server provides an extended set of FTP commands that are nonstandard. One of these commands is called SITE. This command is considered a security risk, and therefore use of the private keyword is also not recommended. In fact, the SITE command is disabled in the default version of wu-ftpd shipped with Red Hat. You have to compile wu-ftpd yourself to enable it, which is not recommended.

```
guestgroup
Syntax: guestgroup groupname groupname . . .
Default: none
```

This keyword specifies the user groups that are to be considered as guest user accounts. See the section "Creating a guest FTP account" in this chapter for more details.

```
autogroup
Syntax: autogroup groupname class [class . . .]
Default: none
```

This keyword enables you to change the effective group ID for an anonymous user if she belongs to one or more classes specified.

INFORMATIONAL CONFIGURATION You can specify an informational configuration using the banner, email, message, and readme keywords.

```
banner
Syntax: banner filename
Default: none
```

You can use this keyword to display the contents of the specified file. Typically, many systems use banners to identify the systems and to also provide user policy and contact information.

Note that if you use the banner keyword to display a file before login, some nonstandard FTP clients may fail to log in, because they are unable to handle multiline responses from the server.

```
email
Syntax: email user@host
Default: email root@localhost
```

This directive sets the e-mail address of the FTP site administrator.

```
message
Syntax: message path {when {class . . .}}
Default: message /welcome.msg     login
  message .message cwd=*
```

Use this keyword to set the name of a file to display when the user logs into the system or uses the `change directory` command to change directories. For example, the first default setting in the preceding code displays the contents of the /welcome.msg file at successful user login. The second default setting shows the contents of the .message file whenever the user changes a directory. Nothing displays when the file to be displayed is missing.

The file to be displayed can contain one or more of the magic cookie strings shown in Table 13-2.

TABLE 13-2 MAGIC COOKIE STRINGS FOR MESSAGE FILES

Cookies	Replacement Text
%C	The current working directory
%E	The maintainer's e-mail address as defined in ftpaccess
%F	Free space in partition of CWD (kilobytes)
%L	The local hostname
%M	The maximum number of users allowed in this class
%N	The current number of users in this class
%R	The remote hostname
%T	The local time (in the form "Thu Nov 15 17:12:42 2000")
%u	The username as determined via RFC 931 authentication
%U	The username given at login time

Listing 13-2 shows the /welcome.msg file I use for my Red Hat system.

Listing 13-2: An example of a /welcome.msg file

```
Hello %U

Welcome to %L.  You are user %N of possible %M users.
You are logging in from %R.

Local time is %T

Feel free to email (%E) if you have
any questions or comments.

Your current directory is %C (Free %F KB)
```

Note that the message file is displayed only once per directory. Also note that if you plan to display message files for anonymous access, use relative paths to the base of the anonymous FTP directory tree.

```
readme
Syntax: readme  path  {when  {class . . .}  }
Default: readme README*  login
        readme README*  cwd=*
```

This keyword is similar to the message keyword discussed previously. However, instead of displaying the contents of the named file, it makes the FTP server notify the user about the existence of the file and also tells the user about the modification date and time of the file.

LOGGING CONFIGURATION   You can specify a logging configuration using the log commands and log transfers keywords.

```
log commands
Syntax: log commands  typelist
Default: none
```

This keyword enables you to log FTP commands for one or more types of users. For example:

```
log commands anonymous
```

This directive logs all the FTP commands performed by all anonymous users.

```
log transfers
Syntax: log transfers typelist directions
Default: log transfers anonymous,real inbound,outbound
```

This keyword enables you to log file transfers to and from the system. The default setting makes the server log both inbound and outbound file transfers for anonymous and real users.

PERMISSION CONFIGURATION   The following keywords enable you to control file/directory permission settings for users.

```
chmod
Syntax: chmod yes|no typelist
Default: chmod no    guest,anonymous
```

This keyword enables or disables the chmod command (site chmod) for user types specified in the list. For example, the default setting disables this command for both guest and anonymous users.

Note that the chmod command is not available by default.

```
delete
Syntax: delete yes|no typelist
Default: delete  no    guest,anonymous
```

This keyword enables or disables the delete (del) command for users specified in the type list. For example, the default setting disables the delete command for both guest and anonymous users.

```
overwrite
Syntax: overwrite yes|no typelist
Default: overwrite no    guest,anonymous
```

This keyword enables or disables the overwriting of files by the users specified in the typelist. For example, the default setting disables file overwriting for both guests and anonymous users.

```
rename
Syntax: rename yes|no typelist
Default: rename  no    guest,anonymous
```

This keyword enables or disables the rename command for specified users in the typelist. For example, the default setting disables the rename command for both guest and anonymous users.

```
umask
Syntax: umask yes|no typelist
Default: none
```

This keyword enables or disables the umask command (site umask) for specified users in the typelist.

Note that the umask command is not available by default.

```
passwd-check
Syntax: passwd-check none|trivial|rfc822 (enforce|warn)
Default: passwd-check rfc822 warn
```

This keyword defines the type of passwords required for anonymous users. The default setting requires the password for an anonymous access to be an e-mail address but does not enforce this rule if the user fails to enter a valid e-mail address. The server just warns the user about the invalid password. When you don't want password checking, set the passwd-check keyword as follows:

```
passwd-check none
```

If you set the checking to be "trivial," the server checks only for the existence of a "@" character in the password.

```
path--filter
Syntax: path-filter typelist mesg allowed_charset {disallowed regexp
. . .}
Default: none
```

This keyword enables you to restrict certain filenames, specifically those used in file uploads by users specified in typelist.

```
upload
Syntax: upload root-dir dirglob yes|no owner group
Default: none
```

This keyword allows you to enable or disable an upload directory. For example:

```
upload  /home/ftp /dropbox  yes root ftp 0600
```

This directive enables the /dropbox directory as an upload directory where files are owned by root and the group ownership is set to "ftp." The uploaded files have a permission setting of 0600. Note that /home/ftp must be the home directory of the user "ftp." If the uploader should not be allowed to create new sub directories under the /dropbox directory, then the preceding upload line needs to be changed to:

```
upload /home/ftp /dropbox  yes root ftp 0600 nodirs
```

On the other hand, if the uploader should be allowed to create subdirectories, then "nodirs" can be replaced with "dirs."

MISCELLANEOUS CONFIGURATION   The following keywords allow you to control miscellaneous settings.

```
alias
Syntax: alias string dir
Default: none
```

This keyword enables you to create an alias for a directory. For example:

```
alias redhat  /pub/linux/distributions/redhat
```

allows a user to type the cd redhat command to change to /pub/linux/distributions/redhat directory.

```
cdpath
```

```
Syntax: cdpath dir
Default: none
```

This keyword adds the specified directory to the search path of the change directory (cd) command. For example:

```
cdpath /pub/linux/redhat
```

Now if a user enters the command cd RPMS, the server first looks for a directory called RPMS in the user's current directory. If it fails to find one, it looks for an alias called "RPMS," and if it fails to find an alias "RPMS," then it tries to change directory to "/pub/linux/redhat/RPMS."

```
compress
Syntax: compress yes|no class [classg . . .]
Default: compress yes all
```

This keyword enables or disables the compression feature for specified classes. The default setting allows the compression feature for the class called "all," which by default covers all real, anonymous, and guest users. When the default is left alone and the ftpconversions file is not modified, all the users who use the FTP service are able to compress files on the fly. For example, a user who wants to get the entire contents of a directory as a compressed file can enter the command "get directoryname.tar.gz," and a compressed tar file is downloaded.

```
tar
Syntax: tar yes|no classg [class . . .]
Default: tar yes all
```

This keyword enables or disables the tar (tape archive file) feature for specified classes. The default setting allows the compression feature for the class called "all," which by default covers all the real, anonymous, and guest users. When the default is left alone and the ftpconversions file is not modified, all the users who use the FTP service are able to tar files on the fly. For example, a user who wants to get the entire contents of a directory as a compressed file can enter the command "get directoryname.tar," and a tar file is downloaded.

```
shutdown
Syntax: shutdown path
Default: shutdown /etc/shutmsg
```

This keyword specifies the file that the FTP server monitors from time to time to detect a shutdown event. You can create this file using the ftpshut command. For example, to shut down the server immediately, you run the following command:

```
ftpshut now
```

However, you can schedule a shutdown in such a way that the logged-in users have some time before the shutdown begins. For example, say the current date is Monday, December 13, 1999, and the time is 1600 (in 24-hour format). To shut down the system in an hour, you can issue:

```
ftpshut -d 30 1700
```

This creates the /etc/shutmsg file as follows:

```
1999 11 13 17 00 0010 0030
System shutdown at %s
```

The format of the first line is as follows:

```
YYYY MM DD HH MM   HHMM HHMM
```

The *YYYY* is the year, *MM* is the month (0–11), *DD* is the day (1–31), *HH* is the hour (0–23), and *MM* is the minute (0–59). The first *HHMM* pair is the offset in time for denying new connections, and the second *HHMM* pair is the offset in time for disconnecting current connections. As you can see, the –d 30 option set the last *HHMM* pair to 0030 in the example file just shown. The deny offset for new connections by default is 10 minutes, but you can change that with –l option. Also note that you can supply a more customized warning message then the default "System shutdown at %s" using one or more of the magic cookies shown in Table 13-3.

TABLE 13-3 MAGIC COOKIES FOR ftpshut WARNING MESSAGE

Magic Cookie	Replacement Text
%s	The time the system is going to shut down
%r	The time new connections will be denied
%d	The time current connections will be disconnected

In addition to these cookies, you can use all the cookies shown in Table 18-2. To create such a message, run the ftpshut command as follows:

```
ftpshut -d MM -l MM HHMM "Shutdown at %s. Be done by %d."
```

Don't forget to replace the *MM*, *HHMM*, and so on with appropriate values. Also note that when you are ready to restart the FTP service, you have to remove the /etc/shutmsg file.

```
virtual
Syntax: virtual address root|banner|logfile path
Default: none
```

If you have multiple IP addresses for your Linux system and would like to offer virtual FTP services, you can use this keyword. See the section "Creating virtual FTP sites" later in this chapter for details.

/etc/ftpconversions

The /etc/ftpconversions file stores the FTP server's conversion database. The default configuration for this file is sufficient for almost all installations. If you need more information, see the man page for ftpconversions.

/etc/ftpgroups

The file /etc/ftpgroups is important only if you allow the nonstandard SITE commands. The Red Hat–shipped wu-ftpd package comes with the SITE commands disabled. This is done to enhance security, as SITE commands have been known to create security holes in earlier versions of the server. For the sake of completeness, I describe the purpose of this file, but I strongly discourage its use.

When a not-so-security-savvy FTP administrator enables the SITE commands, she needs to set up the /etc/ftpgroups file as follows:

```
groupname:encrypted password:realgroup
```

Typically, the SITE GROUP and SITE GPASS commands are used to allow an already-logged-in FTP user to upgrade her group privileges. The /etc/ftpgroups file provides the necessary mapping for a user of groupname to be upgraded to the realgroup when a valid password is entered using the SITE GPASS command. Also note that the realgroup must be a group in the /etc/group file.

/etc/ftphosts

The file /etc/ftphosts is used to control FTP access to specific accounts from various hosts. To allow a user to log in from one or more hosts, use a line such as the following:

```
allow username addrglob [addrglob. . .]
```

This command allows the specified user to log in from the specified hosts. For example:

```
allow joegunchy *.nitec.com
```

Here the user joegunchy is allowed to log in from any machine in the `nitec.com` domain. To deny a user the ability to log into the server from one or more hosts, you can use the following line:

```
deny username  addrglob [addrglob. . .]
```

For example, to prevent joegunchy from logging into the server from the 206.171.50.0 network, you can use:

```
deny joegunchy  206.171.50.*
```

/etcftpusers

The file /etcftpusers specifies the list of users who are not allowed to access the FTP server. The default /etc/ftpusers file contains the following users:

- root
- bin
- daemon
- adm
- lp
- sync
- shutdown
- halt
- mail
- news
- uucp
- operator
- games
- nobody

These accounts are not allowed to log in because they are not real user accounts. If you need to stop a real user from being able to FTP to the server, you can put the username in this file.

At this point you have learned about all the configuration files necessary to run the FTP server. In the following sections I discuss some common FTP server configuration issues.

Because a lot of configuration is needed for proper FTP service, you might want to have a way to verify your configuration files from time to time. You can do this with a utility called ftpck, which you can download from the following FTP site: `ftp://ftp.landfield.com/wu--ftpd/ftpck/`.

Creating an anonymous FTP site

Having an anonymous FTP site could be a mixed blessing. It can be a great medium for distributing files that need to be widely distributed. In fact, all the free software packages (including the Red Hat Linux distribution) that you can download from the Internet are stored in many anonymous FTP sites all around the world. Just think what a nightmare it would be if you needed accounts on each of the FTP servers on the Internet to get access to free software. It is simply not practical. This problem has been solved with anonymous FTP service. However, anonymous FTP service is also a common gateway for hackers to get into a system. So think twice before you decide to create an anonymous FTP server.

Assuming that you have decided to create an anonymous FTP server because you really need it, take a look at what it takes to make one.

Fortunately, Red Hat makes it very easy to create an anonymous FTP server. All you need is the anonftp RPM package. First, query your RPM database to find out if you have already installed the anonftp package. Run:

```
rpm -qa | grep anonftp
```

This command shows you the package name, such as anonftp-2.8-1, if you have already installed the anonftp package as part of your Red Hat Linux installation. If you haven't, however, there is no output from the preceding command. In such a case, get the latest anonftp package from your Red Hat CD-ROM and run:

```
rpm -ivh anonftp-3.0-6.i386.rpm
```

If you want to install the latest version from a Red Hat mirror site, run the following command:

```
rpm -ivh ftp://ftp.cdrom.com/pub/linux/redhat/redhat-\
7.0/i386/RedHat/RPMS/anonftp-3.0-6.i386.rpm
```

Note that your anonftp package name varies with your system architecture and anonftp version. Also note that the anonftp package does not install if you do not already have an FTP server such as the wu-ftpd.

Once you have installed the anonftp package, you have an anonymous FTP server ready to run.

You need to make sure that you have the user account called "ftp" without any password in the /etc/passwd file before you can use anonymous FTP service. The FTP user account line in your /etc/password should look similar to this: `ftp:*:14:50:FTP User:/home/ftp:/bin/true`.

If you are curious to see the installation contents, run:

```
rpm -qlp anonftp-3.0-6.i386.rpm
```

and you see the files the package installed. Note that it has installed all the files under the ~ftp directory (that is, the home directory of the 'ftp' account see the /etc/passwd file). Now consider these files in detail.

Change directory to ~ftp and enter `ls -l`. You see the following directories:

```
[kabir@picaso ~ftp]# ls -l
total 4
d−x−x−x   2 root     root     1024 Nov  5 19:29 bin
d−x−x−x   2 root     root     1024 Nov  5 19:29 etc
drwxr--xr--x  2 root     root      1024 Nov  5 19:29 lib
dr--xr--sr--x  2 root     ftp       1024 Sep 10 17:21 pub
```

Now change directory to the bin subdirectory and run `ls -l` as before; you see something like the following:

```
[kabir@picaso ~ftp/bin]# ls -l
total 313
---x-x-x 1 root   root   15236 Nov  5 20:02 compress
---x-x-x 1 root   root   46356 Nov  5 20:02 cpio
---x-x-x 1 root   root   45436 Nov  5 20:02 gzip
---x-x-x 1 root   root   29980 Nov  5 20:02 ls
---x-x-x 1 root   root   62660 Nov  5 20:02 sh
---x-x-x 1 root   root  110668 Nov  5 20:02 tar
lrwxrwxrwx 1 root   root       4 Nov  5 20:02 zcat - gzip
```

These are the utilities you need to provide an anonymous FTP service. The `ls` utility is used to provide the directory listings, and the compression utilities are used to provide on-the-fly compression/decompression facilities. You might wonder why these files are here, right? Well, when someone accesses the anonymous FTP server, the server performs a `chroot` to the ~ftp directory. The `chroot` program is a facility that allows the server to treat the ~ftp directory as the root directory of the system. In other words, when an anonymous FTP user logs into the server, the server does a `chroot` to ~ftp and thus hides the real file system, showing only what is under the ~ftp directory. This is why you need a copy of the etc, bin, and lib directories with an absolutely minimal number of files. The lib directory contains the system library files needed for the programs in the bin directory. The ~ftp/pub directory is where you should keep the publicly distributable files.

If you need an incoming or dropbox directory where anonymous users can upload files, do the following:

1. Create a subdirectory in the ~ftp directory for uploads. This directory is typically called "incoming," and so I use this name here.

2. Add the following line in your /etc/ftpaccess file:

   ```
   upload  /home/ftp  /incoming yes root ftp 0600 nodirs
   ```

3. Make sure you change /home/ftp to the appropriate directory. For example, if your ~ftp is really /data/ftp, then change /home/ftp to /data/ftp in the preceding line. Also, if you want to allow anonymous users to be able to create subdirectories under ~ftp/incoming, remove the nodirs option in the preceding line.

4. Run the following commands:

   ```
   chown -R root.ftp ~ftp/incoming
   chmod -R 1733 ~ftp/incoming
   ```

   The chown command sets root as the owner and ftp as the group for the incoming directory. The chmod command changes the incoming directory permissions such that root has read, write, and execute (rwx) permissions and the group and the world has write and execute (wx) permissions. It also sets the sticky bit for the directory and all its files. The sticky bit protects the files from being deleted by regular users. Normally when a directory has write and execute permissions set for everyone, any user of that system can delete a file in that directory. The sticky bit stops that by allowing only the creator of the file to delete the file. Because the FTP server writes the file setting root being the owner, no one but root is allowed to delete the uploaded files.

5. Finally, make sure that you have the anonymous user type listed in at least one of the class definitions in your /etc/ftpaccess file. By default real, guest, and anonymous are all included in the default "all" class, so you do not need to do anything unless you have altered the default class definitions.

Once you have taken these steps, you should FTP to the server as an anonymous user and make sure you can upload files in the specified directory only. Because you do not have read access to the ~ftp/incoming directory, you should not be able to see the files you upload using the ls command. However, you are still able to download the uploaded files if you supply the proper filenames.

Creating an anonymous FTP site is already a security risk, and having an upload-able directory is adding more risk. However, many organizations have successfully run anonymous FTP servers for years, so do not be extremely discouraged: just be cautious. Here are some guidelines for enhancing anonymous FTP server security:

◆ Ensure that the ftp account in /etc/passwd is using an invalid password. For example, your ftp account entry in the passwd file should look like:

```
ftp:*:14:50:FTP User:/home/ftp:/bin/true
```

◆ The ~ftp/bin directory should be owned by root and not by the ftp account. The binaries such as ls, compress, and tar that you have in the ~ftp/bin directory also must be owned by the root user. The ~ftp/bin directory and its contents should be executable and no more. You can run:

```
chown -R root.root ~ftp/bin; chmod -R 111 ~ftp/bin
```

to ensure that all files in the ~ftp/bin directory are just executable.

◆ The ~ftp/etc directory should be owned by the root user, and it must be only executable. You can make it so using the following commands:

```
chown -R root.root ~ftp/etc; chmod 111 ~ftp/etc
```

◆ Contents of the ~ftp/etc directory must be only readable and owned by root. Run:

```
chown -R root.root ~ftp/etc; cd ~ftp/etc; chmod 444 *
```

to make sure the permissions are set up correctly.

◆ Do not ever copy your /etc/passwd or /etc/group files into ~ftp/etc direc-tory. The ~ftp/etc/passwd and ~ftp/etc/group files are dummy files needed to satisfy programs that look for them when running under ~ftp as the root directory due to the server's chroot to ~ftp.

◆ Finally, as a general security rule, make sure that no files or directories in ~ftp are owned by the ftp user.

Creating a guest FTP account

A guest FTP account is a real account with a real username and password. However, the only difference between the guest and the real FTP is that when a guest user accesses an FTP server she does not see anything other than her own home directory. In other words, when a guest user logs into an FTP server, the server does a chroot operation to the guest user's home directory, thus making the home directory of the guest user appear as the entire file system. The great advantage is that the user is unable to see anything else, such as system files and other user directories. This security feature is worth spending the time in configuring guest user accounts. Apart from the extra work required to configure guest accounts, the other sacrifice is the redundant use of the disk space. Like an anonymous FTP user, each guest user has to have her own set of binaries for simple things like ls, gzip, and tar. However, considering how the cost of disk space gets lower and lower every day, perhaps disk space is not really an issue for most people. Now learn how you can set up a guest account.

The easiest way to set up a guest account is to use the anonftp package, even if you do not want to provide anonymous FTP service. Just install the package temporarily for the purpose of creating a single guest account. Here are the steps to create a guest account quite easily.

STEP 1: CREATE THE GUEST USER ACCOUNT
Become root and create the guest user account as you create a real user account. I assume this guest user account is called "mrfrog" and that it was created using the usual useradd command as follows:

```
useradd mrfrog
```

Now set a desired password for mrfrog using the following command:

```
passwd mrfrog
```

STEP 2: STOP TELNET ACCESS
Now change mrfrog's default shell to /bin/true using the following command:

```
chsh mrfrog
```

When prompted for the new shell path, enter /bin/true. This command disallows mrfrog from Telneting to the system. Note that you take this step to ensure that mrfrog can't use Telnet to access the server and browse other user files or system files. After all, we disallow all that when this user accesses the system via the FTP server.

Now edit the /etc/passwd file and append /./ to the existing home directory path. For example, if the /etc/passwd file has a line similar to the following:

```
mrfrog:1dev33vylewv.:516:519::/home/mrfrog:/bin/true
```

then change it to:

```
mrfrog:1dev33vylewv.:516:519::/home/mrfrog/./:/bin/true
```

The /./ sequence determines where the chroot() function is performed.

Now edit the /etc/shells file and add /bin/true at the end of the file. This change makes the /bin/true program a valid shell option. Note that the /bin/true program does nothing and exits immediately after it is run. This feature makes it a good candidate for a shell that needs to be validated but denies the user anything and then exits. Because an exit from the shell logs out the user, the user never gets a chance to do anything when attempting a Telnet connection.

STEP 3: INSTALL THE ANONFTP PACKAGE

If you already have the anonftp package installed on your system, skip this step and go to the next one. If you don't have it installed, get the latest anonftp package and install it by running the rpm command:

```
rpm -ivh anonftp-3.0-6.i386.rpm
```

Your anonftp package name varies based on your system architecture and anonftp version. Also note that the anonftp package does not install if you do not already have an FTP server such as wu-ftpd.

STEP 4: COPY THE ANONFTP PACKAGE FILES TO THE GUEST USER'S HOME DIRECTORY

Change directory to ~ftp and use the following command to copy all the files and directories to, for example, ~mrfrog:

```
tar cvf - * | ( cd ~mrfrog ;  tar xvf  -)
```

All mrfrog really needs are the ~ftp/bin, ~ftp/etc, and ~ftp/lib directories. You can delete the ~ftp/pub directory or any other directory from your ~ftp directory.

STEP 5: UPDATE THE ~mrfrog/etc/passwd and ~mrfrog/etc/group FILES

Now edit the ~mrfrog/etc/passwd file and remove the line for the ftp user. Append the exact password line for mrfrog from the /etc/passwd file. However, remove mrfrog's password and replace it with a "*" to make it invalid. For example:

```
mrfrog:1dev33vylewv.:516:519::/home/mrfrog/./:/bin/true
```

Copy this line to ~mrfrog/etc/passwd, and replace the password so that the line looks like:

```
mrfrog:*:516:519::/home/mrfrog/./:/bin/true
```

Now modify the ~mrfrog/etc/group file and add the mrfrog line found in /etc/group. Note I assume that you have not somehow disabled Red Hat's default feature for automatic creation of a private group by the same name as the new user. In other words, when you create a user with the useradd program, it automatically creates a private group for that user with the same name. So when you created mrfrog, you should have also automatically created a group called mrfrog in the /etc/passwd. If you have changed the default behavior of the useradd program or manually created the user, make sure you create a group for this user and add it to the ~mrfrog/etc/group file. Also remove the ftp group from the ~ftp/etc/group file.

STEP 6: SET DIRECTORY AND FILE PERMISSIONS
Change the directory/file permissions as follows:

```
chown mrfrog.mrfrog ~mrfrog
chmod 750 ~mrfrog
```

The `chown` command sets the user and group ownership to mrfrog's user and group. The second command makes the ~mrfrog directory accessible only to the mrfrog user and group.

```
chown --R root.root ~mrfrog/etc  ~mrfrog/bin ~mrfrog/lib
```

This command changes the ownership of the etc, bin, and lib subdirectories under ~mrfrog to the root user and group.

```
cd ~mrfrog
chmod --R 111 *
```

The first command changes directory to ~mrfrog, and the second one makes all the files and directories executable only for everyone.

```
cd etc; chmod  444 *
```

These commands change directory to the ~mrfrog/etc directory and change the file permissions to read-only for everyone.

STEP 7: SET THE GUESTGROUP IN /etc/ftpaccess
Because we want the real user mrfrog to be a guest user, we need to add mrfrog's group (which is also called mrfrog) to the guestgroup group list. For example:

```
guestgroup mrfrog
```

This line allows any member of the mrfrog group (found in /etc/group) to be a guest user. In other words, the FTP server performs the `chroot` operation. For the mrfrog user, the FTP server change root directory to /home/mrfrog.

STEP 8: TEST THE ACCOUNT

Now FTP to the server and log in as mrfrog. If everything is set up correctly, you see nothing other than the home directory of this user. Try to upload a file or create a directory. You should be allowed to do these operations. However, whether or not mrfrog is allowed to delete, overwrite, or rename files depends on the settings for these operations in /etc/ftpaccess. For example, the default /etc/ftpaccess includes the following lines:

```
chmod       no   guest,anonymous
delete      no   guest,anonymous
overwrite   no   guest,anonymous
rename      no   guest,anonymous
```

These lines prohibit the guest accounts from performing chmod, delete, overwrite, or rename operations. If you wish to allow these for the guest accounts, you have to remove the "guest" from the default typelist in these lines and turn them into the following lines:

```
chmod       no   anonymous
delete      no   anonymous
overwrite   no   anonymous
rename      no   anonymous
```

Finally, if you do not wish to keep the anonftp package around or do not want to have anonftp capabilities on your FTP server, you can remove the package files from the appropriate (~ftp) directory, or just run:

```
rpm --e anonftp---3.0-6.i386.rpm
```

Don't forget to use the appropriate filename, because your version or architecture might be different from the description in this line.

Creating virtual FTP sites

If you have multiple domains and need to support separate FTP servers (ftp.domain--1.com, ftp.domain--2.com, and so on), you can use virtual FTP service. Virtual FTP service enables you to share a single-server system for multiple domains. You can configure the wu-ftpd server at least two ways to support virtual FTP service. I discuss both methods here. Because both methods require that you have IP address aliases set up on your system, take a look at the IP aliasing issue first.

CREATING IP ALIASES

In order to have virtual FTP servers, first you need to have appropriate DNS records for each FTP host. You need multiple IP addresses (one per FTP server host) to be routed to your FTP server machine. Using the IP aliasing technique discussed in Chapter 9, you have to create virtual Ethernet interfaces for all the IP addresses. For example, say that I have to create two virtual FTP servers (ftp.client--01.com and ftp.client--02.com) on an FTP server called ftp.nitec.com. Also assume that I have already set up DNS records for each domain such that the following lines are true:

```
; In client--01.com DNS database
ftp.client--01.com.   IN   A    206.171.50.51

; In client--02.com DNS database
ftp.client--02.com.   IN   A    206.171.50.52

; In nitec.com DNS database
ftp.nitec.com.   IN   A    206.171.50.50
```

After setting up IP aliases and routes on the ftp.nitec.com machine per instructions found in Chapter 12, if I run:

```
cat /proc/net/aliases
```

I see the following IP aliases:

```
Device   family   address
eth0:0   2        206.171.50.51
eth0:1   2        206.171.50.52
```

Now take a look at the simplest way of creating virtual hosts.

CREATING A LIMITED VIRTUAL FTP SERVICE

This method is simpler than the other but is also quite limited. Although you will have virtual FTP service, you won't be able to customize it as much. If you want a completely customizable service (like the primary FTP server), then skip to the section "Creating a complete virtual FTP service."

To create this limited version of virtual FTP service, you need to make multiple copies of the anon-ftp package–created file/directory structure. Simply install the anonftp package and make copies of it for each virtual host. For the preceding example, I create two virtual FTP site directories – /home/client1/ftp and /home/client2/ftp – and copy all the contents of the /home/ftp files and directories. One of the easiest ways to make an exact copy of /home/ftp is to run the following commands:

```
cd /home/client1/ ; cp --a /home/ftp .
cd /home/client2/ ; cp --a /home/ftp .
```

These commands copy the /home/ftp file/directory structure in the virtual site directories. Now edit the /etc/ftpaccess file to add virtual keywords as follows:

```
virtual 206.171.50.51 root    /home/client1/ftp
virtual 206.171.50.51 banner  /home/client1/ftp/banner.msg
virtual 206.171.50.51 logfile /home/client1/ftp/xferlog

virtual 206.171.50.52 root    /home/client2/ftp
virtual 206.171.50.52 banner  /home/client2/ftp/banner.msg
virtual 206.171.50.52 logfile /home/client2/ftp/xferlog
```

Don't forget to replace IP addresses and directory paths with those you chose earlier. You should now modify the banner.msg file for each host to reflect any site-specific information you want to display. Also, you do not need the pub subdirectory for your virtual FTP sites, so you can remove it from each site.

Once you create the preceding configuration, your virtual FTP servers are ready for testing. FTP to each of the virtual IP addresses and notice how the banner files are different for each host. Although quite easy to create, this virtual setup lacks the capability to fully customize the look and feel of the server. For example, you cannot use the email keyword in /etc/ftpaccess to point to different e-mail addresses appropriate for the virtual sites.

Note that the ftpshut command supplied with standard wu-ftpd does not support shutdown of virtual sites, because it writes the shutdown message file in only a single location specified by the shutdown keyword in the /etc/ftpaccess file. Also when the time comes to restart the server, you need to remove the shutdown message file manually. To overcome this nuisance, you might want to get the replacement ftpshut/ftprestart utilities from the following Web site: http://www.landfield.com/wu--ftpd/restart. You need to compile and build these utilities yourself.

Now look at the more complete method of hosting virtual FTP servers.

CREATING A COMPLETE VIRTUAL FTP SERVICE

This method requires you to patch the wu-ftpd source and compile it on your own. You can download the source code for wu-ftpd from the following FTP site: ftp://ftp.academ.com/pub/wu--ftpd/private/. You also need the patch file from the following FTP site: ftp://ftp.meme.com/pub/software/wu--ftpd--2.4.2/.

Read the README file that comes with the patch tar-ball and apply the patch to the wu-ftpd source you downloaded earlier. Compile and install the patched wu-ftpd per the instructions provided in the wu-ftpd source package. Install the new FTP server to the default location /usr/sbin/in.ftpd.

The newly patched wu-ftpd program (in.ftpd) now accepts an argument for the -a option. Normally, -a tells the server that you want it to read the /etc/ftpacesss file. Now the patched version allows the server to specify a different path for the ftpaccess file. So this option allows the new server to look at different ftpaccess configuration files that are needed to create virtual FTP sites.

Now modify the /etc/xinetd.d/wu-ftpdfile so that the FTP service is defined as follows:

```
service ftp
{
    flags                    = REUSE NAMEINARGS
        socket_type          = stream
        wait                 = no
        user                 = root
        server               = /usr/sbin/tcpd
        server_args          = /usr/sbin/in.ftpd
        log_on_success       += DURATION USERID
        log_on_failure       += USERID
        nice                 = 10
}
```

This file invokes the FTP server via the TCP wrapper (tcpd). Now modify the /etc/hosts.allow file for each FTP server (that is, the primary server and all the virtual FTP servers) so that the lines are similar to the ones that follow:

```
# For the primary server
ftpd@206.171.50.50 : ALL : twist exec \
/usr/sbin/in.ftpd -l -a /etc/ftp/ftpaccess

# For the virtual FTP server
ftpd@206.171.50.51 : ALL : twist exec \
/usr/sbin/in.ftpd -l -a /etc/ftp/client1.ftpaccess

# For the second virtual FTP server
ftpd@206.171.50.52 : ALL : twist exec \
/usr/sbin/in.ftpd -l -a /etc/ftp/client2.ftpaccess
```

Now create the /etc/ftp directory and move the /etc/ftpaccess file into that directory. Make two copies of the /etc/ftp/ftpaccess file such that you have /etc/ftp/client1.ftpaccess and /etc/ftp/client2.ftpaccess files. Remove any virtual keywords from the /etc/ftp/ftpaccess file used for the mail FTP server. Finally, modify the client1.ftpaccess file so that it has a line such as:

```
virtual 206.171.50.51 root /home/client1/ftp
```

Similarly, modify the client2.ftpaccess file to have a line such as:

```
virtual 206.171.50.52 root /home/client2/ftp
```

Don't forget to replace the IP addresses and the directory path with your own. Now copy the anonftp files in the /home/client1/ftp and /home/client2/ftp directories.

Once you have created the preceding configuration, restart the xinetd server using the following command:

```
killall  -USR1  xinetd
```

That's all there is to it. Now you have two virtual FTP sites that can be accessed via their respective hostnames or IP addresses.

MONITORING TRANSFER LOG

Logging is very important for FTP service because you want to know who is doing what with your files. The wu-ftpd server logs transfers in the xfrlog file, which typically resides in /var/log directory. You can customize logging using the "log commands" and "log transfers" keywords discussed earlier.

If you are interested in monitoring xferlog on a regular basis, you can try Dumpxfer. You can download this package from the following FTP address: ftp://ftp.microimages.com/tools/dumpxfer.1.2.tar.gz.

Using a Commercial FTP Server

The wu-ftpd server is free and provides reasonably good configurability when it comes to providing standard FTP service. However, it is deficient in performance under heavy load and also does not have a very clean and customizable virtual FTP service solution. If you are in need of a high-performance FTP server and do not mind paying for it, you might look into the NcFTPd package. It is a commercial FTP server that has the following interesting features:

- ◆ It does not run via xinetd and therefore has much better startup performance. The xinetd-based processes were never intended for high performance.

- ◆ It has built-in directory listing capabilities, whereas wu-ftpd has to form an ls process per directory listing request. Thus NcFTPd is better at handling directory listings. It can even cache directory listings in memory to provide faster transfer of such listings in a high-volume FTP site.

- ◆ NcFTPd has highly configurable virtual hosting capabilities. Each virtual host can have its own welcome message, anonymous FTP directory tree, password authentication scheme, user limit, and log files.

You can try out this commercial FTP server by downloading it from the following Web site: http://www.ncftp.com/download/.

Note that NcFTPd is free for educational organizations with certain top-level domains such as .edu and .us.

Using a Trivial File Transfer Protocol Server

You may have installed a TFTP server already. It's called the tftpd server. It is really not an FTP server in that it uses the Trivial File Transfer Protocol instead of the File Transfer Protocol. TFTP uses UDP over IP, an unreliable, packet-oriented transfer method. FTP uses TCP over IP, a reliable, stream-oriented transfer method. TFTP has no provisions for security. FTP has user authentication provisions for security.

However, a TFTP server works pretty much the same way an FTP server works. The only big difference is that it is not meant for anything but an anonymous FTP-like file transfer where no authentication is used.

So why use it? Many people use TFTP primarily in conjunction with the bootp protocol to load diskless workstations such as X Windows terminals. The TFTP service can be enabled by creating a file called tftpd in /etc/xinetd.d directory

```
service tftp
{
    flags                   = REUSE NAMEINARGS
        socket_type         = stream
        wait                = no
        user                = root
        server              = /usr/sbin/in.tftpd
        server_args         = /tftpboot
        log_on_success      += DURATION USERID
        log_on_failure      += USERID
        nice                = 10
}
```

Once you have created the above file, restart the xinetd server using killall USR1 xinetd command so that the change becomes effective.

Note that /tftpbook is the directory that TFTP clients can access. Make sure this directory does not contain any files that you don't want to share with anyone. Remember that no authentication is required to access this file, so anyone who can access your server will have access to this directory. You might want to allow only read-only access to files in the directory as well.

Summary

In this chapter, you learned how to configure the wu-ftpd FTP server for standard, anonymous, guest, and virtual FTP service.

Chapter 14

Internet Relay Chat and News Servers

IN THIS CHAPTER

◆ How to set up an Internet Relay Chat server

◆ How to set up a Usenet news server

IN THIS CHAPTER, I discuss two important user services that have become very popular over time. Both of these services are related to user communication. They allow users of your system to communicate with other Internet users in the world using two popular Internet protocols. First I discuss the Internet Relay Chat (IRC) service, which we use to provide real-time communication among multiple users. The next service is a news service that enables users to share information in a multithreaded bulletin board called the Usenet.

Setting Up Internet Relay Chat (IRC) Service

Internet Relay Chat (IRC) is a widely-used multiuser chat service. IRC started in Finland in 1988, and since then it has spread all over the world. There are many publicly accessible IRC servers around the world. Although IRC has been primarily used to enable informal chats among friends, family, and colleagues, it has the potential to provide a valuable service for commercial organizations. For example, using an IRC server, a company can provide real-time communication between support personnel and customers from anywhere around the world. Or companies can use it to hold meetings where members are diversely located. Because IRC is text-based communication, it does not have system requirements for a real-time audio or video conferencing system. In this section, you will learn to install and configure an IRC server on your Red Hat Linux server.

Installing an IRC server

The IRC server is called ircd. When it comes to installing ircd, you have two choices. You can either install an RPM binary package or compile the server from source. However, I notice that the binary RPM for ircd does not include any documentation, so if you would like to have documentation, you need to install the source distribution as well.

You can download the appropriate ircd RPM package from `http://contrib.redhat.com/` or any of its mirror sites. Personally, I prefer to go to a mirror Red Hat site. In this case, you have to go to a Red Hat mirror site that also mirrors the `http://contrib.redhat.com/` site. Check the following URL for a mirror site near you: `http://www.redhat.com/mirrors.html`.

Download the ircd*.rpm packages. Install these packages by using the `rpm -ivh ircd*.rpm` command. This installs the ircd daemon, its configuration file, and a configuration file verification utility program in the /usr/local/lib/ircd directory. The source RPM package installs the source file in compressed tar (.tgz) format in the /usr/src/redhat/SOURCES directory. You need to extract the source by using the `tar xvzf irc source distribution name.tgz` command.

 If you would like to compile ircd yourself, read the doc/INSTALL file in the source distribution.

Now you are ready to configure the IRC daemon.

Configuring an IRC server

The ircd daemon uses a single configuration file called ircd.conf. Listing 14-1 shows an example ircd configuration file in the source distribution.

Listing 14-1: An example ircd.conf file

```
# IRC - Internet Relay Chat, doc/example.conf
# Copyright (C) 1994, Helen Rose
#
#   This program is free software; you can redistribute it
#   and/or modify it under the terms of the GNU General
#   Public License as published by
#   the Free Software Foundation; either version 1, or (at
#   your option) any later version.
#
#   This program is distributed in the hope that it will be useful,
#   but WITHOUT ANY WARRANTY; without even the implied warranty of
#   MERCHANTABILITY or FITNESS FOR A PARTICULAR PURPOSE.  See the
#   GNU General Public License for more details.
#
```

```
#   You should have received a copy of the GNU General Public License
#   along with this program; if not, write to the Free Software
#   Foundation, Inc., 675 Mass Ave, Cambridge, MA 02139, USA.
#
# This is an example configuration file for the IRC server
#
# You only need an ircd.conf (IRC server configuration file) if
# you are running an IRC server. If you are running a standalone
# client this file is not necessary.
#
# This file will explain the various lines in the IRC server
# configuration file. Not all lines are mandatory. You can
# check to make sure that your configuration file is
# correct by using the program "chkconf", provided in the
# server distribution (and when you do "make install" this
# program will be installed in the same directory as the irc
# server).
#
# The options for whether a line is needed or not are:
# MANDATORY: you absolutely MUST have this line
# NETWORKED: you must have this line if you are connecting this irc
#            server to any other server (servers can run standalone).
# SUGGESTED: it is highly suggested that you use this line
# OPTIONAL: it's completely up to you whether to define this or not
# DISCOURAGED: you really should not use this line if at all
#              possible.
# NOT NECESSARY: an old or out of date line that isn't needed.
#
# MANDATORY lines are absolute *must*, that is, if you do
# not have this line then your server will not work properly.
# SUGGESTED lines are close-to-mandatory (that is, the server
# will run without it, but you are highly encouraged to use
# these lines).
#
# Note that "*" in a field indicates an "unused" field.
#
# ================================================================
# NOTE! this entire configuration file is read UPSIDE-DOWN!
# So if you have to put something in a specific order (for
# example, client-connection lines), put them in reverse order!
# ================================================================
#
#
```

```
# M: [MANDATORY]. This line sets your server's name, description,
# and port number. Fields, in order, are:
#
# M:hostname:*:Description Of Your Server:6667
#
M:csa.bu.edu:*:Boston University Computer Science Department:6667
#
# A: [MANDATORY]. This line lists your administrative
# information (contact address, etc). To view this
# information, /admin (server) will show it to you.
#
# The A: line has no set information, in fact, you can
# put arbitrary text in there if you wish (it is encouraged
# that you put at *least* a contact address for a person
# responsible for the irc server, however)
#
A:Boston University CS Department:Main Client Server:Helen Rose <hrose@cs.bu.edu>
#
# Y: [SUGGESTED]. These lines define connection classes.
# Connection classes allow you to fine-tune your client and
# server connections. It is suggested that clients and servers
# be placed in separate classes, and if you have lots of
# server connections (if you do have lots of servers you
# shouldn't be reading this file :-) each set of servers (defined
# arbitrarily by you) should have its own class. If you have clients
# coming in from lots of different sites, you may want to separate them
# out into classes. For instance, you may want to put local
# users in one class, with remote users in another class.
#
# The class numbers are not arbitrary. In auto-connecting
# servers—that is, servers that you have a port number
# (e.g. 6667) on the end of the C: line (see below) the
# higher the number the higher the priority in auto-connecting.
#
# The fields in order are: class number, ping frequency
# (in seconds), connect frequency (in seconds), maximum
# number of links (used for auto-connecting, and for
# limiting the number of clients in that class), and sendq
# (this overrides any value set in include/config.h for #define
# MAXSENDQLENGTH).
#
# Note that it is a good idea to have ping frequency the
# same at both ends of the link.
#
# in this case, connect-frequency is 0 indicating that this
```

```
# is a client class (servers never connect to clients, it is
# the other way around).
Y:1:90:0:20:100000
#
# this is a normal server connection (normal as of March, 1994)
Y:2:90:300:1:600000
#
Y:10:90:0:3:100000
#
# I: [MANDATORY]. The I: lines are client-authorization
# lines. Without these lines, no clients will be able to
# connect to your server. Wildcards ("*") are permitted.
# Passwords are also permitted (clients can be configured
# to send passwords).
#
# Ident (for more information on this, see rfc1413) can
# also be used by# placing a @ in the appropriate fields.
#
# Fields are as follows:
# I:IP-address-mask:optional password:domain-mask::connection \
# class (opt)
#
# With a password..... This will allow anyone from anywhere
# to connect as long as they know the password ("foobar").
# Note listing this I: line first, it will be read *last*,
# meaning it is the "fall-through". That is, anyone who doesn't
# match the I: lines listed below must know the
# password ("foobar") to connect.
#
I:*@*:foobar:*@*::1
# This is a standard vanilla I: line which will permit
# anyone with an IP address starting with 128.197 OR with
# a hostname ending in .bu.edu to connect to the server.
# NOTE, the ircd matches on the *right-most* match,
# so if I connect as hrose@csa.bu.edu (which is
# hrose@128.197.10.3) I will show up on irc as
# hrose@csa.bu.edu since that is the first match it
# found. (Even though the second match is valid).
I:128.197.*::*.bu.edu::1
#
# using ident
I:*@128.197.*::*@*.bu.edu::1
# and you can even specify just certain usernames
# running ident (as long as the client's site is running
# the ident daemon):
```

```
I:NOMATCH::hrose@csa.bu.edu::1
# putting NOMATCH in the first field will stop the ircd
# from matching automatically against the IP address and
# it will force the server to match against the hostname.
# (the "NOMATCH" string is not mandatory, you
# can use any arbitrary text in the first field).
#
#
# O: [OPTIONAL]. These lines define operator access. You
# do not need to have an operator to run a server. A well
# configured leaf site should not need an operator online,
# if its connections are well defined, the irc
# administrator can use kill -HUP on the ircd to reload
# the configuration file.
# The fields are as follows:
# O:hostname (ident "@" permitted):password:NickName
# if the person in "NickName" is not coming from the
# hostname defined in the first field then the person
# will get the error message "No O: lines for your host".
# NOTE that since Crypted Passwords are defined by default in
# include/config.h this text probably will not be
#  plaintext. See ircd/crypt/README for more information.
#
O:*.bu.edu:Zaphod:Trillian::10
#
# and this line forces ident:
O:hrose@csa.bu.edu:Zaphod:Trillian::10
#
# This line is a "local operator", it is specified with
# a lower-case "o"
#-it is the only lower-case type in the ircd.conf file.
#
# this line permits the nickname "jhs" with the password
# of "ITBites" to be a local operator only (be able to
# issue commands locally-can /kill and /squit and
# /connect-but *only* locally)
#
o:*.bu.edu:ITBites:jhs::10
#
# a crypted password line (NOTE that if you have
# crypted passwords, *all* of you passwords must be
# crypted! In fact, if you are getting an error
# "Incorrect Password" it may well be because crypted
# passwords are defined and you have used plaintext.  So
# my example of plaintext and crypted strings in the same
```

```
# IRC server configuration file is an impossibility (but it
# is just theoretical, which is why I explained both).
#
O:rocker@csa.bu.edu:TOeiVgHrqeKTQ:Rocker::10
#
# U: [NOT NECESSARY]. This line defines the default
# server for the IRC client that ships with the server
#—the default client is in irc/irc You should not use
# U: lines but instead use the UPHOST definition in
# include/config.h
U:csa.bu.edu:foobar:csa.bu.edu
#
# C: [NETWORKED]. These lines define what servers
# your server tries to connect to.
# N: [NETWORKED]. These lines define what servers
# your server permits connections to be initiated from.
# C/N lines MUST be used in pairs. You cannot have one
# without the other.
#
# C: lines contain the following fields:
# C:remote server's hostname:passwd:remote server's name:port:conn class
# (connection class)
# N: lines contain the following fields:
# N:remote server's hostname:passwd:remote server's
# name:host mask:conn class (connection class)
# "host mask" is the number of parts in *your* hostname
# to mask to. For instance, with my servername being
# "csa.bu.edu", if I wanted to present my servername to
# be "*.bu.edu" I would have a host-mask portion of "1".
#
# it is *strongly* advised that your C/N line passwords
# be different for security's sake.
#
# ident is allowed in the server's hostname part of the field.
# these lines tell the server to automatically (note the
# port number, that means automatic connection) connect
# to cs-ftp.bu.edu:
C:hrose@cs-ftp.bu.edu:bigspark:cs-ftp.bu.edu:6667:2
N:hrose@cs-ftp.bu.edu:bigalpha:cs-ftp.bu.edu::2
#
# This server's connection lines are more vanilla,
# masking the host to *.bu.edu (as described above):
C:irc-2.mit.edu:camelsrk001:irc-2.mit.edu::2
N:irc-2.mit.edu:andsoarellamas:irc-2.mit.edu:1:2
#
```

```
# K: [OPTIONAL]. These lines define user@host
# patterns to be banned from this particular server
# (with an optional time field). Note that K: lines
# are *not* global, and if you ban a user they can
# still use any other IRC server (unless they have
# specifically been banned there as well).
#
# the fields are defined as:
# K:hostmask:time field:username
# wildcards are permitted in any one of the fields,
# in other words, you can K:*::* if you wanted
# (but your server wouldn't be used much ;-)
#
# This K: line bans the username "FSSPR" (the
# wildcards are used to make sure that any
# ident-checking character will match) on any machine from
# the University of Alaska.
K:*.alaska.edu::*FSSPR*
#
# This K: line bans any users from acs*.bu.edu
# between the hours of 8am and 12pm and 1pm and 5pm
# (the time is always the server's local time):
K:acs*.bu.edu:0800-1200,1300-1700:*
# Note that 24 hour time is used (no "AM" or "PM").
#
# R: [DISCOURAGED]. These lines restrict user access
# based on a more stringent checking system than is
# available in the K: line. It looks for a match (based
# on hostname and username) and then runs an outside
# program (which MUST be specified using a full pathname).
# The output of the program should be a string in the
# form "Y <message>" (which permits access for the user)
# or "N <message>" (which denies access for the user).
# If "Y <message>" is received by the server, the server ignores
# the message and permits access for the user. If "N <message>" is
# returned, the server tells the user that he/she is not permitted to
# access that irc server, and gives the reason.
#
# Again, like K: lines, R: lines are local and thus
# not very effective in blocking certain machines
# from having IRC access.
#
# Use of R: requires that you have defined R_LINES
# in include/config.h
#
```

```
# The fields are as follows:
# R:hostmask:/full/path/to/program:username
# you can use wildcards in either the hostmask
# or username portion
#
R:csl.bu.edu:/home/hrose/bin.sun3/sun3access:*
#
# Q: [DISCOURAGED]. These lines "quarantine" specified
# servers.  Because of the way they operates, the same
# Q: lines MUST be installed by everyone or the net will
# keep breaking. I CANNOT EMPHASIZE THIS ENOUGH.
# Do NOT use Q: lines lightly!
#
# The fields are as follows:
# Q:*:reason why quarantine is in place:servername
#
Q::this server is too slow and lags the net:cm5.eng.umd.edu
#
# L: [OPTIONAL]. These lines "Leaf" specified servers.
# They are only useful if you are a non-leaf site yourself.
# There are two ways you can use L: lines. The first will
# limit one particular site to a particular tree depth
# (including 0, which would mean the server has to connect with
# no servers linked behind it otherwise the connection will fail).
# The second will allow you to be selective about which
# other servers you wish the connecting server to behave as
# a leaf toward.
#
# The fields are as follows:
# L:disallow connections to this hostmask::server name:depth
# For example, this will force kaja.gi.alaska.edu to connect
# only as a leaf (if it is not a leaf, the link will be dropped):
L:::kaja.gi.alaska.edu
# This line will force cm5.eng.umd.edu to have a depth of
# only 1 below it (that is, it is allowed to have only
# leaves connected to it):
L:::cm5.eng.umd.edu:1
#
# This line will prohibit anything matching *.edu
# to be connected behind any server matching *.au:
L:*.edu::*.au
#
# H: [OPTIONAL]. These lines define who you permit
# to act as a "hub" to you (that is, who you permit to
# connect non-leafed servers to you).
```

```
#
# the first field may use wildcards, the third
# field *must* be an exact match for a server's name
# (NOT a server's hostname, if they differ, the server's
# name must be used). If the servername is a wildcard (e.g. *.au)
# that is an acceptable name for the third field.
#
# The fields are as follows:
# H:servers which are permitted entry::hub server
#
# Example, permit cs-ftp.bu.edu to allow any servers
# behind it to connect:
# H:*::cs-ftp.bu.edu
#
# Example, permit irc-2.mit.edu to allow any MIT servers
# behind it to connect:
# H:*.mit.edu::irc-2.mit.edu
#
# T: [OPTIONAL]. These lines allow you to specify
# different motd's for different types of clients. This
# could be used to give *.edu users some informational
# message, while giving *.cl users a pointer to a closer server.
#
# The fields are as follows:
# T:hostmask:pathname
# for example, to give *.edu users the MOTD file /usr/ircd/lib/edu.motd:
# T:*.edu:/usr/ircd/lib/edu.motd
#
# P: [OPTIONAL]. This field allows the server to listen
# on various ports (other than 6667) for connections.
# Any internet domain port that is below 1024 means the
# ircd has to be run from inetd. The server can listen to
# ports in the UNIX domain or the internet domain. If you wish
# to create a port in the UNIX domain you must compile with
# UNIXPORT defined in include/config.h. If you are
# permitting connections to a separate port, you can control
# access to that port by the host field.
#
# The fields are as follows::
# P:hostmask or UNIX socket file:*:*:port number
# for example, an internet domain socket on port 6665 for
# South African users:
# P:*.za:*:*:6665
#
# This line is an example of a UNIX domain socket
```

```
# in /tmp
P:/tmp/.ircd:*:*:6666
```

Notice that this configuration file consists of extensive comments (lines starting with leading "#") and that all configuration lines have the following format:

```
single character record type:colon-separated list of values
```

Now let's discuss the records in detail.

MACHINE INFORMATION RECORD (M)

We use an M record to define the hostname of the IRC server and also to provide information about the geographic location of the server. For example:

```
M:picaso.nitec.com:*:Sacramento, CA, USA.
```

This states that the IRC server hostname is `picaso.nitec.com` and that it is located in Sacramento, California, in the United States. Note that we need to set the second field to "*" as it is unused.

ADMINISTRATIVE INFORMATION RECORD (A)

We use an A record to define administrative contact information. For example:

```
A:Mohammed Kabir:irc-operator@picaso.nitec.com: (916) 555-5555
```

Here, Mohammed Kabir is the administrator for the IRC server. The information you provide here is completely arbitrary. This information is visible to an IRC client via the `/admin` command.

SERVER CONNECTIONS RECORDS (C, N)

We use C records to allow your IRC server to connect to remote IRC servers to establish IRC network connection. We use the N records to allow remote IRC servers to connect to your server. Thus, these two records are crucial in forming an IRC network.

You should have three C records at most. For example:

```
C:192.168.1.30:xiTwD4qLoFM9M:remote-irc-srv-3:6667:1
C:192.168.1.20:xiTwD4qLoFM9M:remote-irc-srv-2:6667:1
C:192.168.1.10:xiTwD4qLoFM9M:remote-irc-srv-1:6667:1
```

Here, ircd tries remote-irc-srv-1.com (192.168.1.10), remote-irc-srv-2.com (192.168.1.20), and remote-irc-srv-3.com (192.168.1.30) to establish a connection. In each case, ircd makes connection attempts on port 6667, and the connection class number is 1. You must define class 1 by using a connection class record (Y) line. The password the server uses to connect to the other hosts is encrypted. You can generate encrypted passwords by using the mkpasswd program in the source distribution. You can also use your standard passwd program or the htpasswd that comes with Apache to generate encrypted passwords. In all cases, you have to copy the encrypted password as it appears in C record lines.

 If you downloaded and installed a binary ircd RPM package, the person who compiled ircd might have chosen to use clear-text passwords. In such a case, encrypted passwords do not work, and you have to use clear-text passwords. If you find you are unable to connect to other allowed servers or other allowed hosts are unable to connect to your server, try using clear-text passwords.

Also note that the server makes connection attempts in reverse order of their appearance as C records in the inetd.conf file. In other words, if you want the server to try to connect to a host first, put the C record for that host as the last C record line.

As mentioned previously, the N records allow other IRC servers to connect to your IRC server. For example:

```
N:192.168.2.100:xixwD4wL3FM9M:my-friends-server.com
```

Here, the server my-friends-server.com (192.168.2.100) can connect to your server by using a password.

CONNECTION CLASS RECORDS (Y)

We use Y records to define classes used for the S and N records. The class definition specifies ping frequency, connection frequency, maximum connections from clients and servers, and so on. For example:

```
Y:2:90:300:1:600000
```

Here the class number is 2. The ping frequency is set to 90. If you use this class (2) in a C line, your server tries every 300 seconds to connect to the host specified in the C line. On the other hand, if you use the class in an N line, your server allows 300 clients from the remote IRC server. Your server allows only one host to connect to itself via this class. Finally, the sendq value is set to 600000, which you should leave alone unless you know what you are doing.

CLIENT CONNECTIONS (I)

The I record allows you to control who (IRC client) can connect to your server. For example:

```
I:*::*::1
```

The preceding line allows everyone to connect to your server. Say that you want to allow only IRC clients that connect from within a single domain called nitec. com. In such a case, the corresponding I record is as follows:

```
I:x::*.nitec.com::1
```

This I record allows all hosts from the nitec.com domain to connect to the server without any password. If you want to require a password, you can insert the encrypted password in the third field. For example:

```
I:x:oiTwD4qLoFM9M:*.csus.edu::1
```

This I record allows hosts from the csus.edu domain to connect to the server by using an encrypted password. In other words, users from csus.edu must know the password to connect to this IRC server.

If you would like to allow connection on a nonstandard IRC port (that is, not 6667), you can specify the port number as well. For example:

```
I:x:oiTwD4qLoFM9M:*.csus.edu:9999:1
```

Here, the IRC clients from the csus.edu domain can connect by using the oiTwD4qLoFM9M password and on port 9999.

OPERATOR PRIVILEGES (O)

The O record defines operator privileges. For example:

```
O:*@picaso.nitec.com:foobar:netrat::10
```

Here, any user logged in from the picaso.nitec.com host with netrat as the nick-name can become an IRC operator by using the /oper command as long as the user knows the clear-text password is "foobar."

EXCLUDED ACCOUNTS (K)

The K record allows you to exclude certain users from using your IRC server. For example:

```
K:*.some-isp.net::baduser:0
```

Here, the user named "baduser" attempting to connect from any host in the some-isp.net domain is disallowed connection. Here is another example:

```
K:*::baduser:0
```

This K record disallows baduser to connect from any hosts.

When you exclude one or more users from your IRC server, they can always use someone else's server to connect to the IRC network unless you happen to be friends with all IRC operators.

EXCLUDED MACHINES (Q)

The Q record allows you to exclude servers from connecting to your IRC server. For example:

```
Q::I do not like you:irc.bad-server.net
```

Here the `irc.bad-server.net` server is not allowed to be a link to your server, and the reason given to the server is "I do not like you."

LEAF CONNECTIONS (L)

The L record allows you to define which servers are leaf servers:

```
# L:disallow connections to this hostmask::server name:depth
```

SERVICE CONNECTIONS (S)

The S record allows you to define a service that acts as a client to your IRC server. However, this feature is only partially implemented, and therefore I do not recommend use of this feature yet.

PORT CONNECTIONS (P)

The P record allows you to define which port (Internet or UNIX socket) the server listens to for incoming connections. For example:

```
P:*:*:*:6669
```

This line instructs the IRC server to listen to Internet port 6669 for incoming connections. You can use the second field to specify an IP mask you can use to control access to your server. For example:

```
P:192.168.1.0:*:*:6666
```

This allows all hosts on the 192.168.1.0 network to access the IRC server by using Internet port 6666.

HUB CONNECTIONS (H)

The H record allows you to define hubs for an IRC network. For example:

```
H:*:*:eff.org
```

Here, the `eff.org` server is defined as the hub for any server. You need to use H records only if you plan to have your IRC server participate in an IRC network.

DEFAULT LOCAL SERVER (U)

The U record allows you to define default connections for local IRC clients (that is, IRC clients running on the IRC server). For example:

```
U:irc.myserver.com::irc.myserver.com:6667
```

This allows IRC clients on `irc.myserver.com` to connect to the IRC server running on `irc.myserver.com` on port 6667.

Once you have configured the ircd.conf file to your liking using the preceding configuration options, you are ready to start your server.

Running an IRC server

To reduce security risks, you must run the IRC server as a regular user. You might want to create a regular user called "ircserver" and run ircd as follows:

◆ Change the ownership and permissions for the IRC server executable and the configuration file to the regular user you want to run it. For example, run chown ircserver.ircserver ircd; chmod 770 ircd.* from the directory where you keep the IRC server and its configuration file.

◆ Use the su ircserver command to change your user ID to ircserver, and run the ./ircd & command from the IRC server directory. This runs the IRC server as the regular user.

Once your IRC server is running, you need to use an IRC client to test your IRC environment.

Installing and using an IRC client

You can install the IRC client that comes with your Red Hat CD-ROM. For example, the IRC client package for the *x*86 architecture is ircii-*x.x-x*.i386.rpm (where *x.x-x* is the version number). Install the appropriate IRC client on your system.

Once you have installed your IRC client, you can run it by entering the following command:

```
irc nickname irc server name [-p port number]
```

Here, the nickname can be an arbitrary name you use to identify yourself, and the irc server name is the hostname or the IP address of the IRC server. You need the

–p port number only if you are connecting to an IRC server running on a nonstandard port (that is, any port other than 6667). Here is an example of the irc command:

```
irc mrfrog picaso.nitec.com
```

Here, the irc program makes a connection to the `picaso.nitec.com` IRC server and allows the user to use "mrfrog" as the nickname. Figure 14-1 shows the initial screen after irc has connected to `picaso.nitec.com`.

Figure 14-1: Connecting to an IRC server using the irc program

 TIP If you would like to add a message of the day (MOTD) file to your IRC server so that it is displayed when a user connects to the server, create a text file called ircd.motd in the same directory of ircd.conf.

As you can see in Figure 14-1, the screen is divided into two unequal sections. The status line just before the last line separates the two sections. The top section is where we display output from the server, and we use the bottom section (the last line) to enter input.

The irc program allows you to communicate with the IRC server by using the following command syntax:

```
/command name   arguments
```

For example, to get help on available commands, you can enter:

```
/help
```

This shows the help screen as in Figure 14-2.

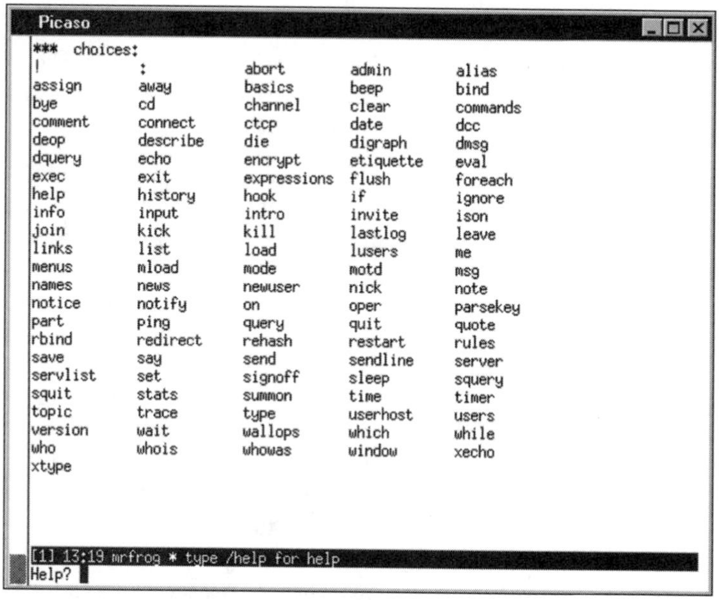

Figure 14-2: Getting help on IRC commands

You can now get help on any of the displayed topics simply by typing the name of the topic (or command). Table 14-1 discusses some basic commands you can use with IRC.

TABLE 14-1 BASIC IRC COMMANDS

Command	Example	Explanation
/join #<channel name>	/join #meeting	This command allows you to join an IRC channel. If the channel does not exist, it is created, and you become the channel operator. In other words, anyone who creates a new channel becomes the channel's operator.

Continued

TABLE 14-1 BASIC IRC COMMANDS *(Continued)*

Command	Example	Explanation

`/topic`
`#<channel>`
`<topic>`
	`/topic #meeting`
	`Sales Meeting`
	`for FormTrack`
		This command allows you to set or change the discussion topic name for a channel.

`/who` `#<channel>`	`/who #meeting`	This command shows the users who have already joined a particular channel.

`/mode`
`#<channel>`
`<options>`
	`/mode #meeting +i`	This command allows you to control the mode of the channel. For example, the +i option in the example makes a channel an invite-only channel. In other words, no one can join this channel at will unless users already in the channel extend an invitation. You can use the mode command to change a channel's mode to secret, invite-only, password protected, and so on. You can also use the mode command to create new channel operators or to ban users from using your channel. You should use the `/help` mode command to find more details on the mode command.

`/invite` `<nickname>`	`/invite mrfrog`	This command allows you to invite a user to your current channel.
`/whois` `<nickname>`	`/whois mrfrog`	This command shows detailed information about a nickname.
`/ping` `<nickname>`	`/ping mrfrog`	This command allows you to measure the message delay between you and the nickname.

`/kick`
`#<channel>`
`<nickname>`
	`/kick #meeting`
	`mrfrog`
		This channel operator-specific command allows the operator to kick out (remove) a user from a certain channel.

`/msg` `<nickname>`	`/msg mrfrog` `Hi there`	This command allows you to send a private message to the nickname specified in the command line.

Command	Example	Explanation
/notify <nickname>	/notify mrfrog	This command allows you to get a notice when the nickname (user) joins or leaves the IRC server.
/quit	/quit	This allows you to exit the IRC session.

Setting Up a Usenet News Service

Usenet newsgroups are one of the most popular services on the Internet. Normally, you run a newsreader program and point it to your ISP's news server to read and post articles on the Usenet. Having Usenet newsgroups on your local server has quite a few benefits, such as the following:

◆ You can control which newsgroups are appropriate for your organization.

◆ You can create suitable expiration policies so that important newsgroups expire as slowly as you want and not-so-important newsgroup articles expire as fast as makes sense.

However, turning your Red Hat server into a full-blown Usenet news feed is a massive undertaking. Consider the following issues:

◆ Usenet consists of nearly 100,000 newsgroups, and the number of groups is always increasing. This means there is a great load on your system and network.

◆ The daily volume of new articles can easily exceed hundreds of megabytes and even gigabytes, which could have serious effects on your disk space and the bandwidth of your network.

Although various software packages such as B news and C news are available to provide news services, InternNetNews (INN) is probably the most popular solution. INN distribution is shipped with your Red Hat CD-ROM. Installing INN is quite simple; use the `rpm -ivh inn-package-name` command to install it on your Red Hat system.

Configuring an INN server

Once you have installed INN, you need to configure it before you can use it. INN configuration can be quite a hairy task. In this section, I show you how to create a simple configuration that allows your INN server to get news articles from a remote news server and allows your users to read news from the local news server. The INN configuration files are kept in the /etc/news directory.

First, you need a news feed. This involves getting permission and access to use someone else's news server as your upstream news feed. For commercial purposes, this someone would typically be your ISP. Ask your ISP to set up its news server to allow your INN server to connect for news. Because transferring large amounts of news requires lots of resources on both ends of the news feed, your ISP might charge additional fees for this service. If such an arrangement is not acceptable, try your luck by posting an article in the `news.admin.misc` newsgroup. Some news administrators might be willing to offer you news service for free or other mutually agreed-upon arrangements. Another place to ask for a news feed is the NNTP news administrator's mailing list, `nntp-managers@colossus.apple.com`. You can subscribe to this mailing list by sending a message to `nntp-managers-request@colossus.apple.com`.

Once you have a news feeder host or IP address, you need to add it to the /etc/news/hosts.nntp file as follows:

```
hostname or IP address:optional password
```

The password field is required only if your news feed host requires a password. For example, if a host called `news.your-isp.net` acts as your upstream news feeder and requires the password "foobar," you can add the following line in the /etc/news/hosts.nntp file:

```
news.your-isp.net:foobar
```

Once your news feed host is set up, it periodically connects to your INN server and offers it any new articles that have arrived since the last connection. The INN server accepts the connection, receives the articles, and queues them.

The next step in configuring your news server is to allow your users to connect to the INN server. We use the /etc/news/nnrp.access file to control access to the INN server. The default version of this file looks as follows:

```
# Default to no access
*:: -no- : -no- :!*
# Allow access from localhost
localhost:Read Post:::*
```

As usual, the lines with leading "#" characters are treated as comments. The first configuration line states that no host is allowed read or post access to the server. This allows you to stop unauthorized use of your news server. The second configuration line allows only the localhost host to read and post articles. This means that to read and/or post articles by using the INN server, users must be connected (via Telnet or other means, such as an xterm) to the news server itself. This is not acceptable for a network of users in which each user wants to run his or her own newsreader program on some other platform such as a Windows 9.x/2000/NT workstation. In such a case, you can add a line such as the following:

```
*.yourdomain.com:Read Post:::*
```

For example:

```
*.nitec.com:Read Post:::*
```

This line allows all hosts in the nitec.com domain to have read and post privileges on the news server. When someone posts articles by using your INN server, the article needs to be sent out to the proper upstream server. You can do this by using a program called nntpsend, which is distributed with the INN package. To save you work, the Red Hat INN package automatically installs a shell script called inn-cron-nntpsend in /etc/cron.hourly directory; this script, in turn, calls the nntpsend program as follows:

```
su - news -c /usr/lib/news/bin/nntpsend
```

Here, you run the nntpsend program by using the user id "news," so make sure you have a user called "news" in your /etc/passwd file. By default, the /etc/passwd file includes this user account, and the /etc/group file includes a "news" group as well.

Once you have news flowing in and out of the system, you have to expire it, or your disks fill up. Article accounting and various other news-related administrative tasks are performed by a script called news.daily, which is also distributed with the INN package. The RPM version of the INN installation also installs a script called inn-cron-expire in /etc/cron.daily that, in turn, runs the news.daily script as follows:

```
su - news -c "/usr/lib/news/bin/news.daily"
```

This allows you to automate article expiration processes along with log file maintenance tasks.

Once you have completed the configuration just described, you can start the INN server using the following command:

```
/etc/rc.d/init.d/innd start
```

If you would like to start the INN server at boot, make sure you have a link to /etc/rc.d/init.d/innd from your default rc run level directory. For example, to start INN in multiuser run level (3), you can add a symbolic link by using the following command:

```
ln -s /etc/rc.d/init.d/innd  /etc/rc.d/rc3.d/S99innd
```

Accessing your INN server

You need a newsreader program to access your INN server. Many newsreader programs are available, including trn, rn, and so on. You can run these programs via a Telnet session, from the console, or from an xterm window. The trn package, a threaded news reader, is my favorite for accessing news directories on the server. You can install it from your Red Hat CD-ROM.

If you have users who would like to access the news server from their own workstations, make sure you include them in your /etc/news/nnrp.access file.

Summary

In this chapter, you learned about two interesting Internet services — IRC and the Usenet news service. Both of these services are quite popular among Internet users and are often a must for an Internet server.

Part V

Setting Up Office Services

Chapter 15

Sharing Files and Printers with Samba

MICROSOFT AND INTEL INITIALLY developed a protocol called Server Message Block (SMB) to allow Windows systems to share resources such as disks and printers with one another. This protocol is now available for many platforms, including Linux. Linux uses a suite of programs called Samba to implement the protocol. Using Samba, you can turn your Red Hat Linux system into an SMB client or a server. In other words, you can make your Linux disks and printers available to users on SMB clients such as Windows 9x, Windows NT/2000, and OS/2 systems. Similarly, you can make disks and printers from SMB servers such as Windows 9x, Windows NT/2000, and OS/2 available for your Linux users. In this chapter you learn to install, configure, and make use of Samba.

Installing Samba

If you chose the DOS/Windows compatibility option during Red Hat Linux installation, the Samba RPM packages were automatically installed. However, if you did not install Samba packages during installation, you can always install them using the rpm command. For example, to install the Samba client/server packages for an x86 Red Hat Linux system, I run the following commands from the /RedHat/RPMS directory of the official Red Hat CD-ROM:

```
rpm -ivh samba-2.0.7-20.i386.rpm
rpm -ivh samba-client-2.0.7-20.i386.rpm
rpm -ivh samba-common-2.0.7-20.i386.rpm
```

As you can see, installing Samba is quite a breeze. Now let's configure Samba to make use of this great package.

Configuring Samba

When you install the Samba RPM package, it installs a configuration file called smb.conf in your /etc directory. Listing 15-1 shows the default /etc/samba/smb.conf.

Listing 15-1: The default /etc/samba/smb.conf

```
/etc/samba/smb.conf # This is the main Samba configuration file. You
should read the
# smb.conf(5) manual page in order to understand the options listed
# here. Samba has a huge number of configurable options (perhaps too
# many!), most of which are not shown in this example.
#
# Any line which starts with a ; (semi-colon) or a # (hash)
# is a comment and is ignored. In this example we use a #
# for commentry and a ; for parts of the config file that you
# may wish to enable.
#
# NOTE: Whenever you modify this file you should run the
# command "testparm"
# to check that you have not many any basic syntactic errors.
#
#======================= Global Settings
=====================================
[global]

# workgroup = NT-Domain-Name or Workgroup-Name
    workgroup = MYGROUP

# server string is the equivalent of the NT Description field
    server string = Samba Server

# This option is important for security. It allows you to restrict
# connections to machines which are on your local network. The
# following example restricts access to two C class networks and
# the "loopback" interface. For more examples of the syntax see
# the smb.conf man page.
;    hosts allow = 192.168.1. 192.168.2. 127.

# If you want to load your printer list automatically rather
# than setting them up individually then you need this:
    printcap name = /etc/printcap
```

```
    load printers = yes

# It should not be necessary to spell out the print system type
unless
# yours is non-standard. Currently supported print systems include:
# bsd, sysv, plp, lprng, aix, hpux, qnx
    printing = lprng

# Uncomment this if you want a guest account; you must add this to
/etc/passwd
# otherwise the user "nobody" is used.
;   guest account = pcguest

# This line tells Samba to use a separate log file for each machine
# that connects
    log file = /var/log/samba/%m.log

# Put a capping on the size of the log files (in Kb).
    max log size = 0

# Security mode. Most people want user level security. See
# security_level.txt for details.
    security = user
# Use password server option only with security = server or
# security = domain
;    password server = <NT-Server-Name>

# Password Level allows matching of _n_ characters of the password
for
# all combinations of upper and lower case.
;   password level = 8
;   username level = 8

# You may wish to use password encryption. Please read
# ENCRYPTION.txt, Win95.txt and WinNT.txt in the Samba
documentation.
# Do not enable this option unless you have read those documents.
;   encrypt passwords = yes
;   smb passwd file = /etc/samba/smbpasswd

# The following are needed to allow password changing from Windows
to
# update the Linux sytsem password also.
# NOTE: Use these with 'encrypt passwords' and 'smb passwd file'
above.
```

```
# NOTE2: You do NOT need these to allow workstations to change only
#        the encrypted SMB passwords. They allow the Unix password
#        to be kept in sync with the SMB password.
;  unix password sync = Yes
;  passwd program = /usr/bin/passwd %u
;  passwd chat = *New*UNIX*password* %n\n *ReType*new*UNIX*password*
%n\n *passwd:*all*authentication*tokens*updated*successfully*


# Unix users can map to different SMB User names
;  username map = /etc/samba/smbusers


# Using the following line enables you to customise your
configuration
# on a per machine basis. The %m gets replaced with the netbios name
# of the machine that is connecting
;   include = /etc/samba/smb.conf.%m


# Most people find that this option gives better performance.
# See speed.txt and the manual pages for details
    socket options = TCP_NODELAY SO_RCVBUF=8192 SO_SNDBUF=8192


# Configure Samba to use multiple interfaces
# If you have multiple network interfaces then you must list them
# here. See the man page for details.
;   interfaces = 192.168.12.2/24 192.168.13.2/24


# Configure remote browse list synchronisation here
#  request announcement to, or browse list sync from:
#   a specific host or from / to a whole subnet (see below)
;   remote browse sync = 192.168.3.25 192.168.5.255
# Cause this host to announce itself to local subnets here
;    remote announce = 192.168.1.255 192.168.2.44


# Browser Control Options:
# set local master to no if you don't want Samba to
# become a master
# browser on your network. Otherwise the normal election
# rules apply
;   local master = no


# OS Level determines the precedence of this server in
# master browser elections. The default value should be reasonable
;   os level = 33


# Domain Master specifies Samba to be the Domain Master
```

```
# Browser. This allows Samba to collate browse lists between
subnets.
# Don't use this if you already have a Windows NT domain controller
# doing this job
;    domain master = yes


# Preferred Master causes Samba to force a local browser
# election on startup and gives it a slightly higher chance of
winning
# the election
;    preferred master = yes


# Enable this if you want Samba to be a domain logon server for
# Windows95 workstations.
;    domain logons = yes


# If you enable domain logons then you may want a per-machine or
# per-user logon script.
# Run a specific logon batch file per workstation (machine).
;    logon script = %m.bat
# Run a specific logon batch file per username.
;    logon script = %U.bat


# All NetBIOS names must be resolved to IP Addresses
# 'Name Resolve Order' allows the named resolution mechanism
# to be specified the default order is "host lmhosts wins bcast".
# "host" means use the unix system gethostbyname() function call
that uses
# either /etc/hosts OR DNS or NIS depending on the settings of
# /etc/host.config, /etc/nsswitch.conf
# and the /etc/resolv.conf file. "host" therefore is
# system configuration dependant. This parameter is most often of
use
# to prevent DNS lookupsin order to resolve NetBIOS names to IP
Addresses.
# Use with care!  The example below excludes use of name resolution
# for machines that are NOT on the local network segment
# - OR - are not deliberately to be known via lmhosts or
# via WINS.
; name resolve order = wins lmhosts bcast


# Windows Internet Name Serving Support Section:
# WINS Support - Tells the NMBD component of Samba to enable
# its WINS Server
;    wins support = yes
```

```
# WINS Server - Tells the NMBD components of Samba to be a
# WINS Client
#    Note: Samba can be either a WINS Server, or a WINS Client, but
NOT both
;   wins server = w.x.y.z

# WINS Proxy - Tells Samba to answer name resolution queries on
# behalf of a non WINS capable client; for this to work
# there must be at least one WINS Server on the network.
# The default is NO.
;   wins proxy = yes

# DNS Proxy - tells Samba whether or not to try to resolve
# NetBIOS names via DNS nslookups. The built-in default for versions
1.9.17
# is yes.
# this has been changed in version 1.9.18 to no.
    dns proxy = no

# Case Preservation can be handy ( system default is _no_
# NOTE: These can be set on a per share basis
;   preserve case = no
;   short preserve case = no
# Default case is normally upper case for all DOS files
;   default case = lower
# Be very careful with case sensitivity - it can break things!
;   case sensitive = no

#==== Share Definitions ====
[homes]
    comment = Home Directories
    browseable = no
    writable = yes

# Un-comment the following and create the netlogon
# directory for Domain Logons
; [netlogon]
;   comment = Network Logon Service
;   path = /home/netlogon
;   guest ok = yes
;   writable = no
;   share modes = no


# Un-comment the following to provide a specific roving
```

```
# profile share the default is to use the user's home
# directory
;[Profiles]
;    path = /home/profiles
;    browseable = no
;    guest ok = yes


# NOTE: If you have a BSD-style print system there is no need to
# specifically define each individual printer
[printers]
    comment = All Printers
    path = /var/spool/samba
    browseable = no
# Set public = yes to allow user 'guest account' to print
    guest ok = no
    printable = yes

# This one is useful for people to share files
;[tmp]
;    comment = Temporary file space
;    path = /tmp
;    read only = no
;    public = yes

# A publicly accessible directory, but read only, except for people
in
# the "staff" group
;[public]
;    comment = Public Stuff
;    path = /home/samba
;    public = yes
;    writable = yes
;    printable = no
;    write list = @staff

# Other examples.
#
# A private printer, usable only by fred. Spool data
# will be placed in fred's ome directory. Note that fred must have
write
# access to the spool directory,
# wherever it is.
;[fredsprn]
;    comment = Fred's Printer
```

```
;    valid users = fred
;    path = /homes/fred
;    printer = freds_printer
;    public = no
;    printable = yes


# A private directory, usable only by fred. Note that fred requires write
# access to the directory.
;[fredsdir]
;    comment = Fred's Service
;    path = /usr/somewhere/private
;    valid users = fred
;    public = no
;    writable = yes
;    printable = no


# A service which has a different directory for each
# machine that connects this allows you to tailor configurations to
# incoming machines. You could
# also use the %u option to tailor it by user name.
# The %m gets replaced with the machine name that
# is connecting.
;[pchome]
;    comment = PC Directories
;    path = /usr/pc/%m
;    public = no
;    writable = yes


# A publicly accessible directory, read/write to all users.
# Note that all files created in the directory by users are owned by
# the default user, so
# any user with access can delete any other user's files.
# Obviously this
# directory must be writable by the default user.
# Another user could, of course,
# be specified, in which case all files would be owned
# by that user instead.
;[public]
;    path = /usr/somewhere/else/public
;    public = yes
;    only guest = yes
;    writable = yes
;    printable = no
```

```
# The following two entries demonstrate how to share
# a directory so that two users can place files there that are owned
by
# the specific users. In this setup, the directory should be
writable by both
# users and should have the
# sticky bit set on it to prevent abuse. Obviously this
# could be extended to
# as many users as required.
;[myshare]
;   comment = Mary's and Fred's stuff
;   path = /usr/somewhere/shared
;   valid users = mary fred
;   public = no
;   writable = yes
;   printable = no
;   create mask = 0765
```

Observant readers will notice that the file has four types of lines as follows:

- ◆ Lines that start with "#" (number sign) characters. These lines are treated as comments and ignored by Samba. Typically, comment lines of this type are used for commentary only.

- ◆ Lines that start with ";" (semicolon) characters. These lines are also treated as comments and ignored by Samba. Typically, these lines are used to disable a configuration line. But you can always use a "#" instead of a ";" character to do the same. Why use two different types of comment lines? Well, the "#" style of comments is very common to all UNIX configuration files, and ";"-style comment lines are common in the Windows world. My theory is that because Samba is the bridge between these two platforms, the Samba developers chose to allow and use both comment styles.

- ◆ Lines that define a section using a pair of square brackets. Lines following a section belong to the named section until another section name is defined. For example:

```
[global]
workgroup = MYGROUP

[homes]
comment = Home Directories
```

Here two sections, global and homes, are being defined. The line workgroup = MYGROUP belongs to the global section, and the line comment = Home Directories belongs to the homes section. Note that the section names are not case sensitive. In other words [Global] is the same as [global] or any other case variant of the same word. Each section describes a particular service. There are two types of services: file and print service. There are three special sections: [global], [homes], and [printers].

◆ Lines that define configuration parameters in the name = value format. For example:

```
workgroup = MYGROUP
```

Here the parameter workgroup is being set to a value MYGROUP. Note that the parameter names (the left side) are not case sensitive as well.

Now let's look at the default configuration. If you remove all the comment lines from the default /etc/samba/smb.conf file, you notice that only three special configuration sections are defined in the file. I discuss these next.

The [global] configuration

The [global] section defines Samba parameters that apply to all other configuration sections (that is, services that they define). The default [global] configuration is as follows:

```
[global]
    workgroup = MYGROUP
    server string = Samba Server
    printcap name = /etc/printcap
    load printers = yes
    printing = lprng
    log file = /var/log/samba/%m.log
    max log size =  0
    security = user
    socket options =  TCP_NODELAY SO_RCVBUF=8192 SO_SNDBUF=8192
    dns proxy = no
```

The first parameter, workgroup, is used to set the Windows workgroup or Windows NT domain name that you want Samba to participate in as a node. For example, I use NITEC as the Windows NT domain name so that I can set workgroup to NITEC. When a Windows 9x or Windows NT system on my network browses the Network Neighborhood, it sees the Samba server under the NITEC Windows NT domain. Set this to whatever workgroup or domain name is appropriate for your LAN. The server string parameter is used to provide a description for the Samba server.

The `printcap name` parameter is used to set the printcap file path. The default value, `/etc/printcap`, should work for you. Use the /etc/printcap file to describe your printer's capabilities. If you have one or more printers attached to your Linux server and you would like to make all your printers available to the Windows systems on your LAN, you need to set this parameter along with the next parameter. The `load printers` parameter is used to tell Samba to make local printers automatically available to any SMB client computer on the network. Set this to `yes` if you want to enable this feature, or if you prefer to specify printer configurations in individual configuration sections, you can set this to no. The `printing` parameter is used to set the `print` command. The default value of `lprng` tells Samba to use the `lpr` command.

The `log file` parameter sets the filename of the Samba log file. The default setting writes a log file per client. This is done using the %m macro, which expands to the client name. For example, if you keep the log file setting as is and access the Samba server from a Windows machine called r2d2, a log file called /var/log/samba/r2d2.log is created. The max log size is used to control the maximum log file size in KB. The default of 0 means unlimited size.

The `security` parameter is the most important one among all the other global parameters. A Samba server uses this parameter to determine how it performs client authentication. The three possible values are `user`, `share`, and `server`.

When you set the `security` parameter to `user`, the Samba server tells the client to supply a username/password pair for authentication. If you use the same username/password pairs on your Windows systems and Linux systems, you should set the security parameter to `user`. For example, if you have a user called joe on an NT server and have the same user on the Samba server with the same password, set this parameter to `user`.

If your Windows systems and the Linux Samba server do not have the same set of username/password pairs, you should set this parameter to `share`. When this parameter is set to `share`, the Samba server expects a password with each request for a service. No usernames are required.

Finally, if you set the `security` parameter to `server`, the Samba server tells the client to supply a username/password pair just like when you set this parameter to `user`. However, the only difference is that the Samba server actually does not verify the username/password pair itself. It uses another SMB server to authenticate the user. For this reason, when you set `security` to `server`, you must also set the `password server` parameter. The `password server` parameter is used to name an SMB server that is responsible for authentication. If you want to centralize your usernames/passwords for SMB activity on a Windows NT server, you can set the `password server` to point to the Windows NT server.

If you use a Windows NT server as your password server to do the authentication for Samba, make sure that you do not have the guest account on the Windows NT system enabled. If the guest account is enabled, any time a username/password pair fails because of an incorrect password, Windows NT still provides a valid response to the Samba server. This is because Windows NT simply assigns guest privileges to the failed authentication attempt and returns a success response to the Samba server.

The default setting for security is user, which means a client has to supply a plain-text password along with a username. The Samba server verifies this username/password pair using the /etc/password file. However, the later versions of Windows 9.x and Windows NT operating systems do not use plain-text (also known as clear-text) passwords by default. Microsoft decided to use encrypted passwords as part of upgrades to its operating system service packs. Because these Windows clients do not supply plain-text passwords, they can't be verified, and therefore the Samba server refuses to service them. To remedy this problem, you have two options: (a) to enable plain-text passwords on Windows systems or (b) to use encrypted passwords for authentication. The first option is acceptable if any of the following conditions is true:

◆ You already allow plain-text-based services such as FTP and Telnet between your Windows machine and Red Hat Linux server.

◆ Your network is not connected to the Internet, and hence use of plain-text passwords does not pose a great threat to your organization.

◆ You just want to get Samba working first and then either deal with encrypted passwords or plan on delegating all authentication tasks to a Windows NT server in the long run.

Because I believe you will probably go for option (a), I am going to discuss how you can use plain-text passwords with Windows clients here and also provide the details of option (b) in a later section (see "Securing Your Samba Server").

If you are using Windows 98, Windows 95 (with Service Pack 3 or above), or Windows NT 4.0 with Service Pack 3 or above, you need to take the following steps to enable plain-text passwords.

1. Run the Windows Registry editor program called regedit.

2. For Windows 9.x, locate the following Registry key:

```
/HKEY_LOCAL_MACHINE
    /System
        /CurrentControlSet
```

```
/Services
    /VxD
        /VNETSUP
```

3. For Windows NT 4.0 with Service Pack 3 or above, locate the following Registry key:

```
/HKEY_LOCAL_MACHINE
    /SYSTEM
        /CurrentControlSet
            /Services
                /Rdr
                    /Parameters
```

4. Once you have located the VNETSUP branch (for Windows 9*x*) or the Parameters branch (for Windows NT) in the Registry tree, select Edit ⇨ New and choose to create a new DWORD value.

5. The Registry editor inserts a new DWORD value called "New Value #1" in the Registry. Rename this new value to EnablePlainTextPassword and double-click this new name.

6. A dialog box pops up to enable you to set a value for the EnablePlainTextPassword you just created. Enter 1 as the value and close the Registry editor as usual.

7. Reboot your Windows 9*x*/NT system.

These settings ensure that your Windows 9*x*/NT system is able to use plain-text passwords for SMB authentication.

By default, the `socket options` in the global configuration section is set to `TCP_NODELAY SO_RCVBUF=8192 SO_SNDBUF=8192`, which enhances Samba performance on certain platforms. You should leave this parameter as is. The final default parameter in the global configuration is `dns proxy`, which is set to `no`. This parameter affects how the Samba suite's built-in Windows Internet Name Server (nmbd) behaves when a Windows system name (NETBIOS name) cannot be resolved to an IP address. In such a case if this parameter is set to yes, the nmbd server treats the NETBIOS name as an Internet domain name and tries to resolve it using the DNS protocol. I recommend that you leave the default as is.

Now let's look at the [homes] section of the default configuration.

The [homes] configuration

The [homes] section is also a special configuration section. It enables you to set up home directory access from Windows systems. In other words, a user with a valid username/password on the Red Hat system can access her home directory on the Linux system from a Windows system.

```
[homes]
   comment = Home Directories
   browseable = no
   writable = yes
```

The first parameter, comment, is just what its name says. The second parameter, browseable, controls whether or not home directories are visible in a browser list (such as the Network Neighborhood) or when the NET VIEW command is used from the Windows command prompt.

The writable parameter controls whether or not a user can write to her home directory. For most practical purposes, this needs to be set to yes. If you set this to no, a user has read-only access to her own home directory.

Finally, the last enabled configuration section in the default /etc/srm.conf file is the [printers] section.

The [printers] configuration

The [printers] section is useful only if you have one or more printers attached to your Red Hat Linux system.

```
[printers]
   comment = All Printers
   path = /var/spool/samba
   browseable = no
   guest ok = no

   printable = yes
```

The comment parameter is exactly what the name says. The path parameter is used to set the directory where printer data files are spooled. The browseable parameter enables you to make the printers appear (or not appear) in a browser (such as Network Neighborhood) or NET VIEW command output. The guest ok parameter allows the printers to be used by anyone without a password. The final parameter, printable, is very important. It has to be set to yes so that printing can occur.

The default configuration includes many commented configuration parameters and additional sections. You should carefully investigate these options and enable anything that you would like to use. However, if you are using Samba for the first time, I recommend that you first get it working using the default configuration. In a later section I discuss some common configuration details that help you create practical Samba configurations for many common scenarios. Now it's time to get ready to test your configuration.

Using GUI Configuration Tools

If you find the /etc/samba/smb.conf file hard to manage manually, you are not alone. Many people find it hard to manage because there are so many options to consider. Because of the demand for a better interface than a text editor to manage the /etc/samba/smb.conf file, quite a few graphical user interface (GUI) tools are available for managing this file. If you are interested, you can try out a few listed in Table 15-1.

TABLE 15-1 GUI TOOLS FOR MANAGING /etc/samba/smb.conf

Tool	Comments/URL
SWAT — Samba Web Administration Tool	This is the official GUI for Samba because it will be packaged with the next major release of Samba. It is a Web-based configuration tool. `http://anu.samba.org/cgi-bin/swat/`
SMBEdit	This is a Windows-based smb.conf editor. `http://us2.samba.org/samba/smbedit/intro.htm`
SMB2WWW	SMB2WWW is a perl-based gateway to SMB from Web browsers. `http://us2.samba.org/samba/smb2www/index.html`
Smbconftool	This is a Java-based tool for smb.conf editing. `http://www.eatonweb.com/samba/`

Among these GUI options, I like only the official SWAT tool. Until it is ready for prime time, however, I prefer my favorite vi editor to do all the editing work.

Testing the /etc/samba/smb.conf configuration

Any time you change a Samba configuration file, make sure you run the `testparm` utility that is bundled with the Samba package. When you run this nifty utility from the command line, it checks the syntax of the /etc/samba/smb.conf file and gives you useful warning and error messages. Because a misconfigured /etc/samba/smb.conf can be a security hole, I highly recommend the use of this utility whenever you modify this file.

Starting, stopping, and restarting the Samba service

Once you have made sure that your /etc/samba/smb.conf file is error free, you are ready to start Samba. Two daemons come with the Samba package. The smbd daemon is the Samba server, and the nmbd daemon is the NETBIOS name server. To start the daemons, run the following command as root:

```
/etc/rc.d/init.d/smb start
```

This command starts the daemons, and then you can start accessing the Samba server from your Windows computers. To stop the Samba server, you can run the same command with a stop argument. You can also restart the daemons using the same command with a restart argument.

If you would like to start the Samba service at boot time, create a symbolic link as follows:

```
ln -s /etc/rc.d/init.d/smb    /etc/rc.d/rc3.d/S91smb
```

This command starts the Samba service when your Red Hat Linux server enters run level 3, which is the default run level for all multiuser systems. Note that if you use an X Window System–based login (using XDM) and want to start Samba automatically, you need to create another link as follows:

```
ln -s /etc/rc.d/init.d/smb    /etc/rc.d/rc5.d/S91smb
```

Now take a look at a few practical uses of the Samba service you just configured and started on your server.

Practical Uses of Samba

Samba is a great way of bringing the Microsoft and the Linux worlds together. In this section I show you a few practical examples of how you can achieve interesting results with Samba.

Using a Linux file server on Windows

This is probably the most common reason why a Linux administrator in a Linux/Windows shop may think about using Samba is to make her Linux server available to Windows users. For example, suppose you want to make a Linux partition (or directory) called /intranet available to a group of Windows users (jennifer, chad, and phil) on your LAN. Here is what you need to do:

1. If you set the security parameter in the [global] configuration section to user or share, create three user accounts (jennifer, chad, and phil) on your

Linux system. These user accounts need to be set up such that the password for each account matches its Windows counterpart. For example, if jennifer's password on her Windows system is set to tsk#tsk then you must set her Linux account with the same password as well. Also create a group called intranet in /etc/group such that users jennifer, chad, and phil are the only members in the group.

2. Now modify the /etc/samba/smb.conf file to add the following:

```
[Intranet]
    comment = Intranet Directory
    path = /intranet
    public = no
    writable = yes
    write list = @intranet
    printable = no
```

The preceding configuration [Intranet] specifies that /intranet is not publicly accessible and write permission is given for the intranet group. Once you have run testparm to make sure that there are no syntax errors in the /etc/samba/smb.conf file, you can restart the Samba service.

Now you can have jennifer, chad, and phil access the /intranet partition or directory from their Windows machine. Now if you want to create a read-only file server, you can set the writable parameter to no and remove the write list parameter from the preceding configuration. To force the file permissions in this shared partition (or directory) to remain the same, you can use the force create mode parameter. For example:

```
force create mode  0750
```

This command makes sure that all files created in the shared space have full access (read, write, and execute) for the owner and read and execute access for everyone in the group. Anyone outside the group does not have any access to these files.

Using a Windows file server on your Linux system

If you have a Windows file server that you would like to make available to your Linux users, you can use the smbfs (SMB file system) to mount Windows disks and directories onto your Linux system. For example, to mount the default drive (C: drive) of a Windows NT server called PLUTO on a Linux Samba server, follow these steps:

1. On the Windows NT system, double-click the My Computer icon to open up the My Computer window. Click the C drive icon once and then press the right button of your mouse to bring up the window shown in Figure 15-1.

Figure 15-1: Selecting disk sharing on Windows NT

2. Select the Sharing option from the list. This selection brings up a dialog box similar to the one shown in Figure 15-2.

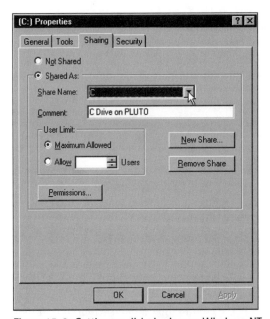

Figure 15-2: Setting up disk sharing on Windows NT

3. Select the Sharing tab (as shown in the figure). Click the Shared As radio button and select a name for the share from the drop-down Share Name list. In this example the share name is C. Write a comment line to help identify the share when browsed from other computers.

4. Click Apply and exit the window.

You have just enabled SMB sharing for the C drive. Now all you need to do is mount this share on your Linux system.

The smbfs file system comes with a command called `smbmount` that allows you to mount an SMB share. The common syntax is as shown here:

```
smbmount //WINDOWS-SERVER/path  /mount-point  \
-U WindowsUser -P WindowsUserPassword
```

Here `//WINDOWS-SERVER` is the Windows system with the share (path), the `/mount-point` is the mount directory on the Linux system, the `WindowsUser` is a user on the Windows system that has at least read access to the share, and `Windows UserPassword` is the password for that user. If your Windows NT system is set up correctly, only the Administrator user (or an equivalent user) should have full access to the entire drive. So in this example, we use the Administrator user to mount the C drive. Here is an example `smbmount` that mounts the C drive from PLUTO:

```
smbmount //PLUTO/c /mnt/pluto-c  -U Administrator -P gowent
```

If you get an error message when you run your version of the preceding command, make sure you have entered the proper password. Also, you might want to try the –I option to specify the IP address of the Windows NT server just in case it does not advertise its IP address. When the command is successful, you see the /mnt/pluto-c in your df listing and you can access all the files from the C drive of your Windows system. If you would prefer to mount the C drive such that only certain users and groups on the Linux system can access the drive, you can use the –u UID and –g GID options. For example:

```
smbmount //PLUTO/c /mnt/pluto-c  -U Administrator -P gowent \
-u root -g admin
```

Here only user root and anyone in group admin have access to PLUTO's C drive, which is mounted on the Linux system under /mnt/pluto-c.

To unmount or remove an SMB file system from the Linux system, you need to run the `smbumount` command. For example:

```
smbumount /mnt/pluto-c
```

This command unmounts the //PLUTO/c share from the Linux system.

Sharing printers between Linux and Windows

Sharing printers is a common benefit of a LAN environment. Using Samba, you can now share printers between both Linux and Windows. Let's first look at how you can share a Windows printer on a Linux system.

SHARING A WINDOWS PRINTER WITH LINUX

On your Windows system attached to the printer, create an account that can use the printer and that also requires no password. For example, on a Windows NT workstation or server you can follow these steps to create such an account:

1. Use the User Administrator program to create an account called printeruser. Do not assign any password for this user and assign only the user to the regular user group.

2. Select your printer from the My Computer folder and click the right mouse button to bring up the printer properties window. Select the Security tab and click Permissions. This dialog box looks like the one shown in Figure 15-3.

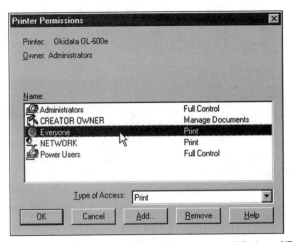

Figure 15-3: Printer permissions for users on a Windows NT system

If you see that "Everyone" has print access, you need not do anything. If you have a setup where Everyone does not have print access, you have to add the printeruser in the list with the privilege to print to the selected printer. Once you have configured the Windows NT account to print, you are ready to test it:

1. From the Linux system use the smbclient program to connect to the printer as follows:

   ```
   smbclient //WINDOWS-SYSTEM/SharedPrinter -U printeruser -N -P
   ```

   Do not forget to replace *WINDOWS-SYSTEM* with your Windows system name and *SharedPrinter* with the printer name. The -N and -P options are used to instruct the smbclient program to use the null password for connection.

2. Once you are connected and in the smbclient program prompt, you can type `printmode text` to set print mode to text and enter a command like `print /path/to/a/linux/textfile` to print the file. If your printer prints the file, you are halfway done.

3. Now you need to configure the Linux side. The easiest way to configure an SMB-based printer is to use the X Windows–based printtool utility that comes with Red Hat. Run printtool from an xterm and click Add. You see a dialog box like the one shown in Figure 15-4. Select the SMB/Windows 95/96/NT Printeroption and click OK to continue. You see a warning message about a remote SMB/Windows 9x/NT printer requiring a username/password. The warning window recommends that if your remote printer requires a username/password, you should make sure the account used is not a real user account. In other words, you should use an unprivileged user account on your SMB/Windows server for your printer. Click OK to continue.

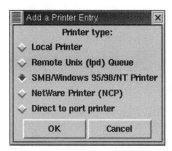

Figure 15-4: Adding an SMB/Windows 9x/NT Printer using printtool

4. You now see a dialog box like the one shown in Figure 15-5.

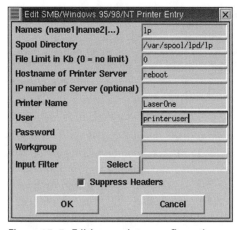

Figure 15-5: Editing a printer configuration

5. If this is your first printer, the name is set to lp. You can change it to whatever you want.

    Print commands such as lpr use this name to identify this printer. The spool directory should also be set to /var/spool/lpd/lp. If you change the printer name, make sure you also change the spool directory path to reflect the name change. The File Limit option should be left as is unless you are setting up the printer in an environment where users can abuse it by sending large files. In such a case, use a reasonable limit, like 2048KB (2MB). The hostname of the printer should be set to the Windows NT system where the printer is attached. The IP address of this host is optional. The printer name is the share name you created for the printer. The username should be the printer user (printuser) you created earlier. The password field should be left blank, as you have not assigned a password to this user.

6. Now click Input Filter Select to modify the input filter. The Configure Filter dialog box is similar to the one shown in Figure 15-6.

7. Select the printer type and printer options as appropriate. Click OK to complete the filter configuration and finally click OK to add the new printer.

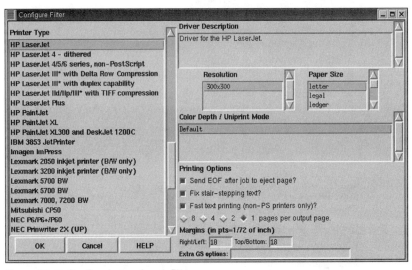

Figure 15-6: Configuring an input filter

8. Now you are ready to test the printer. From the Red Hat Linux Print System Manager screen, select the newly created printer by clicking it once, and then click the Tests menu and select a test option to test your printer. If you get output on the printer, your configuration is working. However, if your output is pretty much garbage, you can go back to the input filter configuration dialog box by editing the printer and making changes to get better or appropriate output.

If you have successfully test-printed in the last step, you are done with printer configuration. Now you can use the printer from your Linux applications. For example, to use the printer to print a text file from the command line, you can use the lpr command as follows:

```
lpr -Pprintername /path/to/file
```

If the printer name is lp and you want to print the /etc/samba/smb.conf file, the command is as follows:

```
lpr -Plp /etc/samba/smb.conf
```

You can use the lpq command to see the print queue and the lprm command to remove print jobs from the queue. Note that when the file being printed is transferred to the Windows print spooler, its status is no longer available to you.

Now let's look at how you can get a Linux printer to be shared on a Windows system.

SHARING A LINUX PRINTER WITH WINDOWS
Modify your /etc/samba/smb.conf file as follows:

1. In the [global] configuration section set the following:

   ```
   printcap name = /etc/printcap
   load printers = yes
   ```

2. In your [printers] configuration section set the following:

   ```
   comments = All Printers
   path = /var/spool/lpd
   writable = no
   printable = yes
   ```

If you would like the printer list to appear in browser list, set the browseable parameter to yes in the preceding configuration. Similarly, if you would like to allow the guest account to use the printer, set guest ok = yes in the preceding configuration. That's all there is to setting up all your printers. However, if you would prefer to make one or more printers privately available to one or more users, you can specify a separate section for each of these users. For example, say that I want to create a private printer (fancyjet) access for a user called bigboss, I can create a configuration such as the following:

```
[fancyjet]
comment = Big Boss Only Printer
valid users = bigboss
path = /home/bigboss/fancyjet
guest ok = no
```

```
browseable = no
writable = no
printable = yes
```

The `valid users` parameter enables you to specify a space-separated list of users who have access to the printer.

Once you have modified and tested the /etc/samba/smb.conf file, restart the Samba service, and you should be able to access the Linux printers from your Windows computers.

Using an interactive Samba client

The Samba package comes with a program called smbclient that enables you to access a Samba resource interactively. For example, say that you want to access a disk share on a Windows system from your Linux system. You can use the smbclient program to access it as follows:

```
smbclient //WINDOWS-SERVER/resource  -U username -P password
```

For example:

```
smbclient //PLUTO/c -U kabir -P mypass
```

Here the smbclient is used to access the C drive on PLUTO as a user kabir. If the authentication is successful – in other words, if PLUTO allows connection – the smbclient displays an FTP client-like prompt and enable you to perform many FTP client commands. You can learn more about the commands by typing "help" or the question mark at any time.

You can use the smbclient to list the available Samba resources on a remote computer. For example:

```
smbclient -L reboot -U kabir
```

Here the –L option specifies the Samba server to be interrogated using username kabir. The example output is shown in Listing 15-2.

Listing 15-2: Example output of smbclient

```
Server time is Sat Aug 13 19:48:03 2000
Timezone is UTC-8.0
Password:
Domain=[NITEC] OS=[Windows NT 4.0] Server=[NT LAN Manager 4.0]
security=user
```

```
Server=[REBOOT] User=[] Workgroup=[NITEC] Domain=[]

        Sharename      Type      Comment
        ---------      ----      -------
        ADMIN$         Disk      Remote Admin
        C              Disk      C Drive on PLUTO
        C$             Disk      Default share
        F              Disk
        home           Disk
        IPC$           IPC       Remote IPC
        Okidata0       Printer   Okidata OL-600e
        print$         Disk      Printer Drivers
        sheila         Disk
        TEMP           Disk


This machine has a browse list:

        Server               Comment
        ------               -------
        PICASO               Picaso Samba Server
        PLUTO
        R2D2                 Nitec Laptop (r2d2)
        REBOOT

This machine has a workgroup list:

        Workgroup            Master
        ---------            ------
        NITEC                PLUTO
```

As you can see, you can use the smbclient program to determine the resources being shared from other Samba-compliant systems.

The smbclient program also allows you to send Windows pop-up messages to Windows computers that have enabled this service. For example:

```
smbclient -M reboot
```

When you run this command, the smbclient enables you to enter text messages from the keyboard that it displays as pop-up messages on the target Windows computer. An example of such a pop-up message is shown in Figure 15-7.

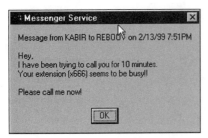

Messenger Service

Message from KABIR to REBOOT on 2/13/99 7:51PM

Hey,
I have been trying to call you for 10 minutes.
Your extension (x666) seems to be busy!!

Please call me now!

OK

Figure 15-7: An example of a pop-up message from smbclient

Securing Your Samba Server

Samba is great. If used correctly, it can turn a mixed environment (Linux/Windows) into a smooth computing environment. However, like any other useful service, when misconfigured, Samba could be a potential source of security holes. This is especially important if your Samba server is in any way connected to the Internet. I do not recommend that you connect a Samba server to the Internet or enable Samba services over the Internet. Here I discuss a few security measures that you can take to reduce risks involving Samba.

Earlier I showed you how to enable plain-text passwords on later versions of Windows 9.*x* and NT systems. This works well but might not be suitable for a LAN or WAN environment where a potential for TCP/IP packet sniffers exists. In other words, if you have reason to believe that your network might be vulnerable to packet sniffers, you can implement encrypted passwords. The encrypted password–based authentication that the SMB protocol permits never transmits any passwords between a Samba client and server. This ensures a higher degree of security and hence is very desirable in high-risk scenarios where security and confidentiality are of utmost importance. You have two ways to go about using encrypted passwords.

USING A WINDOWS NT SERVER AS A PASSWORD SERVER

A Windows NT server, by default, can provide encrypted password services. So if you have a Windows NT server on your network, consider making it your password server. You can centralize all your user accounts on the Windows NT server so that Samba services can be enabled using encrypted passwords. To use a Windows NT server as your encrypted password server, do the following:

1. Create a Windows NT server account for each user who needs Samba access.

2. Modify the /etc/samba/smb.conf file so that you have the `password server` parameter set to the name of the Windows NT server. Also set the `security` parameter to `server`.

3. Run the `testparm` command to ensure that all configuration lines are syntactically correct in the /etc/samba/smb.conf file.

4. Restart the Samba service.

To test your new configuration, use one of the Windows NT server user accounts to access the Samba server.

USING ENCRYPTED PASSWORDS ON YOUR SAMBA SERVER

The Samba package shipped with Red Hat is precompiled with encrypted password support, so there is no need to download the Samba source code and compile it with encrypted password support. All you need to do to enable encrypted passwords is to take these steps:

1. Use the mksmbpasswd.sh script supplied with the Samba package to create a password file for /etc/passwd. Run the following command:

```
cat /etc/passwd | /usr/bin/mksmbpasswd.sh >
/etc/samba/smbpasswd
```

   This command line creates a special password file that has lines such as the following:

```
root:0:XXXXXXXXXXXXXXXXXXXXXXXXXXXXXXXX:XXXXXXXXXXXXXXXXXXXXXX
XXXXXXXXXXX :[U             ]:LCT-00000000:root
```

2. Now use the smbpasswd program to create encrypted Samba passwords for each user. For example, to create an encrypted Samba password for a user called sheila, I can run:

```
smbpasswd sheila
```

3. Once you have created the passwords, modify the /etc/samba/smb.conf file such that you have the following lines in the [global] configuration file:

```
encrypt passwords = yes
smb passwd file = /etc/samba/smbpasswd
```

4. Test your new configuration using testparm, and if the test is successful, restart the Samba service.

Now you are ready to test the Samba service from your Windows systems. Note that if you have modified your Windows Registry to use plain-text passwords, you have to remove the Registry entry you created so that encrypted passwords can be used.

Summary

In this chapter, you learned to use the Samba services to allow Windows clients to access the Red Hat Linux server. You also learned to access Windows resources via the Samba service on your Red Hat Linux system.

Chapter 16

Using NFS File Servers

IN THIS CHAPTER

- How to install and configure the NFS server
- How to install and configure the NFS client
- How to use rdist to distribute files among multiple computers

IN THE PREVIOUS CHAPTER you learned to share files between SMB protocol–compliant systems such as your Red Hat Linux and various Windows operating systems. Network File System (NFS) solves the same file-sharing problem but was designed to handle UNIX semantics from early on. While NFS was designed from the ground up, SMB was implemented first and documented later. In my opinion, SMB feels like an architecture that grew rather than something that was designed from the very start. Because SMB shares a great tie with Microsoft, things can break at any time the company changes it. For example, the service packs (3 or above) for Windows NT 4.0 broke Samba service due to a change in Microsoft's idea of SMB security. NFS, on the other hand, has been around for a long time and has been implemented in just about all the UNIX platforms. In short, if you want to share disk and other resources between your Red Hat Linux and Windows systems, use SMB; if you are planning on sharing disks between multiple UNIX systems, NFS is probably your best choice. In this chapter I show you how to use NFS.

Installing NFS Server and Client Software

You can install the NFS server and client software from the RPM package shipped with the Red Hat CD-ROM. For example, to install the NFS server package for a *x*86 Red Hat Linux system, I can run the following command from the /RedHat/RPMS directory of the CD-ROM:

```
rpm -ivh nfs-utils-0.1.9.1-7.i386.rpm
```

The NFS server package includes the NFS daemons and configuration files necessary to turn a Red Hat Linux system into an NFS server. However, because NFS is based on Remote Procedure Call (RPC), you need another package called the portmap. If you do not have this package already installed (check using `rpm -q portmap`), then you should install it via the `rpm` command from the CD-ROM. Red Hat Linux kernel comes with the NFS module (nfs.o) by default. However, if you wanted to compile a custom kernel and still have NFS support in kernel, you would have to choose NFS file system support when running the kernelcfg utility.

Now look at how to turn your Red Hat Linux system into an NFS server.

Configuring an NFS Server

An NFS server needs to run a program called portmap (also called rpc.portmap), which is usually started at boot time via init. To check if the portmapper is already running, use the following command:

```
ps auxw | grep portmap
```

When you install the portmap package, it also installs an init script in /etc/rc.d/init.d called portmap. This script should also be automatically linked in your default run level (typically run level 3 for a multiuser system) rc directory. Absence of such a symbolic link requires that you run portmap manually. In such a case, I recommend that you run:

```
ln -s /etc/rc.d/init.d/portmap   /etc/rc.d/rc3.d/S11portmap
```

This creates a symbolic link that allows Red Hat Linux to run the portmap program automatically at boot. Similarly you should have another script called nfs in your /etc/rc.d/init.d directory. Use this script to start up the NFS daemons (rpc.mountd, rpc.nfsd) at boot time. This script should also be linked from your default run level directory, or else you have to run these daemons manually.

The next step is to create an /etc/exports file to tell the system what file systems or directories need to be exported to NFS clients. The syntax of this file is as follows:

```
/directory nfs-client-host-ip-or-name (access options)
```

Here is an example of the /etc/exports file:

```
/www         www1.nitec.com(ro) www2.nitec.com(ro)
/www-data    cgi.nitec.com(rw)  fastcgi.nitec.com(rw)
```

Here the /www directory on the NFS server is exported to the `www1.nitec.com` and `www2.nitec.com` NFS clients. Both of these machines are given read-only (ro) access to the exported directory. The second line is used to export the /www-data directory to `cgi.nitec.com` and `fastcgi.nitec.com` client systems. Both of these systems have read/write (rw) access to the exported directory. You can specify NFS clients in any of the following commonly used ways as well.

An NFS client can be specified as an IP address in the /etc/export file. For example:

```
/www        206.171.50.51(ro)
```

Here the machine with the IP address 206.171.50.51 is given read-only NFS access to the /www directory. You can specify an entire IP network as shown in the following example:

```
/         206.171.50.48/255.255.255.240 (rw)
```

Here the entire 206.171.50.48 network (14 IP addresses in the range 206.171.50. 48–206.171.50.63) has been given permission to read and write from and to the root file system of the NFS server. You can also specify a set of hosts using wild cards. For example:

```
/pc        *.nitec.com (rw)
```

Here all the hosts in the nitec.com domain can access the /pc directory on the NFS server. You can also use the ? character as a single character wildcard.

If you want to export a file system or a directory to all the NFS clients in the world, you can omit the NFS client list in the line used to export it. For example:

```
/pub        (ro)
```

Here the /pub directory is exported to any NFS client. Now look at the commonly used access options.

Granting read-only access to the exported directory

If you want to allow only read-only access to any directory or file system you export from your NFS server to the clients, you can use ro as the access option. For example:

```
/master-data   production.nitec.com(ro)
```

Here the production.nitec.com client system has read-only access to the /master-data directory.

Granting read and write access to the exported directory

If you want to allow read and write access to any directory or file system you export from your NFS server to the clients, you can use rw as the access option. For example:

```
/intranet   *.nitec.com(rw)
```

Here all the NFS clients on the `nitec.com` domain have read and write access to the /intranet directory.

Disabling access to a specific directory

When you export an entire file system or a directory, the subdirectories below the exported directory are automatically accessible using the same access options. However, this might not always be desirable. You might want to allow access to a directory called /pub but not a directory called /pub/staff-only. In such a case you need to use the noaccess access option as follows:

```
/pub    weblab-??.nitec.com (ro)
/pub/staff-only    weblab-??.nitec.com (noaccess)
```

Here all the `weblab-??.nitec.com` (where `??` is any two characters) computers have read-only access to the /pub directory, but they are not allowed to access the /pub/staff-only directory because of the noaccess option in the next line.

Mapping users between the NFS server and the clients

One of the issues that comes up quickly after you set up an NFS server is the user mapping between the NFS server and the clients. For example, say that you are exporting a directory called /www that is owned by a user and group called webguru and webdev, respectively. The NFS client capable of mounting this directory has to have a user called webguru or a webdev group to access it. This is not often desirable. In particular, you do not want an NFS client root account to have root privileges on the NFS-mounted directory. This is why the NFS server by default enforces an option called root_squash. This option typically maps the root user (UID = 0) and root group (GID = 0) to user nobody on the client system. You can disable the default mapping of root user and group to 'nobody' by adding no_root_squash when defining your export lines, but I do not recommend it at all unless you have an extraordinary circumstance where both NFS client and server are in a isolated, trusted environment.

If you would like to map the root UID/GID pair to a particular UID/GID, you can use the anonuid and anongid access options. For example:

```
/proj    *.nitec.com (anonuid=500 anongid=666)
```

Here the anonuid and anongid are specified to allow root squashing to UID 500 and gid 666.

If you prefer to squash all the UID/GID pairs to an anonymous UID/GID pair, you can use the all_squash option. For example:

```
/proj    *.nitec.com (anonuid=500 anongid=666 all_squash)
```

Here the /proj directory is exported to all hosts in the nitec.com domain, but all accesses are made as UID 500 and GID 666.

If you would like to specify a list of UIDs and GIDs that needs to be squashed using the anonymous UID/GID pair, you can use the squash_uids and squash_gids options. For example:

```
/proj     *.nitec.com (anonuid=500 anongid=666 \
squash_uids=0-100 squash_gids=0-100)
```

Here all the UIDs and GIDs in the range 0–100 are squashed using the anonymous UID 500 and GID 666.

You can also specify an external map file to map NFS client-supplied UIDs and GIDs to whatever you want. The map is specified using the map_static option. For example:

```
/proj     *.nitec.com (map_static=/etc/nfs.map)
```

Here the /proj directory is exported to all the nitec.com hosts, but all NFS client-supplied UIDs and GIDs are mapped using the /etc/nfs.map file. An example of this map file is as follows:

```
uid  0-100   -  # squash all remote uids in the 0-100 range
gid  0-100   -  # squash all remote gids in the 0-100 range
uid  500    666 # map remove uid 500 to local uid 666
gid  500    777 # map remove gid 500 to local gid 777
```

Now you know all the commonly used options for creating the /etc/export file. Whenever a change is made to the /etc/exports file, however, the NFS daemons need to be told about this change. A script called exportfs can be used to restart these daemons, as follows:

```
/usr/sbin/exportfs
```

Now to make sure both rpc.mountd and rpc.nfsd are running properly, run a program called rpcinfo, as follows:

```
rpcinfo -p
```

The output looks like this:

```
program vers      proto     port
   program vers proto  port
    100000    2   tcp    111   portmapper
    100000    2   udp    111   portmapper
    100021    1   udp   1024   nlockmgr
```

```
100021    3    udp    1024    nlockmgr
100024    1    udp    1025    status
100024    1    tcp    1024    status
100011    1    udp     728    rquotad
100011    2    udp     728    rquotad
100005    1    udp    1026    mountd
100005    1    tcp    1025    mountd
100005    2    udp    1026    mountd
100005    2    tcp    1025    mountd
100003    2    udp    2049    nfs
```

This output shows that mountd and nfsd have announced their services and are working fine. At this point the NFS server is set up, so now set up the NFS client hosts.

Configuring an NFS Client

The NFS client package comes with a program called showmount that gives you information on exported file systems or directories on an NFS server. You can run this command with the NFS server's hostname or IP as the argument to see what hosts are allowed to access the exported file systems or directories. For example:

```
showmount    nfs-server.nitec.com
```

This command displays the list of NFS clients that are allowed to import files from nfs-server.nitec.com. To see the NFS server's export list, run this command with a -e option. To see which client is allowed to import what file systems or directories, run the command with a -a option.

If the showmount command shows that the NFS client you are configuring right now is allowed to import a file system or directory, you are ready to continue with client configuration. If it does not show the hostname or IP of your current NFS client, you must reconfigure the /etc/exports file on the NFS server to allow this client access to whatever directory or file system you wish to import.

To import a directory or file system from an NFS server, you need to mount it using the standard mount command. For example, to mount a directory called /www from an NFS server called nfs-server.nitec.com, I can use the following mount command:

```
mount nfs-server.nitec.com:/www    /www    -t nfs
```

This command mounts the /www directory from the nfs-server.nitec.com system to /www as an NFS file system that is specified using the -t option. However, if you plan on mounting an NFS file system or directory on a regular basis and on boot, you have to add a new line in the /etc/fstab file of your client system. For example, to mount the /www directory from `nfs-server.nitec.com` at boot, I have to add the following line in the /etc/fstab file:

```
nfs-server.nitec.com:/www   /www  nfs
```

To make sure that your NFS client automatically mounts NFS file systems and directories at boot, you should check to see if you have a symbolic link (starting with S*xx* where *xx* is a two-digit number) to the /etc/rc.d/init.d/nfsfs script in your default run level rc directory. Unmounting an NFS file system is exactly the same as unmounting the local file system.

Once you mount the NFS server–exported files on your NFS client system, your users can start using the mounted file systems or directories immediately. Before you allow users access to your NFS exports, consider the following security issues.

Securing Your NFS Server

The portmap, in combination with rpc.nfsd, can be fooled, making it possible to get to files on NFS servers without any privileges. Fortunately, the portmap Linux uses is relatively secure against attack and can be made more secure by adding the following line in the /etc/hosts.deny file:

```
portmap: ALL
```

The system then denies portmap access for everyone. Now the /etc/hosts.allow file needs to be modified as follows:

```
portmap: 192.168.1.0/255.255.255.0
```

This instruction allows all hosts from the 192.168.1.0 network to have access to portmap-administered programs such as nfsd and mountd.

 Never use host names in the portmap line in /etc/hosts.allow because use of host name lookups can indirectly cause portmap activity that triggers host name lookups in a loop.

One other security issue on the server side is whether to allow the root account on a client to be treated as root on the server. By default, Linux prohibits root on the client side of the NFS to be treated as root on the server side. In other words, an exported file owned by root on the server cannot be modified by the client root user. To explicitly enforce this rule, the /etc/exports file can be modified as follows:

```
/www www1.nitec.com(rw, root_squash)
```

Now, if a user with UID 0 (the root user) on the client attempts to access (read, write, or delete) the file system, the server substitutes the UID of the server's "nobody" account. This means the root user on the client can't access or change files that only the root on the server can access or change. To grant root access to an NFS file system, use the no_root_squash option instead.

Note that it is also possible to enhance NFS client security by not trusting the NFS server too much. For example, you can disable suid programs from working off the NFS file system with a nosuid option. This means the server's root user cannot make an suid-root program on the file system, log into the client as a normal user, and then use the suid-root program to become the root on the client, too. It is also possible to forbid execution of files on the mounted file system altogether with the noexec option. You can enter these options in the options column of the line that describes your NFS mount point in the /etc/fstab file.

Now that you have learned how to use NFS to share files among many hosts, look at when NFS is not the right solution. For example, say that you want to distribute a set of files and directories to one or more Linux systems such that each has its own copy of the files. NFS would not be helpful here, because if you make these files available via NFS, the entire client system shares a single copy. This kind of scenario is very easy to find in places like a university computer lab. In most cases, you want the students to have their own copies of files while they work in the lab and at the same time replace the modified files with the originals from a master server for the next batch of students. Both SMB and NFS protocol are not much help in such a scenario. This is where you need a program called rdist.

Distributing Files Using rdist

The rdist program enables you to maintain identical copies of files over multiple hosts. It uses either the rcmd function calls or the remote shell (rsh) to access each of the target host computers.

The easiest way to get rdist working is to create a common account on all the machines involved and create .rhosts files for each target (that is, client) system so that the common user on the master host is allowed to run rsh sessions. Because an example makes this easier to understand, suppose that you want to create a file distribution environment where a master computer called master.an-university.edu contains the master copy of the file and two hosts called student1.an-university.edu and student2.an-university.edu need to get fresh copies of the files on the master on a daily basis. I also assume that each of these three computers shares a common user account called updater. Here is how to set up such an environment.

On each of the student computers, add an .rhosts file in the home directory of the updater user. This file contains a single line such as the following:

```
master.an-university.edu
```

This file must be owned by the root user and be read-only for everyone else. This allows a user called updater on master.an-university.edu to run remote shell sessions on each student system. The next step is to create a file distribution configuration file for rdist. This file is often called the distfile. A distfile is a text file that contains instructions for rdist to perform the file distribution task. Listing 16-1 shows one such distfile, rdist_distfile.

Listing 16-1: The rdist_distfile file

```
#
# Distfile for rdist
#
# This file is used to distribute files from
# master.an-university.edu to student[12].an-university.edu
# systems.
#
# $Author$ (kabir@nitec.com)

# $Version$
# $Date$
# $Id$

# List all the hosts that need to be updated.
# The list is created using user@hostname entries where each
# entry is separated by a white-space character.
#
HOSTS = (updater@student1.an-university.edu \
         updater@student2.an-university.edu)

# List the directories that need to be updated.
#
FILES = ( /csc101)

# List the directories that need to be excluded from
# the update process.
EXCLUDE_DIR = (/csc101/instructor /csc101/secret)

# Here are the commands:
# Install all directories listed in FILES for
# all hosts listed in HOSTS except for the directories
# that are listed in EXCLUDE_DIR
#
${FILES} -> ${HOSTS}
  install ;
  except ${EXCLUDE_DIR};
```

This is really a very simple distfile. It defines a variable called HOSTS that has two entries as values: updater@student1.an-university.edu and updater@student2. an-university.edu. This distfile tells rdist to use the updater user account on both student1.an-university.edu and student2.an-university.edu for connection. The next variable, FILES, defines the directories for rdist to distribute. Here only the /csc101 directory is being distributed.

The third variable is EXCLUDE_DIR. This variable is set to list all the files and directories that we want to exclude from getting distributed. The values that you see in the example are /csc101/instructors (this variable could contain files that only the instructor should have access to) and /cs101/secret (a directory that students should not have access to).

The rest of the file describes a simple command:

```
${FILES} -> ${HOSTS}
  install ;
  except ${EXCLUDE_DIR};
```

This command takes all the files and directories that the FILES variable points to and installs them on the hosts indicated by the HOSTS variable. It also tells rdist to exclude the files and directories specified by the EXCLUDE_DIR variable. To run rdist (as updater) from the command line, do the following:

1. Log in as updater. (If you are root on the master system, you can use su to change the UID to updater as well.)

2. Run the following command as updater:

```
/usr/bin/rdist -p /usr/sbin/rdistd -oremove,quiet \
-f /usr/local/rdist/ rdist_distfile
```

The -p option specifies the location of the rdistd program needed by rdist; the -o option specifies that one or more options are to follow—in this case, remove and quiet. The remove option tells rdist to remove any extraneous files found in the target system in target directories. This provides an easy method for maintaining an identical copy of the files on each student system. The quiet option tells rdist to be as quiet as possible during the operation. The final option, -f, specifies the location of the distfile.

To reduce human error in running this command, create an sh script called rdistribute.sh, as shown in Listing 16-2.

Listing 16-2: The rdistribute.sh script

```
#!/bin/sh
#
# This script runs rdist to update Web servers via the
# non-routable lan an-university.edu. The script is run
# by cron at a fixed interval.
```

```
#
# /etc/rc.d/rc.local starts the script to clean up
# left-over tempfiles that might have been left
# at shutdown. This process also removes the
# log file.
#
# $Author$ (kabir@nitec.com)
# $Version$
# $Id$
# $Date$
# $Status
######################################################################

# If the script is called with an
# argument then

case "$1" in

boot)

  # Since the argument is 'boot' the script is being
  # called at system start-up, so remove all old lock
  # files and logs.
  echo -n "Cleaning up rdistribute.sh tmp files: "
    rm -f /tmp/rdist.lck
      rm -f /tmp/rdist.log
  echo "complete."
  exit 0;
  ;;

  # Since the argument is 'restart' the script
  # needs to clean up as if the system just booted.

restart)
  $0 boot
  ;;

esac

# If the lock file exists then don't do anything.
if [ -f /tmp/rdist.lck ]; then
  exit 0
fi

# Otherwise create the lock file using /bin/touch
```

```
/bin/touch  /tmp/rdist.lck

# Run rdist.
/usr/bin/rdist -p /usr/sbin/rdistd -
oremove,nochkgroup,nochkmode,nochkowner,quiet -f
/usr/local/rdist/rdist_distfile

# Remote the lock file.
rm -f /tmp/rdist.lck

# Write the time and date in the log file.
echo `date` > /tmp/rdist.log

# Exit the script.
exit 0
```

This script is smart enough to detect the in-progress rdistribute.sh process by using a lock file, which can tell when a previous rdistribute.sh is already in progress and continuing. This can happen when a great many files are being updated over multiple servers. The script also accepts an argument called boot that can be used to clean up the lock file and the log file it creates during the boot process. The script should be called from /etc/rc.d/rc.local as follows:

```
/usr/local/rdistribute.sh boot
```

This script can be scheduled to run by a cron entry in /etc/crontab. For example, to run this script every hour, the following cron entry can be added in /etc/crontab:

```
01 * * * * updater /usr/local/rdistribute.sh > /dev/null
```

The cron daemon runs the script as updater. Alternatively, you can create a link to rdistribute.sh from /etc/cron.hourly (or /etc/cron.daily, /etc/cron.monthly, or what have you) as you see fit.

Summary

In this chapter, you learned to use NFS. I showed you how to turn your Red Hat Linux system into an NFS server and a client. You also learned to use rdist to distribute multiple copies of the same files and directories to client systems.

Chapter 17

SQL Database Services

- ◆ How to install and configure an SQL database server
- ◆ How to access the SQL server using a command line SQL client
- ◆ How to access your SQL databases from the Web

EVERY PERSON HAS A need for storing and sorting data, whether it is a large store inventory or a simple way to take telephone messages. Red Hat has the capability to allow fast and easy access to any number of databases, ranging from flat files to full relational databases. You can write simple CGI programs to add database access to your Web site, or you can use simple commands to probe a database for the information you want. Structured Query Language (SQL) is a language of communication with the database server to aid you in finding the data you want. This chapter will give you an introduction to installing and manipulating data inside a SQL database and a few simple programs to use so you can hit the ground running.

What Is SQL?

Structured Query Language is just that, a language. It's a method of communicating requests to a database server to store or retrieve the data you want. The word "Query" in SQL often throws people off. It is a misnomer. With SQL, you can create tables of data, manipulate them, extract information, and make calculations based on what you find. SQL is not just for asking questions of a static database.

The SQL model is made of databases, tables, rows, fields, and elements. An entire set of data is called a database. Each user of your system can have a separate database independent of others. Databases contain tables. Visualize tables as columns of data types and rows of data, as in Table 17-1, with no two rows alike.

TABLE 17-1 SAMPLE SQL TABLE: CUSTOMERS

Name	Address	Telephone	ID
Brian Smith	321 Lincoln Ln.	555-4444	1
Mary Morris	433 Washington St.	555-7777	2
Linda Chadwick	776 Monroe Dr.	555-8833	3
Brian Smith	931 Jefferson Pl.	555-9090	4

If you are paying attention, you'll notice two rows with the name "Brian Smith." When we say the rows cannot be alike, we mean all the data in the row, not just a single cell. Two people can share the same name, and even the same address and telephone number. This is why we make an ID field. With a unique ID number in the ID column, we can ensure no two rows will ever be exactly alike.

It is very easy to learn the simple commands to find and show data from a database. In no time, you can find yourself pulling the data you need from your SQL database. With a simple command like

```
select name, address, telephone from table friends where birthyear >
1950;
```

you can get a simple table of data like the following:

```
+----+----------+------+
| name | address      | telephone |
+----+----------+------+
| Kabir | 123 Any Street | 555-3547 |
| Terry | 77 Lucky Lane | 555-3133 |
| Ian   | 444 Monkey Ave | 555-6302 |
+----+----------+------+
3 rows in set (0.02 sec)
```

Not only do you get the data in an easily readable format, but also you get it quickly. I'll admit that my friend's database isn't as large as it should be, but in 0.02 seconds the database gives me requested information in a pretty table.

SQL is a relational database model. This means it not only stores tables of information but can make relations between tables. The easiest way to grasp this is to think of a simple example.

Imagine that we have a simple mail-order store. We have the following tables of data:

♦ "Products" contains the names, descriptions, and prices of all of our products and a unique product ID number for each.

♦ "Customers" contains the name, address, and telephone number of anyone who has ordered from us, along with a unique ID number for each customer.

♦ "Invoices" contains an invoice number, the customer ID number of the person ordering from us, and the product ID number of each product the customer orders.

The key to the relational aspect is the Invoices table. We don't actually store the information as it appears on the printed invoice; we save only the ID numbers of where to find the information in other tables. Otherwise, we end up storing the same information over and over.

Obviously, SQL isn't the answer for everything. Unless you have quite a large shopping list, I wouldn't stop writing it on the back of your junk mail. SQL is not always the best solution or a wise one. If you have small amounts of data, you may find a text file that best suits your needs. If you have a simple data set, you may look into DBM files.

Installing and Configuring a SQL Server: MySQL

Many SQL servers are available for Red Hat and, among the most popular. Oracle, DB2, Postgres, and MySQL come to mind quickly. I chose to explore MySQL for a number of reasons:

♦ MySQL is free for most uses. MySQL costs nothing as long as you don't sell MySQL to someone, sell a product that is bundled with MySQL, or install and maintain MySQL at a client site. If you're in doubt as to whether you fit within the license parameters, please see the Web site at http://www.mysql.com/.

♦ MySQL supports many programming interfaces, including C, C++, Java, Perl, and Python. Your ability to tailor programs to fit your needs is endless.

♦ MySQL uses very fast methods of relating tables of information to each other. Using a method called a one-sweep multijoin, MySQL is very efficient at gathering the information you request from many different tables at once.

◆ MySQL is widely used. Chances are, many other people have done something similar to what you are doing. If you have questions or problems, you have a wide base of people to go to. You can get advice from others about how to solve your problems, but, most of all, you can get information on what not to do. This saves you from making the same mistakes others have made.

Where to get MySQL

MySQL is available all over the Internet. The best way to get MySQL is to go to http://www.mysql.com/ and find a mirror site close to you.

You have two choices: You can either compile a custom copy of MySQL from the source RPM packages, or you can simply download the binary distribution. In this chapter, I assume you will use the binary distribution. You want to get both the RPM package containing the MySQL server program and the RPM package containing the client programs. To use the example programs in this chapter, you also need to get the RPM package containing the include files and libraries, the Perl DBI module, and the Perl DBD::msql driver modules at http://www.mysql.org/download.html.

Installing the MySQL RPM packages

Installing the MySQL RPM package is simple. Just run `rpm -i mysql-version.rpm`, where *mysql-version.rpm* is the name of the RPM package containing the MySQL server. Next, run `rpm -i mysql-client-version.rpm`, again substituting the name of the RPM package you have. Do the same for the RPM package for the include files and library binaries.

You need to install The Perl modules after you successfully install the MySQL server because the DBD::mysql driver installation typically runs a connectivity test. If you install the standard Perl that comes with the CPAN module on your Linux system, installing the DBI and DBD:mysql is quite simple. Simply run:

```
perl -MCPAN -e shell
```

Use the `install DBI` and `install DBD::mysql` commands within the CPAN shell to install the modules.

Accessing the SQL Server

Once you install the MySQL server RPM package, it starts the server automatically every time you boot your system. You will find a file called mysql in /etc/rc.d/init.d you can use to start and stop the MySQL server by using the following commands:

```
/etc/rc.d/init.d/mysql start
/etc/rc.d/init.d/mysql stop
```

The RPM installation automatically starts the server for you. To ensure that the MySQL server is running, you can ping it by using the following command:

```
/usr/bin/mysqladmin ping
```

You should get a response such as "mysqld is alive" when the server is up and running. If you don't get such a response, use the `/etc/rc.d/init.d/mysql start` command to start the server.

Once the server starts, you need to run the following command to create some required tables:

```
/usr/bin/mysql_install_db
```

By default, the password for the server's administrative account (root) is not set, so use the following command to set the password.

```
/usr/bin/mysqladmin -u root password newpassword
```

Now you are ready to run the MySQL client.

Starting MySQL client for the first time

You can start the MySQL client program by typing:

```
mysql -u username -p
```

where *username* is the username you are using to access the SQL server. If a password is required, you are prompted for it. You should now see something like:

```
Welcome to the MySQL monitor.  Commands end with ; or \g.
Your MySQL connection id is 3 to server version: 3.22.15

Type 'help' for help.

mysql>
```

You are now ready to start laying the framework of your database.

Creating a database

At this point, you have installed the software, but you have no data. In fact, you don't even have a database defined! This should be our next step. We begin by creating a database called `store`. The syntax for this is simply:

```
create database store;
```

You should get a response like:

```
Query OK, 1 row affected (0.02 sec)
```

This generic response shows you that your command has executed. You can confirm this by issuing the command:

```
show databases;
```

If this is the first database you create, you see the following:

```
+-----+
| Database |
+-----+
| store   |
+-----+
1 row in set (0.00 sec)
```

There it is. You now have an empty database named store that contains no data. Now it is up to us to create the tables that store data. We need to define not only the names of all the columns but also the types of data they store. We begin by identifying the database we're going to use by issuing the command:

```
Use store
```

We then issue the following command to make our first table:

```
create table customers (
    name CHAR(40) NOT NULL,
    address CHAR(80),
    telephone CHAR(13),
    id INT AUTO_INCREMENT PRIMARY KEY);
```

Let's take a look at each of these lines and what they do.

```
create table customers (
```

This line tells the SQL server we are trying to create a table called "customers."

```
name CHAR(40) NOT NULL,
```

Create a column named "name" that contains 40 characters of data per item. Additionally, this column can never be blank.

```
address CHAR(80),
```

Create a column called "address" that holds 80 characters of data per item.

```
telephone CHAR(13),
```

Create a column called "telephone" that holds 13 characters. You may wonder why we set this up as a character field instead of making it able to hold a number. Because it is unusual for us to try to add telephone numbers to each other or to perform mathematics functions with them, we can just treat the phone number like any other character data. Plus, it makes it easier to deal with the dashes people put in phone numbers.

```
id INT AUTO_INCREMENT PRIMARY KEY);
```

This is the meat of the table. We are creating a column named "id" that holds whole numbers (int stands for integer). Additionally, this column is the primary key, which means the information we store in this column determines the order in which the database stores data. Lower ID numbers come before higher numbers when we read data out of the database unless we specify some other method of ordering data.

Now that you know the basics of how to create a simple SQL database on the MySQL server, you are ready to interact with your databases by using means other than the MySQL client.

Interacting with the SQL Server Using Scripts

The power of Linux is evident when we see how easy it is to write small scripts to interact with a SQL database. Any command we enter on the MySQL command line can also be entered through a program or script. This allows you to write programs to select, update, delete, or insert items in the database. You can even write programs to create your tables for you! In this section, I show you some examples of simple scripts to read from, write to, and modify data in a table. This isn't a programming book, nor is it a book about the SQL language, so the examples are simple. If you're not a programmer, don't worry; this section is for you too.

These programs are written in the Perl scripting language. Perl is an excellent choice for our SQL tasks because it is simple and efficient. All scripts use the DBI module to handle the database interaction.

The DBI module is an abstraction layer. As in Figure 17-1, this means you ask DBI for data, and the DBI module handles anything specific to the database engine. This saves you from ever needing to learn the subtle differences among the different SQL implementations. With DBI, it is also easy to migrate to a different database. If you need features or performance beyond the capabilities of MySQL, you can install the new database and change a single word in your Perl script; suddenly, you are operating in a whole new environment. Dan Bunce wrote DBI, and you can download it from `http://cpan.perl.org/`.

User

Perl script

DBI

SQL database

Figure 17-1: Using DBM module as an abstraction layer

We also use the CGI module (CGI.pm) to interact with the user through a Web browser. This is an excellent tool for writing CGI scripts; it makes your code easier to read and removes the burden of writing everything from scratch. Lincoln Stein wrote it, and you can download it from `http://cpan.perl.org/`.

Now take a look at a few scripts that interact with the MySQL server by using the modules previously mentioned.

SQL interactions from the UNIX command prompt

Let's create a simple database called test containing a single table called friends to store contact information: name, phone number, address, and age. To create this database and the table, do the following:

- ◆ Use the `mysql -u username -p` command to start the MySQL client.

- ◆ At the mysql prompt, enter `create database test;` to create the test database. Then enter `use test;` to start using this database.

◆ Now enter the following lines to create a table called friends:

```
create table friends (
  name CHAR(40) NOT NULL,
  phone CHAR(13),
  address CHAR(80),
  age INT,
  id INT AUTO_INCREMENT PRIMARY KEY);
```

◆ Once you have entered these lines, enter `describe friends;` to view the description of the table, which should display output as shown here:

```
+------+----------+------+-----+---------+----------------+
| Field   | Type     | Null | Key | Default | Extra          |
+------+----------+------+-----+---------+----------------+
| name    | char(40) |      |     |         |                |
| phone   | char(13) | YES  |     | NULL    |                |
| address | char(80) | YES  |     | NULL    |                |
| age     | int(11)  | YES  |     | NULL    |                |
| id      | int(11)  |      | PRI | 0       | auto_increment |
+------+----------+------+-----+---------+----------------+
5 rows in set (0.01 sec)
```

◆ Now you are ready to insert some example data in the database. Here is an example of a SQL `insert` command:

```
insert into friends (id, name, phone, address, age) values
("0", "Joe Gunchy", "555-5555", "1234 University Ave,
Sacramento, CA 95555", "21");
```

◆ Once you have entered a few records by using the `insert` command, you can exit the client by entering the `exit;` command.

Listing 17-1 shows a relatively simple script to retrieve and print data stored in the database. This program assumes you have a user named terry with a password of asecret1. You need to change the definitions section to match an account with permission to access the database.

Listing 17-1: The cmdline.select.pl file

```perl
#!/usr/bin/perl
# Command line script to select from SQL database

use DBI;

# Definitions - You will need to change these
my $table = "friends";
my $db = "test";
my $user = "terry";
my $password = "asecret1";

# End of definitions

# Tell the script that we will be using
# a MySQL database
my $drh = DBI->install_driver( 'mysql' );

# Establish a connection with the database
my $dbh = $drh->connect($db, $user, $password);

# A simple check to see if we connected
die "Cannot connect: $DBI::errstr\n" unless $dbh;

# Get input from user
print "Name: ";
my $name = <STDIN>;
chomp($name);
print "\n";

# Build and execute the SQL statement
my $SQLstatement = "select name, phone, address, age from $table
where name = \"$name\"";
my $sth = $dbh->prepare($SQLstatement);
my $howmany = $sth->execute;

die "Couldn't match $name in database\n" if $howmany eq "OEO";

print "$howmany matches found in database\n\n";
printf ("%17.14s %13.9s %15.12s   %s \n",
        "NAME", "PHONE", "ADDRESS", "AGE");

# loop through all the matches and print them
for (my $i = 0; $i < $howmany; $i++) {
```

```
my ($SQLname, $SQLphone, $SQLaddress, $SQLage) =
    $sth->fetchrow_array;
printf ("%17.14s %13.9s %15.12s    %2d \n",
        $SQLname, $SQLphone, $SQLaddress, $SQLage);


}
```

This program displays a prompt for you to enter a name and queries the friends table in the test database by using the following SQL `select` statement:

```
select name, phone, address, age from $table where name =
\"$name\"";
```

The `$name` variable holds the name you enter at the command prompt. For example, when this program is run as follows:

```
./cmdline.select.pl
Name: brian smith
```

it shows the following output:

```
1 matches found in database

          NAME         PHONE       ADDRESS    AGE
    Brian Smith      555-2453   1915 11th St   23
```

This program is very crude. You need to supply the full name of your friend for it to find the record in the database. The only time that it finds more than one match is when you have more than one entry with the name Brian Smith. This doesn't help us too much. Listing 17-2 gives us a bit more flexibility. We can use the partial name rather than the complete name to locate all matching records.

Listing 17-2: The cmdline.select.revised.pl file

```
#!/usr/bin/perl
# Command line script to select from SQL database
# Revised to match substrings

use DBI;

# Definitions - You will need to change these
my $table = "friends";
my $db = "test";
my $user = "terry";
```

```perl
my $password = "asecret1";

# End of definitions

# Tell the script that we will be using
# a MySQL database
my $drh = DBI->install_driver( 'mysql' );

# Establish a connection with the database
my $dbh = $drh->connect($db, $user, $password);

# A simple check to see if we connected
die "Cannot connect: $DBI::errstr\n" unless $dbh;

# Get input from user
print "Name: ";
my $name = <STDIN>;
chomp($name);
print "\n";

# Build and execute the SQL statement
my $SQLstatement = "select name, phone, address, age from $table
where name like \"%$name%\"";
my $sth = $dbh->prepare($SQLstatement);
my $howmany = $sth->execute;

die "Couldn't match $name in database\n" if $howmany eq "0E0";

print "$howmany matches found in database\n\n";
printf ("%17.14s %13.9s %15.12s   %s \n",
        "NAME", "PHONE", "ADDRESS", "AGE");

# loop through all the matches and print them
for (my $i = 0; $i < $howmany; $i++) {
   my ($SQLname, $SQLphone, $SQLaddress, $SQLage) =
       $sth->fetchrow_array;
   printf ("%17.14s %13.9s %15.12s   %2d \n",
           $SQLname, $SQLphone, $SQLaddress, $SQLage);

   }
```

When we run the program now, we no longer need to enter the full name:

```
./cmdline.select.revised.pl
```

```
Name: brian
```

```
2 matches found in database
```

```
          NAME          PHONE          ADDRESS    AGE
          Brian         555-9999       433 M St.  29
    Brian Smith         555-2453    1915 11th St  23
```

All of this is because of the modification we made to the following line:

```
$SQLstatement = "select name, phone, address, age from $table
                where name like \"%$name%\"";
```

As a side effect, if we run the program without entering a name, we see every entry in the database. What if we notice someone missing from the database? We need a script that asks us for the contents of each field and then places the new row of data in the database. Listing 17-3 does exactly that.

Listing 17-3: The cmdline.insert.pl line

```perl
#!/usr/bin/perl
# Command line script to select from SQL database
# Revised to match substrings

use DBI;

# Definitions - You will need to change these
my $table = "friends";
my $db = "test";
my $user = "terry";
my $password = "asecret1";

# End of definitions

# Tell the script that we will be using
# a MySQL database
my $drh = DBI->install_driver( 'mysql' );

# Establish a connection with the database
my $dbh = $drh->connect($db, $user, $password);

# A simple check to see if we connected
die "Cannot connect: $DBI::errstr\n" unless $dbh;
```

```
# Get input from user
print "Name: ";
my $name = <STDIN>;
chomp($name);
print "\n";

print "Phone: ";
my $phone = <STDIN>;
chomp($phone);
print "\n";

print "Address: ";
my $address = <STDIN>;
chomp($address);
print "\n";

print "Age: ";
my $age = <STDIN>;
chomp($age);
print "\n";

# Build and do the SQL statement
my $SQLstatement = "insert into $table (id, name, phone, address,
age)
    values (\"0\", \"$name\", \"$phone\", \"$address\", \"$age\")";
my $sth = $dbh->do($SQLstatement);
```

This script simply creates the following SQL insert statement and asks the MySQL server to execute it.

```
insert into $table (id, name, phone, address, age) values (\"0\",
\"$name\", \"$phone\", \"$address\", \"$age\")
```

Notice that the fields in the preceding insert statements are Perl variables that get values from the command line. Let's look at the script in action:

```
./cmdline.insert.pl
Name: Scott Ramshaw

Phone: 555-5828

Address: 1311 26th Ave.

Age: 23
```

This inserts a new record with the given information, which we can search using the cmdline.select.revised.pl script.

What if my friend Brian moves to San Francisco? I need a way to change data when people move or change phone numbers. Listing 17-4 shows a Perl script that does just that. It takes a name from the user, finds any rows of data that match the name exactly, and then asks the user for new information for each row. It allows the user to just hit Enter to keep the existing data.

Listing 17-4: The cmdline.update.pl file

```perl
#!/usr/local/bin/perl
# Command line script to update rows in a SQL database

use DBI;

# Definitions - You will need to change these
my $table = "friends";
my $db = "test";
my $user = "terry";
my $password = "asecret1";

# End of definitions

# Tell the script that we will be using
# a MySQL database
my $drh = DBI->install_driver( 'mysql' );

# Establish a connection with the database
my $dbh = $drh->connect($db, $user, $password);

# A simple check to see if we connected
die "Cannot connect: $DBI::errstr\n" unless $dbh;

# Get input from user
print "Name: ";
my $name = <STDIN>;
chomp($name);

# Build and execute the SQL statement
my $SQLstatement = "select id, name, phone, address, age from $table
                    where name like \"$name\"";
my $sth = $dbh->prepare($SQLstatement);
my $howmany = $sth->execute;
```

```
die "Couldn't match $name in database\n" if $howmany eq "OEO";
print "$howmany matches found in database\n\n";

# Define local variables
my ($i, $input, $SQLname, $SQLphone, $SQLaddress, $SQLage,
$updatestatement);
# loop through all the matching rows,
# ask user for new data, then update
# the row to reflect the changes made
for ($i = 0; $i < $howmany; $i++) {
    ($SQLid, $SQLname, $SQLphone, $SQLaddress, $SQLage) =
      $sth->fetchrow_array;

    printf ("%17.14s %13.9s %15.12s    %s \n",
            "NAME", "PHONE", "ADDRESS", "AGE");
    printf ("%17.14s %13.9s %15.12s    %2d \n",
            $SQLname, $SQLphone, $SQLaddress, $SQLage);

    print "Name [$SQLname]: ";
    $input = <STDIN>;
    chomp($input);
    $SQLname = $input || $SQLname;

    print "Phone [$SQLphone]: ";
    $input = <STDIN>;
    chomp($input);
    $SQLphone = $input || $SQLphone;

    print "Address [$SQLaddress]: ";
    $input = <STDIN>;
    chomp($input);
    $SQLaddress = $input || $SQLaddress;

    print "Age [$SQLage]: ";
    $input = <STDIN>;
    chomp($input);
    $SQLage = $input || $SQLage;

    $updatestatement = "update $table set name    = \"$SQLname\",
                                       address = \"$SQLaddress\",
                                       phone   = \"$SQLphone\",
                                       age     = $SQLage
                        where id = $SQLid";
```

```
        $dbh->do($updatestatement);
}
```

This script uses the following SQL update statement to perform its job of updating an existing record:

```
update $table set name  = \"$SQLname\", address = \"$SQLaddress\",
phone  = \"$SQLphone\", age     = $SQLage where id = $SQLid";
```

Here is an example of how this script works:

```
./cmdline.update.pl
Name: brian smith
1 matches found in database


          NAME          PHONE         ADDRESS        AGE
      Brian Smith       555-2453    1915 11th St    23
Name [Brian Smith]:
Phone [555-2453]: 415-555-9242
Address [1915 11th St.]: 132 Market St. #100
Age [23]:
```

Voila! Brian's new information is now in the database.

Using a CGI script to access a SQL database via a Web browser

So far, the scripts I've shown you are pretty dull. SQL on Red Hat really soars when you incorporate it within a CGI script and display the output in a Web browser. Suddenly, your Web site can show you useful data you want to show your visitors! You can allow your Web users to search data, input their own data, and so on. SQL and CGI really do go together like peanut butter and jelly.

Listing 17-5 shows an example CGI script that uses the core functionality of some of the command line scripts we discuss. Once you install this script in the cgi-bin directory of a Web server, you can run the CGI script by using a Web browser. First, it displays an HTML form. This HTML interface is much more flexible than the interfaces in the previously built command line scripts. This script allows you to retrieve information based on any of the fields in the friends table in the test database you created earlier. You can find people by address, phone number, or age as well as by name. It also allows you to make the search exact or to search for a substring.

Listing 17-5: select.cgi

```perl
#!/usr/bin/perl
#  CGI to select data from a SQL database
use CGI;
```

```perl
use DBI;
my $q = new CGI;

# Definitions - You will need to change these
my $table = "friends";
my $db = "test";
my $user = "terry";
my $password = "asecret1";
# End of definitions

# This is the main branch.  The first time through
# display the form to the user, when the user submits
# the form then we process the input
if ($q->param('field') eq "") {&printform()} else {&results()}

sub printform {

  print $q->header;
  print $q->start_html(-title=>'Friend Database',
                       -BGCOLOR=>'black',
                       -TEXT=>'white');
  print "<CENTER><H1>Friend Database</H1></CENTER><HR>";
  print $q->startform;
  print "Find all my friends whose ";
  print $q->popup_menu(-name    => field,
                       -values  => [("name", "address",
                                     "phone", "age")],
                       -default => "name");
  print $q->popup_menu(-name    => searchtype,
                       -values  => [("is", "contains")],
                       -default => "is");
  print $q->textfield(-name => text,
                      -size => 16), "<BR>";
  print $q->submit;
  print $q->endform;
  print $q->end_html;
}

sub results {

  my $field = $q->param('field');
  my $searchtype = $q->param('searchtype');
  my $text = $q->param('text');
  my @table=();
```

```perl
print $q->header;
print $q->start_html(-title=>'Database Results',
-BGCOLOR=>'black',
-TEXT=>'white');

# Tell the script that we will be using
# a MySQL database
my $drh = DBI->install_driver( 'mysql' );

# Establish a connection with the database
my $dbh = $drh->connect($db, $user, $password);

# A simple check to see if we connected
if (!$dbh) {
   print "Cannot connect: $DBI::errstr<BR>";
   print $q->end_html;
   die;
}

# Build and execute the SQL statement
my ($SQLstatement);
if ($searchtype eq "contains") {
   $SQLstatement = "select name, phone, address, age from $table
                    where $field like \"%$text%\"";
} else {
   $SQLstatement = "select name, phone, address, age from $table
                    where $field = \"$text\"";
}
my $sth = $dbh->prepare($SQLstatement);
my $howmany = $sth->execute;

# Display an error message if we can't find
# any matches
if ($howmany eq "0E0") {
   print$q->h3("<font color=red>Couldn't match $text in ".
               "database</font>");
   die;
}

print "$howmany matches found in database<br><br>";
push (@table,$q->th(["Name", "Phone", "Address", "Age"]));

# loop through all the matches and store
# them in @table
```

```
for (my $i = 0; $i < $howmany; $i++) {
    my ($SQLname, $SQLphone, $SQLaddress, $SQLage) =
        $sth->fetchrow_array;
    push (@table,$q->td([$SQLname, $SQLphone,
                            $SQLaddress, $SQLage]));

}

# print the table of data we got from the
# SQL database
print $q->table({-border => 1, -align => center},$q->Tr(\@table));
print $q->end_html;

}
```

Figure 17-2 shows the HTML form screen in a Web browser.

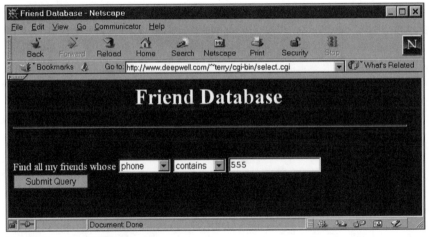

Figure 17-2: The HTML form screen

When you submit the HTML form with the search criteria, the CGI script runs again and retrieves the requested data from the SQL database. Then it formats the data into an HTML table and sends it back to the Web browser where it is displayed. Figure 17-3 shows an example of the resulting output page.

You can also make CGI scripts that perform other functions such as insert, update, and delete from a database. I've modified the cmdline.insert.pl script, discussed previously, to a CGI script as in Listing 17-6. It gives the user an HTML form to enter new data, and when new data are submitted, it displays a status message telling the user that data have been added to the database.

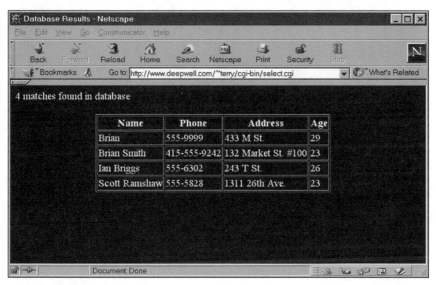

4 matches found in database

Name	Phone	Address	Age
Brian	555-9999	433 M St.	29
Brian Smith	415-555-9242	132 Market St. #100	23
Ian Briggs	555-6302	243 T St.	26
Scott Ramshaw	555-5828	1311 26th Ave.	23

Figure 17-3: The output screen

Listing 17-6: The insert.cgi file

```perl
#!/usr/bin/perl
#  CGI to insert data into a SQL database
use CGI;
use DBI;
my $q = new CGI;

# Definitions - You will need to change these
my $table = "friends";
my $db = "test";
my $user = "terry";
my $password = "asecret1";
# End of definitions

if ($q->param('name') eq "") {&printform()} else {&results()}

sub printform {

  print $q->header;
  print $q->start_html(-title=>'Friend Database',
                       -BGCOLOR=>'black',
                       -TEXT=>'white');
  print "<CENTER><H1>Friend Database</H1></CENTER><HR>";
  print $q->startform;
```

```
      print "Name: ", $q->textfield(-name => name,
                                    -size => 16), "<BR>";
      print "Phone: ", $q->textfield(-name => phone,
                                     -size => 16), "<BR>";
      print "Address: ", $q->textfield(-name => address,
                                       -size => 16), "<BR>";
      print "Age: ", $q->textfield(-name => age,
                                   -size => 16), "<BR>";
      print $q->submit;
      print $q->endform;
      print $q->end_html;
   }

   sub results {

      my ($name, $phone, $address, $age);
      $name = $q->param('name');
      $phone = $q->param('phone');
      $address = $q->param('address');
      $age = $q->param('age');

      print $q->header;
      print $q->start_html(-title=>'Database Results',
                       -BGCOLOR=>'black',
                       -TEXT=>'white');

      # Tell the script that we will be using
      # a MySQL database
      my ($drh, $dbh);
      $drh = DBI->install_driver( 'mysql' );

      # Establish a connection with the database
      $dbh = $drh->connect($db, $user, $password);

      # A simple check to see if we connected
      if (!$dbh) {
         print "Cannot connect: $DBI::errstr<BR>";
         print $q->end_html;
         die;
      }

      # Build and do the SQL statement
        my $SQLstatement = "insert into $table (name, phone, address,
age)
            values (\"$name\", \"$phone\", \"$address\", \"$age\"";
```

```
$dbh->do($SQLstatement);

print "$name added to database<br><br>";
print $q->end_html;

}
```

We have barely scratched the surface of the power of SQL in CGI scripts. Many major online stores use both SQL and CGI for their shopping cart, order tracking, and inventory tracking applications. We can purchase anything through the Web these days, and SQL databases are a major part of this. Whether you are looking for books, CDs, or a car, chances are if you're searching a Web site for a product, you're probably using an SQL database.

The Perl scripts in this chapter are only meant to introduce you to the interaction between a program and an SQL database. There are many things we didn't do, such as making computations based on our search results or building graphs from our data. The possibilities are limitless. I hope you have an idea of the interaction between the user and the database, and I hope you get ideas for future uses of SQL in your Red Hat server.

Summary

In this chapter, you learned to install and configure MySQL, which is a very popular SQL server for Linux. You learned to create simple databases that contain simple tables. Finally, you learned to access data in databases by using methods such as the command line or via CGI scripts. Treat this chapter as a simple introduction to this subject.

Part VI

Securing and Monitoring

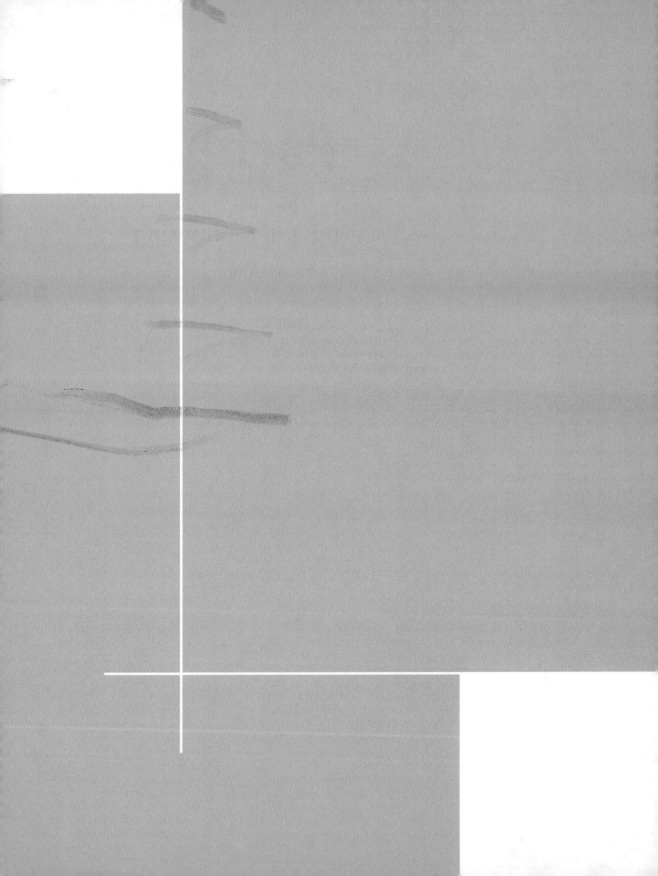

Chapter 18

Security 101

IN THIS CHAPTER

- ◆ How to secure user access
- ◆ How to use shadow passwords
- ◆ How to use pluggable authentication modules (PAM)
- ◆ How to use a file/directory integrity checker
- ◆ How to secure inet-run services
- ◆ How to use a TCP wrapper
- ◆ How to crack passwords
- ◆ How to use COPS

EVERY COMPUTER CONNECTED TO the Internet is potentially at risk of abuse or misuse by anyone. There is no surefire way to ensure complete security, even with the most expensive and advanced security hardware and software solutions available. However, it is possible to reduce security risks substantially by taking preventive measures and keeping an eye on all ongoing developments in the computer security arena. In this chapter I discuss various security issues and solutions that fall under the host security category. In other words, discussions are limited to security issues for a host that is configured as a single entity. Network-level security, which involves how multiple hosts are interconnected, is discussed in the next chapter.

Securing User Access

If you could keep a computer outside the reach of everyone, you might be able to make it completely secure. Of course, such a computer would be useless for anyone, practically speaking. Unfortunately, all security risks are associated with the people (the users) who access your computer. You never hear about a computer attacking another by itself. The attack can come from a user who has rightful access to your computer or someone who acquired access to your computer by illegal means. In most cases, people who have rightful access do not attack the computer they use but often unknowingly aid in attacks that come from people who gain illegal access. So restricting a user's ability to do damage to your system makes perfect sense; such restrictions in turn enhance your system security. In the following sections you learn how you restrict unnecessary user interaction with your system.

Restricting physical access

All security measures fail when someone capable of physically accessing your computer decides to do damage to your computer or the service and data it has to offer. There is virtually no easy way of protecting your computer from such a bad guy. Such a bad guy can pull out the power plug to choke your computer to a screeching halt, or boot the computer with a floppy and steal or vandalize your data, or do anything he wants.

The only way to ensure physical security for your system is to restrict who has such access to your computer. Know the people who can get to your computer. I recommend keeping your server away from public places where it is hard to know who is coming and going at all times. If it is impossible for you to restrict strangers from physically being near your computer, I recommend you do the following:

◆ Password-protect access to the computer's BIOS. You should do this whenever you get a computer for the first time. If your computer is going to be in a public place, be assured that if someone tries to get into the BIOS before you do, they can lock you out by adding a password. Recovering from such a problem could require that you call your computer vendor or open the computer to reset the BIOS by unplugging the battery for a short time. So secure your BIOS by password-protecting it. No one but you should have access to your computer's BIOS.

◆ If your BIOS allows you to disable floppy seek at boot, enable that disable option. Some newer BIOSes allow boot from CD-ROM drives; if you have such a computer, disable that option too. Do not allow your computer to boot from anything but your hard disk.

◆ Create or modify the /etc/shutdown.allow file and list only the users that are allowed to shut down your computer. If you allow only the root user to perform such a task, create an empty /etc/shutdown.allow file. When anyone at the computer console presses the Ctrl+Alt+Del keys to reboot the computer, the computer checks the file to make sure a specified user is logged in at the console before it shuts down. When someone who is not allowed to shut down presses these keys, the computer ignores the request and prints a warning message on the console. Of course this precaution does not stop anyone from pressing the reset button (if your computer has one) or turning off power to shut down the hard way. So make sure you have some way of protecting these switches.

♦ To deter or delay theft of computer equipment, you should also lock your computer to some large furniture in the same way a bike is locked to a bike stand.

Once you have implemented one or more means to restrict physical access to your computer, you can continue to implement other restrictions on user access as discussed in the following sections.

Restricting normal user access

There are two kinds of users on a Red Hat Linux system: normal users and superusers. When a normal user account is used to acquire superuser privileges illegally, bad things start to happen to a computer. So you (the superuser) need to make sure that user accounts have the fewest privileges required to get their jobs done. For example, if you created a Red Hat Linux server to provide e-mail and Web services for your users, you don't need to allow them Telnet access to your server. In order to restrict Telnet (shell) access for users who do not need such service, do the following:

1. Edit the /etc/shells file to insert /bin/false as a valid shell. You can either manually modify the file using an editor such as vi or use linuxconf, as shown in Figure 18-1.

Figure 18-1: Modifying the /etc/shells file using linuxconf

2. Modify each user account with either usermod or linuxconf to set the login shell to /etc/false. Figure 18-2 shows how a user account called kabir is modified using linuxconf.

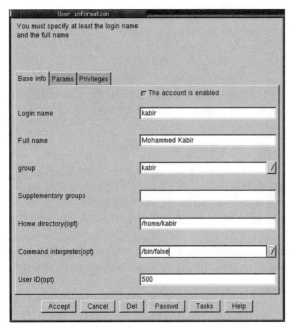

Figure 18-2: Modifying a user account using linuxconf

Once you have completed these steps, the modified account cannot be used for Telnet access. You can also create more restricted user accounts for FTP-only users with the guest account feature found in the wu-ftpd server. A guest FTP account is a real account with a real username and password. The only difference between the two is that when a guest user accesses an FTP server, she does not see anything other than her own home directory. In other words, when a guest user logs into an FTP server, the server does a chroot operation to the guest user's home directory, thus making the home directory of the guest user appear as the entire file system. The great advantage is that the user is unable to see anything beyond her home directory, such as system files and other user directories. See the section "Creating a guest FTP account" in Chapter 13 for details.

Restricting superuser access

Many people mistakenly associate superuser access with only the root account. They think that if you are not the root user, you aren't the superuser. In fact, what makes the root account a superuser is not the name but its user ID and the group ID. The root account's user ID and group ID are set to 0 (zero), which makes it a superuser.

So it is possible to create multiple superuser accounts by assigning them the previously mentioned user and group ID values. Superuser accounts are very powerful and people are prone to abuse them. Thus, superuser accounts should be used infrequently, that is, only when necessary and with extreme care. Just because one has superuser privileges does not mean one should use it at all times. As a superuser you may want to follow these guidelines:

◆ Use superuser accounts only when necessary. In other words, when you are configuring the system or installing systemwide software such as a new version of the Web server software, compiling and installing Perl for the entire system, or performing some similar task, use the superuser account. However, you should avoid using the root account or any superuser equivalent account to do everyday tasks such as sending e-mail, browsing the Web, running an IRC client to talk to friends or coworkers, transferring files via FTP, and so on.

Sometimes new system administrators wonder why they can't Telnet to a system as the root user. This is due to the fact that the /etc/securetty file specifies which tty device can be used for root logins. Typically, /etc/securetty lists tty[0-8] as allowed devices. Because Telnet access uses pseudo tty device ttyp[0-f], root cannot log in via Telnet. You should keep /etc/securetty as is. It's a good thing.

◆ Do not log in as root or an equivalent superuser from anywhere. The preferred method of performing administrative tasks is to log in as a normal user and use the su command to become a superuser (such as root). This method reduces the chances of accidental damage to your system.

Run the su command with - as an argument so that it makes the shell a login shell, which in turn makes the shell read the shell startup files (such as .bashrc). This argument also makes su change directories to the user's home directory.

◆ If you have a situation where others need to have superuser access to perform their jobs, consider using `sudo` instead of giving everyone a superuser account. If others need to run some programs that require superuser access, you can specify these users in the /etc/sudoers file such that they are able to run these programs without being a superuser. The `sudo` command allows a normal user to run only certain commands (specified by the superuser) as a superuser. This limitation is a good mechanism because it is less risky than giving someone full superuser access. The `sudo` command itself runs as a setuid root. This means that when sudo runs, it runs as a root user process, which allows it to run other programs that require superuser privileges. Red Hat Linux does not come with the sudo package, but you can get it from the `ftp://contrib.redhat.com/` site. I typically have a hard time accessing Red Hat's busy FTP servers, so if you are having no luck with their servers, try the `http://www.courtesan.com/sudo/` site. This is the official sudo Web site and has a great deal of information on sudo, including a list of FTP sites for sudo.

The main idea in all of these suggestions is to reduce superuser privileges whenever you can.

Restricting all access in an emergency or attack

In many cases when a system administrator detects an attack or emergency (such as a disk problem), the first task is to disallow user logins until the problem has been resolved or the system has been taken offline. My experience shows that sometimes it takes a bit of thinking before a system can be shut down. In such a case disallowing new logins becomes important. To disallow new logins quickly, just create a file called /etc/nologin with an appropriate message to let users know why you are blocking them and when the system is expected to come back online. The presence of this file disallows any normal user login. Because superusers are allowed to log in only from the console, be sure that you have physical console access to the system, or else you might accidentally log out of your current shell sessions and lock yourself out of the system.

Securing User Authentication Process

Traditionally, all UNIX systems use a basic user authentication scheme. Typically, all the user information such as username, encrypted password, user ID, user's group ID, and default shell, is stored in the /etc/passwd file. This file is consulted by programs that require user information. It is kept as a universally readable file so that any program can access it. For example, if you change the file permissions for /etc/passwd such that it is not world-readable anymore, you notice that a simple program like ls cannot display the username when run with the -l option. This is due to the fact that ls, like many other programs, needs to consult the /etc/passwd file for user information. In this particular case ls needs to map the user's user ID (such as 500) to username (kabir) from a /etc/passwd line such as the following:

```
kabir:PtxWphZQAyH3x:500:500:Mohammed Kabir:/home/kabir:/bin/tics
```

Programs consult the /etc/group file to determine the group name. If /etc/group is not world-readable, programs such as ls that need group information for a user do not function properly.

So what's wrong with keeping the /etc/passwd world-readable? Well, since any program can access a world-readable file, many bad guys (hackers) spend a considerable amount of effort to trick poorly written programs to give them access to this file. For example, bad guys have tricked many poorly written CGI scripts to even send the /etc/passwd file of a system to their own mailboxes! Also anyone who has an account on your system has access to this file. In short, the /etc/passwd file is often very easy to get. Once the file is in the hands of the bad guys, they can run password-cracking programs to detect weak passwords in the file. Because users often choose cute or easy-to-remember passwords, which are typically dictionary words, the cracking becomes fairly easy. The advancements of computer technology such as faster CPUs and cheaper hard drives have made password cracking an affordable hobby for many misguided individuals. For example, it takes 52 kilobytes to store all possible (4,096 per password) combinations of an 8-character password, which is internally stored as a 13-character encrypted string. As you can see, it would not take a very large hard drive to store a couple hundred thousand encrypted passwords to compare with a stolen /etc/passwd file.

So what can you do about this situation? You can shadow your passwords. This technique is described in the following section.

Using shadow passwords

It turns out that only a handful of programs, including login, passwd, and so on, really need the encrypted password field in the /etc/passwd file. All the other programs just need user information such as the user name, user ID, group ID, and shell. But what if you can relocate the encrypted passwords from /etc/passwd to another file and change the programs that need access to encrypted passwords in a way that they can read this file? This file is not world-readable, because the programs allowed access are run as setuid root programs. In other words, these programs run as root user to read the new password file; a package called Shadow Utils does all that for us.

Shadow password support is found in the Shadow Utils package, which is not installed by default. Once installed, this package provides utilities that enable you to convert your /etc/passwd file into a password-free file. The encrypted passwords are relocated in /etc/shadow, which is readable only by root and any program run as setuid root. This setup means that a bad guy who exploits weak programs to get access to /etc/passwd may still get it, but the file does not provide any password information. The shadow utility package provides other interesting features, such as password aging, account expiration, and locking features as well. In the following section you learn about how to use shadow passwords on your system.

INSTALLING THE SHADOW UTILITY PACKAGE

Get the file shadow-utils-*version-release-architecture*.rpm (for instance, shadow-utils-980403-4.i386.rpm) from your Red Hat CD-ROM or the Red Hat FTP site. Install it using the rpm utility as follows:

```
rpm -ivh shadow utility rpm file
```

Once you have installed the package, you need to convert the existing /etc/passwd file into a shadow password-based /etc/passwd file.

CONVERTING /ETC/PASSWD AND /ETC/GROUP TO SHADOW FORMAT

The traditional /etc/passwd file has the following format:

```
username:passwd:UID:GID:full_name:directory:shell
```

It is very simple to convert the /etc/passwd and /etc/group files to shadow format. Just run:

```
/usr/sbin/pwconv
```

to convert your original /etc/passwd to the shadow /etc/passwd format. Once you have converted /etc/passwd, it has the following format:

```
username:x:UID:GID:full_name:directory:shell
```

The second field now has an "x" instead of the encrypted password. You also have another file called /etc/shadow, which has the following format:

```
username:passwd:last:may:must:warn:expire:disable:reserved
```

As you can see, the encrypted password field (passwd) is now in this file. All the fields in the /etc/shadow file are described in Table 18-1.

TABLE 18-1 FIELDS IN THE /ETC/SHADOW FILE

Fields	Description
username	The user name
passwd	The encrypted character password
last	Date of last password change
may	Minimum number of days after which the current password may be changed
must	Maximum number of days after which the current password must be changed
warn	Number of days after which the user is warned about the current password becoming expired
expire	Number of days after which the current password expires and the account is disabled
disable	Number of days since the account has expired

The new fields (everything but the username and passwd) can be used to provide the user accounting functions such as account expiration and password aging. The /usr/sbin/pwconv utility uses the PASS_MAX_DAYS (maximum number of days after which the current password must be changed), PASS_MIN_DAYS (minimum number of days after which the current password may be changed), and PASS_WARN_AGE (number of days after which the user is warned about the current password's expiration) values from /etc/login.defs file. Modify the /etc/login.defs file to set desired values for these fields.

MANAGING USER ACCOUNTS

The shadow utility package installs replacements for utilities such as useradd, userdel, usermod, groupadd, groupdel, and groupmod that are typically used to manage user accounts. You can run the following rpm command to see the files installed when you installed this package.

```
rpm  -q -l shadow-utils-version-release
```

The new and increasingly popular linuxconf utility is also capable of working with shadow password systems. In fact, the Params dialog window, shown in Figure 18-3, becomes available when linuxconf detects the use of shadow passwords.

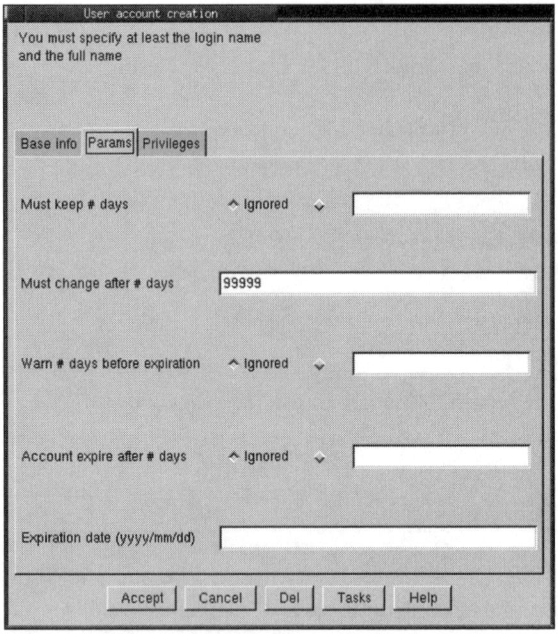

Figure 18-3: A special linuxconf dialog window for a shadow password–enabled system

This dialog window becomes part of the user account creation process and allows you to specify information about password aging, account expiration, and so on. You can also change the default values for PASS_MAX_DAYS, PASS_MIN_DAYS, and PASS_WARN_AGE that are stored in /etc/login.defs using linuxconf. Figure 18-4 shows the dialog window to use for this purpose.

Very careful readers will wonder how programs such as chsh, chfn, ftp, imap, linuxconf, rlogin, rexec, rsh, su, login, and passwd all of a sudden understand the shadow password scheme and use the /etc/shadow password file for authentication. Red Hat distributes these programs with shadow password capabilities. Actually, Red Hat ships these programs with a much grander scheme of authentication support called pluggable authentication modules (PAM). These PAM-aware programs are capable of using not only the shadow password scheme but also virtually any other authentication scheme that you care to implement to enhance your system security. In the following section, I discuss PAM.

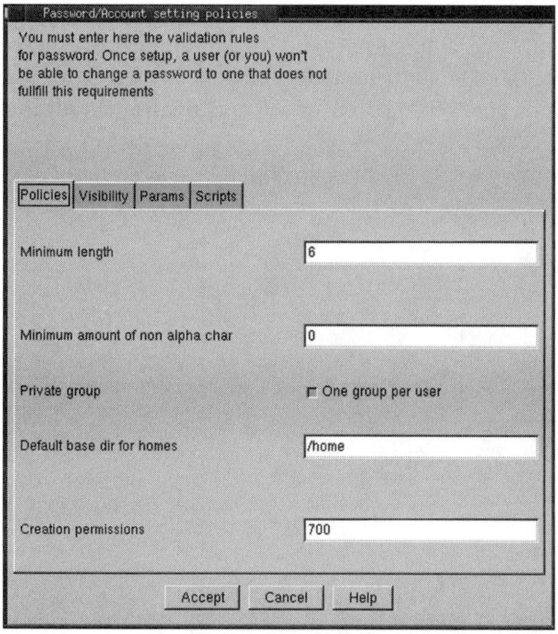

Figure 18-4: A special linuxconf dialog window for changing defaults in /etc/login.defs

Understanding PAM

Traditionally, authentication schemes are built into programs that grant privileges to users. Programs like login or passwd used to be built with necessary code to handle authentication. Over time, this approach proved to be nonscalable, because incorporating a new authentication scheme required that privilege-granting programs be recoded and recompiled. In order to relieve the privilege-granting software developer from writing secure authentication code, PAM was developed. Figure 18-5 shows how PAM works with privilege-granting applications.

When a privilege-granting application such as /bin/login is made into a PAM-aware application, it typically works in the manner shown in Figure 18-5. First a user invokes such an application to access the service it offers (step 1). The PAM-aware application then calls the underlying PAM library to perform the authentication (step 2). The PAM library then looks up an application-specific configuration file in the /etc/pam.d/ directory (step 3). This file tells PAM what type of authentication is required for this application. The PAM library then loads the required authentication module(s) (step 4). These modules can then make PAM communicate with the conversation functions available in the application (step 5). The conversation functions can be used to request information from the user (step 6). For example, the user can be asked to enter a password or look into a retinal scanner. The user responds to the request by providing requested information (step 7). The PAM authentication modules then supply the application with an authentication status message via the PAM library (step 8). If the authentication process is successful, the application grants the requested privileges to the user or informs the user about the failure (step 9).

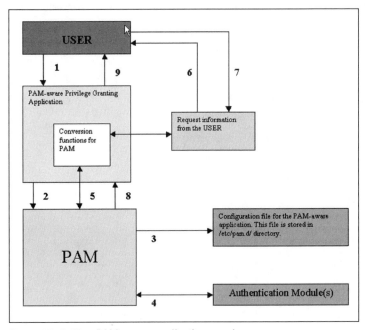

Figure 18-5: How PAM-aware applications work

Think of PAM as a facility that takes the burden of authentication away from the applications and enables you to stack multiple authentication schemes for a single application. For example, the PAM configuration file for the rlogin application is shown in Listing 18-1.

Listing 18-1: The /etc/pam.d/rlogin file

```
auth       required /lib/security/pam_securetty.so
auth       sufficient /lib/security/pam_rhosts_auth.so
auth       required /lib/security/pam_pwdb.so shadow nullok
auth       required /lib/security/pam_nologin.so
account    required /lib/security/pam_pwdb.so
```

```
password    required /lib/security/pam_cracklib.so
password    required /lib/security/pam_pwdb.so shadow nullok \
use_authtok
session     required /lib/security/pam_pwdb.so
```

Here multiple authentication modules from /lib/security are used to authenticate the user. I discuss the details of the configuration files in the next section.

WORKING WITH A PAM CONFIGURATION FILE

In Listing 18-1 you saw what an application-specific PAM configuration file looks like. Lines starting with a leading "#" character and blank lines are ignored. A configuration line has the following fields:

```
module-type control-flag module-path module-args
```

Currently there are four module types, which are described in Table 18-2.

TABLE 18-2 PAM MODULE TYPES

Module Type	Description
auth	This type of module does the actual authentication. Typically, an auth module requires a user to enter a password or provide some other proof to prove that she is who she claims to be.
account	This type of module handles all the accounting aspects of an authentication request. Typically, an account module checks to see if the user access meets all the access guidelines. For example, it can check to see if the user is accessing the service from a secure host or if the user is accessing the system during a specified time.
password	This type of module manages functions that need to be done before and after the user is given access to the requested service.
session	This type of module is used to manage session tasks, such as refreshing session tokens.

The control flag is used to define how the PAM library handles a module's response. The four control flags currently allowed are described in Table 18-3.

TABLE 18-3 PAM MODULE CONTROL FLAGS

Control Flag	Description
required	This flag states that the specified module must return a success value as the response code. When a module returns a response indicating a failure, the authentication definitely fails but PAM still continues with other modules (if any). This is done to ensure that the user cannot detect which part of the authentication process failed, because knowing might aid a potential attacker.
requisite	Using this control flag makes the authentication process abort as soon as a failure response is received by the PAM library.
sufficient	When you use this control flag, PAM considers the authentication process complete if it receives a success response. In other words, there is no need to proceed with other modules in the configuration file.
optional	This control flag is hardly used. It does not put any emphasis on the success or failure response of the module.

The module path is the path of a pluggable authentication module. Red Hat Linux stores all the PAM modules in /lib/security directory. You can supply each module with optional arguments as well.

Now if you look back at Listing 18-1, note that the PAM library calls the pam_securetty.so module, which must return a response indicating success in order for the authentication to be successful. If the module's response indicates failure, PAM still continues processing the other modules so that the user (who could be a potential attacker) is not aware of where the failure occurred. If the next module (pam_rhosts_auth.so) returns a success, the authentication process is complete, because the control flag is set to sufficient. However, if the previous module (map_securetty.so) does not fail but this one fails, the authentication process continues and the failure does not affect the final result. In the same fashion, the rest of the modules are processed by the PAM library. The order of execution follows the way the modules appear in the configuration exactly. However, each type of module (auth, account, password, and session) is processed in a stack. In other words, for the example in Listing 18-1 all the auth modules are stacked and processed in the order of appearance in the configuration file. The rest of the modules are processed in a similar fashion.

USING PAM TO FINE-TUNE THE AUTHENTICATION PROCESS

Now that you know so much about how PAM works, consider an example of how you can use PAM to fine-tune authentication processes for certain services. The very first step you should take is to read the documentation available for all the available PAM authentication modules. All the available PAM modules are stored in the /lib/security directory, and you can find documentation on each module in the /usr/doc/pam-*X.xx* directory, where *X.xx* is your PAM version. Read the documentation for each module and determine which you want to use in building a more restrictive authentication scheme for your system. In this section I show you how you can restrict login access to your server by time.

A module called pam_time (/lib/security/pam_time.so) enables you to control access to services based on time. You can configure this module to deny access to (individual) users based on their names, the times of day, the days of the week, the services they are applying for, and the terminals from which they are making their requests. Its actions are determined with the /etc/security/time.conf configuration file.

Because you want to control login access, you need to modify the /etc/pam.d/ login PAM configuration file. You have to add the following line:

```
account  required  /lib/security/pam_time.so
```

Once you have added this line to the /etc/pam.d/login file, you need to come up with an access policy for login service. In other words, determine when you want users to be able to log in. In the example, I assume that you want to allow users to be able to log in after 6 A.M. and as late as 8 P.M. Now you need to configure the /etc/security/time.conf file. The configuration lines in this file have the following syntax:

```
services;ttys;users;times
```

You can use some special characters in each of the fields. Table 18-4 shows the meaning of the special characters that you can use.

TABLE 18-4 SPECIAL CHARACTERS FOR CONFIGURATION FIELDS IN /ETC/SECURITY/TIME.CONF

Character	Meaning
!	NOT. For example, !login means "not login" or "except login."
|	OR. For example, kabir|ronak means "either kabir or ronak."
&	AND. For example, login&su means "both login and su."
*	Wildcard. For example, foo* means "everything that starts with foo."

Table 18-5 describes the fields in such a configuration line.

TABLE 18-5 FIELDS OF THE /ETC/SECURITY/TIME.CONF FILE

Field	Description
services	A list of services that are affected by the time restriction. For example, to control both login and su using a single rule, you can specify the service to be "login&su" in a configuration line.
ttys	A list of terminals that are affected by the time restriction. For example, to control only pseudo-terminals and not the console terminals, you can specify "ttyp*!tty*" where ttyp* lists all the pseudo-terminals used in remote login via services like Telnet, and tty* lists all the console terminals.
users	A list of users that are affected by the time restriction. For example, to specify all the users, you can simply use the wildcard character "*" in a configuration line.
time	A list of times when the restrictions apply. You can specify time as a range in a 24-hr clock format. For example, to specify a range from 8 P.M. to 6 A.M., you can specify 2000–0600 (for example, HHMM format, where HH is 00–23 and MM is 00–59). You can also specify days using a two-character code such as Mo (Monday), Tu (Tuesday), We (Wednesday), Th (Thursday), Fr (Friday), Sa (Saturday), and Su (Sunday). You can also use special codes such as Wk for all weekdays, Wd for weekends, Al for all seven days. For example, to restrict access to a service from 8 P.M. to 6 A.M. on a daily basis, you can specify a time range as !Al2000–0600.

For the ongoing example, you can create a time-based rule that prohibits login access from 8 P.M. to 6 A.M. for all users who access the system via remote means (such as Telnet) by adding the following line in the /etc/security/time.conf file:

```
login;ttyp*;*;!Al2000-0600
```

This line can be interpreted as the following:

```
If (requested service is login) and
   (access is made from a pseudo ttyp type device) and
   (current time is between 8PM to 6 AM) then

   Access to the requested service is not allowed.

Else
Access to the requested service is permitted.

End
```

Now if you wanted to allow a user called "kabir" access to the system at any time but all others to follow the preceding rule, you can modify the rule as follows:

```
login;ttyp*;*!kabir;!Al2000-0600
```

This is just a single example of how PAM can be used to fine-tune your user authentication process. Again, read the module documentation and experiment with the settings to come up with the most suitable authentication scheme for your system.

Now that you have learned about many ways of controlling user access to your system, let's look at how you can enhance the security of the services your system offers.

Securing Services

Too often a bad guy compromises a system's security because the system administrator did not take the time to weed out unnecessary services. Remember that the more programs you have on your system, the more ways a bad guy can break in. So start the weeding-out process from the very beginning.

Removing unnecessary services during OS installation

Before you install Red Hat Linux on your computer, decide what you want to run on the system. Write down the services needed to accomplish your goals. For example, if you are creating a Web server system, you are not likely to need the POP server or the Gopher server or the NNTP News server. Make a list of server software you want to install. The Red Hat Linux installation program enables you to select individual packages before installation. Take the time to go through all the lists and select only the necessary packages. Sometimes the installation program installs one or more packages that are prerequisite to the packages you have selected. It actually shows you these prerequisite package names once you complete your package selection during the installation process. Write down the names of these packages.

After you have installed all the necessary packages and booted the system for the first time, you can either look at the installation log stored in /tmp or run the following rpm command to get the complete listing of all installed packages:

```
rpm -qa > /tmp/all.packages
```

Carefully go through the /tmp/all.packages file to detect any packages that you do not recall approving for installation. If the package does not show up in your prerequisite list, you may want to find out more about the package using the following command:

```
rpm -qi package_name
```

If the package seems unnecessary, remove it using the following command:

```
rpm -e package_name
```

The rpm command checks to see if the package_name is required by some other package. If it is, you get a warning message and the package is not removed unless you use the -e –force options. You should carefully read what the warning says and decide accordingly. However, if the package is not a dependency for any other package, it is cleanly removed from your system.

I recommend not installing the following types of packages on a computer that you use as a server on the Internet:

♦ Anything related to X-Windows and X-Windows itself.

♦ Any multimedia applications except the real-audio/video server package if you are planning on providing real-audio/video services.

♦ Any interpreter other than that required. I personally use Perl only for scripting and therefore do not install other scripting languages.

♦ Any server software such as NFS, NIS, INN, POP2 or 3, or Samba that you do not need to have.

♦ Any file editor that you do not use. I use only vi and therefore do not install a complex editor like emacs. Of course if you are an emacs kind of person, you would choose this beast over vi. I also do not install various newer vi clones.

♦ Any client program that you do not need. For example, do not install e-mail clients that you do not think will be used by you or your users.

As you can see, the theme is always the same — the less you install, the less you have to worry about.

Now let's take a look at how you can enhance security of various network services.

Securing xinetd-run services

The xinetd daemon is called the Internet "super server" because it is used to provide many such popular Internet services as FTP, Telnet, POP2/3, and finger. The xinetd daemon typically is started at some point during the multiuser boot process. At startup the xinetd daemon reads the /etc/xinetd.conf configuration and listens for requests on all standard ports listed in /etc/services. When a request is received on a certain port, it starts the appropriate service to process the request. Listing 18-2 shows a typical /etc/xinetd.conf file.

Listing 18-2: An /etc/xinetd.conf file

```
#
# Simple configuration file for xinetd
#
# Some defaults, and include /etc/xinetd.d/

defaults
{
        instances               = 60
        log_type                = SYSLOG authpriv
        log_on_success          = HOST PID
        log_on_failure          = HOST RECORD
}


includedir /etc/xinetd.d
```

As in many other UNIX configuration files, the lines starting with a "#" character are treated as comments and ignored along with blank lines. This file sets some default values for xinetd and also makes it read the /etc/xinetd.d directory for service files. Each Internet service managed via xinetd must have a service file in the /etc/xinetd.d directory. For example, the FTP service file /etc/xinetd.d/wu-ftp looks as follows:

```
# default: on
# description: The wu-ftpd FTP server serves FTP connections.
# It uses normal, unencrypted usernames and passwords
# for authentication.

service ftp
{
        socket_type             = stream
        wait                    = no
        user                    = root
        server                  = /usr/sbin/in.ftpd
        server_args             = -l -a
        log_on_success          += DURATION USERID
        log_on_failure          += USERID
        nice                    = 10
}
```

Here the ftp service is defined such that xinetd runs the /usr/sbin/in.ftpd FTP daemon whenever it detects a connection request for FTP service on the FTP port listed in /etc/services. The /usr/sbin/in.ftpd server is run using the server arguments –l and –a as stated in the server_args configuration line.

Now that you understand how xinetd works, you are ready to remove unnecessary services.

REMOVING UNNECESSARY INTERNET SERVICES

If you have installed many Internet services such as FTP, Telnet, Gopher, remote shell (rsh), remove login (rlogin), remote exec (rexec), talk, ntalk, POP3, finger, etc. and find that you do not want to run one or more of them, simply edit the appropriate service file in the /etc/xinetd.d directory and add a line as follows:

```
disable = yes
```

This line will disable the appropriate service run by xinetd. However, before xinetd knows about this change, you must reload xinetd configuration by running the following command:

```
Killall USR1 xinetd
```

If you wish to never run an Internet service, you might want to completely remove the appropriate service file from /etc/xinet.d directory and reload xinetd configuration as mentioned above. This way you are sure that the service is disabled forever.

On the other hand, if you wish to not disable a service completely but partially make it available to a restricted set of IP addresses or networks, you can add:

```
only_from <IP address or network>
```

within a service definition file to control access. You can also use TCP wrapper for the same purpose as discussed next.

USING THE TCP WRAPPER TO SECURE XINETD RUN-SERVICES

As mentioned before the TCP wrapper program can used to control access to xinetd run services. Any xinetd run service can be run via TCP wrapper by modifying the appropriate service file in the /etc/xinetd.d directory. The lines that needs to be added or modified are following:

```
flags           = REUSE NAMEINARGS
server          = /usr/sbin/tcpd
server_args      = /path/to/service_daemin
```

The server_args line needs to be set to the path of the service daemon. For example, to run the FTP service via the TCP wrapper, the /etc/xinetd.d/wu-ftpd service definition file might looks like:

```
service ftp
{
        flags                   = REUSE NAMEINARGS
        socket_type             = stream
        wait                    = no
        user                    = root
        server                  = /usr/sbin/tcpd
        server_args             = /usr/sbin/in.ftpd
        log_on_success          += DURATION USERID
        log_on_failure          += USERID
        nice                    = 10
}
```

The TCP wrapper program enhances security by providing the following services:

◆ Logging service: It can log information about a request using the syslog facility.

◆ Host-based access control: It can provide host-based access control using pattern matching.

◆ Host name and address verification service: It can detect spoofing of host names or addresses when a host is pretending to be some other host.

You can guess how important the TCP wrapper is, as it comes as part of the default Red Hat Linux installation. There is absolutely no reason for not wrapping each of your xinetd services with the TCP wrapper.

Now let's look at how you can restrict host access via the TCP wrapper.

RESTRICTING HOST ACCESS VIA THE TCP WRAPPER   As mentioned before, the TCP wrapper provides a great deal of flexibility in controlling access at an Internet host (or IP address) level. This flexibility can come in very handy for configuring a tight server system. Here I discuss an example of a tightly controlled system based on a system I use daily.

First, decide on the goal of the sample control configuration. Say that you want to create an Internet Web server system that allows only Telnet, FTP, POP3, and HTTP services. Because the Web service (HTTP) is typically a high-demand service, it is not run via xinetd. Let's assume that the Web server is Apache and it is run as a stand-alone service (see Chapter 12 for more about Web service). In this example, then, xinetd manages the rest of the service. Also let's assume that we want to restrict Telnet, FTP, and POP3 access to only a single network whose network address is 206.171.50.0.

Listing 18-3 shows the flags, server and server_args lines for each of these services:

Listing 18-3: flags, server and server_args lines for Telnet, FTP, and POP3

```
# Telnet (in /etc/xinetd.d/telnet)
        flags            = REUSE NAMEINARGS
        server           = /usr/sbin/tcpd
        server_args      = /usr/sbin/in.telnetd

# FTP (in /etc/xinetd.d/wu-ftpd)
        flags            = REUSE NAMEINARGS
        server           = /usr/sbin/tcpd
        server_args      = /usr/sbin/in.ftpd

# POP3 (in /etc/xinetd.d/ipop3)
        flags            = REUSE NAMEINARGS
        server           = /usr/sbin/tcpd
        server_args      = /usr/sbin/in.ipop3d
```

Now you need to restrict access to these services via the /etc/hosts.allow and /etc/hosts.deny files. The /etc/hosts.allow file is used to specify which hosts are allowed access to a xinetd services, and the /etc/hosts.deny file is used to specify which hosts are not allowed access to a xinetd services. Both of these files use the same configuration format as shown here:

```
daemon list : client list [ : shell command ]
```

The daemon list is a list of one or more service process names. For instance, in.ftpd, in.telnetd, and ipop3d are daemon names for this example. The client list consists of one or more host names or IP addresses. You can use the wildcards shown in Table 18-6 in both daemon and client lists.

**TABLE 18-6 WILDCARDS FOR DAEMON AND CLIENT LISTS IN /ETC/HOSTS.
[ALLOW | DENY] FILES**

Wildcard	Meaning
ALL	Always matches.
LOCAL	Matches a local host name like wormhole but not wormhole.nitec.com.

Wildcard	Meaning
UNKNOWN	Matches when the host name or IP address is unknown due to a problem.
KNOWN	Matches when a host or IP address is known.
PARANOID	Matches a host that does not match its IP address. This only works if the tcpd wrapper program is not built with the -DPARANOID option at compilation.

You can also use patterns like the following:

◆ '.nitec.com' matches a host name such as wormhole.nitec.com or picaso.nitec.com. In other words, when a leading dot is used in a pattern, it can be matched from the right side of the host name.

◆ '206.171.50.' matches any hosts with addresses such in the range of 206.171.50.0 to 206.171.50.255. In other words, when a trailing dot is used in a pattern, the matching is done from the left.

◆ '206.171.50.0/255.255.255.0' matches any hosts with addresses in the range of 206.171.50.0 to 206.171.50.255. The pattern is treated as a network/netmask definition.

Also, if you plan to use shell commands to perform some action, you can take advantage of the character expansions shown in Table 18-7.

TABLE 18-7 CHARACTER EXPANSIONS FOR SHELL COMMANDS

Character	Expanded Meaning
%a	The IP address of the client trying to access a service
%A	The IP address of the server
%c	Client information such as host name or IP address, or *user@host* or *user@ip_address*, etc.
%d	The name of the daemon or service
%h	The host name of the client trying to access a service
%H	The host name of the server
%p	The process ID (PID) of the daemon or service

Continued

TABLE 18-7 **CHARACTER EXPANSIONS FOR SHELL COMMANDS** *(Continued)*

Character	Expanded Meaning
%s	Server information such as host name or IP address, or *user@host* or *user@ip_address*, etc.
%u	The client user name if known, or else set to 'unknown'
%%	The % character

Because the goal here is to disallow all the hosts except for the ones belonging to the 206.171.50.0 network, you can create a /etc/hosts.deny file as shown in Listing 18-4.

Listing 18-4: The /etc/hosts.deny file

```
#
# hosts.deny   This file describes the names of the
# hosts that are not allowed to use the local INET
# services, as decided by the /usr/sbin/tcpd program.
#

# Deny all daemon access to all hosts.
#
ALL : ALL
```

As you can see, the /etc/hosts.deny file is set up to deny all hosts. The single configuration line, ALL : ALL, tells the TCP wrapper (tcpd) to deny ALL daemon access to ALL hosts. If it is left as is and there is no /etc/hosts.allow file in the system, no host is able to access any of the three xinetd-run services (Telnet, FTP, and POP3). So you must allow specific hosts, particularly the 206.171.50.0 network, to access these services in the /etc/hosts.allow file. This is done in Listing 18-5.

Listing 18-5: The /etc/hosts.allow file

```
#
# hosts.allow   This file describes the names of the
# hosts that are allowed to use the local INET
# services, as decided by the /usr/sbin/tcpd program.
#

# Deny all daemon access to all hosts.
#
ALL : 206.171.50.0/255.255.255.0
```

Here the single configuration line, `ALL : 206.171.50.0/255.255.255.0`, states that the TCP wrapper (tcpd) allows access to ALL daemons for the specified 206.171.50.0 network. In other words, all the hosts in the IP range of 206.171.50.0 to 206.171.50.255 should have access to the Telnet, FTP, and POP3 services.

That's all there is to configuring the TCP wrapper. Now if you want to allow another network, 208.233.7.48/255.255.255.240, to access these services, the only change needed is in /etc/hosts.allow. You just need to add this network in the client list as follows:

```
ALL : 206.171.50.0/255.255.255.0 208.233.7.48/255.255.255.240
```

As you can see, configuring tcpd using /etc/hosts.allow and /etc/hosts.deny is quite simple. Now take a look at a couple more tcpd configuration examples.

EXAMPLE 1: USING HOST AND DOMAIN NAMES IN /ETC/HOSTS.ALLOW   Let's say that you want to allow all hosts from the `classifiedworks.com` domain to access all the xinetd services except for the `msql.classifiedworks.com` host. The /etc/hosts.deny file has a single line such as `ALL: ALL` to deny all service to everyone not specified in /etc/hosts.allow. The /etc/hosts.allow file has a line such as:

```
ALL: .classifiedworks.com EXCEPT msql.classifiedworks.com
```

EXAMPLE 2: BLOCKING A SERVICE TO A SPECIFIC HOST   In this example, I show you how you can block the FTP service to a single host called `reboot.nitec.com` when all the other hosts in the `nitec.com` domain are allowed to access all the services. The /etc/hosts.deny file has a single line such as `ALL: ALL` to deny all service to everyone not specified in /etc/hosts.allow. The /etc/hosts.allow file has lines such as:

```
in.ftpd: .nitec.com EXCEPT reboot.nitec.com
ALL EXCEPT in.ftpd: .nitec.com
```

The first line states that the in.ftpd daemon is allowed to service all the hosts in the `nitec.com` domain except `reboot.nitec.com`. The next line states that all daemons (that is, services) but the FTP service (in.ftpd) are allowed to service all the hosts in the `nitec.com` domain.

The TCP wrapper can also be configured using an extended host access control language that uses the following configuration syntax:

```
daemon list : client list : option : option : . . .
```

An option can be any of the keywords shown in Table 18-8.

TABLE 18-8 ACCEPTABLE KEYWORDS IN EXTENDED HOST ACCESS CONTROL LANGUAGE

Keyword	Description
ALLOW *client list*	Used to permit access to one or more hosts. Example: ALL : .your-domain.com : ALLOW Here all the hosts in your-domain.com are allowed access to all the xinetd-run services.
DENY *client list*	Used to restrict access to one or more hosts. Example: ALL: .bad-guy-domain.com: DENY Here all the hosts in bad-guy-domain.com are denied access to all the xinetd-run services. ALL: .bad-guy-domain.com : DENY
SPAWN *shell command*	Used to execute a shell command. The command is run such that STDIN, STDOUT, and STDERR are directed to /dev/null. This makes sure the command does not interfere with the client software on the host trying to access a service. The character expansion discussed earlier applies before the command is called.
TWIST *shell command*	Used to execute a shell command. The command is run such that STDIN, STDOUT, and STDERR are directed to the client. The character expansion discussed earlier applies before the command is called. You should use TWIST as the last option in the configuration line. I recommend using TWIST only for TCP-based services.
LINGER *seconds*	Used to make kernel retry data delivery for specified number of seconds.
RFC931 *seconds*	Used to look up user information on the client side when the client is running an RFC 931-complaint IDENT server. The specified seconds are used to time out in case the IDENT server is not responding. This keyword works only for TCP-based services.
BANNERS directory	Used to display a text file to the client. The text file or banner is looked up in the specified directory. The file name must be the same as the daemon name. This command works only for connection-oriented TCP-based services such as Telnet.
NICE *number*	Used to change daemon process priority. The higher the number, the lower the priority.

Keyword	Description
SETENV name value	Sets the *name=value* in the environment process of the daemon. This keyword does not always work, because many daemon processes reset their environment when handling a request using a child process.
UMASK mask	Used to set file permission policy in the same manner as the traditional umask shell command.
USER username.group	Used to specify the user and group of the daemon process.

Now let's take a look at an example that uses the extended access control language.

EXAMPLE 3: USING A SHELL COMMAND IN /ETC/HOSTS.ALLOW   Let's say that you want to block Telnet service for a host called spooky.badguy-domain.com. However, you also want to let the host know that you do not welcome it. In such a case you can create an /etc/hosts.allow configuration as follows:

```
# Everyone but spooky is allowed telnet access.
In.telnetd: ALL EXCEPT spooky.badguy-domain.com

# spooky.badguy-domain.com is made to understand that it is
# not welcome on this server.
in.telnetd: spooky.badguy-domain.com: twist /bin/echo \
You are not welcome here!
```

Or if you want to be notified via e-mail as soon as the spooky host tries to Telnet, you can send yourself a message using the /bin/mail program. In such a case you need an /etc/hosts.allow configuration such as:

```
# Everyone but spooky is allowed telnet access.
In.telnetd: ALL EXCEPT spooky.badguy-domain.com

# spooky.badguy-domain.com is made to understand that it is
# not welcome on this server.
in.telnetd: spooky.badguy-domain.com: linger 5: twist /bin/mail \
-s "%a (%c) tried to access %d (%p)" your@emailaddress <
/etc/badguy-came.txt
```

Here the /bin/mail program is invoked when spooky tries to Telnet in. The mail program is called with the -s option to set the subject line as "%a (%c) tried to access %d (%p)," which expands to "*x.x.x.x* (spooky.badguy-domain.com) tried to access in.telnetd (xyz)" where *x.x.x.x* is the IP address of the host and xyz is the PID of the daemon process.

REPLACING THE R* COMMANDS WITH SECURE SHELL (SSH)

First of all, if you do not use the r* commands including `rlogin`, `rsh`, `rexec`, and so on, consider removing them completely from your system. You learned how to disable services like this in the /etc/xinetd.d directory. These services have been prone to attacks. If you use these services to access your system, consider replacing them with a secured solution called Secure Shell, or ssh. The ssh solution enables you all the benefits of the r* commands and then some. For example, using ssh you can log into a remote system or execute a command on the remote system with a secured, encrypted connection. It provides extensive logging capabilities and works well with syslog. With ssh, you can also create secure remote X sessions. It can provide protection against IP and DNS spoofing, attacks based on the weaknesses in X authentication protocol, and so on. You can get ready to run RPM packages for ssh from the following Web site: `http://www.replay.com/redhat/ssh.html`.

You need the base ssh package, the ssh client package, and the ssh server package. There might be some legal restrictions on ssh due to the U.S. export control laws for encryption software. Please make sure you read the documentation found in the preceding Web site.

Protecting Your Files and File System

Files and file systems are the most important components when it comes to computer system protection. As with everything else in this chapter, the idea is to give the fewest possible privileges to others. If you can get by with granting read access, then don't give write or execute access just because you can. In the following section, I discuss a few such issues.

Mounting file systems as read-only

It is a good idea to mount certain file systems as read-only whenever possible. For example, if you have to maintain a public FTP server where the public files are stored in a separate partition, you can mount the partition as read-only. Let's say that the public files are stored in /dev/sda5 (a partition of a SCSI disk) and automatically mounted on /public via a line the /etc/fstab file as follows:

```
/dev/sda5 /public ext2 defaults 1 2
```

The mount option for the partition is "defaults," which means the following:

◆ Mount the file system read/write (rw).

- ◆ Allow set-UID or set-GID bits to take effect (suid).

- ◆ Interpret character/block devices on the file system (dev).

- ◆ Allow execution of programs (exec).

- ◆ Mount the file system when the system is booted or the mount command is run with the -a option (auto).

- ◆ Prevent anyone but a superuser (user ID = 0, group ID = 0) to mount the file system (nouser).

- ◆ Use asynchronous I/O mode (async) for the file system .

If you are certain there is no need for write permission for this partition, you can change it as follows:

```
/dev/sda5 /public ext2 ro,suid,dev,exec,auto,nouser,async 1 2
```

However, if you further decide that you do not need to allow suid and exec support, you can remove them as well, as follows:

```
/dev/sda5 /public ext2 ro,nosuid,dev,noexec,auto,nouser,async 1 2
```

Use the EXT2 file system's attributes wherever appropriate. The most helpful one I've used is the "immutable" flag, which makes it possible to disallow even root to change some files. Check the chattr(1) and lsattr(1) man pages for details.

Taking advantage of ext2 file system

Many new system administrators do everything as root. This habit is dangerous and can be very costly if one is not very careful. The best advice is to not run root for everything: I can't emphasize it enough. Even if you become root infrequently, it can still be costly. For example, if you mistakenly issue the rm command, many files and directories can be lost forever. I personally made such a serious mistake once. At first I did not believe it, but it did happen. This is what I did. Some years ago, my job required that I manage multiple Linux systems as a remote system administrator. One day I logged into one of these systems as a normal user and became root (using the su command) to do some software installations. Because of some routing problem at an upstream ISP location, the connection was virtually unbearable. I was typing faster than the terminal could echo the characters back at me. At one point, I decided to abandon the software installation and delete the source. So I used the cd command to return to the top directory but because the connection was slow, I was entering cd commands one after another and not seeing the results on the screen. At some point, I thought that I had entered the rm -rf partial_name_of_the_package* command. But unfortunately, due to my inability to see what I was typing, the command I really entered was rm -rf partial_name_of_the_package   (space) *, which meant that all the files in the current directory got wiped out. I had backups of files that got deleted, but getting the backup tape from offsite, finding the files in the tape, and restoring them took the rest of my week. If I had been a bit more patient in this case, this disaster could have been easily avoided.

So the moral of the story is to be very careful with root. In fact, I recommend using some of the Linux ext2 file system features to protect against such disasters. For example, you can use the `chattr` command to provide protection from accidental modification and deletion by even the root user. Here is how.

The ext2 file system used for Red Hat Linux provides some unique features. One of these features allows a file to be immutable by even the root user. For example:

```
chattr +i filename
```

This command sets the "i" attribute of a file in an ext2 file system. When this attribute is set, the file cannot be modified, deleted, or renamed by anyone. No links can be added to point to this file either. This attribute can be set or cleared only by the root user. So you can use this attribute to protect against file accidents. When you need to clear the attribute, you can run:

```
chattr -i filename
```

A few other interesting features of the ext2 system, such as the undelete attribute, are not yet implemented but will become available in a future ext2 file system version. If you start using the `chattr` command, sometimes you notice that you can't modify or delete a file, although you have the permission to do so. This happens when you forget that you have set the immutable attribute of the file using `chattr` earlier, and because this attribute does not show up in the `ls` output, it can be a bit confusing. To see which files have which ext2 attributes, you can use the `lsattr` program.

Unfortunately, what you know now about file and file system security is possibly known by the informed bad guys. Use of tools like `chattr` might just make it a bit harder for the bad guy, but not make it impossible to damage your files or file systems. In fact, if the bad guy gets root level privileges, ext2 attributes provide just a simple hide-and-seek game. One major problem after a break-in is to determine if you can trust your files. You might wonder if the bad guy has installed a Trojan application or embedded a virus to infect new files and possibly provide access to other computers that you access. None of the methods I talked about handles this aspect of a security problem. Well, the solution is to run a file integrity checker program like Tripwire.

Using Tripwire for ensuring file integrity

Simply speaking, Tripwire is a file and directory integrity checker that creates a database of signatures for all files and directories and stores them in a single file. When Tripwire is run again, it computes new signatures for current files and directories and compares them with the original signatures stored in the database. If there is a discrepancy, the file or directory name is reported along with information about the discrepancy.

Now you can see why Tripwire can be a great tool for helping you determine which files were modified in a break-in. Of course for that you have to ensure the security of the database that the application uses. When setting up a new server system, many experienced system administrators do the following things:

1. Ensure that the new system is not attached to any network to guarantee that no one has already installed a Trojan program, virus program, or other danger to your system security.

2. Run Tripwire to create a signature database of all the important system files, including all the system binaries and configuration files.

3. Write the database in a recordable CD-ROM. This ensures that an advanced bad guy cannot modify the Tripwire database to hide Trojans and modified files from being noticed by the application. Administrators who have a small number of files to monitor often use a floppy disk to store the database. After writing the database to the floppy disk, the administrator write-protects the disk and, if the BIOS permits, configures the disk drive as a read-only device.

4. Set up a cron job to run Tripwire on a periodic basis (daily, weekly, monthly) such that the application uses the CD-ROM version of the database.

Now you can have the same level of security using Tripwire. Here is how.

INSTALLING TRIPWIRE   The official Red Hat distribution (the boxed version) sold by Red Hat includes an application CD that contains a version of Tripwire. This version of the software is suitable for a single-CPU, end-user setup. The software comes in two separate RPM packages — one contains the binary distribution and the other contains the source distribution. Unless you are interested in compiling your own copy, you can use the binary distribution. Normally, I compile security software if I can, but because Red Hat packages this software in its product, I have a certain degree of trust in their professionalism and hence I discuss the binary installation here.

As usual, the binary installation is quite simple; you just need to run the rpm command as follows:

```
rpm -ivh tripwire_package.rpm
```

Don't forget to replace tripwire_package.rpm with the RPM package appropriate for your system architecture. Once you have installed Tripwire, you can run rpm -ql tripwire_package.rpm to find out where the files are installed. The default installation directory is /usr/local/bin/tw for Tripwire version 1.3.

I noticed that the RPM package containing the binary distribution of Tripwire did not contain any man pages. However, I found the man pages in the source distribution. So you should install the source RPM distribution of Tripwire, which is also included in the Application CD shipped with Red Hat. Once you install the source distribution using rpm, you can extract the source in the /usr/src/redhat/ SOURCES directory to an appropriate location to access the man pages. If you would like to install the man pages follow these steps:

1. Extract the source distribution tar file in a directory and change directories to the man subdirectory.

2. Edit the Makefile in the man directory and add MANDIR = /usr/man in a line after the comment lines at the top.

3. Run make to install the man pages into appropriate man page locations in your system.

   Once you have completed these steps, you have access to the siggen (8), tripwire (8), and tw.config (5) man pages, which you should read before continuing with Tripwire any further.

Now let's look at how you can configure Tripwire for your system.

CREATING A TRIPWIRE DATABASE   The very first task you need to do to get Tripwire working is to create a database of signatures for all the files and directories you want it to compare against. To do that, you must specify the files and directory names in a configuration file called tw.config, which is also stored in the /usr/local/bin/tw directory. Listing 18-6 shows the tw.config file. The RPM package version of the configuration file is custom-suited for Linux systems. You should modify it after you have read the tw.config man pages and understand the syntax used. Listing 18-6 shows the tw.config I use on a Red Hat Web server system.

Listing 18-6: An example tw.config file

```
# $Id: tw.conf.linux,v 1.1 1994/04/04 00:34:03 gkim Exp $
#
# last updated: 1998/04/17 genek
#
# tripwire.config for linux machines

#  First, root's "home"
/root                   R
/                       R

# critical boot resources
/boot                   R
```

```
# Critical directories and files
#              some exceptions are noted further down
/etc                    R
/etc/xinetd.conf        R
/etc/rc.d               R
/etc/exports            R
/etc/mtab               L
/etc/motd               L
/etc/group              R        # changes should be infrequent
/etc/passwd             L

# other popular filesystems
/usr                    R
/usr/local              R
/dev                    L-am
/usr/etc                R

# truncate home
=/home                  R

# var tree
=/var/spool             L
/var/log                L
/var/spool/cron         L
/var/spool/mqueue       L
/var/spool/mail         L
!/var/lock
!/var/tripwire

# GENE:  /sbin contains binaries critical when in single user mode
/sbin                   R

# other critical directories
/usr/etc                R

# unusual directories
=/proc                  E
=/tmp
```

Because the syntax of such a configuration file is well documented in the tw.config manual page, I do not discuss the file syntax here.

Before you go ahead and create the database file, make sure you are absolutely certain that the files on your current system have not already been modified by bad guys. This is why the best time for creating this database is when your new system has not yet been connected to the Internet or any other network. Once you are certain that your files are untouched, change directory to /usr/local/bin/tw and run Tripwire as follows:

```
./tripwire -initialize
```

Once you have created the database, quickly move it to a read-only medium such as a CD-ROM if possible. You can also print out the entire database content so that you can verify information manually if need be. Once you have created the database, you need to protect Tripwire files too.

PROTECTING TRIPWIRE ITSELF

Bad guys can modify the Tripwire binary (tripwire) or the configuration file (tw.config) to hide traces of their work. For this reason, you can run the siggen utility to create a set of signatures for these files. To generate a signature for the tripwire binary, you can run the following command from the /usr/local/bin/tw directory:

```
./siggen tripwire
```

You see something like the following on the screen:

```
sig0: nullsig : 0
sig1: md5      : Of17oytjSfosJBXXCBZxuo
sig2: snefru   : 2UOlnsPiKYtb5K2DJ0Z06G
sig3: crc32    : 08arMS
sig4: crc16    : 000DFd
sig5: md4      : 2DDym8m3JGRry.Y5WuPzX4
sig6: md2      : 3N7KPOm:A5ynvixPGLCW.O
sig7: sha      : 4AZqq5nq16DM7D6pbaRtMk49wGX
sig8: haval    : O7QMyy6T4EERZw1pMyzZkw
sig9: nullsig  : 0
```

You can keep the signature in a file by redirecting it to that file. You should print out the signature as well. Do not forget to generate a signature for the siggen utility itself also. If you ever get suspicious about Tripwire not working right, run the siggen utility on each of these files and compare the signatures. If any of them do not match, you should not trust these files but replace them with fresh new copies and launch an investigation of how the discrepancy happened.

RUNNING TRIPWIRE TO DETECT INTEGRITY PROBLEMS

You can run Tripwire in two ways:

◆ In the interactive mode, whenever Tripwire encounters a file or directory that has been added, deleted, or changed, you are asked whether to update the database or not.

◆ You can also run Tripwire as a cron job by creating a small script such the one shown in Listing 18-7.

Listing 18-7: The tripwire.sh file

```
#!/bin/sh
/usr/local/bin/tw/tripwire -q | /bin/mail -s "Security report by
Tripwire" your@email
```

The -q allows tripwire to run quietly and send a report via mail to *your@email* address. You can just put a script like this in your /etc/cron.daily directory to run it on a daily basis. Any changes to your files are reported to you every day.

UPDATING THE TRIPWIRE DATABASE   To update the entire Tripwire database, you can run:

```
./tripwire -update
```

or if you want to add a new directory and all the files and subdirectories underneath it, you can run:

```
./tripwire -update  /some/dir
```

This same command works when updating an existing, modified directory or its files. If you just want to add or update a single file, you can use the following syntax:

```
./tripwire -update   newfile
```

WEIGHING SPEED AGAINST A HIGHER LEVEL OF SECURITY   Tripwire employs multiple signature algorithms such as the null signature, Message Digesting Algorithm (MD5) from RSA Data Security, Inc., a Secure Hash Function called Snefru from Xerox, a Cyclic Redundancy Check (CRC-32), CRC-16, MD4, MD2, a Secure Hash Algorithm (SHA), and Haval.

Performing all of these algorithms on each file on a large file system takes a great deal of CPU resources and a long time. To reduce load on the system or to speed up the checking process, you can tell Tripwire to ignore one or more of these algorithms. For example:

```
./tripwire -i  1
```

Here Tripwire is being told to ignore the first algorithm, MD5. You can use the -i command line option to ignore any algorithm as long as you know the corresponding number of the algorithm. The number-to-algorithm map is shown in Table 18-9.

TABLE 18-9 TRIPWIRE ALGORITHMS

-i Option	Signature Algorithm
-i 0	Null signature
-i 1	MD5
-i 2	Snefru
-i 3	CRC-32
-i 4	CRC-16
-i 5	MD4
-i 6	MD2
-i 7	SHA
-i 8	Haval
-i 9	Null signature (reserved for future)

To locate new or missing files without any signature integrity checking, run:

```
./tripwire -i all
```

Playing Devil's Advocate

So far I have talked about various methods that you can use to enhance the security of your system. Most of these methods can be considered good, preventive measures against attacks. Many experienced administrators feel that just taking such measures and hoping that nothing bad will ever happen is purely wishful thinking. In order to get a real sense of security, they feel that a system should be put to real tests. In other words, why not attack your security infrastructure yourself before the bad guy does it? By posing as a potential attacker, you may be able to reveal vulnerabilities yourself before the unfriendly ones find them out. Luckily, you do not have to work too hard to become a "bad guy" these days. There are tools that can help you assume the role of a bad guy quite easily. In this section, I discuss some commonly used tools.

Cracking your own passwords

Weak passwords are typically an easy target for attackers of all ages. Once the bad guy has managed to acquire your /etc/passwd file (if you are not yet using shadow passwords), it is fed to the password-cracking programs to reveal your secrets, the weak passwords. So you can imagine how cool it would be to be able to crack your own passwords before they do. Let's get a simplified understanding of how password-cracking software works.

HOW PASSWORDS ARE CRACKED

The best way to understand the details of this cryptography would be to use an example. If you create a new user on your system with a username called bob and umbrella as his password, you see a line in the /etc/passwd file that looks something like the following line:

```
bob:XoAlxlaiwepBs:Red Hat Linux User:/home/bob:/bin/bash
```

The line may not look quite the same, but the point is that you have a line with bob's encrypted password. The encrypted password is a 13-character-long string that was created by a function called crypt() as follows:

```
Encrypted Password (XoAlxlaiwepBs) = crypt('umbrella', salt)
```

The *salt* is a two-character string chosen from a set of [a–zA–Z0–9./]. This string is used to influence the encryption algorithm in one of 4,096 different ways. The *salt* value is stored in the encrypted password as the first two characters. For example, if XoAlxlaiwepBs is the encrypted password for umbrella, the *salt* value used is "Xo." There is no known way of retrieving the original password from the encrypted version, because the encryption algorithm used is one-way only. However, if the encrypted password is known, then a program can be written to use the two-character *salt* value and encrypt a large dictionary of words with this *salt*. Now if the password happens to be a word in the dictionary, as it is in our example case, it is *salt*ed and a match is found. In other words, when you know that the *salt* value for bob's password is "Xo," you can use this *salt* to write a program to do the following:

```
Encrypted Password = crypt(each dictionary_word, Xo)
```

Now when this program chooses the "umbrella" word, the encrypted password is same as the one stored in /etc/passwd. Too bad, bob's password has just been cracked! Now the program knows which word (umbrella) was used to create the password. This is the simplified explanation of how cracking software works. However, bear in mind that today's cracking software is much more advanced, and as computer hardware becomes more and more powerful, cracking passwords becomes easier and faster.

Now, let's look at how you can crack your own passwords before the bad guys get the chance to crack them.

INSTALLING CRACK

In order to crack your system's passwords, you need a password-cracking program. Crack is one such widely used, free software package. You can download an RPM package version of Crack from many of the Red Hat mirror sites that keep user-contributed software. One such site is `http://ftp.digital.com/pub/linux/ redhat/contrib/`.

You have to go into the directory corresponding to your system's architecture, such as i386 (*x*86 or Intel), sparc (Sun Microsystems), alpha (Digital Alpha), etc., and download the crack-*X.xx-x.*(*architecture*).rpm, where *X.xx-x* is a version number and (*architecture*) is your system's architecture. For example, for an x86 or Intel-based system, you would download crack-4.1f-1.i386.rpm. The version number may vary, as newer versions are uploaded over time.

Once you have uploaded the RPM package, install it as follows:

```
rpm -ivh crack_package_name.rpm
```

Once you have installed the package, you can find out which files were installed by running the following command:

```
rpm -qi crack_package_name
```

Typically, Crack gets installed in /root/Crack-*X.xx*/ directory.

RUNNING CRACK

Once it is installed on your system, you can run the Crack program from the installed directory as follows:

```
Crack /etc/passwd
```

If you use shadow passwords and want to run Crack, you need to use a support script called shadmrg (found in the Scripts directory) to merge the /etc/passwd and /etc/shadow files. The merged output is typically sent to STDOUT, so you have to point it to a file, which you can then use with Crack as the input password file.

Crack starts cracking your passwords. If you have a lot of user accounts in your password file, it might take a long time for Crack to complete the job. That's why Crack automatically runs in the background. You can also specify a few command line options to Crack to control some of its behavior. Just run Crack without any arguments to see a list of command line options.

GETTING CRACK'S OUTPUT

Once you run Crack, it creates output in two files: out.PID and out.(hostname)PID. For example, the output files could be out.5678 and out.picaso.nitec.com5699, where `picaso.nitec.com` is the name of the host running Crack. Listing 18-8 shows an example of a Crack output file.

Listing 18-8: Example Crack output

```
join: User apache (in /etc/passwd) has a locked password:- !!
join: User uucp (in /etc/passwd) has a locked password:- *
join: User operator (in /etc/passwd) has a locked password:- *
join: User ftp (in /etc/passwd) has a locked password:- *
join: User bin (in /etc/passwd) has a locked password:- *
join: User daemon (in /etc/passwd) has a locked password:- *
join: User adm (in /etc/passwd) has a locked password:- *
join: User lp (in /etc/passwd) has a locked password:- *
join: User sync (in /etc/passwd) has a locked password:- *
join: User shutdown (in /etc/passwd) has a locked password:- *
join: User halt (in /etc/passwd) has a locked password:- *
join: User mail (in /etc/passwd) has a locked password:- *
join: User nobody (in /etc/passwd) has a locked password:- *
join: User news (in /etc/passwd) has a locked password:- *
join: Guessed pikeb (/bin/tics in /etc/passwd) [book] NssDRm.TU/EFc
```

I removed the date stamp field that appears right after "Join:" to reduce line width. When Crack reports that a password is locked, it means that the password is set to "*," or in other words, the user account cannot be used to log in. The last line is the most interesting one. It says that Crack has guessed the password (book) for user pikeb!

Once you know which user passwords are crackable, you should lock out the account right away using an "*" as the password and contact the user personally to discuss security. If that's not possible, notify the user to change the password immediately. If the user does not change the password in a given time frame, you should definitely lock out the account and advise your superiors on the matter.

As you already know from our ongoing discussion, passwords are not the only weak points in a system. To find many other potential security holes, you need COPS. In the following section, I discuss this security tool.

Having COPS around

COPS is a set of tools that attempts to locate potential security holes in a system. Among other things, these tools focus on detecting potential security problems that can surface from file/directory/device permissions, passwords, init files in the /etc/rc.d directory, cron configuration, and anonymous FTP setup. Basically, the purpose of COPS is to detect potential security problems and warn you about them. It does not fix any of the problems it detects.

INSTALLING COPS

I have not yet seen an RPM-packaged version of COPS. So to download a general COPS distribution, you have to go to the following FTP site: `ftp://ftp.cert.org/pub/tools/cops/`.

Download the latest COPS distribution and uncompress and extract the files to an appropriate directory on your system.

The COPS distribution includes two versions of the same software. One version is written primarily in C, and the other is primarily in Perl. You can run a version as long as you have either Perl or a C compiler, either of which is practically standard in Red Hat Linux. Here I show you how to use the C version. If you are interested in running the Perl version of the software, read the bundled README files for Perl version. You also find the Perl version of the software in a perl subdirectory of your installation directory.

To configure the C version of COPS, first run the following script from the installation directory:

```
./reconfig
```

This command adjusts a few paths for binaries such as awk in some scripts to match your system. Now you have to modify the makefile in the docs directory to remove the -ms from the ROFFLAGS = -ms line. You do not need to do this if you have installed the -ms package for nroff. Then run:

```
./make all
```

from the installation directory. Now edit the COPS shell script and modify the following lines:

```
SECURE=/usr/foobar
SECURE_USERS="foo@bar.edu"
```

You should change the first line so that the directory is the fully qualified directory name of your installation path. For example, if you have installed COPS in the /usr/local/security/cops directory, then set SECURE to that directory. The second line should be set to your e-mail address where the COPS output will be sent. If you do not want to receive the report in e-mail format, you can modify MMAIL=NO or change the line to be MMAIL=YES to receive the report via e-mail. If you decide not to receive e-mailed reports, you can find the report files in the $SECURE/(short hostname) directory. For example, if your system's hostname is `picaso.nitec.com`, and SECURE is set to /usr/local/security/cops, the report file is stored in the /usr/local/security/cops/picaso/ directory. The report filename is created using the year_month_day format (for instance, 1999_Feb_25). If you plan on using the Crack program as your password-cracking software, you can comment out the line (by inserting a "#" character in front of the line) that starts with "$SECURE/pass.chk," and finally, if you run an anonymous FTP site, you can modify the line that starts with "$SECURE/ftp.chk" to read "$SECURE/ftp.chk –a."

Now you are ready to run COPS.

RUNNING COPS

Running COPS is quite simple; you can run it from the installation directory as follows:

```
./cops
```

Listing 18-9 shows an example COPS report.

Listing 18-9: An example COPS report

```
ATTENTION:
Security Report for Thu Jan 29 10:35:44 PST 1998
from host picaso.nitec.com

Warning!  /dev/fd0 is _World_ readable!
Warning!  /etc/security is _World_ readable!
Warning!  /etc/crontab is _World_ readable!

ATTENTION:
CRC Security Report for Thu Jan 29 10:34:39 PST 1998
from host picaso.nitec.com

replaced -rw-r-r—root    root    Jan 28 23:22:01 1998 /etc/passwd
removed  -r————root      root    Dec 20 13:31:36 1998 /etc/shadow
```

As mentioned before, COPS just finds the problems; it is up to you to investigate and fix them. You should run COPS on a regular basis by setting it up as a cron job so that you get regular reports on potential problems before they are exploited by the bad guys.

Back Up and Backtrack Everything

The most important security advice anyone can give you is to regularly back up all your files. Create a maintainable backup schedule for your system. For example, you can perform incremental backups on weekdays and schedule a full backup over the weekend. I also prefer removable media-based backup equipment such as 8 mm tape drives or DAT drives. Having a removable backup medium enables you to take the backup away from the location and store it in a secure offsite location. Periodically check that your backup mechanism is functioning as expected. Make sure you're able to restore files from randomly selected backup media. You may recycle backup media, but make sure you know the usage limits that the media manufacturer claims. There's more to protecting your system than keeping bad guys out. You want to protect your data from other sorts of disasters as well, and good, periodic backup gives you that protection.

Another type of "backup" you should get used to doing is backtracking your work as a system administrator. Document everything you do, especially work that you do as a superuser. This documentation enables you to trace problems that often arise while you solve another. One of the security precautions I like to take when carrying out system administrator work is keep a large history setting (a shell feature that remembers *N* number last commands), and I often print out the history in a file or on paper. You can also use the `script` command to record everything you do while using privileged accounts.

Get the Latest Security News

Being informed about the security problems are out there in the world helps you keep a step ahead of the bad guys who might want to attack your systems. As soon as you know about a security issue that might affect your system, take immediate action before it is too late. You should subscribe to reputable security alert resources available on the Internet. Here are two.

CERT

Computer Emergency Response Team (CERT) regularly issues advisories on computer security matters. You should subscribe to their mailing list as soon as possible. Visit their Web site at `http://www.cert.org/` for details.

BUGTRAQ

BUGTRAQ is another mailing list that you can subscribe to access daily reports on security issues. Visit their Web site at http://www.securityfocus.com/ for details.

Summary

In this chapter, you have been introduced to the basics of host-level security issues and how to take preventive measures against them. I discussed how you can protect a system by employing various techniques to restrict user access and improving authentication mechanisms using shadow passwords, pluggable authentication modules, and so on. You learned to configure the xinetd-run services using the TCP wrapper to ensure greater control over who accesses network services. I discussed how to locate potential security holes using tools such as COPS and Crack so that you can take care of the problem before anything bad happens. You also learned to protect your files and file systems using native file system features of the ext2 file system and third-party tools such as Tripwire. You learned about how Tripwire, a file integrity checker, can be used to monitor changes in your files on a regular basis. Overall, the theme of this chapter was to get you thinking about host security.

Chapter 19

Network Security

IN THIS CHAPTER

- ◆ How to design a secure network using non-routable IP addresses

- ◆ How to masquerade IP addresses

- ◆ How to use a packet filtering firewall

- ◆ How to use a proxy server to enhance network security

- ◆ How to use SATAN to monitor security of a network

WHENEVER YOU CONNECT A NETWORK to a WAN or to the outside world via the Internet, you need to consider not only the security of each computer but also the security of your entire network. However, by having a method to your network planning, you can limit the damage caused by an attack or a mishap. In this chapter, I examine the different types of firewalls and how they can be used to better insulate your trusted computers from the distrusted outside world. I also talk about how you can monitor your network to see who is using your network and in what ways.

Understanding the Security Problem

When people start thinking of network security, they most commonly think of the outside hacker. Network security is about a whole array of possible problems — some coming from malicious intruders, some from unwitting employees, and some from system misconfiguration. You need to be aware of all the possible risks before taking on the job of network security administrator.

Ethernet sniffing

A hacker or a malicious insider who has access to a computer on your network can easily pick up information about the other machines and users on your network. Ethernet is a broadcast protocol. That means every computer on the network has access to every packet sent. In normal situations all of the hosts on the network are expected to be good neighbors to each other. This means they pay attention only to packets sent to them and ignore all other traffic. Hackers have tools called Ethernet sniffers that watch traffic not going to the local computer. They can set up camp on a machine on your network and watch as information goes flying by. If someone uses FTP to upload a file to a computer on the network, the sniffer can record the username and password they used as well as reconstruct the entire file.

How can you protect against sniffing? You really can't. A few brands of Ethernet interface cards do not have the "promiscuous mode" needed for a sniffer to work, but who's to say a hacker won't bring his own computer in. Another way of slowing the progress of the hacker is to use switching hubs. Switching hubs watch the traffic as it goes by and build a table of network addresses. They learn which network addresses can be reached through a certain port on the hub. The switching hub then directs network specific traffic to the appropriate port of a hub. If each computer has a port on the switching hub, you should be able to cut off the sniffer from getting any information. Recently new tools have been developed that allow a hacker to fool a switching hub into sending the data to a sniffing computer. One such tool is called Hunt. Hunt is a powerful tool that allows sniffing, hijacking, and resetting active TCP connections. If you think you've solved all possible sniffing problems by implementing a switching hub, you should check out Hunt. Hunt was written by Pavel Krauz and can be downloaded from `http://www.cri.cz/kra/index.html`.

IP spoofing

Services such as rlogin, rexec, and rcp rely on DNS for authentication. These services (known as the R services) operate with the idea of trusted hosts. If you have already logged in and authenticated on a trusted machine, you don't have to log in again. This is an incredibly bad idea dating back to a time when the Internet was a small network of generally trustworthy peers. Sad to say, that isn't the case anymore and you shouldn't use these services. Using these services can cause every host on your network to fall prey to hackers as soon as they find a way into one machine.

Hackers use a trick called IP spoofing to make a computer think it is talking to a trusted host. By using the IP address of a trusted host, a hacker can walk right in the front door of your system. Usually the hacker performs a denial-of-service attack against the computer it will impersonate in order to keep it from speaking up during the confusion and revealing that the packets are not in fact coming from the IP address given. With the trusted host effectively offline, the hacker is free to impersonate the IP of the trusted host and start executing commands remotely.

The easiest way to guard against this attack is not to use any of the R services. These services are well known to be a security vulnerability, and secure replacements are available. Instead of running rlogin, you should use ssh, and rcp can be replaced with scp. Another guard against this attack is to use a firewall to disallow any packet from the outside world that says it is coming from one of your IP addresses. This doesn't prevent an internal attack, but the majority of security breeches are from outside, and not inside, your local network.

A bad guy can carry out a number of attacks that do nothing except cause the attacked computer to crash or overload. Sometimes this is used as part of an attack on another system, but most often the bad guy does it simply to cause the machine to stop performing. The bad guy can send packets to your machine directly or can congest your gateway, effectively removing you from the network. Because each packet in itself is valid, there is no way of protecting yourself from an attack of this kind.

Designing a Secure Network

As a network grows it becomes harder to implement security as an afterthought. Users grow accustomed to patterns of usage, poor choices become accepted handicaps, and the administrator must play political games to make changes. These are some of the reasons you must examine network security as a whole as you plan network topology.

Using nonroutable IP addresses

The simplest way of maintaining security on a network is by ensuring that hosts on your network cannot contact, nor be contacted by, the outside world. The easiest way to achieve this would be to never connect them to a public network like the Internet. This security through isolation is not always acceptable. In many situations, complete isolation is not an acceptable restraint. An easy way of allowing your users to reach the Internet while preventing the bad guys from getting to the user machines is by the use of nonroutable IP addresses.

RFC 1918 specifies blocks of IP addresses that may be used within a local TCP/IP network but that cannot traverse Internet routers. These groups of IP addresses are commonly called LAN IP addresses or private IPs. Because these IP addresses do not route across the Internet, you do not need to register to use them. By assigning an IP address from within this range, you effectively limit traffic to and from the computer to the local network. This is a quick and effective way of denying outside access to computers while allowing traffic to flow between your internal computers.

The blocks of nonroutable IP addresses are:

```
10.0.0.0    -  10.255.255.255
172.16.0.0  -  172.31.255.255
192.168.0.0 - 192.168.255.255
```

Now remember that traffic coming from a nonroutable IP is not able to traverse Internet routers. This means any computer assigned a nonroutable IP will be unreachable by computers outside your network, but this approach will also have the effect of not allowing your users to talk to the outside world. IP masquerading is the solution for this.

Masquerading IP addresses

By placing an IP masquerading enabled Red Hat server between your users and the outside world, you can avoid the side effects caused by using nonroutable IPs. As a packet leaves a user computer, it has the "source address" of its own IP. As the packet travels through the Red Hat server toward the outside world, it is transformed. The source address of the packet is changed to the address of the Red Hat server, which is a fully routable IP address. The Red Hat server also makes a note of which source address contacted which destination on the Internet. Now when the packet is sent to the Internet, it is fully capable of reaching its destination and getting a response.

There is one catch. Because the source address of the packet is set to the IP of the Red Hat server and not the user machine behind the server, the response from the foreign computer is sent to the Red Hat server. The Red Hat server then has to search a table to see which machine this packet belongs to. Then, it can set the source address of the packet to the address of the nonroutable user computer and voilà, a round trip across the Internet is made from a machine with a nonroutable IP address. IP masquerading is also known as Network Address Translation (NAT).

Now you are probably wondering what this has to do with network security. From the user standpoint, the user has an Internet connection that appears to be fully routable. The security comes from the table the Red Hat server keeps of which user computers are talking to which foreign Internet sites. If some bad guy wants to gain access to one of your user computers, he can't. The only IP address ever seen by the outside world is the address of the Red Hat server, and not all the addresses behind it. Even if the bad guy sent a packet to the Red Hat server, it would have no way of knowing which user machine to forward it to.

By default, the Red Hat Linux kernel has IP masquerading support built in. However, if you have removed such support earlier or are using a kernel that does not have IP masquerading built in, you need to recompile the kernel, load a few modules, and set a packet filtering rule to allow the address translation to occur. If you are not familiar with how to compile a custom kernel, please read Chapter 20. In order for IP masquerading to work, you need to enable IP forwarding service on the server. You can enable IP forwarding (for the default kernel shipped by Red Hat) by setting FORWARD_IPV4 to `yes` in the /etc/sysconfig/network file and restarting the network using the `/etc/rc.d/init.d/network restart` command. Here I assume that you are using a kernel with the IP masquerading and forwarding support built in and you have also installed the ipchains package on the Red Hat server.

To connect your internal network to the outside world, you need two network interfaces on the IP masquerading server. Use one interface to connect to the internal network, and the other one for connecting the server (and the internal network via IP masquerading) to the outside world. Because such a server has multiple interfaces, it is often called a multihomed server. You can assign a nonroutable IP address to the network card connected to the internal network. For example:

```
/sbin/ifconfig eth1 inet 192.168.1.1 netmask 255.255.255.0
```

This command line assumes your network interface for the internal network is eth1 and you run fewer than 253 user computers within your network. If you are in a situation where you have more than 253 user computers, you may use a netmask of 255.255.0.0, which allows more than 65,000 user computers behind one Red Hat IP masquerade computer. I suggest sticking with the line just given. If you exceed 253 user computers, it would be wise to set up a second IP masquerade computer and divide your network into two pieces.

By configuring your user computers with IP addresses starting at 192.168.1.2 and ending at 192.168.1.254, and by assigning them all a gateway of 192.168.1.1 and a subnet mask of 255.255.255.0, you should now be able to ping the gateway (192.168.1.1) from each user computer.

At this point you have a situation where all of the user machines can talk to each other and the Red Hat server. You still cannot reach the outside world from a client machine until you define a filter rule on the Red Hat server. Once you enter the following commands, you should be able to browse and communicate from a user machine as if you were directly connected to the Internet:

```
/sbin/ipchains -A forward -j MASQ -s 192.168.0.0/24 -d 0.0.0.0/0
/sbin/ipchains -P forward DENY
```

The first command enables IP masquerading service for all IP packets having a destination other than the 192.168.0.0 network. It forwards masqueraded IP packets originating from the 192.168.0.0 network to the default route to the network attached to the other network interface. The second command sets the default forwarding policy to be deny for all packets not originating from the internal network. You want to put these commands into /etc/rc.d/rc.local so that the IP masquerading begins when you boot the Red Hat server.

What Is a Firewall?

Sometimes you don't want the all-or-nothing approach you achieve by using non-routable IP addresses. You may want to give the general public access to browse Web sites on your Web server, but no other type of access. You may have a policy restriction that limits employee use of the Internet to e-mail only. Both of these are examples of situations perfect for a firewall.

A firewall is a computer intended to enforce your policies about the type of traffic allowed to pass from the public network to the private network. Most often a firewall is placed between a private intranet and the Internet to allow traffic that meets certain criteria while denying the rest. Firewalls can be very open, allowing nearly all traffic through, or they can be very restrictive, permitting very limited use. The firewall administrator controls all of this through configuration of rule sets.

It is a wise idea to dedicate a computer solely to the task of being the firewall. If you are relying on your firewall to control access to your internal network, then you need to make sure your firewall is as secure as possible. This machine serves not only as a security checkpoint but also as a gateway from a secured network to the rest of the world. The bad guys know that if they can control your firewall, they can gain access to your internal network. Because of this, you need to shut the windows and lock the doors. Some guidelines for basic firewall security are:

♦ Turn off any unneeded services. There is a good description in the previous chapter on how to disable services in inetd or xinetd. To go one step further, I suggest it's a good idea to disable sendmail, finger, netstat, systat, bootp, and FTP.

♦ Limit the number of people who have shell access to the firewall. If there are only one or two user accounts, the bad guy has to get very lucky to find them.

♦ Don't use the same password on the firewall as you do elsewhere. Sometimes people fall into the trap of using the same password for many different computers. Don't do that here! Otherwise your network may topple like a line of dominos.

♦ Physical security is a huge consideration. While you may find it acceptable to have your desktop machine sitting in an open office or cubicle, you should keep tighter tabs on the physical access people have to your firewall.

Firewalls come in all varieties. Some are software applications, while others are sold as hardware. Many cost in the tens of thousands of dollars, while others are free. Firewalls can usually be classified in one of two categories: packet filter or application level.

Packet filters

Packet filters do nothing more than take each packet, test it against a set of rules, and either allow the packet to reach the other network or deny it the possibility. Packet filters are fast, simple, and effective ways of deciding which traffic passes and which does not. Packet filters exist at the network level and do not concern themselves with the data contained within the packets.

Typically a packet filter has the capability to examine the source IP address, destination IP address, source port number, destination port number, and protocol type. It can also distinguish between the separate network interfaces on your computer. This way, someone forging one of your IP addresses from the outside world can be blocked. Table 19-1 shows the strengths and weaknesses of packet filters.

TABLE 19-1 STRENGTHS AND WEAKNESSES OF PACKET FILTERS

Strengths	Weaknesses
Speed	Inability to log application data
Ease of administration	Inability to control access to specific applications
Ability to count and log packets meeting specific criteria	
Transparency to users	

Because packet filters look at each packet individually, they don't see the "whole picture." For example, packet filters are unable to see which Web page you are looking at or make sure someone is not mailing all the company secrets to the competitors.

Using a basic packet-filtering firewall: ipchains

Red Hat Linux comes with a package called ipchains that enables you to create a packet-filtering firewall.

 Those of you who have used ipfwadm for creating packet filtering firewalls on pre-6.0 Red Hat Linux systems will find that ipfwadm is no longer supported because ipchains is an improved replacement for it.

Take a look at a real-world example of using ipchains to control access to an internal network. Assume that your network provider has given you the IP addresses 206.170.189.1 through 206.170.189.254. You have configured a multi-homed Red Hat Linux server to be the firewall and have included two Ethernet interface cards, eth0 and eth1. You have given the outside Ethernet interface, eth0, the IP address of 206.170.189.1 and the inside Ethernet interface, eth1, the address of 206.170.189.2. Each of the computers in your internal network has been assigned an IP address starting at 20.170.189.3 and continuing up through the remaining 252 addresses. Each of the internal computers has its gateway set to the firewall computer with IP address 206.170.189.2.

First, you want to set a default filtering policy that denies all traffic to and from the firewall system. This becomes the last rule in your set and is the natural way to enforce the security policy "All traffic not specifically allowed by the firewall is denied." You do this by issuing the following three commands:

```
/sbin/ipchains -P input DENY
/sbin/ipchains -P output DENY
/sbin/ipchains -P forward DENY
```

In order, this says that your default policy for incoming packets, outgoing packets, and packet forwarding is to deny anything that is not allowed by an ipchains filter rule.

 Always administer your filter rules from the console of the firewall and not remotely. It becomes very easy to lock yourself out by using a deny rule that also excludes you. These rules become active the moment you press the Enter key. Also, if you flush your ipchains filter rules (using the -F command), you may find that the only rule still existing denies all traffic to or from your firewall. This situation has made for a few middle-of-the-night drives to the office for me. Be careful.

```
/sbin/ipchains -A input -j DENY -i eth0 -s 206.170.189.0/24
```

This rule denies any packets that claim to be from your internal network but have been sent by a computer outside your firewall. In a normal situation this should never happen, but bad guys have been known to place fake headers on packets in order to circumvent firewalls. This method of getting around the firewall is known as packet spoofing.

```
/sbin/ipchains -A input -j ACCEPT -i eth1
/sbin/ipchains -A output -j ACCEPT -i eth1
```

These two rules allow all traffic between the local network and the firewall, enabling any of your machines to talk to one other. They shouldn't have to bounce off the firewall, but it doesn't hurt to add the rules.

```
/sbin/ipchains -A input -j DENY -p icmp
```

This rule may cause some controversy among your users. By setting this rule, you deny all packets that are using the ICMP protocol. This is the protocol used by programs like ping and traceroute. By denying this traffic, you can limit a popular denial-of-service attack called a ping flood in which a bad guy uses the ping program to send packets of an obscenely large size. A ping flood attack does not destroy any data but can be used to consume all of your bandwidth with the ping packets, thus giving no room for legitimate traffic. By disallowing ICMP traffic, you are also restricting your local network from using tools such as ping or traceroute to check the status of machines beyond the firewall. It is a tradeoff you have to contemplate.

```
/sbin/ipchains -A input -j ACCEPT -p tcp -d 206.170.189.3 smtp
```

Here you allow all traffic using the TCP protocol with a destination of 206.170.189.3 to travel to the SMTP port. In this example, 206.170.189.3 is your mail server and you allow any mail from the outside world to the mail server. You can also use the lines

```
/sbin/ipchains -A input -j ACCEPT -p tcp -d 206.170.189.5 www
/sbin/ipchains -A input -j ACCEPT -p tcp -d 206.170.189.9 domain
```

to allow access to your Web server (206.170.189.5) and your DNS server (206. 170.189.6). You can continue this process ad infinitum for any number of hosts and services.

Using an application-level firewall

Situations arise in which you need the ability to control your network at the application level rather than at the network level. You may need to restrict your users from sending e-mail to certain addresses, monitor the Web sites your users are hitting, or get a good idea of the average size of files users are sending through the firewall. When you want this type of information and control, you require an application-level firewall.

Application firewalls work in a manner different from that of packet filters. Application-level firewalls, sometimes called application proxies or proxy servers, work without a direct connection between the local and remote computers. Application firewalls permit no traffic to pass from the inside to the outside. Instead, the local computer queries the firewall for the information it wants. The firewall then examines the request, makes the connection to the outside world, retrieves the information, and passes the information back to the client. As far as the outside world knows, all of the requests for information are coming from the application firewall. With an application proxy you need not worry about unwanted traffic getting into your network. It can't.

Because application firewalls are specific to the protocol they are passing, a separate application firewall is needed for each protocol. You need separate application proxies for FTP, Telnet, or Web traffic. If you don't want your users to have the ability to view Web pages, you can just omit the Web proxy program from your suite of firewall programs. Not only do you get the ability to make rules based on which local IP addresses can see which external IP addresses, but you can make rules based on the protocol with which they're communicating.

Using the Squid Proxy Server

Many different application proxies are available. The most common proxy is for HTTP. By using a proxy for Web traffic, you gain twofold: you get control over which Web sites your clients can see, and you also gain by passive caching. In a normal office environment it is common for two or more people to view the same Web site within a small period of time. Because all Web requests are being funneled through the Web proxy, the proxy can save each Web page or picture as it travels through. Then if someone comes along asking for the same page, the proxy server can give her the local copy instead of going out across the Internet to find it again. This saves bandwidth on your link to the outside world. Some estimates say that in a moderate-sized network (over 75 active users) you can save up to 60 percent of your Web traffic bandwidth. In a large network that could be a significant amount.

Squid is a proxy server that implements caching for the HTTP, FTP, and Gopher protocols. Squid uses access control lists to allow or deny access to locations. Because Squid is so configurable and robust, it takes some time to tailor it to your use, but you may find that it is easy to learn. Best of all, Squid can be configured in a way that your users never even know it is there.

Getting and installing Squid

As of this writing Squid 2.1 is available only as a tar.gz file and not as an RPM. You can obtain the most current version from the FTP site at `ftp://squid.nlanr.net/pub`. Hopefully, by the time this is published there will be a contributed RPM. You can periodically check the contrib subdirectory of the Web site for an RPM version of the software.

I assume that your proxy server has two network interfaces — one to the outside world and one to the internal network. I also assume that you have turned off IP forwarding.

You can make Squid function on only one network interface, but I don't recommend it. This configuration doubles up traffic on your local network and can cause congestion. With the low price of network interface cards and hubs it is well worth the investment even for a relatively small network.

If you plan on using Squid to maintain a cache, you need to consider your hard drive and memory limitations. The nature of a Web cache is to have thousands of small files that you need to serve out to clients both simultaneously and efficiently. The Squid authors recommend at least a 300 MHZ Pentium II CPU, 512MB RAM, and five ultra-wide SCSI disks of 9GB each. I have heard of an entire Internet provider using nothing more than a few 486/66 processors with IDE drives. I suspect most people would be comfortable with something between these two extremes. I recommend using at least a 100 MHZ Pentium CPU, 64MB RAM, and 6GB of SCSI disk. You may find you can get away with using slightly less.

Once you have the tar.gz file, unpack it by using the command:

```
gunzip -c squid-2.1.RELEASE-src.tar.gz |tar -xv
```

This command unpacks the tar file into a directory called squid-2.1.RELEASE. Once inside that directory you run ./configure to check the capabilities of your computer and create the configuration files. When this finishes, type `make` to begin compiling Squid into a usable product. If this finishes without error, type `make install` to put the binary files into place.

Making Squid work for the first time

You need to create the swap directories. You can do this by typing

```
/usr/bin/squid -z
```

Squid can run "out of the box" with one exception. You need to change the configuration file /etc/squid/squid.conf before running it for the first time. The Access Control List for Squid defaults to denying all requests. You can change this by editing the file /etc/squid/squid.conf and adding the line:

```
acl local_net src 192.168.0.1/255.255.255.0
```

where 192.168.129.1 is an IP in your local network, and 255.255.255.0 is the netmask of your internal network. You also need to add the line:

```
http_access allow local_net
```

just before `http_access deny all`. This command defines the group of IP addresses allowed to use the cache.

Now you can type `squid &` to start Squid for the first time. You can verify it is working in a number of ways:

◆ Squid shows up in a ps –x listing.

◆ Running `client www.yahoo.com` dumps Web page text to your terminal.

◆ The files cache.log and store.log in the directory /var/log/squid show Squid to be working.

◆ Running `squid -k check && echo "Squid is running"` tells you Squid is active.

Now for the real test: If you configure the Web browser on a client machine to use the Squid proxy, you should see results. In Netscape Navigator 4.5 select Edit → Preferences and then select Proxies from within the Advanced category. By selecting Manual Proxy Configuration and then clicking View, you can specify the IP address of the Squid server as the http, FTP, and Gopher proxy server. The default proxy port is 3128, so unless you have changed it in the squid.conf file, place that number in the port field.

You should now be able to browse any Web site as if you had no proxy. You can double-check that Squid is working correctly by checking the log file /var/log/squid/access.log from the proxy server and making sure the Web site you were viewing is in there.

Tweaking Squid to fit your needs

Now that you have Squid up and running, you can customize it to fit your needs. At this point it is not restricting your users from accessing any sites. You can define rules in your squid.conf file to set access control lists and allow or deny visitors according to these lists.

```
acl BadWords url_regex foo bar
```

By adding the preceding line, you have defined an ACL rule called BadWords that matches any URL containing the words "foo" or "bar." This applies to http://foo.deepwell.com/pictures and http://www.thekennedycompound.com/ourbar.jpg because they both contain words that are members of BadWords.

By adding:

```
http_access deny BadWords
```

to squid.conf, you block your users from accessing any URLs that match this rule.

Almost every administrator using word-based ACLs has a story about not examining all the ways a word can be used. Realize that if you ban your users from accessing sites containing the word "sex," you are also banning them from accessing www.buildersexchange.com and any others that may fall into that category.

Because all aspects of how Squid functions are controlled within the squid.conf file, you can tune it to fit your needs.

By adding the line:

```
cache_mem   16 MB
```

you allow Squid to use 16MB of memory to hold Web pages in memory. By trial and error you may find you need a different amount.

The cache_mem is not the amount of memory Squid consumes; it only sets the maximum amount of memory Squid uses for holding Web pages, pictures, and so forth. The Squid documentation says you can expect Squid to consume up to three times this amount.

By using the line:

```
emulate_httpd_log on
```

you arrange that the files in /var/log/squid are written in a form similar to the Web server log files. This arrangement allows you to use a Web statistics program such as Analog or Webtrends to analyze your logs and examine the sites your users are viewing.

Some FTP servers require that an e-mail address be used when one is logging in anonymously. By setting ftp_user to a valid e-mail address, as shown here, you give the server at the other end of an FTP session the data it wants to see:

```
ftp_user squid@deepwell.com
```

You may want to use the address of your proxy firewall administrator. This would give the foreign FTP administrator someone to contact in case of a problem.

If you type in a URL and find that the page does not exist, chances are that page won't exist anytime in the near future. By setting negative_ttl to a desired number of minutes, as shown in the next example, you can control how long Squid remembers that a page was not found in a earlier attempt. This is called negative caching.

```
negative_ttl 2 minutes
```

This isn't always a good thing. The default is 5 minutes, but I suggest lessening this to 2 or possibly 1 minute, if not disabling it all together. Why would you do such a thing? You want your proxy to be as transparent as possible. If a user is looking for a page she knows exists, you don't want a short lag time between the URL coming into the world and your user's ability to access it.

```
cache_mgr proxy@deepwell.com
```

By setting this to your own e-mail address, you arrange to receive mail if Squid dies.

```
cache_effective_user nobody
cache_effective_group nobody
```

These two lines are very important! If you are starting Squid while you are root, these commands change the UID Squid runs as to user "nobody." Hopefully the result keeps any bugs in the program from changing or deleting anything they shouldn't.

Ultimately, a tool like Squid should be completely transparent to your users. This "invisibility" removes them from the complexity of administration and allows them to browse the Web as if there were no Web proxy server. Although I do not detail how to do that here, you may refer to the Squid Frequently Asked Questions at `http://squid.nlanr.net/Squid/FAQ/FAQ.html`. Section 17 of this site details using Squid as a transparent proxy.

Also, if you find yourself managing a large list of "blacklisted" sites in the squid.conf file, you should think of using a program called a redirector. Large lists of ACL rules can begin to slow a heavily used Squid proxy. By using a redirector to do this same job you can improve on Squid's efficiency of allowing or denying URLs based on filter rules. You can get more information on Squirm, a full-featured redirector made to work with Squid, from `http://www.senet.com.au/squirm/`.

The cachemgr.cgi file comes in the Squid RPM. It is a CGI program that enables you to view statistics of your proxy as well as shut down and restart Squid. It requires only a few minutes of your time to install, but it gives you explicit details about how your proxy is performing. If you'd like to tune your Web cache, this tool will help.

I have just touched upon the basics of using Squid as a Web proxy firewall. Squid has many features above and beyond what I have discussed here. If you are interested in making Squid function beyond the basics I have shown you, please visit the Squid Web page at `http://squid.nlanr.net/`.

Getting Help from SATAN

It always helps to be on the offensive with your network security. If you actively check the security of your computers on a regular basis, you will be aware of your weaknesses. Few things are as bad as walking in one morning to realize that an intruder has been in your system. SATAN is a tool to probe computers looking for possible weaknesses hackers could exploit to get into your system.

SATAN, the Security Administrator Tool for Analyzing Networks, gained a lot of media attention at the time of its release. Back in 1995 when the tool was released, system administrators went into a frenzy expecting hackers to use it as a lock pick, thereby automating their work. But hackers already had tools like this. Hackers had written and shared many tools for getting into other systems, searching for known weaknesses, and removing their trails. But the hackers weren't sharing. The good guys didn't have access to tools like this. Dan Farmer and Wietse Venema decided to write SATAN to even the odds. By releasing tools like this to the public, they gave access to security tools to everyone, so not only the bad guys had them. With widespread access like this, the administrators can discover the problems and patch the holes before someone else wanders in.

SATAN scans for known vulnerabilities, and when done it walks the user through HTML tutorials explaining how hackers exploit the problem and how to patch it. SATAN uses a Web browser as the user interface so anyone used to surfing the Web can operate it. Satan was designed to be used on a UNIX computer, but you can probe any operating system.

Quoting from the documentation, SATAN tests for the following:

- NFS file systems exported to arbitrary hosts

- NFS file systems exported to unprivileged programs

- NFS file systems exported via the portmapper

- NIS password file access from arbitrary hosts

- Old (i.e. before 8.6.10) sendmail versions

- REXD access from arbitrary hosts

- X server access control disabled

- Arbitrary files accessible via TFTP

- Remote shell access from arbitrary hosts

- Writable anonymous FTP home directory

All of these are old and standard misconfigurations, so don't expect SATAN to tell you anything that a well-seasoned administrator wouldn't catch, but it is much easier and cheaper to install and run the program than explore the systems with a fine comb.

Installing SATAN

You can retrieve SATAN from a number of sites. Remember, as with any security program, to make sure you are downloading from a reputable site. My rule of thumb is, if it's not on the list of mirror sites, I don't trust it. You can find the list of mirrors at

```
http://www.fish.com/~zen/satan/satan.html
```

Although you can get the satan-1.1.1.tar.gz file from the official SATAN site, it requires you to get additional patches from other sites. The cleanest way to compile and install SATAN is to download a source RPM version from `http://contrib.redhat.com/`. Here I assume that you are running Red Hat on an *x*86 system, so you need to get the satan-1.1.1.linux-3.i386.rpm package or a later version. Once you have downloaded the RPM package, run the following command as root user:

```
rpm -ivh satan-1.1.1.linux-3.i386.rpm
```

By default, this command installs the SATAN source distribution in the /root/satan directory.

TIP If you do not want to install and compile SATAN in /root/satan, use --prefix `path` option in the preceding rpm command to install it in a different location.

Note that the compilation process requires that you have the latest version of the GNU C compiler (gcc), glibc support, and C development libraries. You also need a Web browser installed on the system. Because the RPM program automatically compiles and installs SATAN, your next step is start it.

Working with SATAN

Assuming that you have let RPM install SATAN in /root/satan, run it using the following command:

```
/root/satan/satan
```

If you run the preceding command from an xterm (that is, in X Windows), SATAN launches the Netscape Navigator browser (/usr/bin/netscape). If you do not have this Web browser and would like to use the text-based Lynx browser, modify the /root/satan/config/paths.pl script such that the $MOSAIC variable is set to the fully qualified path name of the Lynx browser. Now if you start SATAN, it uses the specified browser. Here I assume that you use Netscape Navigator instead.

One other issue that you might have to tackle depending on your Netscape Navigator version is that when you click links from the SATAN main interface screen, as shown in Figure 19-1, they might not work.

For example, I used Netscape Navigator Web browser version 4.0 and when I clicked any of the links on the SATAN main page, I got a screen such as the one shown in Figure 19-2.

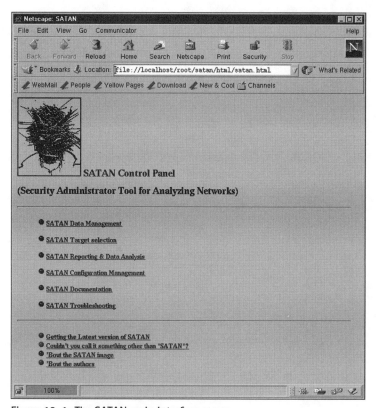

Figure 19-1: The SATAN main interface screen

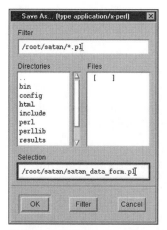

Figure 19-2: Navigator asks to download SATAN scripts.

This screen results from Navigator's inability to run the script due to a miscon-figured or missing MIME configuration. If you have this problem, do the following:

1. From Netscape Navigator's Edit menu, select the Preference option and click Applications as shown in Figure 19-3.

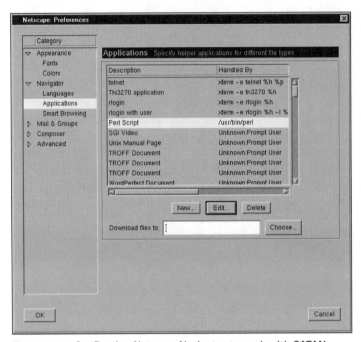

Figure 19-3: Configuring Netscape Navigator to work with SATAN

2. Now click New to associate the .pl extension to /usr/bin/perl (or wher-ever you keep the Perl interpreter). You see a dialog window as shown in Figure 19-4.

3. In the Description field you can type anything you want (such as Perl Script); in the MIMEType field, enter application/x-perl; and in the Suffixes field, enter .pl.

4. Now select Application to assign the handler for .pl files and enter the fully qualified path name of the Perl interpreter in the entry box as shown in the figure.

5. Click OK to complete this process and close the Preference window as usual.

Once you have carried out these steps, SATAN scripts run as expected.

When you start up SATAN, you'll probably be surprised. Most security tools are very short on their user interface. SATAN places a very high priority on user inter-action. Now would be a good time to jump right in to your first network security probe. Click the "SATAN Target selection" link from the main menu screen as shown in Figure 19-1. You are brought to the next screen as shown in Figure 19-5.

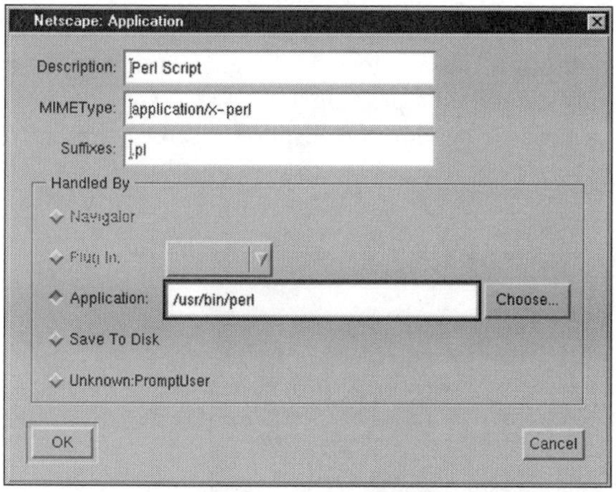

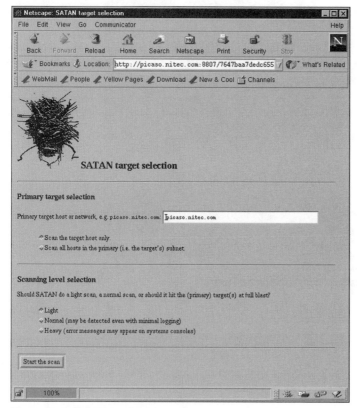

Figure 19-4: Associating .pl with the Perl interpreter

Figure 19-5: Selecting a host to probe

Here you can name the primary host or network at which you want to launch the probe, tell SATAN if you also want to probe other hosts in the subnet, and set the level at which you want to probe. I suggest starting with one host on a light scan. From there you get the feel for SATAN, and you can then branch out into more powerful probes. For a quick test, select a host on your own network; select the "Scan the target host only" option and also select the "Light" option to do a light scan. Now click "Start the scan" to start the probing.

When SATAN finishes probing a host (or network), it displays a screen similar to the one shown in Figure 19-6.

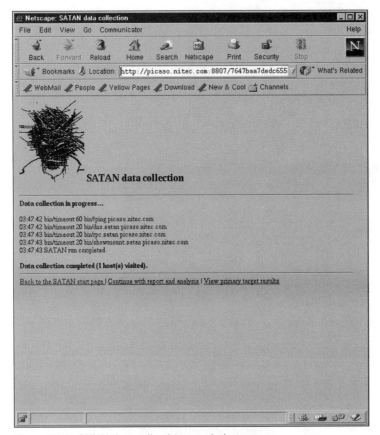

Figure 19-6: SATAN data collection completion screen

To view probe results, click the "View primary target results" link, and you see the results of SATAN's probe in a screen similar to Figure 19-7. Here the figure shows that SATAN has not found any problem in this probe.

The light probe uses fping, nslookup, rpcinfo, and showmount to gather information about DNS, RPC services, and NFS. If the light probe does not detect problems, you should try the normal probe. In addition to the tasks in a light probe, the normal probe tries to determine information on UDP and TCP services, and finger service. However, in Figure 19-8 you see that SATAN has detected a problem with the Trusted host(s) configuration in my test server `picaso.nitec.com`.

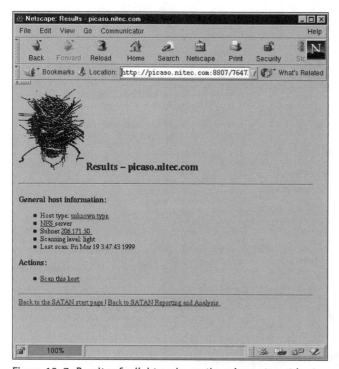

Figure 19–7: Results of a light probe on the primary target host

Notice that in the normal probe, SATAN has found a problem with the trust configuration on my test server. Clicking the "Trusted host(s)" link in the results page shows more details of the problem as shown in Figure 19-9.

Doing a more time-consuming, heavy scan might reveal more problems. As you can see, SATAN provides reasonably good documentation outlining problems SATAN encountered (or lack thereof). You can follow each vulnerability to see how you can make your systems more secure. After you master probing a single target host, you can try scanning all of the hosts in a given subnet. You can also change SATAN's configuration using the "SATAN Configuration Management" link from the home page. If you experience any problem while running SATAN, you can also use the troubleshooting link to learn about commonly asked questions and answers.

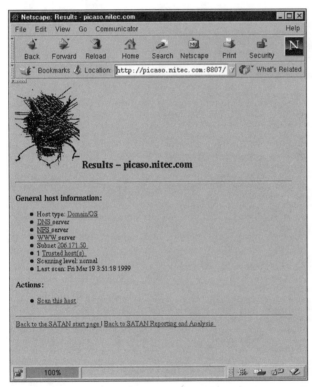

Figure 19-8: Results of a normal probe on the primary target host

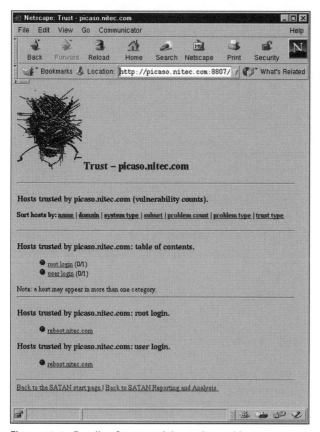

Figure 19-9: Details of a potential security problem

Summary

In this chapter, you learned about network security. I discussed the security problem so that you can better understand what is involved in network security. I then discussed a few popular ways of implementing better security such as the use of nonroutable IP addressees, IP masquerading, and various types of firewall and proxy servers. Finally, I discussed how you can use a security tool called SATAN to preemptively attack your own network so that you can find out about the vulnerabilities before the bad guys do.

Part VII

Tuning for Performance

Chapter 20

Hacking the Kernel

LINUX IS PROBABLY THE only operating system that develops a new kernel every so often. Generally speaking, you can expect a new kernel from Red Hat every two to three months. This should tell you how heavy developmental efforts are in this platform. In this chapter, you learn to upgrade, configure, compile, and install custom kernels.

Linux runs on many hardware architectures, such as *x*86 (Intel), Alpha, and Sparc, among others. It is practically impossible to discuss kernel issues for all platforms in a single chapter, and therefore I assume that, like a majority of Red Hat Linux users, you have an *x*86 (Intel)-based system. However, if you are running Red Hat Linux on a system based on the mighty Alpha processor, you can find useful kernel-related information at the following URL: http://www.alphalinux.org/. Also, for all architectures, you can go to the URL http://www.kernel.org/.

Why Do You Need a Newer Kernel?

The most common reason to upgrade a kernel is to take advantage of new device drivers to handle specific devices. For example, suppose you have a fancy SCSI controller that has a bare-bones driver and you find that a vendor has released a new module or that a driver guru has written one. Another reason you might want to upgrade your Linux kernel is to plug security holes in the kernel or in a module. You should monitor the following Web site for availability of updated packages: http://www.redhat.com/corp/support/errata/index.html.

Of course, many people (perhaps those with lots of time) want to upgrade just to be on the cutting edge of the Linux revolution. If you are such a Linux disciple, my only recommendation is that you keep the latest and the greatest Linux kernel away from any of your production servers. Playing with the latest development-grade Linux kernel on a personal workstation can be quite an amusing task for people who dig it. Let's proceed with the upgrade and customization of your kernel.

What Linux Kernel Do You Have?

Before you do anything else, determine the version of the current kernel in your system. For example, you can run:

```
rpm -q kernel kernel-headers kernel-ibcs \
kernel-pcmcia-cs kernel-source > /current-kernel-pkgs.txt
```

The current-kernel-pkgs.txt file has version information for kernel-related packages. You also need to know the version numbers for mkinitrd (used to create initial ramdisk images), SysVinit (the init package), and the initscripts (the /etc/rc.d scripts) packages that often change with the new kernels. You can run the following command to add version information for these packages to the current-kernel-pkgs.txt file.

```
rpm -q mkinitrd SysVinit initscripts > \
/current-kernel-pkgs.txt
```

By running the preceding rpm commands, you have placed version information for all the typical packages you need for a full kernel upgrade. Table 20-1 lists the names and RPM descriptions of these packages.

TABLE 20-1 TYPICAL PACKAGES NEEDED FOR KERNEL UPGRADES

Package	Description Found in the RPM
kernel-2.x.xx-x.i386.rpm	This package contains the Linux kernel used to boot and run your system. It contains few device drivers for specific hardware. Modules loaded after booting support most hardware.
-kernel-headers-2.x.xx- x.i386.rpm	These are C header files for the Linux kernel, which define structures and constants you need to build most standard programs under Linux, as well as to rebuild the kernel.

Package	Description Found in the RPM
kernel-ibcs-2.*x.xx-x*.i386.rpm	This package allows you to run programs in the iBCS2 (Intel Binary Compatibility Standard, version 2) and in related executable formats.
kernel-pcmcia-cs-2.*x.xx-x*.i386.rpm	Many laptop machines (and some others) support PCMCIA cards for expansion. Also known as "credit card adapters," PCMCIA cards are small cards for everything from SCSI support to modems. They are hot-swappable (you can exchange them without rebooting the system) and quite convenient. This package contains support for PCMCIA cards of all varieties and supplies a daemon that allows you to hot-swap them.
kernel-source-2.*x.xx-x*.i386.rpm	This is the source code for the Linux kernel. It is required to build most C programs, as C programs depend on constants defined here. You can also build a custom kernel that is better tuned to your hardware.
mkinitrd-*x.x-x*.rpm	You can build Generic kernels without drivers for any SCSI adapters that load the SCSI driver as a module. You use an initial ramdisk to solve the problem of allowing the kernel to read the module without being able to address the SCSI adapter. The operating system loader (such as LILO) loads the ramdisk and is available to the kernel as soon as it is loaded. That image is responsible for loading the proper SCSI adapter and allowing the kernel to mount the root file system. This program creates such a ramdisk image using information in /etc/conf.modules.
SysVinit-*x.xx-x*.rpm	SysVinit is the first program the Linux kernal starts when the system boots, controlling the startup, running, and shutdown of all other programs.
initscripts-*x.xx-x*.rpm	This package contains scripts used to boot a system, change run levels, and shut the system down cleanly. It also contains the scripts that activate and deactivate most network interfaces.

Now let's find which kernel you are using to boot the system. One sure-fire way to do this is to take a look at your /etc/lilo.conf file. For example, my /etc/lilo.conf on a Red Hat 7.0 system has the following lines:

```
boot=/dev/hda
map=/boot/map
install=/boot/boot.b
prompt
timeout=50
message=/boot/message
linear
default=linux

image=/boot/vmlinuz-2.2.16-21
        label=linux
        read-only
        root=/dev/hda2
```

As you can see, I am using a single Linux kernel image (/boot/vmlinuz-2.2. 16-21) labeled "linux," and my current kernel is /boot/vmlinuz-2.2.16-21. If you have upgraded your Linux kernel, you might have multiple labels defined in your /etc/lilo.conf file. In such a case, you need to identify the kernel (image=/ boot/vmlinux-2.*x*.*xx*-*r*.*x*) that you use to boot your system. Simply locate the LILO label you use to boot the system, and find the corresponding image=/boot/ vmlinux-2.*x*.*xx*-*r*.*x* line. Note the version number of your kernel, which you need in a later section to create an emergency boot disk. Now that you have identified the kernel packages and the kernel you use, it's time to prepare for the upgrade.

Preparing for a Kernel Upgrade

The official FTP site for the Red Hat Linux updates is ftp://updates.redhat. com/. I can never get into this site unless it is a very odd time such as 3 a.m. or later. Your best choice is to locate a mirror site near you. You can find a mirror near your area by using the following URL: http://www.redhat.com/mirrors.html.

Once you have located a mirror site for the updated kernel RPM packages, connect to the site, and compare versions of the packages you have stored in the /current-kernel-pkgs.txt file earlier.

Download the new packages for the packages in the /current-kernel-pkgs file created previously. If you do not see a new package for one of the packages in the /current-kernel-pkgs.txt file, just ignore it; a new package is not yet available.

Now you have new packages for your kernel upgrade. At this point, I highly recommend that you create an emergency boot floppy just in case something goes wrong with the kernel upgrade.

To create a stand-alone boot floppy, insert a formatted floppy disk in your floppy drive, and run:

```
mkbootdisk 2.x.xx-x.x
```

Don't forget to replace *2.x.xx-x.x* with your current kernel version. Also, if you have multiple floppy drives and do not want to use the default floppy device (/dev/fd0), you can use the --device option to specify your floppy device of choice. For example:

```
mkbootdisk—device /dev/fd1 2.0.36-0.7
```

This command creates the emergency boot floppy on /dev/fd1 by using kernel image version 2.0.36-0.7. Once you have created the boot disk, reboot your system by using this floppy to ensure that the emergency book disk actually works.

Installing the New Kernel

After testing the emergency boot disk, you are ready to install a new kernel. Using rpm, install all the packages you have downloaded. I typically download all new packages to a new directory in a temporary space such as /tmp/new-kernel-pkgs and run:

```
rpm -ivh /tmp/new-kernel-pkgs/*.rpm
```

 TIP If you do not plan to compile the kernel, you may skip the kernel-headers-2.x. xx-x.i386.rpm kernel-source-2.x.xx-x.i386.rpm packages, as you need them only to compile custom kernels.

Once you have upgraded the new kernel and related packages, you need to create the initial ramdisk image file the kernel needs to boot the system. The initial ramdisk image file allows a kernel to access modules such as disk drivers, which you need, in turn, to access the rest of the modules residing on the root file system.

Creating the initial ramdisk

As mentioned previously, you use the mkinitrd command to create the initial ramdisk. Replacing 2.*x*.*xx*-*x* with the version number of your new kernel, run the following command:

```
mkinitrd /boot/initrd-2.x.xx-x.img 2.x.xx-x
```

This creates the /boot/initrd-2.*x*.*xx*-*x*.img initial ramdisk image file. Using the ls utility, confirm that this file is in the /boot directory. Once you have created the initial ramdisk, you need to modify the /etc/lilo.conf file to configure LILO for the new kernel.

Configuring LILO

Configuring LILO is critical to your kernel installation, and you must not reboot the system until you have reconfigured LILO as discussed here. Using your favorite text editor, add a new configuration segment such as the following to your /etc/lilo.conf file:

```
image=/boot/vmlinuz-2.x.xx-x
        label=new-linux
        root=/dev/hda1
        initrd=/boot/initrd-2.x.xx-x.img
        read-only
```

Remember to replace 2.*x*.*xx*-*x* with the appropriate kernel version number for both the image= and initrd= lines. The label= line should be set to an arbitrary string of your choice. The root device should point to your root disk partition. For example, if your current root partition is /dv/sda1, you should make sure the root= line is set to that partition. Once you have modified and saved the /etc/lilo.conf file, run:

```
/sbin/lilo
```

This makes LILO read the new configuration file and update the boot sector of the appropriate root partition. You can use the –v flag with the preceding command to make LILO be a bit more verbose. Once you have run LILO, you are ready to reboot the system.

Booting with the new kernel

Enter the shutdown -r now command to reboot your system as usual. At the LILO prompt, press the Tab key to see your choices. The labels you enter (in the label= lines) for your old and new kernels appear on the screen. Enter the new label (in the preceding example, this label is new-linux) at the LILO prompt to boot the system with the new kernel.

The next step mostly depends on your facial expression after you tell LILO to start the new kernel. If you find yourself smiling, your new kernel is up and running. On the other hand, if you find yourself not smiling but screaming, do not panic. You still have the old kernel, remember? If the system locks, press Ctrl+Alt+Del, or do a hard reboot. Once you get the LILO prompt again, enter the label name for your old kernel. The system should boot up as usual. In such a case, you need to check the steps you have taken, especially check the /etc/lilo configuration file. Make sure you have the new configuration set up correctly. Rerun /sbin/lilo, and try to boot the system with the new kernel. If the problem persists, you need to post the details of your problem (such as what appears on the console when you attempt to boot the new kernel) to a comp.linux news group specific to Linux. If your software license permits, you may also contact Red Hat for help.

In most cases, the new installation should go smoothly without incident. To make sure you are running the new kernel, run:

```
uname -a
```

This displays the kernel version number with other information. Once your new kernel is up and running, you should create a new boot disk by using the mkbookdisk command as you do in the preparation section of this install.

Customizing the Kernel

The only way you can customize a kernel to your liking is via custom compilation. To compile a kernel on your Red Hat Linux server system, you need the kernel header and source RPM packages. If the kernel you are trying to customize is not production grade, there might not be an RPM version available. In such a case, you have to download the source in compressed tar format (.tar.gz). Check the official Red Hat web site for availability of the kernel source and header RPM packages. If you can't find the RPM packages, download the .tar.gz distribution from the official http://www.kernel.com/ site (or any of its mirrors). In this section, I assume you want to customize the latest 2.2.2 kernel and have downloaded the linux-2.2.2. tar.gz source distribution from the site just mentioned.

Installing Linux kernel source

Extract the linux-2.2.2.tar.gz distribution in /usr/src directory by entering the tar xvzf linux-2.2.2.tar.gz command. The source distribution is stored in a subdirectory called linux-2.2.2 in /usr/src. The Linux kernel is traditionally stored in /usr/src/linux. Actually, /usr/src/linux is a symbolic link to the /usr/src/linux-x.x.xx directory. Remove the symbolic link by using rm /usr/src/linux; then create a new symbolic link by using the following command:

```
ln -s /usr/src/linux-2.2.2  /usr/src/linux
```

The series of commands you have to run to arrive at this stage might look as follows:

```
cd /usr/src
tar xvzf linux-2.2.2.tar.gz
rm -f /usr/src/linux
ln -s linux-2.2.2 linux
```

 When I extracted the source distribution in the /usr/src directory, it created a linux subdirectory, and therefore the symbolic link was unnecessary. However, if you plan to experiment with various kernels, I recommend that you keep a particular source distribution in the /usr/src/linux-*x.x.xx* directory and always point a symbolic link (linux) to the kernel you are currently working on.

Although a freshly downloaded source distribution is not going to have stale object files, it is wise to run the following command to clean up such files just in case:

```
make mrproper
```

Now you are ready to configure (customize) the kernel. You have multiple choices as to how you can customize the kernel.

Configuring the kernel the old-fashioned way

To configure the kernel the old-fashioned way, you need to run the following command from the /usr/src/linux directory:

```
make config
```

This is the simplest way to configure a kernel; however, it might not be the most suitable for beginning kernel hackers. Next, I will discuss a sample kernel configuration session using the make config method. However, you should know that as features and support for various devices are added on an on going basis to Linux, the exact steps that make config shows also change. Therefore, what you will see in the following section might not be exactly what you see when you run make config on your system. I discuss the major decision points here. If you find a new configuration question when you run make config, you can simply find more about it by entering the ? character at the prompt, or you can choose to go with the default.

CODE MATURITY-LEVEL OPTIONS
In this section, you have to decide if you want to be asked about features not yet ready for prime time. In other words, you are asked if you want to be prompted for experimental features. You can choose to see (and perhaps use) these experimental

features if you are configuring the kernel for a system where experimentation or down time and crashes are part of the fun and not a burden. The prompt appears as follows:

```
Prompt for development and/or incomplete code/drivers
(CONFIG_EXPERIMENTAL) [N/y/?]
```

The default answer is N or no. You can choose the default answer by pressing the Enter key. Also note that the default answer is always a capital letter.

PROCESSOR TYPE, MEMORY MODEL, AND FEATURES

In this section, you are asked about the processor family, the memory model, the math coprocessor, multiprocessors, and other processor-specific questions. Here is the first:

```
Processor family (386, 486/Cx486, 586/K5/5x86/6x86, Pentium/K6/TSC,
PPro/6x86MX) [PPro/6x86MX]
```

If the default processor architecture is incorrect, you should choose one of the listed ones. In my case, the default is wrong, so I enter "Pentium/K6/TSC" as the processor family.

```
Maximum Physical Memory (1GB, 2GB) [1GB]
```

The default memory model is 1 GB, which should be fine if you're system has 1 GB or less RAM. If you have 2 GB or less, choose 2GB. In my case, I choose the default.

```
defined CONFIG_M686
Math emulation (CONFIG_MATH_EMULATION) [N/y/?]
```

Unless you have a (really old) processor that does not have a math coprocessor built in, you should choose the default by pressing Enter here.

```
MTRR (Memory Type Range Register) support (CONFIG_MTRR) [N/y/?]
```

This is probably the first question that does not quite make sense to you (unless you are an expert in *x*86 CPU design) and to most beginning kernel hackers. So what can you choose here? The default option is often the right one for most cases. Also, you can find what Memory Type Range Register (MTRR) support means by entering the "?" character at the prompt. You get the help screen as shown here:

```
CONFIG_MTRR:

On Intel Pentium Pro and Pentium II systems the Memory Type Range
Registers (MTRRs) may be used to control processor access to memory
```

ranges. This is most useful when you have a video (VGA) card on a
PCI or AGP bus. Enabling write-combining allows bus write transfers
to be combined into a larger transfer before bursting over the
PCI/AGP bus. This can increase performance of image write operations
2.5 times or more. This option creates a /proc/mtrr file which may
be used to manipulate your MTRRs. Typically the X server should use
this. This should have a reasonably generic interface so that
similar control registers on other processors can be easily
supported.

Saying Y here also fixes a problem with buggy SMP BIOSes which only
set the MTRRs for the boot CPU and not the secondary CPUs. This can
lead to all sorts of problems.

You can safely say Y even if your machine doesn't have MTRRs, you'll
just add about 3k to your kernel.

See Documentation/mtrr.txt for more information.

As you can see, this is quite helpful. Because I am configuring this kernel for a
server, I do not care much about the video, so I choose "N" here.

Symmetric multi-processing support (CONFIG_SMP) [Y/n/?]

If you have multiple processors on your system and would like to turn on symmetric multiprocessing support, choose the default. In my case, I do not have a
motherboard with multiprocessors; therefore, I chose "n" to decline SMB support.

LOADABLE MODULE SUPPORT

The Linux kernel uses an innovative method for keeping a low profile. It uses features and drivers implemented as external modules. The modules are dynamically
loaded and unloaded on an as-needed basis. This allows the kernel to require less
memory and to become more hardware independent. Typically, you load the modules by using a program called kerneld, which, in turn, uses another program called
modprobe to manage available modules. Modules can be device drivers, file systems,
binary executable formats, and so on. In this section, you are asked if you want
module-related support or not. The first question is as follows:

Enable loadable module support (CONFIG_MODULES) [Y/n/?]

This really should not be a prompt because you definitely want to have loadable
module support for almost all scenarios. The default is fine.

Set version information on all symbols for modules
(CONFIG_MODVERSIONS) [N/y/?]

When you compile modules with version information, you can reuse them with new kernels without needing to compile them from scratch. However, the preferred method is to compile the modules along with the new kernel to eliminate compatibility problems. Hence the default option to not include the version information is sufficient.

```
Kernel module loader (CONFIG_KMOD) [N/y/?]
```

As I mentioned previously, you load modules by using the kerneld program. This prompt asks you if would like to use a module loader inside the kernel itself to avoid using the kerneld daemon. Either way, modules are loaded automatically, so this does not make much difference.

GENERAL SETUP

In this section, you configure the general options.

```
BIGMEM support (CONFIG_BIGMEM) [N/y/?]
```

If you have more than 1 GB of physical RAM, you need to select 'y' here. If you have not used the 2GB memory model, use the default.value.

```
Networking support (CONFIG_NET) [Y/n/?]
```

This is a dumb question, isn't it? Who wants to run Linux and not have networking support? Perhaps there are a few out there. The default is a must.

```
PCI support (CONFIG_PCI) [Y/n/?]
```

Unless you are on a really old *x*86 system that has only an ISA bus, the default is fine. Note that on Sparc systems you might not need PCI support if you have only sbus cards.

```
PCI access mode (BIOS, Direct, Any) [Any]
```

The default option allows the kernel to detect the PCI configuration by using the direct method; if that fails, it gets PCI configuration from the system BIOS, so the default is fine.

```
PCI quirks (CONFIG_PCI_QUIRKS) [Y/n/?]
```

This option is for motherboards with lousy BIOSes that fail to set up the PCI bus properly. If you don't have such a board, select "n" for no. If you are unsure, you can keep the default.

```
MCA support (CONFIG_MCA) [N/y/?]
```

Unless you have an IBM PS/2 Micro Channel Architecture (MCA)-based system, you do not need MCA support.

```
SGI Visual Workstation support (CONFIG_VISWS) [N/y/?]
```

If you are not using an SGI system, keep the defaults.

```
System V IPC (CONFIG_SYSVIPC) [Y/n/?]
```

Many programs need Inter Process Communication (IPC); therefore, the default is a must.

```
BSD Process Accounting (CONFIG_BSD_PROCESS_ACCT) [N/y/?]
```

This allows a program to ask the kernel to dump information about a process, such as a process owner's UID, creation time, and memory stats. This is not required; answer either way.

```
Sysctl support (CONFIG_SYSCTL) [Y/n/?]
```

This option allows dynamic changing of various kernel parameters in the /proc file system without a reboot or recompilation of the kernel. This is a must for all systems.

```
Kernel support for a.out binaries (CONFIG_BINFMT_AOUT) [Y/m/n/?]
```

Traditionally, the a.out format has been used to create executable and library programs; however, the new Executable and Linkable Format (ELF) has been in use for a while. You might want to keep support in a module instead of making it part of the kernel. Hence, choose the "m" option for module.

```
Kernel support for ELF binaries (CONFIG_BINFMT_ELF) [Y/m/n/?]
```

The ELF support is a must; therefore, the default is fine.

```
Kernel support for MISC binaries (CONFIG_BINFMT_MISC) [Y/m/n/?]
```

If you plan on running Java or DOS executables using interpreters, you might want to have the miscellaneous binary support as a module.

```
Parallel port support (CONFIG_PARPORT) [N/y/m/?]
```

If you plan on connecting a printer or other parallel port devices to your Linux system, select "y" for adding support to the kernel or "m" to have support available as a module.

```
Advanced Power Management BIOS support (CONFIG_APM) [N/y/?]
```

If you are not concerned about saving power, the default is fine.

PLUG AND PLAY SUPPORT

In my personal experience, Plug and Play should really be Plug and Pray (don't know who said it first). I urge you not to enable PNP in something so nice as Linux.

```
Plug and Play support (CONFIG_PNP) [N/y/?]
```

You should know my answer to this prompt. If you have a card that works only in PNP mode, you are likely to encounter problems. The best thing to do is buy hardware that has an option to turn off PNP.

BLOCK DEVICES

In this section, you are asked about disk drives.

```
Normal PC floppy disk support (CONFIG_BLK_DEV_FD) [Y/m/n/?]
```

Because most systems have floppy drives, this should be set to yes.
If you use IDE/EIDE hard disks, an IDE/ATAPI CD-ROM, tape drives, floppy drives, and so on, say yes (or choose the module option) for all of the following questions:

```
Enhanced IDE/MFM/RLL disk/cdrom/tape/floppy support
(CONFIG_BLK_DEV_IDE) [Y/m/n/?]
Use old disk-only driver on primary interface
(CONFIG_BLK_DEV_HD_IDE) [N/y/?]
Include IDE/ATA-2 DISK support (CONFIG_BLK_DEV_IDEDISK) [Y/m/n/?]
Include IDE/ATAPI CDROM support (CONFIG_BLK_DEV_IDECD) [Y/m/n/?]
Include IDE/ATAPI TAPE support (CONFIG_BLK_DEV_IDETAPE) [N/y/m/?]
Include IDE/ATAPI FLOPPY support (CONFIG_BLK_DEV_IDEFLOPPY)
[N/y/m/?]
```

```
SCSI emulation support (CONFIG_BLK_DEV_IDESCSI) [N/y/m/?]
```

SCSI emulation works only for IDE/ATAPI devices that do not have native driver support in Linux. You might want to consider a different drive to avoid emulation.
The CMD-Technologies CMD640 IDE chip and the PC-Technologies RZ1000 IDE chip are common on many 486/P5 motherboards. If your system uses these chips, you need to say yes to the following prompts. If you do not know whether your system uses these chips, saying yes is not likely to cause any problem:

```
CMD640 chipset bugfix/support (CONFIG_BLK_DEV_CMD640) [Y/n/?]
CMD640 enhanced support (CONFIG_BLK_DEV_CMD640_ENHANCED) [N/y/?]
RZ1000 chipset bugfix/support (CONFIG_BLK_DEV_RZ1000) [Y/n/?] n
```

If you use IDE drives on a PCI system, keep the defaults for the following options:

```
Generic PCI IDE chipset support (CONFIG_BLK_DEV_IDEPCI) [Y/n/?]
Generic PCI bus-master DMA support (CONFIG_BLK_DEV_IDEDMA) [Y/n/?]
Boot off-board chipsets first support (CONFIG_BLK_DEV_OFFBOARD)
[N/y/?]
```

If your system is capable of using Direct Memory Access (DMA) for IDE drives, keep the default for the following question:

```
Use DMA by default when available (CONFIG_IDEDMA_AUTO) [Y/n/?]
```

If you would like to enable enhanced support for various IDE chipsets, choose yes for the following question:

```
Other IDE chipset support (CONFIG_IDE_CHIPSETS) [N/y/?]
```

ADDITIONAL BLOCK DEVICES

For most cases, all options in this section are useless, so you can safely accept the default answers here:

```
Loopback device support (CONFIG_BLK_DEV_LOOP) [N/y/m/?] y
Network block device support (CONFIG_BLK_DEV_NBD) [N/y/m/?]
Multiple devices driver support (CONFIG_BLK_DEV_MD) [N/y/?]
RAM disk support (CONFIG_BLK_DEV_RAM) [N/y/m/?]
XT hard disk support (CONFIG_BLK_DEV_XD) [N/y/m/?]
Parallel port IDE device support (CONFIG_PARIDE) [N/y/m/?]
```

NETWORKING OPTIONS

Networking is one of the most important sections. Here, you decide on various networking issues.

```
Packet socket (CONFIG_PACKET) [Y/m/n/?]
```

Applications such as tcpdump use the Packet protocol; therefore, you should accept the default answer.

```
Kernel/User netlink socket (CONFIG_NETLINK) [N/y/?]
```

If you want to use your system as a firewall or want to use the arpd daemon to maintain an internal ARP cache, say yes here.

```
Network firewalls (CONFIG_FIREWALL) [N/y/?]
```

If you would like to use your system as a packet-filtering firewall, set this to yes.

```
Network aliasing (CONFIG_NET_ALIAS) [N/y/?] ?
```

If you have multiple network interfaces for your system, set this to yes.

```
Socket Filtering (CONFIG_FILTER) [N/y/?] ?
```

This feature allows programs to attach filters to sockets and to control how data go through the socket. Unless you use such programs, the default answer is fine.

```
Unix domain sockets (CONFIG_UNIX) [Y/m/n/?]
```

Sockets are standard UNIX mechanisms for establishing and accessing network connections. Therefore, the default answer is fine.

```
TCP/IP networking (CONFIG_INET) [Y/n/?]
```

This is a no-brainer.

```
IP: multicasting (CONFIG_IP_MULTICAST) [N/y/?]
```

Typically, you use IP multicasting for transferring large amounts of data such as real-time, broadcast-quality video that uses large bandwidth connections. Unless you have such needs, the default is fine.

```
IP: advanced router (CONFIG_IP_ADVANCED_ROUTER) [N/y/?]
```

If you intend to run your Linux box mostly as a router (as a computer that forwards and redistributes network packets), press Y.

```
IP: kernel level autoconfiguration (CONFIG_IP_PNP) [N/y/?]
```

This enables automatic configuration of the IP addresses of devices, and of the routing table during kernel boot, based on either information supplied at the kernel command line or by BOOTP or RARP protocols.

```
IP: optimize as router not host (CONFIG_IP_ROUTER) [N/y/?] ?
```

Some Linux network drivers use a technique called copy and checksum to optimize host performance. However, for a machine that acts as a router most of the time and is forwarding most packets to another host, this is a loss.

```
IP: tunneling (CONFIG_NET_IPIP) [N/y/m/?]
```

Tunneling means encapsulating data of one protocol within another protocol and sending it over a channel that understands the encapsulating protocol. This particular tunneling driver implements encapsulation of IP within IP, which sounds kind of pointless but can be useful if you want to make your (or some other) machine appear on a different network than it is physically connected to or to use mobile-IP facilities (allowing laptops to seamlessly move between networks without changing their IP addresses).

```
IP: GRE tunnels over IP (CONFIG_NET_IPGRE) [N/y/m/?] ?
```

GRE (Generic Routing Encapsulation) allows encapsulating of IPv4 or IPv6 over the existing IPv4 infrastructure.

```
IP: aliasing support (CONFIG_IP_ALIAS) [N/y/?]
```

If you wish to attach multiple IP addresses to a single network interface, say yes here.

```
IP: TCP syncookie support (not enabled per default)
(CONFIG_SYN_COOKIES) [N/y/?]
```

Normal TCP/IP networking is open to an attack known as "SYN flooding." This denial-of-service attack prevents legitimate remote users from connecting to your computer during an ongoing attack and requires very little work from the attacker, who can operate from anywhere on the Internet. SYN cookies provide protection against this type of attack. If you choose y here, the TCP/IP stack uses a cryptographic challenge protocol known as "SYN cookies" to enable legitimate users to continue to connect even when your machine is under attack. There is no need for legitimate users to change their TCP/IP software, but SYN cookies may prevent correct error reporting on clients when the server is overloaded. If this happens frequently, you better turn them off. If you choose Y here, note that default does not enable SYN cookies; you can enable them by choosing Y to "/proc filesystem support" and "Sysctl support" below and executing the command

```
echo 1 >/proc/sys/net/ipv4/tcp_syncookies
```

at boot time after the proc file system mounts.

```
IP: Reverse ARP (CONFIG_INET_RARP) [N/y/m/?]
```

If you want your server to provide Reverse Address Resolution Protocol (RARP) service for other computers on your network, you can select yes or set this feature to be a module.

```
IP: Drop source routed frames (CONFIG_IP_NOSR) [Y/n/?] ?
```

Source routing is an IP protocol feature that allows the originating IP packet to contain full routing information for the destination IP address. This is typically the cause of many network security problems, and you should avoid it. The default option is recommended.

```
IP: Allow large windows (not recommended if <16Mb of memory)
(CONFIG_SKB_LARGE) [Y/n/?] ?
```

This option is useful only if you are dealing with 2MB/sec or above bandwidth and long-distance networks.

```
The IPX protocol (CONFIG_IPX) [N/y/m/?] ?
```

Unless you need support for Novell networking, the default answer is fine.

```
Appletalk DDP (CONFIG_ATALK) [N/y/m/?] ?
```

Unless you need AppleTalk networking support, the default answer is fine.

SCSI SUPPORT

If you have SCSI disks, a CD-ROM, tape drives, or other SCSI devices, this section allows you to configure support for such devices. You should answer the following questions based on available SCSI hardware:

```
SCSI support (CONFIG_SCSI) [Y/m/n/?]
SCSI disk support (CONFIG_BLK_DEV_SD) [Y/m/n/?]
SCSI tape support (CONFIG_CHR_DEV_ST) [N/y/m/?]
SCSI CD-ROM support (CONFIG_BLK_DEV_SR) [N/y/m/?]
SCSI generic support (CONFIG_CHR_DEV_SG) [N/y/m/?]
```

```
Probe all LUNs on each SCSI device (CONFIG_SCSI_MULTI_LUN) [Y/n/?]
```

Unless you have a SCSI device with multiple Logical Unit Numbers (LUN), choose no here.

```
Verbose SCSI error reporting (kernel size +=12K)
(CONFIG_SCSI_CONSTANTS) [Y/n/?]
```

The error messages regarding your SCSI hardware are easier to understand if you choose yes here.

```
SCSI logging facility (CONFIG_SCSI_LOGGING) [N/y/?]
```

This turns on a logging facility you can use to debug a number of SCSI-related problems. If you choose yes, you have to enable logging by using the following command in /etc/rc.d/rc.local.

```
echo "scsi log token [level]" > /proc/scsi/scsi
```

Here, *token* can be error, scan, mlqueue, mlcomplete, llqueue, llcomplete, hlqueue, or hlcomplete. The *level* controls the verbosity of the log and can be any positive number, including 0.

The rest of the questions in the SCSI section are specific to SCSI host adapters. You should choose support for only the adapter(s) you have installed.

NETWORK DEVICE SUPPORT

In this section, you configure various network device features.

```
Network device support (CONFIG_NETDEVICES) [Y/n/?]
```

Because you are configuring the kernel for your server, you must say yes to the preceding question.

```
ARCnet support (CONFIG_ARCNET) [N/y/m/?]
```

Unless you have ARCnet network interface cards, the default is fine.

```
Dummy net driver support (CONFIG_DUMMY) [M/n/y/?] ?
```

This driver allows you a dummy network interface device you can use to fool a network client program. Keeping this as a module might be handy; hence, the default is recommended.

```
EQL (serial line load balancing) support (CONFIG_EQUALIZER)
[N/y/m/?]
```

This feature is not useful for most server configurations. The default answer is recommended.

```
Ethernet (10 or 100Mbit) (CONFIG_NET_ETHERNET) [Y/n/?]
```

Yet another no-brainer.

Answers to the following questions depend on what types of network cards you have; respond accordingly:

```
3COM cards (CONFIG_NET_VENDOR_3COM) [N/y/?]
AMD LANCE and PCnet (AT1500 and NE2100) support (CONFIG_LANCE)
[N/y/m/?]
Western Digital/SMC cards (CONFIG_NET_VENDOR_SMC) [N/y/?]
Racal-Interlan (Micom) NI cards (CONFIG_NET_VENDOR_RACAL) [N/y/?]
Other ISA cards (CONFIG_NET_ISA) [N/y/?]
EISA, VLB, PCI and on board controllers (CONFIG_NET_EISA) [Y/n/?]
AMD PCnet32 (VLB and PCI) support (CONFIG_PCNET32) [N/y/m/?]
Apricot Xen-II on board Ethernet (CONFIG_APRICOT) [N/y/m/?]
CS89x0 support (CONFIG_CS89x0) [N/y/m/?]
Generic DECchip & DIGITAL EtherWORKS PCI/EISA (CONFIG_DE4X5)
[N/y/m/?]
DECchip Tulip (dc21x4x) PCI support (CONFIG_DEC_ELCP) [N/y/m/?]
Digi Intl. RightSwitch SE-X support (CONFIG_DGRS) [N/y/m/?]
EtherExpressPro/100 support (CONFIG_EEXPRESS_PRO100) [Y/m/n/?]
PCI NE2000 support (CONFIG_NE2K_PCI) [N/y/m/?]
TI ThunderLAN support (CONFIG_TLAN) [N/y/m/?]
VIA Rhine support (CONFIG_VIA_RHINE) [N/y/m/?]
Pocket and portable adaptors (CONFIG_NET_POCKET) [N/y/?]
FDDI driver support (CONFIG_FDDI) [N/y/?]
Frame relay DLCI support (CONFIG_DLCI) [N/y/m/?]
PPP (point-to-point) support (CONFIG_PPP) [N/y/m/?]
SLIP (serial line) support (CONFIG_SLIP) [N/y/m/?]
Wireless LAN (non-hamradio) (CONFIG_NET_RADIO) [N/y/?]
Token Ring driver support (CONFIG_TR) [N/y/?]
Comtrol Hostess SV-11 support (CONFIG_HOSTESS_SV11) [N/m/?]
COSA/SRP sync serial boards support (CONFIG_COSA) [N/m/?]
Red Creek Hardware VPN (EXPERIMENTAL) (CONFIG_RCPCI) [N/y/m/?]
WAN drivers (CONFIG_WAN_DRIVERS) [N/y/?]
LAPB over Ethernet driver (CONFIG_LAPBETHER) [N/y/m/?]
X.25 async driver (CONFIG_X25_ASY) [N/y/m/?]
```

AMATEUR RADIO, ISDN, AND OLD CD-ROM SUPPORT

I assume that you are not going to use Amateur Radio, ISDN, or old CD-ROM support; hence, the default answers to the following questions are sufficient:

```
Amateur Radio support (CONFIG_HAMRADIO) [N/y/?]
ISDN support (CONFIG_ISDN) [N/y/m/?]
Support non-SCSI/IDE/ATAPI CDROM drives (CONFIG_CD_NO_IDESCSI)
[N/y/?]
```

If you are planning on using an ISDN card to provide Internet connectivity for your server, I highly recommend that you get an ISDN router instead of an internal card. My personal experience with internal cards has made me come to this conclusion. I have tried a few name-brand ISDN cards that do not work very well. On top of the problems with dealing with yet another card (IRQ and I/O address resources are limited on a PC), the price difference between a internal card and an external ISDN router is not significant when considering the fact that dedicated ISDN itself is a fairly expensive service in most parts of the United States.

CHARACTER DEVICES

In this section, you are asked about terminal configuration.

```
Virtual terminal (CONFIG_VT) [Y/n/?]
```

This feature allows you to have virtual terminals. The default answer is required unless you are installing the kernel in an embedded Linux system.

```
Support for console on virtual terminal (CONFIG_VT_CONSOLE) [Y/n/?]
```

This feature allows you to turn a virtual terminal into a system console. This is required for the same reason as the last answer.

```
Support for console on serial port (CONFIG_SERIAL_CONSOLE) [N/y/?]
```

If you would like to use your computer's serial port as the system console, change the default answer.

```
Extended dumb serial driver options (CONFIG_SERIAL_EXTENDED) [N/y/?]
```

Unless you enable the serial port as a system console in the last question, keep the default here.

```
Unix98 PTY support (CONFIG_UNIX98_PTYS) [Y/n/?]
```

This feature provides support for the UNIX 98 pseudo-terminal numbering convention, which is superior to the traditional Linux pseudo-terminal number convention. You should keep the default.

If you keep the default, you are asked the following question to set the maximum number of UNIX 98 PTYs the system can use:

```
Maximum number of Unix98 PTYs in use (0-2048)
(CONFIG_UNIX98_PTY_COUNT) [256]
```

For most cases, the default value should be sufficient.

```
Mouse Support (not serial mice) (CONFIG_MOUSE) [Y/n/?]
```

This feature allows you to use the mouse with terminals capable of using such a device. The default is recommended.

```
QIC-02 tape support (CONFIG_QIC02_TAPE) [N/y/m/?]
```

If you have QIC-02 tape, you can choose to add support for it here.

```
Watchdog Timer Support (CONFIG_WATCHDOG) [N/y/?]
```

If you would like to create a watchdog timer so that it can reboot the system in case of a failure, answer yes here. If you enable this feature, you have to create a special device called /dev/watchdog (major,minor=130,10) by using the mknod program. Then, you can use a watchdog daemon program that writes to this special device every minute. If the kernel detects that the daemon has not written to the device for one minute, it reboots the system.

```
/dev/nvram support (CONFIG_NVRAM) [N/y/m/?]
```

This feature allows you to create the special device /dev/nvram to have read and write access to nonvolatile memory in the real-time clock. Unless you know what you are doing, keep the default.

```
Enhanced Real Time Clock Support (CONFIG_RTC) [N/y/?]
```

This feature allows you to create a special device, /dev/rtc, which you can use to access the real-time clock in your system. Unless you know what you are doing, keep the default.

VIDEO AND JOYSTICK SUPPORT
Because you are configuring a server system, I assume you do not have video-capture hardware or joysticks on the system; therefore, you should accept the default answers for the following questions:

```
Video For Linux (CONFIG_VIDEO_DEV) [N/y/m/?]
Joystick support (CONFIG_JOYSTICK) [N/y/m/?]
```

FTAPE, THE FLOPPY TAPE DEVICE DRIVER
If you have a floppy controller-based tape drive, you need to choose to add support for it here.

```
Ftape (QIC-80/Travan) support (CONFIG_FTAPE) [N/y/m/?]
```

FILE SYSTEMS

In this section, you configure the kernel for various file system-specific features.

```
Quota support (CONFIG_QUOTA) [N/y/?]
```

If you would like to have disk quota support built into the kernel, choose yes here.

```
Kernel automounter support (CONFIG_AUTOFS_FS) [Y/m/n/?]
```

If you would like remote file systems, such as NFS file systems, automatically mounted and unmounted, choose to add direct or module-based support for the automounter here.

Following are various vendor-specific, file-system support questions. Answer them according to your needs:

```
Amiga FFS filesystem support (CONFIG_AFFS_FS) [N/y/m/?]
Apple Macintosh filesystem support (experimental) (CONFIG_HFS_FS)
[N/y/m/?]
DOS FAT fs support (CONFIG_FAT_FS) [N/y/m/?]
ISO 9660 CDROM filesystem support (CONFIG_ISO9660_FS) [Y/m/n/?]
Microsoft Joliet CDROM extensions (CONFIG_JOLIET) [N/y/?]
Minix fs support (CONFIG_MINIX_FS) [N/y/m/?]
NTFS filesystem support (read only) (CONFIG_NTFS_FS) [N/y/m/?]
OS/2 HPFS filesystem support (read only) (CONFIG_HPFS_FS) [N/y/m/?]
```

```
/proc filesystem support (CONFIG_PROC_FS) [Y/n/?]
```

The /proc file system is a must have for any modern Linux system; therefore the default answer is highly recommended.

```
/dev/pts filesystem for Unix98 PTYs (CONFIG_DEVPTS_FS) [Y/n/?]
```

If you choose to add support for UNIX 98 pseudo-terminals, you need to add /dev/pts filesystem support here.

```
ROM filesystem support (CONFIG_ROMFS_FS) [N/y/m/?]
```

Most systems do not need file systems of this type.

```
Second extended fs support (CONFIG_EXT2_FS) [Y/m/n/?]
```

Extended fs is the primary file system for Linux; therefore, the default answer is a must.

Default answers for the following questions should work for most systems:

```
System V and Coherent filesystem support (CONFIG_SYSV_FS) [N/y/m/?]
UFS filesystem support (CONFIG_UFS_FS) [N/y/m/?]
```

Note that the UFS file system support is required if you choose to mount disk partitions created by other operating systems such as Solaris *x*86 or BSD.

NETWORK FILE SYSTEMS
Here, you are able to configure the kernel for advanced network file systems.

```
Coda filesystem support (advanced network fs) (CONFIG_CODA_FS)
[N/y/m/?]
```

The Coda file system is not yet popular enough, and I do not recommend adding it to the kernel; you might choose to add it as a module.

```
NFS filesystem support (CONFIG_NFS_FS) [Y/m/n/?]
```

If you plan to use NFS, use the default answer.

```
Emulate SUN NFS server (CONFIG_NFSD_SUN) [N/y/?]
```

Unless you want your Linux NFS server to behave like a Sun-based NFS server that allows NFS clients to access directories that are mount points on the local file system, leave the default as is.

```
SMB filesystem support (to mount WfW shares etc.) (CONFIG_SMB_FS)
[N/y/m/?]
```

If you would like to mount Windows 9*x*/NT file systems on your Linux system as SMB file systems, you need to choose yes or set this feature to be a module.

```
NCP filesystem support (to mount NetWare volumes) (CONFIG_NCP_FS)
[N/y/m/?]
```

Unless you are planning on mounting NetWare volumes on your Linux system, keep the default answer.

PARTITION TYPES
If you would like to have support for disk partitions based on BSD, Macintosh, Solaris, and so on, answer the following questions accordingly:

```
BSD disklabel (BSD partition tables) support (CONFIG_BSD_DISKLABEL)
[N/y/?]
```

```
Macintosh partition map support (CONFIG_MAC_PARTITION) [N/y/?]
SMD disklabel (Sun partition tables) support (CONFIG_SMD_DISKLABEL)
[N/y/?]
Solaris (x86) partition table support (CONFIG_SOLARIS_X86_PARTITION)
[N/y/?]
```

In most cases, the default answers are sufficient.

CONSOLE DRIVERS

In this section, you are able to set the following:

```
VGA text console (CONFIG_VGA_CONSOLE) [Y/n/?]
```

If you would like to have a VGA text console, keep the default.

```
Video mode selection support (CONFIG_VIDEO_SELECT) [N/y/?] ?
```

If you would like to be able to specify text mode on kernel bootup, set this option, or keep the default.

SOUND

Assuming that you probably do not need a sound card in a server system, you can keep the default answer for the following question:

```
Sound card support (CONFIG_SOUND) [N/y/m/?]
```

KERNEL HACKING

The only option available in this section is the support for the Magic SysRq key. If you enable support for this key by answering yes to the following question, you are able to press SysRq+Alt+PrintScreen to dump status information even when the system has crashed.

```
Magic SysRq key (CONFIG_MAGIC_SYSRQ) [N/y/?] ?
```

This is only useful for kernel developers. You should choose no here.

Once you have answered all these questions, the configuration script creates a .config file in the /usr/src/linux directory. You might want to view the content of this file to ensure that all features are configured as you think they are.

 If you are not interested in finding how else you can configure the kernel but are ready to compile the kernel, skip the next two sections, and proceed to "Compiling, installing, and booting the new kernel."

Using make config to configure the kernel is quite a long process. It is also a bit cumbersome; however, it is quite appropriate if you happen to be configuring the kernel via a Telnet connection on a remote server. The line-based interface may not be elegant, but it works for most scenarios, and you should consider it the default method of configuration when the following two methods are unusable.

Configuring the kernel using make menuconfig

One major problem with the make config-based configuration script is that if you make a mistake, you can't fix it without starting over. Also, you cannot review your choices unless you use a text editor to view manually the /usr/src/linux/.config file.

To remedy these shortcomings (at least for beginning kernel hackers), use the following command:

```
make menuconfig
```

This runs a menu-driven configuration tool that is much more user-friendly than the make config script. The main menu screen is in Figure 20-1.

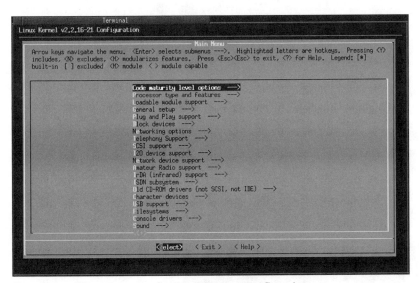

Figure 20-1: The main screen for the make menuconfig script

As you can see, the user interface is quite simple and easy to navigate. However, the configuration questions are exactly the same. This configuration program also allows you to save and load configuration files. In other words, you can create multiple configuration files with different settings and use these configuration files to experiment with various features of the new kernel.

Although the make menuconfig script is quite friendly, it imposes extra requirements on remote kernel configuration. For example, if you plan to configure and compile the kernel over a Telnet connection to a remote server, you have to make sure the Telnet client program on your side is capable of good terminal emulation, which is required for a full-screen menu application. Also, note that make menuconfig is not the fanciest way to configure a kernel. That title goes to the make xconfig script.

Configuring the kernel using make xconfig

As you may have guessed from the script name, this method of kernel configuration requires the X Window system. Because I do not recommend installation of the X Window system on server systems, I can't recommend this method either. However, I must agree that on systems with X Windows, this is the preferred method of kernel configuration. Figure 20-2 shows the main window when the make xconfig script (wish -f scripts/kconfig.tk) is run from X Windows.

Linux Kernel Configuration		
Code maturity level options	I2O device support	Console drivers
Processor type and features	Network device support	Sound
Loadable module support	Amateur Radio support	Kernel hacking
General setup	IrDA (infrared) support	
Plug and Play support	ISDN subsystem	
Block devices	Old CD-ROM drivers (not SCSI, not IDE)	Save and Exit
Networking options	Character devices	Quit Without Saving
Telephony Support	USB support	Load Configuration from File
SCSI support	Filesystems	Store Configuration to File

Figure 20-2: The main screen for make xconfig script

You can click any button to configure a particular section of the entire configuration. For example, Figure 20-3 shows the processor's type and features dialog box.

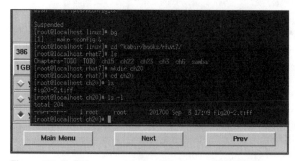

Figure 20-3: Processors type and features dialog box

As you can see, this is quite a user-friendly interface. Another advantage of this interface is that you can open multiple sections by clicking the appropriate buttons. For example, if you are configuring the Partitions Type section and want to confirm that you have enabled UFS file system support in the Filesystems section, you can click the buttons for these two sections and verify your selections.

I hope you are able to determine which method works well for your environment. Now it's time to proceed with the compilation of the newly configured kernel.

Compiling, installing, and booting the new kernel

Before you can compile the kernel, you need to run

```
make dep
```

to make sure all dependencies within the source are set up correctly. This should return without error unless a problem exists with the kernel source code itself. To compile and create a compressed Linux kernel, run the following command:

```
make bzImage
```

If you have configured any part of the kernel as a module during configuration, you have to run the following command to compile the modules:

```
make modules
```

After you have compiled the modules, install them in /lib/modules/2.2.2 directory by using the following command:

```
make modules_install
```

Now you need to copy the new kernel to the /boot directory as follows:

```
cp /usr/src/linux-2.2.2/arch/i386/boot/bzImage /boot/vmlinuz-2.2.2
```

Also copy and rename the new System.map file to the /boot directory as follows:

```
cp /usr/src/linux-2.2.1/System.map /boot/System.map-2.2.2
```

Now remove the existing symbolic link for System.map as follows:

```
rm -f /boot/System.map
```

Finally, create a new symbolic link called /boot/System.map as follows:

```
ln -s /boot/System.map-2.2.2 /boot/System.map
```

You also need to create a new initial ramdisk as follows:

```
mkinitrd /boot/initrd-2.2.2.img 2.2.2
```

The final step before you boot the new kernel is to prepare LILO for the new kernel. See the previous section "Configuring LILO" for details on how you can create a new configuration segment in /etc/lilo.conf for the new kernel. Once you have modified the /etc/lilo.conf file and have run /sbin/lilo, you can reboot the system and attempt to use the new kernel as discussed in the section "Booting with the new kernel."

If all things go well, you have a fresh, new, custom-configured kernel running all your favorite Linux applications from now on.

 Do not forget to make a new boot floppy using the `mkbootdisk --device /dev/fd0 2.2.2` command.

Now that you know how to configure, compile, install, and boot a new kernel from the source, you should also know that often you will have situations when the entire kernel code does not change, only small pieces. This is the time you need to know how to patch your kernel source and create a new kernel.

Patching a Kernel

It is not uncommon to have a situation when you need to patch an existing kernel to get something working the way you want. In such a case, you can simply patch the source and rebuild the kernel. You can patch the kernel source from the /usr/src directory by using the following command:

```
gzip -cd patchXX.gz | patch -p0
```

 If multiple patches are available for a kernel, apply the patches in order. In other words, apply patch01.gz before you apply pach02.gz and so on.

As an alternative, you can use the script patch-kernel to automate this process. Store the patch file(s) in the /usr/src directory, and from the /usr/src directory, run:

```
./linux/scripts/patch-kernel
```

After patching the kernel, follow the instructions for compiling and installing the new kernel as discussed previously.

Because the modern Linux kernel supports modules you can load and unload automatically via the kerneld daemon, you might need to configure one or more parameters for these modules to work properly. You can use kernelcfg for such a job.

Using kernelcfg

All module configuration information is stored in /etc/conf.modules. You can either modify this file manually or use the kernelcfg tool. Figure 20-4 shows the main kernelcfg window.

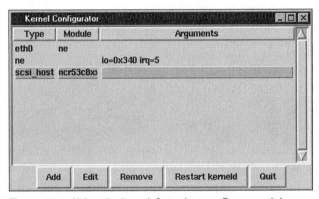

Figure 20-4: Using the kernelcfg tool to configure modules

As you can see, you can add, delete, or modify module configuration information by using this interface. To understand how to configure a module, take a look at the /etc/conf.modules file, which is what the kernelcfg tool manages.

```
alias scsi_hostadapter ncr53c8xx
alias eth0 ne
options ne io=0x340 irq=5
```

To add a new module configuration, click the Add button, and select the module name from the drop-down menu, as in Figure 20-5.

Once you select the module name from the list of available modules, you can click OK to continue. If the module requires any arguments, you can add them in the next screen, as in Figure 20-6.

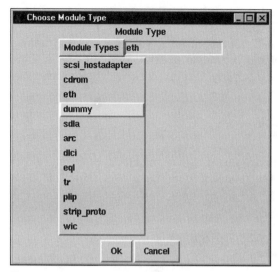

Figure 20-5: Adding a new module configuration for kerneld

Figure 20-6: Adding arguments for the new module configuration

Once you add the arguments and click the OK button in the argument entry window, the new module configuration appears in the main window. You can also edit or delete an existing module configuration by using the appropriate buttons available on the interface. Once you are done making changes, you should restart the kerneld daemon by clicking the Restart kerneld button.

Summary

In this chapter, you learned how to install a new kernel from RPM packages and also how to create a custom kernel by configuring and compiling it yourself from kernel source code.

Chapter 21

Building a Multiserver Web Network

IN THIS CHAPTER

- ◆ How to design a Web network
- ◆ How to use round-robin DNS for balancing load
- ◆ How to use a hardware-based load-balancing solution
- ◆ How to use NFS for sharing disk space among Web servers
- ◆ How to mirror contents among multiple Web servers using rdist

ALL SYSTEM ADMINISTRATORS, AT one point or another, face a server performance issue. After you work very hard setting up your server, you might find it is not powerful enough to handle your workload. What do you do then? You have two choices: Tune your server to the extreme, or get another server to distribute load. The first option is more challenging and time consuming. Fine-tuning the kernel or your server applications might require detailed understanding of the software involved. After you implement all well-known tune-up tricks, it still might not be enough. The second method is more realistic, especially because x86-based computers are getting cheaper and faster every day. It is likely to take less time and effort to set up a second server to distribute load than to try all the tricks in a Linux hacker's bag. For real businesses, I recommend the distributed load approach because at the end of the day it is also the most economical. In this chapter, I discuss a real-life network solution that uses a distributed network architecture.

Distributing load over multiple computers is not new. It just became more affordable because of the low cost of x86 PCs and, of course, Linux! In this chapter, I discuss how you can use Red Hat Linux servers and hardware load distributing equipment to create a high-end Web hosting service. Note that the immediate value of the chapter depends on your situation. If you are looking for a high-end solution involving Red Hat Linux and other hardware, this is a good starting point. However, if you are not in such a situation yet, this chapter provides you with ideas about how to go about building a reliable network of a multitude of services.

Say you are the chief network architect for a consulting company and you have been asked to develop a high-end Web hosting service for a fictitious U.S. company called AMINEWS. Let's look at the client requirements.

Requirements for the Web Network

AMINEWS wants to build a Web hosting service with the following requirements:

♦ One or more Web servers provide a load-balanced Web service for each client Web site. When a Web server is unavailable because of a crash, an application error, or routine maintenance, the remaining Web servers service the Web sites. The Web service should not be interrupted as long as at least one Web server is available to service all the Web sites.

♦ Each client site has a unique domain, and the Web site has the following URL format: `http://www.client-domain.tld/`.

♦ Each client must be allowed to update her Web sites via FTP. Each client receives an ftp.client-domain.tld host as part of the DNS configuration. The client uses this host for updating the contents of her Web site.

♦ Because AMINEWS provides a centralized CGI scripting service via a central cgi-bin directory, clients must be allowed to use this facility. However, because many of the AMINEWS CGI applications write data, a way must exist to synchronize the data among the Web servers. In other words, if a CGI application writes a data file, this file needs to be available to all Web servers so that other CGI applications can share the data.

♦ Clients must be allowed to have virtual SMTP mail service. Each client also has one or more POP3 mail accounts to access mail directly from the POP3 server.

Now that you know the requirements, take a look at how you can design such a network.

Designing the Web Network

The first step in designing the network I describe previously is to develop some diagrams. The first network diagram is quite simple, as in Figure 21-1.

This diagram shows two farms: a Web server farm and a related network services farm. The Web server farm consists of the Web server systems, and the related network services farm consists of the DNS, SMTP, POP3, and FTP servers. These two server farms are interconnected on the same network via an Ethernet hub connected to the router responsible for carrying the Internet traffic to and from the network. Once you have a simple diagram such as this, you can start thinking about ways of load-balancing the Web traffic among the servers in the Web server farm.

One of the easiest ways to distribute load among multiple servers is to use a round-robin DNS configuration, which you learn more about in the following section.

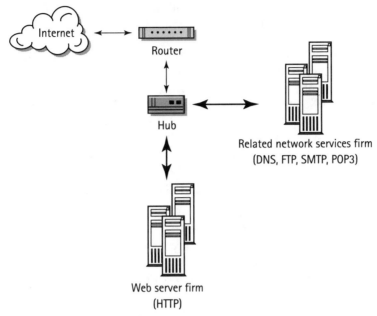

Figure 21-1: A simple network diagram

Considering a round-robin DNS solution

If you have already read the section "Balancing Load Using the DNS Server" in Chapter 10, you know how round-robin DNS works.

Suppose AMINEWS is going to have only two Web servers in the Web server farm — ww1.aminews.com (192.168.1.10) and www2.aminews.com (192.168.1.20). You would like to balance load for the www.aminews.com on these two servers by using a round-robin DNS configuration. In the aminews.com zone file, you can add the following lines:

```
www1 IN   A      192.168.1.10
www2 IN   A      192.168.1.20
www  IN   CNAME  www1
www  IN   CNAME  www2
```

Restart the name server, and ping the www1.aminews.com host. You see the 192.168.1.10 address in the ping output. Stop and restart pinging the same host, and now you see the second IP address being pinged. This is because the preceding configuration tells the name server to cycle through the CNAME records for www. In other words, the www1.aminews.com host is both www1.aminews.com and www2.aminews.com.

When someone enters www.aminews.com, the name server produces the first address once; for the next request, it produces the second address. It keeps cycling between these addresses.

One disadvantage of the round-robin DNS configuration is that there is no way for the name server to know which system is heavily loaded and which is not; it just blindly cycles. If one of the servers crashes or becomes unavailable for some reason, the round-robin DNS still returns the broken server's IP on a regular basis. This can generate chaos because some people are able to get to the sites and some are not. Because this is not acceptable, as I state in the preceding network requirements, you must find a better solution. Consider a hardware-based solution.

Considering a hardware load-balancing solution

In recent years, a great deal of development has taken place in the realm of hardware-based load-balancing solutions. Many name-brand network equipment companies now provide hardware for implementing truly load-balanced networks.

To load-balance the AMINEWS network, you can use a type of hardware called a director. Typically, a director product works as in Figure 21-2.

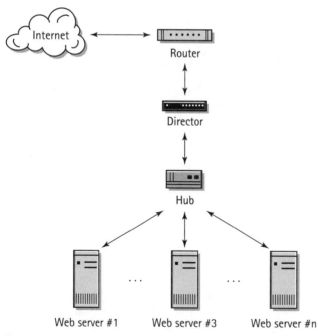

Figure 21-2: How a director works

All Internet traffic destined for Web servers is routed toward the director equipment. The director product then chooses a Web server based on one or more algorithms. For example, a director can choose a Web server because it is the least busy at a given moment. It can also choose a Web server because the rest of the servers are down. In other words, the director uses the availability of the network and service, and also the performance of the server, to choose a Web server.

Many director products are available. You have to research such products and determine which works in this scenario. You should look into the trade magazines related to networking for ideas about what might work; you should also search the Web sites of well-known network hardware vendors. Here I assume you have researched such products and have found the following:

◆ Local Director: The well-known network equipment company called Cisco Systems, Inc. (`http://www.cisco.com/`) offers this solution.

◆ Ace Director: Another well-known network equipment company called Alteon Networks, Inc. (`http://www.alteon.com/`) provides this solution.

◆ Web Server Director: Yet another well-known network equipment company called RADWARE (`http://www.radware.com/`) provides this solution.

Once you have identified a list of products that might work, you need to research how these products perform in real-life scenarios. One of the easiest ways to know how these products rank against each other is to search for customer testimonials and complaints on Usenet. You can post an article in appropriate newsgroups (those related to computer networking, Web servers, and so on) asking people to tell you how they like these products. You might even find a frequently asked question (FAQ) document about load-balancing solutions. You should also call the product company and talk to an engineer (not to the marketing people) about your plans and ask how that person sees the product fitting your solutions. Likely, you will hear how well each product will work in your design. Don't be discouraged by this. Each engineer will try to sell her product, but you will gain information about the exact model number, pricing, and support packages.

Once you have searched the Web and Usenet, have talked to vendors, and have an idea about how these products rank against each other, you are able to make a decision. Personally, when I have to make such a decision, I use the following formula: I give each vendor 100 points at the beginning and then take points off as I find reliable negative information about the product or the company.

For example, if I find that tens of people are complaining about how hard it is to configure a product in my list, I subtract a few points from the total points for that company. If a company's engineering staff is not greatly helpful and does not take time to explain information, I remove more points from the total. If a trade magazine reviews the products in my list and gives a low score to a product, I drop a few more points. Eventually, I might have a clear winner or a situation in which there are potentially no differences in the points. In either case, I base my final judgment on my experience.

Choosing the right load-balancing solution

Here, I have discussed two load-balancing solutions: a round-robin DNS configuration and a director-based hardware solution. Table 21-1 shows a comparison table to help you make your final decision.

TABLE 21-1 COMPARING ROUND-ROBIN DNS AND A DIRECTOR-BASED
HARDWARE SOLUTION

Feature	Round-Robin DNS	Director
Distributes load among multiple servers?	Yes. However, distribution is done in a dumb mode. The servers are selected in a cyclic order.	Yes. A server is selected based on its network load, availability of the underlying application, and even performance.
Fault tolerant?	No. If a server in the round-robin DNS configuration becomes unavailable because of a crash or the application (that is, Web server software) fails for some reason, the DNS configuration still sends traffic to the broken server and hence creates an undesirable situation.	Yes. If a server crashes or the desired application fails for some reason, it is taken out of the server farm and no traffic is directed toward the broken server.
DNS update delayed?	Yes. Any changes to the DNS configuration, such as the addition of a new server in the farm, are not available until the DNS configuration has propagated on the Internet.	No. Because a new server remains behind the director, as soon as the director knows about the server, it can be brought to service.

Feature	Round-Robin DNS	Director
Manageable?	No. There is no way to control or influence the load-balancing scheme.	Yes. You can tell the director to load balance based on network load, the availability of the application itself, and performance. Typically, a director reports statistics and other valuable management-related information to fine-tune the load-balancing scheme.

As you can see, a hardware solution is preferable to a round-robin DNS configuration. If the budget permits, I highly recommend it. In this example, I assume you have chosen the Web Server Director (especially the WSD Pro model) product from RADWARE.

Now look at the new network diagram. Figure 21-3 is a combination of Figures 21-1 and 21-2.

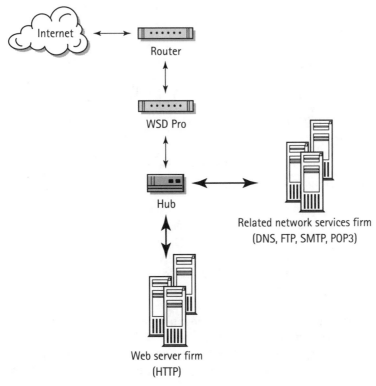

Figure 21-3: The new and improved network diagram

As you can see, the director, WSD Pro, is now between the router and the two server farms. We do this to allow the director to control all traffic. However, if you want to, you can keep the related network services farm outside of the load balancer. However, because AMINEWS might want to load balance these services in the future, it is a good idea to bring both farms under the control of the director. For example, Figure 21-4 shows a highly redundant version of the same network.

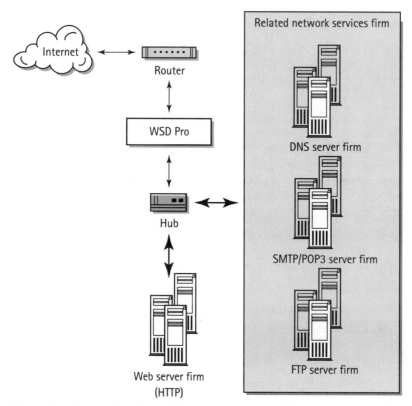

Figure 21-4: A redundant network service diagram

As you can see, the related network services farm can be a collection of service farms such as a DNS service farm, an SMTP/POP3 service farm, an FTP service farm, and so on. However, assume that, for now, AMINEWS wants to use only two Web servers in the Web server farm and only a single server for DNS, FTP, SMTP, and POP3. The idea here is to create a network configuration that works with this minimum number of servers and yet allows an easy integration path for more servers so the network can become highly redundant.

At this point, you have tackled the first requirement of the network. The second requirement states that each client must have its own domain. You can do this simply by providing DNS service for each client. This is really a software configuration issue because you can configure your DNS server to provide DNS service client domains. Hence, these requirements have no impact on the network design. However, the third and fourth requirements do. The third requirement states that clients must be allowed to FTP files into their accounts by using `ftp.client-domain.tld` hosts and that these files need to be available on Web servers in the Web server farm. The fourth requirement states that CGI applications must create files and directories Web servers need to share.

Now that you know the actual server count, we can draw a more realistic network diagram, as in Figure 21-5.

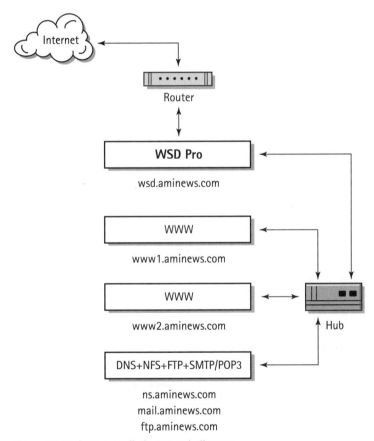

Figure 21-5: A more realistic network diagram

This diagram shows proposed hostnames for each machine. The single server in the related network services farm has multiple hostnames. You use the `ns.aminews.com` hostname for DNS services, the `mail.aminews.com` hostname for SMTP/POP3, and the ftp.aminews.com hostname for FTP service. The Web servers in the Web server farm are called `www1.aminews.com` and `www2.aminews.com`. Finally, the WSD Pro director itself is called `wsdpro.aminews.com`.

Because AMINEWS (for now) use a single server (`ns.aminews.com`) for all related network services, the `ftp.client-domain.tld` hosts must be aliases of this host. If clients have accounts on this machine, how do you bring the files from this machine to the Web server farm? One way is to use NFS. You can mount one or more disks in this server and make the disk(s) available to the Web server via NFS. In other words, you have to turn the `ns.aminews.com` server into an NFS server so that all Web sites become NFS clients. This makes sense for the fourth requirement. If you use the NFS file system to share files, all Web servers running the CGI applications read and write to the data from the same file system and hence do not have data synchronization problems.

However, some performance concerns are associated with NFS. No one disagrees that servicing Web sites from local disks is much faster than servicing them from an NFS-mounted file system. You need to come up with a compromise.

One option for preventing synchronization problems is to NFS-mount only a small file system that Web servers must share. This can be a directory on the `ns.aminews.com` server that hosts the CGI application-specific data files and directories. You must distribute the rest of the Web site-related files via another mechanism. In Chapter 16, you learned about using rdist to distribute files among computers; you can use this technique here. You can use rdist to distribute all Web site files and directories to the Web servers and mount only a central CGI data directory via NFS.

To reduce NFS and rdist traffic that shares the bandwidth with your Internet traffic, you can create a local area network (LAN) as in Figure 21-6.

Here, the NFS and rdist traffic is routed via a separate LAN so that this traffic does not interfere with Internet traffic. Because such a configuration makes the NFS file system unavailable to the outside world, it also enhances server security.

 Using a second LAN for NFS and rdist traffic requires each server to have two network interfaces.

Finally, the fifth requirement is purely a software configuration in that it involves configuring the SMTP/POP3 mail server on `ns.aminews.com`; it is, therefore, not related to network design.

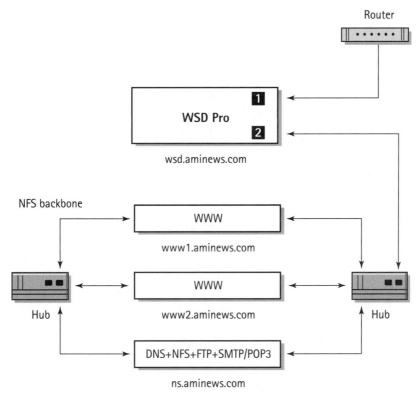

Figure 21-6: Using a LAN for NFS and rdist traffic

At this point, you have developed a network design that works. Now look at the next phase of development – allocating IP addresses for your network.

Allocating IP Addresses

As you know from earlier chapters, each network interface must have an IP address. Because each server computer in this network has two interfaces (one for the Internet traffic and one for the NFS/rdist LAN traffic), each server must have two IP addresses. The WSD Pro director also has two interfaces. Figure 21-7 shows a possible IP address assignment.

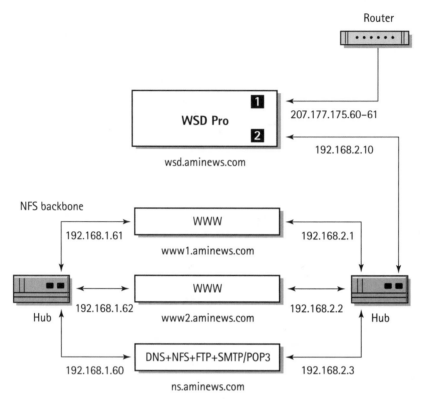

Figure 21-7: A possible IP address assignment

If you look closely, you notice three networks here. The NFS backbone network on the left side of the figure shows a network 192.168.1.0, and the right side of the figure shows a network 192.168.2.0 that interconnects the servers with the WSD Pro director. The WSD Pro's port #1 is connected to the router via network 207.177.175.0.

The two internal networks, 192.168.1.0 and 192.168.2.0, are not routable over the Internet. Other than local servers, no computer needs to see the NFS backbone network 192.168.1.0; therefore, using 192.168.1.*x* addresses poses no problem. The 192.168.2.*x* network is visible only among the server computers and the WSD Pro director. Therefore, it does not need an Internet-routable IP network address. Because this network is also local to the servers and the WSD Pro director, using 192.168.*x*.*x* addresses poses no problem. However, the router and the WSD Pro's network interface #1 need to be on a routable network because Internet packets must travel via this network to the WSD Pro director. Here, I have used the 207.177.175.0 network as an example. In real life, this is whatever IP addresses are available from your ISP.

Notice that the WSD Pro director's #1 network interface has four IP addresses: 207.177.175.60 through 207.177.175.63. Although you can configure WSD Pro to answer up to 512 IP addresses, in this example you need only three IP addresses for this interface. You need one IP (207.177.175.60) for the DNS/FTP/SMTP/POP3 server farm, one IP (207.177.175.61) for the Web server farm, and another IP (207.177.175.63) for the WSD Pro director itself. Because this example is based on a real installation in which four IP addresses are available, I am showing four IP addresses assigned to this interface.

The preceding IP assignments use only three routable IP addresses (207.177.175.60, 207.177.175.61, and 207.177.175.63). This can be a blessing in that many ISPs charge for each IP address you use for your servers. The allocation also benefits from the use of nonroutable IP address in one other way. The current IP allocation allows you to create a total of 253 (192.168.2.1–9,192.168.2.11–254) servers in both the Web server farm and the related network services farm. In other words, you can add new servers in either farm without the need to have the ISP allocate new routable IP addresses for you.

Using Internet-routable IP addresses for the NFS backbone or the network behind the WSD Pro director can be a waste because these networks are not visible to the Internet even with routable IP addresses.

Assuming that you stick to the IP allocation presented here, the next thing to do is to wire the network as desired. Once you have wired the network, you can configure the network.

Configuring the Network

You have three computers to configure: the DNS/FTP/SMTP/POP3 computer and two Web servers. You also have to configure the WSD Pro director. Before you can begin, you need to decide these points:

◆ What domain name do you use for the NFS backbone (192.168.1.0) so that you can create hostnames for each computer on this private network? Because no computer outside this LAN sees the domain, it really does not matter what you call the domain. I call it `aminews-lan.com`; I name the name server host interface `ns.aminews-lan.com` and the Web server host interfaces `www1.aminews-lan.com` and `www2.aminews-lan.com`.

◆ The 192.168.2.0 network is also invisible to the outside world, so you can use whatever domain name you choose here as well. However, when a client connects to the name server machine via FTP, the hostname of the machine is displayed to the client, and therefore you might want to use aminews.com as the domain name. So the name server interface on this network receives the ns.aminews.com hostname, and the two Web servers interfaces receive the names www1.aminews.com and www2.aminews.com, as in Figure 21-7. Note that the WSD Pro director's interface #2 is wsd.aminews.com.

Once you have decided the domain names, you can start configuring the name server computer.

Setting up the network for a name server computer

First, you have to configure the name server's network interfaces. The /etc/sysconfig/network file for ns.aminews.com is in Listing 21-1.

Listing 21-1: The /etc/sysconfig/network file

```
NETWORKING=yes
FORWARD_IPV4=false
HOSTNAME=ns.aminews.com
DOMAINNAME=aminews.com
GATEWAY=192.168.2.10
GATEWAYDEV=eth0
```

Notice that the gateway address is set to the WSD Pro director's #2 interface address. This occurs because all Internet packets must travel to and from the WSD Pro system. Because the eth0 interface is named as the gateway device, this interface has the 192.168.2.3 address in the /etc/sysconfig/network-scripts file, as in Listing 21-2.

Listing 21-2: /etc/sysconfig/network-scripts/ifcfg-eth0

```
DEVICE=eth0
IPADDR=192.168.2.3
NETMASK=255.255.255.0
NETWORK=192.168.2.0
BROADCAST=255.255.255.255
ONBOOT=yes
```

We use the other network interface, eth1, to connect to the NFS backbone network. This interface uses the 192.168.1.60 address. Listing 21-3 shows the /etc/sysconfig/network-scripts/ifcfg-eth1 file.

Listing 21-3: /etc/sysconfig/network-scripts/ifcfg-eth1

```
DEVICE=eth1
IPADDR=192.168.1.60
NETMASK=255.255.255.0
NETWORK=192.168.1.0
BROADCAST=255.255.255.255
ONBOOT=yes
```

Once you have configured the preceding files, you can bring the interfaces up using the ifconfig eth0 up and ifconfig eth1 up commands. If you run the ifconfig command without any argument, you should see output similar to that in Listing 21-4.

Listing 21-4: Output of ifconfig

```
lo        Link encap:Local Loopback
          inet addr:127.0.0.1  Bcast:127.255.255.255  Mask:255.0.0.0
          UP BROADCAST LOOPBACK RUNNING  MTU:3584  Metric:1
          RX packets:156329 errors:0 dropped:0 overruns:0
          TX packets:156329 errors:0 dropped:0 overruns:0

eth0      Link encap:10Mbps Ethernet  HWaddr 00:60:08:CE:0D:8B
          inet addr:192.168.2.3  Bcast:255.255.255.255
Mask:255.255.255.0
          UP BROADCAST RUNNING MULTICAST  MTU:1500  Metric:1
          RX packets:1102949 errors:0 dropped:0 overruns:0
          TX packets:1140982 errors:0 dropped:0 overruns:0
          Interrupt:10 Base address:0xef00

eth1      Link encap:10Mbps Ethernet  HWaddr 00:60:08:CE:0D:C2
          inet addr:192.168.1.60  Bcast:255.255.255.255
Mask:255.255.255.0
          UP BROADCAST RUNNING MULTICAST  MTU:1500  Metric:1
          RX packets:35844834 errors:0 dropped:0 overruns:0
          TX packets:36356899 errors:0 dropped:0 overruns:0
          Interrupt:9 Base address:0xee80
```

Setting up the network interfaces for each Web server

The network interface configurations for each Web server are identical. I discuss only one here because you can replace the IP address and use the same configuration files for the other Web server. Here, I show you the network configuration for www1.aminews.com. The /etc/sysconfig/network file is in Listing 21-5.

Listing 21-5: The /etc/sysconfig/network file

```
NETWORKING=yes
FORWARD_IPV4=false
HOSTNAME=www1.aminews.com
DOMAINNAME=aminews.com
GATEWAY= 192.168.2.10
GATEWAYDEV=eth0
```

As you can see, the gateway is set to 192.168.2.10, which is the IP address of the #2 interface of the WSD Pro director. The /etc/sysconfig/network-scripts/ifcfg-eth0 file is in Listing 21-6.

Listing 21-6: The /etc/sysconfig/network-scripts/ifcfg-eth0 file

```
DEVICE=eth0
IPADDR=192.168.2.1
NETMASK=255.255.255.0
NETWORK=192.168.2.0
BROADCAST=255.255.255.255
ONBOOT=yes
```

The /etc/sysconfig/network-scripts/ifcfg-eth1 file is in Listing 21-7.

Listing 21-7: The /etc/sysconfig/network-scripts/ifcfg-eth1 file

```
DEVICE=eth1
IPADDR=192.168.1.61
NETMASK=255.255.255.0
NETWORK=192.168.1.0
BROADCAST=255.255.255.255
ONBOOT=yes
```

We use this interface for the NFS backbone.

To create the network configuration for the other Web server, use the configuration options just shown. Do not forget to replace 192.168.2.1 with 192.168.2.2 and 192.168.1.61 with 192.168.1.62.

Setting up network interfaces of the WSD Pro director

The idea here is to set up WSD Pro so you can access it via an SNMP (Simple Network Management Protocol) tool called ConfigMaster, which is provided with WSD Pro. The first step is to configure the #1 interface port to answer to the 207.177.175.63 address. As with many outer network devices, the only way you can configure the first IP address is via a serial port available on WSD Pro. You can connect the WSD Pro director to a PC or a laptop that is running a standard terminal program so that you can access a simple, menu-driven interface on WSD Pro. Using this serial port interface, you can configure the first IP address for the WSD Pro director. Once you configure the #1 interface, connect the interface to your router. Now you should be able to ping the 207.177.175.63 address from anywhere. If you are able to ping the IP address, you can perform the rest of the configuration via the ConfigMaster program. The ConfigMaster program runs on Windows 9x/2000 computers; if you do not have a Windows 9x/NT computer available, you can run a Java application on any Java-compliant platform. However, ConfigMaster makes managing WSD Pro really simple; hence, I use it in this example.

Installing ConfigMaster on a Windows NT (or Windows 9x) machine is as simple as installing any Windows software. Once you install and run it for the first time, the ConfigMaster software displays a screen as in Figure 21-8.

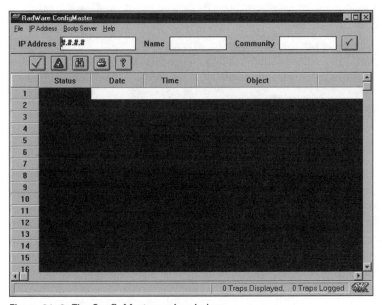

Figure 21-8: The ConfigMaster main window

When you see the screen in Figure 21-8, enter the IP address (207.177.175.63 for the #1 interface) of the WSD Pro director in the IP Address text box, and enter Public in the Community text box. Then click the check mark at the upper right. This allows ConfigMaster to connect the WSD Pro director. Once ConfigMaster makes the connection, a new zoom window appears. This window displays the front of the WSD Pro director, as in Figure 21-9.

Before you proceed, you must read the Using Buttons section of online help. This is a must because RADWARE does not provide a standard, menu-based interface for each screen in ConfigMaster but relies heavily on graphical buttons. Without knowing which button is which, you easily get lost or confused.

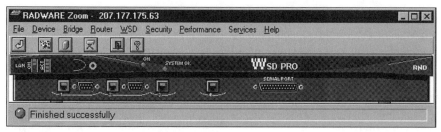

Figure 21-9: The ConfigMaster zoom window

To configure the #2 interface, select the Interface Parameters option from the IP Router submenu of the Router menu, as in Figure 21-10.

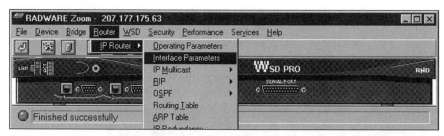

Figure 21-10: Setting an IP address for the second interface

You should see the IP Router Interface Parameters window. This shows the interfaces you have configured: in this case, interface #1. You should move your mouse over the available buttons and see the status line change. Click the Add a new table row button, which displays a screen where you can select the interface you want to assign to the new IP address. Select interface #2, and assign it the 192.168.2.10 IP address. After you have assigned the IP address and sent the new configuration to the WSD Pro director, you should have two interfaces configured, as in Figure 21-11.

	IP Address	Network Mask	If Num	Fwd Broadcast	Broadcast Type
1	192.168.2.10	255.255.255.0	2	Enable	One Fill
2	207.177.175.63	255.255.255.0	1	Enable	One Fill

2 rows displayed

Figure 21-11: IP router interface parameters for WSD Pro

Once you have configured the WSD Pro director to answer to 207.177.175.63 (on interface #1) and 192.168.2.10 (on interface #2), you are done with the basic network configuration and are ready to test it.

Testing the network configuration

Turn on each network interface (eth0 and eth1) on each server computer by using the ifconfig interface up command. Also, run the following commands on each of the servers:

```
route add default  gw 192.168.2.10 dev eth0
route add -net 192.168.1.0 netmask 255.255.255.0 eth1
```

The first route command creates a default route to the WSD Pro director's interface #2, and the second one tells each computer to use eth1 for the 192.168.1.0 network. Run the following command to make sure the routing is set up properly. (Use the -n option to prevent the route command from trying to resolve domain names.)

```
route -n
```

This command should produce output similar to that in Listing 21-8.

Listing 21-8: Output of route -n

```
Kernel IP routing table
Destination Gateway     Genmask        Flags Metric Ref Use Iface
192.168.2.0 0.0.0.0     255.255.255.0  U     0      0   31  eth0
192.168.1.0 0.0.0.0     255.255.255.0  U     0      0   5   eth1
127.0.0.0   0.0.0.0     255.0.0.0      U     0      0   4   lo
0.0.0.0     192.168.2.10 0.0.0.0       UG    0      0   999 et0
```

Once you have added these routes to each of the servers, you should be able to do the following:

1. Ping the WSD Pro director's interface #2 (192.168.2.10) from each server by using the ping 192.168.2.10 command. If you cannot ping from one or more of the servers, make sure you have the preceding routes implemented correctly. You should also check the wiring and the hub connections for faults.

2. Once you can ping the WSD Pro director's interface #2 from each of the servers, you should ping each server from the other by using the ping command and the 192.168.2.*x* addresses.

3. Once you have tested the 192.168.2.0 network, test the 192.168.1.0 network by pinging each server from the other.

Once all of these tests are successful, your basic network configuration is complete, and you can move on to the server software configuration. Start with the name server configuration.

Setting Up the DNS Server

First, you need to set up the name server daemon to act as the primary name server for the `aminews.com` and `aminews-lan.com` domains. The /etc/named.boot file in Listing 21-9 does just that.

Listing 21-9: The /etc/named.boot file

```
;
; a caching only nameserver config
;
directory                                    /var/named
cache           .                            named.ca
primary         0.0.127.in-addr.arpa         named.local


;
; Main domain
;

primary         aminews.com                          aminews.db
secondary       175.177.207.in-addr.arpa             aminews.rev


;
; Non-routable domains
;
primary         aminews-lan.com          aminews-lan.db
primary         1.168.192.in-addr.arpa   aminews-lan.rev
primary         2.168.192.in-addr.arpa   db.192.168.2
```

Here, the name server is set up as the primary name server for the `aminews.com` and `aminews-lan.com` domains. It is also set up to provide primary reverse DNS for networks 127.0.0.0 (the loopback network), 192.168.1.0 (the NFS backbone), and 192.168.2.0, as well as secondary reverse DNS for the 207.177.175.0 network. I assume that AMINEWS does not own the 207.177.175.0 network and that its upstream ISP should do the primary reverse DNS for this network.

 If you are using the latest version of BIND, use the named-bootconf.pl script to convert /etc/named.boot to /etc/named.conf.

Listing 21-10 shows the /var/named/aminews.db file.

Listing 21-10: The /var/named/aminews.db file

```
@       IN      SOA     aminews.com.     hostmaster.aminews.com. (
                        19990223001      ; serial YYYYMMDDXXX
                        7200             ; refresh
                        3600             ; (1 hour) retry
                        604800           ; (7 days) expire
                        3600)            ; (1 hour) minimal TTL


        IN      NS      ns.aminews.com.
        IN      MX      5 mail.aminews.com.


ns      IN      A       207.177.175.60
mail    IN      A       207.177.175.60
www     IN      A       207.177.175.61
wsd     IN      A       207.177.175.63
ftp     IN      CNAME   ns
```

If you have read Chapter 10, you should be able to understand this file quite easily. Remember from the previous network configuration that these IP addresses are not assigned to any of the servers. These are the IP addresses that WSD Pro answers to on interface #1.

Later, you will configure WSD Pro so that when a DNS, SMTP, POP3, or FTP request comes to 207.177.175.60, it will be directed to 192.168.2.3. Similarly, when an HTTP request comes to 207.177.175.61, it will be directed to either 192.168.2.1 or 192.168.2.2.

Listing 21-11 shows the reverse DNS configuration file for aminews.com.

Listing 21-11: The /var/named/aminews.rev file

```
@       IN      SOA     aminews.com.     hostmaster.aminews.com. (
                        19990224001      ; serial YYYYMMDDXXX
                        7200             ; refresh
                        3600             ; (1 hour) retry
                        43200            ; (12 hours) expire
                        3600)            ; (1 hour) minimal TTL


        IN      NS      ns.aminews.com.
        IN      MX      5 mail.aminews.com.


60      IN      PTR     ns.aminews.com.
60      IN      PTR     mail.aminews.com.
61      IN      PTR     www.aminews.com.
63      IN      PTR     wsd.aminews.com.
```

The fake domain used for the NFS backbone has the forward and reverse configuration files in Listings 21-12 and 21-13, respectively.

Listing 21-12: The /var/named/aminews-lan.db file

```
@       IN      SOA     aminews-lan.com. hostmaster.aminews-lan.com. (
                        19990215000     ; serial YYYYMMDDXXX
                        7200            ; refresh
                        3600            ; (1 hour) retry
                        604800          ; (7 days) expire
                        3600)           ; (1 hour) minimal TTL

; Name server amd Mail eXchange records
        IN      NS      ns.aminews.com.


; A records
ns      IN      A       192.168.1.60
www1    IN      A       192.168.1.61
www2    IN      A       192.168.1.62
```

Here, ns.aminews-lan.com is assigned 192.168.1.60, which is the IP address for eht1 on the DNS/FTP/SMTP/POP3 server. The other two IP addresses are also assigned to eth1 interfaces on the Web servers.

Listing 21-13: The /var/named/aminews-lan.rev file

```
@       IN      SOA     aminews-lan.com.              hostmaster.aminews-
lan.com. (
                        19990215000     ; serial YYYYMMDDXXX
                        7200            ; refresh
                        3600            ; (1 hour) retry
                        43200           ; (12 hours) expire
                        3600)           ; (1 hour) minimal TTL


; Name server amd Mail eXchange records
        IN      NS      ns.aminews-lan.com.


; PTR Records
60      IN      PTR     ns.aminews-lan.com.
61      IN      PTR     www1.aminews-lan.com.
62      IN      PTR     www2.aminews-lan.com.
```

You need to configure the /etc/hosts file as in Listing 21-14 so that private networks can work even without a name server daemon.

Listing 21-14: The /etc/hosts file

```
[kabir@ns /etc]# cat hosts
127.0.0.1        localhost
192.168.1.60     ns.aminews-lan.com
192.168.1.61     www1.aminews-lan.com
192.168.1.62     www2.aminews-lan.com

192.168.2.3      ns.aminews.com
192.168.2.2      www2.aminews.com
192.168.2.1      www1.aminews.com
192.168.2.3      mail.aminews.com
```

You should configure the /etc/host.conf file as in Listing 21-15 so that the /etc/hosts file gets higher priority in resolving hostnames. This allows you to troubleshoot things even if the name server is not functioning properly.

Listing 21-15: The /etc/host.conf file

```
order hosts,bind
multi on
```

Start the name server daemon. Once it starts, set up the /etc/resolv.conf file as in Listing 21-16.

Listing 21-16: The /etc/resolv.conf file

```
nameserver 192.168.2.3
```

This tells the name server computer to use the local name server daemon to resolve names. Using the nslookup tool, test your name server configuration. If you can resolve the `aminews.com` and `aminews-lan.com` hostnames properly, you are done with the name server configuration.

Setting Up the NFS Server

Because the CGI applications need to share data space, you need to export a directory or a full partition of your name server computer.

You should follow the instructions in Chapter 16 to learn full details on how to create NFS file systems.

Say you have decided to export the /www/data directory to the Web servers. In such a case, create an /etc/exports file as in Listing 21-17.

Listing 21-17: The /etc/exports file

```
/www/data www1.aminews-lan.com(rw) www2.aminews-lan.com(rw)
```

Here, the /www/data directory is NFS-exported to the www1.amienws-lan.com (192.168.1.61) and www2.aminews-lan.com (192.168.1.62) Web servers via the NFS backbone LAN. Both of these servers have read/write (rw) permission because CGI applications on both servers need full access. Once you have created the /etc/exports file, run the exportfs -a command to make the exported directory available to Web servers. You should verify that the exporting is working properly by running the showmount ns.aminews-lan.com command.

Setting Up the Mail (SMTP/POP3) Server

Because you want the sendmail daemon on mail.aminews.com to handle all mail, you must configure the sendmail daemons on Web servers to relay mail to this server. In other words, the sendmail server on mail.aminews.com has to become the smart host for other sendmail daemons on Web servers. This requires that you add Web servers in the /etc/mail/relay-domain file (or whatever is equivalent in your version of sendmail). You should add 192.168.2.1 and 192.168.2.2 to this file so that sendmail on the mail.aminews.com server allows the other two sendmail daemons to relay mail via this host.

You should add the aminews.com domain in the /etc/mail/sendmail.cw file so that the sendmail daemon handles all mail for aminews.com. You should read Chapter 11 to learn how to test the sendmail daemon. Don't forget to restart the sendmail server after you have changed the configuration files.

The default POP3 server shipped with Red Hat does not require special configuration to work in this environment. All you need to do is make sure it is set up as usual. To learn more about how to set up POP3, read Chapter 11.

Setting Up the FTP Server

Read Chapter 13 to enable the FTP server. Once you have enabled the FTP server, there is no more configuration to do.

Setting Up rdist on the Name Server

You must configure rdist on the name server so that it can distribute all Web-related files from the appropriate directories to the Web servers. For example, if you keep all Web files and directories under the /www partition, you can set up rdist to distribute all files in this partition to the Web servers via the NFS backbone LAN. For example, Listing 21-18 shows a distfile.

Listing 21-18: An example distfile file

```
#
# Distfile for rdist
#
# This is used to distribute files from ns.aminews-lan.com
# to www[12].aminews-lan.com systems.
#
# $Author$
# $Version$
# $Date$
# $Id$

HOSTS = (httpd@www1.aminews-lan.com httpd@www2.aminews-lan.com)

FILES = (/www)

EXCLUDE_DIR = (/www/data )

${FILES} -> ${HOSTS}
        install ;
        except ${EXCLUDE_DIR};
```

You can use this distfile to distribute all files in /www (except /www/data (because it is NFS-mounted for CGI applications) to the www1.aminews-lan.com and www2.aminews-lan.com hosts. Notice that the distfile expects a user called httpd to exist on Web servers whose account is set up with an appropriate .rhosts file to allow the ns.aminews-lan.com host to distribute files. You can use the rdist.sh script in Listing 21-19 to run rdist.

Listing 21-19: The rdist.sh script

```
#!/bin/sh
#
# This script runs rdist to update Web servers via
# the non-routable lan aminews-lan.com. The script
# is run by cron at a fixed interval.
#
```

```
# /etc/rc.d/rc.local starts the script to clean
# up left-over temp files that might have been
# left at shutdown. This process also removes
# the log file.
#
# $Author$
# $Version$
# $Id$
# $Date$
# $Status
###############################################################

case "$1" in
  boot)
        echo -n "Cleaning up rdist_net tmp files: "
        rm -f /tmp/rdist_net.lck
        rm -f /tmp/rdist.log
        echo "complete."
        exit 0;
        ;;

  restart)
        $0 boot
        ;;

esac

if [ -f /tmp/rdist_net.lck ]; then
   exit 0
fi

touch  /tmp/rdist_net.lck

/usr/bin/rdist -p /usr/sbin/rdistd \
-oremove,nochkgroup,nochkmode,nochkowner,quiet \
-f /path/to/distfile

rm -f /tmp/rdist_net.lck

echo `date` > /tmp/rdist.log

exit 0
```

You can use the following cron job in /etc/crontab to update Web servers at (approximately) 10-minute intervals by using the rdist.sh script just shown.

```
0,10,20,30,40,50 * * * * httpd \
/path/to/rdist.sh > /dev/null
```

Here, the cron job is set up to run the rdist.sh script as the httpd user on the ns.aminews-lan.com system. You must make sure this user exists and has access to all files and directories in /www partition.

Once you have set up all the services on ns.aminews.com (same as ns.aminews-lan.com), you are ready to configure the Web servers.

Setting Up Each Web Server

First, you should install the Apache Web server as discussed in Chapter 12. You do not need any special configuration in Apache to make it work in this environment. However, remember to use the 192.168.2.*x* IP addresses when creating virtual hosts for clients using <VirtualHost> directives. In other words, a virtual host on the 192.168.2.1 server uses the following configuration syntax:

```
<VirtualHost 192.168.2.1>
    # virtual host specific configuration goes here
</VirtualHost>
```

You should set up the www.aminews.com virtual Web site on each of the Web servers. Next, you need to set up the Web server computer as a NFS client.

Setting up the NFS client configuration

Because the ns.aminews-lan.com server exports /www/data to Web servers, you can add the following line to your /etc/fstab file:

```
ns.aminews-lan.com:/www/data   /data   nfs
```

Once you have added this line, create a /data directory, and run the mount -a -t nfs command to mount the /www/data from ns.aminews-lan.com to the /data directory. Run the df command to ensure that you can mount the /www/data directory. Among your other file systems, you should see a line similar to the following:

```
ns.aminews-lan.com:/www/data 27728  7588  18705  23%   /data
```

Once you have performed this configuration on both Web servers and can mount the /www/data from ns.aminews-lan.com, you are done with the NFS configuration. Now set up the sendmail daemon on the Web servers.

Setting up sendmail to relay to the smart host

Because sendmail programs on Web server hosts relay SMTP mail only to the mail.aminews.com server using the 192.168.1.0 network, all you need to do is set up the /etc/sendmail.cf file to use the smart relay option. You can add the following line in /etc/sendmail.cf:

```
DSns.aminews-lan.com
```

This line makes sure that the sendmail daemon on the Web server uses ns.aminews-lan.com as a smart SMTP relay. Once you have modified the /etc/sendmail.cf file on both Web servers to reflect the preceding change, restart the sendmail server on each Web server. To test the mail server configuration on Web servers, use the mail command to send mail to some address at aminews.com. Check the /var/log/maillog files on both the Web server you are testing and the mail.aminews.com server to make sure the account on the mail.aminews.com server is receiving mail. If you see a "we do not relay" message, make sure you have added the Web servers in the /etc/mail/domain-relay file (or equivalent file for your version of sendmail).

Astute readers wonder why they need to use the SMTP relay — why not let the sendmail programs on Web servers send mail directly to wherever the destination mail server is via DNS lookup?

Here is why. Remember that each Web server has only nonroutable IP addresses for both interfaces. When a Web server wants to send a IP packet to the outside world via the 192.168.2.0 network interface, the WSD Pro director needs to masquerade it via the Network Address Translation (NAT) protocol. For example, when the 192.168.2.1 Web server wants to ping www.yahoo.com for some reason, the WSD Pro director must use NAT to translate this request so that the outgoing packet has a source IP address of 207.177.175.63 (WSD Pro's #1 interface address). If www.yahoo.com responds to the request, WSD Pro repackages the response package to have the destination address 192.168.2.1.

Because many CGI scripts or other applications the Web server runs might expect to have outside network connectivity, you need to enable NAT translation on the WSD Pro director. When you enable NAT, any mail originating at the Web server and destined for mail.aminews.com is not delivered. When you tell the sendmail server on a Web server to send mail to any e-mail address, such as user@aminews.com, it first performs a DNS lookup to locate the MX record for aminews.com. It finds that mail.aminews.com is the STMP mail server for aminews.com; then, the sendmail server resolves this hostname to 207.177.175.60. It tries to open an SMTP connection (on port 25) to 207.177.175.60. Because of NAT, however, the WSD Pro director cannot connect the Web server to mail.aminews.com. Hence, you must use the smart relay trick, which uses the 192.168.1.0 network to transfer all mail messages to mail.aminews.com.

Setting up rdist for file distribution from ns.aminews-lan.com

To allow the `ns.aminews-lan.com` host to distribute files on Web servers, you need to create the user account specified in the distfile in `ns.aminews-lanc.com`. For example, if you have created a distfile on `ns.aminews-lan.com` to use the httpd account, you must create this account on each Web server and configure the .rhosts file to allow `ns.aminews-lan.com` rsh access. You can do this simply by putting the `ns.aminews-lan.com` hostname in the .rhosts file of each Web server. Make sure only the superuser can modify the file and that everyone else can only read the file.

Once you have configured the account you will use to distribute files, create a directory called /www on each Web server, and ensure that the rdist user can read, write, and execute in this directory. To test your rdist setup, you can run the rdist.sh script from the `ns.aminews-lan.com` server. If you see that all files in the /www partition of the `ns.aminews-lan.com` server are being copied as expected, you are done. If you have any problems, check the /var/log/messages and /var/log/security files for clues on what's not set up properly.

Once you have performed the preceding configuration on each of the Web servers, you are done with all server configuration. Now you are ready to configure WSD Pro.

Setting Up Web Director

Setting up WSD Pro via the ConfigMaster tool is quite easy. Run ConfigMaster, and connect to the WSD Pro director by using the 207.177.175.63 IP address and the "Public" community. Once you are connected to the WSD Pro director, you can create the following configuration.

Creating the Web services farm

As I mention previously, you need to create a Web server farm consisting of two Web servers. This farm has 207.177.175.61 as its published IP address and 192.168.2.1-2 as its physical IP address. When WSD Pro for 207.177.175.61 receives an HTTP request (on port 80), it uses its load-balancing algorithms to determine which of the two Web servers receives the request. To create this Web services farm, follow these steps:

1. Click the Farm Parameters option from the WSD menu. This displays a window as in Figure 21-12.

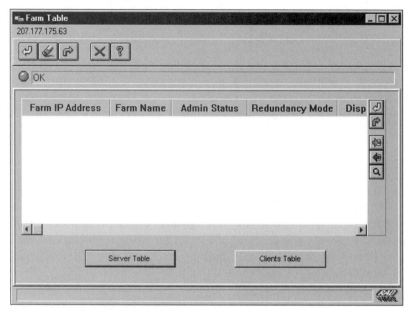

Figure 21-12: The Farm Table window

2. Click the Add a new table row icon (the right arrow). This displays a window as in Figure 21-13.

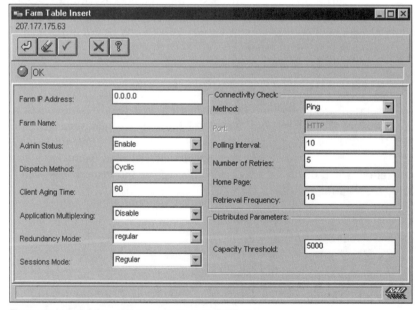

Figure 21-13: Adding a Web server farm to WSD Pro

3. Enter 207.177.175.61 as the Farm IP address; enter a name for this farm in the Farm Name entry box.

4. To enable WSD Pro to start using this farm right away, select the Enable option from the Admin Status menu.

5. If you would like WSD Pro to check your Web server by using ping, select Ping as the Connectivity Check method. Note that if you use ping to check the availability of Web servers, WSD Pro cannot detect if the Web server application is available or not because ping works even if the Apache server is down or not able to respond. To allow WSD Pro to check your Apache server's availability, select HTTP Page as the Connectivity Check method. This makes WSD Pro fetch the home page of www.amienws.com at every polling interval (the default is 10 seconds.).

If the page is not fetched due to a failure, WSD Pro takes the Web server out of service. I recommend that you do not change anything else at this point. The goal here is to get things working first and then to fine-tune them. Click the check mark to complete the farm setup. You see the new Web server farm appear in the Farm Table window as in Figure 21-14.

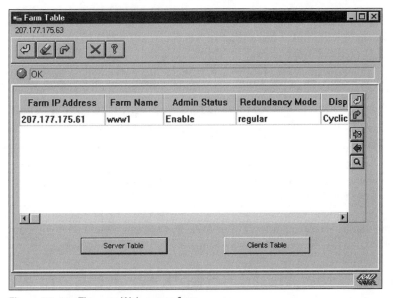

Figure 21-14: The new Web server farm

6. Once you have added the farm, you need to add Web servers to the farm. From the Farm Table window, select the farm you just created, and click the Server Table button. This displays an empty Server Table window. Click the Add a new row button (the right arrow) to add a new server to the farm. This brings up a dialog box as in Figure 21-15.

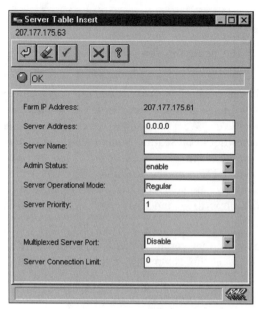

Figure 21–15: Adding Web servers to the Web server farm

7. Notice that the Farm IP Address is set to 207.177.175.61. Enter 192.168.2.1 as the Server Address, and enter a unique name for the server (such as webserver1). To enable the server, make sure the Admin Status is set to Enable. Click the Accept value, and return icon (the check mark).

8. Once you have added the 192.168.2.1 server to the farm, it appears in the Server table. Now add the 192.168.2.2 server in the same manner.

9. Once you have added both Web servers, you should click the Send value to element icon (the right-turn arrow) to let WSD Pro know about the new servers in the farm. Exit from the Server Table window by closing the window.

That's all there is to adding a new Web server farm. Now take a look at how you can add the related network services farm.

Creating the related network services farm

You can create the related network services farm in the same manner as you create the Web server farm. The only difference is that you have to use 207.177.175.60 as the farm IP address and 192.168.2.3 as the only server in the farm. You should also use the ping method to check connectivity in this farm because this farm does not run HTTP servers.

Once you have created the preceding WSD Pro configuration, you are completely done with the configuration. At this point, you should be able to test your configuration. Using a Web browser, access the `http://www.aminews.com/` site. If you do not get the site, check to make sure the Web servers are running the Apache server. You can also use WSD to determine if there is a configuration problem. To find if there is a problem in the WSD Pro configuration, select Application Server Table from the WSD menu. This displays all servers with their statuses. If any server is listed as disabled or shut down, you need to enable it by selecting the row and using the Edit selected row icon (magnifying glass). Check the Admin Status field in the server edit window and make sure it is enabled. Once you have verified that all servers are set up properly in WSD Pro, check for problems in the server configurations in each server. If you find a configuration error, correct it, and restart the server.

Finally, you need to enable the Network Address Translation (NAT) feature from the Global Configuration option under the WSD menu. Set the NAT Operation option to Enable. This allows the Web server machines to access outside Internet sites as usual. Once you have completed these steps, you are finished with the WSD Pro configuration.

Managing the Network

The ConfigMaster program allows you to manage all your servers. Here are some examples of what you can do.

Taking a server out of service

You can take a server out of service as follows:

1. Select Farm Parameters from the WSD menu. From the Farm Table window, select the farm where the server belongs. Click the Edit selected row icon (magnifying glass). This displays all servers in that farm.

2. Select the server you would like to take out of service, and click the Edit selected row icon (magnifying glass).

3. From the Admin Status option, select Shutdown to allow graceful removal of the server from the farm. If any user is using this server, the server still services the user, but WSD Pro does not allow new connections; once all connected users are serviced, the server becomes unavailable. Also, you can disable the server immediately by choosing the Disable option.

4. Click the check mark to return to the Server table. Click Send value to element (the right-turn arrow) to tell WSD Pro about the new configuration.

You are done. To later enable the server, follow the same steps, but instead of choosing the Shutdown or Disable option from the Admin Status menu, select the Enable option.

Prioritizing server selection

You may have some servers that are better at doing what they do than the others. For example, say you have a 500 MHz Alpha box running the Red Hat Alpha distribution and the rest of your servers are 400 MHz Pentium II systems. If you would like to give the Alpha box higher priority, you can edit its configuration from the Server Table window (select Application Servers Table from the WSD menu) and increase the value of the Server Priority field. You can set this to a number between 1 and 10, where the higher the number, the higher the priority.

Monitoring server load and statistics

You can easily monitor how many users connect to a server, the peak load, and so on by using ConfigMaster. You can view the Server Table window to see how each server is performing and also to generate various statistics and display them graphically. For example, Figure 21-16 shows a graph that depicts the number of users served over time.

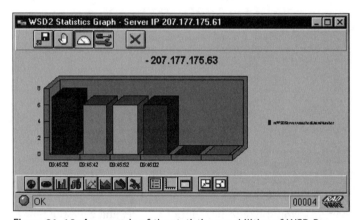

Figure 21-16: An example of the statistics capabilities of WSD Pro

Adding a new Web server in the Web server farm

You have to follow these steps to add a new Web server in the farm:

1. Configure the new server to use the 192.168.1.*x* and 192.168.2.*x* IP addresses as you configure the initial two Web servers. Make sure you can ping 192.168.2.10 (WSD Pro) from the server and also can ping other servers via both networks.

2. Add new A and PTR records for this new host in the DNS configuration files.

3. Modify the /etc/exports file on the NFS server to allow the new server to mount the NFS file system (/www/data). On the new Web server, modify the /etc/fstab file to mount the NFS file system automatically at boot. You also have to create the /www and /data directories.

4. Modify the distfile for rdist so that it services the new server. In other words, you have to include `httpd@wwwN.aminews-lan.com` in the HOSTS line. Replace `wwwN.aminews-lan.com` with appropriate hostname. Create the httpd user account on the new Web server, and also create an .rhosts file for the account that allows the `ns.aminews-lan.com` server to distribute files and directories in the /www directory.

5. Modify the /etc/mail/relay-domains file on the `mail.aminews.com` server to allow the new Web server to relay mail.

6. Using ConfigMaster, add the new server in the 207.177.175.61 farm, and enable its Admin Status.

   That's all there is to adding a new Web server.

Adding Client Web Sites

Adding new client sites becomes quite easy if you use the makesite script discussed in Listing 10-6 in Chapter 10. This script creates the necessary DNS and Apache server configurations. Every time you run makesite, it creates new configurations and appends them to the named.conf and httpd.conf files. If you run the script on the DNS server, you can point it to update /etc/named.conf. However, because you do not run the Web servers on this system, you need to copy the httpd.conf configuration segment for the new site manually onto your httpd.conf files on the Web server systems. You also need to add the client domain in the /etc/mail/relay-domains file in your `mail.aminews.com` server. This allows you to relay mail for this domain.

On the other hand, if you prefer to do everything manually, you have to follow these steps:

1. Create the name server configuration file for the new domain, and put it in /var/named. Add the domain in your /etc/named.conf file so that your name server becomes its primary DNS server.

2. Create the necessary directory structure for the Web site. This could mean that you have to create multiple directories such as /www/client-domain, /www/client-domain/htdocs, and so on. Make sure you set file/directory permissions so that the rdist program can copy the new files and directories.

3. Create virtual host configurations for each Apache server by using the `<VirtualHost www.client-domain.tld></VirtualHost>` containers.

4. Add the domain to your /etc/mail/relay-domains file so that sendmail on mail.aminews.com relays mail for this new domain.

That's all there is to adding new client Web sites. Restart the name server and the Apache servers to start serving the new domain.

When you are setting up a lot of new domains whose DNS configuration has not propagated throughout the Internet because of Internic's inefficiency, you can simply set your test machines to use your name server that services this domain. This allows you to test Web sites that are not available to the rest of the Internet.

Summary

It is very important to realize how you can integrate Red Hat Linux with high-end commercial network equipment so that this great operating system can find its way into the mainstream. This chapter showed you how such an integration is possible. In this chapter, I discussed how you can create a high-end Web network service by using a hardware load-balancing solution.

Chapter 22

Configuring the X Windows System

IN THIS CHAPTER

- ◆ How to install and configure XFree86
- ◆ How to customize your X Windows manager
- ◆ How to use X Windows on MS Windows 9*x*/2000

I AM NO MICROSOFT WINDOWS fan, but on many occasions I have noticed that many novice system administrators unfairly blame Microsoft (MS) Windows for lack of performance. I do agree that on similar hardware, any decent distribution of Linux, such as Red Hat Linux, can easily outperform any Windows operating system. However, many of the novice system administrators fail to realize that when a computer is a server to a network of users and also the desktop computer for the administrator, it may run a little slow — no matter what operating system is being used. The moral here is that if you want to use a computer as your desktop computer, use it as just that. Don't expect great server performance from a computer that is supposed to play the role of a desktop machine as well as a server. So I highly recommend that you do not install the X Windows System on your Red Hat Linux server unless you know very well that the load is going to be minimal; in other words, unless either you use it as a desktop machine very infrequently or the server load is quite low. Of course you can always install the X Windows System on a Red Hat Linux system and use it as a desktop-only computer. That said, I now discuss how you can turn your Red Hat Linux system into an X Windows System desktop computer.

The X Windows System is a hardware-independent, client/server windowing system that provides the base platform for graphical user interfaces (GUIs) for all kinds of applications and utilities. You can even run Microsoft Windows applications under X Windows System using a software emulator such as WINE.

The X Windows System is the end result of research and development in many prestigious computer research organization such as Stanford University, Xerox, and the Massachusetts Institute of Technology (MIT). MIT released a version of the X Windows System in 1984 as part of a project called Athena. The X Windows System is currently developed and distributed by the Open Group. The X Windows System is commonly referred as X Windows, which is what I use throughout this chapter.

What Is XFree86?

XFree86 is a freely distributable implementation of the X Window System. It is developed by the Xfree86 Project, Inc., a nonprofit organization. Although it is based on the Open Group's X Windows System, it has its own development goals. Traditionally, Xfree86 was developed for the Intel *x*86 platform, but it now runs on other platforms, such as Compaq/Digital Alpha processors as well. The official Xfree86 Web site is located at `http://www.xfree86.org/`.

The official Red Hat Linux comes with the latest XFree86 distribution. It is also the topic of this chapter.

Preparing for XFree86

The XFree86 X Windows package requires a lot of system resources to be comfortably usable. Although you can run XFree86 on a Intel 486 with 4MB of RAM, your ability to use such a system would be limited. The following system requirements should be considered before you install XFree86 on any system.

RAM requirements

RAM is a resource you can never have enough of. Having plenty of RAM helps just about everything you do on a multiuser system such as Red Hat Linux. My personal experience shows that having 64MB of RAM with 128MB of swap space provides a very comfortable user experience on a Red Hat Linux system running XFree86 on a regular basis. However, if you would like to run XFree86 while serving Web pages using the Apache Web server and providing NFS or Samba file sharing services, the amount of RAM you need depends on how loaded your server gets at peak hours. At the low end, I recommend that you install 128MB of RAM with 128MB of swap space; as your load increases, you can always add more and more RAM to better your server performance.

Video card requirements

Not all video cards are supported by XFree86, so do not forget to check the XFree86 Web site for a list of supported video cards. I recommend a name-brand PCI video card with at least 4MB of video memory. In this day and age, such a card is practically the low end. The more video memory you have, the better.

Before installing XFree86, you should note the amount of video memory you have on your video card, along with the chipset it uses. You also need the brand and model information.

In the spirit of getting the most recent hardware, you might consider buying the very latest in video cards. Don't. Because XFree86 developers might not have had a chance to tinker with the latest and the greatest video hardware as soon as it is available in the market, it is highly recommended that you stick to S3- or ATI-based video cards that are a bit older than the one that was released yesterday.

Monitor requirements

A good monitor and a good video card can make your XFree86 user experience superb. I recommend a large-screen, name-brand, high-resolution monitor. Although large monitors — 19", 21", or more — are quite expensive, they greatly enhance your day-to-day X Windows experience. The more screen real estate you have, the better. Unfortunately, name-brand large monitors often cost more than a high-end PC.

Disk space requirements

Expect to use roughly 400MB to half a gigabyte of disk space for a full-blown XFree86 installation with all the goodies (applications, utilities, games, and so forth) that come with it.

Now that you know about the prerequisites, let's get started with the installation.

Installing XFree86

When you install Red Hat Linux from the official CD-ROM, you get a chance to install and configure XFree86. If you haven't done that already, you can install XFree86 quite easily using the RPM packages on your CD-ROM. To install XFree86 from the RPMS directory of your CD-ROM, run:

```
rpm -ivh XFree86*.rpm
```

This installs all the XFree86 packages from the CD-ROM. Now continue with XFree86 configuration.

Configuring XFree86

Before you can configure XFree86 for your system, you need to know the following:

◆ How much video memory you have

◆ What kind of chipset your video card uses

◆ The maximum resolution of your monitor

◆ The horizontal and vertical refresh rates, make, and model of your monitor.

If you do not know the information for your video card, you can run an utility called SuperProbe to determine it. This utility is included with XFree86. You can run it as follows:

```
/usr/X11R6/bin/SuperProbe
```

Here is an example of SuperProbe output:

```
WARNING - THIS SOFTWARE COULD HANG YOUR MACHINE.
          READ THE SuperProbe.1 MANUAL PAGE BEFORE
          RUNNING THIS PROGRAM.

          INTERRUPT WITHIN FIVE SECONDS TO ABORT!

First video: Super-VGA
        Chipset: S3 Trio64V+ (Port Probed)
        Memory:  2048 Kbytes
        RAMDAC:  Generic 8-bit pseudo-color DAC
                 (with 6-bit wide lookup tables (or in 6-bit
mode
```

 As the warning message in the output clearly indicates, this program can make your system unresponsive, and therefore you should read the man pages before you run this program.

Once you have the information, you need to decide how you want to configure XFree86. You have three choices. You can use a full-screen, menu-driven utility called Xconfigurator, or you can use a command line, prompt-oriented utility called xf86config, or you can manually create an XF86 configuration file. The XF86Config file is the primary configuration file needed to create a usable X Windows environment in XFree86. The XF86Config file usually resides in the /etc/X11 directory, and typically, a symbolic link (/usr/X11R6/lib/X11/XF86Config) is pointed back to /etc/X11/XF86Config. Because Xconfigurator is the best choice, I discuss only this tool here.

Using Xconfigurator to create an XF86Config file

The Xconfigurator utility enables you to create the XF86Config file quite easily. Run the program as follows:

```
/usr/X11R6/bin/Xconfigurator
```

This command displays a screen similar to the one shown in Figure 22-1.

As suggested in the opening screen, you should read the /usr/X11R6/lib/X11/doc/README.Config file to learn about the latest details on the structure of the file. Click OK to continue. If for some reason the /usr/X11R6/lib/X11/XF86Config symbolic link is broken, Xconfigurator displays the screen shown in Figure 22-2.

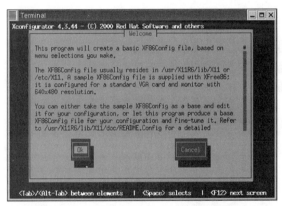

Figure 22-1: The opening screen for Xconfigurator

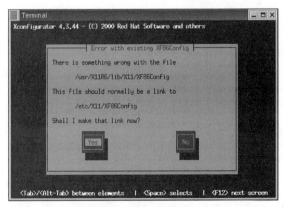

Figure 22-2: Pointing /usr/X11R6/lib/X11/XF86Config to /etc/X11/XF86Config

Click OK to create the symbolic link. If you didn't have the symbolic link problem or just fixed it, you see the screen shown in Figure 22-3 next.

The results of the probing are shown in Figure 22-3, which lists the video card information and the selected X server name. Click OK to continue.

Now you need to select the monitor type, as shown in Figure 22-4.

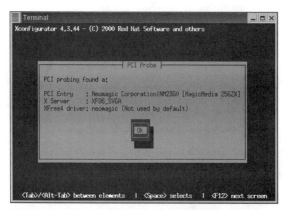

Figure 22-3: The results of probing the video card

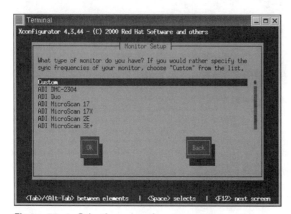

Figure 22-4: Selecting a monitor type

Use the up and down arrow keys to scroll back and forth to locate your monitor brand and model. If you find your monitor in the list, select it and press OK to continue. Figure 22-5 shows that I have selected Viewsonic PS775 as my monitor brand and model.

However, it is quite possible that your monitor might not be listed here. In such a case you have to select the Custom monitor and press OK to continue. You see a screen that tells you that you now need to specify your monitor's vertical refresh rate and horizontal sync rate. You should first consult with your monitor's manual to find these numbers.

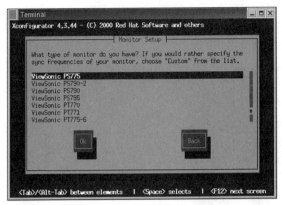

Figure 22-5: Selecting a monitor by brand name

 TIP   If you lost or have thrown away the monitor manual, you might be able to find information about your monitor on the vendor's Web site.

If you still cannot locate information on your monitor, check /usr/X11R6/share/ Xconfigurator/MonitorsDB file. Click OK to proceed with the monitor specification. Now you see a screen as shown in Figure 22-6.

From the list, select the most appropriate resolution and horizontal refresh rate for your monitor. If you do not know what these settings should be, call your monitor or computer vendor to find this information. Do not experiment with these settings unless you care very little about the health of your monitor. Be warned that if you give XFree86 the wrong monitor settings, it might harm your monitor.

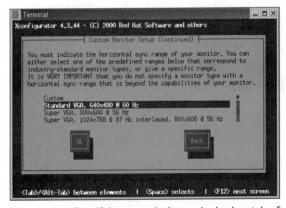

Figure 22-6: Specifying a resolution and a horizontal refresh rate for a monitor

Once you have specified the resolution and the horizontal refresh rate, you can click OK to continue to specify the vertical refresh rate as shown in Figure 22-7.

Figure 22-7: Specifying a vertical refresh rate for a monitor

If Xconfigurator cannot determine how much video memory your video card has; it asks you to specify the amount of video RAM you have as shown in Figure 22-8. Also, Xconfigurator might ask you to specify the clock chip your video card uses as shown in Figure 22-9.

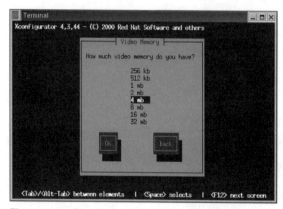

Figure 22-8: Specifying video RAM

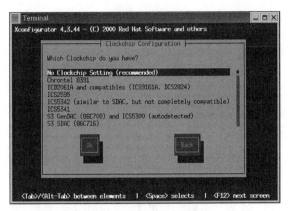

Figure 22-9: Specifying video clock chip

Use the recommended "No clockchip setting" option unless you specifically know your video card clock chip information.

Once you click OK, you see a dialog box stating that Xconfigurator now probes your video card using the selected X server. Click OK to continue. Wait for the probing to complete. As warned by the previous dialog window, the screen might blank a few times as part of the probing procedure. Once the probing is complete (hopefully without any problem), you see a screen as shown in Figure 22-10.

This screen shows the manual default video mode selection options for 8-bit (256 colors), 16-bit (64,536 colors), and 24-bit (16,777,216 colors) modes.

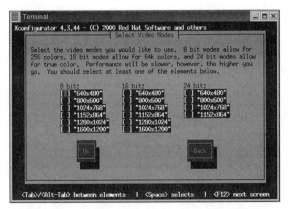

Figure 22-10: Manually choosing default video modes

Using the up and down arrow keys, select an appropriate resolution for each color mode by pressing the Spacebar. You can also toggle a selection using the Spacebar. Once you have selected all the default video modes for each color mode, click OK to complete this step and continue to the next.

A dialog screen confirms the creation of the XF86Config file. Before you start the X server, you should take a look at the XF86Config file.

Understanding XF86Config file

Like any typical UNIX configuration file, the XF86Config file ignores blank lines and any lines that start with leading "#" characters, which are treated as comments. The XF86Config file is divided into multiple sections. Each section provides a particular type of information to the X server. Also, each section starts with the Section "<name of the section>" line and ends with an EndSection line.

FILES SECTION

This section is used to specify font and color database paths. Here is an example of such a section:

```
Section "Files"


    RgbPath     "/usr/X11R6/lib/X11/rgb"
    FontPath    "/usr/X11R6/lib/X11/fonts/TrueType"
    FontPath    "unix/:7100"


EndSection
```

If you add new fonts to your system, you can use the FontPath option to specify the directory for the fonts you installed.

SERVER FLAGS SECTION

This section is used to specify general options to the X server. Here is an example of such a section:

```
Section "ServerFlags"

# Uncomment this to cause a core dump at the
# spot where a signal is received.  This may leave
# the console in an unusable state, but may provide
# a better stack trace in the core dump to aid in debugging
#NoTrapSignals
```

```
# Uncomment this to disable the <Crtl><Alt><BS>
# server abort sequence This allows clients to receive
# this key event.
#DontZap

# Uncomment this to disable the
# <Crtl><Alt><KP_+>/<KP_-> mode switching sequences.
# This allows clients to receive these key events.
#DontZoom

EndSection
```

The NoTrapSignals option should be turned on by removing the leading "#" sign (that is, comment character) only if you are an X Windows developer and know what you are doing.

The DontZap option disallows you to terminate the X Windows server using Ctrl+Alt+Backspace. If you have an X application that requires this key sequence, you can uncomment the DontZap line so that this key sequence can be passed to the application.

The DontZoom option disallows you to switch back and forth between different screen resolutions using Ctrl+Alt+Keypad-Plus and Ctrl+Alt+Keypad-Minus. If you have an X application that requires these key sequences, you can uncomment the DontZoom line so that these key sequences can be passed to the application.

Other commonly used options that you can add in this section are listed in Table 22-1.

TABLE 22-1 OPTIONS FOR THE FILES SECTION OF XF86CONFIG

Option	Use
AllowNonLocalXvidtune	Allows the xvidtune program to connect from a remote host.
DisableVidMode	Disables certain video mode extensions used by the xvidtune program.
AllowNonLocalModInDev	Allows a remote X client to change keyboard and mouse settings.
DisableModInDev	Disables certain input device extensions that can normally be set dynamically.
AllowMouseOpenFail	Allows the X server to start without a mouse.

KEYBOARD SECTION

Use this section to set up keyboard devices. An example of this section is shown here:

```
Section "Keyboard"

  Protocol    "Standard"

  # when using XQUEUE, comment out the above line,
  # and uncomment the following line
  #Protocol   "Xqueue"

  AutoRepeat  500 5

  LeftAlt         Meta
  RightAlt        Meta
  ScrollLock      Compose
  RightCtl        Control

  XkbRules        "xfree86"
  XkbModel        "pc101"
  XkbLayout       "us"

EndSection
```

The Protocol option specifies the keyboard option. It should be set to standard for all Linux systems.

The AutoRepeat option sets the auto repeat delay (first argument) and rate (second argument).

The LeftAlt, RightAlt, ScrollLock, and RightCtl options enable you to map the Left Alt key, Right Alt key, Scroll Lock key, and Right Ctrl key to either Meta, Compose, or Control values.

If you have a non-U.S. 102-key keyboard, you can use the XkbModel option to set it to pc102. Similarly, if you have a Microsoft Natural Keyboard, you can set XkbModel to Microsoft.

If you use any language other than American English, you can set the language using the two-digit language code with the XkbLayout option. For example, to set your keyboard language to French, you can use fr as the XkbLayout option. The default is us.

If you are used to Sun Microsystems keyboards, which have the Ctrl key in place of a regular keyboard's Caps Lock key, you can swap these keys (that is, Caps Lock becomes Ctrl) in a regular keyboard using the XkbOptions option. For example:

```
XkbOptions "ctrl:swapcaps"
```

This command swaps Caps Lock with Ctrl. The default is to leave the keys as is.

You can specify the XkbRules option to specify the rules file. The default rules file is xfree86.

Other commonly used options that you can add in this section are listed in Table 22-2.

TABLE 22-2 OPTIONS FOR THE KEYBOARD SECTION OF XF86CONFIG

Options	Explanation
XkbTypes	Sets keyboard type. The default is "default"; other possible values are: basic, cancel, complete, iso9995, mousekeys, nocancel, pc.
XkbCompat	Sets keyboard compatibility. The default value is "default"; other possible values are: accessx, basic, complete, group_led, iso9995, japan, keypad, misc, mousekeys, norepeat, pc, pc98, xtest.
XkbSymbols	Sets the keyboard symbol. The default value is "us"; the other possible values are: amiga, ataritt, be, bg, ca, cs, ctrl, czsk, de, de_CH, digital, dk, dvorak, en_US, es, fi, fr, fr_CH, fujitsu, gb, group, hu, iso9995-3, it, jp, keypad, lock, nec, no, pc104, pl, pt, ru, se, sgi, sony, sun, th.
XkbGeometry	Sets the keyboard geometry parameters. The default value is "pc"; other possible values are: amiga, ataritt, dell, digital, everex, fujitsu, keytronic, kinesis, Microsoft, nec, northgate, sgi, sony, sun, winbook.
XkbKeycodes	Sets the key codes for the keyboard. The default value is "xfree86"; other possible values are: amiga, ataritt, digital, fujitsu, hp, ibm, sgi, sony, sun.

POINTER SECTION

Use this section to set up the pointer device, which is typically a mouse. An example of this section is as follows:

```
Section "Pointer"

    Protocol    "Microsoft"
    Device      "/dev/mouse"

EndSection
```

The Protocol option sets the protocol for the pointer device. The protocol can be Auto, BusMouse, GlidePoint, GlidePointPS/2, IntelliMouse, IMPS/2, Logitech, Microsoft, MMHitTab, MMSeries, Mouseman, MouseManPlusPS/2, MouseSystems, NetMousePS/2, NetScrollPS/2, OSMouse, PS/2, SysMouse, ThinkingMouse,

ThinkingMousePS/2, or Xqueue. If you do not know what protocol is appropriate for your late-model pointer device, try setting the protocol to Auto.

The Device option specifies the device path. If you use a mouse as your pointing device and have it connected to serial port 1 (cua0) or serial port (cua1), you can specify /dev/cua0 or /dev/cua1, respectively. However, the best method is to create a symbolic link called /dev/mouse that points to your serial port device (cua0 or cua1) and have the device set to /dev/mouse. This way, if you change the port, all you need to do is readjust the link, not the configuration file as well.

Other commonly used options that you can add are listed in Table 22-3.

TABLE 22-3 OPTIONS FOR THE POINTER SECTION OF XF86CONFIG

Option	Explanation
BaudRate	Sets the baud rate for your pointer device.
Port	Same as Device option.
Button	Sets the number of buttons.
Emulate3Buttons	Emulates a three-button mouse with a two-button mouse. When you press both buttons together, you get the action the third button would give you.
Emulate3Timeout	Sets the time-out (in milliseconds) for three-button emulation. The X server waits for the specified number of milliseconds to decide whether or not a third button was pressed when you hold down both of the buttons.

MONITOR SECTION

The monitor section is the most commonly modified. Use this section to describe your monitor. Here is an example of this section:

```
Section "Monitor"

Identifier  "My Monitor"
VendorName  "Unknown"
ModelName   "Unknown"
HorizSync   31.5 - 82.0
VertRefresh 50-100

# This is a set of standard mode timings.
# Modes that are out of monitor spec
# are automatically deleted by the server
```

```
# (provided the HorizSync and VertRefresh lines
# are correct), so there's no immediate need to
# delete mode timings (unless particular mode timings
# don't work on your monitor). With these modes,
# the best standard mode that your monitor
# and video card can support for a given resolution
# is automatically used.

# 640x400 @ 70 Hz, 31.5 kHz hsync
Modeline "640x400" 25.175 640   664   760   800    400   409   411   450

# 640x480 @ 60 Hz, 31.5 kHz hsync
Modeline "640x480" 25.175 640   664   760   800    480   491   493   525

# 800x600 @ 56 Hz, 35.15 kHz hsync
ModeLine "800x600" 36      800   824   896  1024    600   601   603   625

# 640x480 @ 72 Hz, 36.5 kHz hsync
Modeline "640x480" 31.5 640 680 720   864 480 488 491 521

# 800x600 @ 60 Hz, 37.8 kHz hsync
Modeline "800x600" 40 800 840 968 1056 600 601 605 628 +hsync +vsync

# 1024x768 @ 60 Hz, 48.4 kHz hsync
Modeline "1024x768" 65 1024 1032 1176 1344 768 771 777 806 -hsync
-vsync

# 1024x768 @ 70 Hz, 56.5 kHz hsync
Modeline "1024x768" 75 1024 1048 1184 1328 768 771 777  806 -hsync
-vsync

# 1024x768 @ 76 Hz, 62.5 kHz hsync
Modeline "1024x768"  85  1024 1032 1152 1360   768   784   787   823

# 1280x1024 @ 61 Hz, 64.2 kHz hsync
Modeline "1280x1024" 110 1280 1328 1512 1712  1024 1025 1028 1054

# 1280x1024 @ 74 Hz, 78.85 kHz hsync
Modeline "1280x1024" 135 1280 1312 1456 1712  1024 1027 1030 1064

# 1280x1024 @ 76 Hz, 81.13 kHz hsync
Modeline "1280x1024" 135 1280 1312 1416 1664  1024 1027 1030 1064

EndSection
```

Use the Identifier option to set a unique identifier for the monitor. Each monitor needs to have a unique identifier that can be referenced in the Screen section.

Use the VendorName and ModelName options to specify the vendor name and model of the monitor.

Use the HorizSync option to set the horizontal refresh (sync) rate in KHz. If you would like to specify this rate in megahertz or in hertz, use MHz or Hz at the end of the line.

Use the VertRefresh option to set the vertical refresh (sync) rate in Hz. If you would like to specify this rate in megahertz or in kilohertz, use MHz or KHz at the end of the line.

Use the ModeLine options to specify video modes. Each ModeLine option has the following format:

```
ModeLine mode  clk-rate Horizontal-timing Vertical-timing Flags
```

Here, clk-rate is the rate of the pixel clock for this mode. This number is a single positive (integer) number. Horizontal-timing and Vertical-timing are a set of four timing (integer) numbers. Use the optional Flags to specify additional characteristics of the mode. You can write a ModeLine in multiple lines using the mode option. For example:

```
ModeLine "1024x768i" 45 1024 1048 1208 1264 768 776 784 817
Interlace

Mode "1024x768i"
DotClock       45
HTimings       1024 1048 1208 1264
VTimings       768 776 784 817
Flags          "Interlace"
EndMode
```

Both of the preceding video mode descriptions are identical.

GRAPHICS DEVICE SECTION

This section is used to set options for the video card. Here is an example section:

```
# Device configured by Xconfigurator:

Section "Device"
    Identifier  "Trio32/Trio64"
    VendorName  "Unknown"
    BoardName   "Unknown"


EndSection
```

Use the Identifier option to set a unique identifier for the monitor. Each monitor needs to have a unique identifier that can be referenced in the Screen section.

Use the VendorName and BoardName options to specify the vendor name and name of the video card.

Typically, the X server detects the features installed on your video card, including the amount of RAM, the chipset, and so on.

SCREEN SECTION

Use the screen section to specify how the video hardware (monitor and video card) should be used by X server. Here is an example of this section:

```
Section "Screen"
    Driver      "accel"
    Device      "Trio32/Trio64"
    Monitor     "My Monitor"

    Subsection "Display"
        Depth       8
        Modes       "640x480" "800x600" "1024x768" "1280x1024"
        ViewPort    0 0
        Virtual     1280 1024
    EndSubsection

    Subsection "Display"
        Depth       16
        Modes       "640x480" "800x600" "1024x768"
        ViewPort    0 0
        Virtual     1024 768
    EndSubsection

    Subsection "Display"
        Depth       32
        Modes       "640x480" "800x600"
        ViewPort    0 0
        Virtual     800 600
    EndSubsection

EndSection
```

The Driver option sets the driver name. Supported driver names are accel, mono, svga, vga2, and vga16.

The Device option sets the name of the video card that is to be used. The Monitor option sets the name of the monitor that is to be used.

A display subsection specifies a set of parameters for a particular display type. The Depth option sets color depth; the Modes option sets video modes or resolutions; the ViewPort option sets the top-left corner of the initial display; the Virtual option specifies the virtual video resolution. A screen section may have multiple display sections.

You can select or unselect the video resolutions specified as the arguments for a Modes option in a display section with the Ctrl+Alt+Keypad-Plus and Ctrl+Alt+Keypad-Minus keys.

Using X Windows

You can start X Windows in any of several ways. You can run xinit, which starts the X Windows server and also runs the first X client application. The client application it runs depends on the .xinitrc script in a user's home directory. For example, if you run xinit as root, the ~root/.xinitrc script is used to determine what X client application needs to be started after the X Windows server is up and running. If no client application is specified in the command line, or if the ~<user home directory>/.xinitrc file does not exist, xinit uses the following command as a default:

```
xterm -geometry +1+1 -n login -display :0
```

In other words, it starts an xterm session as the sole client application. When this client application exits, the X Windows server also terminates.

In order to provide better user control on what gets started, an sh script called startx is distributed. You can run startx without any argument to start the X Windows server. This script is really a front end for the xinit program.

By default, the startx script looks for .xserverrc in the user's home directory and if such a file is not found, it looks for a systemwide xserverrc file in the /usr/X11R6/lib/X11/xinit directory. The ~<user home directory>/.xserverrc file or the /usr/X11R6/lib/X11/xinit/xserverrc file is used to determine which X Windows server needs to be started. The script also looks for .xinitrc in the user's home directory and if such a file is not found, it looks for a systemwide xinitrc file in /usr/X11R6/lib/X11/xinit directory. The ~<user home directory>/.xinitrc or the /usr/X11R6/lib/X11/xinit/xinitrc file is used to determine which client applications are going to be run after the X Windows server has been started. Note that you can provide command line arguments to alter the default settings found in any of these files. However, if you keep overriding the defaults, you might as well put your chosen settings in these files so that you don't have to type them every time you want to run this script.

If you like, start X Windows in a different color mode by specifying the color mode in the command line. For example:

```
startx--bbp 8
```

This will start X Windows in 256-color mode. To start X Windows in true color mode, use the following command:

```
startx--bbp 32
```

Note that the double dashes are required to pass arguments directly to the xinit program.

When you run startx for the first time, your home directory is not likely to have a preinstalled .xinitrc, and therefore the systemwide xinitrc file is used. To create your own .xinitrc file, run the locate xinitrc command to locate a copy of the file in /usr/X11R6/lib/X11/xinit or in /etc/X11/xinit. Copy this file to your home directory by renaming it with a period as the first character so that the final name is .xinitrc. Now you can configure this file to customize your X Windows environment.

Configuring .xinitrc

As mentioned before, the .xinitrc script is used to launch client applications per a user's preference. When such a script is found in a user's home directory, startx runs it; when the .xinitrc script exits, it terminates the X Windows server. Therefore you must call a client application in the script so that control does not fall through to the bottom of the script (causing it to exit) until you terminate that client application. Typically, you accomplish this by running all but the last client program in the background. The last client program is usually an X Windows manager. Listing 22-1 shows an example of an .xinitrc file.

Listing 22-1: An example .xinitrc file

```
#
# Example .xinitrc
#

# start xclock (in the background)
xclock -geometry 50x50-1+1 &

# start two xterms (in the background)
xterm -geometry 80x50+494+51 &
xterm -geometry 80x20+494-0 &

#
# now start a window manager in
# the foreground
#

# If my favorite GNOME is there, start it
if [ -f  /usr/bin/gnome-session]; then
    exec gnome-session
```

```
# Ok, no GNOME, try KDE
elif [ -f  /usr/bin/startkde]; then
    exec startkde

# Ok, no GNOME or  KDE, try just  twm
else
    exec twm
fi
```

As you can see, instances of X applications such as xclock and xterm are executed in the background using the "&" operator. Only the X Windows manager application is run in the foreground. You should start with a simple .xinitrc file such as the preceding one and modify it to include X applications you need to start by default.

You can decide to run X Windows without a window manager by running xinit directly; however, most people will find window managers must-have tools to work under X Windows. The popular X Windows managers are: fvwm2, fvwm, afterstep, twm, wmaker, and wmx, among others. Each window manager has its own look and feel and thus provides a different appeal to different users. I recommend that you install the popular window managers and try them out.

Because window managers are so numerous, taking full advantage of them requires knowledge of each package, which in turns require a great deal of time on your part. It almost seems, as if you need a manager for the window managers.

Customizing the look and feel of client applications

When you run an X client application such as an xterm or a calculator (xcalc), the default look and feel of the application typically comes from a file in /usr/X1R6/lib/X11/app-defaults. For example, the default look and feel of xcalc (the calculator) comes from the /usr/X1R6/lib/X11/app-defaults/XCalc file. You can modify these defaults to provide a customized look and feel for you and/or your users. Be sure to back up each file you want to modify.

If you are interested only in changing the look and feel of a few applications for yourself, you can create an .Xresources file in your home directory and add lines using the following syntax:

```
<application><resource key>: <resource value>
```

For example:

```
XCalc*bevel.Background:   red
```

Here I have changed the default background color (black) of the digital display of the xcalc program by placing this line in my .Xresources file. To identify which resource is responsible for changing this particular color, I first looked at the /usr/X1R6/lib/X11/app-defaults/XCalc file. Once I located the resource, I copied it in my .Xresources file and prefixed the line with the name of the application (XCalc). If you use an .xinitrc file in your home directory, you should put `xrdb -merge $HOME/` `.Xresources` in it before loading any client applications. Any time you add or modify resources in your .Xresources file, you can run this command from the command line to integrate resource changes to your current X environment.

You have learned to start X Windows using xinit and startx from the command line, but what if you want to boot your system straight to X Windows? The answer is xdm, or X Display Manager.

Using xdm, the X Display Manager

If you would like to provide a GUI-based user authentication interface, X Display Manager, or xdm, is your answer. Using xdm, you can authenticate users via a graphical login screen and take them straight to their X Windows environment. The purpose of this program is to provide services similar to getty and login. You can simply start the display manager as follows:

```
xdm &
```

The xdm configuration files are located in the /usr/X11R6/lib/X11/xdm directory. The file xdm-config is for configuring how the login screen appears to users, and Xsetup_0 is used to tell xdm what programs should be launched when X is started. The default Xsetup_0 is shown here:

```
#!/bin/sh
# Xsetup for Red Hat Linux
# Copyright (c) 1999, 2000 Red Hat, Inc.

pidof -s kdm > /dev/null 2>&1
if [ $? -eq 0 -a -x /usr/bin/kdmdesktop ]; then
  /usr/bin/kdmdesktop
else
  /usr/X11R6/bin/xsetroot -solid "#356390"
fi

# only set the background if the xsri program is installed
if [ -x /usr/bin/xsri ]; then
    /usr/bin/xsri  -geometry +5+5 -avoid 300x250 -keep-aspect \
        /usr/share/pixmaps/redhat/redhat-transparent.png
fi
```

This file starts the xconsole and xbanner programs when a user is authenticated. These are practically useless for most users. Hence you should modify this to whatever is appropriate. For example, you might use the xv program to set the background of the X environment to something appropriate for your organization. Or perhaps you can start up a few applications that are typically run by most users, such as the xmailbox.

The xdm can be run automatically after boot by changing the default run level to 5. To change the run level of your system to 5, modify the following line in the /etc/inittab file:

```
id:3:initdefault:
```

Replace the 3 with 5. And make sure that you have the following lines in the same file:

```
#
# Run xdm in runlevel 5
# xdm is now a separate service
x:5:respawn:/etc/X11/prefdm -nodaemon
```

Because most system administrators work in heterogeneous network environments consisting of Linux, MS Windows 9.x/2000, and other operating systems, it is likely that you will need to integrate Linux and MS Windows 9.x/2000 at one time or another. In the following section, I will discuss how you can incorporate X Windows under the MS Windows 9.x/2000 environment.

Using XFree86 with Windows 9x/2000

Like most UNIX system administrators, most Linux administrators do not enjoy working with MS platforms; some have legitimate reasons, and some just follow their UNIX guru's trends. However, reality checks will show that in most medium- to large-sized organizations there are more MS Windows systems than there are Linux systems. In such a case, the smart Linux administrators will stop fighting the establishment and start converting users to Linux in an indirect way. For example, what if you were able to let MS Windows users use X Windows from their systems? This could certainly give these users a chance to explore the powerful world of Linux without having to install Linux on their own systems. Here is how.

To run X Windows applications on MS Windows 9.x/2000, you need to run an X Windows server on such a platform. Many commercial X Windows server software packages are available for MS Windows 9.x/2000. Here I will use Micro X-Win32, which I have used for over a year and find very easy to install and support.

Getting Micro X-Win32

You can download an evaluation copy of X-Win32 from StarNet Communications Corporation at the following URL: http://www.starnet.com/. The evaluation version of the product runs exactly like the product version; the only limitation is that you can use the evaluation version for only two hours per session. After every two-hour period you have to restart the X Windows server on the MS Windows side. Because none of the features are crippled in the evaluation version, this constraint is not much of a problem. After all, if you use it, you should pay for it.

Once you have downloaded an evaluation copy, which typically comes in a self-extracting executable file, extract the files by clicking the executable; it will automatically start the installation. You will be asked to select a destination directory for the installation. Once it is installed, you are ready to use the X Windows server on MS Windows such that your Red Hat Linux server's X client applications can be run on the MS Windows system running the local X Windows server.

Before you can run an X client from your Red Hat Linux X installation, you need to configure Micro X-Win32 using the X-Util32 program provided with the distribution. Do the following:

1. Run the X-Util32 program, which displays a screen similar to the one shown in Figure 22-11.

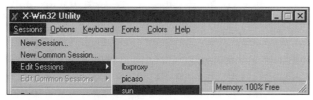

Figure 22-11: The X-Win32 Utility main window

2. From the menu, select Sessions → Edit sessions. From this menu select an existing session entry such as sun. This will display a dialog screen with information on the current session. See Figure 22-12.

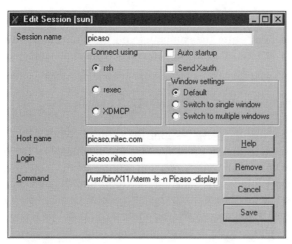

Figure 22-12: Editing an existing session entry

3. First you will need to rename the session entry by typing a new name in the Session name field. This can be any name. Next you will have to select the connection method. You have three choices: rsh (remote shell), rexec (remote exec), and XDMCP (for use with xdm). You should choose the one most appropriate for your Red Hat Linux X Windows environment. For example, if you are running xdm on the Linux side, choose XDMCP.

   If you choose to use the remote shell option, you will have to have a .rhosts file in the Linux user's home directory. This file must contain the hostname or the IP address of the MS Windows system.

   You will also have to make sure you have not disabled the rsh or rexec lines in /etc/inetd.conf. For security, you may want to disallow anyone from using rsh or rexec via the /etc/hosts.deny file and allow only hosts that are specifically allowed such services in the /etc/hosts.allow file. See Chapter 18, "Security 101," for details on TCP Wrapper.

   If you would like to automatically start this session every time you start X-Win32, you can click the Auto startup option. Also make sure the Windows setting is set to the "Switch to multiple windows" option.

4. Enter the hostname of the Red Hat Linux server where the X application will reside.

5. Enter the username in the Login field. If you choose the remote exec (rexec) option, you will be asked to enter a password every time you want to connect your session. If you would prefer to enter the password once, you can enter it in the password field, which appears only when you select the rexec option.

6. In the Command field, enter the command you want to run. Typically, you will want to run xterm here. So you can set this field to this value:

   ```
   /usr/bin/X11/xterm -ls -display $DISPLAY.
   ```

7. Save the modified session and exit the X-Util32 application.

Now you are ready to run the new session. Click the X-Win32 icon in your taskbar and select the Sessions menu. From the Sessions menu, select the modified session name. If you are connecting via rexec, you will be asked to enter the password. Once you are successfully authenticated, an xterm (or whatever application you put in the Command field while editing this entry in X-Util32) will appear on your MS Windows system. If you do not see the application in a few seconds, however, go back to the X-Win32 icon on your taskbar, click the Show Messages option, and try to run your application again. Watch for any permission errors in the message window. If you do get permission errors, either you have forgotten to enable the rexec or rsh service in /etc/inetd.conf, you have forgotten to restart the inetd server after modifying the /etc/inetd.conf file, or you have not yet set up the .rhosts file for rsh-only sessions. Make sure your .rhosts file is writable only by the owner; everyone else should have only read access to this file.

At this point, you should have an X Windows application running under the Micro X-Win32 server. If you prefer to start an X Windows manager such as fvwm2 or openstep and run all X Windows applications as usual (that is, as if you were on the Red Hat Linux system), you should do the following:

1. Using XUtil32, create or edit a session. Enter the hostname, the login username, and the connection method (rsh, rexec) as you did before. Select the "Switch to single window" option and enter the following line as the Command:

```
fvwm2  -display $DISPLAY
```

2. Don't forget to replace fvwm2 with your favorite X Windows manager. Save the new (or edited) session.

Now close any X Windows client sessions that you have already started, and once all X connections are closed, start the new session. You should see a large single window where your favorite X Windows manager is loaded. Now you can use X Windows as if you are running it from the console of the Red Hat Linux system. In case of a problem, read the online troubleshooting information for details.

It is also possible to allow xdm-based authenticated connection using Micro X-Win32.

Summary

In this chapter, you learned to set up X Windows on your Red Hat Linux system. I discussed how you can install and configure the XFree86 X Windows System. You learned to customize and personalize your X Windows environment using various tools, and finally you learned to bring X Windows to Microsoft Windows in a heterogeneous network environment using a commercial X Windows server.

Chapter 23

Using the X Window System

IN THIS CHAPTER

◆ How to configure the GNOME desktop environment

◆ How to use administer Red Hat via X

IN THE PREVIOUS CHAPTER, you learned about how to get the X Window System up and running. In this chapter, I discuss how you can use X Windows.

Unlike Microsoft Windows 9.x/NT/2000, the X Window System gives you the flexibility to choose your own desktop environments. GNOME and KDE are the leading desktop environments available for Red Hat Linux. Since GNOME is the most popular one, I discuss only this environment in this chapter.

Using the GNOME Desktop Environment

The primary purpose of the GNOME project is to provide a complete, user-friendly desktop environment using only open source, freely distributed software. The official Web site for this project is located at the following URL: http://www.gnome.org/.

The official Red Hat Linux CD-ROM comes with GNOME software. However, you can always download the latest RPM packages from the preceding Web site or one of its mirror sites near you. Because GNOME is being developed rapidly, I highly recommend that you visit this Web site to find out about the latest version and download it.

Before you can install the GNOME-related RPM packages, you need to ensure that you have already installed the umb-scheme, xscreensaver, and guile packages from your Red Hat Linux CD-ROM. For example, to find out if you have already installed the umb-scheme package, run:

```
rpm  -q umb-scheme
```

If one or more of these prerequisite packages are not installed, install them from the Red Hat Linux CD-ROM. Once you have installed these packages, you can install all the GNOME packages by running the following command from the gnome directory of your Red Hat Linux CD-ROM:

```
rpm -ivh gnome-*.rpm
```

Once you have installed the GNOME packages, you can run your favorite window manager and load the GNOME desktop by running the following command:

```
gnome-session &
```

If you prefer to load the GNOME desktop by default, modify your .xinitrc file and add the following line just before you load the window manager:

```
exec gnome-session
```

When you start gnome-session for the first time, you see the Help Browser window and the GNOME Panel appear as shown in Figure 23-1.

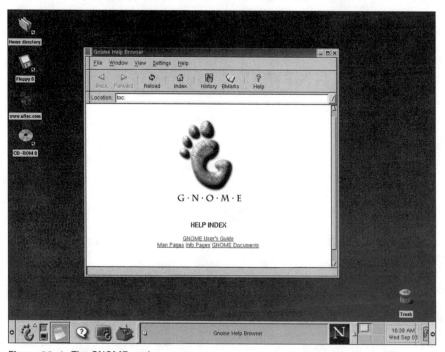

Figure 23-1: The GNOME environment

The stylized foot icon you see on the bottom-left corner of the figure is the main menu button. This menu is embedded in a panel that is the heart of the GNOME interface. The Panel is used as repository of applications, applets, and the main menu.

The Panel is the heart of the GNOME interface and acts as a repository for all of your system applications, applets, and the Main menu. You can start any of the pre-loaded applications by pressing the Main menu button. Figure 23-1 shows the first-level menu options, which can be expanded by selecting one of the options. The left arrow button next to the foot icon (that is, the Main menu button) or the right-arrow button on the bottom-right corner enables you to reduce the Panel to the button itself. You can also configure the Panel to hide itself automatically or move itself to a different edge of the screen using the middle mouse button. The Panel can be configured using the options available under the Panel menu in the main menu. You can also add new panels to your screen. The more you use GNOME, the more you find it highly configurable and user-friendly. To configure your GNOME environment per your needs, you need to run the Control Center program (/usr/bin/ wm-properties-capplet.) Here is how.

Click on the Programs menu option under the Main menu. Select GNOME Control Center under the Settings sub menu. You see a screen as shown in Figure 23-2.

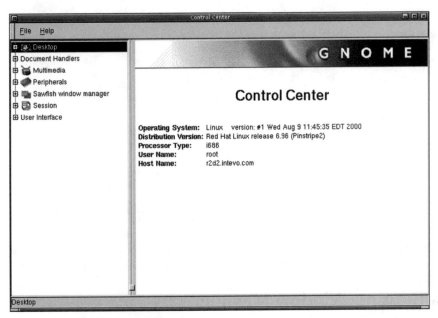

Figure 23-2: GNOME Control Center

The GNOME Control Center enables you to customize your desktop, document handlers, multimedia, peripherals, window manager's session, and user interface. In the following section you learn to configure various aspects of your desktop.

Choosing a Window Manager

To choose a window manager program, click on the Window Manager option under Desktop in the Tree menu on the left side of the window. You see a list of available window manager programs as shown in Figure 23-3.

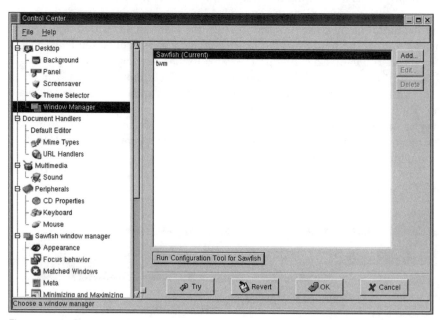

Figure 23-3: Choosing a Window Manager

By default GNOME uses the Sawfish window manager as shown in Figure 23-3. You can install other window manager programs such as fvwm95, fvwm, Another-Level, etc., using an appropriate RPM package found in the Red Hat CD-ROM or by downloading it from the Internet. The other window manager found in the default installation is TWM, which is a very old style window manager. I personally do not recommend it. However, you can always experiment with other window managers and find the one you like. Configuring your desktop is always a personal aspect of computing and can never be standardized without sacrificing someone's comfort.

Configuring Window Manager

The Sawfish window manager can also be configured from within the GNOME Control Center. Click on the Sawfish window manager option in the Tree menu to expand all the options as shown in Figure 23-4.

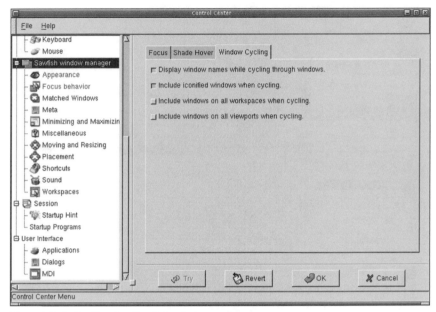

Figure 23-4: Configuring Sawfish window manager

You can configure various look and feel related features of the window manager by clicking on the appropriate option. Since customizing a window is a matter of personal taste, there is no right or wrong approach in changing them. Try out different options and find out what you like. However, one of the features, workspace, might be a new concept for you if you migrated from the world of Microsoft Windows. Workspace is a very powerful feature that enables you to create virtual "desktops" called workspaces on a single monitor screen. Figure 23-5 shows the main GNOME Panel of a typical X Window System desktop.

Figure 23-5: Main GNOME Panel

Notice the six rectangles on the bottom-right side of the screen. Each of these rectangles represents a workspace window. If you click on any of these rectangles, you automatically switch to that workspace. In a workspace, you can run a number of client programs such as Netscape Navigator, xterms, etc. to organize your screen space in the way you like. If six workspaces is not enough, you can create more workspaces using the GNOME Control Center application as follows:

1. Click on the Workspace option under Sawfish window manager option from the Tree menu. You see a screen similar to the one shown in Figure 23-6.

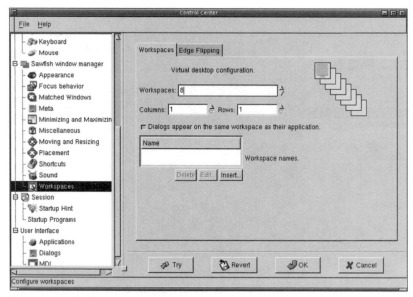

Figure 23-6: Configuring workspace

2. Enter the desired number of workspaces, and even assign a name for each workspace if you wish.

3. Click OK and you should see the workspaces appear in the bottom-right panel as rectangles. Clicking on any of these rectangles takes you to the appropriate workspace.

As you use GNOME Control Center more and more, you become an expert at it. One of the side effects of becoming an expert user is that a few routine things such as startup splash screen, tips or hints, starting the same programs again and again, "Are you sure" types of prompts, etc., become very boring. You can remove these irritations using the session configuration options available under the Session sub-tree. In the following section I show you the session settings I use.

Setting session options for expert mode

Click on the Session option in the Tree menu and you notice the options Startup Hints, Startup Programs, etc. Click on the Startup Hints option and you see a screen like the one in Figure 23-7.

To disable possibly annoying startup hints, ensure that the "Enable login hints" option is not checked.

Now click on the Startup Programs option in the Tree menu and you see a screen as shown in Figure 23-8.

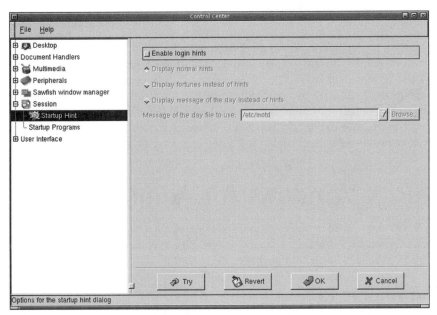

Figure 23-7: Disabling startup hints

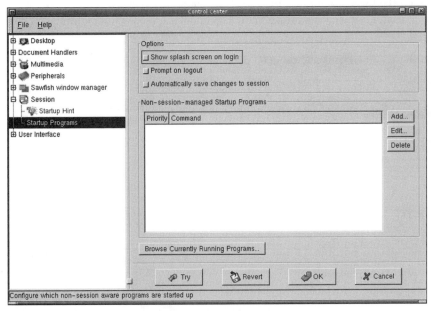

Figure 23-8: Disabling splash screens and prompts

Now make sure that "Show splash screen on login" option is disabled. If you do not want to be prompted for logout confirmation, ensure that the "Prompt on logout" option is disabled. You can also choose to save session-related changes automatically by enabling "Automatically save changes to session" option.

If you wish to start a program every time you start GNOME, you can add it using the Add option under the Non-session-managed Startup Programs option. For example, to run a terminal window whenever you start GNOME, simply add "xterm" using the Add button. If you wish to run multiple programs at startup, you can control the run order using the priority numbering scheme available during the add operation.

Now that you have explored a number of avenues in creating a suitable X Windows environment, let's focus on getting some real work done under X Windows.

Using X Windows for Administration

Some X Windows applications can make it bit easier to perform some system administrative tasks. I discuss a few very interesting ones here. First take a look at how you can manage your RPM packages using a program called GnoRPM .

Using Gnome RPM

This program is really a graphical interface for managing RPM packages. It enables you to install, upgrade, uninstall, verify, and query RPM packages quite easily. To run it, click on the System option in the Programs menu and then click on the GnoRPM option. The program appears as shown in Figure 23-9.

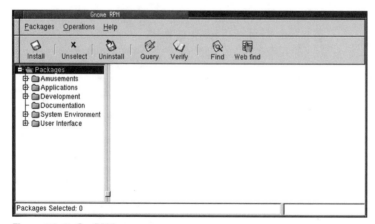

Figure 23-9: GnoRPM screen

To install an RPM package from a CD-ROM, insert the CD-ROM and mount it (GNOME automatically mounts CD-ROM unless you disable this option using GNOME Control Center.) Click on the Install icon or select Install option under the Packages menu (top left.) You see a screen as shown in Figure 23-10.

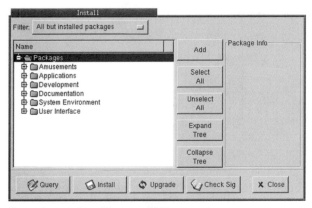

Figure 23-10: Installing new RPMs

GnoRPM reads the CD-ROM and locates packages. By default, GnoRPM only displays packages not installed already. If you click on the Expand Tree button, all the packages are visible as shown in Figure 23-11.

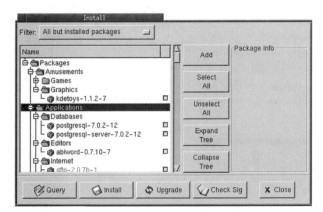

Figure 23-11: Expanding package tree

Select the appropriate packages and click on the Install button to install selected packages.

If you wish to upgrade existing packages using the current CD-ROM, simply change the filter rule (top left) to "All packages" or "Only newer packages" to make it easy for yourself to find appropriate packages. If you are upgrading from an older version of an installed package, use the Upgrade button instead of the Install button.

To verify that an existing package is intact, you can simply select the package and click on the Verify button. For example, Figure 23-12 shows that GnoRPM has found one problem with the installed kernel package.

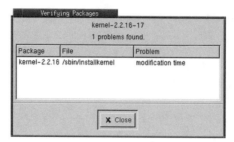

Figure 23-12: Verifying a package

Since the only problem found is the modification date which I know I have changed, there is no need to re-install this package. However, if GnoRPM reports files missing for a package that you have installed, it is best to re-install it.

The Gnome RPM program can also find RPM packages that you need via the Web using the Web Find feature.

Using Update Agent

Whenever new updates become available from Red Hat, their FTP servers often become very busy as a world of Red Hat users connects to get the updates. Red Hat has decided to provide a "first-class" service for the paying customers by creating a network of Web servers available only to paying, priority users. If you have Red Hat priority user account, you can use the Update Agent to update packages via the Web. Run the GUI for Update Agent by clicking on the Update Agent option under Programs → System. The Update Agent appears as shown in Figure 23-13.

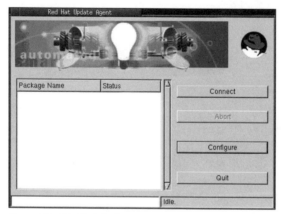

Figure 23-13: Update Agent

To configure the Update Agent, click on the Configure button, which brings up the screen shown in Figure 23-14.

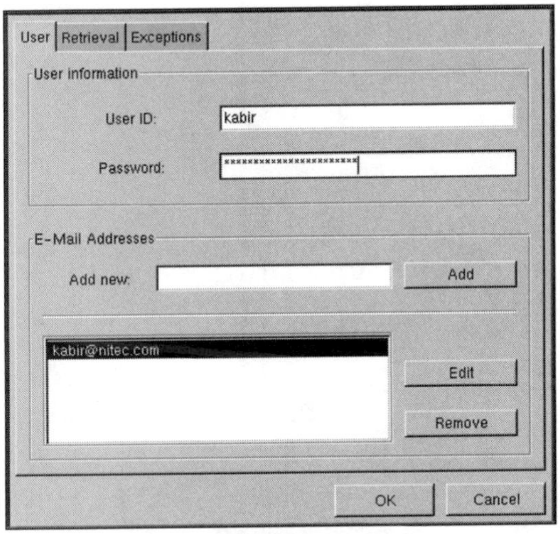

Figure 23-14: Configuring Update Agent

Enter your Red Hat priority user ID, password, and e-mail address in the appropriate data entry boxes. The default Retrieval settings should be fine unless Red Hat specifically informs you of any new settings. Click OK to return to the main screen. You can connect to the Red Hat priority server by clicking on the Connect button.

In addition to the package management tools discussed in the previous sections, you can run an array of GUI front-end applications to manage just about everything from your X Windows System. In the following sections I discuss a few of the more interesting applications. All of the applications discussed in the following section can be run by going to Programs → System.

Using the GNOME System Monitor

The GNOME System Monitor or Gtop enables you to feel the heartbeat of your system. It is a very glorified "top" utility that can be quite a treat for a system administrator who is interested in finding how her system spends resouces such as CPU time, disk usage, and RAM. Figure 23-15 shows a sample screen of a system running Gtop.

Gtop enables you to sort by any column. For example, you can sort all the running processes by their CPU usage by simply clicking on the CPU column. Or, you can sort the processes by their owner (user) by simply clicking on the User column. The resident memory usage information is displayed separately. Click on the Memory Usage (resident) tab to view a screen similar to the one shown in Figure 23-16.

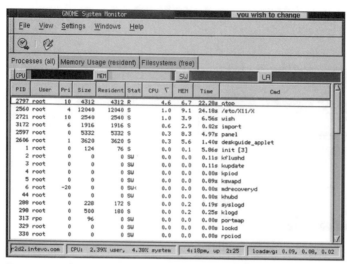

Figure 23-15: Running Gtop

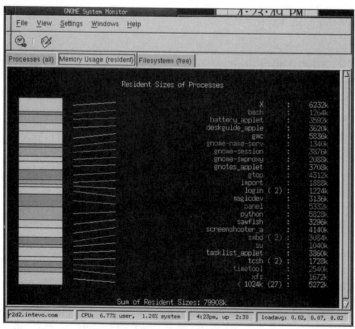

Figure 23-16: Viewing resident memory usage

Using Time Machine

To set system time and date use the Time Tool. This is a very simple tool that enables you to change system time or date. The interface is shown in Figure 23-17.

Figure 23-17: Time Tool

Using netcfg

See the section "Using netcfg to configure a network interface card" in Chapter 9 for details.

Using printtool

See the section "Sharing printers between Linux and Windows" in Chapter 15 for details.

Using the system configuration tool

The system configuration tool that the control panel runs is called Linuxconf. See Chapter 6 for details.

Using the kernel configuration tool

See Chapter 20 for details.

Using the help search tool

The help search tool that the control panel runs is called helptool. It searches online documents including man pages, info files, and random documents in the /usr/doc and /usr/local/doc directories to locate matches for keywords you specify.

Summary

In this chapter, you learned about the GNOME desktop environment and how to use X Window System to administer Red Hat Linux.

Part VIII

Appendixes

APPENDIX A
Linux Resources

APPENDIX B
What's on the CD-ROM

Appendix A

Linux Resources

THIS APPENDIX PROVIDES you with a list of Linux resources. Many Linux-oriented newsgroups, mailing lists, and Web sites are available on the Internet. Although you are likely to discover many more new Linux resources as time passes and as Linux's popularity increases, the following resources are likely to remain in good health at all times. I use these resources on an almost daily basis.

Usenet Newsgroups

The following Usenet newsgroups can be a great place to learn about advances in Linux, to engage in Linux-specific discussions, and also to find answers to questions you might have.

The comp.os.linux hierarchy

Linux has its own hierarchy of Usenet newsgroups. These groups are strictly Linux only. Before you post an article or a question in any of these newsgroups (or any Usenet newsgroup), make sure you know the charter of the group. In particular, when you are looking for answers to questions or solutions to problems, make sure you have read the available frequently asked questions, man pages, and how-to documentation. If you post a question that has been answered in a FAQ or a how-to document, chances are that some people who participate in that group might not take it kindly. Also, be careful when you post the same question in multiple groups (known as cross-posting) in the hope that you are increasing your chances of getting answers. As long as your post is relevant to the group, it is okay.

COMP.OS.LINUX.ADVOCACY (UNMODERATED)
This newsgroup is intended for discussions of the benefits of Linux compared with other operating systems.

COMP.OS.LINUX.ANNOUNCE (MODERATED)
This newsgroup is intended for all Linux-specific announcements. You will find information on new Linux software, bug and security alerts, and user group information here.

COMP.OS.LINUX.ANSWERS (MODERATED)

The Linux FAQ, how-to, readme, and other documents are posted in this newsgroup. If you have a question about Linux, check this newsgroup before posting your question in any Linux newsgroup.

COMP.OS.LINUX.DEVELOPMENT.APPS (UNMODERATED)

This newsgroup is intended for Linux developers who want to discuss development issues with others.

COMP.OS.LINUX.HARDWARE (UNMODERATED)

This newsgroup is intended for hardware-specific discussions. If you have a question about a piece of hardware you are trying to use with Linux, look for help here.

COMP.OS.LINUX.M68K (UNMODERATED)

This newsgroup is intended for Motorola 68K architecture-specific Linux development.

COMP.OS.LINUX.ALPHA (UNMODERATED)

This newsgroup is intended for Compaq/Digital Alpha architecture-specific discussions.

COMP.OS.LINUX.NETWORKING (UNMODERATED)

This newsgroup is intended for networking-related discussions.

COMP.OS.LINUX.X (UNMODERATED)

This newsgroup is intended for discussions relating to the X Window System, version 11, and compatible software such as servers, clients, libraries, and fonts running under Linux.

COMP.OS.LINUX.DEVELOPMENT.SYSTEM (UNMODERATED)

This newsgroup is intended for kernel hackers and module developers. Here you will find ongoing discussions on the development of the Linux operating system proper: kernel, device drivers, loadable modules, and so forth.

COMP.OS.LINUX.SETUP (UNMODERATED)

This newsgroup is intended for discussions on installation and system administration issues.

COMP.OS.LINUX.MISC (UNMODERATED)

This is the bit-bucket for the comp.os.linux hierarchy. Any topics not suitable for the other newsgroups in this hierarchy are discussed here.

Miscellaneous Linux newsgroups

The following newsgroups are mainstream Linux newsgroups. Most of these groups are geographically oriented and typically used for local Linux-related announcements for Linux user group meetings and events.

- alt.uu.comp.os.linux.questions
- alt.fan.linus-torvalds
- aus.computers.linux
- dc.org.linux-users
- de.alt.sources.linux.patches
- de.comp.os.linux.hardware
- de.comp.os.linux.misc
- de.comp.os.linux.networking
- de.comp.os.x
- ed.linux
- fido.linux-ger
- fj.os.linux
- fr.comp.os.linux
- han.sys.linux
- hannet.ml.linux.680x0
- it.comp.linux.pluto
- maus.os.linux
- maus.os.linux68k
- no.linux
- okinawa.os.linux
- tn.linux
- tw.bbs.comp.linux
- ucb.os.linux
- uiuc.sw.linux
- umich.linux

Mailing Lists

Mailing lists provide a good way of getting information directly to your e-mail account. If you are interested in Linux news, announcements, and other discussions, mailing lists can be quite helpful. This is especially true of mailing lists that provide a digest option. Such mailing lists send a digest of all daily or weekly messages to your e-mail address.

General lists

The following Linux mailing lists are general. They provide good general discussions of Linux news and helpful information for beginning Linux users.

LINUX-ANNOUNCE

Subscribe to Linux-Announce by sending e-mail to `linux-announce-request@redhat.com` with the word "subscribe" in the subject line of the message.

LINUX-LIST

To subscribe, send e-mail to `linux-list-request@ssc.com` with the word "subscribe" in the body of your message.

LINUX-NEWBIE

To subscribe, send e-mail to `majordomo@vger.rutgers.edu` with the words "subscribe linux-newbie" in the body of your message.

LINUXUSERS

To subscribe, send e-mail to `majordomo@dmu.ac.uk` with the words "subscribe linux users" in the body of your message.

Security alert lists

The following mailing lists deal with Linux and computer security issues. I strongly recommend that you subscribe to the bugtraq mailing list immediately.

BUGTRAQ

Although BugTraq is not specific to Linux, it is a great bug alert resource. To subscribe, send e-mail to `listserv@netspace.org` with the following as the body of the message: "SUBSCRIBE bugtraq *your-firstname your-lastname*."

LINUX-SECURITY

Red Hat Software, Inc. hosts this mailing list. To subscribe, send e-mail to `linux-security-request@redhat.com` with the words "subscribe linux-security" in your subject line.

Special lists

The following mailing lists deal with two issues: Linux as a server platform and Linux as a desktop platform.

SERVER-LINUX

To subscribe, send e-mail to `listserv@netspace.org` with the words "subscribe SERVER-LINUX" in your subject line.

WORKSTATION-LINUX

To subscribe, send e-mail to `listserv@netspace.org` with the words "subscribe WORKSTATION-LINUX" in your subject line.

Web Sites

Many Web sites provide Linux-oriented information. Here are few good ones.

General resources

The following Web sites are general. Most of these sites act as portal sites:

- `http://www.redhat.com/`
- `http://www.linux.com/`
- `http://www.linuxresources.com/`
- `http://linuxcentral.com/`
- `http://www.linuxcare.com/`

Publications

The following Web sites are official Web sites for various Linux publications:

- `http://www.linuxworld.com/`
- `http://www.linuxgazette.com/`
- `http://www.linuxjournal.com/`

Software stores

The following Web sites offer commercial Linux software:

- `http://www.linuxmall.com/`
- `http://www.cheapbytes.com/`
- `http://www.lsl.com/`

Security resources

The following Web sites deal with computer security:

- `http://www.cert.org/`
- `http://www.rootshell.com/`
- `http://www.replay.com/redhat/`

User Groups

A local Linux user group could be just the help you need for finding information on Linux. You can locate or even register a new user group of your own in your area by using the following URL: `http://www.linuxresources.com/glue/index.html`.

Appendix B

What's on the CD-ROM

THE CONTENTS OF this CD-ROM are copyright © 2000 Red Hat Software, Inc. and others. Please see individual copyright notices in each source package for distribution terms. The distribution terms of the tools copyrighted by Red Hat Software are noted in the file COPYING.

Red Hat and RPM are trademarks of Red Hat Software, Inc.

Directory Organization

This directory is organized as follows:

```
/mnt/redhat
   |--> RedHat
   |    |--> RPMS      -- binary packages
   |    `--> base      -- information on this release of Red Hat
   |                      used by the installation process
   |--> images        -- boot and ramdisk images
   |--> dosutils      -- installation utilities for DOS
   |--> COPYING       -- copyright information
   |--> README        -- this file
   `--> RPM-GPG-KEY   -- GPG signature for packages from Red Hat
```

If you are setting up an image for NFS, FTP, HTTP, or Hard Drive installations, you need to get everything from the RedHat directory from both CDs. On Linux and Unix, the following process will properly set up the /target/directory on your server for installing Red Hat.

Installing

The CD-ROM that accompanies this book contains a special one-disc edition of Red Hat Linux 7. To install, follow the instructions contained in the README file on the root directory of the disc. You will need to create a Linux boot disk; use the rawrite. exe program in the /dosutils folder to do so. Check rawrite3.doc for instructions on how to use it. For documentation, open the file \doc\rhmanual\index.htm.

There are three separate boot images for booting your system; you will need one of them to boot your system into the Red Hat installation and upgrade process. For CDROM and hard drive installs, use the boot.img file (most Red Hat boxed sets include this floppy already; just boot it!). NFS, ftp, and http installations require the bootnet.img floppy, which is available in the images directory. Installs through PCMCIA adapters (such as for PCMCIA CDROM or networking cards) need the pcmcia.img floppy.

Many systems will require additional device drivers that are not available on the boot floppy. The images directory contains a drivers.img file which contains many extra drivers. Put its contents onto a floppy before beginning the installation process, and follow the on-screen instructions.

Support

For those who have Web access, see `http://www.redhat.com`. In particular, you can find access to Red Hat mailing lists at `http://www.redhat.com/mailing-lists`.

If you don't have Web access, you can still subscribe to the main mailing list. To subscribe, send mail to `hedwig-list-request@redhat.com` with subscribe in the subject line. You can leave the body empty.

Obtaining a Red Hat Linux Manual

If you do not receive documentation with this product, you can order the manual from Red Hat Software. You can reach Red Hat Software at:

(800) 454-5502

(888) RED-HAT1

(919) 547-0012

(919) 547-0024 (fax)

`info@redhat.com` (e-mail)

`ftp://ftp.redhat.com` (FTP)

`http://www.redhat.com` (WWW)

Red Hat Software_PO Box 13588
Research Triangle Park, NC 27713

Index

Symbols and Numerics

Continued

Continued

E

GNU GENERAL PUBLIC LICENSE

Version 2, June 1991
Copyright © 1989, 1991 Free Software Foundation, Inc.
59 Temple Place, Suite 330, Boston, MA 02111-1307, USA
Everyone is permitted to copy and distribute verbatim copies of this license document, but changing it is not allowed.

Preamble

The licenses for most software are designed to take away your freedom to share and change it. By contrast, the GNU General Public License is intended to guarantee your freedom to share and change free software – to make sure the software is free for all its users. This General Public License applies to most of the Free Software Foundation's software and to any other program whose authors commit to using it. (Some other Free Software Foundation software is covered by the GNU Library General Public License instead.) You can apply it to your programs, too.

When we speak of free software, we are referring to freedom, not price. Our General Public Licenses are designed to make sure that you have the freedom to distribute copies of free software (and charge for this service if you wish), that you receive source code or can get it if you want it, that you can change the software or use pieces of it in new free programs; and that you know you can do these things.

To protect your rights, we need to make restrictions that forbid anyone to deny you these rights or to ask you to surrender the rights. These restrictions translate to certain responsibilities for you if you distribute copies of the software, or if you modify it.

For example, if you distribute copies of such a program, whether gratis or for a fee, you must give the recipients all the rights that you have. You must make sure that they, too, receive or can get the source code. And you must show them these terms so they know their rights.

We protect your rights with two steps: (1) copyright the software, and (2) offer you this license which gives you legal permission to copy, distribute and/or modify the software.

Also, for each author's protection and ours, we want to make certain that everyone understands that there is no warranty for this free software. If the software is modified by someone else and passed on, we want its recipients to know that what they have is not the original, so that any problems introduced by others will not reflect on the original authors' reputations.

Finally, any free program is threatened constantly by software patents. We wish to avoid the danger that redistributors of a free program will individually obtain patent licenses, in effect making the program proprietary. To prevent this, we have made it clear that any patent must be licensed for everyone's free use or not licensed at all.

The precise terms and conditions for copying, distribution and modification follow.

730

TERMS AND CONDITIONS FOR COPYING, DISTRIBUTION, AND MODIFICATION

0. This License applies to any program or other work which contains a notice placed by the copyright holder saying it may be distributed under the terms of this General Public License. The "Program", below, refers to any such program or work, and a "work based on the Program" means either the Program or any derivative work under copyright law: that is to say, a work containing the Program or a portion of it, either verbatim or with modifications and/or translated into another language. (Hereinafter, translation is included without limitation in the term "modification".) Each licensee is addressed as "you".

   Activities other than copying, distribution and modification are not covered by this License; they are outside its scope. The act of running the Program is not restricted, and the output from the Program is covered only if its contents constitute a work based on the Program (independent of having been made by running the Program). Whether that is true depends on what the Program does.

1. You may copy and distribute verbatim copies of the Program's source code as you receive it, in any medium, provided that you conspicuously and appropriately publish on each copy an appropriate copyright notice and disclaimer of warranty; keep intact all the notices that refer to this License and to the absence of any warranty; and give any other recipients of the Program a copy of this License along with the Program.

   You may charge a fee for the physical act of transferring a copy, and you may at your option offer warranty protection in exchange for a fee.

2. You may modify your copy or copies of the Program or any portion of it, thus forming a work based on the Program, and copy and distribute such modifications or work under the terms of Section 1 above, provided that you also meet all of these conditions:

   a) You must cause the modified files to carry prominent notices stating that you changed the files and the date of any change.

   b) You must cause any work that you distribute or publish, that in whole or in part contains or is derived from the Program or any part thereof, to be licensed as a whole at no charge to all third parties under the terms of this License.

   c) If the modified program normally reads commands interactively when run, you must cause it, when started running for such interactive use in the most ordinary way, to print or display an announcement including an appropriate copyright notice and a notice that there is no warranty (or else, saying that you provide a warranty) and that users may redistribute the program under these conditions, and telling the user how to view a copy of this License. (Exception: if the Program itself is interactive but does not normally print such an announcement, your work based on the Program is not required to print an announcement.)

These requirements apply to the modified work as a whole. If identifiable sections of that work are not derived from the Program, and can be reasonably considered independent and separate works in themselves, then this License, and its terms, do not apply to those sections when you distribute them as separate works. But when you distribute the same sections as part of a whole which is a work based on the Program, the distribution of the whole must be on the terms of this License, whose permissions for other licensees extend to the entire whole, and thus to each and every part regardless of who wrote it.

Thus, it is not the intent of this section to claim rights or contest your rights to work written entirely by you; rather, the intent is to exercise the right to control the distribution of derivative or collective works based on the Program.

In addition, mere aggregation of another work not based on the Program with the Program (or with a work based on the Program) on a volume of a storage or distribution medium does not bring the other work under the scope of this License.

3. You may copy and distribute the Program (or a work based on it, under Section 2) in object code or executable form under the terms of Sections 1 and 2 above provided that you also do one of the following:

   a) Accompany it with the complete corresponding machine-readable source code, which must be distributed under the terms of Sections 1 and 2 above on a medium customarily used for software interchange; or,

   b) Accompany it with a written offer, valid for at least three years, to give any third party, for a charge no more than your cost of physically performing source distribution, a complete machine-readable copy of the corresponding source code, to be distributed under the terms of Sections 1 and 2 above on a medium customarily used for software interchange; or,

   c) Accompany it with the information you received as to the offer to distribute corresponding source code. (This alternative is allowed only for noncommercial distribution and only if you received the program in object code or executable form with such an offer, in accord with Subsection b above.)

The source code for a work means the preferred form of the work for making modifications to it. For an executable work, complete source code means all the source code for all modules it contains, plus any associated interface definition files, plus the scripts used to control compilation and installation of the executable. However, as a special exception, the source code distributed need not include anything that is normally distributed (in either source or binary form) with the major components (compiler, kernel, and so on) of the operating system on which the executable runs, unless that component itself accompanies the executable.

If distribution of executable or object code is made by offering access to copy from a designated place, then offering equivalent access to copy the source code from the same place counts as distribution of the source code, even though third parties are not compelled to copy the source along with the object code.

4. You may not copy, modify, sublicense, or distribute the Program except as expressly provided under this License. Any attempt otherwise to copy, modify, sublicense or distribute the Program is void, and will automatically terminate your rights under this License. However, parties who have received copies, or rights, from you under this License will not have their licenses terminated so long as such parties remain in full compliance.

5. You are not required to accept this License, since you have not signed it. However, nothing else grants you permission to modify or distribute the Program or its derivative works. These actions are prohibited by law if you do not accept this License. Therefore, by modifying or distributing the Program (or any work based on the Program), you indicate your acceptance of this License to do so, and all its terms and conditions for copying, distributing or modifying the Program or works based on it.

6. Each time you redistribute the Program (or any work based on the Program), the recipient automatically receives a license from the original licensor to copy, distribute or modify the Program subject to these terms and conditions. You may not impose any further restrictions on the recipients' exercise of the rights granted herein. You are not responsible for enforcing compliance by third parties to this License.

7. If, as a consequence of a court judgment or allegation of patent infringement or for any other reason (not limited to patent issues), conditions are imposed on you (whether by court order, agreement or otherwise) that contradict the conditions of this License, they do not excuse you from the conditions of this License. If you cannot distribute so as to satisfy simultaneously your obligations under this License and any other pertinent obligations, then as a consequence you may not distribute the Program at all. For example, if a patent license would not permit royalty-free redistribution of the Program by all those who receive copies directly or indirectly through you, then the only way you could satisfy both it and this License would be to refrain entirely from distribution of the Program.

If any portion of this section is held invalid or unenforceable under any particular circumstance, the balance of the section is intended to apply and the section as a whole is intended to apply in other circumstances.

It is not the purpose of this section to induce you to infringe any patents or other property right claims or to contest validity of any such claims; this section has the sole purpose of protecting the integrity of the free software distribution system, which is implemented by public license practices. Many people have made generous contributions to the wide range of software distributed through that system in reliance on consistent application of that system; it is up to the author/donor to decide if he or she is willing to distribute software through any other system and a licensee cannot impose that choice.

This section is intended to make thoroughly clear what is believed to be a consequence of the rest of this License.

8. If the distribution and/or use of the Program is restricted in certain countries either by patents or by copyrighted interfaces, the original copyright holder who places the Program under this License may add an explicit geographical distribution limitation excluding those countries, so that distribution is permitted only in or among countries not thus excluded. In such case, this License incorporates the limitation as if written in the body of this License.

9. The Free Software Foundation may publish revised and/or new versions of the General Public License from time to time. Such new versions will be similar in spirit to the present version, but may differ in detail to address new problems or concerns.

Each version is given a distinguishing version number. If the Program specifies a version number of this License which applies to it and "any later version", you have the option of following the terms and conditions either of that version or of any later version published by the Free Software Foundation. If the Program does not specify a version number of this License, you may choose any version ever published by the Free Software Foundation.

10. If you wish to incorporate parts of the Program into other free programs whose distribution conditions are different, write to the author to ask for permission. For software which is copyrighted by the Free Software Foundation, write to the Free Software Foundation; we sometimes make exceptions for this. Our decision will be guided by the two goals of preserving the free status of all derivatives of our free software and of promoting the sharing and reuse of software generally.

NO WARRANTY

11. BECAUSE THE PROGRAM IS LICENSED FREE OF CHARGE, THERE IS NO WARRANTY FOR THE PROGRAM, TO THE EXTENT PERMITTED BY APPLICABLE LAW. EXCEPT WHEN OTHERWISE STATED IN WRITING THE COPYRIGHT HOLDERS AND/OR OTHER PARTIES PROVIDE THE PROGRAM "AS IS" WITHOUT WARRANTY OF ANY KIND, EITHER EXPRESSED OR IMPLIED, INCLUDING, BUT NOT LIMITED TO, THE IMPLIED WARRANTIES OF MERCHANTABILITY AND FITNESS FOR A PARTICULAR PURPOSE. THE ENTIRE RISK AS TO THE QUALITY AND PERFORMANCE OF THE PROGRAM IS WITH YOU. SHOULD THE PROGRAM PROVE DEFECTIVE, YOU ASSUME THE COST OF ALL NECESSARY SERVICING, REPAIR OR CORRECTION.

12. IN NO EVENT UNLESS REQUIRED BY APPLICABLE LAW OR AGREED TO IN WRITING WILL ANY COPYRIGHT HOLDER, OR ANY OTHER PARTY WHO MAY MODIFY AND/OR REDISTRIBUTE THE PROGRAM AS PERMITTED ABOVE, BE LIABLE TO YOU FOR DAMAGES, INCLUDING ANY GENERAL, SPECIAL, INCIDENTAL OR CONSEQUENTIAL DAMAGES ARISING OUT OF THE USE OR INABILITY TO USE THE PROGRAM (INCLUDING BUT NOT LIMITED TO LOSS OF DATA OR DATA BEING RENDERED INACCURATE OR LOSSES SUSTAINED BY YOU OR THIRD PARTIES OR A FAILURE OF THE PROGRAM TO OPERATE WITH ANY OTHER PROGRAMS), EVEN IF SUCH HOLDER OR OTHER PARTY HAS BEEN ADVISED OF THE POSSIBILITY OF SUCH DAMAGES.

*****End Of Terms And Conditions*****

Professional Mindware™

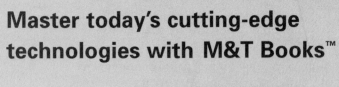

Master today's cutting-edge technologies with M&T Books™

As an IT professional, you know you can count on M&T Books for authoritative coverage of today's hottest topics. From ASP+ to XML, just turn to M&T Books for the answers you need.

Written by top IT professionals, M&T Books delivers the tools you need to get the job done, whether you're a programmer, a Web developer, or a network administrator.

Available wherever the very best technology books are sold.
For more information, visit us at www.mandtbooks.com

my2cents.idgbooks.com

Register This Book — And Win!

Visit **http://my2cents.idgbooks.com** to register this book and we'll automatically enter you in our fantastic monthly prize giveaway. It's also your opportunity to give us feedback: let us know what you thought of this book and how you would like to see other topics covered.

Discover IDG Books Online!

The IDG Books Online Web site is your online resource for tackling technology — at home and at the office. Frequently updated, the IDG Books Online Web site features exclusive software, insider information, online books, and live events!

10 Productive & Career-Enhancing Things You Can Do at www.idgbooks.com

- Nab source code for your own programming projects.

- Download software.

- Read Web exclusives: special articles and book excerpts by IDG Books Worldwide authors.

- Take advantage of resources to help you advance your career as a Novell or Microsoft professional.

- Buy IDG Books Worldwide titles or find a convenient bookstore that carries them.

- Register your book and win a prize.

- Chat live online with authors.

- Sign up for regular e-mail updates about our latest books.

- Suggest a book you'd like to read or write.

- Give us your 2¢ about our books and about our Web site.

You say you're not on the Web yet? It's easy to get started with IDG Books' *Discover the Internet*, available at local retailers everywhere.

my2cents.idgbooks.com

Register This Book — And Win!

Visit **http://my2cents.idgbooks.com** to register this book and we'll automatically enter you in our fantastic monthly prize giveaway. It's also your opportunity to give us feedback: let us know what you thought of this book and how you would like to see other topics covered.

Discover IDG Books Online!

The IDG Books Online Web site is your online resource for tackling technology — at home and at the office. Frequently updated, the IDG Books Online Web site features exclusive software, insider information, online books, and live events!

10 Productive & Career-Enhancing Things You Can Do at www.idgbooks.com

- Nab source code for your own programming projects.

- Download software.

- Read Web exclusives: special articles and book excerpts by IDG Books Worldwide authors.

- Take advantage of resources to help you advance your career as a Novell or Microsoft professional.

- Buy IDG Books Worldwide titles or find a convenient bookstore that carries them.

- Register your book and win a prize.

- Chat live online with authors.

- Sign up for regular e-mail updates about our latest books.

- Suggest a book you'd like to read or write.

- Give us your 2¢ about our books and about our Web site.

You say you're not on the Web yet? It's easy to get started with IDG Books' *Discover the Internet,* available at local retailers everywhere.

CD-ROM Installation Instructions

The CD-ROM that accompanies this book contains a special one-disc edition of Red Hat Linux 7. To install, follow the instructions contained in the README file on the root directory of the disc. You will need to create a Linux boot disk; use the rawrite.exe program in the /dosutils folder to do so. Check rawrite3.doc for instructions on how to use it. For documentation, open the file \doc\rhmanual\index.htm.

Limited Warranty

IDG Books Worldwide, Inc. ("IDGB") warrants that the Software and Software Media are free from defects in materials and workmanship under normal use for a period of sixty (60) days from the date of purchase of this Book. If IDGB receives notification within the warranty period of defects in materials or workmanship, IDGB will replace the defective Software Media.

IDGB AND THE AUTHOR OF THE BOOK DISCLAIM ALL OTHER WARRANTIES, EXPRESS OR IMPLIED, INCLUDING WITHOUT LIMITATION IMPLIED WARRANTIES OF MERCHANTABILITY AND FITNESS FOR A PARTICULAR PURPOSE, WITH RESPECT TO THE SOFTWARE, THE PROGRAMS, THE SOURCE CODE CONTAINED THEREIN, AND/OR THE TECHNIQUES DESCRIBED IN THIS BOOK. IDGB DOES NOT WARRANT THAT THE FUNCTIONS CONTAINED IN THE SOFTWARE WILL MEET YOUR REQUIREMENTS OR THAT THE OPERATION OF THE SOFTWARE WILL BE ERROR FREE.

This limited warranty gives you specific legal rights, and you may have other rights that vary from jurisdiction to jurisdiction.